The Gray Fox

The Gray Fox

George Crook and the Indian Wars

By Paul Magid

University of Oklahoma Press : Norman

Also by Paul Magid

George Crook: From the Redwoods to Appomattox (Norman, Okla., 2011)

Library of Congress Cataloging-in-Publication Data

Magid, Paul.
The Gray Fox : George Crook and the Indian wars / by Paul Magid.
pages cm
Includes bibliographical references and index.
ISBN 978-0-8061-4706-2 (hardcover : alk. paper) 1. Crook, George, 1829–1890. 2. Indians of North America—Wars—1866–1895. 3. General—United States—Biography. 4. United States. Army—Biography. I. Title.
E83.866.C94M34 2015
355.0092—dc23
[B]

2014042989

The paper in this book meets the guidelines for permanence and durability of the Committee on Production Guidelines for Book Longevity of the Council on Library Resources, Inc. ∞

1 2 3 4 5 6 7 8 9 10

To Paul Hedren, whose generosity, hospitality, expert advice, and unfailing support contributed so much to this book and my enjoyment in writing it

Contents

Illustrations

FIGURES

MAPS

Preface

Under the slate sky of a chill November afternoon, the steamer *Ocean Queen* plowed its way through heaving Atlantic swells. A young lieutenant clung to the gangway railing and pulled himself up the metal stairway to the main deck in the hope that fresh air and the sight of New York's receding skyline might relieve the nausea rising in his gut. Emerging topside, he found himself alone, except for a tall, well-built, neatly dressed passenger who strode back and forth across the deck. The lieutenant felt an immediate kinship, recognizing from the stranger's determined pace and the set of his jaw that he, too, was fighting the onset of seasickness. Since they were the only persons on deck, civility demanded some sort of mutual acknowledgment, so the two men began to converse. His fellow passenger made such a vivid impression upon the lieutenant that, years later, he would be able to recall the details of his appearance with an almost photographic precision.

> I should have believed from his looks that he was fully forty and perhaps forty-five years of age, though in point of fact he had barely passed his thirty-sixth birthday. His hair, beard, and mustache were . . . so light . . . that they appeared to be absolutely white, giving a somewhat grizzled look to his countenance and adding several years in appearance to his age. . . . The jaw . . . gave indication of great firmness of character,—a

> positiveness which I afterward learned often approached stubbornness. . . . The eyes, which were bluish gray in color and rather small, when not animated in conversation, or by some pleasant thought, were cold and stern in their expression. . . . He looked to be about six feet in height.

Though the man's bearing was military, his clothing, a suit of blue serge with plain buttons, while neat, gave no hint that he was a soldier. But one article of apparel bespoke his military service—"a black slouch hat of the pattern worn by officers of the Union Army at almost every grade at the close of the Civil War and in the Army of the Potomac, generally known as the Burnside hat."[1]

The young officer, with the cumbersome name of Azor Howett Seldon Nickerson, was nine years younger than the man he described. He, too, had served in the war, and its rigors had impressed themselves upon his face and frame. His full, dark beard did not hide the gauntness of his features, the sadness in his eyes, or a pallor that indicated a long illness.

His shipboard companion was George Crook, a seasoned veteran of the Indian wars and a major general and corps commander in the volunteer army during the late War of Rebellion. He had, as Nickerson admiringly put it, "already written his name high upon the country's history." Now, holding the rank of lieutenant colonel in the much reduced postwar military, he was en route to the western frontier to assume field command of the newly formed Twenty-Third Regiment of Infantry headquartered at Fort Boise, Idaho.[2]

Crook was equally impressed. Not ordinarily given to praise, in this case he saw fit to record his positive impressions in a letter to his close friend and former subordinate Rutherford Hayes. Nickerson, he wrote, "was wounded 4 times & in the battles of Antietam and Gettysburg, was left for dead & his recovery was regarded as almost a miracle. He has now a hole in his chest which you can nearly stick your fist in, & in consequence his health is delicate & at times he suffers terribly from this wound. Notwithstanding all this, his ambition & zeal to do his duty has been . . . great."[3]

He might have added that the lieutenant was a fellow Buckeye, a former captain in a volunteer Ohio regiment during the Civil War. Despite the severity of his wounds, he had received a commission in the regular army following Appomattox. Assigned to the Fourteenth Infantry as a second lieutenant, he was quickly promoted and requested duty on the frontier. He was now en route to the Pacific coast via the Isthmus of Panama, accompanied by Nellie, his new bride.[4]

During the voyage, the respect and admiration the two men felt for one another grew, and on his arrival in San Francisco at the end of November, Crook was moved to ask General Henry Halleck to reassign Nickerson to the Twenty-Third. Halleck, as chief of staff of the army during the Civil War, had known and commanded Crook from a distance. Now, as general in charge of the Division of the Pacific, overseeing the Departments of California (California, Arizona, and Nevada) and the Columbia (Oregon, Washington, and Idaho), both officers were under his command. Aware that the Fourteenth Infantry, to which Nickerson had been assigned, was being reorganized and that one of its battalions had already been transferred to form the nucleus of the Twenty-Third, Halleck willingly granted Crook's request and reassigned Nickerson to his command.[5]

The assignment of the two officers to Fort Boise would place them on the front lines of what historians usually refer to as the Indian wars, over thirty years of hostilities between white men and Indians that flared across the West from the 1860s to 1890. To describe George Crook's role in these wars, I have, for convenience's sake, divided them into two phases, each the subject of a different work. The current work is set in the decade following the end of the Civil War, culminating with the surrender of the Sioux in 1877. Fighting during this period was directed at forcing the nomadic western tribes to abandon their traditional lifestyle and accept confinement on reservations set aside for them by the government. These wars called upon the more aggressive aspects of Crook's character and his skills as a military leader as he waged war in three separate arenas against dissimilar tribes inhabiting radically different terrains spanning the West. During this period he pursued his enemy with such single-minded ferocity that to the Apaches, his fiercest enemies, he became the Gray Fox, a herald of ruin or "impending death" in their culture.[6] Yet it was also a time when the more humanitarian aspects of Crook's personality began to emerge. And although the Indians continued to fear him, they also came to view him as an officer on whom they could rely to represent their interests fairly and sympathetically.

The second phase of the Indian wars, to be covered in a succeeding work, marked the last decade of the general's life. It was a period during which the Indian peoples, their spirits broken, had been exiled to reservations across the West, often in remote, barren, and disease-ridden areas; a time marked by sporadic conflicts almost exclusively precipitated by government mismanagement, corruption, and indifference. As the causes of confrontation changed, so too did Crook's priorities. Moved by compassion and a sense of honor, he would become an advocate for the rights of his former foes.

My previous book, *George Crook: From the Redwoods to Appomattox*, covered Crook's youth, his service on the Pacific coast, and his Civil War years, experiences that provided him with a combination of talents and military skills, and an appreciation of Indians, that made him a rare commodity in the army. At the outset of the Indian wars, most army officers, whether educated at West Point in Napoleonic strategy or bloodied on the killing fields of the Civil War, lacked the knowledge of their enemy's customs and habitat essential to successful Indian warfare. While a number of company and field-grade officers had served on the frontier, most regarded Indians and Indian fighting with scorn and had little inclination to acquire the knowledge and skills involved.[7] Crook was an exception. During his nine-year stint in the Pacific Northwest, he accumulated a wealth of knowledge about the Indians and how to fight them, a familiarity that in the opinion of many of his contemporaries enabled him to think like an Indian. He honed his skills in the Civil War while countering the guerrilla tactics of Confederate partisans and bushwhackers.[8] Consequently, he set out for Idaho Territory with a well-earned reputation as a seasoned, aggressive, and innovative officer who, his superiors anticipated, would become a force to be reckoned with in the West.

Although Crook has been widely credited by historians as having played a significant role in the Indian wars, he has hardly garnered the attention he merited. Several factors may explain this gap in scholarship, chief among them, the nature of the man himself. Few were able to penetrate his uncommunicative and often remote demeanor, leading to mistaken assumptions about his reasoning and motivations. His personality, an assortment of seemingly contradictory aspects, made understanding and writing about him a challenge. Although he ostentatiously eschewed the trappings and protocol of rank and even the uniform of an officer, he harbored strong ambitions for recognition and promotion. He put a premium on honor and veracity, but could be vindictive, insensitive, and spiteful in his dealings with his fellow officers. To his officers and men he appeared self-confident almost to the point of arrogance, though his interactions with women and his sensitivity to criticism betrayed hidden wells of insecurity. And most intriguing, his aggressiveness on the battlefield belied a compassion for his enemy that would come to dominate his dealings with his former foes during his later years.

Unlike many of his contemporaries—Sheridan, Miles, and Custer come to mind—Crook left behind neither letters nor diaries that might have provided clues to the riddle of his personality. What does survive is a barebones memoir that contains only flashes of revelation, almost no insights into his feelings and motivations, and very little of the context that would help the reader to understand the scope of his achievements. To supplement this often murky and ungrammatical autobiography and untangle the skeins of his character requires sifting through limited and often enigmatic sources. These include his abbreviated, frequently cryptic official correspondence and the often conflicting observations and opinions of his contemporaries. These circumstances—Crook's complex personality, his reticence, and the paucity of and frequently contradictory source material—may well account for the reluctance of historians to write about him in any depth, despite his importance. Notwithstanding these difficulties, I have found my thirteen-year immersion in George Crook's life to be richly rewarding and endlessly absorbing. Ultimately, I have come to believe that his role in the settlement of the West has made the effort well worthwhile. I hope that as you read on, you will come to agree.

The Gray Fox

CHAPTER ONE

Changing the Old System of Warfare

December 1866–December 1867

The two officers' journey to remote Fort Boise began in a deceptively agreeable manner. Boarding the Central Pacific Railway, Crook and Nickerson enjoyed an easy passage from San Francisco to the railroad's then-terminus, the hamlet of Cisco, high in the Sierras.[1] There, they left the train and proceeded east via Overland Stage, luxuriating in the relative comfort afforded by springs and padded seats, while delighting in the majestic scenery that unfolded outside the open windows of their coach—a succession of snow-covered peaks, girded by towering stands of Ponderosa and Lodge Pole pines, their craggy summits outlined against cerulean skies. At intervals, the mountains receded as the road descended into grassy vales, partly covered in this season with a patchwork of early snow against which Crook's hunter's eye picked out herds of grazing deer and elk. That night, they slept in a fine hotel on Donner Lake, not far from Tahoe, savoring creature comforts for what they knew would be the last time in a great while.

The next day, the realities of frontier travel intruded. The landscape abruptly changed as they descended from the Sierra foothills onto the alkali flats of the Great Basin. Here, they exchanged the coach's padded interior for the hardwood seat of a "dead-axe" wagon that the war-damaged Nickerson found a torment. Having "neither springs nor any other convenience for the comfort of the traveler," he lamented, "it was all one could do to cling to his seat when he was wide awake and in the full possession of all his strength and faculties; but when tired out, exhausted, and sleepy, it was next to an impossibility."[2]

The clumsy vehicle jolted along the rough trail for six days and nights, stopping only briefly at intervals to permit a change of horses at way stations, rude dugouts excavated into the sides of hillocks that rose like outsized prairie dog mounds in the monotonous desert terrain. At these stops, the two men purchased the only food available—an unvarying fare served regardless of time of day—doughy bread and half-fried, fatty pork, washed down with tea brewed with the bitter alkaline water of the region.

The scenery, only dimly visible through billowing alkali dust, perfectly complemented the accommodations—barren ground, broken only by withered stands of sagebrush. The dust was everywhere, "permeating the beard, hair, eyes and ears. . . ." Nickerson, a keen observer, noted that Crook, normally "a model of personal cleanliness," did not bother to wash it from his face. Asked why, the colonel (for he preferred to be addressed by his current rather than his brevet, or honorary, rank) informed his companion that when the alkali mixed with water, it became lye, which, he advised, would "endanger my eyesight, take the skin from my face, and make me an altogether undesirable traveling companion." For the remainder of the trip, the lieutenant meekly followed his colonel's example, avoiding water and removing such grit as he could with a dry handkerchief.[3]

A succession of drivers relieved the tedium by regaling the officers with lively accounts of the atrocities committed by the Indians of the region. Their tales of depredation were familiar to Crook, and indeed, it was to correct this situation that he had been assigned to Fort Boise. Still, the drivers' narratives provided an impressive litany of dead miners, settlers, and hunters, mutilated corpses, stolen horses and cattle, and burned-out farms and mining camps.[4] One story vividly imprinted itself on Nickerson's mind, an attack on about a hundred or a hundred fifty unarmed Chinese laborers en route to one of the many mining claims in the area. Slaughtered to a man in what the driver callously described as a Mongolian picnic, their unburied bodies were found strewn for six miles along the trail.[5]

To avoid falling victim to similar "festivities," Nickerson wryly noted, whenever the wagon passed through country that seemed a likely spot for an ambush, the two officers descended, double barreled

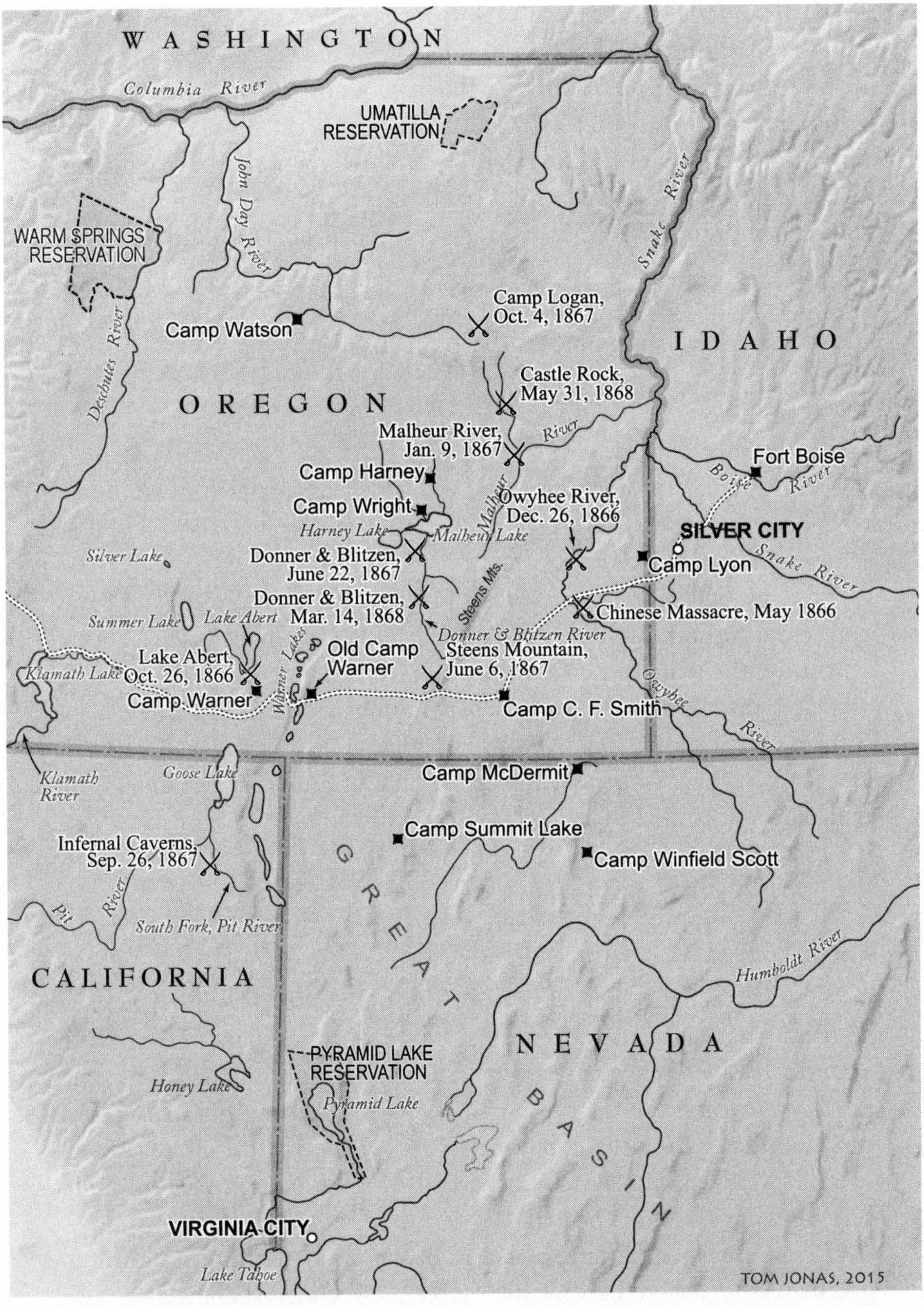
WASHINGTON
Columbia River
UMATILLA RESERVATION
John Day River
WARM SPRINGS RESERVATION
Deschutes River
Snake River
Camp Logan, Oct. 4, 1867
Camp Watson
IDAHO
OREGON
Castle Rock, May 31, 1868
Malheur River, Jan. 9, 1867
River
Fort Boise
Boise River
Camp Harney
Camp Wright
Malheur
Owyhee River, Dec. 26, 1866
Harney Lake
Malheur Lake
SILVER CITY
Silver Lake
Donner & Blitzen, June 22, 1867
Camp Lyon
Snake River
Steens Mts.
Donner & Blitzen, Mar. 14, 1868
Chinese Massacre, May 1866
Summer Lake
Lake Abert
Donner & Blitzen River
Lake Abert, Oct. 26, 1866
Old Camp Warner
Steens Mountain, June 6, 1867
Klamath Lake
Warner Lakes
Camp Warner
Camp C. F. Smith
Owyhee River
Klamath River
Goose Lake
Camp McDermit
Camp Summit Lake
Infernal Caverns, Sep. 26, 1867
Camp Winfield Scott
Pit River
South Fork, Pit River
GREAT BASIN
CALIFORNIA
Humboldt River
NEVADA
PYRAMID LAKE RESERVATION
Honey Lake
Pyramid Lake
VIRGINIA CITY
Lake Tahoe
TOM JONAS, 2015

The Great Basin (eastern Oregon, Idaho, and California's Pitt River Country), 1868–1871.

shotguns in hand, and "acted as skirmishers, [Crook] on one side and I on the other, until the danger point had been passed. We intended that, if the Indians proposed adding a Buckeye picnic to their list of entertainments, we would endeavor to furnish part of the music."[6] Notwithstanding the dire tales of their drivers, the trip proved uneventful, and Crook and Nickerson, who had begun to form an enduring relationship through shared hardship, arrived safely at Fort Boise on December 11, 1866.

The post, an unprepossessing scattering of log structures and a single sandstone edifice that housed the post quartermaster, had been built in dry, treeless surroundings on a creek that flowed into the Boise River some forty miles from where it joined the rushing waters of the Snake. Established to guard the Oregon Trail and the miners prospecting in the area, the fort afforded protection from the Indians, and a rough mining town had grown up beside it, its dusty streets lined with saloons and dry goods stores.[7]

The civilian population of Boise and its surroundings, having endured almost a decade of Indian warfare, welcomed Crook enthusiastically, their interest aroused by an article appearing just before his arrival in the *Owyhee Avalanche*, a paper published in nearby Silver City. Informed of Crook's Indian-fighting experience prior to the Civil War as a young officer in the Pit River country of northern California, the *Avalanche* concluded that he was "a splendid Indian exterminator, and if he will only do half as well as a General [*sic*] as he did as a Lieutenant, the Lo family may expect much trouble."[8]

Crook set to work immediately. Though not quite the bloodthirsty "Indian exterminator" described by the *Avalanche*, he began to formulate plans for the aggressive campaigning that he fervently believed would bring peace to the region. Aware that good intelligence was essential to the success of such operations, he spent his first week calling upon members of the military and civilian community to assess the situation, determine the extent of his resources, and fix upon a course of action. As would become his habit, he listened attentively throughout, but kept his own counsel.

He soon learned that the massacre of the Chinese miners, the Mongolian picnic referred to by his driver, was widely believed to have been perpetrated by one of the small, autonomous bands of Northern Paiutes who, together with related Bannocks and Shoshones, occupied this vast, arid territory. Frontier whites, who had little interest in distinguishing among the various tribes or learning their proper names, collectively referred to them simply as Snakes, in accordance with a common custom of naming tribes after the nearest river.

John C. Frémont, one of the first whites to enter the region, christened it the Great Basin, as he was struck by the land's resemblance to a huge bathtub: a depression, hemmed in on all sides by high plateaus and mountain peaks and drained by streams that flowed inward from its rim toward its center. Frémont's seemingly benign appellation failed to capture the area's daunting nature. Subject to subzero temperatures and raging blizzards in winter, the Great Basin in summertime saw temperatures that often reached one hundred degrees. Far from flat, its surface was broken by ravines and jagged mountain ranges that made travel arduous. And its low annual rainfall and alkaline soil ensured that few varieties of plants and animals could survive in this barren landscape.[9] Nevertheless, the tribes that made it their home had adapted to its peculiarities and eked out a satisfactory, though precarious, existence through a carefully balanced nomadic lifestyle. Generally peaceful peoples, they fished, hunted small game, and gathered grasshoppers, roots, nuts, and berries as these became available during their seasonal migrations.[10]

The white man first intruded into this simple way of life in the 1840s. "They came like a lion, yes like a roaring lion," recalled the daughter of a Paiute chief, a youngster at the time.[11] But their rapaciousness was not immediately evident. And for a time, white and red man coexisted, aided by the fact that the first intruders were merely transiting the country en route to the Pacific. But before long, the Basin revealed its enormous mineral wealth, and immigrants began to settle in the region, their numbers soon rivaling the Indian population.[12] Inevitably, relations between the two peoples deteriorated.

The army was keenly aware of both the reasons for and the consequences of the growing conflict, but held little hope for a solution beneficial to the Indians. As General Halleck perceptively described the situation to the secretary of war, the infertile character of the Basin demanded that the Indians range over a large area throughout the year to meet their minimum food requirements. But the settlers and miners had seized "all the good lands in the valleys and on the borders of the lakes and streams," killed off the game, chopped down the trees, and claimed the best habitat for the natural bounty the Indians required. "Almost their only means of subsistence now," he wrote, "are fish and the few rabbits, quails, and small birds and grasshoppers, which they can find upon the barren sage-brush plains and deserts. And even here, . . . they are pretty certain to be shot down without notice or inquiry. . . ." "Hence," he concluded, "these Indians are almost forced into collision and hostilities with the whites, . . . which will be ended only with [their] removal or entire destruction."[13]

In 1860, a harsh winter and the wanton killing by whites of two young Paiute girls brought the situation to a head, igniting what became known as the Paiute or Pyramid Lake War.[14] Unable to end the war by force of arms, white volunteers negotiated an agreement that allowed the rebellious Paiutes to return peacefully to their homeland around Pyramid Lake in northern Nevada. But the discovery of gold and silver, some of it on Indian land, drew a fresh influx of miners into the area. The Indians responded with guerrilla warfare. Three separate bands of Paiutes, joined by disaffected Bannocks and Shoshones, each raided within a defined area under its own chief.[15] The regular army, preoccupied by the Civil War, left the protection of this frontier to volunteer units composed of miners and settlers. Many were rough and bloodthirsty Indian haters who made little effort to distinguish between hostile and friendly Indians or, for that matter, between warriors and their wives and children. Their conduct exacerbated a bloody cycle of violence and revenge.[16] For their part, the Indians stole livestock and arms, and when the opportunity presented, murdered whites, including women, and savagely mutilated the dead, before disappearing into the trackless landscape as effortlessly as they had arrived.[17]

The frontier folk who met with Crook at Fort Boise had lost family, friends, and property as a result of these raids and were untroubled by the brutality of the volunteers. Indeed, many favored extermination as the only solution to the "Indian problem." Local newspapers like the *Owyhee Avalanche*, which had lauded Crook as an Indian exterminator, fanned these sentiments with detailed accounts of Indian atrocities and scorching editorials advocating annihilation of the "bi-ped hyenas" and "red rapists."[18]

When the Civil War ended and volunteer enlistments expired, responsibility for frontier defense returned to the regular army, which now underwent a radical shift in outlook. Prior to the war, when government policy toward the Indians was still in flux, regulars had served as a buffer between the Indians and settlers. During the 1850s, Crook and many of his contemporaries sympathized with the Indians. Observing that rapacious settlers and miners often initiated the violence, they often strove for evenhandedness, sometimes defending the Indians, sometimes the whites. Following the war, to satisfy a pent-up demand for land and wealth, the army, at the government's behest, refocused its energies on the subjugation and removal of the Indian as an obstacle to expansion into western lands. General Sherman, who would become the commanding general during the Grant administration and was by no means the most virulent Indian hater in the military, described this new mission in chilling terms. "The more we can kill this year, the less will have to be killed in the next war, for the more I see of these Indians the more convinced I am that they all have to be killed or be maintained as a species of paupers. Their attempts at civilization are simply ridiculous."[19]

In 1866, Major General Fredrick Steele, a West Point graduate and veteran of the Mexican and Civil Wars, was given command of the Department of the Columbia, which included the Great Basin.[20] To garrison this vast area, he was given a force of only 870 volunteers, whose enlistments were to expire shortly. They were replaced by regular infantry of indifferent quality, a force drawn disproportionately from among unskilled workers, the urban poor, and recent immigrants, who, for one reason or another, had difficulty thriving in civilian life. As a whole, the new recruits reflected a marked decline in ability, physical health, and motivation when measured against the men who had served in the Civil War. And neither they nor their officers, a mix of West Pointers and veterans of Civil War volunteer regiments, had much, if any, experience fighting Indians. Suddenly, experienced Indian fighters like Crook became an important and scarce asset.[21]

Steele consolidated the bulk of the troops in his department in the Great Basin, creating a new Military District of Boise administered from Fort Boise, but extending west into Oregon, where most of the depredations were occurring. He appointed Major L. H. Marshall, then in command of the Second Battalion, Fourteenth Infantry, to head the district.[22] To strengthen Marshall's hand in dealing with the

Indians, Steele requested, and was given, reinforcements, particularly cavalry, as foot soldiers were considered virtually useless in this kind of warfare.[23]

In May, six months before Crook's arrival, the major, eager to demonstrate his martial ardor, engaged a large Paiute band believed to have been responsible for the massacre of the Chinese miners. But after trading fire ineffectually with the Indians for four hours, Marshall precipitously withdrew from the field, losing his only artillery piece and most of his provisions and abandoning four of his soldiers. His performance sparked an outpouring of mockery in press accounts, which Crook undoubtedly found illuminating.[24]

Not only were the local citizens contemptuous of the regulars' ineptitude on the battlefield, but they had become increasingly resentful of the troops' undisciplined off duty behavior, conduct that included public drunkenness and theft of civilian property.[25] Besieged with complaints, General Steele grew so weary of Marshall's performance that, in September, he named Crook to replace him. The latter, en route to California by sea at the time, had not been aware of the full extent of the problem or that he would be charged with correcting it until his arrival at Fort Boise. Now his investigations disclosed a situation even more perilous than he anticipated. "That whole country . . ." he later recalled, "was in a state of siege. Hostile Indians were all over the country, dealing death and destruction everywhere they wished. People were afraid to go outside their own doors without protection. There was scarcely a day that reports of depredations were not coming in." Further, he learned, "the feeling against Marshall and many of his officers was very bitter. They were accused of all manner of things. One thing was certain: they had not, nor were they, making headway against the hostile Indians."[26]

Surveying the limited resources he had to deal with the situation, he noted that he had only a few outposts, spread too thinly over a huge landscape,[27] and they were garrisoned with drunken, dissipated officers and apathetic troops indifferent "to the proper discharge of duty." His transportation system was in a sorry state. In contrast to an enemy known for their superb horsemanship, mounted on sturdy ponies, faster and more durable than cavalry mounts, many of his own city-bred troopers had difficulty mounting a horse. Moreover, his pack mules were in such a state of exhaustion that they could barely carry their loads.[28] Notwithstanding these shortcomings, military patrols had been out looking for and sometimes even attacking raiding parties. But the Indians' superior mobility allowed them to evade the soldiers with ease, creating the unfortunately accurate impression that the army was having no impact on either the number or severity of the raids.

Within a week of Crook's arrival, Indians attacked near the mouth of the Boise River, not twenty miles from the camp. The colonel immediately seized the occasion to go on the offensive. As he recorded in his autobiography, "I took . . . one change of underclothes, toothbrush, etc., and went to investigate matters, intending to be gone a week. But I got interested after the Indians and did not return there again for over two years."[29]

John Bourke, who would later serve as Crook's aide, described his colonel's plan of action as "simple and comprehensible: to get into the center of operations, and thence to move as necessity dictated, in any and every direction, securing the advantage of operating on interior lines, and of conducting movements which would allow the enemy no rest."[30] Dogged pursuit of an enemy, depriving them of any respite, and engaging them at every opportunity, became the hallmarks of his campaigning from this time forward, meeting with varying degrees of success.

Given the state of his forces, Crook had few expectations regarding his initial foray. He intended to use the opportunity to discipline and harden his officers and men, and to demonstrate to them that military operations could be carried out even in the severest season of the year.[31] Not surprisingly, his decision to campaign during this season raised a storm of protest. It was December and the weather was already showing signs of a harsh winter. His troops, demoralized by past patrols that produced few results, were none too eager to leave the relative comfort of their warm barracks for such meager rewards. But Crook ignored their grumbling and busied himself preparing for the field.

Winter campaigning was not unknown in the West. General Steele had ordered continuing patrols shortly before Crook's arrival at Fort Boise, despite the onset of wintery conditions; and Crook and others had campaigned in the winter months in California and Oregon. Nevertheless, the subzero temperatures and fierce storms of the Basin made taking to the field in cold weather a risky business. But, as Nickerson accurately predicted, "the old system of warfare is to be changed."[32]

The first snows would no longer signal the end of the fighting season in the Great Basin or elsewhere on the frontier.

By luck, good judgment, or perhaps because he had known many of these men from his cavalry service during the last year of the Civil War, Crook selected forty-five veterans from Company F of the First Cavalry for his first expedition. He was particularly fortunate with respect to their commander, Captain David Perry, a twenty-six-year-old Connecticut Yankee and Civil War veteran. He had been in Idaho since mid-1866 and had demonstrated sufficient promise that Steele had been persuaded to appoint him to replace Marshall as interim commander of the Boise garrison pending Crook's arrival.[33] In addition to Perry's troopers, in what would soon become a cornerstone of his campaigns, Crook took along ten Warm Springs Indians under two civilian scouts.[34]

Crook tracked the perpetrators of the Boise River raid to their rancheria on the Owyhee River.[35] Intending a dawn attack, by now an established tactic in Indian warfare, he marched his men through Christmas night and caught the unsuspecting Indians at sunrise, "chastising them severely." The Paiutes, led by Chief Howluck, one of the principal chiefs of the tribe, put up a fight; but thirty of his warriors died for their trouble and all of the band's stock was captured. Crook's losses amounted to a single soldier killed and another wounded.[36] Howluck escaped, but among the dead was the chief's wife, attesting to the unrestrained nature of the fight. On the other hand, Crook took nine women and children prisoner, indicating that he had no intention of bending to the extermination policies favored by whites in the territory, including his commanding officer, General Steele.[37]

Rather than return to Fort Boise following the fight, Crook led his column back up the Owyhee, passing a point where he had previously spotted the tracks of mountain sheep. An inveterate hunter with almost legendary skills as a woodsman, he was unable to resist temptation. Sending his command, together with his mount, ahead to make camp, he set off confidently, alone and on foot, in pursuit of the sheep. The tracks soon led him up a steep ridge overlooking the Owyhee River, where he lost the trail. As the sun set, he found himself hiking along the edge of a bluff with a drop-off of over a thousand feet to the river below. His path was frequently crossed by ravines and, in the failing light, as he contemplated the prospect of falling into one of them, a thick mist, accompanied by sleet, began to roll in over the landscape. Clad in only a thin coat that rapidly soaked through and with no means to build a fire, he had no choice but to keep moving. Carefully he began picking his way down the steep slope in the general direction of the camp, guided by only a cursory knowledge of the terrain and the direction of the wind on his face. Around midnight, having fallen into a number of narrow defiles, he decided that if he continued on in this manner, he would either break his neck or pass the camp in the dark. So, seating himself in a clump of sagebrush, he crossed his arms with his hands under his armpits for warmth and knocked his knees together to restore circulation. He was prepared to spend the night in this manner, but as luck would have it, within two or three hours, the sky cleared. The moon rose and by its light, he saw the camp not far below him. Within minutes he had descended to the welcoming warmth of a campfire. Without awakening his sleeping troopers, he curled up in his blanket and slept soundly through the remainder of the night.[38]

Hoping to keep up pressure on the Indians, Crook continued northeast along the Owyhee to the Snake River, where he camped to await resupply from Fort Boise. Thoroughly disgusted with the incompetence of one of his scouts, he dismissed him and sent a courier to the fort for a detachment of what he called Boise Snakes, members of the Shoshone tribe under the command of a mixed-blood named Archie McIntosh. When the Shoshones joined Crook, they were accompanied by two additional contingents from the Warm Springs Reservation. Though not Northern Paiutes, these Indians spoke the same language and shared many of the same customs. Their use by Crook in this operation was perhaps the first time he deployed scouts related to the people he was fighting. He would do this often in the belief that being hunted by their own kin had a demoralizing effect on the Indians being pursued.[39]

Crook was not the first to use Indians as scouts and fighters. Employing Indians in that capacity was a tradition dating back to the colonial period, particularly during the French and Indian wars, when both European powers had allied themselves with different tribes whom they pitted against each other. In recent memory, while Crook had served on the Pacific coast, his commanding officer, Captain B. R. Alden, had enlisted local tribesmen to help protect settlers during the Rogue River War. And Nez Perces had fought alongside the army in

Washington Territory in 1856 and again in 1858.[40] Indian units had even fought in the Civil War. Notwithstanding this long history, it was only a year before Crook's arrival in Boise that Congress had authorized the formal recruitment of independent Indian units, "a force of Indians, not to exceed one thousand, to act as scouts." The warriors were to be uniformed, armed, and in some cases mounted at government expense, and paid as soldiers. In the Boise District, as elsewhere, they were officered by mixed-blood and white scouts given the rank of lieutenant and later, captain.[41]

Their use was not universally applauded. Some disliked the idea of Indians operating as independent detachments. As one officer put it, "their manner of warfare is repugnant to our civilization, and they would be a constant source of anxiety and perhaps trouble to the commander of the expedition."[42] But most came to respect and like the warriors who rode with them. Shortly before Crook's arrival in the Department of the Columbia, General Steele had warmly welcomed the services of a contingent of seventy-four scouts from the Warm Springs Reservation.[43]

Though forced to share the same reservation, the warriors from Warm Springs were not of a single tribe. Those who volunteered were Wascos and Deschutes, two bands that shared a common enmity with the Paiutes, but did not get along well with each other. Hence, the army wisely enrolled them in separate detachments, each commanded by a leader who had the complete trust and respect of their men and of the army officers with whom they served.[44] The Wascos, thirty-eight in number, were led by John Darragh. Though a transplanted New Yorker, he had an encyclopedic familiarity with the country. He had worked for some time as a miller on the reservation, and spoke the language of his men and knew them well. The Deschutes were commanded by William McKay, a mixed-blood from the Pacific Northwest, who been trained as a doctor and served on the reservation in that capacity. He, too, knew his men intimately and was fluent in their language.[45]

Archie McIntosh's Boise Snakes completed Crook's scout contingent. These Shoshones had been engaged in "temporary" service, meaning that their unit was not formally enlisted under the law of 1866.[46] As such, they were not as well equipped as the Warm Springs, being armed with older, muzzle-loading Harpers Ferry muskets, rather than the breech-loading carbines given to the Warm Springs warriors. Despite the awkwardness inherent in the use of single-shot, long-barreled guns while on horseback, the Shoshones were formidable fighters.[47]

On the trail from January 3 to the 20th, Crook's small force pushed west into Oregon, up the Malheur River in search of Paiute raiders. It was rough country. Jagged mountains alternated with steep ravines, making it difficult for the command to close quickly enough with their quarry to engage them. Eventually, the scouts located a Paiute encampment and Crook ordered an attack. But, at the last moment, Crook wrote, "by the misbehavior of the chief of scouts," the Indians were alerted to their presence and escaped into a nearby bottomland, marshy and overgrown with willows and wild rose bushes. In this tangled undergrowth, they were inaccessible to Crook's men, who now found themselves on open ground, exposed to fire from the concealed Indians with darkness rapidly coming on. As Crook paused to mull over this precarious situation, one of his men took a bullet in the chest. Incredibly, he escaped injury when the ball was deflected by a horseshoe in his shirt pocket. Crook used the incident as an excuse to suspend operations for the night. The next morning, a delegation of Paiutes entered his camp professing a desire for peace. Crook was suspicious, believing that no Indian undefeated in battle would surrender his arms without a fight. Moreover, as he later recalled, these Indians "had been depredating all over the country and never had been punished. . . . They were entirely too independent and saucy."[48]

Knowing that a frontal assault on their stronghold would be costly, and unwilling to follow the urgings of some of his officers to kill the Indians while they were in his camp under a flag of truce, he devised a strategy that relied on trickery, but would not, if successful, result in a bloodbath. He ordered his soldiers to infiltrate the village under the pretext of trading with the Indians, leaving their rifles behind as a show of peace, but wearing their pistols. Following his command, the troops entered the compound, mingling with the Paiutes. The Indians, suddenly aware of the number of armed soldiers in their midst, realized that they had been outwitted and their defenses breached. At that point, their demeanor abruptly changed; they surrendered their weapons and consented to return with the troops to Fort Boise.[49]

With his captives in tow, Crook proceeded south down the Owyhee toward Camp Lyon, planning to drop them off and resupply his men for further operations. His route ran across a high plateau where he suddenly found his column enveloped in a blizzard that obscured all landmarks and reduced visibility to little more than fifty yards. Crook turned to the more experienced McIntosh, seeking confirmation that it would be preferable to go into camp to wait out the storm. But, instead, the scout boldly offered to move forward, though aware that a deviation of even ten degrees from his course on this featureless plain would lead them into a series of impassable canyons where they would become hopelessly lost. At this point, the colonel was not entirely familiar with McIntosh's ability, but he decided to gamble on his instincts while keeping a wary eye on him.[50]

It was a wise decision. McIntosh, tall, slender, with dark brown skin and markedly Indian features, was an experienced woodsman. The offspring of a Scot who worked in the Hudson's Bay fur trade and a Chippewa woman from Ontario, Archie had been raised in the wilderness. When the elder McIntosh was slain in an ambush, Archie, his mother, and three sisters escaped and made their way to Vancouver, British Columbia, where he attended school. He went on to Edinburgh University in Scotland and on his return to western Canada, clerked for Hudson's Bay and then scouted for the U.S. army in the Rogue River War. Liking the work, during the Civil War he had served with the Oregon Volunteers.[51]

As night cloaked the plateau, the wind picked up and the troopers found themselves riding into a gale so strong that the men were almost torn from their saddles. With visibility limited to a few feet, Crook called a halt, hoping that the wind would soon abate. The command huddled on the open plain, protected by only a single flimsy tent and a few clumps of sagebrush. The Paiute captives, though less warmly clad than the soldiers, contentedly hunkered down alongside their captors.

Dawn brought no slackening of the blizzard. But with no alternatives—remaining where they were would only result in death—they resumed their trek. Then, in the late afternoon, in a feat of navigation that drew Crook's undisguised admiration, McIntosh found the sole path leading off the plateau to the banks of the Owyhee, which they found "serene and lovely."[52]

While the weather may have improved, the detachment's arrival at Camp Lyon presented Crook with new challenges. The post, commanded by Captain J. C. Hunt, was garrisoned by a company of First

Cavalry troopers who, like so many on the frontier, had taken to drink to relieve their boredom and isolation. Crook had been raised under the strict tenets of the Dutch Reform Church and though not overly religious, had retained enough of its teachings to maintain a lifelong abstinence from alcohol. So, predictably, he was displeased to find the post manned by soldiers whose "normal condition" was "drunkenness and sloth."[53] To whip the troopers into shape, he ordered Captain Hunt and the entire disgruntled Fort Lyon garrison to accompany him into the Owyhee River country in search of a Paiute band whose trail he had picked up while riding into Camp Lyon. Captain Perry was ordered back to Fort Boise with the Indian captives.

The trail Crook had identified led to the base of a formidable peak in southeastern Oregon known as Steen's Mountain. There, on January 28, Crook's scouts unearthed his quarry. Slowing the rate of march to arrive at the village just as the sun was coming up behind them, Crook deployed his force in a line of battle covering the flanks and rear of the camp to trap any warriors who might try to escape. He stationed himself to the rear of his troops to "see that the men did their duty." But his plan went awry when, agitated by the sights and sounds of battle, his horse took the bit between its teeth and carried him straight through the encampment at the forefront of the charge, his excited troopers firing over his head. He only regained control when he reached the far side of the village where, throwing himself off the horse, he turned back on foot to join in the fray. Joining a civilian from Silver City named Hanson, he approached a wickiup that seemed occupied. Ignoring Crook's warning, Hanson incautiously barged into the hut and was shot in the heart by an Indian hiding just inside the doorway, the only fatality incurred by the command. Before the Indian could turn his gun on Crook, he was slain in a burst of fire from the troopers.[54]

The casualty statistics from this engagement make plain the brutality of this type of warfare and the devastation wreaked on the tribes. While themselves losing only one man, the soldiers killed over sixty Paiutes, including all but two of the band's warriors. Of the women and children, twenty-seven were slain and only thirty survived to be taken prisoner. They would be sold into slavery by the scouts.[55]

Casualties among noncombatants were expected and even welcomed by some. Governor Woods had ordered the scouts to kill all Indians "without regard to age, sex or condition." Steele himself was reported to have issued an "extermination" order, instructing the scouts to take no prisoners.[56] But, if such an order existed, Crook ignored it. Instead he enjoined his troops to spare women and children whenever possible. Yet to him and most officers, such losses were often considered unavoidable; and they made no apologies, despite the obvious truth that sometimes the killing was deliberate and unnecessary.[57] Few civilians on the frontier were troubled by this bloodshed. One exception, the wife of one of Crook's officers, disgusted by the slaughter, angrily wrote home that "This persecution of the Indians goes against the grain with me. . . . The poor creatures are hunted down like wild beasts and shot down in cold blood."[58]

After the battle at Steen's Mountain, Crook moved southward along the Owyhee River toward Camp C. F. Smith, attacking a second, much smaller, camp along the way that he believed responsible for prior depredations. His men killed five Indians and captured the rest. Among the prisoners was a Paiute who had been captured earlier and released on his promise to refrain from further hostilities. With no apparent hesitation, Crook had him shot for violating his parole.[59]

Camp C. F. Smith, Crook's destination in early February, was situated on a high plateau in the southeast corner of Oregon. He did not linger there, but instead, turned west to Camp Warner on February 22. During this leg of the journey, about one hundred miles, he casually recalled that "several small bands of a few Indians each were cleaned up along the way."[60]

The weather proved more dangerous than the Indians. Once more, the command found itself caught in a blizzard, crossing yet another plateau in whiteout conditions. And again, Archie McIntosh proved his mettle. Crook insisted that the command push forward through the storm. Although not yet comfortable enough with the colonel to openly oppose his decision, Crook observed that McIntosh "showed by his actions that he did not approve of moving."[61] But choosing to ignore his scout's nonverbal communication, he insisted on riding on. Making the best of a bad decision, Archie led the half-frozen troops and their mounts forward into the teeth of the storm. Doggedly, the men pushed forward into the howling gale, their eyes, ears, and noses filling with snow, their hair and whiskers freezing into a mass of ice. Their path led them into drifts that sometimes reached heights in excess of fifteen feet, composed of powder so fine that they moved through it like a ship through water. By nightfall, the troops were in an advanced state of exhaustion. Crook, who had dismounted to rest his horse, slumped on a snow bank, unable to continue on foot and dazed by the incessant wind, which, he declared, had blown "the vitality out of him." As he watched his column march past, a rider-less mule appeared, and he managed to slide from the snow bank onto its back. The beast soon delivered him to the fort, which McIntosh providentially recognized when he glimpsed roof peaks poking out of the drifts along the trail. His navigational instincts were all the more remarkable as he had only visited the camp once and was drunk at the time.

The camp's location, in a deep snow pocket, made it unsuitable for winter campaigning. Though the post could not be relocated during the winter months, Crook made up his mind to do so as soon as the weather improved. For the present, he took advantage of his presence in the area to send McIntosh on a scout to the south and west of nearby Lake Warner in search of a more suitable site. When the scout finally returned after several days, he sought to explain his tardiness with an improbable tale of Indian fights. But, from his demeanor and possibly by the reek of his breath, Crook surmised that the man "was drunk the greater part of the time, and the hostiles he saw and slayed [*sic*] were mostly in his mind." Though personally disgusted, the colonel took no action, reconciling himself to the reality that heavy drinking was all too common on the frontier, and acknowledging that, in view of the scout's talents, it would be better to overlook it in his case.[62]

Snowed in at Camp Warner for the remainder of that long cold winter, Crook set his men to work constructing a causeway across Lake Warner at a point where it narrowed to about three or four hundred yards. The project kept the soldiers busy and would later save supply trains from the east a hundred-mile journey around the lake.[63]

In March, Crook made a series of forays in search of Indians who were rumored to be in the Dunder and Blitzen country to the north. Most patrols came up empty-handed, but on one, the Indians found them first, stealing their horse herd and leaving Crook's small command afoot. Unable to pursue the raiders through deep snow, they trudged back to Camp Warner, their equipment and supplies on their backs. Further campaigning was out of the question until the horse herd could be replenished with stock from California, giving Crook and his men a much-needed respite. He used the time to investigate the lake, which was of substantial size, paddling awkwardly in a dugout canoe carved out of a pine log. With his favorite shotgun close at hand, he contentedly hunted waterfowl and collected eggs, enjoying the peaceful seclusion afforded by his solitary explorations.[64]

In May, when fresh horses and mules finally arrived, he resumed his scouts in the area around the camp. But once again, the results were meager. As the historian Michno aptly described it, Crook's situation was like that of a man in the middle of a prairie dog town. As he approached one hole, the prairie dog would disappear, only to reappear, yapping at him from another hole he had just left. Yet his troops were making a dent in the problem. The war of attrition had eroded the Indians' manpower, and their war parties were becoming increasingly smaller.[65] At the same time, military patrols, including several carried out by the Warm Springs scouts, prevented the bands from engaging in their normal food-gathering pursuits. Starvation and fatigue were taking their toll.[66]

Crook sensed that the time was ripe for a major thrust that would finally break the back of Paiute resistance. While preparing for it, Crook kept the pressure on. McIntosh and his Shoshones made an independent patrol in June, reportedly killing twelve Indians (how many were women and children was not stated). While not an overwhelming victory, it posed a threat that continued to keep the Indians on the move, depriving them of the rest and time needed to replenish their food stocks after the hard winter.[67]

Despite an initial resistance to Crook's use of Indian auxiliaries, General Steele had come to endorse the practice enthusiastically, writing in his annual report to the secretary of war in August 1867:

> [They] have done most valuable service. Being armed [not always with the best weapons], mounted, and supplied, and backed by troops, they cheerfully lead the way into the middle of their enemies. They have also proved themselves very efficient when acting alone; they are very useful as guides and spies and in destroying the spies of the enemy. It is my opinion,

> that one hundred, in addition to those now employed, would exterminate the hostile bands before next spring.[68]

Further up the chain of command, Halleck seconded Steele's statement, claiming that he could "employ at least a thousand on this coast . . . ," adding with undisguised racism, "they would save the more valuable lives of many white men."[69] Halleck also bestowed extravagant praise on Crook as an Indian fighter. "Most of the troops engaged in hostile operations in this district [Columbia] have been under the command of Brevet Major General George Crook, of the 23rd Infantry, who has exhibited skill, bravery, and the most untiring energy."[70] Clearly, the senior ranks in the military had their eye on Lieutenant Colonel Crook.

CHAPTER TWO

A Summer and Fall Campaign

July–November 1867

The readers of the July 27, 1867, edition of the *Owyhee Avalanche* were treated to a colorful description of the force gathered at Camp C. F. Smith in anticipation of Crook's culminating campaign in the so-called Snake War. Garishly painted Indian scouts, some of them waving fresh scalps from their rifle barrels, sun-reddened cavalry veterans, a thousand head of horses and half-tamed mules and their bearded packers and drovers crowded the small post in a turmoil of dust and noise. It was, the writer commented, "the liveliest place I've seen in the upper country since the early days of the Boise Basin."[1]

The reporter, Joe Wasson, had only just arrived at the camp by stage from Silver City, a booming mining center in the Owyhee region, with high hopes of being allowed to accompany the campaign in the field. Whether Wasson would be granted his wish was entirely up to Colonel Crook. The army had no rules governing whether journalists could join troops on military expeditions or, if they did, whether they could use army couriers to carry their dispatches. These decisions were left up to the commander in the field.[2] Though newsmen had been in the front lines of conflicts since the Crimean War, reporters filing stories on the Snake and other Indian wars had previously received their information from military and civilian participants in the comfort of a local newspaper office or saloon. If permitted to accompany Crook's column, Wasson would become one of the earliest newsmen to cover an Indian campaign firsthand and the first to observe Crook as an Indian fighter.

Wasson was young, relatively well educated, fit, and possessed of a strong sense of adventure. At twenty-six, his most salient physical characteristics were a sturdy frame and a mop of red hair and matching mustache.[3] John Bourke, who came to know him some years later in Arizona, thought that the reporter "approached every duty with the alertness and earnestness of a Scotch terrier."[4]

Born in Wooster, Ohio, Wasson had trained as a printer until, at the age of nineteen, bored with printing and eager to experience the frontier, he decided to follow Horace Greeley's advice and go west. During the journey, the wagon train that he accompanied was attacked by warriors, turning the young man into a confirmed Indian hater, a bias that often colored his writing and the tone of the paper that he and his brother, John, established in Silver City.

Running the first newspaper in the Idaho Territory, Wasson spent his days setting type in the back room of a drafty clapboard building, a job ill-suited to either his temperament or his health. So when word reached him that Crook was mounting an expedition into Paiute country, he experienced a powerful urge to go along, anticipating both a newsworthy experience and the restorative powers of the great outdoors.[5] As Wasson did not record his initial conversations with the colonel, we do not know the arguments he presented to convince Crook to take him along. But he succeeded, inaugurating what was to be Crook's enduring association with the press.

Reporters would soon become such a common feature of Crook's campaigns that one writer concluded that more correspondents traveled with him than with any other general,[6] an anomaly for such an intensely private man. To explain the phenomenon, some point to Crook's experiences during the Civil War, which led him to conclude that it is not what a person does, but what he gets credit for doing that builds his reputation and allows him to advance through the ranks.[7]

Whether this somewhat cynical conclusion accurately reflected Crook's relationship with the press remains to be seen. In his published articles, Wasson made it clear that while Crook permitted him to join the column, the colonel did nothing either to arrange or encourage it. On the contrary, as Wasson was quick to point out, far from being a favored guest, he was viewed as a tolerated visitor who could be asked to leave the column at any time. And, while he accompanied the troops, they made no effort to spare him any of the hardships or dangers to which they were exposed.[8] Crook, himself, rarely disclosed his reasons for doing anything, so his precise logic in allowing the newsman to accompany him remains a mystery. But in all probability, he anticipated a successful campaign and thought that a little firsthand coverage of the fighting would not hurt his image. It is equally likely that he admired the man's openness and pluck.

By later standards, the force that Crook had assembled was modest, three troops of the First Cavalry and a detachment from one company of the Twenty-Third Infantry (mounted), a total of about 150 soldiers.[9] The regulars were joined by the two detachments of Warm Springs scouts under McKay and Darragh, and McIntosh's Northern Shoshones.[10] The expedition, responding to various scouting reports, would be targeting Paiutes who had been raiding stock throughout southern and central Oregon. Initially, they would march southwest along the Oregon-Nevada line.

The night before the column left Camp C. F. Smith, the wild war songs of the Warm Springs kept Wasson awake. Rather than toss and turn fitfully in his tent, he left his blankets to seek out Crook's officers to learn something of the colonel's methods of operation. In his first dispatch, he recorded the results, a compendium of knowledge Crook had acquired fighting Indians on the Pacific coast and Confederate guerrillas in West Virginia during the War.

"Crook wants to get as near the Indians as possible and is satisfied that a good cleaning out where he is going will put a damper on their raiding out in the settlements and along the highways. A surprise accompanying a defeat of Indians is said to sicken them more than double the amount of destruction in a pitched battle. They don't like to be beat at their own game of stealth. The expedition going out tonight will travel altogether in the nighttime and endeavor to camp during the day in places as unobservable as possible. It will go hard, this turning night into day and vice versa, but I know some who have been practicing lately and may be specially adapted to the service forthcoming."[11]

On the evening of July 20, as the sun dipped below the horizon, Crook's force quietly departed Camp C. F. Smith. As few Paiutes were in the immediate vicinity of the camp, Crook's night departure seemed unnecessary. But, a great believer in the benefits of training, he undoubtedly saw an opportunity to acclimate his men to traveling in complete darkness.[12]

The column had a motley appearance, the soldiers dressed for the most part in faded army blue, while the scouts wore as much or little as they liked, some favoring buckskin with scalps interwoven in the fringes of their shirts. The civilian packers, clad in flannel shirts, tucked their pants in their boot tops and sported broad brimmed hats that shadowed their heavily bearded faces.[13]

Crook deployed his scouts in a protective screen, at all times keeping two detachments fanned out at a distance of up to fifty miles to the front and sides of the main column. The regulars rode in a column, each soldier armed with a seven-shot Sharps repeater, its short barrel making it easier to use on horseback, though less accurate than the older rifled muskets issued since the 1840s.

The pack train that trailed the column under the watchful eyes of the troopers numbered some two hundred animals, mostly mules, managed by twenty-two civilian packers. Many of the mules were half wild, not yet thoroughly broken to the work, a circumstance accounting for the delays experienced during the column's second day out as packers and scouts combed the brush in search of animals that had broken loose and wandered away from the camp during the night. Despite their orneriness and cost—in the two years following the war, mules averaged $75 apiece in an army that paid its privates $13 a month—Crook favored them over the more traditional army wagon. Mules could go more places—faster and without breaking down—than wagons, giving his troops greater mobility in the broken terrain of the Great Basin.[14]

Crook's love affair with the mule—he even preferred one as a mount on a campaign—was not typical of the officer corps. Despite providing valuable service on campaigns against the Seminoles in the Florida swamps and during the recent war with Mexico, the beast was generally not highly regarded by soldiers of the time. A sterile cross between a jackass and a horse, it was commonly looked upon as "an outrage against nature, a monstrosity, unapproachable in devilment, fathomless in cunning," and dexterous only in its ability to kick its handlers or throw off its gear. Crook, however, was untroubled by either the mule's inelegant pedigree or its fractious nature, possibly because he had more in common with the creature than he cared to admit. Like the mule, he came from unpretentious parentage, was far more interested in the practical than the flamboyant and, as many of his fellow officers discovered to their regret, could be as prickly, stubborn, and unresponsive to direction as any beast of burden in his pack train.[15]

While there is no record of Crook's introduction to the sturdy hybrid, his father undoubtedly used mules on the family's farm in southwestern Ohio. In his autobiography, which made no mention of his childhood, Crook first referred to mules when describing his crossing of the Isthmus of Nicaragua to the Pacific en route to California. On that occasion, he and his fellow passengers had ridden the animals over a twelve-mile trail that he described as "one gigantic mudhole." The mud was so deep in places, he insisted, that both mule and rider often sank from sight. But his own familiarity with the animal allowed him to make the trip with relative ease. The young lieutenant's appreciation for mules blossomed on the Pacific coast, where they were used not only to carry supplies but as mounts for the infantry. Though intractable in the hands of inexperienced troops, if managed properly, they proved agile, strong, and capable of going farther and carrying more at a faster pace, while eating less, than either of their parents. The mule was also smarter, more adept at sensing and avoiding danger, and when used hard, recuperated faster than the horse.[16]

Mules rose even higher in Crook's estimation during the Civil War when, during his service with the army of the Cumberland, he observed their ability to navigate the rugged terrain of Tennessee. After transferring to West Virginia, he used mules on long-distance raids on steep mountain trails where the going was rough and fodder scarce. He found that they thrived far better than horses. Crook's high regard for the animals moved his longtime aide, John Bourke, to remark that the general became so enamored of mules that he "made the study of pack trains the great study of his life."[17]

While he closely attended to the qualities and training required to maximize the effectiveness of his animals, Crook paid equal attention to the proper design and loading of their packsaddles. The *aparejo*, the packsaddle he favored, first came to the attention of Americans during the Mexican War. It was a simply a grass-filled blanket that conformed snuggly to the mule's back, evenly distributing the weight of the load placed on it without slippage. Campaigning in the Great Basin, Crook used the *aparejo* in place of the traditional cross-tree packsaddles, which tended to rub sores into the mules' backs.[18]

Handling mules was not a job for amateurs. Expertise was required to coax them out of their natural bad tempers and stubbornness and to provide the care needed to prevent them from breaking down on the trail. In California, it was only when the army replaced untrained soldiers with professional civilian packers that pack trains began to function efficiently. Crook carried this lesson with him to Idaho, and on this campaign, despite the cost—an experienced packer earned about $60 a month—insisted on hiring twenty-two civilian packers to accompany the column and was said to know "every packer by name, what his peculiarities were, and how he cared for his animals."[19]

For all of Crook's attention to detail, planning, and tactical sophistication, the campaign produced few results, frustrated by the superior mobility of his enemy and their intimate familiarity with the terrain. But there were some successes. By the time the column arrived at Camp Warner, a week after leaving C. F. Smith, the troops had fought a series of small but brutal engagements, killing a total of forty-six Indians and taking a number of prisoners.[20] At Warner, the column was joined by more troopers from the First Cavalry and a company of mounted infantry from Crook's Twenty-Third Regiment, many of them recent immigrants from Germany and Ireland, largely untrained and inexperienced.[21] The cavalry was commanded by Lieutenant William Parnell, an Irish veteran of the Crimean War and one of the few survivors of the charge of the Light Brigade. A large man, his body so heavyset that, in the saddle, he was said to "try the powers of his horse quite heavily," Parnell was happily welcomed by Crook, who had observed his abilities firsthand during Sheridan's 1864 Shenandoah campaign.[22]

After resupplying his men, Crook pushed west to Goose Lake, and from there north into the snowcapped Cascades, pausing periodically to rest the horses and allow the scouts to search for signs of Indians. Again, the Paiutes managed to avoid the troops. In the absence of combat, Crook occupied himself with fly rod and rifle, adding fish and game to his officers' diet of salt pork and beans.[23] But he had a job to do, and this unproductive campaigning had accomplished little. Rather than continue pursuing will o' the wisps, he returned to Camp Warner, where he set about relocating the post to a less snowbound location, as he had planned the previous winter. He had already found a suitable location at nearby Lake Warner. Now, he revisited the lake to identify the exact site on which to build the post.[24] He soon found an ideal spot. At an elevation five hundred feet lower than the old camp, it was warmer, received less snowfall, and was "in a well sheltered place where there is plenty of timber, grass, and water." It was a confluence of favorable elements unusual for the region.[25]

In a clumsy attempt to curry political favor, Crook proposed naming the new camp after Governor Woods of Oregon, punning in a dispatch to Halleck that "it is the only *Woods* in all the country."[26] General Halleck, unimpressed by either Crook's suggestion or his attempt at humor, pointed out that military posts were not ordinarily named after civilians. Instead, he opted to retain the name of the former camp. So, Camp Warner it became.[27] Meanwhile, Crook's aides engaged in a little apple polishing of their own, naming a nearby mountain after their colonel, after deciding that it was the only unnamed landmark in the country suitable for the honor.[28]

While his troops labored to construct the new post, Crook pondered on the location of the other military garrisons under his command, noting that the present camps were poorly situated to prevent Indian raids, most of them in areas remote from depredations. In August, he wrote a long report to Steele presenting him with a plan to close some posts and reposition others to areas of greater Paiute activity and redefining his area of operational responsibility.[29] Camp closures were no more popular in the nineteenth century than they are today. Consequently, Steele received his recommendations with little enthusiasm, particularly after outraged citizens angrily filed a petition opposing one closure in their neighborhood.

Though Crook failed to close any camps, he did win approval to redraw the boundaries of the Boise District to create a new Military District of the Lakes, which was to be under his command. He could now focus his efforts in an area where he believed Paiutes were concentrated, rather than wasting his time supervising garrisons haphazardly scattered over the entire Great Basin.[30] The new district covered most of Oregon between the Klamath and the Warm Springs Reservation in the west and Steen's Mountain to the east, with Camp Warner at its center. Crook's strategy seems to have been premised on the assumption that the Paiutes were committed to remaining permanently in that area, a supposition that was far from certain.[31]

After submitting his suggestions to headquarters, Crook, with Wasson and a small detachment of soldiers and scouts in tow, set off northward toward Harney Lake, seeking a site for yet another post. They rode through an unwelcoming landscape of rocky outcroppings and sagebrush, with the little water available so alkaline that it tasted like "secondhand soapsuds."[32] Somehow, amid all that desolation, Crook found a grassy valley watered by several streams abounding in trout. Despite its unpromising name, Rattlesnake Canyon, he found the locale ideal. When one of his lieutenants attempted to name it Camp Crook, Crook declined the honor, proposing instead that it be called Camp Steele, another bit of pandering possibly intended to gain favorable consideration for his other recommendations. Halleck again rejected his selection and named the post Camp Harney after the nearby lake.[33]

Having realigned his resources to the extent military and local politics allowed, Crook turned his attention to his enemy's source of supply. During his winter and spring campaigns, he had observed that, despite constant harassment by the army, the bands he pursued never seemed to run short of munitions or warriors. To Crook, this indicated support from an outside source. In the Great Basin and later in Arizona and on the Platte, the army suspected that agency Indians provided supplies and refuge to so-called wild bands who lived off the reservation, enabling them to continue their depredations indefinitely. In this case, Crook believed that the Achumawis, whom whites called Pit Rivers, were the Paiutes' source of supply. Their country lay in the Pit River valley in the remote northeast corner of California, an area that Crook knew well, having campaigned there during the 1850s.[34] Returning to Camp Warner from Harney in late August, he assembled a substantial force of 360 men—three troops of cavalry and an infantry company, supported by McIntosh and McKay's scouts, and a mule train and packers. Prior to their departure, the cavalrymen received a shipment of Spencer carbines to replace their old Sharps repeaters. The latter were passed on to McIntosh's Indians, who now gladly retired their heavy rifle muskets.[35]

The command left in darkness on August 30, peering nervously into the shadows thrown by the surrounding brush. Only days before,

McIntosh's scouts had engaged a strong band of hostiles near the post. Outnumbered and with inferior weaponry (probably one reason Crook had reequipped them with Sharps rifles), they had been "whipped back." But the victorious attackers had long since faded into the countryside, and the command now proceeded on its way unmolested.[36]

En route, the expedition passed through the Camas Prairie, a source of the camas root, a starchy tuber that formed an important part of the diet of the local Indians. They camped on the prairie for several days while the scouts fanned out in search of Indian signs. While awaiting their return, Crook instructed his troops in the fine art of locating and digging for the roots, a practical lesson that added some variety to their menu. When the scouts returned, they confirmed that, as the colonel had suspected, the hostiles were headed for the Pit River country. On receiving their report, Crook held a council of war to consider his next move. Lieutenant Bourke described his method of doing so with a mixture of fascination and frustration:

> He never asked any one for an opinion, never gave one of his own, but, taking his rifle in hand, strolled a short distance away from camp, sat down under a rock, crossed one knee over the other, clasped his arms about his shins, and occasionally rubbed the tip of his nose with the back of his right hand. This last was the infallible sign by which the troops afterwards learned to know that one of Crook's councils of war was in progress.[37]

Having sorted through his options in magnificent isolation, Crook announced his intention to split his command. Two cavalry troops accompanied by McKay and Darragh's scouts would go north in case the Indians had turned in that direction. Crook would take the remainder of the force south into the Pit River country. Wasson, figuring that Crook would go where the action was, accompanied the colonel.[38]

Their trail led through rocky, heavily timbered country past clear, trout-filled lakes. The woods teemed with game, including a number of grizzlies. To avoid exposing his position to the enemy, Crook banned the discharge of weapons. But shortly thereafter, one of his lieutenants ran into an old she-bear, which he later claimed he mistook for the hairy and unkempt chief pack master. The colonel, under no such misapprehension, blasted the hapless bear and her cubs. The following day, he again violated his own order, shooting an antelope. These incidents, Wasson noted, "confused the men," and soon all attempts at fire discipline disappeared and the hills resounded with the echoes of gunshots. Whether the Indians were alerted is not known, but as the column neared the California line, and, as "Indian signs began to get plentiful and interesting," Crook reinstated his order and took other measures to conceal the column's presence.[39]

Concealment became more difficult as the country now opened into a plain of lava beds and juniper. On the evening of September 22, fires flared on the surrounding ridges to the west. Crook dispatched McIntosh and a civilian guide named Wilson to investigate. Wilson, a braggart, but not much of an Indian fighter, stumbled on the Indian camp. Instead of returning silently to report his findings, he panicked, discharged his weapon, and fled into the underbrush. The Indians immediately scattered; and the column, its horses played out, were unable to pursue them. Only Parnell's intervention prevented the angry soldiers from lynching the scout, whom Crook fired on the spot.[40]

The next morning, hoping to mislead the Indians into thinking he had given up the chase, the colonel led his command down an old wagon road toward a post he had occupied in the 1850s. They marched for two days under a rainy sky through mountainous country scored with canyons. While they flushed out an occasional warrior, woman, or child, and observed increasingly fresh indications of large numbers to their front, the main body continued to elude them. On the night of the 25th, they made camp in a heavily wooded canyon in a cold rain. Increasingly depressed by his failure to catch up with his quarry, Crook seated himself against a lone pine tree. In an effort to put on a brave front so as not to further demoralize his men, he pulled out his knife and began to whittle, whistling a tune for effect. But he was a poor actor and his long face broadcast his belief that the campaign had failed.

During their months together on the trail, a relationship had developed between the colonel and Wasson. Wasson was impressed by Crook's abilities as a woodsman and Indian fighter, and Crook delighted in the company of the plucky redhead and admired his personal courage. An element of personal affection, at least on Wasson's part, had entered into their relations. So, when the journalist spied "the old man," seated in disconsolate isolation beneath the tree, he was moved by his lonely vigil. The reporter badly wanted to cheer him up with an offer of a warm supper of camas roots. But ultimately, deterred by Crook's reticent and austere demeanor, he later admitted that he "was afraid to indulge."[41]

The next day, the colonel's mood improved markedly. The detachment at last made contact. As the main body of the command headed north into a valley formed by the South Fork of the Pit River, Archie McIntosh spied an Indian encampment less than half a mile to the east, occupying a fortified position on a lava bluff. The Indians—thirty Achumawis, several Modocs, and a band of seventy-five Paiutes—had gathered for a peaceful feast and celebration. They had not expected soldiers, but fired defiantly as the troops rode up the valley toward them.[42]

The Indians had chosen to hold their gathering at an old Achumawi stronghold used in the past as protection against raiders from enemy tribes.[43] The fortification combined natural features with clever stonework. It was tucked into a shelf that formed a natural basin a little more than halfway up a lava formation that rose precipitously seven hundred feet above the valley floor, overlooking a deep ravine. Access to the sides of the fortress was limited by the steep slope of the bluff, which was littered with huge boulders. Behind these, the Indians could fire at those trying to get at them from below. As an additional defense, the Achumawis had constructed stone rifle pits along the basin's rim and had strengthened two promontories on its southeast corner by adding chest-high breastworks to their summits. At the edge of the shelf, facing south over the ravine, they had built a large redoubt with walls eight to ten feet high. To reach this fortress within a fortress, the soldiers would have to descend to the bottom of the ravine and then advance up a forty-five degree slope to the rock bench, all the while under fire from embrasures and loop holes that the Indians had built into the redoubt's walls. To add to his woes, though Crook was unaware of it at the time, more barriers lay scattered about the interior of the basin, while the basin itself was honeycombed with caves and tunnels from which the Indians could fire in all directions. The configuration of the fortress and the hellish battle that would soon unfold around it earned it the name, "the Infernal Caverns."[44]

Crook's plan of attack called for Parnell to charge from the south across the ravine with his dismounted cavalry, while the infantry, under a young lieutenant, John Madigan, made an assault up the ridge on the north. McIntosh was to take his warriors to the top of the bluff, a vantage point from which they could fire down on the defenders.

The soldiers' blue uniforms made them easy targets against the gray rock, while their foes, by virtue of their natural coloring and dusky clothing, blended into the background. Unable to see their targets, the troops fired blindly into the rocks, while crawling forward through a storm of bullets and arrows. During the initial attack, one soldier was killed and three wounded, one mortally. Crook, on foot, was everywhere, reconnoitering the fortress under enemy fire, narrowly avoiding several well-aimed shots.[45]

At nightfall, as the evening chill set in and lightning flickered across the blackening sky, Crook called a halt to the attack. By this time, the men had inched within yards of the inner fortress and had formed a tight ring around it to prevent escape. There, they lay under cover, taking turns making their way back down into the valley to wolf down a hasty meal of salt pork and hardtack, their first food since departing camp at five that morning. Above the rumble of thunder, they could hear a medicine man's eerie exhortations, and the clatter of stone on stone as the defenders reinforced their breastworks. Parnell, learning from one of the other officers that Lieutenant Madigan was in low spirits, crawled around to his position to offer comfort. The lieutenant had become convinced that he would die in the next day's fighting. To calm him, Parnell gave him a drink of whisky before returning to his position. But neither the alcohol nor Parnell's encouraging words could dispel the lieutenant's morbid premonition.[46]

Unwilling to risk a lengthy siege, Crook decided to attack at dawn. An hour before sunrise, he called in his pickets and formed the men into a line for the attack. Speaking to them in fatherly tones, he quietly instructed them to rise quickly at the command "forward," and "go with a yell and keep yelling, and never think of stopping until they had crossed the ditch, scaled the wall, and broke through the breastworks—and the faster, the better."[47]

As the order to go forward reverberated against the walls of the redoubt, the men, Wasson among them, rose and clamored forward over huge boulders down the ravine's outer slope, making for the fort's towering wall. They were met by "a perfect hailstorm of arrows" and rifle bullets. Protected to some extent by the angle of the slope, they made their way up the other side of the gulch and gained the stone balcony at the foot of the wall. Up to this point, they had taken no casualties. But as they attempted to scale the wall, one of the sergeants, peering through a loophole, was shot through the head at close range. A private nearby was killed in the same manner, and another soldier took a bullet in the wrist that shattered his carbine stock and sent him hurtling off the wall into the ravine. Lieutenant Madigan, who had momentarily stopped in an exposed position to assess the situation, was struck down as he had predicted. A rifle bullet pierced his brain. Despite their casualties, the troopers continued to push forward up and over the rock wall. From the top of the parapet, the men fired into the fort, "using revolvers and clubbed carbines on the skedaddling Indians." Wasson, while engaged in heavy fighting, nevertheless had time to observe that "[Crook] makes few mistakes with that long Spencer of his." Parnell credited the colonel with bringing down the band's leader, a Paiute chief named Si-e-ta, severing his spine with a single well-aimed shot.[48]

The warriors who had been driven from the walls did not attempt to escape the fortress as the soldiers had anticipated. Instead, they disappeared lizard like among the rocks.[49] Crook now realized that the capture of the fortress was what he termed a "'white elephant' prize." The surviving warriors were able to take advantage of the scattered boulders and caves and tunnels that provided them with cover from which they could shoot at the soldiers from all directions without exposing themselves to return fire. As a result, by sunset, after a long afternoon of bitter fighting, the troops had taken additional casualties, but were no closer to driving the enemy from their positions. As they had done the night before, at Crook's command, they cordoned off the area to prevent escape, ate a frugal meal, and settled in for another sleepless night. The next morning, Crook later confessed, he was profoundly relieved to find that his quarry had disappeared. Using hidden tunnels carved in the rock, they had passed beneath the ring of soldiers, emerged in the rear of Crook's position, and slipped away in the darkness.[50]

Archie's scouts captured an Achumawi woman who, facing a choice of talking or being hung from a nearby tree, revealed that the defenders had suffered sixteen killed and nine wounded, an estimate impossible to verify in the maze of the tunnels and caves. Crook put his own losses at four, including Lieutenant Madigan, together with nine wounded.[51] The woman also divulged that the Paiutes who had joined the feast at the caverns had been on the warpath since early spring and had stolen over a thousand horses in raids against settlers and miners in Oregon and Idaho. The body of a dead warrior provided grisly confirmation of her testimony. He wore a cap adorned with pigtails apparently cut from the scalps of Chinese miners. Large amounts of ammunition and powder were also found in the caves, together with a few rifles, most of which were antiques probably received from white traders in exchange for stock stolen by the Indians during raids in Oregon.[52]

The command interred its dead some distance from the battlefield, concealing the graves to avoid their desecration at the hands of the Paiutes, who were known to mutilate enemy corpses. As was customary with slain officers, special care was taken with the body of Lieutenant Madigan. He was buried with ceremony a day's ride from the battle site, though his grave, too, would be obliterated.[53]

Controversy would attach to the manner in which Crook fought this engagement. Some twenty years after the battle, the California historian Hubert Howe Bancroft opined that Crook unnecessarily sacrificed his men "in an endeavor to achieve what the public expected of him." Gregory Michno, who has written extensively on the Snake War, agreed, citing Wasson. The latter had reported that prior to the engagement, Crook had said that "if his venture on this southern tour failed to in any way meet public expectations, the blame should fall upon him alone." In Michno's opinion, Crook was keenly aware of the scorn recently heaped upon Major Marshall by the Idaho newspapers for his retreat after receiving only one casualty. The historian speculated whether the colonel might not have been persuaded that his "reputation could only be secured with victories written in letters of blood."[54]

Bancroft also criticized the colonel's tactics. Had he "let his Indian scouts do the fighting in Indian fashion, while he held his troops ready to succor them if overpowered, the result might have been different."[55] Whether he meant to imply that the scouts would have fought more effectively or that victory could have been achieved with fewer white casualties was not clear.

Crook's frank recognition that he would be held responsible if his forces were defeated may not necessarily have implied that he was willing to sacrifice his men for the sake of public acclaim. As previously established, the colonel had a keen appreciation of the importance of public opinion to his career. But though some officers had no hesitation trading the lives of their men to achieve acclaim, there is little evidence that Crook was one of them. Certainly, he had no reluctance in committing troops to a fight when necessary. But he was not known as one who sought glory at the expense of the lives of his men. On the contrary, his tactics were usually designed to avoid unnecessary casualties. In the Caverns fight, his decision to make a frontal assault on such a heavily fortified position was a deviation from his usual mode of operation, apparently the result of a carefully calibrated determination that weighed the cost in casualties against the significance of the results. Sometime before the battle, he had stressed to Wasson the importance of success in such an engagement. The journalist quoted him as saying "it had become a chronic thing for soldiers to follow Indians into rocks and leave them, [so] the moral effect of such an affair [on the Indians] would be worth several ordinary victories."[56] By attacking and reducing this seemingly impregnable stronghold, he would demonstrate his soldiers' tenacity, courage, and superior fighting ability. The resulting demoralization of the enemy would, he believed, hasten the war's end.

Whatever doubts historians may have had after the fact about Crook's tactics in this battle, his men seemed not to have shared them. Wasson recorded that "I heard no man complain of the charge, but rather that the whole siege was conducted and finished on the cheapest plan, and there was a universal feeling of regret that the savages knew all about the rocks and we didn't."[57]

While Crook campaigned in the Pitt River country, his wife, Mary, who had endured a year-long separation from her husband, had journeyed from her parents' Maryland home to unite with him in the Great Basin. Traveling by sea to California, she then joined the wives and children of other officers in Crook's command on an arduous journey across high mountains and alkali deserts to join him in late October.[58] Wishing to personally escort her on the last stage of her journey to their new home, the colonel, having just returned to Camp Warner following the battle at Infernal Caverns, immediately turned about and rode the 140 miles to Camp Harney to welcome her. He found her in the company of Julia Gilliss, the wife of the recently appointed quartermaster at Camp Warner. No stranger to the frontier—she had lived at various military posts for the past two years—Mrs. Gilliss promptly pronounced Camp Harney the dirtiest place she had ever seen. Crook, embarrassed by the women's dismay, hastily assured them that Camp Warner, which would be their home for the next year, was "far pleasanter."

On November 4, they finally reached the new fort and learned that he had spoken the truth. Though remote, Warner was a vast improvement over Harney—in Julia's words, "the prettiest post on this coast."[59] But the accommodations were far from impressive. Even by frontier standards, the fort was a primitive affair. Living arrangements for Crook and his men consisted of cabins built atop twelve-by-sixteen-foot pits dug to a depth of about three feet in the hardened soil. The only opening, besides the door, was a small outlet on one side for a fireplace, vented by a chimney of poles daubed with mud. The absence of windows meant that "[the] only light by day was through the roof," a tent canvas; and when the canvas ran out, sapling bows and mud, neither covering offering much protection from the subzero temperatures of the now approaching winter.[60] For the remainder of that fall and winter, Mary and her colonel shared their cabin with Crook's hunting dog, Jim, an odiferous, golden haired part-spaniel, whose aptitude for locating game had earned him a place of honor in Crook's heart.[61]

The diet of both officers and men during that winter consisted of a soldier's normal fare—salt pork, beans, hardtack, flour, coffee, and a little salt and sugar. As snow often drifted "about the post ten or fifteen feet deep, and the thermometer was below zero a great portion of the time," it was impossible to supplement their rations with additional supplies from other forts in the area. As a result, three days' supply of food often had to last for five. They eked out their meager supplies with "a few tough old steers . . . with their ribs and hip bones prominently sticking out" and whatever game they could bag in the snow-covered landscape. Crook shot a few snowshoe hares, and served them up to his bride with a garnish of wild onions and a weed known as lamb's quarters thought to prevent scurvy. Lieutenant Parnell, impressed with Mary's stoicism in the face of this hardship, gallantly declared that she and the other spouses at post constituted "an illustration of heroism on the part of women unsurpassed since the days of the Revolution."[62]

But life was far from grim. Mary, though still in her twenties, exhibited great maturity and leadership in making the post habitable for the officers and their families. Though childless, she was particularly attentive to the welfare of the little ones and their anxious mothers. When spring came and the snow melted away, she and Julia went on long rides through the beautiful and now secure countryside, which Julia poetically described as "a little valley . . . green as an emerald, flecked with golden sunshine and laced with a network of little streams, bordered by an amphitheater of hills." Mary gave a "brilliant little party" for her birthday, for which the officers wore full dress uniforms, unusual for her husband, and arranged for the shipment of a croquet set to the post. An officer even started a subscription to build a theater, and a small band was formed. Musical entertainments and amateur theatricals soon became a common occurrence. The colonel, though undoubtedly bemused by these goings-on, cooperated fully. Having experienced the privations of frontier duty for several years, he recognized the need to relieve boredom and keep up the morale of his men and their officers, and where families accompanied his officers, their contentment as well.[63]

CHAPTER THREE

Winter Campaigning

December 1867–March 1868

Crook did not spend much time at Camp Warner during the winter season. Under orders from General Steele's successor, General Lovell H. Rousseau, to keep the pressure on the Paiutes, the colonel mapped out a winter campaign that would take him into the Donner und Blitzen valley.[1] The valley, carved into the landscape by a river of the same name, ran from Steens Mountain north into Malheur Lake, about a hundred miles northeast of Fort Warner. In the past, the Paiutes found the relatively sheltered country ideal for a winter camp. There, they could rest in the warmth of their tipis, living off their summer harvest of dried fish, venison, and camas root, while gathering strength for the coming spring. But constant harassment by the soldiers during the past summer had prevented them from laying in their usual stock of food. Scarce supplies and a harsh winter had left many bands destitute. With their families facing starvation, a growing trickle of warriors here and throughout the Great Basin chose to surrender to the army. The settler population, formerly vociferous advocates of annihilation as the only solution to the Indian problem, now awakened to the possibility that this situation offered a cheaper and more effective way of ending the long and bloody conflict.[2] To hasten the process and avoid the risk of a resurgence of hostilities in the spring, Crook planned a ruthless campaign. He would seek out the Paiutes "in their winter homes, kill the bucks, capture their women, and destroy their supply of provisions, and so cripple them that they would be glad to surrender and beg for peace."[3]

But the campaign could not be launched immediately. The horses and mules, exhausted by the prolonged fall expedition, badly needed rest and recuperation. In addition, time was needed to recruit new scouts to replace the Warm Springs, whose enlistments were expiring and whose thoughts now turned more and more to home and family and the division of the spoils from previous patrols, rather than renewed fighting.[4] Crook's reliance on Indian scouts was such that he had no qualms about delaying his winter expedition to recruit these replacements. The new scouts, fourteen Boise Shoshones, did not arrive until early February, providing the respite needed to fatten the horses and mules for the trail.[5] At last, on February 11, Crook departed Camp Warner, accompanied by one company of Parnell's reliable First Cavalry, thirty men from the Twenty-Third Infantry (mounted), and the Shoshones.[6]

As with previous expeditions, this one was also attended by hardship and failed expectations. Five days' march brought them to the Donner und Blitzen valley. The valley was layered with an eighteen-inch layer of snow with a hard crust that broke under the weight of the horses, bloodying their legs. Their progress was further hampered by radical fluctuations in the weather. One day, the temperature dropped well below zero, with a fresh snowfall that reached their horses' bellies; the next, warmed by Chinook winds, it rained, melting the snow, turning the surrounding countryside into a quagmire. The horses' hooves sunk into the viscous mud where sharp stones, lurking below the surface, slashed their already injured legs and further slowed their advance.[7]

Finally, the Shoshone scouts discovered a village about five miles down the valley that they believed belonged to We-ah-wee-wah, a principal chief of the Paiutes. Crook ordered a night march so his troops would be in place for a dawn attack. But in the dark, they blundered into another, smaller village, and the ensuing firefight alerted the larger encampment to their presence. At dawn, with the temperature at ten below, they found that camp deserted, its former occupants leaving no trail. Unable to ascertain the whereabouts of the Indians, running low on supplies, and with men and mounts exhausted from the hard riding, Crook aborted the campaign and returned to Warner.[8]

One historian concluded that the rapid depletion of the column's supplies indicated a weakness in Crook's logistical planning.[9] But winter campaigning for an army dependent on livestock for transportation was always problematical. Military horses required a daily ration of grain to keep up their strength, and both horses and mules consumed enormous quantities of hay or forage, particularly in cold weather. From late spring through the fall, grazing could satisfy this need; but in the winter, this was impossible, requiring the army to load the pack mules with so much fodder that they were unable to carry sufficient quantities of ammunition and rations to sustain troops in the field for any great length of time. In this instance, Crook probably anticipated resupplying at Camp Harney, a post not far from his area of operations. But he reported that he had decided to return to Warner instead, because the Indians had been alerted to his presence and he wanted to give them time to settle down before resuming his offensive.[10] Whatever his reason for quitting the field, the problem of forage and rations would continue to dog military expeditions, particularly, as we shall see, during the Sioux War.

Crook mounted a second expedition from Warner on March 9, this time with a larger force and enough supplies to allow him to remain out for a month. Within a week, they encountered an Indian band camped in a narrow canyon. While the soldiers inflicted some casualties, most of the Indians escaped over ground made swampy by the spring thaw. Pursuit by mounted troops was hopeless. Three days later, the command rendezvoused with a column that had left Camp Harney a month before. Patrolling in the same direction in which Crook planned to travel, they had come up with nothing. Rising temperatures, coming on the heels of this bad news, convinced the colonel to once again abandon his campaign. The spring thaw had turned the countryside "into a mass of water. . . . The . . . noonday sun sent the melting snow down into the flat country in great streams. . . . Every man had to dismount and lead his horse, sometimes for several miles across the flats." Plainly, hunting Indians under these conditions was impossible.[11]

The column's frustrations were compounded when the Paiutes took advantage of a dark and rainy night to creep in among the column's stock, kill or wound several animals, and steal others, including Crook's own horse, Old Buckskin, an incident the general failed to mention in his memoir. It became evident that the raiders had been motivated by hunger when the stolen livestock, dead and partially butchered, was found lying by the trail. Parnell thought that the Indians might be desperate enough to return to retrieve the meat. Crook agreed. So, the next morning, a patrol doubled back to the site and found several of the Paiutes at work cutting up the dead animals. Catching them unawares, the soldiers killed all but one. Then, to deprive the Indians of sustenance, they sprinkled flour on the dead animals to make them think they had been laced with strychnine, a method favored by frontiersmen to poison Indians.[12]

The Paiutes continued their horse-stealing raids, driven by a scarcity of game and the urgent need to feed their families after the long winter. As the weather warmed, they attacked herds throughout the Great Basin. In one bold move in April, they even raided the Camp Warner herd and ran off a dozen mules.[13] For its part, the army kept up the pressure, killing Indians wherever they could be found and hitting villages without warning. Reports of these actions tell a tale of ruthless and indiscriminate campaigning. In one instance, a column attacked a sleeping village near the Malheur River and, without losing a single soldier, killed thirty-two Indians, twenty of them women and children. The raid netted three beef cattle, a horse, and five thousand pounds of salmon, which the soldiers burned, hoping that the smell of roasting fish would have a demoralizing effect on any survivors left in the area. In another attack, in late May, a patrol of enlisted men struck a village at dawn near the Owyhee River ferry. Again, no soldiers were killed, but thirty-four Indians were slain, twenty-seven of whom were women and children, a bloody toll possibly resulting from the absence of the restraining influence of officers.[14]

By mid-year 1868, Crook had personally led approximately a dozen scouts through Indian country and fought in six engagements. His troops had "kept the Paiutes and other hostile bands constantly on the run for a year and a half and forced them into combat on some forty occasions. . . . In all, the troops reported 329 Indians killed, 20 wounded, and 225 captured."[15] To these small nomadic bands, such losses were catastrophic.

Crook, as a young officer in 1857, had employed aggressive tactics against the Pit River Indians that had drawn criticism from his superiors, who considered them too punitive.[16] Now, perhaps as a measure of the sea change in army policy, he received only praise from his superiors. Halleck's 1868 report to the secretary of war lauded him for his "skill, bravery, and the most untiring energy."[17] Steele, his previous departmental commander, was equally enthusiastic. Though he complained of Crook's tendency to act without orders and his habit of going over his commander's head when disagreements ensued, he lauded his effectiveness as an Indian fighter. Perhaps exaggerating for effect, he opined that "the hostile Indians have been pursued so vigorously and punished so severely during the past year that an officer with ten or fifteen good men might visit any spot in the department with impunity."[18]

Crook's aggressiveness, persistence, willingness to lead his men in the field, and growing popularity on the frontier made him a leading candidate to fill the vacant brigadier position created by the retirement of General Joseph Hooker in the fall of 1878. Politicians from California and Oregon, soon joined by Crook's old friend Rutherford Hayes, now governor of Ohio, and Arthur Ingram Boreman, governor of West Virginia during the war, clamored for his appointment.[19] But the War Department was not prepared to promote a lieutenant colonel over the heads of full colonels ahead of him on the promotion list. Instead, they recognized him with an appointment as acting commander of the Department of Columbia, temporarily replacing General Rousseau when, in March 1868, the latter was reassigned to Louisiana.

Under ordinary circumstances, as the departmental commander, Crook would have moved to Portland, far from the front lines of his war against the Paiutes. But he would have none of it. Because of poor communications he had not heard about his appointment until late April. Even then, preoccupied with Indian depredations, he delayed setting out for Portland until May 1, remaining only briefly in the city before returning to Warner. As a kindness to Nickerson, whose young wife, Nellie, had recently died at Fort Boise, he allowed him to remain at the Portland headquarters to take care of departmental paperwork.[20] In July, Nickerson was promoted to captain, undoubtedly at Crook's urging.[21]

Returning to Warner, Crook found clear signs that in his absence, the tide had begun to turn. On May 31, a patrol from Fort Harney fought and decisively won a minor engagement against Egan, a prominent Paiute chief, at Castle Rock in Oregon. Though the action amounted to little more than a skirmish, it came on the heels of four years of unremitting warfare and proved to be the proverbial straw that broke the camel's back. Within weeks, Egan let it be known that he wanted to talk peace and had sent word to other chiefs in the region to come in for that purpose.[22] At the same time, We-ah-wee-wah, principal chief in that part of the country, announced that he, too, was done fighting.[23] Though chiefs of the western tribes only spoke for their individual bands, Egan, We-ah-wee-wah, and some of the other headmen commanded great respect among the Paiutes. Crook knew that if they were willing to talk peace, it could mean the end of a long and costly war.

As Halleck had decreed that no officer should conclude a treaty in the Division without the division commander's prior approval, Crook wrote him requesting authority to conduct peace negotiations. Then, aware that time was of the essence, without awaiting a reply, he sent word to the chiefs to bring their people to Camp Harney on June 30 to discuss surrender.[24] Even delaying the peace talks until the end of the month entailed a substantial risk. At the news of a possible Indian surrender, vengeful citizens had already gathered, seeking the return of stolen stock and threatening harm to the Indians. One settler let it be known he would pay a thousand dollars apiece for scalps. The chiefs, fearing such reprisals, appealed to the soldiers for protection, while at the same time trying to restrain their own young warriors who, unaffected by peace fever, continued raiding throughout June.[25] While the troops did what they could to protect the Indians, and the chiefs worked to calm their young men, Crook knew that the smallest spark could reignite the war. So, tensions mounted as the month slowly crept by.[26]

On the 29th of June, as he trotted down the narrow canyon leading to Camp Harney, past the temporary wickiups of some fifty restless warriors and their families who had come to attend the council, his nerves must have been stretched to the breaking point. With him rode a small detachment that included officers Parnell and Nickerson, and, in a demonstration of his faith in the peace process, his wife, Mary, her friend Julia Gilliss by her side.[27] After a restless night, he appeared the next morning on Harney's broad parade ground, resplendent in his full dress uniform, removed from storage for the occasion. Accompanying him were Mary and Julia.[28] Facing the Indians, erect and stern-faced, the colonel placed the women to his immediate rear and behind them, his troops. With the two women peering from over his broad shoulders, his face betraying no emotion, he watched the Paiute chiefs and their warriors, "very imposing in their full panoply of war," ride their prancing ponies onto the parade ground. The lack of unanimity among the warriors, all of whom were fully armed, was evident in the sullen expressions and threatening gestures of some and the efforts of others riding through their ranks, to calm them. While the Indians swirled about him, Crook quietly murmured that the two women must remain as calm and indifferent as possible, making no movement that would betray their nervousness. Then he faced the turbulent throng "immovable as stone," while the women, in Julia's words, "stood close behind him, *apparently* as unsuspicious as if we were receiving at a ball" (Gilliss's italics).[29]

When the tumult had died down sufficiently to allow his voice to be heard, the colonel informed the chiefs through an interpreter that he would not enter into discussions until the warriors had laid down their arms. For what seemed an eternity, the Indians continued their warlike demonstrations. But it was all show. The Northern Paiutes had been badly beaten and they knew it. This soon became apparent when, in ones and twos, they dismounted and reluctantly came forward to place their weapons at Crook's feet before squatting in a large semicircle in front of him. After they were seated, Chief We-ah-wee-wah approached Crook, his hand extended in the white man's greeting. To his surprise, the colonel clasped his hands behind his back, addressing the old chief. Nickerson recorded their conversation.

> "Tell him," said Crook through his interpreter, "that I did not come here to shake hands with him. He has been too bad an Indian; murdered too many people. I came to hear what he has to say for himself."
>
> Old We-ah-wee-wah was very much nonplussed at first, but managed to say that he and his warriors were tired of war and wanted to make peace. The general replied:
>
>> I am sorry to hear this. I was in hopes you would continue the war, and though I were to kill only one of your warriors while you kill a hundred of my men,

> you would have to wait for those little people [pointing to the Indian children] to grow to fill the places of your braves, while I can get any number of soldiers the next day to fill the place of my hundred men. In this way, it would not be very long before we could have you all killed off, and then the Government would have no more trouble with you.
>
> But We-ah-wee-wah insisted that they did not want any more war, but wanted peace and had "thrown away their ropes," an important concession signifying his band's pledge to give up horse stealing.
>
> After a little more parlay on similar lines, the general consented to make peace, though, apparently, very reluctantly.[30]

In future years, such peace treaties were merely a prelude to banishing Indians to reservations. But in 1868, memories of the hardships suffered by the Pacific coast tribes following their confinement to a reservation were still fresh in Crook's mind.[31] If he could avoid it, he wanted no part of the broken promises, famine, sickness, and despair that characterized the government's policy of removing Indians to areas remote from their homelands. So, after their surrender, he allowed We-ah-wee-wah's people to return to their traditional hunting grounds, fortuitously located on land not as yet coveted by the whites. In return, the chief would have to restore stolen stock and prevent further depredations against the settlers and miners of the region by what Crook termed the "strolling bands" of young warriors. "If molested by the white man," the colonel said, the tribe should seek out the military for help and would "receive all the protection in our power." If they were unable to secure food, the army would supply them with rations. But—and Crook was very explicit about this point—receiving rations would be a privilege, not a right, contingent on their good behavior. The tribe would be held collectively responsible for failure to abide by these terms as it would be impossible for the army "to distinguish the innocent from the guilty."[32]

Finally, Crook asked the chief to provide several warriors to accompany the troops as scouts on an upcoming expedition against the Pit River Indians, who were suspected of recently murdering several white settlers. His objective was to obtain knowledgeable guides for his troops and, more importantly, to test the tribe's commitment to peace. Crook also anticipated that the presence of Paiute scouts among his soldiers would demoralize the Achumawis, demonstrating the army's power to turn their erstwhile allies into enemies. The chief assented, knowing that, though it meant turning against former allies, it would give his young men an opportunity to demonstrate prowess in battle, crucial to their status within the tribe. And so, after the formalities were concluded, ten men were selected and provided with army uniforms, to participate in the coming campaign.[33] Crook's ruthless and unremitting campaigns had not only broken the will of the Northern Paiutes but transformed them from a dangerous and elusive enemy into a valued ally.

However, more than the subjugation of the Indians was required to maintain the peace. The settlers and miners would also have to be brought into the equation. Despite the surrender of the Paiutes, there remained in the frontier settlements and mining camps of the Great Basin a smoldering hatred for the Indians that threatened to reignite the war. Over thirteen hundred miners and settlers had been killed or wounded, and many families had faced financial ruin as the result of the hostilities.[34] The relatives, friends, and neighbors of the dead and the economically devastated thirsted for revenge. As if to underscore this looming threat, on the very day he concluded his negotiations with the Paiutes, Crook was confronted by a mob gathered at Camp Harney, threatening vengeance on the now pacific Indians. Emphasizing to the angry crowd that he had not made peace with the tribe out of friendship, but so that the "citizens could develop the country," he was able to calm and disburse them.[35] But his troops could not be everywhere. To prevent violence on a broader front, he turned to the civilian authorities for help. In a letter to D. W. Ballard, governor of Idaho, he laid out his case.

> The only thing I fear now is that white men will commit outrages on the Indians in retaliation. If this thing can be controlled, I feel satisfied that the bloody scenes of the last four years are at an end, and we will have permanent peace with the Indians.
>
> It occurs to me that you can do more towards preventing renewed hostilities than any other person I know of in

> the country. Get the newspapers in your territory to interest themselves in this matter, and enjoin upon all good citizens the necessity of refraining from retaliation. Give the Indians a chance to show their hand on the peace side of the question, and I feel satisfied that our troubles with them are over.[36]

Ballard, an easterner appointed by the Grant administration, was more sympathetic to Crook's arguments than many on the frontier. He caused the letter to be published in Portland's *Daily Oregonian*, with some positive effect.[37]

Having done what he could to tamp down white hostility, Crook then appealed to his military superiors to deal with a second potentially inflammatory issue, another winter of starvation among the Paiute bands. Though, generally, Crook disapproved of providing subsistence to the Indians out of concern that it would create dependency on the government, in this case he had promised it and, moreover, considered it justified. The Indians had come a great distance to Harney to make peace, consuming valuable time they would have otherwise devoted to gathering food supplies for the winter. For that, they should be compensated. And, he argued, issuing rations would have the effect of causing the Indians to remain in the vicinity of Camp Harney over the coming winter. Their proximity would allow the army to establish "more friendly relations with them, as many of these Indians have never been friendly to the whites and know nothing of them."[38] Unfortunately, as Crook had foreseen, providing rations to the tribes was a two-edged sword. While pacifying them, it did increase their dependence on the whites, and in future years contributed to the destruction of their initiative, self-esteem, and cultural identity.

Following the surrender of the Paiutes, Crook turned to the Pit River country, the only remaining trouble spot in his area of command. Hoping to resolve the situation peacefully, he rode into the Achumawis' territory backed by two companies of cavalry, a demonstration meant to overawe the small bands of the region. He called for a parley and, reluctantly, the Indians assembled in council.[39] Addressing them with intimidating brusqueness, he asked them if they remembered him from his expedition against them eleven years before. Yes, they boldly responded, they had pounded him. To which Crook recalled responding, "I told them if they didn't stop lying, I would give them another opportunity of pounding me right then and there, whereupon they changed their tactics."[40] Recalling the fight at the Infernal Caverns, the Achumawis became submissive. They confessed that, indeed, some of their warriors had killed whites, but those men had fled into the surrounding mountains. Nevertheless, they would try and catch them. Responding as he had to the Paiutes, Crook demanded that the Achumawis lay down their arms, and made the entire tribe collectively responsible for apprehending the miscreants and maintaining the peace. His firm and uncompromising tone shocked the Indians, and they accepted his terms. Taking their pledge at face value, Crook confidently returned to Idaho.[41] Several months later, his confidence was rewarded when the chiefs surrendered the killers to the army, allowing Crook to pronounce the "Indian War in this country . . . closed." "With care and proper management," he confidently informed his superiors, the Indians would remain at peace.[42]

A year later, Crook asked Nickerson to draft a letter of instruction to the commanding officer of Camp Harney. In it, he laid out what he meant by "proper management" of Indian peoples. It contained fundamental precepts that he and the officers under his command would observe for the remainder of his career. First, he advised, "while you must at all times do everything in your power to preserve [peaceful] relations with [the Indians], they must not be allowed to get the impression that you are anxious to do so. They must fear or they will not respect you." Fear alone, however, was inadequate, unless accompanied by consistency and conduct that inspired trust. To achieve consistency, "[Indians] must be made to feel . . . while they do right, the officers . . . will do all they can for their good, but if they do wrong their punishment will follow as speedily as it will be sure." Trust could be earned only by making promises that are "fulfilled to the letter; for no matter how important the matter involved may seem or how plausible the excuse for failure . . . an Indian never understands or forgives it."[43] To Crook, the promise was sacred. More than a decade afterward, Nickerson observed that,

> Crook made few promises and none that he could not keep; and the peace [with the Snakes] . . . lasted, to my knowledge, for a period of ten years; and when broken, as in 1878 (by the

> Bannocks), . . . I am not so sure that it was not the fault of the white man, but one thing is certain, it was not caused by the failure to keep any promises made to them by General Crook.[44]

Unfortunately, Crook's word was only as good as the government's willingness to honor it. Though in the case of the Idaho bands, he had promised that they would remain "free as the air" as long as they kept the peace, the Bureau of Indian Affairs, which assumed responsibility for the supervision of the tribes after their defeat by the army, had a different agenda. To control the Indians, and not incidentally to nullify their title to lands coveted by whites, they were to be moved onto remote reservations.[45] Accordingly, in the fall of 1868, the Bureau informed Chief We-ah-wee-wah that he and his people were to be placed on reservations in western Oregon. Not surprisingly, the chief refused to submit to the agent's authority. The Bureau then turned to the army and Crook to enforce compliance. In a display of independence and open support for the Indians, he refused to participate, declaring that to do so would precipitate an uprising. "For the reason that I have [the Indians'] confidence," he wrote, ". . . I will do or order only what is best and right, both for themselves and the government."[46] His objections were ignored, and the Northern Paiutes would follow their brethren in the Pacific Northwest into confinement on the reservation.

The army chose to overlook Crook's insubordination in view of his qualities as an Indian fighter. They had plans for the colonel, who was now entering his fortieth year, his sixteenth on active duty. In the meantime, his work of pacification completed, he commanded, albeit temporarily, the now quiescent Department of the Columbia. There, he remained until relieved by General Edward R. S. Canby in August 1870.[47]

CHAPTER FOUR

Assignment to Apacheria

1871

The post–Civil War period was a time of wrenching change for the American military. In March 1869, a coalition of legislators hostile to the concept of a peacetime standing army and resentful of the army's role in Reconstruction passed legislation severely pruning military spending. Clothed in economic arguments, the measure forced a radical reduction in the number of regiments from a postwar high of forty-five down to twenty-five, requiring the discharge of more than 17,000 men from military service. A year later, Congress enacted a second bill making further cuts, resulting in the need to release a total of nearly nine hundred officers from active duty, a number too great to be reached by either attrition or retirement. To cut deeper, the army created so-called Benzene Boards.[1] Named for an industrial solvent used to remove grease from weapons, the boards were tasked with eliminating incompetents, drunkards, and other unsuitable dregs from the officer corps. In August 1870, Crook, who consistently inveighed against alcoholism and stupidity in the military, received an interim posting to a Benzene Board in San Francisco, a duty he undoubtedly relished.

Prior to this assignment, while still in Portland, Crook had been approached by his division commander, Major General George Thomas, General Halleck's replacement, with an offer of command of the Department of Arizona, where the army was bogged down in a frustrating and brutal struggle against the Apaches. Departmental commands were commonly reserved for full colonels of the line. Crook, still a lieutenant colonel, knew that previous efforts to promote him had failed because forty such colonels were currently waiting impatiently for such a command, men who would have to be passed over to give him the position.[2] Concerned about making so many enemies among his fellow officers, Crook turned down the offer. For the record, he claimed that he "was tired of the Indian work, that it only entailed hard work without any corresponding benefits," and pled health concerns related to the climate. The offer was renewed by Thomas's successor, Major General John Schofield, and again, Crook rejected it. But the issue refused to go away.[3]

While serving on the Benzene Board, he was approached once more, this time by Anson P. K. Safford, the governor of Arizona Territory. The governor liked what he had heard about Crook's aggressive, no-nonsense approach to Indian warfare and saw him as a desirable replacement for the current commander, major general of volunteers, now colonel, George Stoneman. A cloud of opprobrium had settled over Stoneman after he had moved the headquarters of his fight against the Apaches from the heat and dust of Arizona to the comfort of a base in southern California. He had further alienated Arizonans by setting up stations throughout the territory to feed Apaches willing to give up raiding. The settler and merchant population of Arizona viewed that policy as coddling the natives. The last straw for Safford had come when Stoneman had closed several military posts.[4]

Crook continued to resist the Arizona assignment, but Safford proved more persistent and far less heedful of military protocol than either Thomas or Schofield. Ignoring the chain of command, the governor forwarded his request directly to President Grant, circumventing the army's commanding general, William Tecumseh Sherman, and Secretary of War William Belknap, both of whom adamantly opposed bypassing the colonels to give the command to an officer of lower rank. The governor's brashness paid off. In May 1871, the adjutant general (AG) wrote the secretary of war: "The President directs me to inform you of his desire that Lieutenant Colonel George Crook be assigned on his Brevet Rank to relieve Colonel Stoneman in command of the Department of Arizona until the new arrangement next fall." The AG then wrote to Crook informing him that the assignment, which he had never requested and did not want, was only temporary, and that "a new deal would be made" in the fall. This clumsy attempt to placate the colonels must have been galling to Crook, already disgruntled at being manipulated into the position and dismayed by the prospect of alienating a host of his fellow officers.[5]

Were it not for the scarcity of command opportunities in the post–Civil War army, Crook's assignment would hardly have excited much envy among his fellow officers. Whether referring to Arizona's current Indian problems or to its generally inhospitable nature, General Sherman tersely summarized the military's prevailing attitude toward the Territory: "We had one war with Mexico to take Arizona, and we should have another to make her take it back."[6]

The region that Sherman dismissed so disparagingly lay in the northwest corner of a vast and dramatic landscape that the Spaniards, the first Europeans to attempt to colonize it, called Apacheria, an assuredly unintended tribute to the warlike tribe that dominated the territory. Bounded by the Grand Canyon to the north and the formidable Sierra Madre in Mexico a thousand miles to the south, and stretching from the Colorado River to the Rio Grande, Apacheria was a far-reaching and potentially dangerous land.

A perceptive few who came into the country held a contrary view, seeing it as a garden of fantastic natural beauty. Herds of antelope and deer grazed in the tall grass. Flowers bloomed in wild profusion in the spring, and mountain passes offered vistas of alpine meadows and pine forests. At lower elevations, its landscape was scored by deep, varicolored canyons carved in the desert floor by ancient rivers and spectacular wind-scoured buttes and mesas that rose high above the sandy terrain, giant sculptures bathed in sun and shadow. But beneath the lavish scenery lurked ever-present danger. As Nickerson would wryly comment, "hostility appeared to be the normal condition of everybody and everything, animate and inanimate."[7]

Crook, who had passed from southern California to Tucson in 1860 on a trip east, was less than enamored by Arizona's climate and scenery and worried by concerns about his future assignment. Bumping across its desert reaches, he saw, not a garden but a monotonous landscape of shifting sands, broken only by the occasional wiry presence of a mesquite bush or desert willow. Even if the view appealed to him, discomfort prevented any appreciation of it. As Martha Summerhayes, a young bride who accompanied her officer husband to the Territory at about the time of Crook's assignment, commented, "One cannot enjoy scenery with the mercury ranging form 107 to 122 in the shade."[8] In June, when Crook arrived at his new post, heat enveloped the traveler in an oven-like haze so unremitting that, even at midnight, sleep was impossible. Archie McIntosh, whom Crook would bring with him as a scout, sidestepped the problem by remaining "stupid drunk" throughout most of the trip, a solution unavailable to the abstinent general.[9]

Even for the rare passenger indifferent to heat, little was visible through the clouds of alkaline dust that sifted through the floorboards of the rumbling coach. During occasional rest stops, a few hardier souls, upon descending from their cramped conveyance, might observe a sampling of the flora and fauna that fed Nickerson's paranoid view of the terrain. Beneath rocks and in innocuous burrows and crannies lay coiled rattlesnakes, keeping company with "black and venomous" gila monsters, often three feet in length, tarantulas as big as a hand, and the smaller, but no less unpleasant, centipedes and scorpions—all prepared to protect their privacy with poisonous bites or painful stings.[10] An equally threatening array of flora, cacti of all shapes and sizes, dominated the arid slopes and canyons, shredding clothing and embedding their spines in the skin of unwary travelers tempted to stroll in the countryside.

On June 2, Crook had begun his daunting journey aboard a steamer that ran down the coast from San Francisco to Wilmington in southern California, where he was to call upon Colonel Stoneman at his departmental headquarters at nearby Camp Drum. Accompanying the general were McIntosh, Azor Nickerson (to be Crook's aide de camp in Arizona), and a private named Andrew Peisen, a soldier who served as the commander's "striker," or body servant. The latter, called Peisy by the Crook family, was a thirty-one-year-old recruit with light complexion and pale eyes characteristic of his native Schleswig-Holstein who would go on to serve Crook for many years.[11]

While Peisy stowed the general's bags in his cabin, Crook moped about the deck. Aside from his normal uneasiness at finding himself once more at sea, he was deeply resentful of his new assignment, dreaded his upcoming meeting with Stoneman, and was lonely for Mary, who had recently departed for Maryland to reside with her parents until he established himself in Arizona. His state of mind was certainly not improved when McIntosh arrived at the dock so inebriated that he had to be escorted aboard the ship under guard.[12]

Disembarking at Wilmington, Crook gloomily contemplated his obligatory dinner at the Stoneman residence. The criticism that had dogged Colonel Stoneman throughout his tenure in Arizona and his abrupt replacement by an officer junior to him in rank had surely left him in a prickly mood. Under the circumstances, while the colonel was bound to be correct in his manner, Crook, never entirely comfortable in formal social situations, was confident that the event would be awkward, if not downright unpleasant. His dour appraisal proved correct. Without Mary's softening presence, Mrs. Stoneman's insincere attempts at polite conversation made the already tense atmosphere all the more distressing. It was obvious even to Crook, unschooled in the ways of women, that "she would like to tear me to pieces." Feeling a bit sorry for himself, he later mused that, "if she only knew how I hated to go to Arizona, she might feel differently. This assignment had made me the innocent cause of a great deal of heartburning and jealousy." But the two officers somehow made it through the evening, and the next day, a relieved Crook departed for Tucson, leaving Nickerson at Camp Drum for several weeks to deal with paperwork.[13]

The general traveled by stage, crossing into the Arizona Territory at bleak Fort Yuma, the military supply depot for Arizona. There, he unenthusiastically transferred to a military ambulance that would jolt him over the remaining three hundred fifty miles of gravelly desert to Tucson.[14] Arriving at the town on June 19, he found it most unpromising. While John Bourke may have described Tucson as the "Mecca of the dragoon, the Naples of the desert," a less romantic contemporary described it as "a city of mud-boxes, dingy and dilapidated, cracked and baked into a composite of dust and filth; littered about with broken corrals, sheds, bake-ovens, carcasses of dead animals, and broken pottery; barren of verdure, parched, naked and grimly desolate in the glare of a southern sun."[15] Built by the Spanish as a presidio or military garrison on the site of an ancient pueblo, it had passed to the Americans after the Mexican War as part of the New Mexico Territory. Fifteen years later, it became the capital of the newly formed Territory of Arizona. As such, and despite its scruffy appearance and lack of amenities, it was the residence of Governor Safford and the home of Arizona's political and business elite.

Crook stepped off the stage, carrying only a small valise and a shotgun "without which he never travelled anywhere." Left to his own

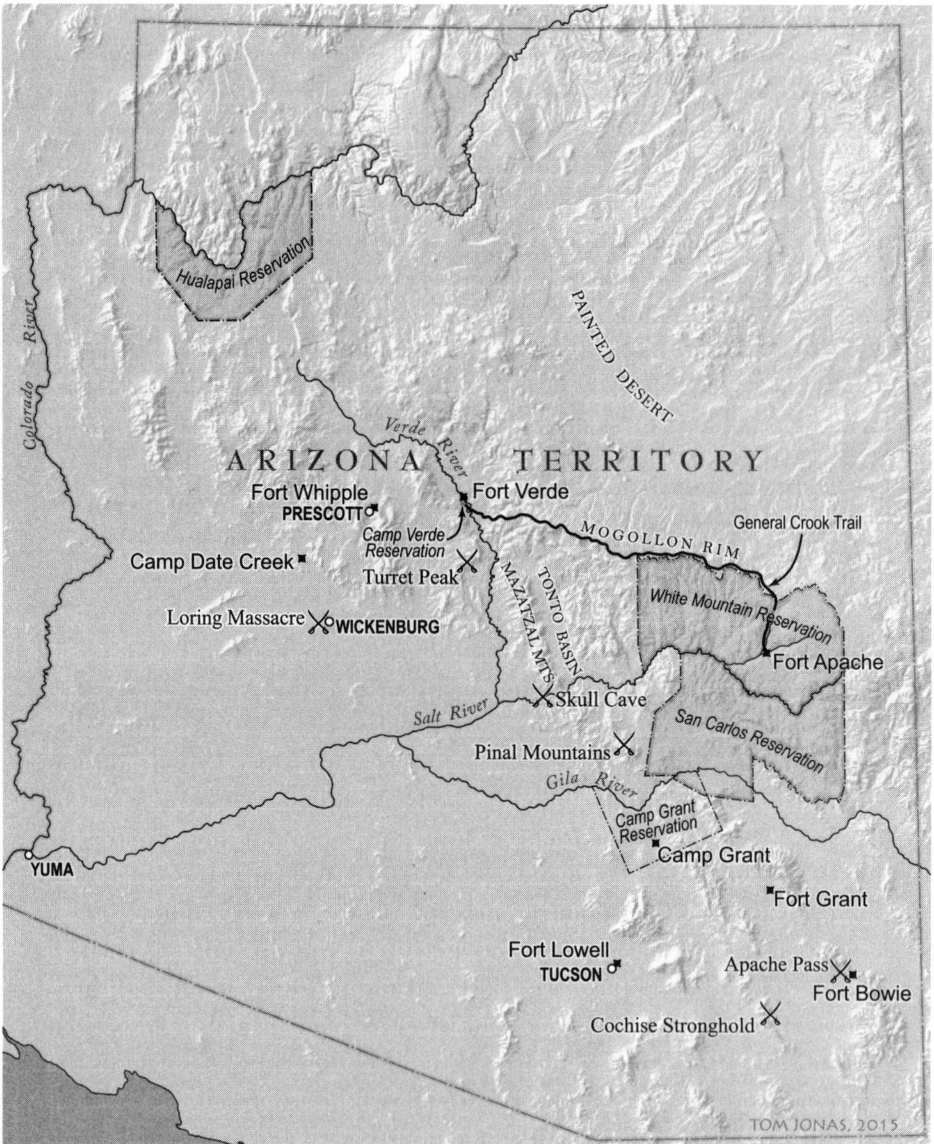

Arizona, 1871–1875.

devices, he found his way to Safford's residence where he took his lunch with the governor, who undoubtedly entertained him with a litany of the bloodshed and destruction inflicted by the Apaches on the good citizens of the Territory. Crook probably listened attentively, but formed no preconceived notions as to the best means to deal with the "Apache problem." To round out the information provided by the governor, he knew he would have to seek out other reliable sources. Accordingly, before the sun had set behind the mountains that cast their evening shadows over Tucson, he had sent out couriers summoning "every officer within the limits of what was then called the southern district of Arizona . . . to report to him" on the conditions prevailing in their areas of command. For the next several weeks, baking in the blazing heat of an Arizona summer, he occupied a temporary headquarters at Camp Lowell outside of Tucson, extracting from all available informants "every . . . item of interest a commander could possibly want to have determined," to assist him, as he put it, in "organizing operations against the Apaches."[16]

The new commander soon learned that the Apaches were universally hated and feared by the local population—Anglo, Mexican, and Indian alike. While the tribe referred to itself simply as N'de or Dine, meaning "the people," other tribes of the Southwest knew them as Apaches, a variant of the Zuni word, *Apiche*, used to denote an enemy.[17] Though possessed of a common language and related customs, over time, the N'de had divided into seven distinct tribes, each carving out its own homeland in Apacheria, a territory extending from Arizona to Texas and down into northern Mexico.[18] Two of these tribes were of primary concern to Crook, the Chiricahuas and the Western Apaches, both of which occupied portions of Arizona. Neither was a single political unit. Instead, to survive in the harsh environment of the desert Southwest, they, like the Paiutes, formed smaller autonomous groupings usually affiliated by blood. Varying in size from thirty-five to two hundred people, they were led by local chiefs, or nantans, who attained their position of authority by demonstrating leadership skills, commonly in warfare, ruling through moral suasion and force of character.[19]

Long before the coming of the white man, the Apaches had adapted to their spare environment by choosing the path of warrior nomads. Similar to the Indians Crook had pursued in the Great Basin, they moved about the land, culling its meager resources according to the season of the year. But in country too arid to provide consistent support, in lean times they survived by raiding their more sedentary neighbors.[20] Few in number, they nevertheless dominated these agrarian peoples by virtue of their superior fighting skills, their genius for concealment and surprise, and their reputation as pitiless combatants. Well before the coming of the white man, the less aggressive inhabitants of the desert Southwest—the Papagos, Maricopas, Pueblos, Zunis, and Pimas—feared these hardened warriors far out of proportion to their numbers. The mere presence of a handful of the Dines in the vicinity of a pueblo would, like a man-eating tiger on the prowl, paralyze entire communities.[21]

The Apaches' warlike habits put them at odds with any peoples within striking distance of their raiding parties. When the Spanish arrived in the sixteenth century, their introduction of cattle and, of even greater interest, horses, to the region attracted the attention of the Apaches. But for the Apaches, unlike the Plains Indians, the horse did not alter either their culture or style of warfare, because they found that in the heat and rough terrain, mounts quickly broke down. Rather, the Dines viewed both cattle and horses as a plentiful and tasty alternative source of protein in a land where meat was scarce. Soon, livestock rustling assumed pride of place in their raiding repertoire.[22]

The Spanish found that extermination, their usual policy of dealing with indigenous populations, was ineffective against the Dines. Their efforts, and those of their successors, the Mexicans, to eliminate the Apache menfolk and enslave their women and children, failed because neither had the manpower or military prowess to defeat this fierce and elusive enemy. Alternative efforts to placate them with offers of sanctuary and trade were inconsistently applied and, therefore, proved equally ineffective, as did an attempt to induce a dependency through a reservation system surprisingly similar to the one that would be adopted by the United States. Treachery became the weapon of choice, augmented by a bounty system that offered rewards for Apache scalps—one hundred pesos (about one hundred dollars) for the scalp of a warrior fourteen years or older, fifty for a woman, and twenty-five for a child.[23] But for the Apaches, revenge was a prime motive for warfare. So, murder and enslavement only compounded the problem and rendered peaceful relations a remote possibility. By the 1840s, when the Americans came upon the scene, whole sections of the desert Southwest had been depopulated by Apache depredations.[24]

In 1848, the United States acquired Arizona and New Mexico by treaty from Mexico after a war of conquest. With the land, the Americans now inherited responsibility for dealing with the Apache "problem," including the seemingly impossible task of diverting the tribe from its long-standing tradition of raiding the Mexican pueblos of Chihuahua and Sonora.[25] Prior to this, Anglo-Dine relations had been generally amicable. While Apacheria remained in Mexican hands, to the Apaches it appeared that the Americans had no interest in remaining on their lands and, in fact, aided the Apache economy by offering guns and whisky for their stolen stock. But with New Mexico and Arizona now American territory, prospectors and ranchers became a permanent presence and a temptation. Raiding and stock theft were so deeply ingrained in the Apache culture that they could not resist an occasional foray against an American ranch or mining camp. In their dealings with the Mexican population, the Apaches were far less restrained.

The Americans were ill-equipped to handle the problem. In the years prior to the Civil War, the army lacked the manpower to adequately garrison the huge territory of the desert Southwest. Nor did the government have a clear policy for dealing with the Indian problem, both in Apacheria and more generally throughout the West. During the Civil War, Apache depredations went unchecked, until the Lincoln administration sent General James H. Carleton, with a force of volunteers known as the California Column, to resolve the issue through a policy of annihilation. As they had with the Spanish and Mexicans, the Apaches responded with an increase in the number and ferocity of their attacks.[26]

After the Civil War, the situation worsened when the Apaches were joined by two bands of the Yavapais. An Arizona tribe consisting of four distinct bands, the Yavapais occupied country in central Arizona too arid and forbidding to be coveted by outsiders. Consequently, they had previously remained aloof from the whites. But as they began to experience pressure from miners drawn to their inhospitable territory by its mineral wealth, two of the bands, the eastern branches of the tribe, allied themselves with the Apache clans with whom they shared the country. Meanwhile, their western cousins attempted to accommodate themselves to the Anglos.[27]

During the immediate postwar period, preoccupied with Reconstruction and reduced in strength, the army was hard-pressed to protect the frontier. In Arizona, they mounted patrols aimed at killing as many Apaches as possible, but their quarry easily eluded them. Frustrated, some post commanders attempted to pacify the Dines by creating feeding stations around their posts where those who tired of life on the run could live peacefully under the protection of the military. Once they were on these informal reservations, the army could keep an eye on them and provide them with rations, obviating their need for raiding. But this concept proved politically premature, opposed not only as a waste of money by Congress, but by local residents who saw no benefit in "coddling" the Apaches.[28]

Colonel Stoneman had been the most recent in a succession of officers to struggle with the problem. Inadequately supported by the War Department, he and his predecessors were constantly harangued by a civilian population convinced that if left to its own devices, it could wipe out the Apache menace far more efficiently than the military. A month before Stoneman's arrival in May 1870, the army, in true bureaucratic fashion, resorted to reorganization to solve the problem. It established a new military department by carving Arizona Territory and a slice of southern California from the military department of California, creating the Department of Arizona, headquartered at Fort Whipple, near the mining center of Prescott. By eliminating a bureaucratic layer between the Department and the Division of the Pacific, the army hoped that the departmental commander could make decisions more rapidly in response to events as they occurred.[29]

Stoneman was not the man to take advantage of this opportunity. Though his military career prior to his assignment to Arizona had been similar in many respects to Crook's—he learned Indian fighting in pre–Civil War California and Oregon and rose to the rank of major general commanding cavalry during the Civil War—his combat service had been problematic, clouded by a lackluster performance at Chancellorsville that suggested a want of aggressiveness and decisiveness that now reappeared in Arizona.[30] Unlike Crook, by temperament a field commander, Stoneman was not an officer who enjoyed leading his men on campaigns. Plagued by hemorrhoids, he was never comfortable in the saddle, preferring to command from behind a desk.[31] Consistent with this inclination, instead of using his posting to Fort Whipple to mount hands-on operations, he moved his headquarters to the more comfortable Drum Barracks in San Diego, as far away from the Territory as he could get without leaving the department.

Though not a fighting officer, by all accounts Stoneman was a competent administrator and a thoughtful man who had a clear view of the problem, if not its solution. The Indian, he reported, "must either starve, steal or be fed; and as they are unwilling to do the former, it becomes simply a question as to which is the best policy, feed them or continue to endeavor to prevent them from stealing." But unfortunately, like his superiors, he seemed unable to answer the question he posed. So, he tried both options, but committed wholly to neither. From his perch on the Pacific, he gave half-hearted support to the establishment of some feeding stations at which Apaches who had given up their warlike ways were provisioned, and directed campaigns against those who did not. His troops, energetic and brave, had killed two hundred Apaches by the fall of 1870, but failed to make a serious dent in the depredations.[32]

As an administrator, Stoneman had a more profound impact. He closed ten of the eighteen posts in the Territory, consolidating his troops and improving the forts that remained operational. He also constructed a rudimentary system of roads connecting them. His next step proved politically unwise. By dismissing a number of superfluous civilian employees and canceling contracts aimed at bilking the government, he undoubtedly increased the efficiency of his operations. But in doing so, he angered beleaguered ranchers and miners, the targets of Apache depredations, while alienating the merchants of southern Arizona who thrived on army business. When taken together with his apparent vacillation between feeding and killing the Indians and his decision to move his headquarters to Drum Barracks, Stoneman managed to bring down upon his head the combined wrath of the entire Territory.[33]

Criticism only increased Stoneman's indecisiveness. Worries about appearing too soft on the Indians seem to have been uppermost in his mind when, during the winter of 1871, he received a request from the commander of Camp Grant, a new post built on the site of one of the original military forts in Arizona, northwest of Tucson.[34] The camp's temporary commander, Lieutenant Royal Emerson Whitman, from Maine and a veteran of the late war, wanted permission to resettle and provision five hundred Aravaipa (Pinal) Apaches on a rancheria near the post.[35] Possessed of what one historian termed "a New Englander's courage and stubbornness, and . . . integrity and inherent democracy of spirit," Whitman defied frontier prejudices and established friendly relations with the band and its chief, Eskiminzin.[36] When they had come to Camp Grant and offered to settle peacefully in its environs, he had requested Stoneman's approval and, in the interim, had allowed them to remain near the fort, cutting hay and wood for the post and nearby ranches. In return, they agreed to cease raiding, give up their arms, and submit to being counted regularly to ensure that they did not use the camp as a base from which to attack settlers in the area.[37]

While ranchers and prospectors in the vicinity of the camp found the Aravaipa settlement to be entirely peaceful, Whitman's efforts were strongly opposed by the citizens of Tucson and Tubac, victimized by frequent raids and only seventy-five miles away from Camp Grant. Aware of popular sentiment, Stoneman avoided responding to Whitman's request. After a six-week delay, he replied through his clerk that no approval would be forthcoming because the lieutenant had improperly failed to summarize the contents of the enclosure on the envelope bearing his message.[38]

Though the Aravaipas remained peaceful, raids by other Apache bands continued in the Tucson vicinity. While little credible evidence linked Eskiminzin's people to the troubles, they served as a convenient substitute for the real culprits, long gone into the mountains.[39] Powerful citizens in Tucson who supplied the army and thus had a vested interest in the continuation of war with the Apaches, sent a delegation headed by William Sanders Oury, a "pillar of Tucson society" and a leading advocate of military action against the Apaches, to ask Colonel Stoneman to clean out the band.[40] The colonel, ambivalent as usual, refused, arguing that he had insufficient troops to spare. He then added, in what was probably intended as an offhand comment, that the citizens of Tucson, the most populous settlement in southern Arizona, ought to be able to protect themselves from the Indians.[41]

Oury and his cohorts took Stoneman's comment as authority to raise a force of 140 Mexicans, Papago Indians, and a few Anglos to wipe out the "murderous Apaches." Leading the way, the club-wielding Papagos, bitter enemies of the Apaches, swept into the sleeping village in a dawn assault. According to Oury, "within half an hour, not a living Apache was to be seen, save children taken prisoners and seven Indians who escaped by being up and ahead of our skirmish line."[42] The assault, from the outset aptly termed a massacre, cost the lives of not less than eighty-five Indians, for the most part women and children.[43] Many of the women showed evidence of having been raped and nearly all the dead were mutilated, including an infant of some ten months, shot twice and with one leg nearly hacked off.[44] Twenty-seven children who survived the massacre were carried off and sold into slavery.

Word of the attack spread quickly. Predictably, throughout the West, the news evoked enthusiasm. The newspapers lionized the killers—within a month, three of the ringleaders were elected to high office in Tucson—and attacked Lieutenant Whitman, while incidentally blaming Colonel Stoneman for his supposed encouragement of lenient treatment for the Apaches.[45] Elsewhere, particularly in the East, the slaughter was greeted with widespread horror and indignation. An infuriated President Grant demanded that the perpetrators be tried, threatening to do so by court-martial should the civil authorities fail to act.[46]

Whether the Camp Grant affair influenced Grant in his decision to replace Stoneman is not clear, but it was only a matter of weeks after the massacre that the president finalized Crook's appointment, an action Arizonans interpreted as a toughening of the government's policy toward the Indians. After all, it was Crook's skills and aggressiveness as an Indian fighter that had attracted Governor Safford's attention in the first place.

Whether Camp Grant had influenced his appointment, the massacre certainly drew Crook's attention. Perhaps even before his meeting with the governor, he had formed the opinion that Stoneman's failure to firmly control the relations between his officers and the Indian population had been a critical factor in the killings. He considered the issue of such importance that one of his first official acts was to issue an order that "no officers in the Department will make peace with, or issue rations (except when in close confinement) to any Indians in this Department now hostile without authority from these headquarters or from higher authority."[47]

CHAPTER FIVE

A March into the Country

By early July, Crook felt that he had accumulated sufficient intelligence from available sources to undertake a reconnaissance in force across the length and breadth of Apacheria, passing through the rugged homelands of tribes considered among the most dangerous in the West. Under conditions that prevailed in Arizona in 1871, any officer contemplating leading such an expedition after less than a month in the Territory might have been considered impulsive and foolhardy. The new departmental commander was neither. A veteran of numerous Indian campaigns in rough and unexplored terrain, he was confident of his ability to command the venture. Moreover, he considered that the need for such a reconnaissance far outweighed the risks. As vigorous campaigning would be required to subdue the Apaches, he knew that the opinions and information he received at Fort Lowell would not be provide a sufficient basis to mount such an offensive. He would have to leave the confining and biased atmosphere of Tucson and personally engage the country and its native inhabitants.[1]

Accompanying him on this mission would be five companies of the Third Cavalry, which he now referred to as his "Destroying Angels," totaling slightly more than two hundred men and supported by a train of pack mules.[2] The Third was officered by a number of seasoned veterans, and included among its ranks a young, intellectual second lieutenant named John Gregory Bourke, whom Crook had recently come to know during his sojourn in Tucson and nearby Fort Lowell. Despite obvious differences in their backgrounds and personalities, Crook, the retiring, frontier-schooled veteran, and the urbane Bourke would soon form a bond based on mutual interests and regard. Their surprisingly complementary relationship would endure for the next two decades and alter the lives of both.

It was Bourke who would chronicle Crook's first scout into Apacheria, recording the details of the expedition in his diary and, of even greater interest, his impressions of the general, often with a fervor that approached idolatry. Relying on a series of journals that he meticulously kept throughout his career, he would later publish a work on his time with the general that for decades would enshrine him as an authentic American hero. For that reason alone, he deserves a detailed introduction.

Bourke was born in 1846 in Philadelphia to well-to-do Irish-born parents who provided him with a comfortable and devoutly Catholic home life. He received a formal Jesuit education and spent his childhood steeped in classical learning. His father, a bookseller, was conversant with Greek, Latin, French, and Gaelic, and had an abiding interest in Irish folklore, while his mother had been well educated in English literature, history, and belles lettres. As a result of their combined influence, John grew into a literate and intellectual young man. But he was no bookworm.[3]

Though only sixteen when rebel forces fired on Fort Sumter, a thirst for adventure, and perhaps idealism, moved him to leave his comfortable youth behind and enlist as a private in the Fifteenth Pennsylvania Volunteer Cavalry. He served with distinction in the war—in 1887 he was retroactively awarded the Medal of Honor for gallantry at Stones River—and because of his record, won an appointment to West Point after Appomattox.[4] Following his graduation, he was commissioned second lieutenant in the Third Cavalry and assigned to Fort Craig, New Mexico Territory. In March of 1870, his unit was transferred to Old Camp Grant in Arizona, where he served under the command of First Lieutenant Howard Bass Cushing, an outstanding officer of whom Bourke wrote, he "killed more savages of the Apache tribe than any other officer or troop in the United States Army had done before or since."[5] Under Cushing's tutelage, Bourke spent many months in the field, gaining considerable firsthand experience tracking and fighting the Apache bands that raided in the vicinity of the post. In May

1871, just before Crook's arrival, Bourke was transferred to Fort Lowell, while Cushing, whom Bourke had come to revere, remained in the field. Within days, the young man received the crushing news that Cushing had been killed in an Apache ambush.[6]

Lieutenant Cushing's death left a void in Bourke's life that he now proceeded to fill through a worshipful attachment to Crook, an adulation that remained largely untarnished despite a later break in their relationship, and lasted well beyond the general's death in 1890. A few months following Crook's funeral, Bourke published *On the Border with Crook*, a memoir that contained many passages about the general that clearly demonstrated the extent of Bourke's attachment to him, including an idealized description of Crook at the time the young lieutenant first met him in Tucson. The forty-three-year-old officer was, as the young lieutenant saw him, "straight as a lance, broad and squared-shouldered, full chested, and with an elasticity and sinewiness which betrayed the latent muscular power gained by years of constant exercise."[7] Though visibly austere in demeanor, Bourke discerned within Crook's Olympian physique a kindly soul, "always interested in the career and progress of young officers under him, and glad to listen to their plans and learn their aspirations." A bit of a prig, Bourke was also delighted to discover that Crook was "a man who never indulged in stimulant of any kind—not so much as tea or coffee—never used tobacco, [and] was never heard to employ a profane or obscene word."[8]

Bourke romantically described Crook's talents as an Indian fighter and woodsman, comparing them to those of the iconic frontiersman, Daniel Boone. Like Boone, he was indifferent to danger, cool under fire, possessed of an inner knowledge of the "wiles and tricks of the enemy, yet modest and disinclined to play the hero." And, also like Boone, or Cooper's Hawkeye, Crook possessed almost superhuman sensibilities. "His keen, blue-gray eyes would detect in a second and at a wonderful distance the slightest movement across the horizon; the slightest sound aroused his curiosity, the faintest odor awakened his suspicions. He noted the smallest depression in the sand, the least deflection in the twigs or branches; no stone could be moved from its position in the trail without appealing at once to his perception."[9]

Crook never read these words and, for his part, during their association rarely mentioned his loyal aide outside official communiques, a practice, which in all fairness, he adhered to with respect to almost everyone close to him, including his spouse. Nevertheless, early on, whether consciously or unconsciously, he recognized in the young lieutenant the consummate publicist, a man who could articulate his qualities in a manner Crook, himself, could not: a Boswell who could ensure that his achievements received their proper due. In addition, while never acknowledging it, he had chanced upon an officer of unquestioned fealty, a worthy and discreet confidant, and an intelligent and sophisticated officer of proven courage and ability, whether in garrison or on the field of battle. In short, Crook had discovered in Bourke a suitable replacement for his old Civil War subordinate and comrade, Rutherford Hayes.[10]

And in the army, where appearances counted, Bourke looked every inch the soldier—five foot ten inches in height, trim, muscular, with "deep set gray eyes under bushy eye brows, a prominent nose and heavy mustache."[11] He was intelligent, and though quick to judge others, a trait he shared with his colonel, he could change his opinion with equal felicity should the individual later measure up. In character, he mirrored Crook's abstemious habits and shared the latter's modesty and taciturnity concerning his own accomplishments. Yet he was an entertaining companion, outgoing, witty, and possessed of a ready Irish charm; and he was widely acclaimed as the "best story teller in the army," a talent that Crook prized.[12] Finally, he grew to share his commander's empathy for the Indians and an interest in their culture, an interest so strong that he would eventually publish several ethnological tracts on the Indians of the Southwest.[13]

While Bourke and his fellow officers remained in the dark about his intentions, Crook laid plans for his reconnaissance. The route he devised would take him through the lands of Apaches and Yavapais, the latter erroneously referred to by whites as the Apache-Yumas and Apache-Mojaves.[14] Ignoring rumors of an impending peace initiative emanating from Washington, Crook conceived of the expedition as a "practice march" in preparation for the aggressive campaigning he was sure would follow. Of equal importance, he hoped that it would demonstrate to the hostile tribes the army's strength and tenacity of purpose.[15]

Initially, he informed his superiors, it would be "against Cochise's band [the Chiricahuas] that I purpose concentrating all my energies for the present." Numbering between eighty and three hundred warriors, they were, Crook had come to believe, the most warlike and menacing of the Apaches.[16] So, they would be the first of several Apache bands he would encounter on a path he had laid out in the shape of a fishhook placed east to west across the south and central Arizona landscape. Tucson, his point of origination, was the barb of the hook that curved eastward into the Chiricahua and Dragoon Mountains before looping north toward Fort Apache, home of the Western (White Mountain) Apaches. From the White Mountains, he would pursue the shank of the hook westward, along the Mogollon Range, a wild, uncharted plateau scored by deep canyons. This region and the adjacent Tonto Basin were the rugged wilderness home of the Tonto Apaches, identified by Bourke as "the fiercest band of this wild and apparently incorrigible family," and the Yavapais, fearsome warriors in their own right.[17] The expedition would last for over six weeks and cover a distance of 675 miles before ending at Camp Verde, Fort Whipple, and the nearby mining town of Prescott.

To guide him through this as-yet-unmapped territory, Crook raised and equipped a body of scouts that he put under the command of Archie McIntosh. They were a mix of Indians and Mexicans that Lieutenant Bourke characterized as "a fair sample of the social driftwood of the Southwest." The Mexicans had been selected on the dubious recommendation of Tucson's governing class, who regarded them as endowed with a superior knowledge of the country and "the habits and modes of Indian warfare," based upon their performance during the Civil War.[18] The Indians, for the most part drawn from tribes traditionally hostile to the Apaches, were chosen because the general's previous experience had convinced him that Indians were best suited as guides and trackers. These tribesmen were a temporary expedient. Crook hoped to replace them soon with Apaches. The scouts departed the post the day before the troops, with orders to scour the countryside for signs of Indians.[19]

At 6 A.M. on July 11, the summer heat already building under the early morning sun, Crook rode out of Tucson at the head of his column. Arizonans who assembled by the dusty road to view his departure might have been forgiven their quizzical glances as they watched him ride past. Contemporary photos show the general with his hair clipped short to combat the desert heat and dust, and his heavy sandy beard parted and braided into two forks. Eschewing the heavy blue wool uniform of an army officer, he wore a tan canvas jacket and pants, cooler and more resistant to cactus thorns; and, in place of the kepi or slouch hat ordinarily worn by troops of that era, he favored a cork sun helmet, purportedly of Japanese origin, that perched on his head like an inverted soup bowl.[20] In lieu of a horse, he rode a powerful mule named Apache and carried his shotgun at the ready across the pommel of his saddle. All in all, he presented an undeniably eccentric appearance for the leader of a military expedition.

As the temperature rose to a sizzling 110 degrees Fahrenheit in the shade, the command proceeded through desert terrain 110 miles to Apache Pass, a crucial passage through the Chiricahua Mountains used by stagecoaches traveling between the United States and California. It was a favorite haunt of the Chiricahuas, so the column's scouts ranged widely to the sides and front, alert to the possibility of an ambush.[21] Meanwhile, Crook's officers continually reported to the general on the topography of the surrounding country and any Indian sign along the trail. In response, he peppered them and the scouts with questions about the names, uses, and habits of each species of flora and fauna encountered, amazing them with his almost complete retention of the information they imparted. Young Bourke was awed by his commander's attention to detail. "Nothing was too insignificant to be noted, nothing too trivial to be treasured up in our memories."[22]

The column reached Fort Bowie, the post guarding Apache Pass, on July 14th. Three days later, they headed north, cautiously delaying their departure until nightfall to conceal their movements.[23] They were now in the heart of Chiricahua country, but at first saw no sign of their recent presence. On the second day, however, as they rode down the Sulphur Springs valley, they sighted dust in the distance. Convinced that it signaled the presence of Indians, Crook decided to set an ambush at a spring that he believed to be the band's destination. He assigned one of his officers, Captain Alexander Moore, to carry out his plan. Disregarding the need for concealment, Moore led his troop straight into the valley, which, as Crook sarcastically noted, brought him in plain sight of the Indians. The band faded quickly into the mountains rather than confront a superior force. In his memoir, the general contemptuously recalled that Moore was deficient in "one of the most essential qualities of a soldier," a reference to his lack of courage, as Crook believed that the captain had deliberately revealed his presence to the Indians to avoid a fight.[24] Lacking evidence to support his supposition, however, Crook did not court-martial Moore, an act of forbearance that would not be repeated when, five years later, on the Powder River, the officer again ignored orders to save his neck.[25]

Following the near encounter with the Chiricahuas, the column continued north to Camp Apache, home of the White Mountain or Coyotero Apaches, arriving there on August 12. The White Mountains had traditionally maintained good relations with the Anglos, and now they welcomed the general. Initially dubious that any Apache could be considered friendly after hearing the tales of bloodshed and torture told by the citizens of Tucson, Crook was soon won over by the professions of friendship offered by their chiefs, Miguel and Pedro, and their apparently sincere desire to "put themselves 'on the white man's road.'"[26]

The colonel responded to their overtures with a brief lecture on the dire consequences of resistance to the white man and the benefits of assimilation to his culture. He intended, he told the bemused chiefs, to end the war against the white man and "to start out in person and see to it that the last man returned to the Reservations or died in the mountains." Strangely, despite Crook's belligerent tone, Bourke noted that the Indians listened attentively, "at intervals expressing approbation . . . by heavy grunts and the utterance of the monosyllable 'Inju' (good)."[27]

Crook was sufficiently impressed by the White Mountains that he chose this moment to dismiss his Mexican scouts, who had fallen far short of his expectations, and to replace them with Coyoteros. It was a felicitous choice. They would serve initially as guides and trackers, but soon proved so trustworthy that they became his shock troops in his war against other Apache bands. They would receive the same pay and allowances as white troops, an article of faith with Crook, who held that providing Indian scouts with benefits equal to those of Regulars was worth more to them than "all the blankets and promises Government could heap upon them."[28]

Crook's ability to recruit Indian scouts to fight other Indians, especially Indians with whom they had formerly been allied, seems almost counterintuitive. Vincent Colyer, who would soon arrive in Arizona on a peace mission from President Grant, contended that the White

Mountains were coerced, believing "that they had to enlist in the service or be considered enemies." The long, uninterrupted, and loyal service of the tribe seems to belie this notion.[29]

Several factors made military service in the scouts attractive to the warriors on the reservation. Economic necessity clearly played a major role. Regular rations and a soldier's pay appealed greatly to a people living on the very edge of subsistence, particularly after the Anglo invasion had deprived them of their traditional sources of supply, raiding and hunting. From a cultural perspective, enlistment provided the only means for agency Indians, trained as warriors from childhood, to achieve rank and status in their society and yet remain within the parameters set for them by the government. Finally, as one historian noted, given their cumstances, it was not that difficult to recruit Indians to scout or fight against their own people. Indians of the time, unlike whites, did not have the same sense of racial identity that allowed Anglos to make common cause against "Indians." They had little compunction about helping the whites make war on tribes and even clans other than their own. This was especially true among the Apache bands steeped in the culture of revenge. Motivated by blood feuds and unresolved enmities, warriors eagerly sought opportunities to avenge themselves on other clans and even, on occasion, factions within their own band. So, for example, Crook was able to recruit White Mountains by taking advantage of a long-standing animosity between them and their Tonto neighbors.[30]

Under the leadership of Corydon Eliphaler Cooley, Civil War veteran, former prospector, and husband to two of Chief Pedro's daughters, the White Mountain recruits formed a nucleus around which Crook built a cadre of scouts. Among the thirty or so men originally enlisted was Alchesay, Pedro's son, about eighteen at the time, who would become one of Crook's most valued allies.[31]

So that "there could be no mistake in future as to who were our friends and who our enemies" in the upcoming campaigns, Crook took a census of all Apaches on the White Mountain Reservation. He then "enrolled" them, providing them with identity tags—an idea Whitman had adopted at Camp Grant—which they were required to carry while off the reservation.[32] Enrollment allowed reservation agents to account for rations and, if need be, prove that their Indians had not been involved in depredations. But the practice was considered degrading by the Indians, who felt more like prisoners than protected allies. Later, as warfare in Apacheria intensified, Crook introduced even more stringent controls, requiring Indians to move within a mile of the post and report daily to be counted or be considered a prisoner of war. This aroused such deep discontent among these loyal allies that he was forced to rescind his decision.[33]

As Crook prepared to embark into the Mogollon Range, the most dangerous leg of the journey, he found his departure from Camp Apache delayed. Prior to leaving Tucson, he had heard, but thought little of, rumors that President Grant had embarked on an initiative to resolve the Apache problem through peaceful means. Now, in mid-August, after several weeks on the trail and out of touch with recent developments, he discovered that, while he had been preparing for his campaign, Vincent Colyer—Grant's point man for the peace initiative—had arrived in the Southwest and had begun peace talks with the Chiricahuas on their temporary reservation at Cañada Alamosa, New Mexico. Crook first learned of this when a delegation composed of a Mexican official and several Chiricahua warriors, whom the White Mountains identified as among "Cochise's worst men," rode into Camp Apache as he was about to depart. They carried a letter from Colyer that identified them and described their mission—to summon Cochise to the Cañada Alamosa peace talks. To Crook, the idea of a negotiated peace with the Chiricahuas was preposterous and a threat to his efforts to win the peace by subjugating the Apaches on the battlefield. The general knew that without Cochise's presence, Colyer's peace talks would collapse. So, to prevent his attendance, Crook treated the delegation as spies, peremptorily ordering their return to Cañada Alamosa, guaranteeing Cochise's absence and thus effectively undermining, at least for the present, the peace talks.[34] He later tried to justify his action by asserting that Cochise's warriors lacked any commitment to peace and were merely using the Cañada Alamosa Reservation as a base and a place to dispose of stolen property. Under these circumstances, Crook insisted, he had every reason to arrest the envoys, but had refrained from doing so only because he "did not want even a semblance of interference with the Peace Department."[35]

Having done what damage he could to Colyer's efforts, Crook resumed his journey into the heart of Apacheria. For this stage of the expedition, he split his command so as to cover both the Tonto Basin and the Mogollon Plateau. Three cavalry troops and a contingent of White Mountains, under Captain Guy V. Henry, one of Crook's more experienced officers, were assigned to scout the Basin. Anticipating that this area would be the scene of intensive campaigning in the near future, Crook's purpose was to acclimate Henry's officers and men to conditions in the area and to test the capabilities of the newly recruited scouts. As Henry crossed the Basin, Crook and the remainder of his column would march across 216 miles of uncharted wilderness that was the Mogollon Plateau, roughly paralleling the captain's route.[36]

Crook's party had no sooner mounted the plateau than the general, riding in the lead with Bourke and several other officers, received fire from a party of Tontos. The officers hastily dove for cover, but the Tontos broke off the action when they saw the size of the column coming behind the officers. They continued to avoid the troops for the remainder of the march, allowing the colonel to fully concentrate his energies on traversing what turned out to be exceedingly harsh terrain.

As Crook's troops proceeded west toward Fort Whipple, their ultimate destination, they found their route confined to a narrow strip of terrain that hugged the extreme rim of the plateau, wedged between a precipitous escarpment on their southern flank, and to their immediate north, country broken by steep canyons. No trails existed and his scouts were unfamiliar with the area, forcing Crook to rely on Archie McIntosh's instincts, as they hacked a rudimentary track along the rim. Their task was complicated by a lack of drinking water for men and animals, a surprising circumstance in country green with stands of pine, juniper, and oak. Fortunately, a providential thundershower and the discovery of a clear spring, later named General Springs in honor of Crook, resolved what could have been a serious problem. After leaving the spring, the column, guided by little more than McIntosh's intuition, veered to the southwest and eventually hit a supply road to Prescott that General Stoneman had built during his tenure. Following it, on August 27 they arrived without further incident at Camp Verde, just east of Fort Whipple.[37]

The route that Crook pioneered was widened the following year to allow its use by wagons and became known as the Crook Trail. It evolved into a vital supply line connecting Forts Whipple and Verde in western Arizona to Fort Apache in the east; and, during the Tonto campaign, it was patrolled by Crook's troops, preventing the Tontos from escaping the Basin onto the Plateau. Because of its importance, it would be designated Arizona's first state historic trail.[38]

Aside from blazing a significant route across the Mogollon Plateau, Crook's expedition served several important purposes. It demonstrated to the people of Arizona that, unlike Colonel Stoneman, he was willing to go into the field to attain his objectives; it familiarized his troops with the topography of much of that portion of Arizona in which he planned to campaign over the coming year; it confronted the Apache in his lair, thereby diluting his fearsome reputation and instilling confidence in the minds of his soldiers; and finally, it provided the opportunity to recruit and test a new ally, the White Mountain Apaches, whose participation would be invaluable in the campaigns to come.

CHAPTER SIX

The Sword and the Olive Branch

At Verde, Crook received a dispatch pouch containing his accumulated mail. Mixed in with correspondence needing his attention were copies of the local papers from the past several weeks, which reported the details of Colyer's arrival in Arizona. The news stories confirmed Crook's worst fears and were a source of monumental frustration since, up to this point, he had believed that he would have a free hand in bringing about a military solution to the Apache problem. That autonomy now seemed about to evaporate, superseded by a presidential initiative that had its origins in the Camp Grant Massacre, rumors of army brutality in dealing with the Indians, and growing evidence of endemic corruption in the reservation system. These issues had moved the Grant administration, at least for the time being, to resolve the Indian problem by peaceful means rather than military force.

Incompetence and corruption in the reservation system transcended the situation in Apacheria, involving tribes throughout the West, dating back to 1849 when management of Indian affairs, previously vested in the army, had been transferred to the Department of the Interior's Indian Bureau. Under Bureau management, with little oversight from Interior, the reservations had become a rich source of patronage appointments. Indian agents chosen for their political connections profited from their positions by contracting with corrupt suppliers who provided inferior and adulterated goods at inflated prices to the Indians and shared the resulting largesse with the agents. The alliance

the act of giving away money

of government agents and private contractors, sometimes referred to as the Indian Ring, redoubled its profits when the Indians, driven to desperation by short rations and shoddy merchandise, returned to the warpath. This further enriched the Ring's participants, who then became suppliers to the army. The situation in Arizona, where there were as yet no reservations, was slightly different. As aptly summed up by General Ord, "almost the only paying business the white inhabitants have . . . is supplying the troops. . . . If the quartermasters and paymasters were to stop payment . . . , a great majority of the white settlers must be compelled to quit. Hostilities are, therefore kept up with a view to supporting the inhabitants. . . ."[1] Thus, in the Territory, the Ring opposed peace (and a reservation system) as a threat to the profits they reaped supplying the military.[2]

Following the Civil War, corruption on the reservations became so prevalent and led to such suffering that the government initiated an investigation of the Bureau, exposing many of the Ring's practices. Public outrage, mostly in the East, moved Congress in 1869 to authorize the appointment of a Board of Indian Commissioners to exercise oversight over management of the reservations. The board diligently pursued its work in the belief that ending the abuses would reduce tribal unrest, and convince the Indians to accept life on the reservations and assimilate into white, Christian society. Its vigorous public championing of Indian rights made Americans who lived far from the frontier more aware of abuses in the system.[3]

While fairly popular in the East, the Board's work was widely ridiculed in the West, though it adhered to the frontier objective of removing the Indian as an obstacle to untrammeled exploitation of their lands. The commissioners differed from the frontiersmen only as to means, preferring subjugation through the benign influence of civilization, rather than by force and in some cases extermination, solutions favored by citizens on the frontier.[4] Soldiers like Crook, who had been fighting Indians for decades, also preferred the reservations to genocide. But they broke with the Board over the best method of achieving their objective, convinced that military action was a necessary precursor to the civilizing process.

As recently as 1867, President Grant had taken the position that the western tribes ought to be destroyed or made prisoners of war.[5] But perhaps influenced by his old friend and advisor, Eli Parker, a Seneca sachem whom he appointed head of the Indian Bureau, he became a proponent of what became known as his peace policy. This new initiative, sometimes referred to as the Quaker Policy because of the influence of the Society of Friends in its conception, called for the appointment of men of the cloth in place of political appointees as agents and staff on the reservations. Such men, it was thought, would end corruption, and hence unrest, while their Christianizing influence would hasten the Indians' progress toward civilization. For those tribes for whom reservations had not yet been established, including most of the Apache and Yavapai bands, peaceful negotiations would replace force in inducing them to settle on lands identified as suited to their needs. The Friends envisioned military action only as a last resort.[6]

Though the president had sent Crook to Arizona to carry the sword to the Apaches, a tribe regarded by most military men as incorrigible, Grant was so outraged by the Camp Grant Massacre that he now veered toward application of his peace policy to the desert Southwest. He selected Vincent Colyer from New York, a Quaker and secretary of the Board of Peace Commissioners, to carry the olive branch. For that purpose, Grant clothed him with full authority "to take such actions as in your judgment may be . . . most proper for locating the nomadic tribes of those Territories upon suitable reservations, bringing them under the control of the proper officers of the Indian department and supplying them with necessary subsistence and clothing, and whatever may be needed."[7]

The man upon whom Grant bestowed such broad powers was not a popular figure in the West. Hubert Bancroft, the California historian, sourly commented that the New Yorker was "fully imbued with the belief that the Apaches were innocent victims of oppression, and that the whites were wholly to blame for past hostilities . . . he would listen to nothing not confirmatory of his preconceived views, scorning to seek information from rascally citizens, the bloody-minded officers, or anybody else who knew anything about the real state of affairs."[8] Most Arizonans subscribed to that view. To them, the peace commissioner represented eastern politics at its most ignorant and despicable. The newspapers nurtured and intensified this animus. In Prescott, John Marion, an obsessive Apache hater and owner/editor of the *Arizona Miner*, editorialized, "We ought, in justice to our murdered dead, to dump the old devil [Colyer] into the shaft of some mine and pile rocks upon him until he is dead."[9] Crook sarcastically referred to him as "Vincent the Good." Governor Safford viewed him as simply deluded.[10]

By all accounts, Colyer, though inflexibly devoted to his opinions, did not deserve this abuse. He was in fact a man of unquestioned integrity and uncommon decency. During the Civil War, he had abandoned a lucrative career as an accomplished landscape artist to accept leadership of the United States Christian Commission, caring for the wounded. Later in the war, he devoted his energies to the support of newly freed slaves, and after the government authorized the formation of colored units, he recruited and trained a black regiment.[11] When the war ended, he continued his work with freedmen, and from there moved on to the Indians. Imbued with confidence that he was doing God's work, Colyer treated the scorn heaped upon him in Arizona with serene indifference. Addressing complaints that he had failed to consult with white citizens in his report, as well as the numerous threats against his life, he commented that he took slight notice of them "as the business for which he was sent was accomplished" and he trusted that his vindication would come with time.[12]

Crook agreed with Colyer that the Apaches were not incorrigible enemies of civilization and his belief that they could be pacified by resettlement on reservations. While not minimizing their warlike nature, he ascribed what he termed their "villainies" to the imperative of survival in the harsh environment of Arizona. "Living in a country the natural products of which will not support him, [the Indian] has either to cultivate the soil or steal, and as our vacillating policy satisfies him we are afraid of him, he chooses the latter, also as requiring less labor and being more congenial to his natural instincts."[13] The reservation system would rescue the Indian from the bonds of savagery by affording him relief from the single-minded pursuit of survival. On the reservation, Crook believed, even the most warlike tribes could evolve into productive members of civilized America through the introduction of Christianity, Western education, and modern farming. The idea that the Indian might not see a benefit to abandoning his culture and traditional lifestyle was considered irrelevant. Once he saw the advantages of assimilation, he would gladly come along. These views, formed through the prism of Crook's observations on the Pacific Coast and in the Great Basin, were based on the current anthropological theory that all societies evolved along a continuum from savagery (Indian) to civilization (Euro-American). Today, the destructive impact of the reservation system is widely recognized. In Crook's day, it was an enlightened alternative to genocide.[14]

As with the frontiersmen, the crux of Crook's opposition to the work of the Peace Commission, and to Colyer in particular, was a dispute over means rather than objectives. To him, and others in the military, it seemed obvious that the warlike nomadic tribes would not passively surrender their traditional freedoms in return for confinement on a small patch of barely habitable land. First, they would have to be convinced of the hopelessness of resistance. And to the career officer, the peace commissioner's religious zeal was no substitute for the carbine given the task at hand. Because he viewed Colyer's advocacy of peaceful persuasion as so inherently unrealistic, Crook mistrusted the commissioner's motives and was unfairly persuaded that he was a tool of the Indian Ring. The passage of time never caused him to alter this patently unfair assumption. Years later, he would insist that "Vincent Colyer had been sent out by the 'Indian Ring' to interfere with my operations . . . , and was coming to [Camp] Apache . . . to make peace with the Apaches by the grace of God."[15]

Despite Crook's lack of faith in the commissioner's mission, he knew that if he continued his campaigning and Colyer failed, he, not Colyer, would take the blame. Accordingly, he countermanded all orders "looking to active operations against the hostiles," and directed his officers to render the Quaker representative "all assistance within their powers in the carrying out of his peace policy."[16] Among the operations he suspended was the enlistment of Apache scouts, a determination the optimistic Colyer thought "[spoke] much for his humanity and good sense."[17]

Having done what he could to protect his political flanks, Crook repaired to Fort Whipple on the outskirts of Prescott, previous capital of the Territory, to await the outcome of events. With streets lined with American-style homes behind neat picket fences, Prescott formed a striking contrast to the Mexican ambiance of Tucson. But nostalgia for the East played no role in the general's decision to relocate to the "ramshackle, tumble-down palisade of unbarked pine logs" that was Fort Whipple in 1871. Having abandoned Camp Drum, Crook preferred this post for his headquarters over Tucson because it was nearer to California, his source of resupply and the communications hub for the military in the West.[18]

Crook was not idle during this period, using the unavoidable hiatus in his operations to prepare for the campaign that he was convinced would follow the inevitable collapse of the peace initiative. Simultaneously, he continued to warn of the consequences he believed woud flow from Colyer's efforts. To his aides he said, "the distrust of the savages for the white man, and all he said and did, had become so confirmed that it would take more than one or two pleasant talks full of glowing promises to eradicate it."[19] To his superiors he predicted, "if the Indians don't soon break out in open hostilities, they will do what is much worse, that is, while their old and decrepid [*sic*] women and children (who are their only encumbrances in the shape of baggage) are being protected and supplied on Reservations, the warriors will . . . keep up their bloody work and, when followed, will glide over the rocks and mountains like birds and make their . . . subjugation next thing to an impossibility." On the other hand, he wrote, "if this entire Indian question be left to me, with my present arrangements and knowledge, I have not the slightest doubt of my ability to conquer a lasting peace with this Apache race in a comparatively short space of time and a peace which will not only save the Treasury millions of dollars, but will save the lives of a good many innocent whites and Indians." To give substance to his claim and demonstrate the breadth of his knowledge, he laid out the disposition, approximate strength, and degree of enmity of every tribal entity in eastern and central Arizona that his proposed campaign might involve, whether as allies or foes.[20]

Though convinced of his ability to make good on his word, Crook understood that it would not be an easy job given the "inaccessibility and extent of [the Apache's] country."[21] While he awaited the failure of Colyer's mission, he planned his campaign, concentrating on overcoming the Apaches' two main assets, their mobility and clever use of terrain. Using Captain Henry's expedition into the Tonto Basin and his own experiences on the Pacific Coast and in the Great Basin as models, he hit upon a deceptively simple tactic. He would employ independent columns (he called them "expeditions"), concentrating on one hostile band at a time, coming at them from multiple directions, remaining in the field until the band was so exhausted that it would "surrender on any terms."[22]

He was confident that he had sufficient troops for the task, but additional horses and mules would be needed, as the hardships of campaigning in the desert and rough mountains of Arizona had rendered over one-third of his stock unserviceable.[23] His preference in the dry, rough country of Arizona was for the mule rather than the horse, and the pack mule rather than the wagon. Wagons, he had learned, were ill-suited to the rugged trails of the region. And those currently available had been built in the humid Pacific Northwest. In the hot and dry desert climate, their frames and wheels would shrink, causing the wagons to fall apart.[24] To remedy this defect, he asked that replacements be constructed at Fort Yuma of timber seasoned in the desert climate.[25]

But it was the mules and pack trains that absorbed his obsessive attention. By now, his knowledge of mule power was so refined that he knew the exact size and weight of the animal best suited to the terrain, and even its proper age range.[26] And he was just as well versed in the arcana of pack train management, from the details of weight and distribution of loads to the knots used and the qualifications of his packers. When his superiors complained about the use of scarce funds to hire civilian packers, he quickly pointed out that, based on his experience, soldiers could not readily be trained to the task. Professional packers were essential to maximize efficiency.[27] He had tested the abilities of such professionals during the recent expedition and had come to know them well. Each night, he sat by their campfires, "listening intently to their 'reminiscences'" and gauging their individual qualities, strengths, and weaknesses.[28] His pack master, or chief packer, was Tom Moore, a Virginian who had accompanied him from Idaho. He trusted the man's character and ability completely. Moore, who had originally come to California in '49 to mine for gold, would become such an expert in pack train management that he would ultimately write a treatise on it that would become the pack masters' bible.[29]

While Colyer worked to complete his peace negotiations, Crook kept his packers on the payroll, sending them out constantly to carry supplies to the various outposts. Because these practice runs gave his men valuable experience while toughening their mules, he brushed aside the complaints from his superiors about the cost and from private haulers who lost business as a result of his preference for mules over wagons.

The bedrock of any campaign against the Apaches would be his troops. Their health and welfare figured prominently in Crook's correspondence during this period. As Camps Verde and Grant were located in malarial areas, he asked that they be moved to more healthful ground. He noted that conditions in Arizona were particularly hard on soldiers' clothing and shoes and therefore requested that their clothing allowance be increased. And he asked his superiors for authority to construct improved accommodations for the men, pointing out that many were currently forced to sleep permanently in tents, while barracks, where they existed, were adobe shacks, dusty and full of bugs and scorpions in the hot season and leaky and muddy in the rains. Finally, aware of the value of prompt communications when fighting a mobile foe, he lobbied for the extension of telegraph service from California to the Territory.[30]

As Crook prepared for war, Vincent Colyer sought to avoid it. Using his delegated authority, he created reservations on lands he judged appropriate to the needs of the Indians, yet, to avoid friction, as remote as possible from transportation routes and areas of white habitation. After visits to the Chiricahua and the White Mountain bands, he traveled to Camp Grant to meet the 250 survivors of the Aravaipa massacre and their chief, Eskiminzin. He was warmly received.[31] But not long after his arrival, his hosts took fright when a large body of armed townspeople from Tucson was reported traveling toward the camp, their intentions unknown. Fearing the Aravaipas might flee into the mountains or, even worse, become the victims of a second bloody confrontation, Colyer asked the post commander, Captain William Nelson, to order the whites to turn back. Reluctantly, the captain obeyed, and Colyer later asserted that his prompt action prevented a repeat of the massacre.[32] Crook took a different view. Though in the past he had voiced sympathy for Indians victimized by settlers, he was incensed when he learned of this incident. Keenly aware of the anti-Apache sentiments in the Mexican and Anglo communities, he believed that Nelson's action would only provoke further hostility toward the military and the Indians and heighten the risk of another Camp Grant Massacre. In a sharply worded message to the post commander, he rebuked him for blocking civilians from using a public road.[33] Like his General Order forbidding his post commanders from establishing feeding stations for the Indians without his express consent, calling Nelson to task demonstrated Crook's sensitivity to frontier animosity toward the Indians and his interest in heading off white vigilantism whenever possible.

Similar concerns seemed to have been at work in his ongoing vendetta with Lieutenant Whitman, Camp Grant's controversial protector of the Aravaipa Apaches.[34] Southern Arizona's outrage at Whitman's advocacy of the Aravaipas' cause found expression on the editorial page of Tucson's *Arizona Citizen.* On September 2, the paper published a scurrilous article excoriating the lieutenant's character and accusing him of improper conduct, alleged to include drunken carousing and a fondness for "dusky maidens." While such charges, if proven, might have genuinely upset the puritanical Crook, his more pragmatic side saw an unparalleled opportunity to remove a polarizing officer from the scene. Before taking any action, he properly declared his intention to investigate the accuracy of the charges. If they were accurate, he intended to convoke a court-martial to rule on the lieutenant's fitness for military service. Unfortunately, his "investigation" was woefully superficial, consisting of no more than an interview with the editor of the *Citizen*, and a request that he retract his remarks unless he believed he could substantiate them.[35] When the editor stood by his story, Crook preferred charges against Whitman and a court-martial was convened in December.

Whitman asked that the charges be dismissed, claiming that they were motivated by malice and had no foundation in fact. Though subsequent events indicated that there may have been some basis to several of the allegations—Whitman did, on occasion, drink to excess and when drunk, tended to behave in an outrageous manner[36]—the court-martial panel agreed that the editor's evidence was questionable and his motives suspect. Accordingly, they dismissed the charges without hearing testimony.[37]

Crook angrily refused to endorse the panel's decision, declaring that its failure to entertain testimony had deprived the lieutenant of an opportunity to vindicate his honor and, conversely, had prevented the service from having a chance to remove an unworthy officer. But since the panel's officers had transferred to other posts, the case could not be retried, and Crook reluctantly ordered Whitman restored to duty at

Camp Grant.[38] Then, learning that the lieutenant's regiment was being transferred to the Department of the Missouri, he rescinded his order and directed Whitman to depart with his unit, thinking that he had finally rid himself of the problem.[39] Much to his chagrin, his superiors reversed his decision and returned Whitman to Camp Grant. Without further legal recourse, a frustrated Crook fired off a final protest to the assistant adjutant general in San Francisco. "There is an intense feeling against this officer and against the conduct of affairs at the Reserve, which his removal would certainly allay . . . ," he wrote. "To retain him here is to keep up the excitement, to complicate matters still more, and embarrass me with his constant turmoil with its citizens, which is liable to culminate in another outrage similar to that which took place in May."[40] For the time being, his complaints fell on deaf ears, but he had by no means given up his quest to remove the lieutenant from the Territory.

Colyer, meanwhile, continued his mission, creating reservations for the Tontos and Yavapais in addition to the one for the Chiricahuas.[41] Then, satisfied that he had successfully completed his task, on October 4 he concluded his Arizona assignment with a courtesy call on the department's commander at his Fort Whipple headquarters. Crook rose to the occasion, receiving the New Yorker "quite cordially," making available his own quarters to ensure the commissioner's comfort.[42] Colyer would later blandly report that "the general and I differed somewhat in opinion as to the best policy to be pursued toward the Apaches, but as these differences were honestly entertained and kindly expressed, it did not lessen the cordiality of our intercourse. . . ." In truth, the visit was somewhat less harmonious. Crook had urged that the two men speak frankly. Colyer agreed and opened by expressing regret at Crook's reprimand of Captain Nelson. He then tried to balance his criticism by complimenting Crook for his overall support of the peace initiative. Less inclined to diplomacy, Crook tartly responded that he had no confidence in the peace policy; but since the commissioner had come to Arizona clothed with superior authority, he had given him his full support, "so that in case his policy was a failure, none of it would be laid at my door."[43] Despite the tension evidenced by this exchange, the two men were able to agree on at least one point. The transfer of one of the Yavapai reservations would be delayed until the following spring to avoid any friction the two men agreed might be anticipated were the tribe moved during the winter, as Colyer had originally proposed.[44]

On October 7, Colyer, having concluded his business at Whipple, departed for Washington. En route, he met with General Schofield at his San Francisco headquarters, smoothly reassuring him that relations between the commissioner and the department commander couldn't have been better. No one appears to have been deluded by this charade. Within three days of Colyer's departure, Crook wrote to Schofield, complaining that the commissioner was simply a stalking horse for the Peace Party, which sought to prove that the military was the main stumbling block to peace with the Apaches. In a paranoid outburst, he claimed that their objective was to provoke him into a war against the Apaches, so that he "would be abused as the great North American Butcher."[45] For his part, Colyer wrote Columbus Delano, secretary of the interior, declaring "Crook's retention as department commander 'jeopardizes the success of the President's Indian policy here.'"[46]

To preclude possible sabotage of his negotiations, Colyer speedily obtained presidential endorsement of the reservations he had established. With the president's backing, Secretary of the Interior Delano could now issue orders relocating all roving bands onto the lands designated by the peace commissioner. There, they would be protected and fed so long as they remained peaceful.

Notwithstanding Crook's grumbling, Colyer's mission had produced some, if not all, the results the New Yorker had hoped for. Most importantly, though the reservations he created would later be abandoned for other locations, the principle had been established: the Apaches who wished to give up the warpath now had a place to retire to safely. According to one source, "those who are settled on the reservations represented fully one half of all Indians who have been at war with the Americans. They numbered about four thousand souls."[47] This left the more difficult task to the army—to ensure that the remaining Indians found their way onto their assigned reservations.

Of some comfort to Crook was the administration's decision to appoint army officers as Indian agents until suitable civilian replacements could be found, a determination that guaranteed him some control over Indian policies in Arizona, at least in the short term.

Regarding Indians who refused to come in, Crook's troops had only limited authority. The army could track down and punish only those directly linked to specific depredations. With respect to the rest, Indians who refused to submit to the reservation system, for the time being, the military would have to rely on peaceful persuasion to induce them to surrender.[48]

CHAPTER SEVEN

The Wickenburg Massacre

November 1871

Scarcely a week had elapsed following Colyer's return to Washington when a violent incident occurred that cast a long shadow on the commissioner's assertions regarding the peaceful nature of the Indians of Arizona and threatened to throw Grant's peace policy into confusion. On November 5, near Wickenburg, a mining town in the southwestern corner of the Territory, a stagecoach was attacked and six of its eight passengers killed, one of whom was scalped. The mailbag had been rifled, but most of its contents, including several large-denomination bills, were left behind, giving the appearance that the attack had been made by Indians, generally believed to be unaware of the value of paper money. Among the dead was Fredrick W. Loring, a Boston journalist and a well-known and respected member of New England's intellectual community, a constituency heretofore unstinting in its support of the president's peace policy. Loring had just completed work as the secretary of a surveying expedition that had explored the upper reaches of the Colorado River and was returning to San Francisco, anticipating no danger from the Indians.[1]

Newspapers across the country headlined the tragedy. Some included a report from a survivor asserting that the attackers were without a doubt Yavapais from the nearby Date Creek Reservation.[2] As soon as news reached him, Crook dispatched Captain Charles Meinhold from Fort Whipple to investigate. Despite some contradictory evidence, Meinhold submitted a report concluding that the perpetrators were, indeed, Date Creek Yavapais.[3] Unconvinced by the captain's observations, Crook directed the Date Creek camp commander, Captain R. F. O'Bierne, to investigate further.[4] O'Bierne turned up additional evidence that several Yavapais had greenbacks in their possession and that one reservation Indian had been seen with the metal hoop from a mail bag. Further, Iretaba, chief of an unrelated (Mohave) band camped near the reservation, claimed that certain Indians at Date Creek had bragged about the attack, an allegation that was corroborated by Indians of yet another band. Though Iretaba was known to be feuding with the Date Creek band, O'Bierne considered his statement credible when taken together with the other information he had unearthed. So he issued a report supporting Meinhold's conclusions.[5]

With the two officers' accounts pointing to Yavapai responsibility in hand, Crook happily concluded that he had evidence that definitively undermined Colyer's claim to have resolved the Indian problem in Arizona. "'Vincent the Good' [Colyer] has been virtually decapitated," he crowed in a letter to his friend Rutherford Hayes. Yet beneath his apparent optimism, he remained doubtful whether the peace lobby had really been neutralized. There was still "great danger of others popping up in his [Colyer's] place," he wrote Hayes. "The fact is there is too much money in this Indian business."[6] So he waited uneasily for instructions that would allow him to initiate offensive action against the Indians.

It was a short wait. Wickenberg had generated public outrage that for the first time reached deep into the pro-peace faction of the eastern establishment. On this occasion, they had lost one of their own. Without their restraining influence and responding to countervailing pressure from the general population and the military, the administration quickly agreed to allow Crook to take measures to punish the culprits. Within four days of the Wickenburg attack, Sherman had wired General Schofield, instructing him to reassure Crook that "whatever measures of severity" he employed to quell resistance would be supported by the War Department.[7] Schofield, in turn, supplied Crook with a list of harsh measures he was to take. All roving bands were to be immediately confined to reservations under the management of military officers; those who resisted were to be punished as hostiles. On the reservations, post commanders were to make lists of all males of an age to be considered warriors, verifying their presence by daily head count.

Those listed were required to carry documents at all times indicating that they and their families were properly registered. While the entire tribe would not be held responsible for the bad acts of individuals, the families of absent males would be held hostage for the return of errant relatives. Hostiles would be vigorously pursued by the military, employing Indian scouts, while peaceful Indians on the reservation would receive rations and protection from white vigilantism. Crook had full discretion to decide how he would carry out these actions and to establish a timetable for their implementation.[8]

Responding to Schofield's instructions, Crook issued his own General Order on December 11, putting into effect the boundaries of the reservations that Colyer had designated for the various bands, including those for temporary reserves at Date Creek, Beale Spring, and Camp McDowell. A second order two weeks later fixed February 15, 1872, as the date on which "all Apache Indians found outside of these Reservations, will be considered and treated as hostile."[9]

Rather than being cowed by the military's tough stance, the Yavapais and Apaches went on the offensive. Over the twelve months following Colyer's departure, there would be over fifty separate attacks against whites, resulting in the death of three soldiers and forty-one civilians and the loss of hundreds of head of livestock.[10] Among certain bands, particularly the Tontos, response to the army's ultimatum was so minimal that on February 7, Crook issued a reminder that they had only a week more to comply. But he knew, as he warned the War Department, that his much anticipated campaign would now be unavoidable.[11] The Department responded with promises of additional troops and a request for appropriations to construct the telegraph line to the Territory that the commander had requested earlier. Crook, now aware that he was in Arizona for the long haul, advised his friend Hayes that he expected "Mrs. Crook to join me soon."[12]

During the winter months, Crook prepared his troops for the upcoming campaign, not sparing himself. At the end of February, Thaddeus Stanton, an army paymaster who would soon become a close friend and admirer, met the general for the first time in the midst of a blizzard deep in the Juniper Mountains. Crook, who had just walked twelve miles in the storm to meet his troops, was clad in civilian clothing—"one would have taken him for the master of transportation rather than the Commanding General of the department." He had been in the mountains for several days organizing a company of scouts. Though Crook asked few questions and talked little, Stanton found him "full of decision and energy." In passing, Stanton mentioned to him that this was the paymaster's eightieth day on the trail and that he was becoming rather weary. "'Why bless you,' Crook replied, 'I have been at this sort of thing for twenty years and more.'"[13]

In March, Crook was ready to launch his operation. He would begin with the apprehension of the perpetrators of the Wickenburg killings. To that end, accompanied by his newly appointed aides, Lieutenants John Bourke and William Ross, he was en route to Date Creek to effect their arrest when he was pulled up short by a telegram from General Schofield. President Grant had decided to send another envoy to Apacheria to try and peacefully resolve the situation. In the meantime, Crook was to prevent "possible collision between troops and Indians."[14] The frustrated general grudgingly passed on Schofield's instructions to his commanders, but pointedly reminded them of their concurrent duty to protect the settlers, "using every exertion of force at your command to recover stolen stock."[15]

CHAPTER EIGHT

The Last Peace Offensive

Aware of Colyer's shortcomings and consequent unpopularity on the frontier, the president selected someone of a different stripe for this last peace initiative, General Oliver Otis Howard. A West Pointer, brigadier general, and hero of the Civil War, Howard had a more practical bent than Colyer and was more inclined to give weight to the military's point of view. Yet he, too, was animated by humanitarian zeal, religious conviction, and a similar single-mindedness of purpose.[1]

A Mainer by birth, Howard had demonstrated great industry and intelligence from an early age. He put himself through Bowdoin College by teaching school and then attended West Point, graduating fourth in his class. While Crook had spent his early career fighting Indians on the Pacific Coast, Howard had served more than half of his time as a professor of mathematics at the Academy and was contemplating joining the ministry when the war intervened. Putting aside his religious aspirations, he resigned from the regular army and joined the Maine Volunteers. As a volunteer officer he managed to achieve a record that one historian called "one of the great paradoxes of American military history; no officer entrusted with field direction of troops has ever equaled Howard's record for surviving so many tactical errors of judgment and disregard of orders, emerging later not only with increased rank, but on one occasion, the thanks of Congress."[2] Though battlefield operations may not have been his forte, his courage was unquestioned. After losing an arm at Fair Oaks, he returned to command less than three months later and, as a corps commander at Gettysburg, received the Medal of Honor for rallying his troops at Cemetery Hill. Through it all, his religious convictions were so pronounced and he was so given to displaying them publicly that he became known as the "praying" or "Christian" general.

At the war's end, Howard's political connections and reputation as a dedicated abolitionist secured him appointment as commissioner of the Freedman's Bureau, a job at which he failed miserably. Plagued by poor administrative skills and a trusting nature, he turned a blind eye to the dishonesty and inefficiency of subordinates, undermining the Bureau's accomplishments and reputation. By 1872, agency corruption and Howard's precocious initiatives on behalf of blacks, including an attempt to integrate the Congregationalist Church, had made him so controversial that it was rumored Grant selected him for the mission to Apacheria as much to get him out of Washington as because of his personal integrity and humanitarian instincts. Whatever the reason for his appointment, like Colyer before him, Howard arrived in Arizona with a sweeping mandate from Secretary Delano "to induce [the Indians] to abandon their present habits of life and go upon permanent reservations."[3] Unlike his predecessor, Howard had the added advantage of outranking Crook.

After calling on General Schofield in San Francisco, Howard entered the territory through Yuma and had his first meeting with Crook at nearby Fort McDowell. As he had with Colyer, Crook cannily welcomed him with apparent warmth and civility. Howard was aware of Crook's war record and his service as an Indian fighter, but had only a slight personal acquaintance with him from their days at the Academy (they were two years apart). However, optimistic by nature, he was hopeful that the two men would be able to establish a cooperative relationship. Before even meeting Crook, he had written Grant, "I would ask no better officer to work with me."[4] And, following their initial meeting, his optimism remained undimmed. As he informed Grant, "General Crook disclaims emphatically being an extreme war man. I believe he fully agrees with me and you know what that means."[5] The two men did in fact have similar views regarding the common humanity of the Indians, and shared a belief that "good Indians" were often blamed—and punished—for the deeds of the "bad" ones.[6] They also agreed that the "bad" Indians could only be subdued by military action.[7] But despite their shared convictions and similar backgrounds, Crook and Howard were sufficiently different in character and personality as to preclude an easy working relationship.

Initially, Howard found Crook "very candid" and desirous of executing the "orders he receives with discretion and fidelity." But he soon discovered that the Ohioan's candor masked a reticence that made him "difficult to gauge." His eyes, Howard decided, "were really no open and transparent windows to his soul. There was no way to divine his thoughts or purpose until his plans were completed and he was ready for action." But despite Crook's opacity and prickly nature, Howard, like many others who had occasion to work with him, learned to respect him, finding him a man of his word and "uniformly just and kind."[8]

For his part, though overtly supportive of Howard's efforts, Crook was repelled by the general's piety and messianic self-importance, the same traits that he had mocked in Colyer. While he concealed these feelings during Howard's visit to Arizona, he was unsparing in his autobiography. "I was very amused at the General's opinion of himself," he wrote. "He told me that he thought the Creator had placed him on earth to be Moses to the Negro. Having accomplished that mission, he felt satisfied his next mission was with the Indian. . . . I was at a loss to make out whether it was his vanity or his cheek that enabled him to hold up his head in this lofty manner." Nor did he trust Howard, believing, without apparent justification, that rather than confront Crook with his opposition to his policies, Howard intended to go behind his back, first by undermining his authority with the Indians, and then by tempting Crook's subordinates to oppose his views with offers of duty in the East.[9] But for now at least, Crook held his resentment in check and played the cooperative role Howard envisioned for him. Accordingly, after conferring with the general at McDowell, he assigned two trusted aides, Lieutenants Bourke and Ross, to escort him to Camp Grant, site of the massacre. As they rode, the two officers, probably acting on Crook's instructions, pointedly identified Anglo and Mexican ranches and mines along the route that had been ravaged by Apache "treachery and bloodshed."[10]

At Camp Grant, Howard found Lieutenant Whitman, the reinstated post commander, absent and the situation tense. Howard soon learned that Whitman had again been placed under arrest and was now being held in Tucson. The allegations made against him included the failure to enroll and make a daily count of those male Apaches at Camp Grant old enough to go on the warpath, a requirement that Crook considered central to his reservation policies.[11] Of less moment, he was also charged with hiring butchers to kill beeves before giving the meat to the Indians, a violation of Crook's directive that beef be issued on the hoof. Finally, and probably most offensive to his commander, he was accused of being drunk on duty and keeping "one or more disreputable women at the post for purposes of prostitution and did cohabit with them."

As the Indians revered Whitman, Crook must have known that arresting the lieutenant and removing him from Fort Grant risked precipitating unrest among them. But the opportunity to rid himself of Whitman once and for all proved too tempting. Nevertheless, he handled the matter cautiously. To avoid any hint of personal animus, rather than bring formal charges himself, he reported the allegations to General Schofield, confident that his commander would act upon them. As expected, Schofield promptly authorized Whitman's apprehension and prosecution, and Crook ordered him to report to Tucson under arrest, pending a court-martial.[12]

Whitman had been replaced by a civilian named Edward Jacobs, and the Aravaipas, already living in a state of paranoia, became convinced that he was part of a plot against them.[13] Consequently, as soon as Howard arrived, they demanded that Whitman be returned to them before they would engage in any talks. Howard, unaware of the history between Crook and the lieutenant, believed he was calming the situation. The general was only too glad to comply. He had looked forward to seeing Whitman, a relative by marriage and an old friend, the two men having grown up together in Maine not twelve miles from one another.[14]

Howard ordered Whitman's temporary release from custody and transfer back to Camp Grant.[15] Predictably, Crook interpreted Howard's action as undermining his authority. But he held his tongue for the time being.

Two days later, after Whitman had returned to Camp Grant, Howard convened the Indians at the Agency's ramshackle adobe headquarters to discuss their grievances. The meeting was almost derailed when the general inadvertently terrorized the Indians by suddenly falling to his knees and praying loudly. Dispersing in all directions "like partridges when they see a hawk," the Aravaipas timidly returned to the building only after an amused Whitman explained that Howard was not indulging in witchcraft, but was engaging in ritual that he employed when embarking on any sort of undertaking—"just as you spit on your hands when you go to draw a bow."[16]

Eskiminzin, quickly recovering his aplomb, voiced his people's desire for peace and then launched into an enumeration of their woes. Foremost was the return of the children taken during the massacre, followed by concerns about the unhealthy nature of the reservation set aside by Colyer and its proximity to hostile Mexican and Anglo population centers. Finally, indifferent to Howard's argument that government policy mandated that Whitman be replaced by a civilian, the chief expressed his fear that Whitman, whom the Aravaipas regarded as their sole protector, would be denied them as a permanent agent.

Howard was impressed with Eskimizin's apparent desire to conclude a formal peace with all of his enemies and resolved to help the chief address his concerns.[17] Pleading a need for time to sort out the issues, he announced that a second council would be held in twenty-five days to discuss a permanent peace. He then departed for Prescott to consult with Crook. Aware that such a peace required the involvement of a number of parties, he stopped at Tucson on his way to secure the participation of Governor Safford, local business leaders, and the chiefs of tribes hostile to the Apaches—the Pimas, Maricopas, and Papagos—at the coming council. Not only did all parties agree to attend, but they consented to bring with them any Aravaipa children who remained with families in the town, a key element to any peace with the band.[18]

Howard reached Prescott in late April and found Crook in a conciliatory mood, keeping to himself his irritation with Howard over his interference in the Whitman affair. As he had with Colyer, Crook graciously offered Howard the hospitality of his home, now presided over by Mary, who had recently rejoined her husband, in company with her brother, John Dailey. Though Dailey had been among the Confederate partisans who had kidnapped Crook during the War, by all accounts the two men enjoyed a warm relationship.[19] The presence of Mary and John seemed to have a salubrious effect on Crook, for Howard later wrote that he was delighted "to find himself at his table, particularly when his genial wife presided at the head of it."[20]

Relations between the two officers improved further when, on May 9, after hearing about renewed depredations in the countryside, Howard presented Crook with a letter authorizing him "to deal with [those who refuse to settle on the reservation] with vigor according to your discretion until the murderers and robbers and those who sympathize with them [are] . . . made to feel the power of the Government to punish crimes."[21]

On May 14, both men proceeded to Camp Grant for the council with the Aravaipas. Crook attended with a mixture of resentment and anxiety. He did not share Howard's faith in Eskiminzin's sincerity and continued to brood about the general's restoration of Whitman to oversight on the reservation. Before talks began, he paced about in the dappled sunlight of the cottonwood grove on Aravaipa Creek, where Howard had chosen to hold the council. As he wandered through these bucolic surroundings, his path led him among groups of warriors armed with lances and guns, "a more saucy, impudent lot of cut-throats I had never seen before. . . . They would walk through our camp in that defiant, impudent manner, as much as to say, 'I would like to kill you just for the fun of it.' I was afraid of them," the hardened Indian fighter confessed, "and kept close to camp for fear some of them would want to be a hero at my expense."[22]

Crook's fears were not wholly illusory. Eskiminzin could be a dangerous and pitiless foe. He had fled to the mountains a year before after being accidentally fired upon by troops. On his way, he had called at the home of rancher Charles McKinney (also referred to as Alex McKinzie), with whom he had struck up a friendship. After taking a meal with him, Eskiminzin had shot McKinney down in cold blood, later explaining that he had done so to convince his people that they could no longer be friends with the white man. After this murder, he had unsuccessfully attacked an army wagon train and had only reluctantly returned to the reservation in September at Whitman's urgings.[23] The chief may also have nursed a personal grudge against Crook, as Whitman had told Howard that Crook was in sympathy with the Tucson residents involved in the massacre and may have repeated the tale to Eskiminzin.[24] Crook's mood continued to darken after he observed Howard and Whitman walking about the post arm in arm. Unaware of their previous history, Crook saw this display of affection as designed to further undercut his authority.[25]

The council took place on the morning of May 21. A large crowd gathered among the cottonwoods, a combustible mix of over a thousand Apaches, many of them armed, in uncomfortable proximity with delegations of their bitterest enemies, Indian, Anglo, and Mexican, among whom were leaders and participants in the massacre of their people.[26] Crook was seriously concerned that an incident might set off a melee. But despite his misgivings, Howard would later credit him with making a genuine effort to defuse tensions with his "frankness and God's help."[27]

In Crook's opinion, the meeting did not begin auspiciously. Eskiminzin, whom he regarded as "'head center' of the cut-throats," began the proceedings with a "half-quizzical, half-contemptuous and defiant manner, as much as to say 'Go to hell.'"[28] The *Arizona Citizen*, which covered the event, provided a more detailed and less jaundiced account.[29] According to the paper, the council's tone was established by Eskiminzin's father, old chief Santos, the first to speak. He placed a rock on the ground in front of Howard and declared that he was for "a peace that will last as long as that stone lasts." Succeeding speakers all indicated that the symbolism of the stone worked for them, providing their former foes also acted in good faith.

When it came time for Crook to address the assemblage, he abandoned metaphors for a more blunt and pragmatic approach. He wanted no repetition of the Camp Grant Massacre, he declared. Then, with a likely glance in Whitman's direction, he noted that registering all Indians on the reservations and counting them daily would go far toward achieving that purpose. Turning to Eskiminzin, he announced his intention to make war on those bands that refused to make peace, referring to them as "bad Indians." As a gesture of good faith, he wondered whether the chief would provide warriors for such a campaign, not to fight the bad Indians, but to find them. Eskiminzin said he would. Extolling the benefits of peace, Crook concluded, "It does not look well, when passing through this country to see you perched upon high points in the mountains, a long distance from water, like so many crows; and to be fearful of being attacked every night. As soon as all the Indians are peaceable, you can go to bed and sleep without fear of danger."[30]

The atmosphere, which had been amicable up to this point, abruptly changed when Howard introduced the emotionally charged issue of the captive children. Though initially he had been determined to return the children to their families, he had become aware that, in the intervening year, most were beyond reach, having had been sold into slavery in Mexico. Only six remained, and were present at the council. The Mexican families who had taken them in adamantly opposed their return, claiming they had been integrated into their families as foster children. Crook supported their position, convinced that many of these youngsters "identified with their new associates, and had correspondingly become weaned from their people, in fact, dreaded going back to the Indians."[31]

Confronted with hostility from both the Indians and Tucson's Anglo and Mexican communities, Howard tacked from point to point, finally managing to finesse the issue with a solution that pleased no one. The children would remain at Camp Grant in the custody of the Indian agent (Whitman), until the Great White Father in Washington made a final decision as to their future.[32] In the meantime, the agent would "provide for a Christian woman to take care of and teach them," and to allow their friends and relatives to visit them freely, "both Mexican and Apaches."[33]

The decision to defer the issue of the captive children allowed the talks to proceed to a positive conclusion. Though Eskiminzin continued to irritate Crook by his use of the by now shopworn "as long as the stone lasts" metaphor, he remained true to his word. His people would never violate the commitments made at Aravaipa Creek. They would remain at peace and, as promised, furnish warriors to serve as scouts in Crook's future campaigns. Notwithstanding these undeniable facts, Crook remained unforgiving, convinced that the conference had been a failure. Of Eskiminzin, he later wrote, "the rascal . . . hadn't promised anything, and didn't intend keeping the promise if he had." Crook would neither forgive nor forget that "when we left, he [the chief] was very profuse in his demonstrations of friendship and good will towards General Howard, but he scarcely noticed me, didn't even offer to shake hands with me."[34]

After the council ended, the officers returned to their camp, where Crook lost no time in attacking Howard for his failure to understand frontier sensitivities on matters concerning the Apaches and for what really bothered him, Howard's conduct with respect to Lieutenant Whitman. Howard, Crook later recalled with ill-disguised satisfaction, was so shocked by this sudden and unanticipated outburst that, unable to sleep, he had remained awake and in prayer until three o'clock the following morning.[35]

As part of the accommodation reached at the council, Howard had agreed to remove the Aravaipas from the unhealthy environs of the post to the San Carlos Reservation, where they would join the White Mountain Apaches on the Gila River.[36] In August, after a brief visit to Washington as escort for a White Mountain and Aravaipa delegation that met with President Grant, Howard returned to Arizona to complete his mission, arranging a peace with Cochise and his Chiricahuas, the most warlike band in the Territory. The details of his efforts may be read elsewhere, but it bears mention that he acted with personal courage and tact in convincing the venerable chief to accept reservation life for his people. His intervention was well timed. Both sides had by this time become weary of a war that had lasted for a decade, and Cochise's willingness to settle on a reservation in their traditional homeland in the Dragoon and Chiricahua Mountains was welcomed, as it brought an end to depredations, at least for the time being, in southern Arizona.[37]

While residents of the Territory lauded Howard's agreement with the Chiricahuas, Crook and others in the military did not share their enthusiasm. Crook remained unconvinced by Cochise's protestations of friendship, aware that the chief had on several occasions agreed to peace only to resume raiding a few months later. Even now, Cochise's warriors continued to conduct raids south of the border, much to the consternation of the Mexican government. These attacks were conducted with the chief's tacit consent. Having made his agreement with the Americans, he saw no inconsistency in allowing his young men to pillage livestock herds and attack villages in Mexico. Crook wrongly believed that Cochise's followers were nothing more than "outlaws and the disaffected of the different adjacent tribes, confederated together for the purpose of murdering and robbing."[38] As such, he did not believe that they could be controlled by one individual, even Cochise. He and many of his fellow officers continued to believe that only a decisive defeat on the battlefield would bring the Chiricahuas to heel.

In the meantime, the general shared with his counterparts in Mexico a concern about the reservation's boundaries. Drawn by General

Howard during his negotiations with Cochise, its southern boundary lay hard against the Mexican border and outside military control, facilitating the raids into Sonora. Crook correctly surmised that this was an issue that he would have to deal with long after Howard's departure. But now, in the fall of 1872, he had more immediate concerns, and had neither the time nor the resources to deal with the Chiricahuas. His attention was focused elsewhere in Apacheria.

CHAPTER NINE

The Tonto Campaign

September 1872–April 1873

General Howard's mission had thrown Crook's pursuit of the suspected culprits in the Wickenburg Massacre into limbo. It will be remembered that just prior to Howard's arrival in the Territory, Crook had obtained evidence from his spies, both Indian and white, that convinced him, whether correctly or not, that Yavapais (known to whites as Apache Mohaves) from the Date Creek Reservation had carried out the attack.[1] He had been en route to the reservation to arrest the suspects when word of Howard's initiative had abruptly forced him to cancel the movement.[2] Now, authorized to pursue offensive operations against any Indians who resisted resettlement on reservations, Crook's first order of business was to arrest those he considered to be the perpetrators of the Wickenburg attack.

On September 6, he left Prescott to meet with his original informant, Irataba, a Mohave chief who claimed he could identify the attackers. The previous spring, the chief had come to Crook with tales of Yavapais at Date Creek overheard bragging about their role in the ambush. He now alleged that he knew the identities of the Indians involved. He named fifteen warriors under the leadership of Ochocama, a dissident Yavapai chief, as the primary culprits, and another fifteen warriors he said had waited close by in reserve.[3] The Indian agent at Date Creek supported Irataba's allegations, as did several friendly Hualapais. Relying on these sources, Crook called for a council of all the Yavapais on the reservation, claiming as a pretext, a desire to recruit some of their number and to distribute rations. He instructed Irataba's Mohaves to circulate among the Indians present and identify the perpetrators by giving each a tobacco leaf, a stratagem he had used years before on the Pacific Coast.[4] His mule packers and a company of soldiers would fan out among the crowd and, at Crook's signal, simultaneously seize the guilty parties.[5]

When Crook arrived at Date Creek, he found that less than one-third of the Indians who were supposed to be at the Agency were actually present. Many had fled into the mountains, some because they feared Crook's retribution and others simply to hunt or escape the unhealthy conditions that prevailed at the reservation during hot weather. Crook described those present as "uneasy and suspicious, and in very bad temper, appearing with their arms and war paint."[6] Nevertheless, he convened the council; and the Mohaves, as agreed, passed out the tobacco to those they claimed were involved in the massacre. Then the situation began to unravel. When a soldier attempted to grab one of the designated warriors, an Indian standing behind him sank his knife into his back. Crook reported that "in an instant firing commenced on both sides," and what the Irishman Bourke characterized as a "perfect Kilkenny fight" broke out. Though Crook and his officers tried to stop the shooting, it ended so quickly that their intervention had little effect.[7] In the course of the melee, Crook's aide, Lieutenant Ross, observing an Indian take aim at the general, shot and killed him, undoubtedly saving Crook's life, an incident the general never mentioned in his official account of the incident.[8] Contrary to his usual practice, his official report also made no reference to the number of casualties among the Indians, which fortunately did not include women and children, as they had not been invited to the meeting.[9] According to one of the packers, seven or eight warriors were killed, an unknown number were wounded, and many fled into the mountains. The supposed leader of the miscreants, Chief Ochocama, was captured, but later escaped.[10]

Though Crook would later claim that the incident had the positive effect of subduing the Yavapais, the tone of his report, particularly his omission of Indian casualties, when taken together with his subsequent actions, indicate that he regretted the affair, unusual for this supremely self-confident officer. In the report, he lamented the fact that the arrests were not "made without trouble," tacitly acknowledging the unnecessary bloodshed. His contrition was still evident when, a month later, he met with some of the Yavapais to discuss their enrollment as scouts. These men had been at the Date Creek council, but had not been implicated in the massacre. In an effort to mend relations with them, Crook ordered his soldiers to return guns confiscated from the Yavapais in the aftermath of the council. When the Indians complained that the troops had rendered the weapons inoperable before returning them, Crook ordered the post commander to distribute new army rifles and ammunition to them. These actions, particularly the issuance of ammunition, virtually unobtainable by the Indians at the time, were widely viewed as an apology and an attempt to atone for putting innocent men at risk. The gesture also demonstrated a level of trust that went far toward restoring the Yavapais' confidence in Crook and greatly facilitated his efforts to enlist them as scouts.[11]

Not long after the Date Creek fracas, Crook demonstrated that the affair had in no way altered his commitment to a military solution to the Apache problem. In his annual report for the year 1872, submitted on September 21 of that year, he attacked the Colyer and Howard missions for failing to bring real peace to Arizona. Under the rules of engagement following the peace agreements with the tribes, Crook pointed out, he had been restricted in his operations to the "pursuit and punishment of [only those Indians] actually engaged in massacre of citizens, or depredations upon their stock. . . . [Meanwhile] Indians on some of the reserves, ostensibly at peace and feeding upon government stores, have been accomplices and in some cases principals in robberies and murders. . . ." To document his assertion, he appended a list of killings and thefts that he attributed to these "very Indians."[12] Having declared the peace initiative dead, he went on to announce his intention to "proceed to carry out the remainder of my instructions which require me to punish the incorrigibly hostile."[13] This section of the report reads less like a request for authority to proceed than a declaration of war. And, true to his word, within the week, he went on the offensive.

Learning from an anonymous source that a group of the Date Creek fugitives had gathered at the headwaters of the Santa Maria River and were making plans to resume raiding, Crook dispatched a column of troopers under Captain Julius Mason on what would be the first of a series of aggressive forays into Indian country.[14] The column was accompanied by a contingent of eighty-six Hualapai scouts, members of a tribe formerly allied with the Yavapais. They were commanded by Albert Sieber, Crook's twenty-eight-year-old, German-born chief of scouts. Sieber, a lean man with a bushy mustache and frank, piercing gaze, spoke with a thick Rhineland accent, having arrived from Germany in America as a teenager. Though his Teutonic inversions contrasted oddly with his buckskin attire and frontier mannerisms, giving him a somewhat comic air, he was a man to be reckoned with. A Civil War veteran wounded at Gettysburg, Sieber had come west in the late 1860s to make his fortune prospecting for gold, but became an Indian fighter and scout instead. Crook originally enlisted him as a packer and then selected him as chief of scouts because of his familiarity with Apache culture, language, and character. He was known to work well with his scouts and instill fear in his adversaries.[15]

Mason's force struck the Date Creek fugitives at dawn on September 25. The Yavapais had thought themselves safe in four rancherias tucked away in a mountainous region so riven by deep ravines that it was called *Muchos Cañones*. But the Hualapais found them, and they were taken completely by surprise. Forty warriors were killed in the fight, a number of women and children were captured, and any food supplies that might have helped those who escaped survive the winter were destroyed.[16] The fury and unexpected nature of the attack and the participation of the Hualapais, their erstwhile allies, so shocked and unnerved the Yavapais that within days, they presented themselves at the Date Creek Reservation, "begging to be allowed to return under any condition."[17]

For Crook, Mason's victory was irrefutable confirmation of his oft-repeated conviction that a resounding defeat on the battlefield would induce the most hostile Indians to abandon the warpath and retire peacefully to the reservation. In October, equally impressed by the results of Mason's attack, General Schofield now cast his lot for "vigorous and unremitting persecution of the war, until they [the Apaches] are completely subdued. . . . "[18] Crook's view seemed to have carried the day.

But was the peace policy indeed dead in Arizona? Crook remained skeptical. Twice he had planned campaigns only to be reined in at the last minute. This time, he was determined to carry on regardless of which way the political winds blew. As he laid out his winter offensive, supremely confident of victory, he later recalled that he resolved to "disobey any order I might receive looking to an interference of the plan which I had adopted, feeling sure if I was successful my disobedience of orders would be forgiven."[19]

The previous year, General Schofield had issued General Order No. 10, declaring that all Indians not settled upon a designated reservation could be regarded by the army as hostile. While it was held in abeyance during Howard's peace mission, Crook now resurrected the directive as his authority for the coming operation.[20] His plan would involve the Twenty-Third Infantry Regiment, which he had commanded during the Paiute fighting, and elements of the First and Fifth Cavalry, veteran troopers fresh from the Indian wars on the Great Plains.[21] He divided this force into nine independent highly mobile commands, each large enough "to prevent disaster" but "small enough to slip around out of sight of the hostiles."[22] All columns were to operate simultaneously and continually, each independent of the others, giving the Indians no respite while driving them steadily inward toward the center of their refuge in the Tonto Basin, two hundred square miles of what Crook had identified as "some of the roughest country in the United States and known only to the Indians."[23] The columns would mount attacks whenever contact was made, killing or capturing as many warriors as possible and destroying their rancherias to deprive them of food and shelter. Each column would have its own contingent of scouts, ranging from thirty to one hundred in number, as well as a pack train. Every packer and mule would be carefully vetted, painstakingly trained, and thoroughly conditioned under Crook's watchful eyes.[24] The soldiers carried only the minimum amount of clothing and gear needed to sustain them on the trail. Many of the troopers emulated their commander, leaving behind their heavy woolen uniforms and wearing instead canvas clothing designed to resist the wear and tear of the rough country.[25]

Given the broken and largely unmapped terrain in which the operations would be carried out, Crook regarded his Indian scouts as key to success. They were drawn from a number of tribes, Yavapais from the Verde and Date Creek Reservations, Aravaipas and White Mountain Apaches from Camps Apache and Grant, and Hualapais, who made their home in the Tonto Basin and were chosen for their familiarity with the country. Their ranks were supplemented by Mohaves, Pimas, Maricopas, and even Paiutes, the latter from Utah. Of all the tribes, Crook considered the Apaches (and we can suppose by that term he meant to include the Yavapais) the most effective. As Bourke wrote, "They were wilder and more suspicious than the Pimas and Maricopas, but far more reliable and endowed with a greater amount of courage and daring."[26] Also, as Bourke the budding ethnologist would learn, while all tribes had a cleansing ritual after slaying an enemy, the Apaches exhibited the greatest flexibility in this regard. While the Pimas and Maricopas underwent a lengthy and time-consuming ceremony after each killing, the Apaches deferred their cleansing until after the campaign ended, thus avoiding time-consuming delays.[27]

To ensure discipline and loyalty among his Indian allies, Crook appointed some of the most experienced scouts in the Southwest to lead them.[28] In the days ahead, commanded by such seasoned veterans as Al Sieber and Archie McIntosh, the Indians would range a day or so ahead or on the flanks of the columns, locating and guiding the troops to long-established strongholds and hidden redoubts deep in the interior of the Basin, so ingeniously concealed that the soldiers on their own would never have found them. They would often be the first to make contact with the enemy and just as frequently, unable to resist a good fight, would bear the brunt of the combat.

The several commands all marched under the same standing orders. Unit commanders were to make every effort to induce the Indians to surrender, but as Bourke put it, "where they preferred to fight, they were to get all the fighting they wanted, and in one good dose instead of in a number of petty engagements, but in either case they were to be hunted down until the last one in hostility had been killed or captured." The killing of women and children was to be avoided, and prisoners were to be well treated so that, where possible, they could be recruited as scouts. Campaigning would be arduous. "No excuse was to be accepted for leaving the trail; if horses played out, the enemy must be followed on foot, and no sacrifice should be left untried to make the campaign short, sharp, and decisive."[29]

The offensive was set to commence in mid-November, the onset of winter in the Tonto Basin and elsewhere in the Arizona high country, when temperatures often plunged well below zero and heavy snows could be expected. While the snow might impede mobility and cause suffering to the troopers and their mounts, it insured a sufficient supply of drinking water in an otherwise arid landscape. And any hardships suffered by the troops were more than compensated for by the impact of a winter campaign on the Indians. The Tontos and Yavapais' most secure haunts lay at higher elevations. But in winter, they usually moved down to lower altitudes to avoid the freezing temperatures. Crook's constant campaigning would deprive them of these warmer refuges, pushing them back up into the less accessible but colder regions, while denying them the warmth of fires that might give away the location of their camps. Winter also reduced the availability of game, forcing the Indians to rely on food they had put aside in warmer seasons. These irreplaceable foodstuffs, stored in caves and caches, would become prime targets for the soldiers to seek out and destroy, leaving the Indians near starvation. Though winter war was a cruel and nasty business, Crook favored it on the theory that it would force the Indians to a swift realization of the hopelessness of continued resistance, thus shortening operations, which, in turn, would reduce the suffering of the Indians and the danger to his troops and scouts.[30]

Crook had no intention of managing the campaign from the relative comfort of his departmental headquarters. He planned instead to move constantly about the periphery of the Basin, giving general direction to the columns and personally supervising their logistics. But, as was his custom, he allowed his officers the autonomy to conduct their movements in the field in accordance with exigencies as they arose. Now, in his forty-fourth year, he was still possessed of the energy and stamina required to lead troops in the field. Early in the campaign, he had demonstrated his endurance to his troops, completing a march of twenty-six hours over extremely rough terrain, a journey that left the rest of his command "pretty well tired out." While his troops laid out their bed rolls and started their cook fires, he had taken his shotgun, remounted his mule and, following a nearby stream for a mile or two, shot "a fine mess of reed birds" for breakfast. Bourke boasted that "no private soldier, no packer, no teamster . . . could 'down the old man' in any work, or outlast him on a march or climb over the rugged peaks of Arizona."[31]

On November 16, Crook set his operation in motion. From Camp Hualapai, a temporary post established to guard the road to Prescott, he dispatched three columns and a detachment of scouts from Date Creek in pursuit of the Yavapais. A fourth column marched out of Verde, the first of several that would patrol along the western and northern edge of the Tonto country and the Yavapai heartland, using Camps Verde, Whipple, and McDowell as their base of supply. Their task was to push the Indians southeast toward the center of the Basin.[32]

Leaving Nickerson in charge in the west, Crook moved eastward across the Mogollon Plateau to Fort Apache and then to Camp Grant, "to organize similar expeditions from those posts," enlisting White Mountains and Aravaipas respectively as guides for columns pushing out from the east.[33] The situation he found at the two reservations disturbed him and may have helped to justify in his own mind the harsh campaign upon which he was about to embark. Angrily, he reported that as far as he could tell, "the whole peace system among the Apaches was a fraud." The Indian agents had failed to hold the regular head counts that Crook regarded as essential. As a result, by his computations, the Indian Bureau furnished rations for 1,400 Indians on the Fort Apache reservation, whereas the military could verify the presence of only 1,100. Of greater concern was his finding that "stolen stock was coming and going constantly on the reservation . . . but that it was almost impossible to fix responsibility on the guilty parties." At Camp Grant, the situation was the same, if not worse.[34] To end the livestock raiding, he issued draconian orders requiring all Indians in the area to move within one mile of the agency and to submit to daily head counts. Any violation of the order would result in arrests and treatment of the offenders as prisoners of war.[35] Notwithstanding these harsh measures, Crook found the Indians on both reservations willing and even eager to enlist in his campaign. Enrolling these expert trackers and fighters as scouts, he now dispatched three columns, one from Apache and two from Grant, eastward into the Basin. He then departed to monitor the progress of his troops, leaving only small detachments to guard the posts.

The Tonto campaign was as terrible for both the Indians and their pursuers as Crook had predicted. In April, after his troops had been five months in the field, Crook publicly commended their performance, enumerating the hardships they had endured—"rigorous cold in the mountains, followed in quick succession by intense heat and arid waste of the desert, not infrequently at dire extremities for want of water . . . ; and when their animals were stricken by pestilence or the country became too rough . . . they left them and carried on their own backs such meager supplies as they might, they persistently followed on, . . . in lava beds, caves and canyons."[36]

For the Indians, the campaign was no less painful. The Tonto chief, Eschetlepan (Cha-lipan or Charley Pan to the white soldiers), described their suffering when he surrendered himself and three hundred Tonto and Yavapai followers at Camp Verde in April. He had not come in out of love for Crook, he explained, but out of fear. His people

> could not go to sleep at night, because they feared to be surrounded before daybreak; they could not hunt—the noise of their guns would attract the troops; they could not cook mescal or anything else, because the flame and smoke would draw down the soldiers; they could not live in the valleys—there were too many soldiers; they had retreated to the mountaintops, thinking to hide in the snow until the soldiers went home, but the scouts found them out and the soldiers followed them.[37]

Crook's columns had crisscrossed the Tonto Basin in a series of converging and diverging marches that when mapped at the conclusion of the campaign produced "such a complication of eccentric and concentric trails [as] were never displayed upon parchment."[38] Each column fought a series of skirmishes, attacking the rancherias of small, and occasionally larger, groups of Indians unearthed by the scouts. These attacks resulted in the deaths of a few warriors and, unavoidably, some women and children. But most importantly, they destroyed food supplies and shelter, keeping the Indians constantly on the run so that they could neither rest nor replenish the resources they needed to survive in the winter months. Only two engagements were fought that could be said to qualify as battles in terms of casualties (almost entirely on the Indian side) and their impact on the overall campaign. These engagements involved the commands of Captains William H. Brown and George M. Randall and give a sense of the cruel nature of the fighting.

On December 11, Brown's column, accompanied by aides Bourke and Ross and a detachment of Apache scouts under Archie McIntosh, rode out of Camp Grant with sufficient rations to keep them supplied for thirty days in the field. They headed northeast into the mountainous country that formed the southern rim of the Tonto Basin.[39] Delche and Chuntz, two chiefs regarded as especially elusive and savage leaders, were their primary targets. Delche, probably of mixed Yavapai and Tonto parentage, was a formidable presence, "being an exceptionally large Indian with broad shoulders set high, which gave the impression that he stooped." He wore a single pearl button in the lobe of the left ear, because, as he explained it, "one in the right ear would interfere with his bow or rifle while shooting."[40] By 1872, his reputation was such that every raid or murder linked to the Indians of the Tonto Basin was laid at his door and, to some extent, Crook appears to have been influenced by this psychology. He singled out the chief as having "the worst reputation amongst all the Indians for villainry [*sic*] and devilment," and referred to him as "the Liar," believing that only Eskiminzin rivaled him in lack of trustworthiness and broken promises.[41]

By Anglo standards, there is little doubt that Delche lived up to his reputation. But like most Apaches, he had good reasons to hate and distrust the whites. An army surgeon had shot him in the chest without apparent provocation, while soldiers had killed his brother while "attempting to escape."[42] And, though he led his band on raids against settlers and ranchers, he had on several occasions made honest attempts to find an accommodation that would achieve peace for his people. But each time he had surrendered, some action on the part of his captors had overwhelmed him with anxiety and he had bolted the reservation and resumed raiding.[43] Chuntz, the second chief targeted by Brown's column, had a similar reputation for treachery. Most recently, he had been accused of murdering a young Mexican boy in cold blood near Camp Grant, an act said to be typical of his cruel and homicidal nature.[44]

On Christmas Day, Brown's troops, deep in the Mazatzal Mountains, were joined by a detachment of forty soldiers from Fort McDowell under Captain James Burns and a contingent of Pima scouts. Burns had captured a six- or seven-year-old Yavapai boy, whom he named Mike, who knew of a hideout in the Salt River Canyon country where Delche might be. Mike had divulged this information though the group included many of his relatives, in the mistaken belief that the band had by now long since fled the area. The two columns set out the next day, and Brown's scouts soon struck a trail that they believed would lead the column to the Yavapai lair, located in a cave carved into the sheer wall of the Salt River Canyon and believed by the Indians to be impregnable.[45]

On December 27, at nightfall, the force camped on a ridge five or six miles from the cave. Attacking the enemy position required a climb on foot down a steep incline into the canyon and then up the mountainside to the cave, all on a narrow rocky trail in pitch darkness. Only the fittest soldiers were selected. The remaining troops stayed behind to guard the horses and mules. The assault force, guided by a Yavapai scout, set out at about eight o'clock that evening, carrying only their weapons and ammunition, a day's rations, a canteen, and a blanket roll. Many wore Apache-style moccasins, allowing them to move noiselessly over the loose shale on the trail. After climbing for several hours in increasingly bone-chilling weather, the troopers reached the rim of the precipitous cliffs overlooking the Salt River gorge. Peering into the gloomy abyss below, it seemed to the more biblically inclined that they were staring into the Valley of the Shadow of Death.[46]

While the troops silently positioned themselves just below the ridgeline, scouts edged upward on a steep trail etched into the canyon wall, seeking the cave entrance. Moments later, they reappeared to report several horses and mules tethered at a wide spot on the trail ahead, indicating that the cave was nearby. Captain Brown sent Lieutenant Ross forward to follow up on the scouts' report and soon, the waiting troopers heard "a noise equal to that of a full battery of six-pounders going off at once." A startled Brown immediately ordered Bourke and a detachment of troopers to identify the source. Hurtling down the slippery path, Bourke rounded a sharp bend and suddenly, the reason for the din became clear.

When Ross had earlier turned the same corner, he had abruptly come upon the cave, a shallow depression in the rock face of the canyon only a short distance away. On an open shelf-like space in front of the cave, the lieutenant could make out the figures of dancing warriors, their shadows silhouetted by flickering firelight against the cave walls. To the soldiers, they seemed to be celebrating their return from a raid, but they could as easily have been trying to keep warm. Several women were visible crouched nearby preparing food. Exposed on the trail and fearing the Indians would become aware of their presence, Ross ordered his men to open fire, immediately killing six of the dancers. The echoes of this volley off the canyon walls had been what Brown's men had heard on the canyon rim.

The Indians, stunned by the suddenness of the attack, momentarily failed to return fire, and the rest of the command, taking advantage of the moment, fell into position beside Ross, forming a firing line that blocked escape. The defenders who by now had recovered from the shock of the attack, responded with shouts of defiance and volleys of arrows fired from behind a stone barrier at the cave entrance. Brown, mindful of Crook's orders to spare women and children whenever possible, offered the band the opportunity to surrender, to which they responded with "shrieks of hatred and defiance." Brown then proposed to accept the surrender of the women and children. This overture, too, was met with jeering and invective. Feeling that he had done his humanitarian duty, Brown ordered his men to resume firing. The results were horrific. In a frenzy, "every man in the command opened and closed the breechblock of his carbine as rapidly as his hands could move. . . . The bullets striking against the mouth of the cave seemed like drops of rain pattering upon the face of a lake." Many of their rounds ricocheted off the stone roof of the cave into the huddled mass of warriors, women, and children crouched behind their meager fortification. Soon, the piteous cries of the women and children, their bodies torn by flying lead and shards of splintered rock, reverberated off the canyon walls. Appalled, Brown again ordered a ceasefire to give the band another opportunity to surrender. Again, the Indians responded with defiance, and a dozen warriors, singing their death chants, charged into the troopers' guns, but were cut down before they reached the soldiers' lines. While carbine fire raked the front of the cave, a detachment of troopers made their way to the top of the bluff above the redoubt and shot downward into the opening and, adding to the slaughter, hurled huge boulders down upon the exposed survivors below.

By noon, return fire from the cave had ceased and the screams had faded to an occasional moan. As the troopers cautiously advanced into the dust-filled cavern, they found it littered with the mutilated bodies of men, women, and children, dead or writhing in agony on the cave floor. With the exception of about thirty dazed and badly injured Indians pulled from the wreckage (of whom only eighteen survived their injuries), and a handful of young men who escaped, the band had been wiped out. Strewn about the cave were the torn corpses of seventy-six men, women, and children. Brown lost only one man in the engagement, a Pima warrior whose body was recovered by the soldiers as they withdrew from the canyon. The slain Yavapais were left where they had fallen. Delche was not among them.

After bringing the wounded survivors to Camp McDowell, Brown's column mounted a patrol into the Superstition Mountains south of the Salt River Canyon. They encountered little resistance from the demoralized, half-starved, and ragged bands. Traumatized by news of the cave fight and the army's demonstrated ability to ferret out their most secluded hideouts, they soon began emerging from cover in groups of twos and threes, pathetically addressing the troops as "siquisn" (brother), before meekly joining a line of prisoners that lengthened behind the column. By the time they returned to Camp McDowell, the troops had 110 captives in hand, 25 of whom Crook recruited as scouts.[47]

But these surrenders did not penetrate the hard core of Indian resistance. So strong was suspicion and hatred of the white man among these holdouts that overwhelming force and privation failed to extinguish their burning will to continue the fight. On March 11, a band of Tontos attacked a party of three whites near Wickenburg. Killing two, they took the third, a young Scotsman, to a secluded spot and shot 150 arrows into his body, taking care not to hit a vital spot. They then finished him off in a manner that one observer found "so excruciating and beastly that I could not . . . hint of the method of his final taking off." Continuing their rampage, they hit several ranches in the area before slipping back into the Tonto Basin.[48]

Crook could not let this challenge go unanswered and immediately dispatched three columns to bring them to justice. One of these columns, a combined force of soldiers from the Twenty-Third Infantry and Fifth Cavalry under the command of Captain Randall and guided by a contingent of White Mountain Apaches, completed the task. On foot because an epidemic of epizootic, an equine influenza, had decimated the horse and mule population in Arizona, Randall's men combed the rough country for seventy-four days. At last they captured a woman who, under questioning, informed them that the Tontos had gone to ground at Turret Mountain east of Wickenburg.[49] Guided by their scouts, the troops sighted the mountain on March 26. As its name implied, it was a daunting steep-sided lava butte with a flattened summit crowned at one end by a rocky outcrop rising against the sky like a dark medieval castle. Knowing that anyone approaching in daylight would be immediately visible from the peak, Randall decided to wait for nightfall to make his approach. As darkness descended, using only starlight for illumination, the men moved forward at a crawl, up a stony creek bed and then laboriously up the side of the mountain on their hands and knees, their feet and knees wrapped in gunnysacks to protect them from the jagged stones that littered the narrow trail. After midnight, the exhausted men reached the summit and, peering over the rocky escarpment, observed the enemy's flickering campfires scattered across the flat mountaintop before them. Silently, they settled into position to await the dawn.[50]

When the sky had lightened sufficiently for the soldiers to see their sleeping foes, Randall gave the order to fire. Crook later reported that, "so secure did [the Indians] feel in this almost impregnable position that [completely surprised by the attack] they lost all presence of mind. . . . Some of them jumped off the precipice and were mashed into a shapeless mass.[51] Between twenty-three and thirty-three Indians were killed, while about ten were captured. So complete was the element of surprise that Randall's force suffered no losses.[52] But again, neither Chunz nor Delche was among the casualties.

For the overwhelming majority of the remaining Tonto and Yavapai resisters, already severely stressed by the relentless winter campaign, Turret Mountain and the penetration of their most impregnable and hidden redoubts was the last straw. Sensing the moment, Crook released captives into the Tonto Basin with the message that he was prepared to extend the "olive branch" to any hostiles willing to give up their depredations forever and move onto the reservation.[53] The first response came on April 6, when Cha-lipan straggled into Camp Verde with three hundred followers, representatives of over twenty-three hundred members of the resisting bands in central and western Arizona. Crook greeted the chief from a chair placed on the post commander's porch. "Had it not been for their barbarities," he later reflected, "one would have been moved to pity by their appearance. They were emaciated, their clothes in tatters, some of their legs were not thicker than my arm."[54] Cha-lipan explained that the soldiers' "copper cartridges" and the efforts of the scouts had done their work. His people were finished as a fighting force. Crook then rose and took the chief's hand, telling him that if he promised to live in peace, "he [Crook] would be the best friend he ever had." But, he warned, this peace would have to be permanent, and must include not only the Americans, but the Mexicans and Indian tribes as well.[55]

Cha-lipan's surrender, though it signaled the end of resistance in the Tonto Basin, was, for Crook, only a first step on the white man's road, the path to peace and the integration of the Apache peoples into American society. The reservation system would be the means toward that end, a framework for the implementation of theories that, while they seem ethnocentric and patronizing to the modern reader, were considered enlightened by the standards of his time. And they did not imply that Crook regarded the Indians as less intelligent or able than whites. Concerned that his men might be misled by the Indians' apparent lack of sophistication, he cautioned his officers "to treat them as children in ignorance, not in innocence."[56]

The initial task was to bind these former nomads to the land the government assigned to them. No Indian would be allowed beyond the boundaries of the reservation without permission; and, until all of their comrades had joined them, they would wear identity tags and submit to frequent head counts. On the reservation, they were expected to abandon their more brutal customs, such as the practice of cutting off the noses of unfaithful spouses and their Tiswin drunks, which often resolved into violence.[57] Renouncing these "savage practices" was to be the first phase in weaning the Indian away from tribalism, which Crook considered the primary obstacle to the assimilation of the Indian into the white world. Tribalism, in his mind, was antithetical to progress. It focused the attention of the individual on the interests of the community rather than on his own advancement and forced conformity of the beliefs of each member to those of the whole. Only if "liberated" from this force, could the Indian become the individualist he would need to be to succeed in a capitalist system. And to Crook, steeped in the dogmas of nineteenth-century America, capitalism was an essential milestone on the road to civilization.

Hard work would be required. "Idleness," he admonished Cha-lipan, drawing deeply on his Methodist heritage, "was the source of all evils, and work was the only cure." Henceforth, he announced, the chief and his people would become farmers. For the foreseeable future, only those who became scouts would avoid this destiny. While the people worked the land, the army would protect them and provide rations until they became self-supporting.[58]

For Crook, his Indian scouts were not only critical to success in waging war, but were essential contributors in the breakdown of tribal loyalties.[59] On the reservation, scouts, who had served initially as guides for the soldiers, would be transformed into a native police force and become pathfinders for their people. Initially responsible for keeping the peace on the reservation, they would gradually evolve into the "nucleus for the establishment of civil government." Introduced by the post commanders to procedures for peaceful dispute resolution "according to the usages of civilization," they would show their fellow tribesmen their "benefits as contrasted with their own barbarous forms and customs." These procedures, simple at first, but increasing in complexity as the Indians' understanding and acceptance of them grew, would be tailored to the practices of each tribe, and would, in time, ready the Indian for self-government and citizenship. The underlying weakness in this scheme was, of course, the patently ethnocentric assumption that the native peoples' own system of governance was ineffective and that they would eagerly embrace the white man's practices despite radical differences in the two cultures.

Yet for all his faith in the uplifting influence of white civilization, at this stage at least, Crook was not naïve about his former hostiles' commitment to reservation life. A substantial element in the Anglo and Mexican population of Arizona shared Crook's wariness, though not his faith that these so recently relentless foes could be transformed into peaceable neighbors. The sight of Apaches wearing uniforms and carrying guns made them uneasy. To allay these concerns, Crook assured Arizonans that his peace policies would endure only so long as the Indians remained on the reservation and in compliance with the government's regulation. As to any "renegades still at large," if they failed to join their comrades on the reservation, post commanders would force them to do so or destroy them.[60]

Two weeks after Cha-lipan's surrender, Delche, who had successfully eluded capture by the troops sent after him, raised the white flag after he and the remnants of his band were cornered by Randall's troops in the Mazatzal Mountains. To his captors, he mourned the fact that his men "used to have no difficulty in eluding the troops, but now the very rocks had gotten soft, they couldn't put their foot anywhere without leaving an impression by which we could follow, that they could get no sleep at night for should a coyote or a fox start a rock rolling during the night they would get up and dig out, thinking it was we who were after them." Initially, Delche and his followers were assigned to the White Mountain reservation, but fearing retaliation from the Coyoteros for the killing of one of their scouts, in August they fled to the Verde reservation, where Crook allowed them to remain.[61]

Following the surrenders of Cha-lipan and Delche, Crook optimistically told his men that "an Indian war that has been waged since the days of Cortez" Had been brought to a close. Days later, he announced to his superiors that "the war is virtually at an end so far as all the tribes in this Territory are concerned, except perhaps Cochise's band."[62] His failure to include the Chiricahuas was significant. They continued to be a burr under his saddle. In July, still chafing from the effects of Howard's agreement, which effectively removed the tribe from his control, he fretted that the Indians on the San Carlos and White Mountain reservations "are . . . impressed with the idea that the troops are afraid of Cochise or they would not permit him to raid on Mexico."[63] In his annual report that fall to the secretary of war, he again expressed uneasiness about the Chiricahuas, blaming them for creating unrest among the other bands, "goading them with the example of their own lawless irresponsible position."[64] In early February 1874, he sent a delegation to call on the chief under the guise of seeking to learn the details of the Howard treaty, the terms of which, he continued to publicly insist, were unknown to him. Undoubtedly, Crook intended the mission, which included Lieutenant Bourke, to also assess the tribe's strength and fortifications and perhaps convince Cochise to curb his warriors. While they may have gathered some intelligence, the envoys' efforts failed to change the tribe's behavior. Though the great chief treated the officers with consideration and reiterated his promise to keep the peace with the Americans, he considered the Mexicans an entirely separate matter. While he personally had not accompanied raids into Sonora, he had little inclination to stop his young men from doing so.[65] Crook, precluded by Howard's agreement from using his troops to end the depredations, continued to badger his superiors with suggestions on how to deal with the threat. Acknowledging that intervention by his own troops might reignite war with the Chiricahuas, he proposed, perhaps with tongue in cheek, that the government consider letting the

Mexicans cross the border to redress their grievances. Unsurprisingly, this proposal met with resounding silence from Washington.[66]

Notwithstanding unresolved issues with Cochise, the army high command was ecstatic over Crook's performance. In late April, General Schofield officially expressed appreciation "to Brevet Major General George Crook . . . and his gallant troop[;] for the extraordinary service they have rendered in the late campaign against the Apache Indians, the Division Commander extends his thanks and his congratulations upon their brilliant successes. They have merited the gratitude of the nation."[67] In Arizona, the local papers anointed General Crook "the Napoleon of successful Indian fighters."[68]

Ironically, the end of hostilities coincided with the arrival of the telegraph in the Territory. In early September, in a ceremony at Fort Whipple, Mary Crook broke ground for the first telegraph pole on Arizona soil; and on October 29, the line was completed. The first message tapped over it came from General Schofield, notifying Mary's husband of his promotion to the rank of brigadier general to fill the vacancy created by the retirement of Brigadier General St. George Cooke.[69] Responding to popular pressure, President Grant had finally overruled War Department opposition and, breaking with military tradition, promoted Crook two ranks, from lieutenant colonel to brigadier over the heads of a number of more senior officers. Some of these men, Nelson Miles in particular, would not forget what they regarded as a slight to their own achievements. But endorsements, including a resolution passed by the California legislature, overcame their objections, and Crook's promotion was swiftly confirmed by the Senate. The oath of office was administered to him on December 4, 1873, in Prescott.[70]

Crook's Tonto Campaign had been something of a tour de force. As one noted historian wrote, "As an exercise in guerrilla operations against an unconventional foe, [the Tonto Basin offensive] had been classic in conception, almost flawless in execution, and decisive in results."[71] Drawing upon his operations against the Paiutes and the Pit River Indians, and perhaps counterinsurgency experiences during the Civil War, Crook had designed and executed a successful campaign in the most inhospitable terrain imaginable against a foe renowned for endurance, elusiveness, and fighting skills. He had attained his objectives through a well-thought-out blend of innovative and imaginative elements that left little to chance.

Not the least of his innovations was his use of scouts drawn from the ranks of his enemy, the only force capable of ferreting out their places of concealment. The employment of scouts to hunt down their own people pierced the veil of tribal unity and by so doing, devastated the hostiles' morale. But their efforts alone could not have succeeded without the highly mobile columns of disciplined and committed troops deployed by Crook; his reliance on commanders of proven intelligence, maturity, and initiative; and the support of mule trains well prepared and conditioned, and managed by professional packers and mule skinners. Nor would these columns have been as effective had Crook not kept them in the field for extended periods, ceaselessly combing the wild country of central Arizona to deny the enemy any opportunity for relief, respite, or resupply. A final indispensable ingredient of Crook's success was his decision not to conduct the campaign from behind a desk. Remaining in the field throughout, he supervised and directed the movements of each independent column while, at the same time, allowing the officers the freedom to deal with exigencies in the field as they arose.[72] It was probably during his conduct of the campaign that he earned the name by which he was known to the Indians of Arizona, Nantan Lupan, or Chief Gray Fox, likely a reference to an animal Apaches regarded as an omen of impending death.[73]

The campaign was certainly extremely harsh in its execution, as indeed Crook had intended. But as he had foreseen, its very cruelty brought it to its rapid conclusion. He could now report with considerable satisfaction, "Although we may have some scattering depredations in some parts of the Territory, I feel that the main work is over, and the necessary corrections can be made by the post commanders." But, he warned, "I expect to be kept busy for several months to come, watching that the Indians on the various reservations settle down in the right grooves."[74] He would be, indeed.

CHAPTER TEN

"Their Future Depended Very Much upon Themselves"

April 1873–March 1875

The newly appointed brigadier now turned his attention to creating a pathway for the adaptation of the Apaches and Yavapais to the reservation system, a task that he clearly welcomed. At Verde, within a week of their surrender, he proudly noted, the Indians were put to work digging a five-mile-long irrigation ditch under the supervision of an officer with some engineering experience. Using old worn-out tools, shovels, picks, and axes, and where tools were not available, fire-sharpened sticks, Tontos and Yavapais laboriously but willingly hacked away at the hard desert soil. Soon, their efforts were rewarded. Watered by the canal, fifty-seven acres of melons and produce sprouted on the formerly barren plain. Additional land was cleared and, the following year, produced a harvest of 500,000 pounds of corn and 30,000 pounds of beans.[1]

But the road to "civilization" was not smooth. As Crook had predicted, a number of the Indians now settled on reservations did not share his enthusiasm for the white man's path. Some of the old resisters—Chunz, Delche, Cochenay, and Chan-Deisi were singled out by Crook for special mention—had surrendered with their people and had been granted amnesty for past misdeeds. But in Crook's eyes "they had no real intention of remaining on their reservations but simply viewed them as a convenience upon which to secure supplies of arms and ammunition." While these elements remained quiescent during the summer of 1873, a sizable number of holdouts who had refused

Crook's terms of surrender continued hit-and-run attacks on ranches and travelers and now occupied his troops in their pursuit.[2]

These irreconcilables were but one source of unrest. The Indian Bureau supplied its own brand of mischief. Following the establishment of the reservation system in Arizona and the surrender of most of the hostiles, responsibility for the management of the reservations was transferred from the military to the Bureau, which, despite the reforms instituted by the Grant administration, remained plagued by corruption. Agents received their positions based on political connections rather than merit. Although some were honest and well intentioned, they were for the most part easterners, wholly ignorant of their Indian charges. Inexperienced and naïve, they proved to be inept administrators. And because of poor pay and bad working conditions, the recruitment of good men was difficult. In their place came individuals who saw the job as an opportunity for graft. Together with merchants seeking government contracts, these agents helped perpetuate "the Indian Ring," bent upon getting rich by cheating both the Indians and the government. Crook was quick to recognize the problem. "As soon as the Indians became settled on the different reservations, gave up the warpath, and became harmless," he later wrote, "the Indian agents, who had sought cover before now, came out as brave as sheep, and took charge of the agencies, and commenced their game of plundering."[3]

One of the more egregious examples of such graft occurred on the Beale Spring Reservation, home of the Hualapais, a tribe that had rendered valuable service to the military during the Tonto campaign. Upon transfer of the management of the reservation to the Indian Bureau, Crook had ordered Captain Thomas Byrne, an officer well respected by both his commander and the tribe, to keep an eye on matters. Byrne soon received angry complaints of short rations from the Indians. Upon investigation, he quickly discovered fraud on a massive scale, ascertaining that, "Beef cattle weighing in reality but 300 pounds each, were issued to the Indians upon scales that made them with the unprecedented weight of 1300 & odd pounds each." Had the commanding officer not put a stop to the practice, Crook warned, an outbreak would have been a certainty.[4] When the Indian Bureau ignored Byrne's findings, Crook convened a court of inquiry that further disclosed that the Indian agent and the beef contractor were selling wagonloads of stolen meat to nearby miners.[5]

As Crook had warned, Bureau corruption resulted in violent outbreaks during the spring and summer of 1874, one at Verde and another at San Carlos. The unrest at San Carlos was unquestionably the result of the machinations of the Indian agent. The first civilian agent on the reservation, George Stevens, had been incorruptible and well liked. Unsurprisingly, the Indian Ring viewed him as an impediment to their interests. Using manufactured evidence of corruption, they managed to have him replaced by a more malleable agent, a retired army officer named Charles F. Larrabee, a man of integrity but inexperienced in Indian affairs.[6] Pending Larrabee's arrival, the Ring connived to have Dr. H. R. Wilbur of Tucson appointed temporary agent.[7] By all accounts, Wilbur, who arrived at San Carlos in February, was "a thoroughly bad man." The doctor played off one Indian faction against another, relying on known malcontents like Chuntz and Cochinay to stir up rivalries. With the two factions vying for the agent's favor, Wilbur concentrated on maintaining "his position at the San Carlos trough."

When Larrabee finally assumed his position on the reservation in March, at Wilbur's urging, one of the factions attempted to undermine the new agent's authority, eventually planning to murder him. The inexperienced Larrabee, unaware of Wilbur's intentions, attempted to placate the rebels, which only encouraged them. Growing frightened by their increasing insolence and threats, the agent sought protection from the military. Captain Brown, commander of nearby Fort Grant, hastened to the agency, sized up the situation, and recommended that the agent arrest Chuntz. But Larrabee could not bring himself to do so and, instead, continued his attempts at appeasement. Frustrated, Brown departed, grimly predicting that the next time he returned to the reservation, it would probably be to bury the hapless agent. Unwilling to leave the man entirely to his fate, he ordered his subordinate, a young lieutenant, a Quaker named Jacob Almy, to remain with Larrabee, warning him to exercise extreme caution and "strike a blow in case he was called upon to act." Tragically, Almy failed to heed this advice.

The Aravaipas at San Carlos were by now so fearful of imminent trouble that their leaders, Eskiminzin and Chiquito, fled into the mountains with their people, sending back spies to monitor the situation. Two weeks after Brown's departure, one of these men overheard Chunz plotting to kill the agent and then go on the warpath.

He informed Larrabee, who set out with Lieutenant Almy and a small detachment of soldiers to confront the miscreant chief. It was ration day and a large and unruly crowd had gathered to receive their allotments. Lieutenant Almy foolishly approached the hostile gathering alone and unarmed. As he disappeared into the throng, a shot rang out and he staggered back, shot in the side, moaning "Oh, my God." His horrified soldiers watched helplessly as a second shot shattered the young Lieutenant's skull, killing him instantly. In the melee that followed, the Indians, both guilty and innocent, decamped to the mountains. Many of the Indians not involved in the plot returned shortly to the reservation, but Chunz and his allies remained at large. Larrabee, badly frightened by the events, resigned.[8]

The news of the outbreak and the death of young Almy infuriated Crook. He was not slow to blame the affair on the Indian Ring and, somewhat illogically, on General Howard for failing to rein in Lieutenant Whitman, whose "rottenness," he declared, was somehow responsible for Wilbur's machinations at San Carlos.[9] He promptly issued orders that none of the Indians currently off the reservation would be allowed to come in until "they shall have delivered up, dead or alive, all the murderers."[10] He used Larrabee's resignation as a means to regain control of the reservation, replacing the civilian agent with Captain Brown. Brown's mandate was almost biblical in tone. "Impartial justice to all who do well, the olive branch to all who desire to be at peace, but certain punishment to the wrongdoers. . . . Let no Indian profit by his own misdeed, but let it be unprofitable to the last degree to the willfully persistent wrongdoers."[11] But despite Brown's diligent efforts, the miscreants continued to elude capture.

Meanwhile, at Camp Verde, a disaffected faction among the reservation Yavapais and Tontos slipped away from the agency to raid nearby ranches and farms, returning each time to receive their rations. These rebels found a leader in Delche, whom Crook had allowed to remain at Verde. Under Delche's direction, his followers plotted a mass exodus into the Tonto Basin. At this time, the acting Indian agent at Verde was Lieutenant Walter Schuyler, a twenty-three-year-old son of a prominent New York family who had become one of the general's favorites, having distinguished himself by his courage and good sense.[12]

By late summer, Schuyler and his scout, Al Sieber, sensed that something was amiss on the reservation. Although uncertain of the exact nature of the problem, they were convinced that Delche was behind it. When the lieutenant reported his concerns to Crook, the general advised him to arrest the dissident immediately, avoiding trouble if at all possible but, if necessary, not to hesitate to kill the ringleaders. In a rare display of fatherly concern, Crook concluded his letter on a personal note. "I shall feel very anxious about you until I hear from you again."[13]

Delche must have been tipped off to Schuyler's intentions because when the lieutenant went to arrest him at an agency head count, the officer discovered that someone had unloaded his gun. Defenseless, his small detachment was quickly surrounded by a crowd of hostile Indians. Only the intervention of a Yavapai chief, whose warriors outnumbered Delche's, saved the soldiers from Almy's fate. The Yavapais, fearing retribution should Schuyler be murdered, convinced Delche to return to his rancheria and remain there until summoned by Schuyler. Without waiting for the lieutenant's call, Delche decamped into the mountains with about forty of his supporters.[14]

The number of Indians on the run grew when, in January, Eskiminzin and some of his Aravaipas took flight from San Carlos after the new post commander, Captain Randall, ordered the chief arrested for unspecified reasons.[15] Crook now faced the same situation that he had in the winter of 1872–73, but on a lesser scale, as small bands of disaffected Apaches and Yavapais scattered throughout the mountain wilderness of central Arizona. With another winter approaching, he again loosed a number of columns into the Tonto Basin and nearby mountain ranges in weather he described as "the most inclement and rigorous ever experienced in Arizona since American occupation." Rain-swollen streams and rivers blocked the troops at every turn, and thick mud bogged down their pack trains.[16] But the Apaches, who had taken to the mountains without supplies or shelter, suffered even more. Hounded by Crook's troops, most of the Indians from San Carlos wanted only to return quickly to the reservation. But flooding on the Gila River blocked their way and prevented the troops from reaching them. So, when Chunz and his confederates infiltrated the camp and got the Indians drunk on Tiswin, the soldiers were helpless to stop him. Before long, drunk on the fermented corn beverage and inflamed by taunts from the hardcore dissidents, a group of young warriors fell upon a nearby wagon train carrying supplies for the troops. Murdering the teamsters, they plundered the wagons and headed into the Pinal mountains. Though the troops soon ran them to ground, killing or capturing most of the warriors, Chunz and his ally, Cochinay once more eluded capture. In a second engagement in early April, thirty-one more hostiles were killed and fifty taken prisoner. But again, the ringleaders escaped.[17]

While Captain Randall hunted Chunz and Cochinay, Lieutenant Schuyler and Al Sieber pursued Delche and Eskiminzin into the Aravaipa Mountains. Despite Crook's distrust of him, Eskiminzin had never been an enthusiastic holdout and voluntarily returned to San Carlos in late April. But Delche escaped onto the Mogollon Rim. Crook plaintively offered a lame excuse for his failure to capture or kill the wily renegades, saying they "were so encamped with their followers that in almost every case of attack by the troops and allies . . . the blow fell upon the latter and the leaders got away."[18]

Frustrated and undoubtedly embarrassed, Crook now resorted to desperate measures that, while greeted warmly in Arizona, must have raised eyebrows among humanitarian groups in the East. In the late spring of 1874, groups of Indians from both Verde and San Carlos, worn out by the fighting and near starvation, straggled into their respective reservations to give themselves up. Crook, adhering to the policy he had adopted after Almy's murder, at first refused to accept their surrender, but then offered them a bizarre trade-off. He recalled years later, "I finally compromised by letting them stay, provided they would bring in the heads of certain of the chiefs who were ringleaders, which they agreed to."[19] A similar message was conveyed to the bands still at large in the mountains.

Nickerson, Crook's aide, sardonically noted that the alacrity with which the former dissidents accepted Crook's offer was "almost magical."[20] Cochinay, of the San Carlos holdouts, was the first to go, killed in June by scouts at a hideout only three miles from Tucson, and his head delivered to the agency.[21] Days later, Crook happily reported to Schuyler at Verde that Chan-Desi (John Daisy to the general, who believed him responsible for Lieutenant Almy's murder) had been killed and his head forwarded to Camp Apache.[22] That, he fairly crowed, "leaves only Chunz's head on his shoulders of all the proscribed from

San Carlos." Then, referring to the Verde renegades, Crook wrote "the more prompt these heads are brought in, the less liable other Indians in the future will be to jeopardize their heads."[23]

Not long afterward, an Apache named Desalin, variously described as either a White Mountain or a recently surrendered Tonto, hunted down Chunz and six of his followers in the Santa Catalina Mountains, again, not far from Tucson. He brought the seven heads back to San Carlos, where they were neatly displayed on the post parade ground.[24] A month later, the indefatigable Desalin triumphantly brought in yet another head, declaring that it belonged to Delche.[25] He was a little late. Some nights previously, three Tontos had delivered a dirty folded rag to the tent of the Camp Verde surgeon, Dr. Corbusier. Unwrapping the cloth, Dr. Corbusier found "a whole scalp with the left ear hanging to it, in the lobe of which [was] tied a pearl shirt button." Scouts at the agency recognized the scalp as Delche's.[26] Crook, confronted by an embarrassment of riches, hit upon a conclusion that would have pleased King Solomon. He declared that Delche had two heads, and "paid both parties."[27]

In his annual report for 1874, Crook concluded that the elimination of the chiefs, whom he termed outlaws, "closes out all the leading elements of disturbances at Verde, San Carlos and Apache, and if the Indians on these reservations are properly managed, kept at work, furnished with seeds and implements and their present interest in raising stock and making themselves houses encouraged, there will be no further trouble with them and they will gradually become self-supporting."[28] And perhaps, if Crook's prescriptions for peace had been followed, this hope might have been realized.

CHAPTER ELEVEN

Removal

No more than three months after Crook had assured the War Department that the Apaches and Yavapais were peacefully settled on their reservations and headed toward self-sufficiency, the Office (Bureau) of Indian Affairs announced plans to close the Verde Reservation and relocate its residents to San Carlos, two hundred miles to the east. The move was to be the first step in the implementation of the Interior Department's so-called concentration policy, aimed at consolidating the Western Apaches and allied tribes at San Carlos, described by one Chiricahua warrior as "the worst place in all the great territory stolen from the Apache. If anybody had ever lived there permanently, no Apache knew of it."[1] General Howard had first proposed relocation to San Carlos as a cost-cutting measure, an important consideration for a government in the grip of a severe depression. If the Indians could be confined to fewer reservations, a smaller number of soldiers would be required to police them, fewer agents would be needed, and rations could be supplied more cheaply and efficiently. Not incidentally, closing reservations would make the land on which they were located available to settlers, ranchers, and miners, a matter of some interest to Howard, who had early on favored reducing the boundaries of existing reservations to exclude valuable ore deposits.[2] Ironically, Verde had become attractive because of the irrigation system, installed at Crook's direction, which increased the arability and hence desirability of the land to nearby white farmers.

In addition to the government and land-hungry settlers, the notorious Indian Ring, also stood to profit from consolidation. These merchants opposed Crook's effort to make the Verde Indians more self-sufficient, concerned that it would reduce the Indians' dependency on contractors' supplies. Tucson businessmen, in particular, being closer to San Carlos than Verde, lobbied Indian Affairs officials in support of the move. Cannily, they calculated that the barren and soon to be overcrowded San Carlos would remain dependent on their trade goods, creating numerous future opportunities for graft.[3]

As a young second lieutenant on the Pacific coast, Crook had experienced the tragic impact of forced removal following the Rogue River War.[4] But, though keenly aware of the human cost of implementing the policy, he did not oppose it in every case. As a soldier, he knew security was of primary importance, inclining him toward removal when it demonstrably reduced the threat to frontier whites. And though he understood the Indians' spiritual attachment to their lands, as the son of a generation of pioneers who willingly abandoned homesteads to move westward in search of new opportunity, he viewed tribal devotion to their native lands as a vestige of tribalism. As such, it would disappear as the Indians advanced to a higher level of development and assimilated into white society. Whatever could be done to hasten this process was desirable, as Crook and other proponents of assimilation saw communal ties to the land as a stumbling block to societal advancement. If private ownership replaced communalism, Indians would be more likely to become entrepreneurial farmers and stock raisers, smoothing their integration into white society. Where removal seemed a useful first step in this progression and could be peacefully effected without harming the economic interests or the health of the Indians, Crook could and did support it.

The removal of the Date Creek Yavapais was an example of a relocation he favored. Despite the tribe's vigorous opposition to being uprooted from their home territory, Crook favored moving them to Verde because of Date Creek's proximity to a major travel route, which Crook considered an open invitation to robbery and murder. At the same time, the move to Verde would ultimately benefit the tribe. The infertile and parched land around Date Creek would never support crops, while at Verde, the land was rich and fish and game were abundant.[5] And, after some initial opposition, the Indians did indeed make the transition peacefully, though not without hardship. Disease decimated the tribe during their first six months at the new agency. Nevertheless, after moving to healthier climes on the reservation, they had adapted reasonably well to their new home.[6]

Perhaps somewhat chastened by the Date Creek experience, Crook took a contrary position when, in September 1873, the Indian Bureau proposed to move the Hualapais from their home at Beale Springs to the Colorado River Reservation on the desert floor, a move to a climate known to be far more unhealthy than Verde. Again, the tribe strongly opposed the move. As Crook had greatly valued their service during the Tonto campaign, he was far more likely to support their cause than had been the case with the Date Creeks, who had actively opposed him. For that reason and because he believed that the transfer posed a threat to the health of the Hualapais, he actively campaigned in their behalf. Probably aware that the threat of violence might carry more weight with the government than health considerations, he warned, "I shall exceedingly regret if [the] Hualapais' attachment to their old hunting grounds causes them to rebel."[7] Despite his efforts, the Indian bureau proceeded with the move and, as Crook had predicted, the Hualapais fled the reservation and commenced raiding nearby ranches and farms. They were eventually recaptured and forced to return to the Colorado River Reservation where, as Crook had foreseen, many perished in the desert heat. Then, the rains failed, resulting in the death of half of their horses from starvation, and loss of their crops, leaving them dependent on inadequate government rations for the duration of the winter.[8]

The following spring, Crook successfully blocked an attempt to force the Yavapais and Tontos to join the Hualapais on the Colorado. In a letter to the War Department, the general described the reservation on the Colorado River as "rotten with loathsome disease." The Yavapais told him, he said, "they would rather die than go to the Colorado."[9] With the Hualapai catastrophe still a fresh memory, the Interior Department canceled plans for the move. Yet only another five months would elapse before the Department announced plans to move the Verde Indians to San Carlos. Crook again fought the move, arguing that relocating the Yavapais would place them among bands traditionally hostile to them. While the same argument might apply to Verde, there peace was preserved by a sizable contingent of troops.

At San Carlos, the Indians would be spread out over a large area and could not be adequately defended. Further, he pointed out, conditions at Verde had vastly improved over the past year. Sicknesses had almost entirely disappeared, and the Indians had constructed a "fine irrigating canal, have built an excellent storehouse and are making for themselves comfortable homes." Finally, he raised an ethical consideration, a factor not usually given much weight by the government in its dealings with the tribes. Involuntary relocation would "break the faith after forcing the Indians to that reserve which they were given to understand was to be their permanent home." The Indian Bureau, which one historian described as run by men who either "stole the livery of heaven to serve the devil in," or were "errant fools," remained obdurate.[10] In February 1875, Interior Department bureaucrats ordered the immediate removal of all of the Arizona bands at Verde to San Carlos, a decision Crook predicted would result in "turning 1500 Apaches [*sic*] loose upon the settlers of Arizona. . . ."[11]

Transporting the entire population of the reservation, some 1,400 Indians, across the mountainous terrain between Verde and San Carlos in winter was an ambitious—some would say foolhardy—endeavor. Men, women, young children, and old people would be forced to travel 180 miles over rough terrain in extreme weather. Adding to the difficulty, the move would place two traditionally hostile tribes—the Tontos and the Eastern Yavapais—in close proximity for a considerable period of time under stressful conditions that could be expected to exacerbate tensions. To handle this delicate situation and superintend the move, the Bureau, with unerring stupidity, chose Edwin L. Dudley, recently retired Indian commissioner of New Mexico.

It is difficult to conceive of a more inappropriate choice than this singularly insensitive individual, a man with no discernable empathy for the Indians whose lives he was about to disrupt. Upon his arrival, Dudley immediately got off on the wrong foot. As he appeared before the anxious Indians to inform them of their impending dislocation, his manner was so rude and erratic as to convince Dr. Corbusier, the post surgeon at Verde, that he was drunk. Exhibiting callous indifference to his charges, he selected a route to San Carlos with complete disregard for their welfare. A relatively flat road linked Verde to their destination; but Dudley reckoned a trail through the mountains would shorten the journey. When Dr. Corbusier and Lieutenant Schuyler attempted to dissuade him, pointing out that the mountain route was too steep and rough for wagons to carry the infirm and the aged, Dudley nonchalantly replied, "They are Indians. Let the beggars walk."[12]

As the Interior Department now controlled the reservation system, Crook had no choice but to assist Dudley. But he was a reluctant accomplice. While freely providing wagons to carry supplies and those too weak to make the journey on foot, he refused to allow his troops to be used to coerce the Indians should they refuse to move.[13] However, though Crook was reluctant to use force, according to at least one source, he appeared disposed to lie to the Indians to get them to move peacefully. Mike Burns, the young Yavapai who had guided soldiers to the Salt Cave two years before, wrote that the general assured the tribe that they would be going to San Carlos only temporarily to learn to live as farmers. Once they had demonstrated their adaptation to a white lifestyle, they would be returned to Verde, probably in no more than ten years. Of course, the government had no such intention, and the tale of Crook's alleged perfidy soon became enshrined in Yavapai and Tonto tradition. It may explain why, in 2005, one Tonto at Fort Apache told the author that Crook was widely hated by the Tontos because "he lied to us." Yet no other source has corroborated Burns's story. Corbusier, who was at Verde at the time and was sympathetic to the Indians, makes no mention of the incident. Nor do others involved in the removal. So the tale, though widely believed, must remain questionable.[14]

Fearing that the Indians would be frightened by a show of force, Crook assigned only a small detachment of troops to accompany them. He named George Eaton, a young but sensible second lieutenant not long out of West Point, to head the escort, which consisted of only a sergeant, two corporals, and twenty privates of the Fifth Cavalry.[15] When Eaton asked the general what he should do in the event fighting broke out between the different bands, he recollected, much after the fact, that "[Crook] dropped his head a moment and then said slowly and reflectively, 'Well, if they want to fight wholly among themselves when we are doing our very best for them, then let them fight, but if it comes to a point where government property and the safety of your command is endangered, you will of course stop it if you can.'"[16] The Indians, who trusted few whites other than Dr. Corbusier, had demanded that the surgeon accompany them. Dudley refused to allow it, believing that the doctor's presence was unnecessary. But Crook overruled him, and Corbusier joined the escort.[17]

On February 27, 1875, "a long, silent, and sad procession," fourteen hundred souls, from tribal elders to babes in arms, the lame, and the pregnant, set out on the rough trail to their new home. They "had to carry all their belongings on their backs and in their V-shaped baskets, old and young with heavy packs. One old man placed his aged and decrepit wife in one of these baskets with her feet hanging out, and carried her on his back . . . almost all the way."[18]

As feared, traditional animosities, aggravated by chronic hunger and hardship, made an outbreak of violence inevitable despite efforts to keep the tribes apart. Ten days after the Indians left Verde, hostilities erupted when a game between young Yavapai and Tonto boys escalated from verbal abuse into armed conflict among their menfolk.[19] If Crook had indeed ordered him not to intervene, Eaton ignored the command. Courageously, he interposed himself and his troops between the opposing forces, preventing what could have become a terrible slaughter. Despite his swift intervention, as many as seven warriors died, and ten were wounded in the melee.[20] Only the timely arrival of supplies from San Carlos prevented a second clash during the last grueling days of the march; and a week after the fight, bedraggled and exhausted, they reached San Carlos at last, dragging their wounded on makeshift litters.

Following Crook's transfer from the Department, the Indian Bureau would continue its policy of concentrating the Apaches and Yavapais at San Carlos. The White Mountain band was moved from the Fort Apache Agency in the summer of 1875, and the Chiricahuas followed a year later. These forced transfers sowed the seeds for Apache outbreaks over the next decade and eventually prompted the War Department to return Crook to Apacheria. Of the Yavapais and Tontos, Crook would later sadly write, "Their removal was one of those cruel things that greed has so often inflicted on the Indian."[21]

CHAPTER TWELVE

Final Days in Arizona

October 1874

In the fall of 1874, the Indians more or less peacefully settled on their reservations, and with his Arizona tour drawing to a close, the general and Lieutenant Bourke embarked on an inspection tour of the department's posts and reservations, a journey that included a visit to the spectacular Grand Canyon country. At San Carlos, Crook found that under the strict discipline of his officers, who had taken charge of the reservation pending the arrival of the Bureau agent, the Indians had settled into a pacific, if highly regimented, lifestyle. The Apaches had erected their brush wickiups in rows along streets laid out with military precision, which were policed daily and inspected by the officers on Sundays to ensure that garbage had not accumulated around the quarters.[1] Every morning the Indians were formed into details and sent off to make bricks, work in the fields, or attend to their duties as policemen. To Bourke, the 875 residents of the reservation seemed happy, healthy, well fed, and eagerly in search of opportunities to enter the cash economy to purchase the white man's goods.[2] This latter observation was particularly edifying to Crook, as it boded well in his view for the Apaches' journey toward integration into white society.[3]

John Clum, a young, self-confident easterner, had recently arrived to serve as the new Indian agent. Bourke thought him a "good man," which to the lieutenant probably meant that he was honest and cheerful, and accepted the military's methods of handling the Apaches.[4] Clum's early impressions of life at San Carlos were decidedly less rosy than

Bourke's. "Of all the desolate, isolated human habitations! Wickipups, covered with brush and grass, blankets, or deerskins, smoky, smelly. Lean dogs, mangy, inert. A few Apaches strolling around, as wild and vicious as the inmates of an old folks home." But despite his initial glum assessment, the young man would come to "like the place."[5]

Leaving San Carlos, Crook, Bourke, and his party visited Camp Apache, riding over the trail he had marked out in 1871, a route that only months before would have been too dangerous for such a small group of travelers. As was often his habit, Crook took advantage of the journey to indulge his love of the hunt, seriously eroding the squirrel and turkey population to supply his men with fresh meat.[6] As at San Carlos, he was pleased to find Camp Apache's White Mountain reservation managed with strict military discipline under the firm and incorruptible hand of Major Randall.

From Camp Apache, the detachment proceeded north into the canyon country above the Mogollon Rim, home of the Moquis (known today as the Hopis). The Moquis, an agricultural society with strong entrepreneurial instincts, had established a trading network extending from northeastern Arizona well into New Mexico. Most recently, they employed it to supply the Apaches with weapons and ammunition they acquired from the Utes and Mormons.[7] Officially, the visit was intended to pressure the tribe to abandon its participation in this trade. As departmental commander, Crook could have assigned this straightforward task to an officer on his staff. But given their shared interest in ethnology, it is obvious that neither he nor Bourke would have given up this opportunity to observe firsthand the Moqui culture in its exotic homeland.

Agriculturists and traders of ancient lineage, the Moquis resided in a series of seven pueblos "perched like old feudal castles upon the very apex of a precipitous sandstone acclivity, rising hundreds of feet," surrounded by cultivated fields of maize and melons and peach trees, their limbs at this season bowed with ripening fruit. The two officers eagerly approached the settlement on an overcast fall day that hinted of snow and enhanced the mystery of the place. The Moquis, some of whom had learned rudimentary English from their Morman contacts, offered friendly greetings. And, before guiding them to their homes, they invited their visitors to water their mounts at an ingeniously designed tank of walled stone accessible by a broad ramp intended for sheep and goats.[8]

Determined to dispose of business quickly, Crook lost no time in expressing the government's displeasure at the gun trade and impressing upon the Moquis the consequences if they failed to stop the practice. The response was immediate and gratifying. Smugly, he later wrote that "the fright we gave them put an end to it."[9] In an atmosphere of prevailing goodwill, Crook then satisfied his hosts' entrepreneurialism by negotiating the purchase of forage for his animals and fresh fruit and vegetables for his men. He and his troops found the peaches particularly succulent, and his men began helping themselves in the orchards. That night, the Moquis tactfully put an end to the thievery by discreetly harvesting the remaining peaches from the orchards nearest to the soldiers' camp.[10]

The next four days were spent exploring the pueblos, observing the dress and habits of the people, and trading for foodstuffs and artifacts as any modern tourist might under similar circumstances. And, like tourists, the general and his aide paid visits to the Petrified Forest, Painted Desert, and Cataract Canyon, all in close proximity to the pueblos and, of course, did some hunting. Both men were fascinated by the richness of the Moqui culture, Bourke meticulously recording his observations in his diary. The adventure sparked an interest in the Pueblo culture of the Southwest that he would pursue throughout the remainder of his life, recalling this particular visit as among "the most pleasant trips of our military career."[11]

Returning to Prescott, Crook devoted his remaining time in Arizona to tending to the needs of the Indians on their reservations and overseeing the improvement of roads and military posts throughout the territory. On March 12, 1875, after completing the distasteful task of assisting in the removal of the Indians from Verde, he was notified that General Sheridan had decided to appoint him commanding general of the Department of the Platte. His replacement in Arizona was to be an old friend and classmate, August Kautz, now a colonel with the Eighth Infantry.

The announcement of his departure prompted an outpouring of affection and gratitude from the people of Arizona and throughout the United States. Though modest in his demeanor, Crook undoubtedly derived considerable pleasure from the accolades that now rained down upon him. Governor Safford opened the January 1875 session of the territorial legislature by announcing that Crook's "subjugation of the Apache . . . deserves the lasting gratitude of our people."[12] Anticipating Crook's departure, the legislature responded by passing a formal resolution thanking the general and his officers and men for their efforts.[13] The legislative action was accompanied by a chorus of demands for his presence at a variety of local entertainments in his honor. Carried away by the notoriety of their favorite son, his old hometown's newspaper, the *Dayton Journal*, on hearing of his lionization, exuberantly touted his nomination for president in '76, because "he has a superb record as a man and soldier; has an abundance of brains and is as resolute and silent as GRANT."[14]

In weather that makes the early spring such a delight in Arizona—clear blue skies, gentle breezes, and mild temperatures—the town of Prescott and his Fort Whipple headquarters prepared to bid farewell to their favorite general. A ball was planned in his honor, and a delegation of Prescott's prominent citizens requested that they be allowed to hold a reception so that "the great throng of his admirers [may have] an opportunity of manifesting their deep sense of his integrity, valor and ability as a true gentleman and soldier.[15] Crook graciously consented, and on the evening of March 23, with Mary at his side, the somewhat embarrassed general seated himself on a carpeted dais "hung with a festoon of Flags" and adorned with his portrait with the words, "Brave, Generous, and True" spelled out in evergreens. Beside him on the dais were Colonel Kautz and members of both officers' staffs. The affair, held at Hatz's Hall, Prescott's newest brick building, featured flowery speeches, music by the Eighth Infantry band, and that most grueling of social gauntlets, the reception line. Bravely, the reticent general stood beside his proud wife and stiffly shook the hands of every one of the three hundred notables in attendance.[16]

The following night, the bemused outgoing commander was feted at Fort Whipple by his officers at a "farewell hop." Bourke, intoxicated by the presence of so many ravishing young women and the lavishness of the menu, pronounced the affair one of the "grandest successes" he had ever attended. Amid fluttering guidons, sabers, and the heavy scent of evergreens, the party stretched on until two o'clock in the morning, when the general, aware that he would be departing early the next morning for the West coast and probably chafing in his unaccustomed dress uniform, called a halt to the proceedings.[17]

Somehow Crook assembled his traveling party, which included Bourke, Nickerson, and the latter's second wife and young daughter, for departure at nine the next morning. Unhappily, Nickerson had found duty in Arizona both arduous and damaging to his already fragile health. Earlier that spring, Crook had made an unsuccessful effort to help him transfer to a less physically taxing assignment in the adjutant general's office in Washington, enlisting the aid of his old friend Rutherford Hayes. But on this occasion, his efforts had been to no avail, and Nickerson was now accompanying him to the Platte, where he would continue to provide valued and dedicated service to his chief.[18]

CHAPTER THIRTEEN

Department of the Platte

A Pretext for War

Bent over the wash basin in his spartan room in Omaha's Grand Central Hotel, the newly arrived commander of the Department of the Platte splashed the dust and trail grit from his face and hands in a hurried attempt to make himself presentable for the welcoming throng, some of whom were even now mounting the stairs to his room. From the street outside, the strains of the recently composed *General Crook March*, played by his own Twenty-Third Regimental Band, wafted through the window, opened to admit the light spring breeze.[1] Needless to say, he was deeply gratified by the warmth and ceremony accorded him, though he may not have communicated his feelings to those assembled to greet him. Perhaps he secretly delighted in the ironic circumstance that this latest accolade had come through the efforts of General Sheridan, whom Crook blamed for denying him credit for his achievements during the Shenandoah campaign. Years later, writing of his relationship with his former West Point classmate, Crook would refer to him with bitterness, but for now,· their relationship appeared, at least outwardly, on a solid footing.[2]

Sheridan had been promoted to lieutenant general in 1868 and awarded command of the Military Division of the Missouri. By 1875, his troops had crushed the Indians of the southern plains, freeing him to turn his attention north, where he believed war was imminent with the fractious Sioux and their allies, the Northern Cheyennes and Arapahos. These tribes roamed over a vast, rolling grassland watered by great rivers—the Platte, the Yellowstone, and the Missouri and their numerous tributaries. It was an area so large that the military had carved it into two Departments, the Platte and Dakota, extending from Nebraska Territory to the Canadian border, encompassing what are today the states of Nebraska, Wyoming, Montana, and North and South Dakota.

In preparation for the clash he considered inevitable, even desirable, Sheridan had decided to replace the current commanding general of the Department of the Platte, General E. O. Ord, whom he regarded as an opportunist who viewed his professional duties through a prism of personal benefit. Worse still, in Sheridan's opinion, Ord regularly ignored the chain of command, bypassing his commander to direct his communications to Sheridan's boss, Sherman.[3] To replace Ord, the lieutenant general's gaze naturally fell on Crook, an officer of suitable rank, a friend—he thought, and a man in whom he had had confidence since their days at the Academy.[4] Crook had served successfully as Sheridan's subordinate during the war, in both the Shenandoah and Appomattox campaigns, and now enjoyed a growing reputation as one of the most competent and experienced Indian fighters in the army. His appointment would offset the inexperience of Brigadier General Alfred Terry, commander of the Department of the Dakotas, the other military district likely to see fighting in the event of war with the Sioux. Moreover, Crook was well regarded by Grant and Sherman, insuring that his appointment would not meet opposition from Washington.[5] Finally, in his former schoolmate, Sheridan thought that he had an officer who shared his philosophy of Indian warfare. Like Crook, Sheridan believed that the Indians must "be soundly whipped" to achieve peace. On the southern plains, the lieutenant general had defined what he meant by that. He had proposed that "the ringleaders in the present trouble [should be] hung, their ponies killed, and such destruction of their property as will make them very poor."[6] He had loudly praised Custer's winter attack on Black Kettle's Southern Cheyennes at the Washita, though a more thoughtful and less prejudiced officer might have found it to have been an excessive use of force against a peaceful village.[7] And he regularly encouraged his troops to bring fire and sword to the Indians as he had in the Shenandoah Valley during the Civil War. To Sheridan, Crook's aggressiveness in the Pacific Northwest and more recently in Idaho and Arizona seemed to confirm that the brigadier shared his commander's views. And to some extent, at the time, he was not too far off the mark.

Crook arrived in Omaha on April 25 after completing a five-week triumphal tour that included visits to Los Angeles and San Francisco, where he was feted by powerful men who controlled the military, political, and economic affairs of the West. When his onward journey to Nebraska was interrupted by bad weather, he spent two weeks in Salt Lake as a guest of the Mormons. There, he and his aides met Brigham Young. Unlike Bourke, Crook's generally tolerant attitude toward religion led him to eschew comment on Mormon practices and the character of its hierarchy. His only public comment on the visit was that he had been "treated royally" by Young and his cohorts, while his aide, a staunch Roman Catholic, later expressed revulsion at some of the practices of the Latter-day Saints, particularly polygamy. As to Young, Bourke found the Mormon leader to be intelligent but cold-blooded and grasping, his face betraying his "strong animal passions."[8]

Crook paused in Omaha for less than a week, basking in the warmth of his welcome by officers with whom he had shared years of hardship and battle. Then, on May 1, accompanied by Lieutenant Bourke, he left for Chicago to be briefed by Sheridan on the growing threat of war with the Sioux. Before departing, he reappointed Nickerson and Bourke as aides de camp, and Nickerson as acting assistant adjutant general of the Department, a post the captain had held in Arizona.[9]

At the time Crook assumed command of the Department of the Platte, he had yet to acquire the familiarity with the Sioux nation that he now had with respect to the Apaches. He soon learned that as Plains Indians, the Sioux nations had quite a different culture and tribal organization. Those Sioux tribes who made their homes on the Great Plains formed the western branch of a loose confederation of linguistically related bands that had migrated from Minnesota in the late eighteenth century. How they were viewed by surrounding tribes can be gathered from the fact that the name by which they were known, Sioux, probably derived from a corruption of an Objibwa term, "Nadousessioux," meaning a treacherous snake.[10] They referred to themselves as Lakota, meaning "friend" or "ally."

Divided into seven tribes—the Oglalas, Brules, Miniconjous, Two Kettles, Sans Arcs, Hunkpapas, and Blackfoots—the Western Sioux, or Tetons, like other native peoples who preceded them onto the plains, acquired horses and adopted a nomadic lifestyle centered on the buffalo.[11] Numbering between fifteen and twenty thousand souls, they became a powerful force, dominating their neighbors, the less numerous Crows, Arikaras, Pawnees, and Flat Heads, among others, and taking their territories when it suited them. Dispossessed and vulnerable to Sioux predation, these weaker tribes allied themselves with the white man for protection.

The Tetons guarded their newly conquered lands jealously and viewed with anger and alarm the increasing encroachment of white migrants moving into and across their territory. Particularly worrisome was the approach of the iron rails that cut buffalo herds' migration routes and frightened off the game. In 1866, their concern turned to fury when the whites carved a shortcut, which they termed the Bozeman Trail, from the North Platte River across prime Sioux hunting grounds to recently discovered goldfields in western Montana, building three forts, Reno, Phil Kearney, and C. F. Smith, to guard it. Under the leadership of Chief Red Cloud, the Oglalas promptly declared war on these outposts. During the ensuing conflict, known as Red Cloud's War, they scored a decisive victory, luring a brash young lieutenant and his entire command of eighty men into an ambush and wiping them out, an incident that became known as the Fetterman Massacre.[12]

Realizing that the post–Civil War military did not presently have the strength to take on the Sioux nation, in 1868 Congress authorized President Johnson to negotiate peace with them. As a precondition, at Red Cloud's insistence, the army abandoned its forts along the Bozeman Trail, which the Indians promptly burned to the ground. The peace agreement ultimately concluded, with the Sioux and their Northern Cheyenne and Arapaho allies, became known as the Fort Laramie Treaty. Like the terms imposed at Versailles after World War I, rather than bringing peace, the treaty carried within it the seeds of future conflict that would spell an end to the nomadic culture of the Plains Indians and destroy the hegemony of the Sioux nation.[13]

The government's objective was to remove the Indians as an obstacle to westward expansion by convincing them to relinquish their nomadic lifestyle in return for a reservation representing a fraction of the territory over which they had previously roamed freely. Though the lands offered represented only a portion of their former domain, it was, by modern standards, a huge area, encompassing what is today that portion of the state of South Dakota west of the Missouri.[14] To convey the concept of durability, the commissioners inserted a provision requiring that reservation land could be alienated by the tribe only by deed "executed and signed by at least three-quarters of all adult male Indians occupying or interested in the same."[15] This clause would come back to haunt the government in the coming years. On the land thus granted them, the Sioux were expected to make the transition from nomadic hunter to farmer. To facilitate this transformation, the treaty provided that for a period of four years, the Sioux would be furnished rations of beef and flour. Thereafter, the provision of food would be at the discretion of the government, giving it a convenient whip hand to keep the Indians in line.

To mollify those Lakotas who, under the leadership of Sitting Bull and Crazy Horse, wanted no part of white civilization and desired only to pursue their traditional lifeways, a special proviso was crafted setting aside a large area west of the reservation as the hunting preserve of the Sioux nation. Known as the unceded Indian territory, it was neither included in the reservation nor surrendered by the Indians to the government.[16] Instead it was granted to the Sioux for their exclusive use "so long as the buffalo may range thereon in such numbers as to justify the chase." The cynicism implicit in this language is readily evident in hindsight. At the moment it was inserted, the government was actively abetting the slaughter to extinction of the once vast buffalo herds.[17] Under a provision that was probably not called to the attention of the Indians, the United States also reserved the right to build railroads, roads, and even military posts (the latter, the cause of Red Cloud's War) in the territory, projects that would ensure that the destruction of the herd would proceed apace.[18] But to the Plains Indians in 1868, unable to conceive of a time when the buffalo would no longer exist in its teeming millions, the treaty proviso appeared tantamount to granting them the unceded country in perpetuity.

Like most treaties entered into with the western tribes, this one, whether unintentionally or by design, ignored a fundamental reality of Indian culture. No chief could bind other members of his band or tribe to any course of action other than by moral suasion. Hence, though the United States could boast that the agreement evidenced the consent of 159 chiefs from ten different Sioux tribes, its terms were essentially nonbinding. Furthermore, unaware of the treaty's finer nuances and implications, Red Cloud and his adherents, mainly Oglalas and Brules, "touched the pen" without realizing that in return for a reservation and promises of largesse, they were surrendering a way of life. Like Red Cloud, most viewed the treaty as merely an agreement to end the war and restore their ability to trade at the white man's forts. Certainly, the complexities and contradictions inherent in the agreement were never fully understood by them or, for that matter, by most whites. This was most likely a deliberate strategy on the part of the treaty negotiators to secure signatories to the agreement.[19]

Though neither fully understood nor accepted, the treaty unhappily divided the Sioux nation into two factions, the agency Indians under Red Cloud and Spotted Tail, who accepted reservation life, and the northern roamers, who renounced the treaty and elected to continue to follow their nomadic traditions on the unceded lands. The roamers proclaimed their solidarity and, in a departure from Sioux custom, anointed Sitting Bull as supreme chief of the nonreservation Sioux, a position that previously would have been inconceivable.[20] As the treaty had no relevance to them, the chief and his adherents for the most part ignored it.

CHAPTER FOURTEEN

Rails to Riches

1873–1874

For those Tetons who chose life on the reservation, the adjustment was uneasy and fraught with tensions. The government's plan was to settle them by tribe at agencies along the Missouri River at sites that could be supplied by steamer and were remote from white settlements. The Oglalas and the Brules were assigned to the Whetstone Agency in the far southeastern corner of the reservation. Neither tribe wished to relocate there, as game was scarce, a circumstance that would force them—as the government intended—to survive by farming, an anathema to these warrior hunters. The Brules reluctantly agreed to settle around the new agency, but soon, under the leadership of their forceful and sophisticated chief, Spotted Tail, were able to pressure the government to allow them to settle to the west, closer to their traditional hunting grounds. Red Cloud achieved a similar success. Accordingly, two agencies, each named for the respective chiefs, were built on the White River, both inexplicably located outside the southern boundary of the reservation in western Nebraska.[1] But unrest continued and the turmoil at both Red Cloud and Spotted Tail Agencies would lead Sheridan to establish a military post at each in 1874—Camp Robinson at Red Cloud and Camp Sheridan at Spotted Tail.[2]

As Sheridan likely pointed out to Crook at their meeting in early May, continued discontent among the Sioux was stoked by white America's awakening interest in the Black Hills, land iconic to the Lakotas that clearly lay within the boundaries of the reservation. *Paha*

Sapa ("hills that are black" in the Lakota language) was a pine-studded mountain range, enfolded by the waters of the Belle Fourche and Cheyenne Rivers. It rose dramatically out of the pale grasses of the surrounding plains in the southwestern corner of the Dakota Territory. The Lakotas had only acquired dominion over the area in the early years of the nineteenth century after expelling the Crows and Kiowas, who had previously occupied it.[3] In the years since, the region had assumed great value to the Sioux nation, a reality to which the government, and even Crook, for all his vaunted understanding of the Indian mentality, seemed oblivious. In 1875, the latter dismissively characterized the Black Hills as a place where the Sioux seldom went because of its terrible storms and deep snows.[4]

From the Lakotas' perspective, as the Hunkpapa chief, Sitting Bull, described it, Paha Sapa was the commissary of his people.[5] The herds of game that grazed its hillsides were an invaluable food source in times of need, while stands of lodge pole pine adorning its mountain slopes provided straight, sturdy poles for their tipis. Its grassy meadows where their ponies fed and sheltered, and its well-watered valleys, ideal for winter camping, were a perpetual resource, as eternal and immutable as the buffalo. The Great Spirit's decision to put this verdant paradise in the midst of the arid plains gave the Hills a spiritual significance that transcended even its economic value, only enhancing its value to the Sioux. But that significance was lost on whites, blinded by greed and an ethnocentric worldview that they saw as conferring on them a superior claim to the land.[6]

The white man's growing interest in the Black Hills was fueled by its perceived strategic value, its proximity to the corridor chosen for the Northern Pacific Railroad, and lastly and most importantly, by rumors of quantities of gold in its streambeds. These elements lured a steady stream of whites into its verdant valleys like yellow jackets to a picnic.

Facilitating construction of the Northern Pacific Railroad had been one of the chief motivations for negotiating an end to Red Cloud's war. As permitted by the treaty, the plan was to run its tracks through the reservation and into the heart of the unceded territory. So, parties of surveyors with heavy military escorts began making summer trips into the Black Hills, raising the specter among the Indians of iron rails that would drive away the last of the great buffalo herds. As the Sioux

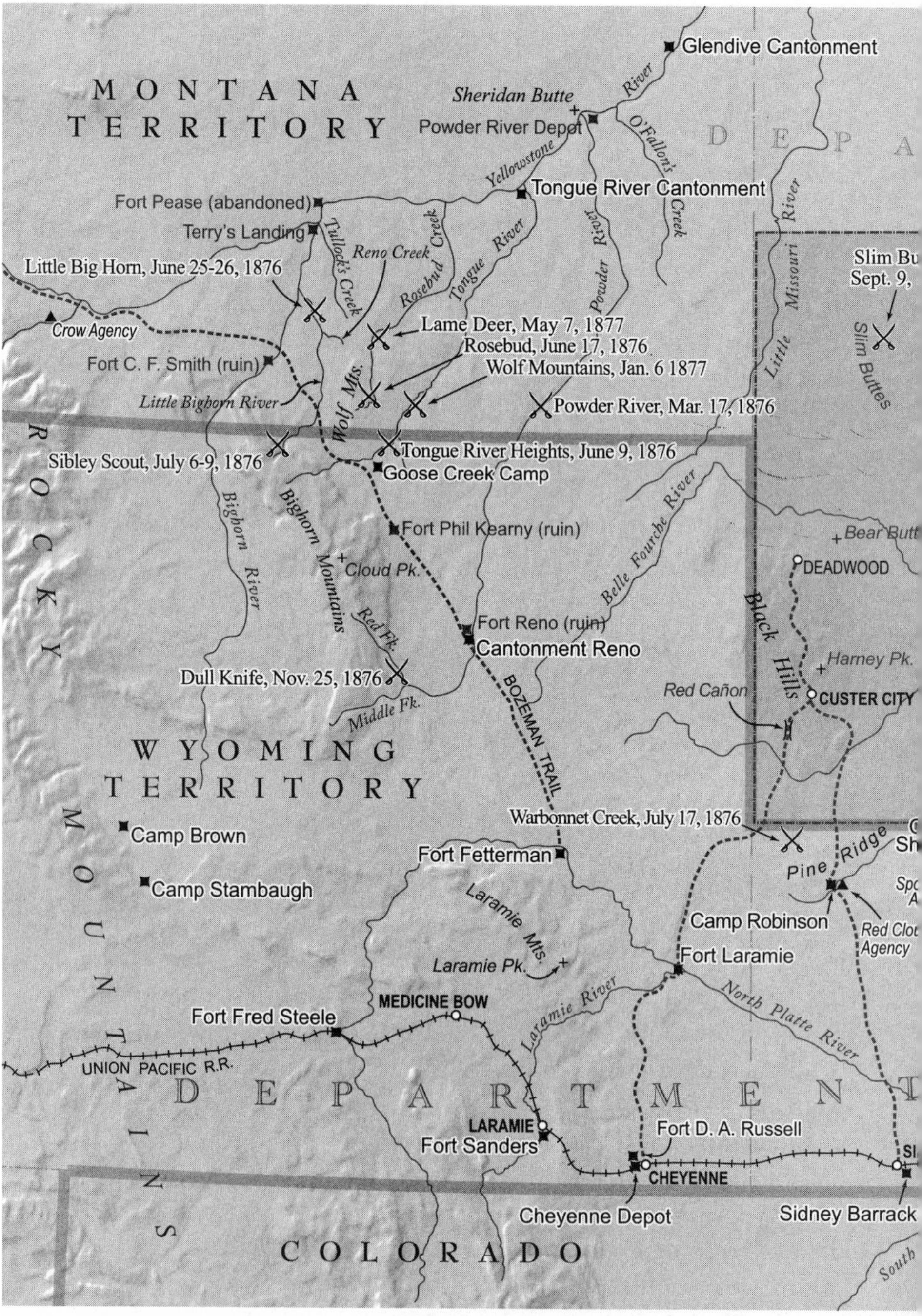
MONTANA TERRITORY
WYOMING TERRITORY
COLORADO
ROCKY MOUNTAINS
DEPARTMENT
Glendive Cantonment
Sheridan Butte
Powder River Depot
Yellowstone River
O'Fallon's Creek
Tongue River Cantonment
Fort Pease (abandoned)
Terry's Landing
Tullock's Creek
Reno Creek
Rosebud Creek
Tongue River
Powder River
Little Missouri River
Little Big Horn, June 25-26, 1876
Crow Agency
Lame Deer, May 7, 1877
Rosebud, June 17, 1876
Wolf Mountains, Jan. 6 1877
Fort C. F. Smith (ruin)
Little Bighorn River
Wolf Mts.
Powder River, Mar. 17, 1876
Slim Buttes
Sibley Scout, July 6-9, 1876
Tongue River Heights, June 9, 1876
Goose Creek Camp
Bighorn River
Bighorn Mountains
Fort Phil Kearny (ruin)
Cloud Pk.
Belle Fourche River
Bear Butte
DEADWOOD
Black Hills
Harney Pk.
CUSTER CITY
Red Cañon
Red Fk.
Fort Reno (ruin)
Cantonment Reno
Dull Knife, Nov. 25, 1876
Middle Fk.
BOZEMAN TRAIL
Warbonnet Creek, July 17, 1876
Camp Brown
Camp Stambaugh
Fort Fetterman
Laramie Mts.
Pine Ridge
Camp Robinson
Red Cloud Agency
Fort Laramie
Laramie Pk.
North Platte River
Laramie River
MEDICINE BOW
Fort Fred Steele
UNION PACIFIC R.R.
LARAMIE
Fort Sanders
Fort D. A. Russell
CHEYENNE
Cheyenne Depot
Sidney Barracks
South

Sioux Country, 1875–1878.

well knew, the Union Pacific had split the once unified western herd, dooming its southern portion to extinction, to be slaughtered for their hides, for sport, and to feed the workers on the railroad. The Northern Pacific portended a similar fate for the remainder of the herd.[7] Suddenly in 1873, the threat from the railroad disappeared when a financial panic brought railroad construction to an abrupt halt in the middle of Dakota Territory.[8] But other concerns supplanted the railroad and the invasion of the Hills continued.

The army's interest in Paha Sapa was strategic, a matter of securing the safety of the whites living in proximity to the reservation. Sheridan had long wanted to control the Sioux by completing a ring of forts enveloping the reservation, separating the Indians from their white neighbors. By 1873 the encirclement had almost been completed, leaving only a gap on its western edge where the Black Hills were situated near the unceded lands. Building a fort in the Hills would close this opening and "make it a little hot for the villages and stock of these Indians if they attempted to raid on the settlements."[9] In late 1873 Sheridan sought permission to send George Armstrong Custer to reconnoiter the hills to find a suitable site.

But strategic considerations were minor compared to the lust for gold that now swept the country. Rumors had long floated throughout the West about the presence of rich mineral deposits on treaty lands, particularly in the mysterious vales of the Black Hills. Scheduled for the summer of 1874, Custer's expedition was officially charged with determining a feasible location for a military post in the Hills.[10] But gold was an important, if unacknowledged, objective. A gold strike would alleviate the pressures of an economic depression that gripped the nation, and news of a discovery would likely precipitate a stampede of miners into the territory, providing an excuse to take over the region. It was therefore no coincidence that the expedition included two professional prospectors, two geologists, and three journalists.[11]

In the minds of most Americans, the provisions of the Fort Laramie Treaty excluding whites from the area were a temporary aberration. The *Cheyenne Daily Leader* voiced a popular sentiment when it editorialized that the "Indians must stand aside or be overwhelmed by the ever advancing and ever increasing tide of emigration. . . . To attempt to defer this result by mawkish sentimentalism in favor of the savages is unworthy of the spirit of our age."[12]

The expedition's prospectors did indeed find gold, no surprise to the hundreds of miners already digging away in the creek beds of Paha Sapa.[13] Custer promptly dispatched a courier to trumpet the news. With thousands out of work, the nation was electrified.[14] Miners soon streamed into Sioux country from as far away as Australia and Europe, while patriotic Americans called for the removal of the Indians and the opening of the Hills for exploitation.

Having unleashed the tide, the government now sought to play King Canute. Grant, unhappy over such a blatant violation of the sanctity of the Laramie Treaty, called on the army to expel the miners from their illegal holdings while he explored alternatives to induce the Indians to surrender their rights to the land. The army's initial efforts to remove the gold seekers during the winter of 1874–75 were predictably feeble, foiled by the reality of a northern plains cold season. Temperatures of twenty to forty below froze rations and drinking water and turned the earth to stone, and eventually, the troops had to be rescued.[15] Any miners who were removed in the process simply filtered back into the Hills almost as soon as they were released.[16] By summer 1875, Crook, newly arrived on the scene, estimated that no fewer than twelve hundred prospectors were working Paha Sapa's streambeds.[17]

Grant's accompanying plan to purchase the land from the Sioux was equally ineffective. The Indians were divided about whether to sell. A faction led by the militant northern roamers opposed the alienation of Paha Sapa under any circumstances. Though in the minority, their position was strengthened by the Treaty's requirement that three-quarters of all adult males of the signatory tribes had to approve alienation of reservation lands.

Grant resorted to threats. The treaty was now in its fifth year, one year after the Lakotas' entitlement to rations had expired, leaving the distribution of food to the government's discretion. A delegation of Sioux chiefs invited to Washington to discuss the sale was bluntly told by the president that any resort to hostilities over the Black Hills "would necessarily lead to withholding rations."[18] In any event, he informed them, he would not be able to keep the miners out of the Hills indefinitely. Shocked and offended, the chiefs dug in their heels and refused to discuss the matter further.

Ignoring for the moment the obvious reluctance of the owners to sell, the president moved to determine a "fair" price for the Hills, which in turn required an evaluation of its mineral wealth, particularly important in view of skepticism in some quarters as to its actual worth.[19] So, yet another expedition into the Hills was arranged, this one to be led by Professor Walter Jenney, an eminent but relatively inexperienced twenty-six-year-old geologist from the Columbia School of Mines in New York. Jenney's entourage included a number of highly qualified scientists and miners and, anticipating resistance, a strong military escort. To ensure the widest possible dissemination of the results, reporters from the *New York Herald* and *Chicago Inter-Ocean* were invited along.[20]

Sheridan thought the venture ill conceived. Untroubled by the fact that his authorization of the Custer expedition was largely responsible for the current problem, he now claimed uneasiness over the government's contradictory policy of encouraging the rush for gold and then ordering the army to turn back the miners who responded. For the record, he complained to Sherman, "to expect me to keep miners out of the Black Hills, while the Indian Bureau, by this examination, is affording an opportunity for skillful and practical miners to ascertain the minerals in it, and newspaper correspondents to publish it to the world, is putting on me a duty which my best skill and most conscientious desire to perform it, with the means I have at hand, will make a failure of."[21] When Sherman ignored his syntactically mangled plaint, Sheridan dutifully ordered Crook to provide Jenney with a military escort. The new departmental commander complied, furnishing two companies of infantry and six of cavalry, over four hundred men, commanded by Lieutenant Colonel Richard Irving Dodge, an old Arizona hand. To keep an eye on developments, he also assigned Lieutenant Bourke to accompany the escort as "expedition engineer."[22] As both Dodge and Bourke were indefatigable diarists and shared an interest in their natural surroundings, including the customs and habits of the Indians, the two got along famously. Bourke considered the colonel, a twenty-seven-year veteran, an officer "of great natural sagacity in matters military and otherwise,"[23] while Dodge described the young lieutenant as "an intelligent energetic ambitious officer [who] will make his mark in the world yet."[24]

Dodge was an interesting choice. He was a year older than Crook, and somewhat similar in appearance—tall, strapping, and richly bearded, with a "Grecian profile" and soldierly bearing.[25] And like Crook, he was in most respects a sensible leader, who relished life on the frontier. He had succeeded Crook as commander of the Twenty-Third Infantry, and shared his predecessor's high regard for the Indians as scouts, trackers, and warriors, and wrote about them extensively, usually with a degree of perceptivity. But on the matter of their humanity, the two officers clearly diverged. As a North Carolinian "of a good old stock," Dodge shared the southern aristocrat's obsession with race and class, and regarded Indians as savages, having "the ordinary good and bad qualities of the mere animal, modified to some extent by reason."[26] His aristocratic sense of superiority extended to packers, mule skinners, enlisted men, indeed to anyone he considered of a lower social class than himself. This snobbery caused him to resent Crook's egalitarianism. He thought that the general spent entirely too much time fraternizing with such riffraff when he should have attended to his social interactions with officers and gentlemen. Despite the colonel's elitism, maintained amicable relations with Crook. Crook, in turn, never forgot that Dodge had given him some sound career advice when, as a young captain, he had returned east to fight in the Civil War.[27] Their shared obsession with hunting and fishing and love of the card game whist may also have had something to do with their generally congenial association.

Departing from Fort Laramie in late May, the expedition penetrated deep into the Hills, ultimately confirming Custer's findings. Gold was present, but in modest quantities, allowing a diligent miner to produce from five to seventy dollars' worth of dust per day. Even that, Bourke predicted, was rich enough to "cause Cheyenne, Omaha, Sidney, and Sioux City to hum like a swarm of angry bees."[28]

While Crook had given Dodge the ancillary task of mapping the Black Hills, work the colonel relished, he had given him no instructions about expelling the miners, probably intentionally. Consequently, Dodge left them undisturbed where he found them, noting that "my force is too small for the subdivision which would be required to send all these parties in to Fort Laramie."[29] In any event, as he freely admitted, he was sympathetic to their cause, making it easy for him to conclude that his escort duty "exonerates me from obedience to the general order [to arrest and remove miners from the Hills]."[30] His neglect of this duty was regarded with indifference by an administration less concerned with Indian rights than with the mineral wealth the miners would eventually produce.

An indefatigable reporter of his surroundings, Dodge soon proved to be something of a diplomat as well. Initially, he had considered Jenney "a crazy man" and "very weak, very jealous, and very much disappointed that he was not in Military Command of the expedition."[31] But he overcame his jaundiced view, winning the prickly geologist's trust with a combination of firmness and tact, and soon had him securely under his wing.[32]

The command moved unmolested about the hills in small detachments, untroubled by the Sioux, though the troops broadcast their presence, blasting away with abandon at the numerous deer, elk, and game birds they encountered.[33] An elderly Sioux who appeared along the trail informed Dodge that "the Indians never come here except occasionally to hunt . . . or in the fall the squaws come in to cut & trim lodge poles." Perhaps the old man was seeking to mislead the soldiers, but Dodge seemed satisfied to accept this explanation.

On June 3, as Jenney's gold seekers wound their way through the Black Hills, General Sheridan, now a portly senior officer of forty-four, contracted a late marriage to Irene Rucker, the twenty-two-year-old daughter of General Daniel Rucker, assistant quartermaster general of the army. The wedding took place in Chicago, a simple ceremony followed by an ice cream social. In attendance were Sheridan's superior and close friend, General of the Army William Tecumseh Sherman, together with George Crook and his fellow departmental commanders Alfred Terry, John Pope, and Christopher Augur.[34] These men, unlike General Ord, conspicuous in his absence, had Sheridan's trust and confidence. Crook, though he privately continued to harbor bitter feelings from perceived slights dating back to the Civil War, had the good sense to keep them to himself.[35] As in the Shenandoah campaign, outwardly at least, he remained his chief's loyal subordinate.

After the wedding and before departing for a planned three-month honeymoon, a tour of Sheridan's old military haunts in the Pacific Northwest, the lieutenant general assembled his commanders for a briefing. It was probably at this meeting that, in obedience to administration policy, Sheridan assigned Crook the task of ousting the miners who had flooded into the Black Hills in response to Custer's reports of gold, a chore Crook accepted without enthusiasm. Like Dodge, his sympathies lay firmly with the miners, who, he later told Sheridan, were not wealthy speculators, but ordinary men "who have all they have in the world invested in their outfit [and] have no means to live outside of the claims they have made."[36] In contrast, for the Sioux whose rights he was supposed to protect, at this point, he had little but contempt. They had, he noted, "violated the [Fort Laramie] treaty hundreds of times . . . by predatory incursions, whereby many settlers were utterly ruined . . . and this by Indians fed, clothed and maintained in utter idleness by the Government."[37]

But a good soldier does as he is told. So, in early July, he set out for the Black Hills, accompanied by a party whose small size and composition belied any concern for the "predatory" Sioux. His companions included the Department's paymaster, Major Thaddeus Stanton, who would soon become a close friend, as well as several civilians, businessmen from New York and Washington. Their military escort consisted of only one company of infantry under the command of Captain Edwin Pollock. It would be that officer's unpleasant duty to round up and remove any miners who refused to leave the Hills voluntarily.

On July 27, Crook's party rendezvoused with Dodge at Camp Harney, Jenney's base camp. His arrival appears to have taken the miners by surprise and a number of them, fearing immediate removal, fled into the surrounding woods. But on learning that he did not intend to arrest them on the spot, they trickled back into camp to resume their mining operations and learn more about the army's intentions.[38] Initially hostile, they were soon disarmed by Crook's demeanor. Instead of the overbearing officer most had expected, they found a sympathetic, kindly man clad in dusty civilian clothes, who circulated among them, listening to their concerns and addressing them individually in a fatherly manner. "I got them to come and have a talk," he later explained, "[and] explained the whole affair to them, that I was merely executing an unpleasant duty and that I had no feeling in the matter, and advised them to go peaceably."[39] Though he did not mention it in his memoirs, one reporter described him "wash[ing] out a pan of dirt that yielded seventy cents, and obtain[ing] $6 in gold from one cubic foot of sand," a gesture guaranteed to further ingratiate him with the prospectors.[40]

Having convinced the miners of his good intentions, on the 29th, he and Dodge drafted a proclamation intended to induce the miners to voluntarily leave the Black Hills without the need for military intervention.[41] The document set a deadline of August 15 for them to vacate the Hills and the Powder River and Big Horn regions. Such a bald ultimatum by itself might well have inflamed the miners and precipitated open defiance and perhaps bloodshed. To avoid that result, Crook worded the order to make it appear that the miners' expulsion was a temporary expedient, acknowledging the obvious truth that the abrogation of Indian rights to the Black Hills was just a matter of time. The eviction, the proclamation announced, would only last "until *some new treaty arrangements have been made with the Indians*" (emphasis added).[42] This qualifier sent a clear signal to the miners that their right to return to their claims at some time in the (near) future had been sanctioned by the government. However, since the miners' occupation of the Black Hills was illegal, any claims they staked could be invalidated by their departure. To safeguard against this, Crook added language to the proclamation suggesting that the miners convene prior to their departure and draft "resolutions, to secure to each, *when this country shall have been opened*, the benefit of his discoveries and the labor he has expended" (emphasis added).[43]

Impressed by Crook's obvious regard for their welfare, the miners accepted the document with good grace, expressing "full confidence in [the general] and believing [him] to be a man whom we can trust." Their faith in him was such that they asked him to intercede with the president to allow seven men to remain in the Hills to safeguard their property as an exception to the expulsion order. Though doubtful that it would be approved, Crook agreed to present their request to General Sheridan with his endorsement and allowed them to keep a delegation in the Hills awaiting the outcome of his recommendation.[44] At the same time, heedful of administration policy, he had Pollock build a stockade to confine miners who refused to leave voluntarily on August 15. Ultimately, as Crook had forecast, on the Department of the Interior's recommendation, the miners' request was denied.[45]

Satisfied that his task had been completed, Crook, accompanied by Dodge and several other officers and civilians, embarked on a hunting trip. For the next two days, they made serious inroads in the region's game population, bagging a total of twenty-nine deer, one mountain sheep, and an elk, distributing the meat to the troops and teamsters. Then, on August 1, Crook departed for Omaha, leaving Dodge exhausted from the whirlwind of activity.[46]

On August 10, as Crook had suggested, about five hundred miners in the immediate environs convened at the site of the new town of Custer City on the edge of the Black Hills and resolved "to cease all mining until such times as a treaty shall be made and evacuate the country. . . ."[47] As Crook had recommended, the miners used the occasion to attempt to secure their claims. But Dodge, on reviewing their efforts, found them sadly lacking. Moved by their situation, he nevertheless refrained from redrafting a more suitable document, fearing that he might jeopardize the army's "neutrality" and noting, "there were too many reporters about."[48] After the gathering had concluded, Dodge reported to Crook that "the miners went out in excellent humor . . . much gratified by your courteous and considerate treatment," which probably avoided "great trouble, perhaps bloodshed."[49] Then, eager to complete his explorations, he too departed, leaving behind a company of troopers from the expedition's escort to reinforce Captain Pollock's stockade detachment.[50]

For his part, Pollock, an officer known for his difficult personality, reined in his overbearing nature and performed his duties with an admirable mix of sensitivity and firmness. Only a few rambunctious prospectors had to be confined to the stockade, and even fewer were put in irons after becoming "more contrary and troublesome." In October, Pollock abandoned the stockade and returned to Fort Laramie with the miners in his charge.[51] But the entire exercise made little difference in the overall situation. As even Crook admitted in his August 16 report to the AAG [assistant adjutant general], "the number of miners and prospectors now in the mining country will not fall far below twelve hundred at least."[52] And this number would swell in the months ahead as the government, despite its public ban on miners entering the Hills, discontinued its efforts to stem the tide. But the Grant administration knew that this situation could not remain long unresolved.[53]

CHAPTER FIFTEEN

Prelude to War

September 1875–February 1876

On September 20, 1875, the Allison Commission, an assemblage of politicians and army officers tasked by President Grant to negotiate the purchase of the Black Hills, met with its owners, several thousand Sioux, Arapahoes, and Cheyennes dressed in full regalia. Conspicuously absent were Sitting Bull and Crazy Horse and most of the northern roamers who, though invited, declined to attend.[1] In their stead, they sent four hundred warriors who circulated through the crowd, stirring up opposition to the sale.[2] Crook, who had also declined to attend for reasons he chose not to disclose, sent Nickerson in his place.[3]

The negotiations came to nothing. The Commission's offer was rejected out of hand, as even the chiefs who favored a sale could not agree among themselves on a purchase price. The final denouement occurred when the parties reassembled to discuss the matter. As Red Cloud rose to speak, Little Big Man, Crazy Horse's representative at the gathering, dramatically interrupted. Naked, but for a breech clout, moccasins, and war bonnet, his body glowing with war paint, he galloped his horse in between the chiefs and the commissioners, waving a pistol in the air and shouting, "I will kill the first Indian chief who speaks favorably to the selling of the Black Hills." Only the Brule chief Spotted Tail's intervention prevented what could have become a massacre. Recognizing that this was not all theater, he and his men moved into the milling crowd of ponies and irate warriors to calm the situation, allowing the commissioners to scuttle for safety.[4]

Personally humiliated, their mission in ruins, the commissioners returned to Washington. Announcing that further efforts at negotiation would be dangerous and futile, they recommended that Congress simply fix a price for the land and pay it to the Sioux whether they liked it or not. The agency Indians, equally alienated, retired to their tipis, persuaded that the government had no intention of offering fair compensation for the Black Hills. And the northern roamers proudly journeyed back to the Powder River country to report that they had beaten back the government's attempts to steal Paha Sapa.

Grant now concluded that only force could resolve the matter. An attack on Red Cloud and Spotted Tail's accommodating reservation Indians would be inexcusable and politically untenable. However, Sitting Bull's people fell into an entirely different category. They could be blamed for undermining the work of the Allison Commission. Furthermore, their obstinate preference for a nomadic life on the unceded land and their adamant refusal to move onto the reservation, though clearly sanctioned by the Treaty, remained an open challenge to the government and a disruptive force on the reservation. Acting as a magnet for the agency Indians, they drew them out to the unceded lands for the spring and summer buffalo hunts and were thought to entice young men to join in raids on nearby farms and ranches. Of equal importance, they occupied country that had become increasingly attractive to the settlers and miners drawn west by the lure of gold and cheap land. At a stroke, a war against the northern tribesmen would break the back of their resistance, force them onto the reservation, and cow the reservation Indians. With their subjugation, resistance to the sale of the Black Hills would collapse, and the unceded lands would be opened to the railroad and white occupation. With these thoughts in mind, the president called together the politicians and military leaders who would prosecute such a war for a meeting in Washington.[5]

Sheridan received his invitation to attend in early October while still honeymooning in San Francisco. Stopping at Omaha to pick up Crook, he hastened east in response to Grant's summons.[6] His decision to bring Crook with him, probably to give the president a firsthand assessment of conditions on the ground, was an affirmation of his continued belief that he and his old West Point roommate still shared common views on the means to resolve the Sioux problem, a realistic assumption at the time. Crook's communications had been filled with tough talk against the Indians and empathy for the miners. His ordinarily sympathetic perspective on Indian rights had been eroded by what he saw as the insolent defiance of Sitting Bull's people. The solution, he had concluded, not for the first time, was a sound licking on the battlefield.

The other attendees who met with Grant at the White House on November 3 were equally hawkish. Foremost among them were Secretary of War Belknap, a staunch supporter of Sheridan's efforts to subdue the Indians by force, and Zachariah Chandler, former boss of the Michigan Republican machine chosen by Grant to replace Columbus Delano as secretary of the interior. Chandler, unlike his predecessor who vigorously opposed the army's intervention in Indian affairs, had a distinctly promilitary bent and a record of militancy on Indian affairs. Grant could clearly count on him for support.[7] The Indian commissioner, E. P. Smith, also present at the meeting, was a Delano holdover. Anticipating his own removal, he had little motivation and no occasion to question any plan put forward by his president.[8]

No official record of the meeting has survived and none of the attendees mentioned their discussions in their memoirs, but a clear picture of the strategy agreed upon emerges from the events that unfolded following the conference. And these events bely Crook's bland later reference to the months of November and December 1875 as a period when "nothing of importance occurred. . . ."[9] For it was precisely during these months that the government initiated the series of occurrences needed to create the pretext for armed action against the Sioux and abrogation of the Fort Laramie Treaty, a sequence of events that must have been planned during the November meeting.

The first step was to unleash the miners. As Sheridan informed General Terry a week after the meeting, Grant had decided that, while the orders forbidding the miners access to the Black Hills would not be rescinded, "no further resistance by the military should be made to the miner going in. . . ." Hence, continued Sheridan, "Will you therefore quietly cause the troops in your Department to assume such attitude as will meet the views of the President in that respect."[10] Lifting military restraints on mining in the Hills, a clear retreat from the terms of the Treaty, triggered an immediate increase in the number of gold seekers into the Hills; and the Sioux reconnoitering the Hills soon noted that mining works polluted streams and log and wood frame cabins replaced rude tents, cluttering pristine valleys only recently teeming with game.[11] Grant anticipated that this stepped-up invasion of Paha Sapa would stir reaction on the reservation, enabling the government to retaliate by withholding rations, an action that would incite the agency Indians, spread fear throughout the settlements, and generate pressure for military action and occupation of the Black Hills.[12]

The second stage of the plan, the military seizure of the unceded lands, would require an entirely separate set of circumstances. While the actual measures to be employed may not have been agreed to on November 3, subsequent developments suggest otherwise. The army could not wait for the Black Hills scenario to unfold to mount a campaign into the Powder River country. That would take too long. The time for a winter expedition, required to catch the elusive nomads snowbound in their villages, was rapidly slipping away. So an immediate casus belli was required.

As if by magic, on November 9, only a week after the White House meeting, the so-called Watkins report conveniently appeared, providing precisely the justification needed. The author, Erwin Watkins, had political ties to Interior Secretary Chandler and military connections that reached back to Generals Sheridan and Crook. His shared history with key participants in the formulation of Grant's Black Hills plan seems hardly coincidental. Now an inspector in the Indian Bureau, he had just completed an inspection of the Indian agencies in Montana and the Dakotas. But his report, rather than discussing matters related to his inspection, contained instead an extensive and inflammatory exposition on the supposed threat presented by the northern roamers. Describing a defiant and insolent people who moved freely over what was probably the best hunting ground in the United States, he affected outrage at "the occupation of this 'paradise' by these savages, independent of government restraint and defiant of law and authority." Their very existence, he declared, impeded the government's civilizing mission and emboldened "the young warriors on the reservation anxious for an opportunity to prove their prowess in battle."[13]

Watkins's report concluded with a bellicose flourish worthy of, and probably approved by, General Sheridan. "In my judgment, one thousand men under the command of an experienced officer, sent into their country in the winter, . . . would be amply sufficient for their capture or punishment . . . for their incessant warfare on friendly tribes, their continuous thieving and their numerous murders of white settlers and their families, or white men found unarmed."[14]

The report rapidly made its way to the top of the Interior Department's bureaucracy and then down the military chain of command, ending up on Sheridan's desk with a request that the general assess his division's preparedness for a war against the Sioux. The lieutenant general wasted no time contacting Crook and Terry, the departmental commanders who would lead Watkins's "thousand men" in battle. Crook, well aware that such a move had been afoot, had been discreetly preparing his troops for a winter campaign. Thus, he responded without hesitation that operations would be undertaken whenever the Indian Bureau deemed necessary.[15] Terry, though he may have had an inkling of the events taking place, had made no such preparations. He nevertheless reported that a winter campaign was possible if mounted quickly and in secrecy so as not to alert the Sioux. Should the Indians flee their camp, he opined, snow and subzero temperatures would preclude a lengthy pursuit.[16]

Crook's reference to the Indian Bureau may have reminded the army that the Interior Department now had primary jurisdiction over Indian affairs. Hence, military intervention could only be initiated pursuant to a request from Interior to the War Department. It was up to Chandler to invent a reason to make such a request, the Watkins Report being too general in nature for that purpose. To Chandler's annoyance, notwithstanding the dire language of his inspector's account, the Department's own annual report to Congress for 1875 had concluded that "during the year passing in review there has been less conflict with the Indians than for many previous years."[17] Reports from army officers in the West seemed to corroborate this conclusion. Those depredations that had been reported faded to nothing on closer examination.[18]

Now, with November snows already starting to fall, the northern tribes had settled, as was their custom, into their winter camps somewhere in the Powder River country, precluding any chance of an incident before spring. To justify the army's intervention, Chandler would need an alternate provocation, one that did not involve open hostilities.

Someone suggested an ultimatum, a certain date upon which the Indians would have to come onto a reservation or be treated as enemy combatants. This was a hoary device used by Sheridan against the

Southern Cheyennes and by Crook to initiate the Tonto campaign in Arizona. Other than the self-serving declarations of the Watkins Report, there was no immediate rationale for such an ultimatum. Nor did the Fort Laramie Treaty permit it. Nevertheless, popular demand to open up the Black Hills and the Powder River country was such that no one questioned its legitimacy.

On December 3, Chandler directed his Indian commissioner to inform the Indians in the unceded lands that unless they placed themselves within the bounds of the reservation on or before January 31, they would be deemed hostile and treated accordingly. The same day, Chandler sent a note asking the War Department to use force, if necessary, to compel compliance with the ultimatum.[19]

Word was to go out to the northern villages by couriers. But in late December, many of them found their way blocked by heavy snows that impeded travel. Several runners did not return to their agencies before the end of January. In other instances, the message was never delivered. Had it been, compliance under prevailing wintery conditions would have been next to impossible. And if feasible, even Sheridan thought that Sitting Bull and his people would regard the demand as "a good joke,"[20] which was how the Indians treated it.

The northern roamers, well supplied with buffalo meat, had no incentive to leave the comfort and warmth of their tipis for the difficult journey to the reservation, where they knew only hunger and an end to their freedom awaited them. Further, rumors reached the north that the government planned to confiscate the guns of the Indians already on the reservation. Even so, several villages sent messages back that they would come into the agencies when spring came and their ponies fattened enough to make the trip.[21] But none thought the army's deadline of January 31 was meant to be taken seriously.[22] As the government had predicted, the date came and went with few northerners appearing on the reservation. As intended, the failure of the overwhelmingly majority to appear triggered Chandler's request for military intervention. Within a week Sheridan received word to proceed with his offensive, an eventuality he had both anticipated and prepared for.[23]

CHAPTER SIXTEEN

Preparing for Battle

February–March 1876

Sheridan's original plan called for three independent columns to seek out the northern roamers in their winter camps in the Powder River country. The first, under General Terry, would drive west from Fort Abraham Lincoln in the Dakotas to the Yellowstone. A second, led by Colonel John Gibbon, would push east from Fort Ellis in Montana along the course of the river, while Crook's column would head north from Fort Fetterman on the Platte and follow the Powder River north toward its confluence with the Yellowstone. Sheridan knew that the nature of the country precluded the three columns from operating in concert, or even communicating with each other on a regular basis. But he supposed that one or another would find Indian villages and destroy them or perhaps drive the bands into the waiting arms of the others.[1]

Winter snows thwarted the plan before the operation even got started. Terry called off his movement from Fort Lincoln after a blizzard rendered travel impossible. Weather also delayed Gibbon's men until April, and even then, they would be slowed by deep snow along the Yellowstone, and suffer intensely from frostbite and snow blindness. So, in the end, only Crook was able to take to the field before spring. His objective, as he outlined them to a newsman who would accompany the expedition, was, first and foremost, to demoralize the Indians by striking at them in a season when they always considered themselves safe from attack, demonstrating that the Powder River and

Big Horn regions were no longer a safe haven. He did not believe that these attacks would end the war, noting that a secondary purpose of the expedition was to condition his men for the serious campaigning that he anticipated would actually come in the spring and summer.[2]

On February 18, 1876, he boarded a Union Pacific car for the thirty-six-hour ride from his Omaha headquarters to Cheyenne. From there, he would continue his journey by wagon to Fetterman, where his forces were assembling for the campaign. He had left behind the canvas pants and jacket, the pith helmet, and moccasins of his Arizona days, but continued to adhere to the ostentatious scruffiness that by now had become his trademark, an undoubtedly intentional counterpoint to the fringed buckskin dandyism of Custer and William "Buffalo Bill" Cody. For his campaigns on the Great Plains, he adopted a shirt of heavy brown wool worn under an enlisted man's faded blouse, and brown corduroy pants, their campfire-singed cuffs stuffed into ancient army-issue cavalry boots. A slouch hat had replaced his cork headgear. Postwar versions of this type of headgear, often referred to as a Kossuth hat, were of notoriously bad quality, the felt dissolving when exposed to rain. The army issued a new, more durable, model in 1876, and photos of Crook during this period show him wearing what appears to be a slightly modified civilian version, already battered in appearance.[3] To cut the cold wind that scoured the plains, he added "an old army overcoat lined with red flannel and provided with a high collar made of the skin of a wolf he had shot, "crossed at the diagonal" by a leather belt that held forty or fifty copper cartridges.[4] On occasion, he probably donned his formal brigadier's uniform, causing the Plains Indians, at least those who did not refer to him as Chief Gray Fox, to name him Three Stars, a reference to the general's stars on each shoulder of his uniform blouse and a third, perhaps on his hat.[5]

Dressed in his distinctly unmilitary attire, Crook walked the streets of Cheyenne, a town that had boomed since his last visit six months before. Gold fever had the settlement firmly in its grip. New brick buildings had replaced old clapboard shacks, and the number of saloons, gambling halls, and dry goods stores catering to miners had grown exponentially. The rough interiors of these shops were crammed with men frantically exchanging rumors, the prospect of war with the Sioux vying with news of nearby gold strikes for attention.[6] These men, mostly prospectors headed for the Hills, complicated Crook's preparations for his winter campaign by creating an insatiable demand for scarce supplies. He found, for example, that most of the wagons he needed to carry forage for his expedition were already in use, transporting gold seekers to the Black Hills.

But the real impediment to his planning was the lack of hard intelligence concerning the strength of his enemy, evident from the wildly divergent estimates current at the time. In his report to Congress the previous September, Secretary of the Interior Delano had fatuously concluded that "it is not probable that as many as five hundred Indian warriors will ever again be mustered at one point for a fight," leading him to confidently predict that "such an event as a general Indian war can never again occur in the United States."[7] Estimates from individuals closer to the action were markedly less optimistic. John "Portuguee" Phillips, a former scout and owner of a ranch that Crook visited while preparing the expedition, told the general that he expected that out-migration from the reservations during the spring and early summer would swell the number of Indians in the unceded lands to around eighteen to twenty thousand, a population that could field some four thousand warriors.[8] Journalist Robert Strahorn (see below) informed readers of the *Rocky Mountain News* that, according to "the best authority" (obviously not an employee of the Department of the Interior), the number of Indians who would oppose the advance of Crook's expedition was likely "from twelve to fifteen thousand, including men, women, and children. Of these, at least three thousand can be counted upon as being first-class fighting braves. . . ." Strahorn's figures, like Phillips's, included an educated guess of the number of young warriors who would leave the reservation to join the spring hunt rather than face the inevitable shortage of government rations.[9]

The number of Indians remained unresolved at the conclusion of the campaign. Bourke, who before the expedition had estimated that the army would confront about five hundred warriors, would later throw up his hands and admit that "the number of Indians out in the country was absolutely unknown to our people, and all guesses as to their strength were wildly conjectural." Thaddeus Stanton, who would cover the expedition for the *New York Tribune*, upon his return to Fetterman, hazarded that the enemy numbered "probably not 2,000 all told," noting that during the campaign, the command "has not seen over 600 Indians."[10]

Ascertaining the enemy's strength paled in comparison to the challenge of finding them. During the winter, Sheridan's intelligence located Sitting Bull's people on the banks of the Little Missouri. But that was old news, and by March they had moved west into the northern plains, a vast rolling prairie broken by pine-covered buttes and drained by a series of northward-flowing rivers—the Powder, Tongue, Rosebud, and Big Horn. Each of these emptied into the Yellowstone, their courses carving out valleys separated from one another by high country divides, while their tributaries etched steep ravines or coulees into the surrounding landscape. In the winter months, the region was virtually inaccessible, buried under deep snow and scoured by arctic winds that drove temperatures to impossible lows. Sheltered from the savage cold, the Sioux camped in small bands, huddled against bluffs along the rivers and creeks, feasting on dried buffalo and venison, while their ponies grew lean on a diet of cottonwood and willow bark. Finding these camps required an intimate knowledge of the tribes' migratory patterns and the ability to follow trails made by small hunting parties who fanned out from the winter villages in search of fresh game, a familiarity normally possessed only by the Indians themselves.

As he had in Arizona, the Gray Fox meticulously prepared for the expedition, and by February, he had assembled almost seven hundred officers and men at Fort Fetterman on the south bank of the North Platte. The force included ten companies of cavalry, drawn equally from the Second and Third Cavalry Regiments. Experienced veterans, these troopers were supported by one battalion (two companies) of the Fourth Infantry, the regiment in which Crook had begun his career, the latter detailed to guard the column's wagon train.[11]

Building on past experience with winter campaigning, Crook strained his departmental budget to outfit his men to better withstand the subzero temperatures they would encounter. Bourke described their elaborate equipage in his diary.

> Commencing with the feet, first a pair of close fitting lamb's wool socks . . . [under] Indian moccasins of buckskin reaching well up the leg. . . . Then comes the overboot, of buffalo-skin, hair side inward. . . . For under clothing, first put on a suit of lamb's wool or merino, then one of buckskin perforated to permit the escape of exhalations. Over this a heavy suit,

> the heavier the better. Finally a loose dark overshirt of thick texture or a heavy blanket blouse. . . . If cold winds prevail, nothing will afford the body complete protection except a coat of beaver or buffalo skin, reaching to the knees or below. . . . For the head, a cap, loosely fitting over the cranium . . . with leather visor to protect the eyes and a border . . . of beaver fur to turn down when required over the ears.
>
> "Pulse warmers" about six inches long will preserve the wrists and fur gloves or gauntlets extending well toward the elbow and worn in wet weather over tightly fitting woolen gloves, are the only adequate safeguard for hands and fingers. An India rubber covering . . . will effectively shield both rider and horse from rain and snow."[12]

While such paraphernalia would keep the troops relatively warm on the trail, Crook was fully aware that it would be too restricting in a fight. During at least part of the coming campaign, the soldiers, including himself, would have to march light, carrying only their weapons, ammunition, and a single robe or blanket, and wearing only a bare minimum of clothing.

The infantry was armed with the 1873 model Springfield rifle, a breech-loading, single-shot, .45 caliber weapon firing a metallic cartridge. Criticized as no match for the Winchester repeaters carried by some of the Plains Indians, the Springfield was, nevertheless, a formidable weapon, capable of firing thirteen rounds per minute and accurate at up to a thousand yards, almost eight hundred yards farther than the Winchester.[13] The cavalry, the bulk of Crook's force, carried the carbine version of the infantry Springfield, with a shorter barrel that made it easier to fire on horseback.[14] The horse soldiers also carried the famous Colt "Peacemaker," a six-shooter of the same caliber as the Springfield. Sabers were left behind. Still part of a cavalryman's standard equipment, but archaic in the age of repeating rifles, they were too cumbersome and apt to clank when silence was required, making them unsuitable for Indian fighting.[15]

Crook reckoned that the column would need sufficient forage and supplies for forty days. To carry these bulky supplies, the general had carefully selected and outfitted a mule pack train managed by professional packers, many of whom he had brought with him from Arizona.

As in Apacheria, each cavalry battalion would have its own mules, allowing them to maneuver independently. Tom Moore continued to supervise the overall operations of the pack train, and a column of eighty wagons and five ambulances for the sick and the wounded.[16] Trailing the wagons would be a herd of forty-five beef cattle whose meat was expected to supplement the men's rations.[17]

Crook attributed much of his success in Arizona to the use of Indian auxiliaries, particularly those drawn from the very tribes he pursued. But the weather and the circumstances of this campaign unhappily conspired to deny him this invaluable resource. The traditional enemies of the Sioux—and there were many in the region, including Crows, Shoshones, Gros Ventres, Blackfeet—were snow-bound at this time of year and, in any event, were reluctant to take to the warpath in winter. Conventional wisdom held that enlisting reservation Sioux would be counterproductive. Surprise was essential to the success of the campaign, and relations between the reservation Indians and Sitting Bull's people were such that it was assumed any reservation scouts with the column would eagerly share any of the expedition's plans with their northern cousins.[18]

As an alternative, the general recruited a corps of thirty white and mixed blood scouts, "men who were supposed to know all about the country, and had good judgment."[19] Rounded up by Azor Nickerson, and vetted by Crook, they were a colorful assortment of characters who hailed from the Fort Laramie area and the Indian agencies. Most were the progeny of French fur traders and their Indian wives, with a sprinkling of local ranchers, trappers, and frontier ruffians with varying degrees of familiarity with both the Powder River country and the Lakota bands.

Bourke thought that most were "as sweet a lot of cut throats as ever scuttled a ship." And some lived up to Bourke's description, ending their lives in jail, hanged for horse thieves, or shot down in gunfights. But the lieutenant managed to identify "a respectable minority . . . of great previous experience and likely to come of inestimable use in any sudden emergency."[20] Ben Clark, who joined the campaign on General Sheridan's recommendation, was among them. Habitually clad in "a pair of worn out jeans tucked into his boots, a greasy hat and a week's growth of beard," Clark was often mistaken for "a second-rate cowboy who couldn't make enough to keep up appearances."[21] But first impressions on the frontier could mislead, and this modest, unassuming man had scouted for the army since the 1850s. Though quick to admit his unfamiliarity with the northern plains, he possessed a natural facility for absorbing the lay of the land, which became an invaluable asset to the expedition.

Others performed their duties in such an outstanding manner that they would remain with Crook for many years, including Baptiste Pourier (Big Bat), a French speaker from St Louis who had resided in the Laramie country for eighteen years and scouted for the army since 1870; Baptiste Garnier (Little Bat), a mixed blood who had also spent years scouting for the army; and Louis Richard (also spelled Richaud or Reshaw). The latter was the son of one of the first settlers in the Laramie region, who headed a group of several men regularly performing scouting and interpreting functions at Fort Laramie, where Crook first came to know them.

But among the most talented—and controversial—of the recruits was a swarthy, muscular, twenty-six-year-old named Frank Grouard. Over six feet tall and weighing about two hundred thirty pounds, the man had black hair and a dark complexion that led some to assume he was a full-blooded Sioux. Others claimed he was the mixed-blood son of a creole or black father and Oglala mother. But the truth was even more fanciful. Grouard was the son of a Mormon missionary from New Hampshire and his Samoan or Sandwich Islander (Hawaiian) wife, whom he had wed while preaching to the natives in the South Pacific. The family moved to California when the boy was still an infant, and when Frank's mother returned to the islands, his father gave him to a Mormon farm couple in Utah to raise.[22] At fifteen, bored with farm life, Frank ran off to the Montana Territory, where he ended up at age nineteen riding for the Pony Express.

In one version of his life, appearing in the *Bismarck Tribune* in 1876, Grouard stole some Pony Express horses and sought refuge with the Indians, ending up with the Hunkpapas and Oglalas.[23] Grouard, who dictated his life story to a journalist named Joe DeBarthe, had his own story.[24] In his account, sometime in January 1869 while running mail between Fort Hall and Fort Peck, he was attacked by a Sioux war party that included Sitting Bull. The chief intervened and spared his life for reasons that remain obscure and took the young man into his lodge. Called "Grabber" or "Standing Bear" because of his size and the thick buffalo coat he wore at the time of his capture,[25] he soon became fluent in the Lakota tongue, adopted Indian customs, and learned the Powder River country better than any non-Indian before him. He did not exaggerate when he told DeBarthe that "I fairly carried a map of the country in my mind and could close my eyes and travel along and never miss a cut-off or a trail. Night or day, light or dark, it made no difference to me; I always knew where I was going."[26]

By 1873, Grouard became friendly with the troops at the Fort Peck Agency, infuriating Sitting Bull. Unsafe with the Hunkpapas, Frank fled to the Oglalas and sought the protection of Crazy Horse, remaining with his people for two years.[27] During the fall of 1875, because of his connections to the northern roamers, he was asked by members of the Allison Commission to carry an invitation to Crazy Horse and Sitting Bull to attend the Black Hills negotiations. That, and his performance of interpreter functions at the council, caused the northerners to view him with suspicion. Fearing that he was wearing out his welcome, Grouard did not return to the tribe. Instead he remained at Fort Laramie, gradually reassuming his white man's persona, abandoning his Indian garb, and relearning English. When the opportunity arose, he interviewed for a scouting position with General Crook's expedition.[28] As Frank recalled it, their meeting was brief and to the point.

> [Crook] asked me if I was acquainted with the country and I told him I was. Wanted to know if there was any possible show of jumping Indians there in the winter time. I told him if he worked it right there might be. He said he would give me one hundred and twenty five dollars a month from the time I left the ranch. He said if I would furnish my own horse he would give me one hundred and fifty dollars; but I didn't have a horse, and told him that he would have to furnish the horse. . . . He said that he expected to start out the first of March.[29]

Robert Strahorn, a reporter for the *Rocky Mountain News* who later claimed he was present at the interview, added an additional twist to the story. He recalled that Grouard had been reluctant to leave Crazy Horse's village and work for the army, not only because he feared for his future safety, but because he planned to wed a white captive of the Oglalas. According to Strahorn, Frank only agreed to scout for Crook after the general promised to "support him to the limit in recovering the girl."[30]

Initially, Crook's suspicions may have been aroused by tales that Frank had joined the Sioux voluntarily and fought with them against the whites on several occasions, making his allegiance to the white man suspect.[31] But his doubts, if any, were quickly overcome by the man's obvious abilities. As Bourke later described him: "No Indian could surpass him in his intimate acquaintance with all that pertained to topography, animal life, and other particulars of the great region between the head of the Piney, the first affluent of the Powder on the west, up to and beyond the Yellowstone on the north; no question could be asked him that he could not answer at once and correctly. His bravery and fidelity were never questioned; he never flinched under fire, and never growled at privation."[32]

While Grouard's experience and skills qualified him to be lead scout on the expedition, army protocol required that a military officer hold the title of chief of scouts. Crook's choice, Major Thaddeus H. Stanton, was an odd one, though, as it later developed, fortuitous. Stanton was paymaster for the Department of the Platte, a forty-one-year-old army veteran with a thirst for adventure not usually found in one holding such an administrative position. In the 1850s he had written for and edited a small town abolitionist newspaper in Iowa and then joined antislavery forces in Bleeding Kansas. During the war, he had initially enlisted for a three-month stint, then briefly held office in the Iowa legislature, before reenlisting in the volunteer service. Finding the military to his liking, after Appomattox, he remained in the army, serving as a paymaster rather than a field officer. Soon, his adventurous spirit led him to accept an assignment to Arizona, where he briefly met Crook, and then on to the Platte. He was a bluff, good-natured man with a tough constitution who, like the general, preferred civilian clothing to the uniform except when actually performing his duties as paymaster.[33]

Stanton arrived at Fetterman to pay the troops just as Crook was casting about for a journalist who could provide sympathetic coverage of his campaign. To that end, the general had wired Whitelaw Reid, then editor of the *New York Tribune* and a fellow Ohioan. As Reid had written extensively on Crook's role in the war, the general took the liberty of requesting a "Tribune correspondent to go with us, as I wanted the country to know what would be taking place." Reid had been unable to find anyone willing to go, but suggested that if Crook had no objection, he ought to take Major Stanton along in that capacity.[34] Possibly recalling his contact with Stanton in Arizona, Crook liked Reid's suggestion, but was aware that War Department rules prohibited carrying an officer on the expedition rolls simply as a journalist. Having no need for a paymaster and knowing that his scouts could function perfectly well without experienced leadership, he circumvented the regulation by giving Stanton the nominal title of chief of scouts despite his complete lack of qualifications for the position.[35]

The appointment worked well for both men. Stanton was a congenial companion and a natural campaigner. He had the good sense to allow the scouts to do their work unhindered, but showed no hesitation in a fight. He shared a tent with Crook on the trail and ultimately they became fast friends. Stanton's display of courage and endurance throughout the Sioux War not only cemented their relationship, but earned him the title of "Crook's Fighting Paymaster."

While Stanton only wrote occasional articles for the *Tribune*, Robert Strahorn provided the main coverage for the expedition. Writing under the nom de plume "Alter Ego," he was employed by Denver's *Rocky Mountain News*, but provided stories on the side to a number of other papers, including the *Chicago Tribune* and the *New York Times*. He was introduced to the expedition by Stanton. The year before, impressed by Strahorn's articles, the paymaster had invited the young reporter to accompany him on his disbursing rounds to the frontier forts. Strahorn had accepted and the two got along famously. So, the following February, Stanton, who may have felt uncomfortable as sole journalist on the expedition, asked the reporter to join him in covering the campaign. Strahorn jumped at the chance.[36] At the time, he was boyish, solidly built, and at the age of twenty-four already a veteran newsman. A journalist since he was fourteen, he had worked first in Illinois and then, diagnosed with tuberculosis, he sought a cure in Colorado, where he was hired by the Denver paper in 1871.[37] Strahorn, like Stanton and Wasson, soon joined a fast-growing coterie of hardy and engaging newsmen with whom Crook formed enduring friendships.

Despite his careful preparations for the campaign, Crook experienced a growing uneasiness about the prospects for its success. Following his resounding victories in the Southwest, he had initially displayed great confidence in his ability to deal with the Sioux who, unlike the Apaches, he thought too vested in their material possessions to put up much of a fight.[38] But, on the eve of this, his first campaign against the Teton Sioux, he was having second thoughts. He had no doubt but that he could beat them on the battlefield. It was finding them that worried him, that and the weather. In his report on the campaign, written two months after it concluded, he frankly admitted that he "had almost come to believe that operations against these Indians were impossible in the rigors of this climate during the winter and early spring."[39] In a letter to Rutherford Hayes written on the eve of his departure, he wrote with uncharacteristic pessimism, "I am here on an expedition against the famous 'Sitting Bull of the North.' . . . I don't feel very sanguine of success, as they have so much advantage over us."[40] The advantage he referred to lay in the intimate familiarity the northern roamers had with the Powder River region. Absent Indian scouts, he shared a concern voiced by Bourke that "we have not the same knowledge of the country which proved so invaluable in [the Arizona] campaign, nor the same unerring Indian auxiliaries who led us into the dens and fastness of the enemy with clock-like accuracy."[41]

Perhaps his doubts about the outcome of the campaign accounted for his decision not to command the expedition, but rather to accompany it as an observer. In a fuzzy statement in his official report, he stated that he believed a winter operation to be impossible, and that he "wished to demonstrate, by personal experience whether this was so or not."[42] Possibly, he determined that going along as an observer would free him from the day-to-day issues of command and allow him to objectively assess the impact of the weather on the success or failure of the campaign. But the very vagueness of this rationale makes it suspect. Likely, his real motive lay elsewhere.

While announcing his own role as an observer, Crook named Colonel Joseph J. Reynolds of the Third Cavalry as his operational commander. A white-haired fifty-four-year-old career officer with an impressive fringe of side-whiskers framing a stubborn jaw, Reynolds had attended West Point with General Grant. During the Civil War he, like Crook, had distinguished himself in the fighting in western Virginia, and like Crook, had thereby drawn the attention of General Rosecrans, who commanded that military sector at the time. When Rosecrans assumed leadership of the Army of the Cumberland, he brought both men to Tennessee to aid him in his campaign to capture Chattanooga. Reynolds, a major general, was given command of the Fourth Division, and Crook, a brigadier, served under him as one of his brigade commanders. In that capacity, the two men fought together during the Tullahoma campaign, particularly at Hoover's Gap, where Reynolds turned in a credible performance and Crook played a minor role. Later, at Chickamauga, with Crook no longer under his command, a notably less impressive side of Reynolds's character came to the fore. In the face of a successful breach of the Union lines by Confederate forces, he exhibited a lack of self-confidence and steadfastness that led him to advocate a hasty, some would say panicky, withdrawal for reasons that later were deemed insufficient by his superiors. Because of his defeatism and poor tactical decisions in the face of the enemy, he did not receive another battlefield command for the remainder of the war. During Reconstruction, his career suffered a further blow when, seeking to enter politics, he exhibited extremely poor judgment by involving himself in partisan political infighting in Texas.[43] His postwar service was further stained by feuds with his subordinates and even a whiff of corruption. Ranald Mackenzie, with whom he frequently clashed, accused him of involvement in some of the Indian agent scandals of the Belknap era.[44] With these clouds hanging over Reynolds's career and his reputation for contentiousness, it did not help that he had very limited experience as an Indian fighter and was, at fifty-four, considered elderly for active campaigning.[45] All in all, Reynolds seemed rather a poor choice to command the expedition. But Crook was loyal to his friends and, according to his aides, looked upon the appointment as an opportunity for the old warhorse to redeem himself.[46] The risk, after all, seemed minimal. If Reynolds succeeded, the colonel would receive the credit; but if he began to evidence weakness in command, Crook could step in and take charge.

On February 27, as the column prepared to move out, several Arapaho bands passed through Fetterman on their way to the Red Cloud Agency, seeking to avoid the coming conflict. They reported that Sitting Bull's people were camped on the lower Powder River.[47] When asked the size of the village, their chief, Black Coal, allowed there were "many lodges, mak'um tired count 'um." He also disclosed that informants from the reservation had at this point already "conveyed intelligence of an anticipated move by the military to the northern tribes."[48] This information could only have deepened Crook's pessimism. If Black Coal was to be believed, the element of surprise had been lost, giving the Sioux ample time to prepare for an attack or flee.

Adding to Crook's sense of foreboding, he also learned from Fort Laramie that insufficient appropriations and an influx of Indians into the Red Cloud Agency meant that rations on the reservation would be exhausted by March 1.[49] This meant, as Crook well knew, that after that date, as the weather warmed, young braves would be driven by hunger to leave the Agencies to join the hunting bands in search of food. Their numbers would augment the fighting strength of Sitting Bull's people. Though Crook expected that Gibbon and Terry would be marching into the Powder River region, he knew that he could not count on them as reinforcements. As he indicated in a telegram to Custer and as Sheridan had predicted, a lack of hard intelligence about the territory and the location of the Indians made it impossible to plan an operation in concert with either column.[50]

On February 29, the sky darkened and snow soon blanketed the camp. But any hopes the troops might have entertained that the march would be delayed were squelched when it was announced that the column would depart the next day. For Crook, it was axiomatic that "the worse it gets, the better; always hunt Indians in bad weather."[51] So, on March 1, ironically a brisk clear spring day, the column, muffled from head to toe in fur, filed out of Fort Fetterman, crossed the frozen North Platte, and set out on the Bozeman Trail. As Crook and Bourke had delayed their departure for a day to await the mail, Reynolds led the way, soon passing another band of Arapahoes hurrying toward the Agency. The officers observed that their ponies were "as fat as stall-fed cattle,"[52] indicating the onset of an early spring. The soldiers would have to move rapidly to have any hope of catching the Indians in their snowbound villages.

At two in the morning of the second day, only thirty-three or so miles out of Fetterman, the sound of war whoops and rifle shots awakened the sleeping men. Reynolds had failed to post an adequate guard, and Indians ran off the beef herd, wounding one of the herders. At daybreak, the embarrassed colonel sent a detachment after the thieves. It was led by Captain Moore, whose disregard of orders in Arizona had caused Crook to question his courage.[53] To the surprise of no one who had served with the man, he soon returned empty-handed, claiming that the herd appeared headed back to Fetterman. Though the loss of the cattle would deprive the column of fresh meat, Crook, unable to resist taking charge under the circumstances and unwilling to delay further, decided to abandon efforts at recovery. Bourke loyally put a positive spin on the incident, describing it as a valuable lesson in the "need for unceasing vigilance."[54]

Even without the loss of the herd, glimpses of warriors stalking their flanks and intermittent puffs of smoke rising from the surrounding hills were sufficient to alert the troops that they were under constant observation. On the evening of the 5th, the Sioux again struck. From surrounding woods, the Indians poured fire into the soldiers' camp on the banks of the Powder, aiming at the lights of dozens of campfires, now hastily extinguished by troopers as they dove for cover. Unruffled by the attack, Crook lounged on a buffalo robe in his tent, greeting his excited officers' pleas for instructions calmly and succinctly. "The plan of the Indians was simply to stampede a portion of our stock. . . . The early firing of the sentry had completely frustrated their scheme. . . . We would hear no more of the Indians that night," he concluded with finality.[55] His analysis was borne out in every detail. The troops suffered but a single casualty; and when the firing abated, after assuring that guards had been properly posted, the general wrapped himself in his robe and immediately fell asleep.[56]

The previous day, the troops had ridden into the teeth of a cold northwest wind and driving snow. But the morning after the attack dawned clear, affording a fine view of the white peaks of the distant Big Horn Mountains. By noon, the temperature had become almost balmy, and the men sweated in their heavy winter outfits. By late afternoon, however, a chill set in as the column made camp on the Crazy Woman Fork of the Powder. After the tents were pitched, Crook gathered his officers and, ignoring Reynolds's now largely symbolic command, "made known his wishes and expectations from each one in authority." The wagons would be sent back to Reno, while the horsemen would move forward with only the barest essentials, traveling light and fast in the hope of getting ahead of their watchers and catching the Indians unawares in their villages. Each man, from Crook to the lowest private, would be equipped with only the clothing he wore, a robe or two blankets, a shelter half, and a hundred rounds of ammunition. Pack mules would carry fifteen days' rations—hard tack, bacon, coffee, and sugar—and another hundred cartridges per man, in addition to the twenty-five thousand pounds of grain required for the horses.[57] At Reynolds's suggestion, the infantry would retire with the wagons, a move intended to confuse the Indians of the column's intentions.[58]

With the scouts fanning out ahead of them, the expedition proceeded along the Bozeman Trail past Fort Phil Kearny, site of the Fetterman Massacre, through deserted Indian campsites, before turning due north up the Tongue. The latter presented a particular challenge as its winding course required the troops to cross and recross it—at one point, eighteen times on a twenty-mile stretch—on ice thick enough to hold the horses but dangerously slick under their worn shoes.[59] As the column proceeded north, the temperature fell steadily until their only thermometer registered twenty-six degrees below zero, at which point the mercury retreated into its bulb, assuming a curdled appearance.[60]

Though the clothing protected them from frostbite, the extraordinary cold posed novel problems for the command, particularly the cooks. Rising before dawn, these hapless souls began their day hacking away at slabs of bacon, frozen so solid it broke knife blades, and thawing bread, beans, and even coffee that had become "hard as flint" during the night. While the cooks whittled away at their rations, the men warmed their cutlery in the fire, lest it stick painfully to their tongues.[61] Water for man and horse alike could only be drawn from streams after cutting through a layer of ice eighteen to thirty inches thick. To warm the frozen ground on which they slept, Crook and the scouts taught the men to brush away the snow and build fires on the bare earth, allowing them to burn for an hour or more before clearing the embers away. The warmth generated lasted until dawn, permitting a decent rest. One evening, Crook and Stanton amazed the troops by moving their blankets into an abandoned beaver lodge in an old streambed, spending a night in relatively comfortable hibernation.[62] For Bourke, the inveterate diarist, the cold exacted a special revenge. He had carefully husbanded a bottle of ink in his pack all the way from Omaha. Though it was frozen most of the day, he thawed it in the evening by the campfire. But, on the night of March 13, the temperature hovering around thirty degrees below zero, the bottle suddenly exploded, leaving him to record the rest of his journey in pencil.[63]

The expedition's officers and scouts were convinced that Crazy Horse's winter camp was somewhere ahead, and the possibility of capturing or killing this famed warrior lent a certain imperative to the expedition, for Crook believed that his removal from the scene might end Sioux resistance. The scouts, with the exception of Frank Grouard, maintained that the village was either on the Tongue or the Big Horn, two valleys to the west. Frank insisted that it was to the northeast on the Powder.[64]

At dusk on the 15th, after searching north along the Tongue to its confluence with the Yellowstone without encountering any Indians, the scouts returned crestfallen to Crook's camp. They now agreed with Grouard, that the village lay east, probably along the Powder, a supposition corroborated by Indian trails leading in that direction, while game tracks headed the opposite way. Accordingly, the column turned toward the Powder, marching twenty miles over a series of steep pine-covered ridges and narrow ravines that divided the two streams, and then descending into a valley carved out by Otter Creek, a tributary of the Powder.[65] While making his way down the steep mountainside into this valley, Grouard spied two Indians on horseback, trotting without apparent haste along the streambed. The scouts set off in pursuit, but the men quickly disappeared into the thick woods. As Indians, in this case probably hunters, would not wander far from home in such inclement weather, Crook suspected that their village was nearby. Fearing that they might alert their people and cause them to flee, and having Grouard's assurances that the camp was no more than a night's march away, he decided to attack without delay.[66]

Because snow and intermittent thaws had made the terrain rough and slick with ice, the general worried that the pack train would slow the attack force, as the mules could not safely navigate at the speed maintained by the cavalry horses. So he decided to divide his command. The mule train would remain in camp under a strong guard, while a force comprised of three squadrons of cavalry, about three hundred men, would advance immediately against the village, hopefully attacking at daybreak the next morning.[67]

Consistent with his decision to give Reynolds command of the expedition, Crook now assigned him responsibility for leading the attack force. It was a decision that, according to Strahorn, required the general to repress "that most striking of his characteristics—'to be there.'"[68] Both Bourke and Strahorn, who were present on the occasion, recorded that Crook put Reynolds in charge to give his former Civil

War commander, in Bourke's words, "every chance to make a brilliant reputation for himself and retrieve the past," a reference to Reynolds's problems in Texas. Strahorn was even more specific, writing that the general wished "to retrieve an uncomfortable position he [Reynolds] had gotten into in Texas."[69] As he had done with his original command decision, Crook elected to obfuscate the reasons for his decision. Reynolds, he wrote in his report on the battle, led the attack and he, Crook, remained behind "to the end that the command might not be embarrassed by any division or appearance of such on the field, and the commander himself might feel free from all embarrassment that he might otherwise feel if the Departmental Commander were present."[70] Perhaps in offering this rationale, he sought to conceal his true reason. Given Reynolds's history, putting him in command might have appeared in hindsight a poor choice simply to help a friend's career.

Although Reynolds would later deny it, Crook gave him instructions prior to his departure that, while perhaps lacking in detail—he believed in allowing his commanders latitude in the field—nevertheless, were clear and unequivocal. The attack offered an unparalleled opportunity to replenish the expedition's badly depleted rations and replace worn-out mounts with Indian ponies. So, with impeccable logic, he expressly ordered Reynolds to capture the pony herd and seize all available food, packsaddles, and robes that the ponies could carry. These measures would allow his command to remain in the field for some time after the attack, "after the manner of General Sherman from Atlanta to the sea."[71] Crook then instructed Reynolds to rendezvous with him after the attack at the mouth of Lodge Pole Creek. Whoever reached the creek first would await the other.[72]

Reynolds and his six troops of cavalry and their scouts, accompanied by Bourke, Stanton, and the intrepid Strahorn, none of whom could bear to miss out on such an opportunity, left the camp at Otter Creek at sundown on the 16th . In the pitch dark of a moonless and stormy night, Grouard and two other scouts took the lead, striking matches from time to time to light the trail and often dropping to their hands and knees like hounds to sniff out the faint moccasin prints left by the Sioux hunters in the powdery snow.[73] The troopers followed, struggling forward in temperatures that dipped well below zero, floundering over steep hillsides and plunging into ravines and frozen gullies in darkness and stinging snow. Often, they were forced to lead their mounts on account of the broken and icy ground, frantically hurrying to keep pace with the swiftly moving scouts.[74]

By 4 A.M., exhausted and numb, the command had reached a point only a few miles from the Powder. While Grouard and his fellow scouts moved ahead to reconnoiter, the soldiers took shelter in an arroyo, awaiting the scouts' return. Fighting sleep that could mean death in this extreme cold, the men huddled "like bees in a hive" for warmth and mutual protection, and consumed the few remaining crumbs of their rations.[75]

Two hours later, an eternity to the suffering soldiers, Grouard reappeared, reporting that he had located the village ahead and was confident it belonged to Crazy Horse's Oglalas. "Knew every horse that was there," he would later declare.[76] A ride five miles to the east brought the troopers to the crest of a high bluff overlooking the Powder River. Though a haze of fog and smoke blanketed the valley below, the sky had lightened sufficiently to allow them to discern the tops of tipis emerging from the mist along the riverbank. Only the faint tinkle of bells from the pony herd broke the early morning stillness.[77]

The Indians had chosen the location carefully. The hundred or so lodges were scattered about in a grove of cottonwoods and willows in a general north-south configuration beside an old riverbed adjacent to the river, whose waters guarded the village's eastern flank. To the north and west, additional security was afforded by an arc of rocky, brush-covered bluffs that rose upward in a series of benches to the steep slopes of two large hills.[78] South of the encampment lay an open plain on which the pony herd browsed.

Grouard indicated two ravines that appeared to lead down the hillsides toward the village. One seemed to curve around to the north behind some hills while the other led down to the flat plain where the ponies grazed. The scout assured Reynolds that soldiers descending these ravines could approach the encampment unseen until they had reached a point at or very near the village. Grouard and Major Stanton proposed that Reynolds divide his command, sending detachments down both ravines to attack the village from two directions. Both men later recalled that Reynolds appeared befuddled and unsure of what to do.[79] Their recollections seemed consistent with other descriptions of the colonel's behavior, both at this time and during the battle, suggesting that his judgment might have suffered from the effects of cold and fatigue on his aging constitution. Nevertheless, after some initial indecisiveness, he accepted his scouts' recommendations, and made the necessary troop dispositions to carry them out.[80]

Captain Egan's troopers were to descend the south ravine together with Noyes's command. The latter was to capture the pony herd while Egan's men charged the village, their blazing guns driving the frightened Indians toward its northern end. In the meantime, Captain Moore's company would descend the northern ravine far enough to trap the villagers fleeing Egan's charge and prevent them from escaping onto the rocky hillside.[81] Having achieved control over the village and the horse herd, the command would then seize the Indians' meat and supplies, burn the tipis, and rejoin Crook at the rendezvous point the next day. That, at least, was the plan.

But from the outset, it began to unravel. The ravines, which from the vantage point of the ridge above appeared to offer relatively easy and concealed access to the valley floor, proved unexpectedly difficult to navigate. Picking their way "down icy canyons, through fallen timber, and over dangerous rock-strewn chasms," Egan's men found the southern ravine particularly slow going. Yet they managed to complete their descent without being seen by the Indians. However, upon emerging into the valley below, they discovered that the village was not immediately to their front as they had been told, but about a mile away. To reach it, they would have to ride through the herd across the exposed plain in full view of any Indians who might be awake. Halting for a moment, they inspected their weapons a final time, strapped their overcoats to their saddles, and advanced their exhausted horses at a cautious walk, threading their way around the nervous ponies.[82]

Incredibly, though it was nine o'clock in the morning, the Indians had yet to emerge from their warm tipis, remaining wrapped snuggly in their buffalo robes, unaware of the looming threat. The day before, they had received word of the command's presence from the returning hunters and had put out scouts to warn of its approach. But these pickets had missed the trail of the attacking force and so failed to alert the village. At last, as Egan's troopers rode through the herd, one of the young herdsmen spied them and let out a shrill warning. The troopers could delay no longer. On command, they forced their mounts into

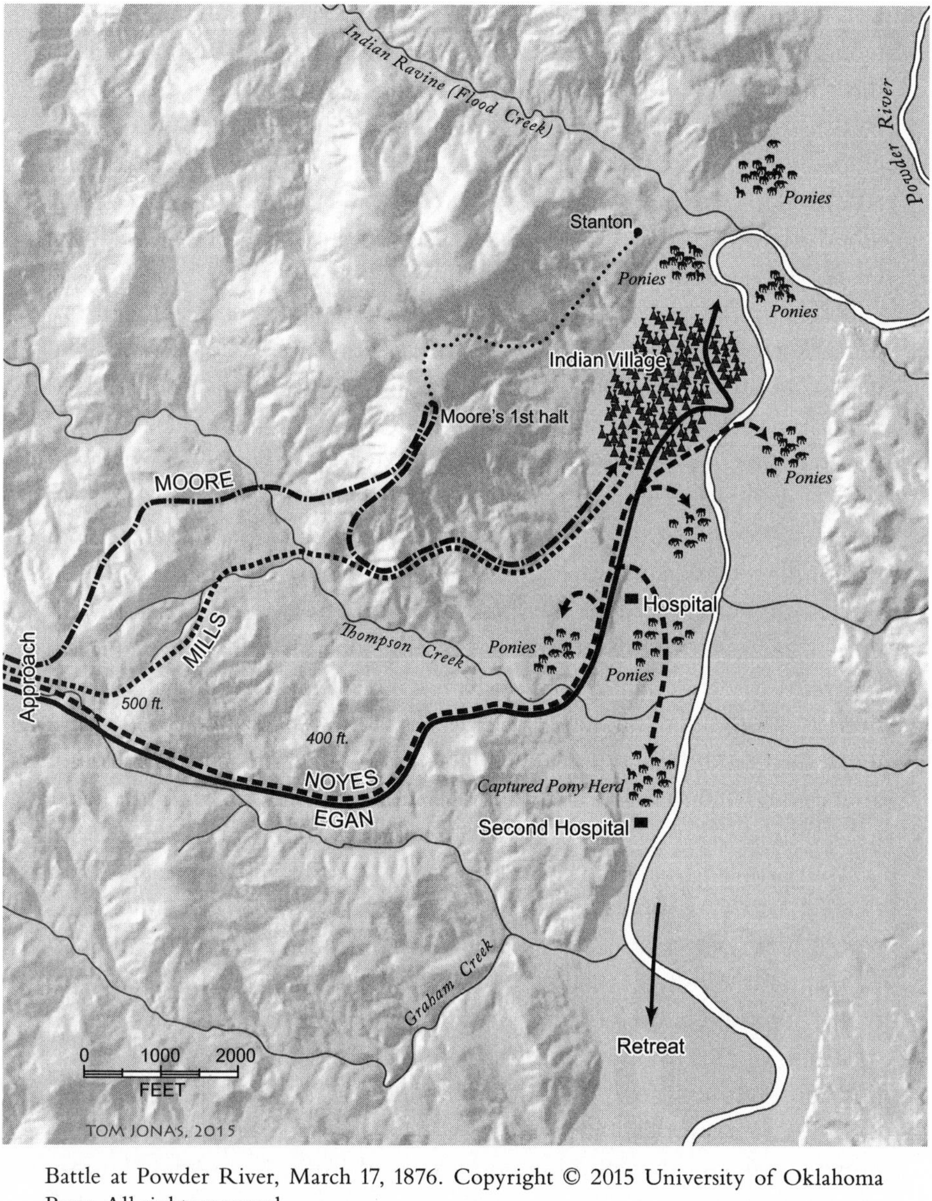

Battle at Powder River, March 17, 1876. Copyright © 2015 University of Oklahoma Press. All rights reserved.

a trot and charged, firing their pistols into the swarm of Indians who now emerged from the tipis. While the women and children fled into the thick brush and rocks on the hillsides, the warriors, near naked in the frigid temperatures, formed a line and fought a skillful rear-guard action, concentrating their fire on the soldiers' horses to slow the attack. Hampered by the rifle fire and by quantities of downed cottonwoods that the Indians had felled for fuel and feed for their ponies, the troopers dismounted and proceeded more slowly on foot.[83]

Moore, who before the battle had boasted that he intended to spill "a bucketful of blood," failed to reach his assigned position. Like Egan, he had found the descent into the valley far more awkward and dangerous than expected, and he and his men had to advance on foot, leading their mounts over slick rocks and steep arroyos to the lower ridges of the escarpment. But, unlike Egan, he did not complete his descent. When he reached a ridge still about a thousand yards from the village, he halted, well short of the north end of the village and out of rifle range of the defenders. Despite pleas from Major Stanton, he refused to advance any further, claiming that the Indians would see him if he moved closer. His inaction effectively nullified his value as a blocking force and, as Stanton pointed out, prevented him from giving Egan's outnumbered troopers covering fire. Frustrated, the major angrily snapped that Moore might as well be in Cheyenne [Wyoming] for all the good he would do so far from the village.[84]

Two hundred or more warriors now burrowed into the low hills that Moore was supposed to have occupied, pouring fire on Egan's troops, who only managed to hold their position after being reinforced by Captain Mills's company, now falling in on their flank. To support them, Stanton commandeered some of Moore's troopers, posting them on a ridge closer to the fighting to direct suppressing fire on the Indian positions. During the skirmishing that followed, the villagers killed four troopers, while suffering two casualties of their own, only one of which proved fatal. But the combined firepower of Mills, Egan, and Stanton, though inaccurate, drove the warriors back out of rifle range, and left the troopers in control of the encampment, at least for the time being.

While Egan and Mills cleared the village, Noyes's company swept up the horse herd, an estimated seven hundred ponies, mules, and horses, driving them across the river about a half mile south of the village. Then, thinking that Reynolds planned to camp overnight in the area, he allowed his men, who had no respite since the day before, to dismount and brew coffee. He would later be criticized for rendering his troops unavailable should their presence become needed.[85]

As the firing died down, Reynolds rode in to inspect the scene. Conferring with Captain Mills, he learned that huge quantities of buffalo meat, both dried and fresh (frozen), had been found, as well as hundreds of robes, a quantity of ammunition and gunpowder, and a large number of pack saddles—in fact, everything needed to resupply the column. Mills suggested that the command make camp in the village, send for General Crook, and upon his arrival, pack up everything they needed and destroy the balance. Reynolds, concerned about the continued pressure from the Indians, asked whether Mills thought that the command could hold the village, and Mills responded affirmatively. Mills later recollected that Reynolds agreed to his recommendation and withdrew to a position above the camp. But, as the captain began collecting meat and robes, Reynolds's aide rode up and announced that the colonel had changed his mind and that everything should be burned.[86] Evidently, as at Chickamauga, in the face of a determined and aggressive enemy, Reynolds lacked the resolve and self-confidence to stand his ground. Overcome by doubt, he decided that his force was not strong enough to hold the village until Crook arrived, or for that matter, even for the time required to gather and load the plunder on Indian ponies so they could be carried off by his troops.

Many of Reynolds's officers, particularly Mills, Stanton, and Bourke, later declared that they had opposed the colonel's decision, confident that they could have safely packed and transported the much needed food and robes back to the command. Egan flatly stated, "There were not enough Indians there to endanger our holding the village the day and night of 3/17." But to defy the colonel's orders in the face of the enemy was inconceivable, and there is no evidence that such an idea ever crossed their minds.[87]

As the Indians watched aghast from the hillsides, Mills and Egan ordered the burning of what was estimated to be in excess of twenty thousand pounds of meat, together with a host of leather and canvas tipis and their contents, the entire wealth of the community. The task was arduous and dangerous, as the troopers were exposed to rifle fire from the hills and the danger of exploding gunpowder that the Indians had amassed and stored in the lodges. As the tipis burst into flame, echoing blasts tore through the camp, sending huge lodge poles rocketing into the air.[88] The soldiers performed their hazardous work in temperatures that now hovered at thirty below, without their coats, which they had shed before the attack. Many would later suffer from frostbite.[89]

While burning the lodges, the troopers came upon an old woman wounded in the attack and left behind by her fleeing relatives. According to Grouard, who interpreted her words, she claimed the village belonged to Crazy Horse's Oglala band, which had been hosting a few Miniconjous and some forty lodges of Cheyennes from the Red Cloud Agency.[90] If this was indeed her story, history has proved it inaccurate, perhaps fabricated to conceal the identity of her people from the soldiers. Alternatively, it may have been the result of a faulty translation, or even an effort by Grouard to lend credibility to his original claims that this was an Oglala village. Subsequent interviews with other occupants of the village later disclosed that the inhabitants were predominantly Northern Cheyennes, a band that had left the Red Cloud Reservation the previous fall under Chiefs Old Bear, Little Wolf, and Two Moon. They had fled to the Powder River country fearing that the army would confiscate their guns and horses and that the government planned to remove them to Oklahoma.[91] A small contingent of Oglalas under Crazy Horse's close friend, He Dog, and several Miniconjous had been present at the time of the attack, most likely to trade with the Cheyennes. It may have been their ponies that Grouard saw when he had scouted the camp.[92] This would not be the last time the Cheyennes would be victimized in the mistaken belief they were Crazy Horse's people. But at the time, Crook and his troops were convinced, based on available intelligence, that they had attacked the village of the second most powerful of the Northern Sioux chiefs.

As the morning wore on and the destruction of the village proceeded apace, the valley filled with the odor of burnt meat, mixing with the acrid smells of black powder and burning leather. Through the smoky haze, the crackle of rifle fire rose in volume as the Cheyennes and their Sioux guests, now recovered from the initial shock of the attack, regrouped and maneuvered closer to the camp under cover of the rocks and brush on the steep hillsides. The slow progress of the burning and the growing audacity of the warriors fueled Reynolds's anxiety. Counting the forces he had on hand, he reckoned that almost one-third of his men were occupied guarding the pony herd and as horse holders, leaving him with only a little over two hundred men to complete the destruction of the village and protect the command from counterattack by an almost equal number of Indians. By noon, fatigue, freezing temperatures, and the enemy's increasing boldness spurred the nervous colonel to abruptly order his command to prepare for an immediate retreat from the village.

Despite his orders, the work of destruction continued to occupy the men for another two hours, and they did not finally assemble for departure until around 2 P.M. By that time, the soldiers had set fire to a quantity of meat sufficient to feed the entire command for almost a week, retaining only a few dried scraps for personal use. Quantities of coffee, flour, beautifully tanned buffalo robes, saddles, and delicately beaded clothing and moccasins had been consigned to the flames or had been blown to smithereens by exploding powderkegs.[93]

Though at least one of his officers described Reynolds as calm and cool during the attack, he now betrayed the depth of his anxiety.[94] In his haste to escape the village, he peremptorily denied Mills's request for time to allow the soldiers to go into the surrounding hills to retrieve their overcoats. This decision meant that many of his exhausted and frozen troopers were condemned to ride the twenty miles to the Lodge Pole Creek rendezvous exposed to subzero weather, wearing only their thin sack coats or blouses.[95] More disturbing was his abandonment of three dead and at least one wounded cavalryman. The latter, a private named Ayers, fell into Indian hands as the troops withdrew from the camp. He was last seen surrounded by Indians and later reported killed and scalped.[96] Egan, who volunteered to retrieve the wounded private, later testified that Reynolds told him, "if you go back [to rescue the wounded] you will renew the engagement and lose twenty men. You must move on."[97]

Crook's instructions to Reynolds had emphasized the importance of capturing the pony herd. It was a basic tenet of Indian warfare that the loss of their mounts would destroy a band's mobility and hence its capacity to fight. But, according to Grouard, Egan, and Stanton, among others, Reynolds seemed utterly indifferent to this consideration as he beat a hasty retreat at the head of his column. He had earlier relieved Noyes of responsibility for the herd and now casually transferred it to the care of his fatigued scouts. When the scouts asked for assistance in driving the six to eight hundred ponies under harassing fire from pursuing Cheyennes, the colonel refused, instructing them to shoot the mounts if they couldn't manage the job.[98] When informed that they didn't have enough ammunition, the colonel shrugged and told them to let them go. Again, Egan stepped into the breach, ordering his troopers to assist in caring for the herd. Slowed by the fractious ponies and Indian fire, the herders did not reach the rendezvous point until about nine that night, well after the rest of the command. Only then did they learn that Crook had yet to make an appearance.[99]

The camp at Lodge Pole Creek was a miserable affair, so grim that Reynolds's officers sardonically named it "Camp Inhospitality." The troops' evening meal, the first since their meager repast prior to the attack, consisted of a few cracker crumbs they salvaged from their saddlebags and a bare mouthful of half-cooked meat scraps roasted in the ashes of their campfires. After finishing off their unsatisfying dinner, the soldiers bedded down on the frozen ground. Soon covered by a layer of blowing snow, they fell into a fitful sleep.[100]

That night, disregarding a lesson he should have learned when he lost the beef herd a day out of Fort Fetterman, Reynolds again neglected the security of his livestock. When Grouard suggested assigning guards to the herd, the colonel refused. Worried about the poor state of his men, he conveniently concluded that the Indians presented little threat and the weather was too foul to bother mounting a watch overnight. Addressing Grouard's concerns, he told him, "they [the ponies] would be perfectly safe turned loose, or . . . the scouts could guard them until morning." Unwilling to assume sole responsibility for the safekeeping of the herd, Grouard made sure his men tied up their own horses and set the rest loose, as Reynolds had ordered. They then turned in, and when they awoke, a portion of the herd was gone.[101]

According to Indian accounts of the battle, after the troops withdrew from the village, only about ten warriors among the Cheyennes still had mounts. This small group rode off in pursuit of the column, hoping to recover as many of the ponies as possible. They shadowed the blue coats to Lodge Pole Creek, and when darkness fell, crept up on the herd. Elated to find that it was unguarded, they had no difficulty stealing silently up to the ponies and reclaiming their best animals.[102]

At dawn, Stanton reported the missing ponies to Reynolds, who reacted with a figurative shrug, casually commenting that they had probably strayed. But Stanton's scouts soon reported the stock being driven by Indians over a ridgeline not more than a mile and a half from the camp. Reynolds remained unmoved, refusing to send the cavalry after them, though he unenthusiastically agreed to allow the scouts to take on the task if they were of a mind.[103] Five men, including Grouard, pursued the Indians and the sixty or seventy ponies they had recovered. Though outnumbered, the scouts were able to recapture a few after a brief skirmish before rejoining the column.[104]

Reynolds's actions with regard to the pony herd, like his decision to burn the village, created the beginnings of a rift among the officers of the command, which, as we shall see, had a lasting impact on unit morale. While his partisans vigorously defended his actions, Crook loyalists, including John Bourke, considered the failure to safeguard the herd an "exhibition of incompetency" that had turned victory into defeat. In an unusual condemnation of a fellow officer, the lieutenant confided to his dairy, "Reynold's imbecility is a very painful revelation to many of us."[105]

After the scouts dashed off in pursuit of the pony herd, the colonel became increasingly anxious as morning waned without any sign of Crook. At Mills's suggestion, Reynolds sent troops out to search for the general, but as noon approached, he had still received no word of his whereabouts. The weather continued bitterly cold; the horses were without forage; and the men, particularly the wounded, suffered cruelly from the low temperature and hunger. Possibly, the cold, hunger, and fatigue magnified Reynolds's brooding pessimism, for he soon convinced himself that he "had to do something to save ourselves–we could not stay there." So, sometime around midday, he gave orders to prepare to move south toward Fort Reno, where the supply train had been parked. Overcome by his negativism, the colonel was poised to violate Crook's explicit instructions to remain at the Lodge Pole Creek rendezvous until the general had arrived.[106]

On the evening of March 16, as Reynolds's column departed in search of the village, Crook's four remaining cavalry troops had posted pickets and bedded down for the night, intending to travel to the rendezvous point at Lodge Pole Creek the following day. The next morning, the troops proceeded toward the Powder River, moving at a leisurely pace, in no hurry as their guides had mistakenly told Crook that the creek was little more than twenty miles away. As a result, by late afternoon, they had only reached a point about half a mile from the Powder, well short of their destination. Suddenly, the general, riding as usual at the head of his column, reined in his horse and sat immobile for several moments. His keen eyes had picked out an Indian in the distance, riding along the river. Suspecting that a village was nearby, he backtracked his men down the trail to avoid alerting its occupants and made camp. By now, having traveled more than thirty miles, Crook realized his guides' error and knew that he would not arrive at the rendezvous until the following day.[107]

The next morning, as the column resumed its journey, a cloud of dust appeared to their front. It soon became clear that several Indians, unaware of the soldiers' presence, were driving a herd of ponies in their direction. Without hesitation, Crook dismounted and fired on them, wounding one. Absorbed in their efforts to rescue their comrade, they abandoned some of the ponies, which Crook's men recaptured. With these mounts in hand, they then completed their journey to Reynolds's campsite, arriving just as the colonel was preparing to decamp for Fort Reno.[108]

The colonel lost no time in apprising Crook of the events that had transpired since the two detachments separated, including the destruction of the village and the loss of the pony herd. Pleased that what he supposed was Crazy Horse's village had been annihilated and undoubtedly exuberant over his recapture of the ponies, the general listened to Reynolds's tale with apparent calm. He then turned to Egan and Noyes, congratulating them on their roles in the battle. He did not question Reynolds about his obvious intention to leave Lodge Pole Creek before Crook's arrival, in direct defiance of the latter's orders.[109]

Gradually, however, as the details of the engagement began to emerge during his conversations with Bourke and others, the consequence of Reynolds's actions began to sink in, and Crook grew angry. The destruction of the meat, ammunition, and warm robes, and the loss of the pony herd, meant that the opportunity to remain in the field for some additional time had evaporated. Crook now knew he would have to abandon the campaign for the time being and return to Fort Fetterman. Though he was now determined to punish Reynolds for his insubordination, mismanagement, and perhaps even cowardice, he decided to defer action until the column reached the Fort. Leaving the colonel in command, he even accepted Reynolds's suggestion to move the force a few miles south to provide the livestock with better pasturage.

That night, at the new site, the exhausted troopers of the reunited column enjoyed their first satisfying meal in three days, devouring rations that arrived with the pack train. While they bedded down for the night, the brooding general rode out alone about half a mile on the back trail to meet the scouts returning from their pursuit of the horse herd and guide them back to the campsite.[110]

Over the next several days, the column's progress on the 180-mile journey back to the North Platte was slowed by the pony herd and continued harassment from a few Indians who shadowed them in the hope of recovering their mounts. Unwilling to countenance the delay, Crook grimly ordered the slaughter of young ponies and brood mares, as their presence encouraged pursuit by the Indians and their slow pace delayed the column. The grisly slaughter took place over two days and filled the air with the "dismal trumpeting . . . of the dying creatures." At first the soldiers used axes and knives, but when that proved too awful, they dispatched the remainder with more merciful shots to the head.[111] As Crook had foreseen, with their horses slain, the Indians abandoned the chase, and the hungry troopers, overcoming an initial distaste for horseflesh, devoured the fresh meat with gusto.

Reuniting with the supply wagons and its infantry escort at old Fort Reno, Crook sent a message by courier to General Sheridan trumpeting the news of the destruction of "the village of Crazy Horse near mouth of Little Powder River." In hindsight, his account was inaccurate in several respects, inaccuracy that unfortunately magnified the importance of the fight and bolstered the government's case regarding the hostile intentions of the Sioux. It is doubtful that Crook set out to deceive Sheridan. He seems to have honestly believed, as he told his commander, that the village was composed primarily of Crazy Horse's Oglalas, with a sprinkling of Northern Cheyennes and Miniconjous. But he embroidered his conclusion with the wild estimate that it contained "probably in all one half of the Indians off the reservation." He also claimed that "every evidence was found to prove these Indians to be in co-partnership with those at the Red Cloud and Spotted Tail agencies," an assertion that weakly rested on the presence of trade goods in the village. He then described the village as preparing for war, having "a perfect magazine of ammunition, war supplies, and general supplies," items the Cheyennes would later credibly claim were needed for buffalo hunting, not war. Based on this "evidence" he "urgently recommend[ed] the immediate remove of the Agency Indians to the Missouri River" to prevent more reservation Sioux and Cheyennes from joining Sitting Bull and Crazy Horse in the Powder River country.[112]

As events transpired, Crook's recommendation had come too late. The moment when this could be safely done had passed. As will become apparent, the situation at the two agencies had already deteriorated to the point that any attempt to follow his recommendations now would have ended in bloodshed. In some measure, the unrest was attributable to Crook's attack on the Cheyenne village. While the Indians at Red Cloud and Spotted Tail may not have harbored intentions to join Sitting Bull in his battle with the white man before the Powder River attack, many certainly did now. The Cheyennes, in particular, considered the attack to be a declaration of war on their people and soon flocked to the northerners' banner. The army would soon pay for these consequences of the Powder River campaign.

Sheridan found Crook's characterization of the Powder River engagement as a victory less than convincing. "Too much attention was paid to the destruction of the Indian village and not enough to the destruction of the Indians . . ," he grumbled to Sherman. "There was too great a desire to receive orders . . . too much of a desire to be supported when there was no necessity for support. The affair is shamefully disgraceful."[113]

Despite his glowing report, Crook, too, recognized that the campaign was far less successful than described. He directed his anger and disappointment at Colonel Reynolds, whom he undoubtedly felt had betrayed the general's efforts to rehabilitate his career. He had no intention of taking the blame for Reynolds's bungling.[114] The day after his return to Fetterman, he summoned the colonel to the headquarters of Major Alexander Chambers, the post's commanding officer. There, he wasted no time bluntly advising him that the "expedition had been a failure when it should have been a success," and that he intended to hold him accountable by court-martial. Chambers, who kept a record of the confrontation, reported that, without naming names, Crook went on to say that it was his understanding that one of Reynolds's officers "went to cooking coffee during the battle." The flustered colonel admitted that had been the case. But when Crook mentioned another officer who had failed to do his duty, a clear reference to Moore, Reynolds claimed to know nothing about that. Having warmed to his subject, the general then upbraided Reynolds for planning to leave the Lodge Pole campsite for Fort Reno before the arrival of Crook's men, a move that would have left them stranded deep in Indian country. At that, the colonel grew defensive, vowing that "such an idea never entered his head, that he would have put his hand in the fire and burned it off before thinking of such a thing.[115] What Crook, who put a premium on truth, thought of this obvious prevarication can only be imagined. But he calmed himself and offered Reynolds a few days' respite to gather evidence to rebut the allegations made against him. When the colonel failed to do so to the general's satisfaction, Crook ordered a court-martial convened.

Given Crook's pointed remarks about Noyes, Reynolds felt he had no option but to bring charges against the officer for the "cooking coffee" incident, an action the colonel charged had rendered the captain's vulnerable to attack and unprepared to respond to orders when he was called upon to come to Egan's aid in the village.[116] The first to be tried, Noyes's case was heard that April at Fort Russell. Though Reynolds had brought the charges, at the outset of the trial, he attempted to derail the proceedings by objecting to the qualifications of the court-martial panel. He based his claim on a military regulation that prohibited an officer from bringing charges against a soldier and then appointing the panel assigned to hear those charges. Reynolds alleged that Crook had forced him to court-martial Noyes and was therefore disqualified from selecting the members of the court. Crook took the stand, denying that he had pressured Reynolds, a statement corroborated by Chambers, who had witnessed the entire exchange in his office. In a ruling decisively undercutting Reynolds's credibility, the court found his motion unsupported by the evidence. The case then proceeded and Noyes was found guilty. Because the officer was generally well regarded, Crook immediately released him from arrest following his conviction and returned him to duty, allowing him to serve in the ensuing campaign.[117]

Following Noyes's conviction, Crook vigorously lobbied for Reynolds's immediate court-martial, fearing that if he were not tried quickly, he might play an active role in the coming expedition. For his part, the colonel appeared confident that he would participate and went about preparing his cavalry companies for action.[118] Word soon reached Crook at his Omaha headquarters that rumors that Reynolds was going to be allowed to remain in command were having a deleterious effect on morale among the veterans of the Powder River fight, men who would form the backbone of the upcoming campaign. These men, it was said, feared that the colonel would use his political connections to escape punishment and remain in command. The extent of their demoralization was evidenced by increasing drunkenness in the ranks and the desertions of a number of men who claimed they would not fight under Reynolds because of his abandonment of dead and wounded on the Powder.[119]

Deeply concerned, Crook wrote to Sheridan requesting that Reynolds's court-martial be convened immediately to allay his troops' anxiety. While Sheridan was sympathetic, he was unable to recruit the number of officers required for the panel, and so was forced to postpone the trial, which would not take place until the following year.[120] Crook then took the matter into his own hands, removing Reynolds from command, placing him under arrest, and confining him to the post pending his trial. In his stead, he appointed Lieutenant Colonel William B. Royall as interim commander of the Third Cavalry. Tactlessly, Crook ordered Royall, an officer in the colonel's regiment, to carry out Reynolds's arrest. Royall obeyed, but with considerable resentment, as he thought the affair a stain on the Third Cavalry's reputation. His anger opened a rift between himself and his commander that would widen over the next several months and contribute to disunity among the officers of Crook's command.[121]

By the time of Reynolds's court-martial, finally convened in January 1877, partisans of Crook and Reynolds, having served together for nine trying months in the campaign against the Sioux and Cheyennes, had reached a stage of open warfare. Many officers from both sides were called as witnesses, publicly airing their opinions. Strahorn, a staunch Crook advocate, wrote to Mrs. Crook during the trial, complaining that Reynolds and Moore bombarded the court with letters charging the general's faction with lying on the stand. The Crook partisans, he said, were up in arms. But the general tried to calm the waters, laughing off the attacks and assuring his loyalists that "the more [the

Reynolds-Moore faction] stirs up this affair the worse it will be for them if a higher investigation is made."[122] As Reynolds's supporters continued to press their case, Bourke noted in his diary that they became so vociferous that they were "really guilty of intimidating witnesses."[123] Strahorn bragged that he and his friends gave as good as they got, "indulg[ing] in some lingual cremation about thirteen times a day." However, when Strahorn, Bourke, and Stanton threatened a public letter attacking the opposition, the general firmly intervened and had a fatherly chat with Strahorn, from which the reporter emerged "mild as a kitten." And the letter never appeared in print.[124]

The charges and supporting specifications against Reynolds covered five printed pages. They included disobedience to orders (Reynolds's destruction of the food and robes in the village and his decision to depart from Lodge Pole Creek before Crook's arrival); his abandonment of the dead and wounded in the village; and a catchall charge of "conduct to the prejudice of good order and military discipline," which focused on his failure to protect the pony herd, his lack of support for Egan in the village, and his allowing Noyes to unsaddle his men while guarding the ponies. The court (probably at Crook's insistence) added a count of perjury, related to Reynolds's claim that Crook had forced him to bring charges against Noyes, and an additional specification of conduct unbecoming an officer for lying to the general about his decision to leave the Lodge Pole Creek campsite before Crook's arrival.[125]

Reynolds conducted his own defense, which amounted to little more than a denial that he had received orders from Crook to preserve the food and supplies taken from the village, and a personal attack on Crook who, the colonel alleged, was using him as a scapegoat to protect the general's own reputation. He countered charges that he had been responsible for the failure of the expedition by blaming the general for dividing the command and failing to cooperate with Reynolds. Many of his arguments bordered on the spiteful. Some, like his persistent claim that Crook had not ordered him to preserve the food and supplies found in the village, were flatly contradicted by numerous witnesses.[126]

Toward the end of his presentation, perhaps sensing that his case was crumbling, Reynolds abruptly mounted an entirely new line of attack. He "invit[ed] the attention of the court to [the] fact that a non-combatant paymaster [Stanton] was taken from his legitimate duties to act as a newspaper correspondent, and under the smiles and encouragement of a Department Commander [Crook] denounced in the public print as cowards and imbeciles his fellow officers, both his superiors and inferiors in rank. . . ."[127] Crook had anticipated this issue when he had appointed Stanton chief of scouts for the expedition, but named him anyway, knowing that it was not uncommon during the Indian wars for junior and senior officers to write letters or articles from the field for publication in the papers.[128]

But the court-martial panel, probably upset by some of Stanton's journalistic criticisms of his fellow officers, chose to see the paymaster's appointment for what it surely was, a sham perpetrated by Crook to gain press coverage for the campaign. As the army had never formally condoned the practice of officers acting as reporters and since the allegation had been raised, the panel could not ignore it. Stanton, they found, "was not only permitted to write and publish criticisms upon the military operations then going on, but . . . he accompanied the expeditions, with the knowledge and by the authority of his commanding officer, knowing that he was engaged as correspondent."[129]

Throughout the trial, witnesses on both sides went to great lengths to claim credit for their own contributions and discredit the actions of others. Yet despite inconsistencies, the court determined that the clear weight of witness testimony demonstrated that the colonel had turned the battle into an embarrassing failure. He was found guilty on all counts, including his false allegation that Crook had compelled him to court-martial Noyes. His sentence, which the War Department affirmed almost in its entirety, was relatively mild—suspension from rank and command for one year. But President Grant remitted even this slap on the wrist out of regard for Reynolds's prior service. But the trial and attendant publicity had ruined the man's career. As a consequence, he retired on account of disability in June 1877 and lived in obscurity until his death in 1899.[130] For his part, Crook received a formal reprimand for allowing Stanton to accompany the column in the duel role of chief of scouts and war correspondent. The court noted that it "regard[ed] such a practice as pernicious in the extreme and . . . unsoldierly and detrimental to the efficiency and best interest of the service."[131]

Captain Moore's case was heard after Reynolds's conviction. After an equally rancorous trial, he was acquitted of the damning charge of cowardice, but convicted of failing to cooperate in the attack on the village. He was suspended from command for six months, but because of his war record, his sentence, too, was remitted by the president. Like his commander, he subsequently resigned his commission.[132]

Tactically, Moore's failure to advance to the north end of the village had been the blunder that partially undermined the effectiveness of the attack. It allowed the Indians to escape into the foothills with minimum casualties, and from there, mount harassing fire on the soldiers occupying the village. Their vigorous defense was a critical factor in convincing the irresolute Reynolds to destroy rather than confiscate the contents of the village and abandon the field in such haste that the dead and wounded were left behind. But while Moore may have been culpable for his stupidity and/or cowardice, it was Reynolds's lack of firm leadership and his loss of resolve under fire that ultimately caused the command to fail to attain its objective, the destruction of the village as an effective fighting force.

Aside from Reynolds's vacillating leadership, the troops' poor showing can be attributed to their physical and mental condition at the time of the attack. They had been on half rations for several days, were fatigued from their forced march of the night before, and were weakened by the extreme cold. Not surprisingly, without strong leadership, they did not fight well and demonstrated a lack of discipline in the face of the Indians' determined and courageous opposition.[133] On one occasion, several troopers defied an officer's orders and abandoned a prominent defensive position, allowing the Indians to capture it and then pour fire into the troops. Some soldiers also engaged in looting, and several assisted in carrying off dead or wounded comrades as a means to escape from the line of fire. In one instance, for example, six men were seen transporting one body off the field.[134] Among the troops, marksmanship was generally poor. During four hours of combat, surrounded by Indians, the soldiers managed to kill only one warrior, wound another, and shoot an old woman in the thigh. This low casualty rate was achieved despite a high rate of fire. Cavalrymen in one company were reputed to have fired an average of sixty rounds each during the engagement, and officers repeatedly reprimanded their troops for wasting ammunition.[135]

Conversely, the Cheyennes and their Sioux allies proved a formidable foe, a fact that was largely unremarked upon by the participating officers, an underestimation for which the army would later pay dearly.

Far better shots than the soldiers, they made able use of cover and terrain to press the troopers out of the village, and attacked with boldness and vigor, despite being disadvantaged by the element of surprise, inferior weaponry, and a general paucity of ammunition. In an aggressive pursuit of the enemy, they even managed, though vastly outnumbered, to recover many of their horses.

While the Powder River fight divided and demoralized the blue coats, it had an opposite effect on the Indians. The unexpected attack on their sleeping village was interpreted by the previously neutral Cheyennes as a declaration of war on their tribe, spurring them to seek protection in an alliance with the more militant Northern Sioux.[136] Under the leadership of their chief, Two Moons, the band, inadequately dressed for the cold and with little food, fled the ruins of their village to seek shelter in the camp of Crazy Horse's Oglalas. Most were afoot, many without moccasins. Their grim <u>hegira</u>, in driving snow and temperatures that soon plunged well below zero, lasted three days. On the fourth, they reached their objective and were warmly and generously welcomed by the Oglalas. Once there, they proposed an alliance with their stronger and more numerous neighbors that they hoped would result in a body of warriors powerful enough to frighten the whites from their country. Crazy Horse accepted their offer on the condition that the Hunkpapas agreed to join the coalition. Together, the two bands traveled to Sitting Bull's camp to seek his approval. The Hunkpapa chief did not disappoint them. Having long anticipated a defensive war against the Wasichus (whites), he welcomed the Cheyennes, and under his direction, the united bands now moved to an area near the Tongue River where the new grass could support a large gathering. There, they convened a council of the nonagency Sioux—Oglalas, Hunkpapas, Miniconjous, Sans Arcs, Blackfeet, and even a few lodges of Santees, all of whom agreed to ally themselves with the Northern Cheyennes against the white invasion. Though their chiefs repeatedly emphasized that the coalition was for defensive purposes, everyone knew that among the young warriors, many welcomed the opportunity for war.[137]

While the bands in the unceded lands could not field over a thousand warriors, they anticipated correctly that their ranks would soon swell as large numbers of agency Sioux and Cheyennes left the reservation to participate in the spring buffalo hunt. While they awaited

flight to a desirable place (margin note)

their arrival, the roamers moved often, as the grass and game could not long sustain such a large congregation of Indians. On these moves, the Northern Cheyennes took the lead, an acknowledgment of their status as the principal aggrieved party in the coalition. In return, the Cheyennes offered the bounty of their own traditional hunting grounds to the Sioux.[138] Crook's attack on the Powder River camp had become the catalyst for the greatest Indian confederation ever mounted against the white invader.[139]

Lieutenant Colonel Crook in his slouch hat, 1866. Courtesy of Mark Kasal.

Alchise, White Mountain scout and Medal of Honor winner. Courtesy of National Archives and Records Administration (83140).

Al Sieber, Crook's German-born chief of scouts in Arizona, in the company of unidentified Indian scouts and a peculiarly costumed representative from Washington, 1883. Courtesy of National Archives and Records Administration (89501).

Eskiminzin, chief of the Aravaipa Apaches, the victims of the Camp Grant Massacre, here posing with his children. Courtesy of National Archives and Records Administration (83714).

Fred W. Loring, taken about forty-eight hours before he was killed by Apaches near Wickenburg, Arizona, in November 1871. Courtesy of National Archives and Records Administration (165-WA-145).

George Crook, photographed in San Francisco while en route to his assignment as commander of the Department of the Platte in 1875. Courtesy of Mark Kasal.

Crook posing with aides Lieutenants John Bourke and Azor Nickerson in 1875. Courtesy of Sharlot Hall Museum.

General Crook in 1876 at outset of the Sioux War, wearing overcoat with Wolf collar and Kossuth-style campaign hat. Courtesy of Mark Kasal.

General Crook's headquarters in the field during the Hunger March, 1876. Photograph by Stanley Morrow. Courtesy of National Archives and Records Administration (165-FF-2F-112).

Colonel Joseph Reynolds, ill-fated commander of the attack on the Cheyenne village on the Powder River in March 1876, photographed as a major general during the Civil War. Courtesy of Paul Hedren.

Frank Grouard (center) posing with Indian scouts and unidentified whites. Known to the Sioux with whom he lived for some years as "Grabber," he was Crook's chief of scouts during the Sioux War. The son of a Polynesian mother and Mormon missionary father, Grouard was a problematic figure. Courtesy of the Nebraska State Historical Society.

Captain George M. Randall (standing), veteran of Crook's Arizona Tonto Campaign and commander of the Shoshone and Crow contingents at the Rosebud, and Major Thaddeus Stanton (seated), appointed chief of scouts on the Powder River campaign of March 1876 and commander of civilian irregulars during the Big Horn and Yellowstone expedition. The officers are modeling the winter clothing worn during the Powder River campaign. Courtesy of Paul Hedren.

Spotted Tail, chief of the Brule Lakotas. Courtesy of National Archives and Records Administration (87731).

Red Cloud, chief of the Oglala Lakotas. Courtesy of National Archives and Records Administration (85730).

Young Man Afraid of His Horse, Oglala warrior and confidant of Crazy Horse. Courtesy of National Archives and Records Administration (85714).

Baptiste "Big Bat" Pourier, noted scout who acted as a guide for General Crook during the Sioux Campaign and on hunts thereafter. Courtesy of the Nebraska State Historical Society.

General Crook and staff gather around the flag prepared for his headquarters by his officers during the Yellowstone and Big Horn expedition. Crook is seated on a stump wearing a light-colored campaign hat. Lieutenant John Bourke is kneeling to his right with his hand on his hip, while Major Stanton stands to the right (the viewer's left) of the flagstaff wearing a vest and holding a rifle. Photograph by Stanley Morrow. Courtesy of Mark Kasal.

Headquarters staff of the Department of the Platte, 1878. General Crook is seated on the left. Lieutenant Colonel Eugene Carr, Indian fighter and aspirant to command of the Fifth Cavalry, is standing third from left, and to his right, Major Thaddeus Stanton, the fighting paymaster. Courtesy of Mark Kasal.

Colonel Ranald Mackenzie, Fourth Cavalry, served with Crook on the Powder River Expedition. Mackenzie rivaled Crook and Miles in reputation as an experienced and skilled fighter of Indians until mental illness ended his career. Courtesy of the Nebraska State Historical Society.

Colonel Nelson Miles, who competed with Crook for military rank and honors during and after the Sioux War. Photograph by Stanley Morrow at his studio at Fort Keogh in the 1870s. Courtesy of Paul Hedren.

This photograph of Crook at Cheyenne was taken by D. S. Mitchell, circa January 1877, at the time of the Reynolds court-martial. Courtesy of Paul Hedren.

CHAPTER SEVENTEEN

The Big Horn and Yellowstone Expedition

April–May 1876

As March faded into April, opportunity was slipping away from General Sheridan. The three-column campaign he had hoped to launch in February to trap Sitting Bull's people in their winter camps had fizzled. The Sioux and Cheyennes were loose upon the northern plains, unencumbered by deep snow, their ponies fattening on new grass, and their numbers swelling daily with the spring influx of agency Indians. Their enhanced mobility made them an elusive quarry for the slow-moving columns of soldiers and their lumbering wagons, which only now were beginning to assemble for the spring offensive. Colonel John Gibbon, his Montana column delayed by snow, was still struggling east along the banks of the Yellowstone. Meanwhile at Fort Abraham Lincoln on the Missouri, General Terry's force remained frozen in place by spring blizzards. Then, just as rail lines to the east began to open up, allowing supplies to reach his column, George Armstrong Custer, the shining star whom Sheridan chose to lead Terry's troops against the Sioux, became embroiled in political scandals involving corruption in the War Department. He had implicated President Grant's brother, Orville, in testimony before a Senate committee investigated scandals on the Indian reservation. The irate president, thinking that allowing Custer to assume command of Terry's troops might be seen as an endorsement of the man's credibility, relieved him of the assignment and placed him in detention. Terry, an honest and self-effacing officer, was keenly aware of his own inexperience in Indian warfare, and felt that Custer rather than himself ought to lead the campaign. Sheridan, his boss, who had an exaggerated notion of Custer's abilities, shared that assessment. Both beseeched the angry president to relent. Though Grant reluctantly agreed, he demanded as a precondition that Terry, not Custer, command the column in the field. He also instructed Sherman to tell Terry to ensure that Custer does "not take along any newspaper men who always make mischief. . . ." Resolving this brouhaha delayed Terry's departure until the 17th of May.[1]

While weather and politics stalled Terry and Gibbon, from his Omaha headquarters Crook labored to assemble and outfit another column to return to the Powder River country. But he, too, was beset by problems, primarily unrest at the Red Cloud Agency, caused in part by near-starvation conditions among the agency Sioux. In April, Crook visited the reservation and found the situation as bad as rumored.[2] Moved by a mix of humanitarian concern and military pragmatism, he fired off a telegram informing Sheridan, "Indians of Red Cloud on verge of starvation owing neglect in forwarding supplies. . . . Unless Beef arrives soon, Indians will be compelled to raid or leave to join hostiles to keep from starving."[3] He considered the situation so desperate, he asked permission to lend army beef to the Indian agents to feed their charges. But Sheridan, reluctant to intervene in a matter he considered the responsibility of the Interior Department, vetoed the suggestion, suggesting instead that agency officials purchase beeves on the open market if the promised cattle did not arrive soon.[4]

If hunger made the Indians desperate, the government's failure to fulfill its promise to keep the miners out of the Black Hills fanned their despair into open resistance. The coming of spring saw the road from Cheyenne to the Hills thronged with gold seekers, while Custer City, a new mining settlement situated in the Hills themselves, had burgeoned into a sprawling boomtown.[5] Crook's unprovoked attack on the Powder River Cheyennes had added kindling to the smoldering fire. It instilled both a desire for revenge and, even more disturbing, contempt among the young warriors for the soldiers' fighting abilities. The latter viewed the fight as a defeat for the army.[6] Fueled by an incendiary mix of desperation, anger, and scorn, young men from the Red Cloud and Spotted Tail Agencies began attacking travelers along the roads that bordered the reservation and raiding nearby settlements, stealing livestock and killing whites who got in their way. By mid-April, the papers were full of lurid tales of stock theft, murder, and mutilation, sometimes the work of outlaws seeking to blame the Indians for their own misdeeds, but more often traceable to the reservation.[7]

Popular outcry prompted Wyoming governor John Thayer to request military protection for travelers on the Cheyenne–Custer City road. Though occupied with preparations for the coming campaign, Crook had developed a sufficiently keen nose for frontier politics to realize that the problem required his prompt attention. And news reports trumpeted his dispatch of a detachment of cavalry to the rescue within thirty minutes after receiving Thayer's plea. At the same time, he commanded Colonel Bradley at Fort Laramie "to allow no parties of less than fifty well armed men to pass there for the gold fields." Despite these measures, conditions continued to worsen and reinforcements were required. Even with this added manpower, by the beginning of June, raids forced suspension of nearly all travel on the Custer City road.[8]

As yet, few Indians appeared to be joining Sitting Bull. On April 27, Crook wired Sheridan, "No Indians have left except Cheyenne who went south."[9] But in May, hunger and outrage swelled the trickle to a torrent, and he reported that a force of six hundred Indians had headed north to the ceded lands.[10] In early June, Captain William Henry Jordon, commander at Camp Robinson, reported his belief that two thousand Indians had joined the roamers since May 10.[11] Among those leaving were many Oglalas, including Red Cloud's own son, Jack, as well as Hunkpapas, Miniconjous, Sans Arcs, and Northern Cheyennes. Only Spotted Tail managed to hold most of his Brules in check.

But neither these defections nor problems with depredations distracted Crook from his preparations for his Big Horn and Yellowstone campaign, as it had now come to be called. A steady stream of orders emanated from his Omaha headquarters, summoning men and supplies to Fort Fetterman, again selected as the jumping-off point for the expedition. Sheridan's plan for a three-pronged offensive had at last begun to take shape. Colonel Gibbon's troops patrolled eastward along the Yellowstone to block Sitting Bull's people from moving north of the river. General Terry's column, about 925 officers and men, twelve companies of the Seventh Cavalry under Custer, three companies of infantry, and a detachment manning three Gatling guns, was poised to depart from Fort Abraham Lincoln in mid-May. The column would march west toward the Yellowstone, where Terry hoped to rendezvous with Gibbon somewhere around the Tongue. Meanwhile Crook would drive north from Wyoming. As previously stated, rough country and intervening Indians made coordination impossible, requiring that each of the columns act independently as exigencies required.[12]

Crook's command was the most powerful of the three, as formidable as Terry's and Gibbon's forces combined—fifteen troops of the Second and Third Cavalry, with a still resentful Colonel William Royall replacing Reynolds as their commander. They were joined by five companies of infantry from the Fourth and Ninth Regiments, led by Major Alexander Chambers. Absorbing about half of the available fighting force in Crook's department, the column numbered over fifty officers and a thousand men drawn from cavalry and infantry regiments stationed at posts in Wyoming and along the Union Pacific line in Nebraska.[13] To feed and supply them, Crook had assembled a train of 106 wagons, manned by 116 teamsters, and 250 pack mules under his longtime pack master, Tom Moore. Though natural forage for the livestock would be available along the route, they still carried almost 400,000 pounds of grain, required for the cavalry horses, in addition to thousands of pounds of rations, arms, and ammunition. To supplement the game that Crook eagerly anticipated shooting along the way, a herd of two hundred beef cattle would be driven behind the column.[14]

Of paramount importance to Crook were the Indian scouts he hoped to recruit for the expedition. Following his return from the Powder, he had discharged his mixed-blood and white scouts except for Richard, Grouard, and Big Bat, and now counted on persuading Red Cloud's Oglalas to act as trackers, guides, and scouts in the war against Sitting Bull. Based on his experience in the Southwest, he knew that the presence of Indians familiar with the country and the traditional haunts of their people would save the expedition a good deal of time and labor. The enlistment of agency Indians would also, he hoped, deter young warriors from raiding or joining Sitting Bull by providing an alternative means to vent their martial ardor. But uppermost in his mind was the psychological advantage he had enjoyed in Arizona. Using tribesmen to hunt down their own would erode tribal unity and undermine their chiefs' leadership. Most of all, as he put it to Bourke, it would demonstrate "to the intractable Uncpapa [Bourke's spelling] Sioux that their line of communication with the agencies was cut off and that when this present force of men and supplies was destroyed or reduced, there would be no alternative but an unconditional surrender."[15]

On May 9, the general departed Omaha for the Red Cloud Agency to recruit Oglalas for the expedition. He was in good spirits and optimistic about his prospects in the coming expedition. Chatting freely with Bourke as they rode across the prairie, he expanded upon his expectations for the upcoming campaign. His ramblings, faithfully recorded in Bourke's diary, reveal that he seriously underestimated the spirit of resistance that animated the Sioux and Cheyennes. While expressing admiration for their courage and boldness, he repeated his conviction that, unlike the Apaches, they would be unable to withstand the military pressure he planned to bring to bear against them. In contrast to the spartan desert peoples of Arizona, he reckoned that the Plains Indians, living on the game-rich prairies, had accumulated so much wealth and property (ponies) that they would feel their loss too deeply to keep fighting for very long.[16]

At Camp Robinson, adjacent to the Red Cloud Agency, the general received disquieting news. Paymaster Stanton reported to him that Spotted Tail, a staunch ally of the Wasichus, had expressed deep cynicism about the military's ability to defeat Sitting Bull after its poor showing on the Powder River. Sarcastically, the chief had told Stanton, "If you don't do better than you did the last time, you had better put on squaws clothes and stay at home."[17] If Red Cloud's Oglalas entertained similar views, Crook knew they would be far from eager to join his expedition.

To sound out the mood of the Oglala leadership, he asked that Red Cloud and the other paramount chiefs meet with him at the fort. To his disappointment, neither Red Cloud nor the Indian agent, James Hastings, showed up at the appointed time. In their stead, three chiefs who favored accommodation with the whites—Three Bears, Rocky Bear, and Sitting Bull of the South—appeared. While they were almost obsequious in their eagerness to impress the general with their willingness to help him, Crook realized that the real authority lay with Red Cloud, whose absence, he suspected, was due to Agent Hastings's interference. The agent had been infuriated by Crook's report of a large stock of arms and ammunition in the Cheyenne village on the

showing servile complaisance or difference

Powder, claiming it had come from the Red Cloud Agency and evidenced collusion between the northern roamers and the reservation Indians. Hastings had vigorously denied this charge.[18]

Forging ahead despite Red Cloud's absence, Crook told the three chiefs that he had come to enlist warriors for the campaign, not to fight, but "to follow along with the soldiers, point out where the villages are, and gobble up the ponies and things of that kind." While he could always get Crows to do this work, he preferred the Sioux. Why should the Crows get the ponies of the Northern Sioux when Red Cloud's people could have them, he argued. Pointing out that since they would soon be faced with the stark choice of living on the reservation or being killed off, "they may as well be our friends and help us as be our enemies." Sitting Bull of the South, an old man who had visited Washington and seen the teeming hordes of white men, was so eager to please the general that he personally volunteered to go and fight.[19]

In the late afternoon, when Hastings finally showed up, Crook received a far chillier reception. The agent was accompanied by seven of the primary Oglala chiefs, among them Red Cloud, Little Wound, and Sitting Bull of the South. Young Man Afraid of his Horse, whom Crook considered critical to his mission because of his influence over the young warriors, did not attend, a circumstance that the general again attributed to Hastings's malevolent influence.[20]

At the outset, Hastings declared that he would not interfere with any Indians who wished to accompany the expedition. But he opposed the army's recruitment effort and refused to recommend that any warriors enlist. Red Cloud, whose words were recorded by Bourke, seemed not to need any instruction from Hastings. Already angry about the situation in the Black Hills and incensed by Crook's efforts to recruit his young men to fight their own people, he aggressively confronted the Gray Fox.[21] He asked who had ordered the general to go after the northerners. When Crook replied that it had been the president and the secretary of the interior, Red Cloud snapped that the president had ordered Red Cloud's people not to make war and that since then, the agency Sioux had maintained a "peaceful house." But Crook, he said, had stirred up trouble by attacking the Cheyennes on the Powder River. When Crook repeated that he was acting under the authority of the administration in pursuing the northerners, Red Cloud declared, "the Great Father told us to stay here. I don't want to go to War anymore." To that, Little Wound added that he did not believe Crook's assertion that he was acting on orders from the Great Father. He, Little Wound, had been to Washington twice and the president had personally told him not to go to war anymore. Crook did not take kindly to anyone questioning his veracity. He abruptly closed off the discussion, announcing that he had nothing else to say. It was stunningly clear at this point that his mission had been a total failure. Red Cloud had no intention of allowing his warriors to scout for the army against their northern cousins. The meeting concluded on this sour note with a furious Crook convinced that Hastings had engineered the chiefs' refusal. But since he could do little to force the issue, he hastily gulped a face-saving glass of "cool champagne" at the post trader quarters before retreating to Camp Robinson empty-handed. Not one Oglala warrior would accompany him on the expedition, though Sitting Bull of the South would subsequently honor his promise and provide scouts later in the year.[22]

Apparently, there were elements at the Red Cloud Agency whose hostility toward Crook went beyond merely denying him scouts. The day following his meeting with Red Cloud, Crook departed Camp Robinson in the predawn darkness with a substantial escort of some sixty-five troopers headed for the rendezvous with his forces at Fort Fetterman. As the sun rose, some of the soldiers, glancing back toward the post, observed a puff of smoke drifting upward from the bluffs in back of the Agency. Concerned, but not unduly worried because of the size of their force, the detachment made camp at noon at the head of a creek, taking note of a lone mail wagon that passed them heading toward the fort. The reporter, Strahorn, who had joined Crook's escort, unsaddled his horse and set out to explore the environs on foot, ignoring warnings that there might be unfriendly Indians about. As he wandered in a stand of willows by a small pond, a snapping twig alerted him to a file of Indians, creeping through the brush not fifty yards behind him. Avoiding detection, he hurried back to the camp to warn the soldiers. As the command assumed defensive positions, the Indians, bearing a white flag, coolly rode into the camp, flaunting a letter from Agent Hastings giving them permission to be off the reservation to check beaver traps in the area. After carefully looking over the command, they departed as abruptly as they had appeared. That evening, a courier from Camp Robinson roused Crook with a dispatch notifying him that the previous noon, not long after passing the general's escort on the road, the driver of the mail wagon had been murdered by Indians at a spot not ten miles from the post. It was later surmised that the smoke seen that morning had signaled Crook's departure from the Agency, part of a plot to assassinate him. The scheme had been abandoned after the plotters observed the size of the general's escort and its state of readiness, and they had murdered the mail carrier instead.[23]

Thwarted in his effort to enlist the Sioux, Crook turned to the Crows and Shoshones to supply his needs. The army could usually count on help from the Crows, or Absarokees, as they called themselves, in a campaign against their traditional enemies, the Sioux.[24] Accordingly, before leaving Camp Robinson, he had wired Fort Ellis, requesting that the tribe send him scouts. If they agreed, they were to meet his column at old Fort Reno on the Bozeman Trail. Crook sent a similar request to the Shoshones at the Wind River Agency. The tribe was well known to him through assistance they had provided during his campaigns in Idaho and eastern Oregon, and had traditionally allied themselves with the whites against the more powerful Sioux. In return, they had received the grant of a reservation in the Wind River valley and military protection through the establishment of nearby Camp Brown. By 1876 their leader, Chief Washakie, a great friend to the army, had reached the advanced age of seventy-eight. Despite his years, he remained a vigorous, unchallenged ruler of a band that he led by dint of his personality and skill as a warrior.[25] He had a reputation as a wise but despotic ruler, often compared by whites, both in appearance and statesmanship, to George Washington. And he seems to have lived up to their expectations. Though he had now reached an age when most warriors were content to retire to the warmth of their tipis, the chief would prove a formidable and reliable ally in the coming campaign.[26]

CHAPTER EIGHTEEN

March to the Rosebud

May–June 1876

At Fetterman, as General Crook assembled his troops for the campaign, a number of journalists flocked to join him. Some historians have claimed that this was the result of a shameless effort to curry favor with the press in order to further Crook's ambitions for higher rank. Such speculation is based on a lesson that Crook himself confessed he had drawn from his Civil War experience. "I learned too late," he wrote in his autobiography, "that it was not what a person did, but it was what he got the credit of doing that gave him a reputation and at the close of the war gave him position." At the time, his remark was directed at General Sheridan, whom he believed, with considerable justification, had robbed him of the recognition he thought he had earned at the battles of Winchester and Fishers Hill.[1]

Some officers, most notably Custer, were indeed known to exploit the press, as well as their own writings, to further their careers. Crook, who shared Custer's aspirations for higher rank, was as keenly aware as his fellow officers of the value of publicity and was not above using the press to promote his own agenda. Sometimes it was to further policies he favored and, perhaps on occasion, for personal advancement. With respect to the latter, however, experience had taught him that news coverage could be a two-edged sword, often eliciting praise, but sometimes opprobrium, particularly when the officer and the journalists did not share the same political point of view.

Newspapers of the time were blatantly partisan. Editors made choices about covering campaigns with an eye to the slant they wished to put on events and based on which generals were likely to generate the most favorable news for the party of choice. And they were likely to hire and assign reporters who favored the paper's editorial leanings. So, officers who hoped to garner favorable publicity for themselves were dependent on which papers chose to cover their campaigns. Further, journalists, then as now, were an independent bunch, not easily given to manipulation. At least during the Sioux War, Crook seems to have figured this out, as there is scant evidence that he tried to influence which papers covered his campaign or the reporters assigned.

At least one historian disagrees, alleging that Crook cultivated reporters and newspapers most likely to provide him with favorable coverage and ostracize those who were hostile.[2] In truth, Crook enjoyed the company of journalists and they, his. Several became among his closest and most durable friends. But there is little to support the notion that he attempted to exploit these friendships to further his ambition for higher rank. Nor did he shun reporters unfriendly to his cause. And his most persistent critic, the *Herald* reporter Reuben Davenport, while he certainly incurred the enmity of Crook partisans among the officers, never complained of ostracism by the general himself or at his direction. (See below.)

Nevertheless, it would be naïve to think that Crook did not attach importance to press coverage of his activities. In this respect, he was fortunate to have the highly literate John Bourke to act as his representative to the newsmen who covered his campaigns. While allowing him good press coverage, this stratagem also permitted him to gain credit for his achievements while maintaining his image as a modest and unassuming officer. And it gave him a reputation as an enigmatic and unconventional leader, aspects of his character that he certainly exaggerated, but that were, nevertheless, too consistently displayed to be other than real aspects of his personality.[3]

During the Sioux War, it appears that newsmen sought out Crook rather than the reverse, a solitary exception being his active solicitation of coverage from the *New York Herald* previously discussed in connection with his campaign into the Powder River country in March 1876. Though at the time he asked the *Herald* to furnish him a reporter, it does not appear that he was doing so for personal reasons. Rather, he seems to have wanted a writer sympathetic to the military to counter the negative portrayal of the army's role in the Indian wars typified by the coverage of Custer's Washita campaign by the eastern press in 1868. Had personal ambition been his objective, he probably would not have appointed Colonel Reynolds to lead the expedition, knowing full well that it would mean that credit for its success would have devolved upon the colonel rather than Crook.

In any event, the journalists who gathered at Fort Fetterman in May 1876 were clearly not there at Crook's connivance. The Sioux War, though it competed for attention with the nation's Centennial celebrations taking place that summer in Philadelphia, was nevertheless big news, an attractive and colorful story guaranteed to attract the attention of the competitive urban press. But covering the war presented the papers with a logistical challenge, involving, as it did, three widely separated military columns operating in remote and generally inaccessible territory. Editors had to decide which of the three columns would produce the best story and, of equal importance, the means to get that story quickly from the field to the paper. To editors, John Gibbon's column would have presented the greatest difficulty since his area of operation lay in the heart of Sioux country at a considerable distance from any existing lines of transportation or communications. The Terry/Custer column was a logical alternative—anything to do with Custer seemed to be good press—but few papers were eager to pick a fight with General Sherman—notoriously averse to journalists—who, in accordance with Grant's instructions, had forbidden Custer to bring along any newsmen. For those who might be tempted to defy Sherman, Wilbur Storey, the eccentric but innovative owner of the *Chicago Times*, offered his own rationale for not doing so. When his reporter asked for permission to accompany Custer and the Dakota column, he flatly refused, declaring that "Crook, who knows more about the Indians, is likely to do the hard work. Custer is a brave soldier—none braver—but he has been out there some years already and has not succeeded in bringing the Sioux to a decisive engagement. . . . It is settled that you go with Crook."[4] Likely, other editors leaned toward Crook's column because it offered the added advantage of rail access to Cheyenne, Crook's point of departure, and a telegraph office at Fort Fetterman, the nearest such facility to the battlefront. So, in the end, only one reporter, Mark Kellogg, a former telegrapher and reporter for the

Bismarck Tribune, would ride with Custer. The rest flocked to the reticent but heretofore successful General Crook. Their work would be supplemented by the scribblings of several officers who, in addition to their military duties, would provide the press with firsthand reports from the field—Captain Andrew Burt and Lieutenant James Foster among them.

The first civilian correspondent to attach himself to Crook was Robert Strahorn. He had been with Crook's column at the Powder River at the invitation of Major Stanton, the fighting paymaster. Now, he was so eager to cover Crook that he had braved a lonesome ride from Cheyenne through Indian country to join the general on his futile recruiting mission to the Red Cloud Agency and was with him on the ride from Camp Robinson.[5] He would remain with the column throughout the campaign, covering it for the *Rocky Mountain News* in dispatches that he signed with his nom de plume, "Alter Ego," as well as for the *Chicago Tribune*, the *New York Times*, and occasionally, the Cheyenne and Omaha papers. Having received a commendation from the secretary of war for his courage during the March 17 fight, he fit in easily with the command, enjoying the respect and comradeship of many of its officers and men.

The remaining reporters arrived by rail in Cheyenne a week after Crook's departure from Red Cloud, purchased mounts, and joined the general on the Platte in late May. Among them was Reuben Briggs Davenport, who would become Crook's most persistent and sharpest critic. An intense young man, Davenport proudly advertised his affiliation with the *New York Herald* by plastering his paper's name on every conceivable piece of his equipment. According to a sarcastic fellow reporter, "He has not branded his horse '*Herald*' but has got him so he looks like a *Herald* horse."[6] Of medium height, pale complexion, with black hair, a thin bearded face, and pale gray eyes, at twenty-four he had already acquired some exposure to frontier reporting. The previous year, he had accompanied the Jenney expedition into the Black Hills, but had failed to make a very good impression. Colonel Dodge concluded that while he "writes well & has the regular reporter knack of pumping people . . . , he is green as a gourd, as credulous as a ninny."[7] Dodge's disparaging comment referred to Davenport's propensity to believe the words of any trooper or scout and record them in print, a weakness that drew frontier veterans to him with the most outrageous tall tales. The camelquo yarn ranks among the most famous. The camelquo, firmly rooted in the fertile soil of frontier imagination, was reputedly the product of the union of a camel, introduced by the army in Arizona during the Civil War, and a Rocky Mountain elk. Davenport dutifully recorded the existence of the splendid beast in a four-column article. It had, he recorded to his everlasting regret, "the stature of the giraffe, the antlers of the elk, the hump of the camel, the fleetness and endurance of both parties, and the unconquerable ferocity of the tiger."[8] Though his credulity might have endeared him to some, Davenport had an irritating, nitpicking personality and a superior attitude that, together with his carping criticisms and intrusive interrogation techniques, succeeded in alienating the officers of Crook's command, several of whom would publicly impugn his courage.[9] Yet he developed into an accomplished journalist with a clear style and a fine eye for detail.[10]

Another of the reporters who joined the expedition from Cheyenne was Thomas MacMillan (sometimes spelled MacMullan, or McMillan), who had also covered the Jenney expedition, in his case for the *Chicago Inter-Ocean*. In contrast to the *Herald* reporter, Dodge found MacMillan to be "of an entirely different stamp—very gentlemanly, hard to stuff, & with excellent good sense & tho this is the first time he has been on the plains he takes to it so kindly & well, as to win the liking and respect of everyone."[11] MacMillan, like Davenport, was in his mid-twenties, fragile in appearance, slender, and pale. He was a Scott, a Congregationalist with strong religious convictions that translated into a fanatic regard for truth.[12] Though he may have given Dodge the impression of an easy adjustment to the plains, in actuality, having suffered from ill health since childhood, he was much affected by the heat, fatigue, and dust of the march, often coughing far into the night.[13] But despite his problems, he remained steadfast in his coverage of the expedition.

Joe Wasson had covered Crook's campaigns in Idaho and Oregon for the *Owyee Avalanche*. Now nine years older and writing for the more sedate *New York Tribune*, *San Francisco Alta California*, and *Philadelphia Press*, his reporting had become considerably less flamboyant, and his stories more abbreviated. He remained the inveterate geologist, apparently more interested in gold exploration than in the military aspects of the campaign.[14]

But the "gem of the lot," at least according to Captain Charles King of the Fifth Cavalry, was John F. Finerty. Of him it was said, "If Davenport is always hungry—for news—Finerty may be said to be always thirsty—for liquids and news, and he can hold any quantity of either." He was red-faced and lanky, so tall he was often addressed as "Long John." When seated astride a horse, he was forced to bend his knees to keep his feet from dragging on the ground, a veritable Don Quixote. Despite his awkward appearance, Finerty was no greenhorn. A native of Ireland and the son of a newspaper editor, his youthful involvement in Irish politics led him to flee to America in 1864, where he promptly enlisted to fight in a New York regiment. For eight years following the war, he had been a reporter and editor, writing local news for three Chicago papers. Though ultimately, Finerty would become a life-long admirer and personal friend of Crook, he did not sacrifice objectivity for sentiment, or lend himself to manipulation by clever army officers. It was he who had asked Storey of the *Chicago Times* to be allowed to accompany the Terry/Custer column. Disappointed, he had accepted Storey's refusal and joined Crook.[15]

Like Wasson and Strahorn, Finerty typified the Henry Morton Stanley school of journalism, reporters who made their reputations as adventurers, covering the frontiers of Western civilization in the nineteenth century. They carried guns and expected to use them. In Finerty's case, his martial instincts were so pronounced that the sight of him in the forefront of a charge, carbine in hand, pipe firmly clamped between his teeth, had earned him the title of the "Fighting Irish Pencil Pusher." But his zest for combat in no way interfered with his journalistic instincts, and he was widely respected for the faithfulness of his written portrayal of life on the campaign trail. His reporting was marred somewhat by his unflinching belief in the superiority of the white race and a willingness to stretch an occasional stray fact for drama, both common attributes in writings of the day. But usually, he meticulously recorded only what he saw and what he experienced, believing that unless he shared hardships and danger with the troops, he would be unable to accurately represent events as they happened. His style was relatively free of the clunky, pretentious vocabulary of the era, though he was known to garnish his copy with the occasional classical reference.[16]

Finerty's first meeting with Crook took place in Omaha on the eve of the expedition's departure. Describing the general in terms by now familiar to the reader, he depicted "a spare but athletic man of about forty, with fair hair, clipped close, and a blond beard which seemed to part naturally at the point of his chin. His nose was long and aquiline, and his blue-gray eyes were bright and piercing." To Finerty, "he looked every inch a soldier, except that he wore no uniform." Brusque at first, Crook warmed to the reporter after reading a letter of introduction from Sheridan. Genially, he inquired whether Finerty could ride and shoot well, to which the latter replied, "I can ride fairly, general. As for shooting, I don't know. I'd engage, however, to hit a hay-stack at two hundred yards." Crook laughed and, on that note, ended the interview by instructing the reporter to make his way to Fort Russell and join one of the cavalry contingents preparing to depart for Fetterman. At Russell, Finerty was further instructed to "never stray from the main column and never trust a horse or an Indian." He then joined MacMillan and Davenport and set out for Fetterman.

On May 27, after almost drowning in the rain-swollen North Platte River, the reporters arrived at the post sunburned and trail-worn, much to Crook's amusement.[17] However, the general's apparent good humor was a façade that concealed a deepening worry about his Indian allies, the Crows and Shoshones. Though the remainder of his force had assembled at the post, the whereabouts of the all-important scouts remained a mystery. On May 21, he had sent a patrol out along the Powder River under Frank Grouard, ostensibly to look for a good crossing, but with instructions to watch for the Crows. The mission proved an ordeal. The scout was forced to travel by day through country alive with Sioux, who eventually ambushed his men. They barely escaped with their lives. Grouard would later claim that the incident was the closest call he ever had.[18] Only a week later, underscoring the importance he attached to Indian auxiliaries, Crook sent out a second patrol, two companies of the Third Cavalry, to ride north to old Fort Reno to meet the Crow scouts and hold them there until the column arrived.

At noon on the May 29, unable to delay longer, Crook ordered the column's departure. Thankfully, the wind that had howled down from the north over the past three months had abated, replaced by the welcome chirp of the meadowlark, a herald of approaching summer. But within a day, the lark's predictive powers were put to the test. The temperature plummeted, the men donned their overcoats, and by the following evening, the first of summer, were chipping ice from their water buckets and kindling fires for warmth.[19] After making camp, Crook dispatched Grouard to the west, ostensibly in search of a better trail to the Powder, but once more, with orders to look out for the Crows.[20]

On June 2, camped among the desolate, fire-blackened ruins of old Fort Reno, the command was rejoined by the Third Cavalry patrol, which had encountered no sign of the Crow scouts.[21] To add to the general gloom, on the same date, the column incurred its first casualty. A private accidentally discharged his carbine, the ball striking his thigh and moving upward to lodge in his bowel, a wound that would soon prove mortal.[22]

Though concealing his concerns from his fellow officers and maintaining a stoic silence on the subject, Crook's anxiety about the whereabouts of his Indian allies drove him to deprive his column of the services of his only experienced scouts. He ordered Richard, Grouard, and Big Bat to ride through Sioux-infested territory to the Crow Agency to personally fetch the warriors he so desperately needed. In the scouts' absence, he would act as both military commander and guide in country little known to whites and overrun by hostile Indians. Besides indicating the critical importance he attached to Indian allies, this decision exemplified his self-confidence and perhaps his low opinion of the skills and ferocity of his enemy. Grouard, who had lived with the Sioux and was under no such illusion, told Crook to expect his return in fourteen days—if he was still alive.[23]

Following the scouts' departure, Crook pushed north on the Bozeman Trail past the ruins of Fort Phil Kearny, planning to site his base camp along Goose Creek, a tributary of the Tongue. On the march, he maintained stringent camp security at night, corralling his wagons every night and posting pickets on surrounding high points around his campsites.[24] Yet he manifested a puzzling laxness on the trail, ignoring his own demand for fire discipline to take pot shots at game, while exposing Captain Noyes and a small detachment of only ten troopers to considerable risk by sending them ahead of the column to search out a suitable campsite. And, though he had passed over this same route in

March, he somehow managed to miss Goose Creek, crossing instead into an adjacent valley, where he made camp on a stream known as Prairie Dog Creek. It was a mistake that perhaps was due to his use of a War Department chart originally drawn up in 1860 that failed to show the creek. It also may have been the case that the area looked substantially different in June than it had in March. Nevertheless, Noyes, a far less experienced woodsman, did manage to locate the right creek and, emulating the general, remained there for a day, fishing, before returning to the column. Noyes does not appear to be the only officer who recognized that they were in the wrong valley. But no one appeared willing to correct the stern commander, particularly as there was always the chance that he had camped on Prairie Dog Creek on purpose, a possibility that, given his penchant for secrecy, would be hard to overlook. When Noyes rejoined the column at the Prairie Dog Creek camp, he too prudently refrained from raising the issue.[25]

However, next day, undoubtedly realizing his error, but certainly not admitting it, the general broke camp and pushed the column down the creek to its confluence with the Tongue. The weather had changed again, growing hot and sultry, with thunder growling in the distance. By the time Crook called a halt, the men were tired and depressed. But their mood lifted as they made themselves at home in their new campsite with its good water, plentiful grass and timber, and "charming scenery."[26] Unfortunately, from a strategic perspective, the new location was a disaster. It lay on a spit of land protruding into a bend of the Tongue, at this juncture a swiftly flowing stream about sixty yards wide, its banks covered with a thick growth of cottonwoods and thick underbrush. Overlooking the encampment to the north across the river, bluffs rising perpendicularly several hundred feet seemed to invite attack. But the illusion of security pervaded the camp so strongly that Crook shrugged off the fatigue and dust of the trail "with Indian-like stolidity" and rode blithely off into the bush in search of game, seemingly indifferent to the possibility that his gunfire might draw any Sioux in the vicinity. Finerty would later ascribe the general's survival to pure luck.[27]

The column would remain at this site for several days while Crook continued to anxiously await the Crows' arrival. As usual, he shared his thoughts with no one but his closest aides.[28] Fully aware that his reticence mystified the column, he reveled in his inscrutability, deriving puckish delight in baffling those around him. One officer remarked that the general "has a faculty for silence that is absolutely astonishing. . . . Grant is loquacious when compared to him." The same officer commented, "We all put this up as the permanent camp, but nobody knows but General Crook, and he won't tell. The general doesn't make any confidants. If an officer asks him a question he doesn't 'sit on' him, as we call snubbing out here, but just looks pleased at the interest manifested in the affairs by the inquiring officer, and sometimes gives him an answer which leaves the questioner more completely in the dark than before, [or] generally simply says, 'I don't know,' which answers the purpose just as well."[29]

After retreat sounded on the evening of their June 7 arrival on the Tongue, the officers and men gathered soberly to lay to rest the body of the trooper who had accidentally shot himself. The service, which was conducted with great ceremony, and a granite boulder was rolled over the grave to protect it from Indians and wild animals.[30] That night, well after the troops had turned in, the camp awoke to the yipping of coyotes, a signal often used by Plains Indians when approaching an enemy encampment. Then the voice of an Indian was heard calling out from the bluff across the river. Other cries echoed from the hillside. Crook awakened Ben Arnold, a frontier roustabout assigned to the column, who was fluent in Lakota. Arnold determined that the language spoken was not Lakota but, as far as he could make out, the Indians were asking whether the Crows had come into camp. Whether this was a taunt or a serious request for information remained unclear. Arnold responded in Lakota and was greeted by silence, infuriating Crook, who believed that the Indians carried a message from the Crows, and that the response in Sioux had frightened them off. The next morning, a stray pony and the tracks of about fifteen Indians were discovered near the camp, heightening tension.[31]

At dawn on the 9th, a courier arrived from Fetterman with the welcome news that 120 Shoshone warriors would be joining the column within the next couple of days. Not as welcome was an accompanying report that many young warriors at the Red Cloud Agency for the Powder River country had left the reservation to join Sitting Bull's people.[32] To meet this threat, Sheridan had ordered eight companies of the Fifth Cavalry, men who had served under Crook in Arizona, to advance to Red Cloud to prevent future defections and to disarm any warriors returning to the Agency.[33]

Though this news might have disturbed some of the officers, many still behaved as if the expedition was merely an outing organized for their amusement. According to one lieutenant, the majority of his fellow officers thought that the Indians had left their immediate area and were miles away on the Yellowstone, either watching Gibbon or skirmishing with Terry.[34] They were soon to be disabused of this fantasy.

That evening, at about 6:30, as a number of officers rose from dinner and their men curried their horses on the picket line, a shot echoed across the camp, followed immediately by a volley of rifle fire. The firing came from the crest of the bluff across the river, where a band of Indians in breechclouts clustered, their rifles aimed at the encampment. Mistakenly believing that most of the troops had retired for the night, they concentrated their fire on the soldiers' tents. Consequently, tent poles, stovepipes, and canvas absorbed the brunt of the attack, while the troops and their livestock suffered little damage. The soldiers returned fire, but the distance was too great for their Springfields to have much affect. Crook, who regarded the shooting as a waste of ammunition and feared that it might be interpreted by the Indians as an indication of panic among the troops, quickly put a stop to it. To clear the Indians from the bluffs, he sent a mixed detachment of infantry and cavalry under Captain Anson Mills to engage them. The troopers charged across the river, dismounted, and laboriously climbed the steep slope beyond. By the time they reached the summit, the Indians, mounted on ponies as fleet and agile as deer, had darted across an open plateau toward a second ridgeline. Beyond the ridge, the hills were cut by numerous rocky defiles, making it ideal terrain for an ambush. Suspecting that the Indians intended to lure them into a trap, Mills called off the chase and returned to camp.[35]

The prevailing mood was euphoric. The troops, many of whom had never heard a shot fired in anger, had now received their baptism by fire, suffered only two casualties, both lightly wounded, and performed well. The officers, who regarded the affair as a welcome break from an otherwise monotonous routine, valued the incident as a means to accustom their raw troops to enemy fire and increase the alertness of the command. Many, however, continued to regard the expedition as a picnic.[36] The skirmish had left them even more smugly confident than before.

Crook read the situation differently. He thought that the bold daylight attack might have been meant to cover the withdrawal of a nearby village, and regretted the absence of Indian allies and his mixed-blood scouts, who might have confirmed his suspicions. Clearly, the incident demonstrated that Crazy Horse (whom he believed responsible) was now aware of his strength and location. The vulnerability of the present campsite had been demonstrated, and the column's huge livestock herd had by now depleted the surrounding grass cover, leaving the general with little choice but to move to a new location.[37]

On June 11, with thunder rumbling in the background, the command finally found itself on the banks of Goose Creek, a spot that now lies in downtown Sheridan, Wyoming. The site was ideal—well watered, with good grazing and plenty of wood and, in the wide, clear streams that flowed through the camp, excellent trout fishing. A warier Crook now put in place a strong system of outlying patrols and pickets to guard against another surprise attack. But in most respects, his officers and men continued to treat the occasion as a spring outing, enjoying the excellent hunting and fishing afforded by the surrounding countryside. For his part, their commander opted to pursue his ornithological interests, gathering specimens for his growing collection.[38]

But an undercurrent of tension was beginning to exert its influence. Crook's reluctance to discuss his plans with any but his closest aides had created an air of uncertainty among his officers, a concern heightened by the continued absence of the three scouts who had gone off to fetch the Crows. Their return was overdue and their fate was the subject of much speculation. Though he kept his own counsel, Crook's anxiety was becoming apparent to all.[39]

Then, on the afternoon of June 14, twelve days following their departure, Frank Grouard and Louis Richard finally reappeared, riding into camp with a huge Indian in tow. They were immediately engulfed in a swarm of excited troopers. As the country between Fetterman and the Crow Agency on the Yellowstone was thick with Sioux, the scouts had traveled by night, following a circuitous route to avoid detection. They had finally reached the banks of the Big Horn. There, they observed a gathering of warriors on the opposite bank. The two parties exchanged gunfire, mistaking each other for Sioux. Then, the warriors forged into the river, shouting their war cries in preparation for an attack. Big Bat, who had lived for some time among the Crows, immediately recognized their yells. Calling out their name for him, *Left Hand*, he managed to get their attention and the shooting died away. The Indians, as relieved as the scouts, put aside their weapons and enveloped the scouts in what Grouard described as a "great American hand-shaking tournament." They had been searching for Crook's column and, in fact, it had been members of their party who hailed the camp on the Tongue, frightened off, as Crook had suspected, when Arnold had addressed them in Lakota.[40]

Though pleased to see Big Bat, the Crows were not eager to engage the Sioux and were more interested in laying a supply of buffalo meat for the next winter. Besides, they, like Spotted Tail, appeared to have grown skeptical of Crook's fighting spirit after hearing of the debacle at the Powder River. But Grouard spent two days cajoling them and eventually won over a respected chief named Old Crow. Influenced by the chief, a sizable contingent of warriors finally agreed to join the campaign.[41]

The scouts and their reluctant recruits made their way back to Crook's former campsite on Prairie Dog Creek only to find it abandoned. Signs indicated that the column had moved toward Goose Creek, in the opposite direction from the Sioux, reinforcing the Crows' suspicion that the blue coats lacked stomach for a fight. Nevertheless, urged on by Grouard, they followed the trail to the soldiers' camp. Then, at the last moment, they refused to enter it, fearing treachery. After much palavering, they finally agreed to send one chief into the camp with Grouard and Richard, holding Big Bat as a hostage to Crook's good intentions. Crook responded by sending Captain Andrew Burt to bring them in. Burt, formerly commander of Fort C. F. Smith, adjacent to the Crow Agency, was well known to the Crows. Reassured, they staged a dramatic entrance, handsomely dressed in elaborately beaded buckskins, their hair tied up and plumed, flourishing carbines and more traditional weaponry. "Quick as lightning," Finerty wrote, "they gained the center of our camp, dismounted, watered, and lariated their ponies, constructed their tipis, or lodges, and like magic the Indian village arose in our midst."[42]

As the Crows settled down to their evening meal, the Shoshone auxiliaries appeared. Eighty-six in number and organized in two companies, they rode into camp in columns of twos, cavalry-style, each led by a warrior bearing an American flag. In command were the sons of the venerable Washakie, their paramount chief, and Captain Tom Cosgrove, a Texan and Confederate cavalry veteran, who had taught the Shoshones military drill.[43] Every warrior was armed with a government-issue breech-loading rifle, a revolver, and a lance, the brightly polished surfaces of their weapons flashing in the reflected light of the soldiers' campfires. Like the Crows, their clothing was fantastically decorated with beads, brass buttons, bells, strips of scarlet cloth, and feathers. Their martial bearing and colorful adornment called to the mind of one observer a band of Don Cossacks in war bonnets. They drew up smartly in file before General Crook, who was so impressed by their presentation and so relieved by their arrival that he immediately conducted an impromptu formal review of their lines.[44]

Later that evening, the Shoshone and Crow warriors, wrapped in their multicolored blankets, gathered around a huge, crackling blaze, their eyes glittering in the reflected firelight. As one, they voiced their hatred of the Sioux and pledged their arms to the campaign against them, asking only that they be allowed to scout in their own manner, a request that so accorded with Crook's own views that he granted it without hesitation.[45] There followed a nightlong orgy of dancing, drumming, and chanting to invoke the blessing of the Great Spirit on the enterprise before them. The troops looked on spellbound or lay awake in their tents listening to the unearthly sounds until a persistent drizzle sent everyone off to sleep.

The arrival of their Indian allies infused Crook and his command with renewed confidence, but with them came unsettling news. The Crows had last seen Gibbon's Montana column a month before at the confluence of the Rosebud and the Yellowstone, facing, but failing to attack, a strong Sioux band on the south bank of the river.[46] The presence of a large body of the enemy between his column and Gibbon and Terry meant that Crook would have to confront the Sioux without reinforcements. But the self-confident general had no doubt that his force could handle the situation. With the arrival of the Crows and Shoshones and some sixty-five miners who had joined the column en route, he now had over thirteen hundred men, more than enough, in his opinion, to soundly thrash the Sioux and their Cheyenne allies. Though estimates indicated that there might be as many as three thousand warriors arrayed against him, Crook was confident that the Indians would be unable to concentrate for long in one encampment because their ponies would deplete the forage in the surrounding area in only a few days. Nor could he envision these bands, each under a different chief, acting in concert against a common enemy. If the Indians broke up into several smaller encampments, which he believed inevitable, Crook thought that if he could find them, he could defeat them in detail.

The primary difficulty lay in finding them. Even with the aid of Crow and Shoshone scouts, the search would not be easy. Intelligence brought in by the Crows was scanty and old. They vaguely reported a large Sioux village on "the Tongue or some of its tributaries," at a distance of somewhere between seventy and one hundred and thirty five miles away." They believed that if found, it could be taken by surprise.[47] Crook was skeptical. Grouard, in whom he placed great trust, had stated flatly that he "supposed [the village was] on the Rosebud," west of the Tongue.[48] As for surprising them, given the number of Sioux hunting parties in the area, the general felt that he had lost that advantage some time ago.[49]

As the last notes of the evening bugle call faded into the night air, the general assembled his officers in the open space before his tent to give them the orders they had long awaited. He clearly favored Grouard's opinion regarding the location of the village. Consequently, he tersely informed the gathering that he planned to move quickly into the valley of the Rosebud, and if possible, attack before his presence became known. In the interests of speed and mobility, "the command would cut loose from wagon and pack-train on the morning of the 16th, taking four days' rations in the saddle-bags."[50] They would travel light—one blanket, the clothes on their backs, one hundred rounds of ammunition, lariats and sidelines, no tents. Soldiers too sick or disabled to accompany the column would be left behind. Supplies currently carried by the mules would be transferred to the wagons, which would remain at Goose Creek, under guard by packers and teamsters. The mules would then be used as mounts for the infantry to allow them to keep pace with the cavalry.[51] Twenty packers and miners who elected to accompany the soldiers would ride with the cavalry led by chief packer Tom Moore.

The next day, under sunny skies, two hundred infantrymen filed tentatively onto a flat plain bordering Goose Creek where a like number of unbroken pack mules awaited them. A crowd of cavalrymen and Indians gathered to watch the spectacle, and they were not disappointed. As experienced troopers saddled the unaccustomed mounts, "a cloud of mule-heels, shod in iron" and a cacophony of squeals and shrill neighs erupted, striking terror into the hearts of the watching foot soldiers. With the order to mount, the "mule rodeo" began. To the reporter Strahorn, "no circus ever furnished a better show in its mule riding department." "The entire valley for a mile in every direction was filled with bucking mules, frightened infantrymen, broken saddles, and applauding spectators." After much effort and not a little pain and embarrassment, at the end of what must have seemed a very long day, the battered infantry regulars had transformed themselves, at least temporarily, into a mounted force.[52]

Before dawn on the 16th, the men, jarred awake by the loud incantations of Crow and Shoshone medicine men, hastily downed a breakfast of hard tack and black coffee, and as the sun pushed over the horizon, rode out of the Goose Creek campsite, newly rechristened Camp Cloud Peak. The column headed in a northwesterly direction across the Tongue and up its park-like valley. Moving quickly, the Indian allies in advance, they traveled north and then west toward the Rosebud, the Indian allies, like wolves on a scent, becoming increasingly agitated at the growing signs of the presence of a large buffalo herd. Trotting forward through fields of wild roses and blue phlox, the column crested a hill on the treeless prairie and was abruptly confronted with an immense sea of buffalo, stretching in undulating brown waves to the horizon. Crook, still holding on to the faint hope of surprising the Sioux, ordered his officers to steady their men to prevent them from charging off, guns blazing. But he dared not attempt to impose a similar discipline on his Indian allies, the latter, entirely without inhibition, ripped off their outer garments with wild shrieks and charged into the herd, discharging their rifles into the fleeing animals with utter abandon. When questioned by the officers why they killed far more than they could possibly eat, a custom more peculiar to the white than the red man, they responded, "better kill buffalo than have him feed the Sioux!"[53] Crook, his already limited aspirations of a surprise attack on the enemy a fading dream, angrily watched the wild foray, but held his counsel. Straight-backed and grim, he led his column past the bloody trail of buffalo carcasses into the valley of the Rosebud just as the setting sun brought closure to the slaughter.[54]

Aware that the Sioux must now be near, Crook bivouacked his fatigued troops on the south fork of the Rosebud and put out his pickets.[55] Though he forbade his own men to light fires, the Indians blithely ignored such caution, happily roasting their buffalo humps and ribs on blazing campfires and feasting well into the night. The general struggled to contain his ire, undoubtedly contrasting their undisciplined behavior with the spartan self-control of the Arizona Apaches.[56] His anger was hardly allayed when he asked the Crows to send out scouts to locate the Sioux and they refused. A few Shoshones and the Laramie scouts stepped into the breach and soon reported a Sioux hunting party not far from the camp. Grouard claimed that when spotted, the hunters had fled in the direction of the Rosebud, confirming Crook's belief that their village lay somewhere on that stream.[57] With thoughts of the imminent possibility of battle the next day, the weary troops wrapped themselves in their single blankets against the night chill and sank into exhausted slumber.

CHAPTER NINETEEN

The Largest Battle

June 17, 1876

The soldiers awoke before dawn, driven from their blankets by the cold. Around them, in the thick fog that had settled over the campsite, the Crows and Shoshones, sobered by the prospect of impending battle, quietly saddled their ponies and readied their equipment. As the sky lightened, they formed a scouting party and trotted out of camp in search of the enemy, swiftly passing like shadows into the mist as they crested the nearby hills.

As Crook had correctly assumed, the Sioux and Cheyennes were well aware of the soldiers' presence. During April and May, Sitting Bull's Hunkpapas, joined by the Oglalas under Crazy Horse and the Cheyenne survivors of the Reynolds attack, had drifted steadily west from the Powder, across the Tongue, into the upper reaches of the Rosebud searching for buffalo while avoiding contact with the bluecoats. Along the way, they gathered into their midst other roaming Teton bands, a sprinkling of their eastern cousins, the Yanktonais and Santees, and numbers of reservation Indians, Cheyennes, Brules, and Oglalas. By the 15th of June, 461 lodges had come together in a series of tribal circles on the south fork of Reno Creek, a tributary of the Little Big Horn, or Greasy Grass, as the Indians had named the river, about twenty-two miles northwest of the head of the Rosebud.[1] By coincidence, Little Hawk, the same Cheyenne wolf (scout) who had found Crook's camp on the Tongue, now blundered upon the bluecoats on the Rosebud. He had set out from the great village with a small band of warriors to steal horses from the white soldiers. Instead, they encountered the same buffalo herd that had thrown the Crows and Shoshones into their killing frenzy. Having slain a bull, they were casting contemplative eyes on a fat cow nearby when they suddenly spied riders on the horizon. Thinking they were Sioux, one of the Cheyennes decided to give them a scare by sneaking up on them. While his friend crept toward the Indians, Little Hawk climbed an intervening hill, cautiously peered over the crest and, with a jolt, realized that the valley below was black with soldiers. With wildly beating hearts, the young warriors scrambled onto their ponies, and after making a short run to the south to throw their enemy off the scent, sped west to warn the Reno Creek camp, probably arriving in the late afternoon or early evening of June 16.[2] The riders they had seen were Grouard and the Shoshones whom Crook had sent out from his bivouac that evening. The young warriors' initial feint toward the Rosebud undoubtedly formed the basis for Grouard's mistaken assumption that the village lay in that direction.

When Little Hawk reported the soldiers' presence to the council of chiefs, they were at first inclined not to attack unless the army attacked first. But self-confidence and an air of invincibility pervaded the camp, fed by a vision that had come to Sitting Bull during a Sun Dance ceremony a few days before that portended a great victory over the white soldiers. According to some sources, the young warriors, bolstered by this sense of indestructibility and spoiling for a fight, impetuously ignored the chiefs' cautious approach and intended to force a fight. Others, including several elderly Cheyennes who were in the village at the time, later asserted that the chiefs accurately concluded that the Gray Fox would move north against the village, and so they decided to mount a preemptive attack.[3]

Whatever the reason, the council decided to go on the offensive, and the warriors from the gathered bands hurriedly painted and adorned themselves and their mounts in preparation for engaging the blue coats. A force that Indians present later estimated to be between five and fifteen hundred warriors then set out up the south fork of Reno Creek toward Crook's encampment.[4] Among them were some of their most formidable chiefs, including the Sioux leaders, Crazy Horse and Sitting Bull, the latter still in pain from the ordeal of the sun dance, and the Cheyenne notables, Chiefs Little Wolf and American Horse.

Left behind were older chiefs and warriors charged with protecting the women and children.[5] Through the night, the war party rode toward the soldiers' encampment, twenty-two miles to the southeast, stopping only once, just before dawn, to let their ponies rest. Then they remounted, not halting until they reached the foot of a large hill beyond which lay Crook's column. As Sioux and Cheyenne outriders ascended the hill, Crow and Shoshone scouts appeared on its crest and exchanged shots with them. The battle was about to be joined.[6]

In the soldiers' camp at about 6 A.M., long after the allied scouts had disappeared into the predawn fog, the rest of the command began their advance up the Rosebud, Crook and his aides in the lead, certain that Crazy Horse's village lay not far ahead. Behind the general rode the infantry, followed by the cavalry and the civilian volunteers. The going was difficult. Following the stream, which at this point snaked through surrounding bluffs, required passage over rocky, uneven ground with many twists and turns, each with its own potential for ambush. As the sun climbed, the temperature rose with it, and the horses, already tired from the previous day's travel, began to show signs of the strain.[7]

At eight o'clock, after about five miles on the trail, the Crow scouts to their front signaled the column that they had seen Sioux warriors. Crook called a halt to await further intelligence and rest the horses. Although he ordered pickets placed on the hills to the north, he did not consider an attack imminent, supposing that the reported sightings referred only to herders from the Lakota village ahead.[8] So peaceful was the moment that many of the officers and men thought Crook intended to bivouac in this spot, make a night march against the village, and attack it at dawn.[9] Possibly he may have considered such a plan, as he ordered the troopers to unsaddle and remove the bridles from their horses so they could graze freely, though he took the precaution of having them hobbled to prevent a stampede in case of an attack. The soldiers took advantage of the halt to brew coffee and erect rude shelters to shade themselves from the sun.[10] Ominously, the Crow warriors who had remained with the column were far from nonchalant. Agitated, they stripped down for battle, sang their war songs, and kicked their ponies into short charges to build their wind for the anticipated fight.[11]

The command was now stretched midway between two bends in the Rosebud, which at that point veered west from its southerly course, bisecting a depression surrounded by bluffs on almost every side. To give their mounts room to graze, the battalions spread out east and west along both sides of the creek in the order of their arrival. The Third Cavalry, which had earlier passed the slower infantry on the trail, halted along the south bank of the stream, with Captain Anson Mills's battalion on the right and Captains Frederick Van Vliet and Guy Henry to his left. The Second Cavalry, under Noyes, dismounted opposite Mills, on the north bank, and infantry and packers tethered their mules west of Noyes along the stream. Crook and his aides established an impromptu headquarters not far from the scouts and packers, adjacent to a spring at the mouth of Kollmar Creek, a small tributary that ambled down a broad valley from the northwest to join the Rosebud. After seeing to their mounts, in keeping with the casual atmosphere that pervaded the column, they sat down to a game of whist.[12]

A half hour later, the peaceful mood was suddenly broken by Anson Mills's servant, a man known for his exceptional hearing, who ran to tell the captain that he heard shouting in the distance. Mills, seeking the source, climbed a nearby rise and spied to the northeast about two or three miles away, "great numbers of moving objects, looking somewhat like distant crows silhouetted on the clear sky. . . ."[13] At roughly the same time, Finerty and the officers around him heard shooting to their north. At first, they thought that the gunfire signaled yet another Crow buffalo hunt. But as the firing came from several directions, the combat veterans among them quickly became aware that this was not the case.[14] Scarcely had the soldiers come to this realization, when Crow and Shoshone riders came pouring over the northern ridgeline, heading pell-mell for the troops' position, yelling "Heap Sioux! Heap Sioux!"[15] Mills shouted a warning to Crook on the opposite bank. The general shouted back that Mills should mount his men and ride out to meet the enemy.[16]

After making initial contact with the advance elements of the Cheyenne/Sioux war party, Crook's greatly outnumbered Crow and Shoshone allies had quickly turned tail, whipping their ponies back over the ridge to rejoin the column. The enemy rode close on their heels. In a short time, "every Hill appeared to be covered with their swarming

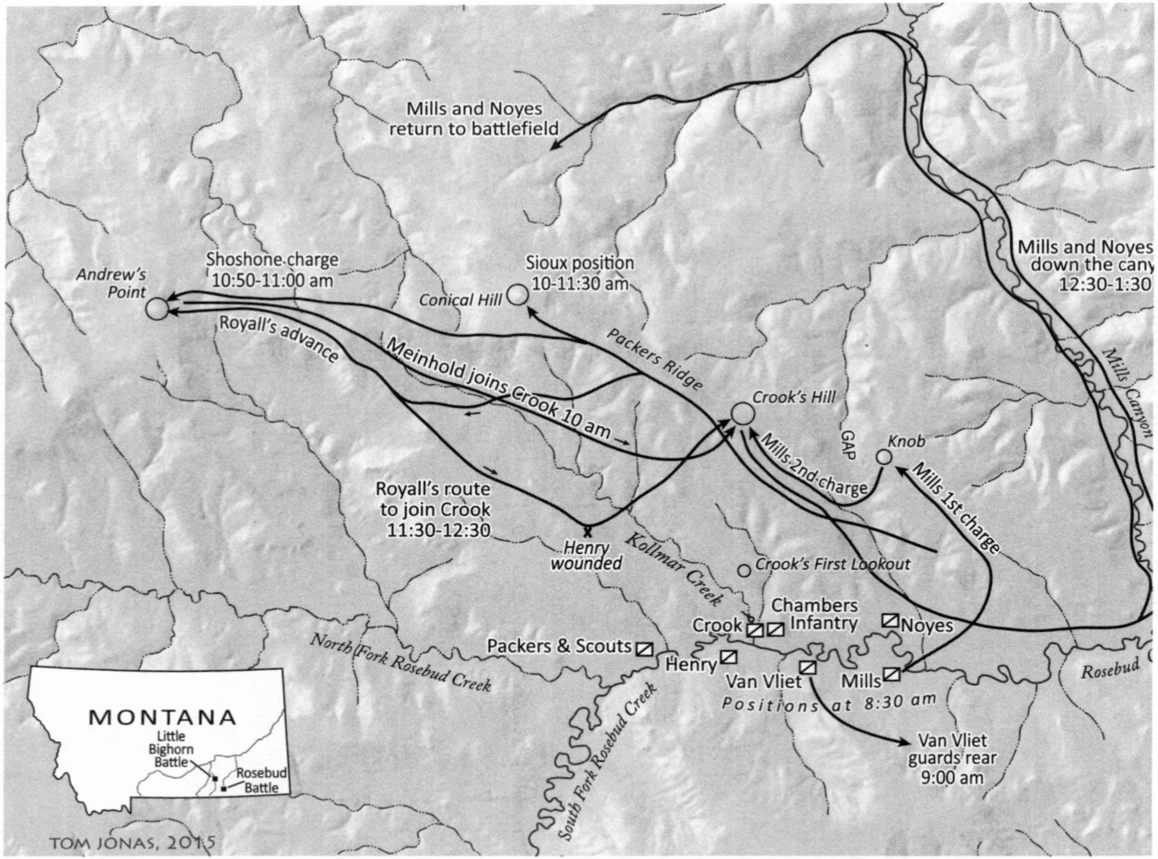
Mills and Noyes
return to battlefield
Shoshone charge
10:50-11:00 am
Andrew's
Point
Sioux position
10-11:30 am
Conical Hill
Mills and Noyes
down the cany
12:30-1:30
Mills Canyon
Royall's advance
Meinhold joins Crook 10 am
Packers Ridge
Crook's Hill
GAP
Knob
Mills 2nd charge
Mills 1st charge
Royall's route
to join Crook
11:30-12:30
Henry
wounded
Kollmar Creek
Crook's First Lookout
Chambers
Infantry
Crook
Noyes
Packers & Scouts
Henry
Van Vliet
Mills
Positions at 8:30 am
Rosebud
North Fork Rosebud Creek
South Fork Rosebud Creek
Van Vliet
guards rear
9:00 am
MONTANA
Little
Bighorn
Battle
Rosebud
Battle
TOM JONAS, 2015

Battle on the Rosebud, June 17, 1876.

legions, and up from every ravine, and out of every little vale, more seemed to be coming."[17]

Crook hastily deployed his infantry along the foot of the north slope to meet the onslaught and shield the cavalry troopers while the latter frantically struggled to control and saddle their panicked mounts. Meanwhile, the Crows and Shoshones still in camp, led by Captain George Randall, chief of scouts, raced up the hillside to reinforce their beleaguered fellow tribesmen and the few pickets who now bore the brunt of the enemy charge. Forming a defensive line stretching from east to west across the high ground, they engaged the oncoming hostiles in hand-to-hand combat, buying precious time to allow the troopers to prepare for battle. Grouard would later state that were it not for this heroic action by the Indian allies, "the Sioux would have killed half of our command before the soldiers were in a position to meet the attack."[18]

During the hiatus provided by his Indian allies, Crook, his view obstructed by a hill to his front, sought a clearer vantage point by climbing a bluff above Kollmar Creek, a move that temporarily put him out of contact with his officers. From there, he saw at a glance that his men were being attacked from the north and northwest by a huge number of Indians who held the advantage of the high ground. As he watched the battle develop to his north, a band of warriors circled around his troops to their left, positioning themselves for an assault against his western flank, threatening to engulf the command. Fortunately, Major Andrew W. Evans, the Third Cavalry commander, alert to this new danger, assumed temporary command to meet it. Deploying two companies of cavalry under Captain Van Vliet to the south to meet any attack from the rear, he ordered two additional companies under Captain Henry to move left to counter the Sioux flank attack. These deployments temporarily neutralized the threat from this quarter.[19] Without awaiting orders, Colonel Royall, Crook's overall commander of cavalry, joined Henry with two additional companies; and, in a series of charges, he and Henry drove the attackers northwest over a succession of ridges.

It soon became apparent that the Indians' withdrawal was a tactic aimed at drawing the troopers away from the rest of the command. At the crest of each ridge, they would face about and throw themselves upon the ground, "reopening their fire while their well-trained ponies grazed or stood fast . . . upon the reverse of the slope." By repeating this maneuver again and again, they succeeded in luring Royall's men westward onto a high plateau about two miles distant from the rest of the column and separated from it by the broad valley carved out by Kollmar Creek.[20]

Mindful of the intense, lopsided struggle waged by the Crows and Shoshones on the northern plateau overlooking the camp, Crook, who had by now resumed overall command, directed the infantry north up the hillside in a skirmish line to drive the Sioux from the heights. Just below the crest they were able to surprise the oncoming warriors with "withering fire at less than a hundred and fifty yards," breaking their charge and causing them to flee "as fast as 'quirt' and heel could persuade their ponies to get out of there."[21] But this retreat, too, was tactical. Crazy Horse, who commanded the Indian force, had used a similar ploy to draw Fetterman's command into an ambush years before, and he now used it against the infantry, hoping to divide the soldiers into small units in the broken terrain of the Rosebud valley. Under his direction, his warriors conducted an orderly withdrawal, moving from ridge to ridge, keeping just out of rifle range of the charging soldiers. On each crest, they would ride back and forth "slapping an indelicate portion of their persons at [the soldiers] and beckoning [the infantrymen] to come on," in an effort to lure the troops into isolated ravines where they could be cut off and destroyed piecemeal.[22] Crook eventually realized the futility of these repeated charges and halted them. The Indians, interpreting the soldiers' failure to pursue them as a sign of weakness, then countercharged their line. This abrupt change of tactics might have succeeded, but for the Shoshones who galloped their ponies furiously into the midst of the enemy and broke up the attack. They did so without the benefit of covering fire from the soldiers, who were afraid to shoot, unable to tell friend from foe in the dust and smoke of the ensuing melee. To avoid casualties from such friendly fire, Crook ordered the outnumbered Shoshones to withdraw. Again, the Sioux saw this as a sign of weakness, and renewed their attacks with vigor.[23]

To the beleaguered troops, the charging warriors presented a savage and frightening spectacle. "Many wore the long Sioux war bonnet of eagle's plumes, which floated and fluttered in the air . . . while others wore half masks of the heads of wild animals with ears and sometimes horns, still protruding, giving them the appearance of devils from the nether world, or uncouth demons from the hills of Brocken." They charged, not in a line, "but in flocks or herds like the buffalo," uttering their bone-chilling cries, while leaning forward alongside their horses' necks and firing from beneath them, making an impossibly small target.[24]

But charging against massed infantry produced unacceptable casualties and, while brave, these warriors were not suicidal. So they abandoned their costly frontal assaults and took positions at the crest of a hill to the east of a dip in the ridgeline, later called the gap. There, concealed behind boulders and folds in the rough ground, they poured flanking fire into the troops. Crook countered this new threat by ordering Mills's four cavalry troops to sweep the enemy from their position. Finerty, who accompanied the charge later, described the action in vivid, if decidedly racist, terms for his readers. "We went like a storm," he reported, "and the Indians waited for us until we were within fifty paces. We were going too rapidly to use our carbines, but several of the men fired their revolvers, with what effect I could neither then, nor afterward, determine, for all passed like a flash of lightening, or a dream. . . . Our men broke into a mad cheer as the Sioux, unable to face that impetuous line of the warriors of the superior race, broke and fled with what white men would consider undignified speed."[25] Driven from the gap, the Indians withdrew to another ridge beyond it, later known as Crook's Hill, and resumed their firing. Again, Crook ordered Mills to dislodge them, and once more he complied, pushing them off Crook's Hill and forcing them to retreat to a high point about 1,200 yards further to the northwest, later named Conical Hill.[26] Realizing the futility of continuing these charges, Crook halted Mills's at Crook's Hill and hurried to join him. It was now a little before ten o'clock.

Because of the elevation of Crook's Hill, for the first time that morning the general was able to look west across the battlefield, enabling him to see for the first time that Royall's troops had been cut off from the rest of the command. The colonel's repeated charges had carried his five cavalry troops, some 225 men, to the extreme western edge of the battlefield. There, separated from the main force by the Kollmar Creek valley and under attack from three sides, his position had become increasingly precarious.

Davenport of the *Herald* rode with Royall's cavalry during the battle. He reported that at that moment, "the troops were going forward with ardor and enthusiasm . . . [when] their officers were surprised to observe that they were receiving no support from the centre, which was yielding ground and permitting the enemy to turn their fire against [Captain Henry's] right flank."[27] This new threat to Royall's right was an unintended consequence of Crook's order to Mills to cease his advance and consolidate with the infantry on Crook's Hill. That action had removed pressure on the Sioux on Conical Hill, allowing them to refocus their attention on Henry's troopers. Because Royall had been beyond his line of sight, Crook had been unaware of the potential threat when he had given Mills the command. Royall's position grew still more tenuous when another band of warriors, which, heretofore, had been preoccupied with an attack against Tom Moore's packers, now also turned their guns on Henry's men.

Despite the threat to Royall's force, Crook was convinced that he had successfully stabilized his position and would emerge from the battle victorious. The majority of his force, comprised of regulars and their Indian and civilian auxiliaries, firmly held the northern heights, and Van Vliet protected his rear. Certainly, he had been surprised—perhaps shocked—earlier that morning by the sudden appearance of an attacking force of unprecedented size. No attack of such magnitude had ever been mounted by Indians on the western frontier. Nor had one ever been launched against such a large force of soldiers. And he was taken aback by the tactical sophistication and feats of horsemanship displayed by his opponents on the battlefield. Nevertheless, he had kept his wits about him and, up to this moment, had successfully countered attacks from every quarter, and believed that he still had the upper hand. Now, he thought, was the time to deploy part of his command against the Sioux village, his primary objective, which he was convinced lay northeast of his present position, not more than six to ten miles up the narrow valley carved out by the Rosebud as it flowed northward to the Yellowstone.[28]

Before attacking the villages, however, Crook hoped to reunite Colonel Royall's companies with the main force. To accomplish that task, he dispatched the intrepid Azor Nickerson through Sioux lines with orders that Royall abandon his exposed position and join the general on Crook's Hill. Royall must have misunderstood the command. In his report after the battle, he asserted that Crook had directed him "to extend my right and connect with the left of the main body occupying a portion of the highest crest (Crook's Hill)."[29] Apparently, rather than move his entire force eastward to join the bulk of the command on Crook's Hill, Royall thought that Crook intended that he merely lengthen his line in that direction so as to form a continuous front with the rest of the force. To accomplish this maneuver, he sent only one company of cavalry under Captain Charles Meinhold east across the Kollmar valley to connect with Captain Noyes, who held the extreme left, anchored on Crook's Hill.[30] The rest of his command, he held in place. The effect of Meinhold's departure severely attenuated Royall's lines, already weakened by the cavalry practice of assigning one in four troopers as horse holders for the troopers now fighting on foot. Under increasing pressure from the Sioux and Cheyennes, he withdrew his men to a more defensible position to the southeast, *in the opposite direction* from Crook's force. There he remained until about 11:30 A.M.

From his perch on the crest of Crook's hill, the general viewed Royall's delay in complying with his orders with mounting impatience. Earlier in the morning, his horse had been shot in the leg, throwing the general to the ground. Though Crook was unhurt, the incident unsettled him.[31] His agitation may have been further heightened by the hit-and-run tactics of the Sioux and Cheyennes, causing him to ignore the possibility that they were fighting an offensive action. Rather, the Indians' behavior encouraged him to believe that they were simply trying to buy time to allow the village to flee.[32] Given his mindset, and his erroneous perception that the village was close by, it is clear that Crook felt an urgent need to attack it before his foe scattered to the four winds.

Considering haste to be paramount, he was convinced that there was no time to dispatch scouts to ascertain the exact whereabouts of the village or to delay the attack until Royall had safely joined him on Crook's Hill. Instead, he sent a second message to the colonel ordering him to move promptly to reunite with the command. Then—it was about 12:30—he summoned Mills to his side. As Mills later recollected, the general ordered him to join with Noyes's command, a total of eight troops of cavalry, and "proceed down the canyon and take the village, which he said he had been reliably informed was about six miles down the canyon." He was to "hold it until [Crook] came to [Mills's] support with the rest of the command."[33] Crook believed that once the Indians became aware of Mills's intentions, they would abandon the field and rush to defend the encampment to defend the village, allowing

Royall's force to safely rejoin the rest of the command. Then, as the tribesmen gathered to protect their village, the massed weaponry of disciplined troops would overwhelm the Indians' individualistic fighting style and lead to a signal victory.

But Mills's deployment produced an entirely different result. Because the village was in reality a considerable distance from the battlefield in the opposite direction, the Indians saw the captain's departure as a retreat. As one of Crook's officers later put it, "Nothing inspired a Plains Indians [*sic*] so much as seeing the backs of their foes." Energized by Mills's apparent show of weakness, the Cheyennes and Sioux now turned the full fury of their martial ardor on Royall's command, which at that moment was preparing to fight its way to the general's position on Crook's Hill.[34]

When Royall received Crook's second message, his troopers were fighting on foot, with every fourth soldier a horseholder. Consequently, their fighting strength was reduced and their progress slowed as they withdrew over open ground through a gauntlet of mounted Indians.[35] It was at this time that the command suffered most of its casualties. Six soldiers were cut off and killed when trapped crossing a hollow. One of the troopers, a raw recruit, attempted to surrender to a warrior by handing him his carbine. The warrior disdainfully threw it to the ground and bashed in the young private's skull with a tomahawk. Other soldiers died at the hands of mounted Sioux who rode so close to their victims that the powder from their revolvers "blackened the flesh."[36]

It was during this fighting that Captain Guy Henry suffered a grievous wound, a bullet striking under his left eye, passing through his mouth and emerging below his other eye. Vomiting blood, he fell from his horse and would have been killed on the spot hand had he not been rescued by Shoshone and Crow warriors whom Crook had sent in response to a desperate plea from Royall for support. To further aid the beleaguered colonel, Crook also directed the infantry to provide covering fire with their long-range rifles.[37]

The deployment of Mills's and Noyes's troops into the canyon had stripped half the strength from the center of Crook's line at a time when the Cheyennes and Sioux were redoubling their efforts against both Royall and the center. To fill the gap left by Mills's and Noyes's departure, Crook summoned Van Vliet from his rearguard position on the southern heights. En route to Crook's Hill, Van Vliet's troops were able to drive off a Sioux attack aimed at the Shoshone pony herd tethered at the column's original halting point on Rosebud Creek. Though they saved the herd, one Shoshone, a young herder, was killed, perhaps the only allied Indian slain that day.

On Crook's Hill, firing became so intense that the sound of bullets striking the hard ground on all sides reminded Strahorn, standing beside the general on the crest, of rain spattering on pavement. The hail of gunfire prompted Captain Burt of the infantry to ask Crook how he felt under fire. Crook coolly responded, "How do *you* feel?" To which Burt answered, "Why, Just as though, if you were not in sight, I'd be running like Hell." "Well," Crook replied, "I feel exactly that way myself."[38]

While the fighting swirled about Crook, Mills's command made its way down the valley of the Rosebud to a point where the riverbed bent north toward the Yellowstone and the valley began to narrow. Here, Noyes, who had followed Mills off the battlefield, caught up with him; their combined force then turned northward following the creek, which here was little more than a rivulet. Forming into two files, one on either side of the stream, they rode down the valley, which increasingly narrowed as they passed into it, until it became a canyon, its rocky, timbered slopes rising higher and more precipitously against the sky.[39] Grouard was convinced that the Indians were just waiting until the troops got deeper into it before bushwhacking them. The sight of barricades made of fallen timber and cut brush along the rocky slopes only confirmed his suspicions.[40]

By Mills's reckoning, he had ridden six miles down the valley—almost to where Crook had predicted the village would be located—when the sound of firing to the west attracted Grouard's notice. As he called out to draw Mills's attention to it, galloping hoofbeats approaching from their rear caused them to turn in their saddles to see a horseman dashing up the length of the column. "Dressed in buckskin and wearing a long beard, originally black, but turned temporarily gray by the dust," was Azor Nickerson, riding once more into harm's way to deliver an urgent message from Crook. Fighting for breath, he delivered a litany of bad news to the incredulous Mills. "Royall is hard pressed and must be relieved. Henry is badly wounded, and Vroom's troop is all cut up. The general orders that you and Noyes defile by your left flank out of this canyon and fall on the rear of the Indians who are pressing Royall."[41]

Mills, sure that he was within a mile or so of the village and that he could take it easily, later claimed he was stunned by the sudden reversal of orders. But, having no alternative, he turned his column and exited the valley by means of an opening in the bluffs that fortunately appeared to his left. This path brought him to the rear of the Sioux who were pressing Royall from the north; and he immediately directed a charge against the attackers, who just as promptly retreated like the wind to the northwest. Their fleet ponies easily outdistanced the troopers' jaded mounts, giving them time to scoop up their wounded, and all but thirteen of their dead. It was about 2:30 in the afternoon. The battle, which had begun at 8:30 that morning, had come to an end.[42]

As the Sioux and Cheyennes fled the field, Mills joined Crook at his hilltop headquarters. Burning to know the reason for his recall on the brink of what he had thought was certain success, he angrily asked the general, "Why did you recall me? I had the village and could have held it." "Well, Colonel," he quoted Crook as replying, "I found it a more serious engagement than I thought. We have lost about fifty killed and wounded, and the doctors refused to remain with the wounded unless I left the infantry and one of the squadrons with them. I knew I could not keep my promise to support you with the remainder of the force."[43]

Though willing to admit he had too few troops to hold the field in Mills's absence, Crook seemingly used the surgeon's demand for troops to protect the wounded as an opportunity to excuse what he surely knew had been an error in judgment. By sending Mills and Noyes against the village, he had placed his command in jeopardy—divided and facing a foe more numerous, aggressive, and tactically skillful than he had anticipated. Fortunately, unlike Custer a week later, he was able to rectify his mistake, recalling them at the last minute. He tacitly acknowledged as much in his original telegraphic report of the battle, stating, "I tried to throw a strong force through the canyon but I was obliged to use it elsewhere before it had gotten to the supposed location of the village."[44]

The troops were exhausted. They had fought a six-hour engagement under the burning sun, with little rest over the preceding two days and no food since their hasty breakfast at dawn. But Crook, reckoning that destruction of the Sioux encampment was still within his grasp, demanded one last effort. Forming his troops into a column screened by his Indian allies, he led them into the valley, bent on attacking the village before the Indians could scatter. As they rode forward, Frank Grouard, who remained convinced that the canyon was a trap, prevailed upon Crook to turn back. "They will kill your whole command if you go through there," he warned, pointing out that the command no longer had sufficient ammunition to oppose an enemy force of any size. Nickerson emphatically supported Grouard. Though Crook had great respect for the judgment of both men, he remained skeptical. But finally, according to Grouard, after polling his officers and confirming that supplies of ammunition were indeed low, he reversed course and returned to the battlefield.[45]

His decision was probably heavily influenced by the behavior of his Indian auxiliaries. As they rode toward the bend in the Rosebud, the Crows, in particular, displayed growing anxiety. They finally halted at the point where the valley narrowed, and refused to advance farther, telling Crook that to enter the canyon "would be certain death." Fellow tribesmen had once made the mistake of following the Sioux into this very defile, which they termed "the Valley of Death," and had been massacred for their trouble. They had no intention of repeating that mistake.[46] After the column turned back, Strahorn asked Crook why he had suddenly altered his plans. The general soberly replied, "Well, with what I have been noting of signs of an ambuscade clearly in sight, all these dead and wounded on our hands, and half the ammunition gone, I won't take the men down into that hole." Three days later, in his after-action report, he gave what was probably a frank appraisal of the elements that led to his decision: the Crows' refusal to enter the canyon, lack of rations, and the condition of the wounded.[47]

Crook and others in the column remained convinced for the remainder of their days that by turning back, they had escaped a massacre.[48] But it is not at all certain that that was the case. Crazy Horse, as he said in a *Chicago Times* interview in 1877, may have intended at the outset of the battle to lure Crook into a tight place where he could not maneuver and then crush him. But this plan, if it did exist, was ruined at the outset when the Crow and Shoshone scouts spotted the Sioux before they ever got a chance to get into position for such an ambush.[49] Moreover, most of the Sioux and Cheyenne participants interviewed in later years said that by two in the afternoon, their warriors were in no shape to mount such an ambush.[50] They had suffered what for them were substantial losses, including over 150 horses, leaving many of their fighters afoot; and, like the soldiers, they were probably short on ammunition.[51] Physically, they were played out. They had ridden through the night to reach the battlefield and then fought a six-hour engagement under the hot sun with neither food nor rest. As John Stands-in-Timber, a Cheyenne historian and descendant of participants in the battle, succinctly summed it up, "They were tired and hungry, so they went home."[52] So, according to Indian informants, by the time Crook's column rode into the valley in mid-afternoon, the hostiles had withdrawn out of range and simply "watched [the soldiers] a long time from the hills. . . ." After observing the blue coats turn back from the ravine, the warriors wheeled their ponies northwest, and rode back toward their camp on Reno Creek, leaving behind only a few scouts to watch the troops.[53]

The Sioux observers shadowed the command as it made its way back to the place on the banks of the Rosebud where the battle had begun, made camp, and went about the grim task of caring for the wounded and collecting the dead. The bodies of nine soldiers were recovered, and an estimated twenty to forty others had been wounded. Of these, the injuries of twenty-one were deemed serious enough to list the troopers' names in Crook's preliminary report on the battle.[54] Regardless of the exact number of casualties on either side, they were amazingly light considering the vast expenditure of ammunition, the length and ferocity of the engagement, and the number of combatants involved. Finerty estimated that 25,000 rounds were fired by the soldiers alone, remarking that "it often takes an immense amount of lead to send even one Indian to the happy hunting grounds."[55] Obviously, the combat marksmanship of the troops was nothing to brag about.

As evening shadows lengthened over the battlefield, dispirited soldiers lit fires for their evening meal, and soon the aroma of wood smoke, frying bacon, and coffee mingled with the sweet odor of wild plums and the lingering stench of black powder and blood. Sleep did not come easily to the troops, as the night was filled with the moans of the wounded and the unearthly wailing of the Shoshones and Crows, mourning their dead.[56] There was much to occupy Crook's mind as he lay in his blankets on the stony ground. The day had not gone well. At sundown, he had counciled with his scouts, trying to persuade them to join a night advance against the Sioux village, followed by a dawn attack. But the Crows refused. They and the Shoshones had enough of fighting and scalp collecting for the time being.[57] Without his Indian allies, his rations and ammunition depleted, and with over twenty wounded to care for, Crook felt that he had no option but to retire to Goose Creek to rest and resupply his men.

His men awakened well before dawn, downed an unappetizing breakfast of hard tack, undercooked bacon, and coffee, and stiffly mounted their horses. The night before, the dead had been interred in a dry creek bed beneath large stones. Now, to further obscure the graves, the column drove their horses and mules over the site to conceal its location from vengeful Indians and hungry varmints, a task that must have distressed many.

Out of concern for the wounded, Crook selected a route of return that covered the most even terrain possible. Six troopers were assigned to attend each of the injured soldiers, who were transported on travois, litters constructed from poles with blankets or robes slung between them and dragged behind a mule or horse. Though seemingly crude, they actually provided greater comfort than sitting astride a horse or lying in a wagon bed.[58] But despite all efforts, the wounded endured excruciating pain during the jolting ride back to Goose Creek. Captain Henry seems to have had the worst of it. With severe facial injuries, he bumped along on his litter in agony, wondering if perhaps "death would have been preferable," an alternative that was almost realized when, crossing a particularly rugged mountain, his mule "shied and pitched the captain headlong down among the rocks some twenty feet below." By some miracle, he survived, despite receiving a savage kick in the face delivered not long afterward by the thoroughly unrepentant animal and then, within sight of the end of his ordeal, almost drowning in the Platte.[59]

As the column progressed, the Crows became increasingly agitated. Nearing the fork of the Little Big Horn, the boundary of their own country, they announced to Crook that it was time for them to go home. They had wounded to return to their families and rituals to perform, and feared an attack on their village by vengeful Sioux.[60] But it was also known that they were disgruntled by what they perceived as a lack of support from the soldiers during the battle, particularly during its initial phase. They departed with a promise to return in fifteen days, a commitment Crook doubted they would fulfill. The Shoshones rode off not long after.[61]

On the 19th, the command, sans allies, rode into the Cloud Peak encampment, where Crook intended to remain until the arrival of reinforcements that he now requested. After a hot meal and a bath in the creek, the men settled down for their first night under canvas in what seemed a lifetime. Two days later, the wagons left under strong escort for Fetterman to bring back fresh supplies. They carried the wounded, as well as *Inter-Ocean* reporter MacMillan, whose health had deteriorated during the campaign, and the exhausted Azor Nickerson. His constant exertions during the battle had opened old wounds and dislocated several ribs. As he departed, Crook had asked him to use his recuperation period to recruit Pawnee tribesmen to replace his Crow scouts. Stanton also joined the wagons in obedience to Crook's order that nonessential personnel leave the camp as "subsistence could not be furnished to them."[62]

While the troops licked their wounds on Goose Creek, the Sioux and Cheyennes moved their village west into the valley of the Little Big Horn. Their scouts soon reported that Crook had camped at Goose Creek and no longer presented a threat. The northerners believed they had achieved their objective. They had won a great victory that they hoped would discourage further attacks by the blue coats. Now they prepared to shift their growing encampment again, seeking better forage for their ponies and fresh hunting grounds. On June 23, responding to news of great antelope herds to the west, the village, its population now swollen by hundreds of additional warriors from the agencies, made a short eight- or nine-mile trek down the valley of the Little Big Horn. On the west bank of the river, across from a ravine called Medicine Tail Coulee, they erected their tipis in an immense campsite that extended almost two miles along the river, turning their vast pony herd loose to graze on the high ground of the valley floor. They were aware of the movements of Terry and Gibbon along the Yellowstone, and so knew that soldiers were in their hunting grounds. But as the greatest gathering of peoples ever recorded on the Great Plains, they anticipated no further problems from the white soldiers.[63]

CHAPTER TWENTY

The Rosebud Revisited

Even today, Crook's handling of the battle generates controversy. It has become almost a cliché to say that while the engagement may have been a tactical victory, it was a strategic defeat. Tactically, Crook can be said to have fought the Indians to a draw, incurring minimal casualties, no small achievement considering the damage inflicted on Custer's command only a week later. But strategically, the outcome was subject to an entirely different interpretation. In hindsight, it was the Sioux who achieved strategic success, neutralizing Crook as an effective element in Sheridan's three-pronged plan of attack. Little Phil may have recognized this when he bluntly opined to Sherman that "the victory was barren of results."[1]

Crook tried to put the best face on the outcome by persistently claiming that his forces had triumphed on the field and, even in his later years, ignoring the longer-term consequences. In his June 20th official report of the action, he defiantly asserted, "The command finally drove the Indians back in great confusion following them several miles."[2] Four months later, he repeated his contention in an interview at the Red Cloud Agency. "Not withstanding this disparity of forces, the troops under my command, about 1,000 in actual strength, at the battle of the Rosebud, thrashed these Indians on a field of their own choosing and completely routed them from it."[3] But as an experienced Indian fighter he would hardly have overlooked the bigger picture. As Sheridan had pointed out, driving hostiles from a battlefield represented a hollow victory. Capture of territory in Indian warfare was meaningless. Success depended upon destroying the enemy or so soundly defeating him that he would be deprived of the will and ability to wage war. At the Rosebud, the foe emerged with his strength intact, his morale high, and, most importantly, having denied Custer 1,300 additional troopers who could have turned the tide at the Little Big Horn.

As Crook's force languished at Goose Creek in the days following the battle, another consequence of the engagement became apparent. The rift among the officers of Crook's command, opened in the aftermath of the Powder River fight, deepened as they began to take opposing positions regarding the general's management of the battle. Bourke, of course, vigorously defended Three Star's honor. "This engagement gives us the morale over the boastful Dacotahs," he declared, while lavishly praising the conduct of both soldiers and their Indian allies. Years later, in his memoir, *On the Border with Crook*, his respect for Crook undiminished, he elaborated. "We had pursued the enemy for seven miles and had held the field of battle, without the slightest resistance on the side of the Sioux and Cheyenne."[4] Nickerson expressed a similar view. In an article published in the *New York Times* immediately after the battle, he loyally asserted, "We won the fight and camped on the field."[5] And following the Little Big Horn, President Grant pointed out Crook had saved his men from a massacre, noting that, "when he finds himself outnumbered and taken at a disadvantage, he prudently retreats."[6]

But naysayers like Captain Mills were unimpressed. The captain took "little pride in our achievement." In his opinion, "we had been humiliatingly defeated."[7] His view, as might be expected, resonated with Colonel Royall and the troops who had fought alongside him on the western edge of Crook's battle line. These men had received the roughest treatment on the field, suffered the greatest number of casualties, and borne the worst of the fighting. Already resentful over Crook's court-martial of Reynolds and having himself been criticized for allowing his force to be isolated from the rest of the command, Royall would soon figure among the most prominent of Crook's critics. Ultimately, in an interview published in the Omaha papers in 1886, he publicly blamed Crook for the failure at the Rosebud. The general was furious and, in a rare display of public temper at a dinner at his home, he confronted the colonel, his anger goading him to unfairly include Nickerson in his rebuttal:

> For ten years, I have suffered silently the obloquy of having made a bad fight at the Rosebud, when the fault was in yourself and Nickerson. . . . I sent word for you to come in, and waited two hours, nearer three, before you obeyed. . . . I had the choice of assuming the responsibility myself for the failure of my plans, or of court-martialing you and Nickerson. I chose to bear the responsibility myself. The failure of my plan was due to your conduct.[8]

Controversy over Crook's leadership was not confined to his command. As we shall see, his superiors, both Sheridan and Sherman, were highly critical of his performance, though, as they were military men, their conversations were held in private. But public commentary, particularly after Custer's defeat, quickly spread by wire across the country. Debates raged in the editorial pages of papers from California to New York about whether the engagement was a victory, a draw, or a defeat, and subsequently, about the degree of Crook's responsibility for the Little Big Horn debacle. Among Crook's defenders were almost all of the journalists who had been on the battlefield—Strahorn, Finerty, Wasson, and MacMillan. Strahorn was predictably partisan. "The whole adventure [the Rosebud fight] was so clearly a crowning triumph and lasting testimonial to the ability of Crook as an Indian fighter that I can only wonder at any divergence of opinion." MacMillan, Finerty, and Wasson also expressed positive views of Crook's management of the engagement, though in less effusive language.[9]

Of the reporters on the field, only Reuben Davenport, writing for Gordon Bennett's antiadministration, pro-Custer *New York Herald*, attacked the general's handling of the battle. Davenport's first dispatch was fairly moderate. Agreeing with Crook, he asserted that "[the Sioux] have been severely crippled" by the engagement, a conclusion he quickly revised after learning of Custer's defeat. Having ridden with Royall during the battle, he adopted the colonel's criticism of Crook's attempts to reunite Royall's troops with the rest of the command in the face of the enemy's ferocious attacks, and his deployment of Mills and Noyes into the valley at the height of the battle. That decision, the reporter correctly concluded, had exposed Royall to the full force of the Sioux. However, in the same article, damning by implication Crook's use of Indian scouts, Davenport mistakenly berated the Crows and Shoshones. Characterizing them as cowardly and unreliable, he attributed the Lakotas' ability to surprise Crook's command to Crow indiscipline.[10] In the weeks following the Little Big Horn, the *Herald*, under Bennett's guidance, grew more strident. On July 6, the paper printed an editorial accompanying Davenport's description of the battle. It depicted Crook's conduct as "such an example of ineptitude as to warrant his immediate removal to a subordinate capacity."[11]

The *Herald* was not alone in attacking Crook's generalship. Some papers, particularly in the South, openly mocked his claim of "victory." On June 30, the *Augusta (Georgia) Chronicle* crowed that "George Crook had had a severe struggle with the Sioux and does not seem to have come off first best. It is true that the Indians retired in one direction, after four hours' fight, but the Government troops retired quite as rapidly, and much further, in the opposite direction." Another Georgia paper gleefully reported "that George Crook was very snugly thrashed in his recent engagement with the Indians." But after hearing of Custer's defeat a week later, the *New York Times* countered that the Rosebud "is, in light of the recent events, considered to be a victory."[12]

While Crook's claims of victory may deservedly be regarded with raised eyebrows, his tactics on the field that day deserve more mixed reviews. Preserving the integrity of his command that day against a well-armed and skillful foe on extremely difficult terrain was no small feat. He successfully countered Sioux efforts to split and defeat his force in detail, limiting his casualties and demonstrating both tactical skill and coolness under fire.[13] His gravest tactical error seems to have been his decision to divide his command by sending Mills and Noyes to attack the village, a decision that left Royall's force exposed to the full force of a Sioux assault. In his defense, it must be kept in mind that he believed that the village was nearby and vulnerable, and that its destruction was crucial. Further, he was unaware of Royall's predicament until after he had sent Mills and Noyes on their way. Finally, he must be credited with acting quickly once he realized the threat, recalling Mills and Noyes to the field and saving Royall's force from destruction.

Crook was also criticized for having been caught unawares by the Sioux attack. This assessment, too, appears to have merit. When he dismounted his men on the Rosebud and settled down to a game of whist on the morning of June 17, he did so despite evidence from his Indian scouts that Sioux were in the vicinity and signs that the scouts anticipated of an impending fight. His negligence can only be attributed to his overconfidence in his ability to divine his opponents' intentions and in his own troop strength, bolstered by his low opinion of Sioux tactical nd fighting skills. In some respects, his confidence was merited. His force was one of the largest ever fielded against Indians in the West, and he, himself, was a seasoned veteran with over twenty years of combat experience marked by repeated successes on the battlefield. He failed, however, to consider that these victories had been won in fights against small bands rarely numbering more than one hundred warriors almost always preoccupied with defense and evasion rather than offensive action. Having had little experience with the more aggressive Sioux, Crook, like Custer, relied on tactics intended on preventing the escape and dispersal of the enemy, ignoring the possibility that he faced a foe bent on the offensive and equipped with the necessary skill and daring to attain their objective.

CHAPTER TWENTY-ONE

Paralysis at Cloud Peak

June 20–August 5, 1876

Crook's decision to remain at Goose Creek pending the arrival of reinforcements produced an interlude that had a distinct air of unreality. Described by one participant as resembling a picnic far more than an expedition against hostile Indians, it was to extend from June 20 to August 6. During that time, Crook submerged his wounded pride and his anxieties about the future of the campaign in an orgy of hunting and fishing. Bourke later wrote that his notebooks for the period "seem to be almost the chronicle of a sporting club, so filled are they with the numbers of trout brought by different fishermen into camp."[1] For those not inclined to fish, a variety of game birds and elk, deer, bear, mountain sheep, and of course buffalo awaited slaughter by any officer or enlisted man with a taste for blood sport and the courage to go into the surrounding hills. The less bloody-minded panned for gold or simply explored the countryside, heretofore virtually unknown to the white man.

With an army of more than a thousand men and the hostile village within a few days' ride, historians, and indeed, many of his contemporaries, were justifiably mystified that this notably aggressive commander spent seven weeks, during the prime season for campaigning on the northern plains, hunting and fishing rather than pursuing the enemy. Crook's own explanation, offered to Captain Burt, who provided occasional pieces for the *Cincinnati Commercial*, was far from satisfying. Convinced that only a force outnumbering his own could have defeated him at the Rosebud, he told Burt, "I could fight and satisfy this clamor, but what would be the results? A lot of my good people killed and a few dead Indians. But I am not out here to make a reputation or satisfy a foolish personal pride. I am here to do my duty to others, and to knock the bottom out of these Sioux when I do hit them." It was a rationale that, as the *Herald*'s Davenport observed, was unhappily reminiscent of the stratagems of General McClellan, whose fantastic overestimation of Confederate strength had paralyzed his will to fight during the Civil War.[2]

Crook was plagued by similar illusions. Initially, he reckoned that he was outmanned two to one. Shortly, he would revise the estimate upward, telling Sheridan, "The best information I can get from my front is that the Sioux have *three* fighting men to my one" (emphasis added). In reality, historians have determined that the Sioux and Cheyenne strength at the Rosebud probably amounted to less than a thousand warriors. In fairness, many officers at the time, including his superiors all the way up to General Sherman, and even the general public, shared Crook's opinion.[3] Only an overwhelming Indian presence, it was thought, could explain Crook's inability to trounce them. Even Sheridan ascribed to this belief, responding to his general's anxious wires with repeated offers of reinforcements and warnings that he should not march against the Indians until he felt "strong enough."[4]

Even if the inflated numbers had been accurate, as a commander during the Civil War, Crook was no stranger to being outmanned on the battlefield. Further, it was a common assumption in the Indian-fighting army that any white command could defeat an Indian force of greater size due to superior discipline, tactical ability, and weaponry. So some factor other than sheer numerical superiority must have been at play. And that may well have been Crook's stunning realization that he had misjudged the fighting capabilities of the Sioux. Indeed, Davenport perceptively pointed out, "[Crook] seems to have formed his estimate of the Sioux from his experience of the Apaches and the surprise which he suffered on June 17 was the first awakening from this delusion." The journalist cited several instances occurring on the trail from Fetterman to the Rosebud that indicated Crook's overconfidence prior to the battle. "The march has been unguarded; the camps have not been compact enough . . . ; the scouting has been without system; and the troops, . . . raw recruits, have scarcely been drilled." Despite these shortcomings, the young journalist generously concluded, now that the general had some experience fighting the Sioux, his performance might improve.[5]

Another factor contributing to Crook's evident paralysis at Goose Creek was his total lack of information about the whereabouts of the enemy. With the departure of the Crows and Shoshones, Crook's intelligence-gathering capabilities had dried up almost completely. He was operating blindfolded. He had no idea where Terry's column was or where the Sioux were in relation to it. Aware of the critical need for such information when fighting a highly mobile guerrilla force, in his western campaigns he had relied heavily on his Indian scouts, while during the Civil War he had recruited locals for the same purpose. A good intelligence-gathering operation had greatly enhanced his self-confidence and consequent aggressiveness. In the absence of his Indian allies, he no longer had his accustomed eyes and ears. As Richard, who knew the Sioux well, had been dispatched to Red Cloud to recruit additional mixed-blood scouts, only two scouts remained in camp, Big Bat and Grouard. Both were highly competent, but two men, acting alone, could not possibly cover the enormous territory to their front despite herculean efforts to do so.

Speculation regarding the psychological state of the long dead is an exercise fraught with uncertainty, particularly with respect to a figure as fanatically devoted to concealing his inner self as George Crook. Yet it would be safe to hazard that, caught unawares by an enemy he had seriously underestimated and, for the first time in his career denied a victory against an Indian foe, the engagement at the Rosebud had dealt a violent blow to the general's considerable ego.

The erosion of his self-confidence could only have been exacerbated by the criticism that ensued in the months after the battle. A particularly cruel example appeared in the *Helena (Montana) Daily Independent* on June 30, a paper that probably found its way to Cloud Peak. The article quoted officers at Fort Laramie who spoke "in terms of unmeasured condemnation of General Crook's behavior, and denounce[d] his retreat in the face of the savage enemy as cowardly." The writer repeated a camp rumor that the Crows "refused to stay with Crook any longer, and have gone off in a body to Gibbon." Crow scouts, the article claimed, called Three Stars the "Squaw Chief," "and say he's afraid to fight." Twisting the knife, the story concluded "the idea of two regiments of American cavalry being stampeded by savages and having to rally behind friendly Indians is regarded as incredibly revolting to the pride and honor of the Army."[6]

Attacks of this nature would have been devastating. Unable to respond, he brooded alone, isolated physically and psychologically from any source of support, encircled in his mind and probably in fact by an elusive foe bent on his destruction. Characteristically, he responded by withdrawing into himself and burying his self-doubt in the familiar rhythms of field and stream. The pain of reliving this time may account for his later decision to abruptly conclude his memoir at the moment the battle ended. Forgoing the opportunity to present his own version of that event and later controversies and leaving his readers to draw their own conclusions, he terminated the work with an unrevealing and awkward sentence: "The next morning, we took up our line of march, but were not molested on our march [to Goose Creek]."[7]

Thus we find Crook on the banks of Goos Creek, his self-confidence shaken by his failure at the Rosebud and completely in the dark as to the current numbers and location of his foe. For several days after their the column's return to Goose Creek, very little information penetrated the camp's picket lines, and there was no word of the whereabouts of Terry and Custer. Communication with the outside world was temporarily restored on June 23 when Lieutenant Walter Schuyler of the Fifth Cavalry rode into camp accompanied by couriers from Fort Fetterman. Crook warmly greeted the young lieutenant, having grown fond of him during their days together in Arizona, and promptly made him an aide de camp.

From Schuyler, the column heard its first news from the outside world since the battle. In addition to regaling the camp with tales of a close brush with the Sioux, the lieutenant brought troubling reports that 1,800 warriors had left Red Cloud Agency to join Sitting Bull.[8] He also carried a dispatch from Sheridan written before the lieutenant general had received word of the Rosebud engagement. In it, he informed Crook that Lieutenant Colonel Eugene Carr, commanding elements of the Fifth Cavalry, had been transferred to Fort Laramie, where he could be called upon to reinforce the campaign should Crook need him. Colonel Wesley Merritt was en route to the frontier to replace Carr as commander of the contingent. In the meantime, Sheridan had ordered Carr to act as a blocking force on the Powder River Trail to prevent any more Indians from leaving the reservation. "This will stir things up and prove advantageous in the settlement of the Indian question," he breezily assured Crook.[9] Crook was familiar with both Merritt and Carr, having served with the former in the Shenandoah during the war, and with the latter in Arizona. Pleased by the availability of reinforcements, he was further heartened to learn that his old friend and Civil War subordinate, Rutherford Hayes, had won the Republican nomination in the 1876 presidential election. But any warmth this information might have generated was offset by the chill of accompanying newspaper articles, several of which already contained pointed criticisms of his conduct on the Rosebud.[10]

Over the next several weeks, a mood of boredom and uncertainty settled over the camp as the command awaited reinforcements and news of Terry's column. Daily, Crook moved the campsite closer to the Big Horn Mountains to ensure good grazing, plentiful firewood, and the continued availability of trout. But magnificent fishing and stunning scenery did little to relieve the oppressive monotony of camp life. As one day merged into the next and camp movements became routine, Crook spent much of his time roaming through the country, relying as he always had on the healing powers of the wilderness. During the three-week period from June 21 until July 10, when Crook finally received word of the Little Big Horn fight, the general was to spend at least ten days fishing or hunting, a likely response to the grim reality of his situation.[11]

CHAPTER TWENTY-TWO

The Last Stand

June 25, 1876

While Crook's troops waited in uncertainty at Camp Cloud Peak, Terry camped on the Yellowstone. He had been searching in vain for Sitting Bull's village, which he now suspected lay somewhere on the Rosebud or the adjacent Little Big Horn, one valley to the west. Though Terry and Crook were never more than several days' ride apart, communication between them was almost, if not entirely, impossible. The country between the Rosebud and the Yellowstone was alive with hostile Indians.[1] Crook's only means of alerting Terry of his engagement at the Rosebud or his plan to remain on Goose Creek until reinforced had been through his official report to Sheridan, which he had sent by wire on June 19, assuming that Sheridan would forward it on. Unfortunately, there was a delay in Terry's receiving the report, as the telegraph line to Fort Ellis, the post nearest his position on the Yellowstone, was down, requiring the dispatch to be carried by courier instead. As a result, when, on June 22, Terry had ordered Custer and the Seventh Cavalry south along the Rosebud in search of Sitting Bull's village, he did so in ignorance of Crook's June 17 engagement. Consequently, neither he nor Custer had any warning of the size and aggressiveness of the force arrayed against them or that they could expect no assistance from the Wyoming column in the event they found what they were looking for.

Custer's force consisted of 31 officers and approximately 566 enlisted men.[2] His orders were to locate the Sioux and hold them in place or, alternatively, drive them into the waiting arms of Terry's column, which would be positioned on the Little Big Horn to block their escape. After Custer departed, Terry marched west to join Colonel Gibbon's column at Fort Pease on the Yellowstone. Then, his combined column turned southwest toward the valley of the Little Big Horn, where Terry had told Custer he would be on the 26th.[3]

During the afternoon of June 25, as Terry's force crossed the divide into the valley of the Little Big Horn, his scouts reported heavy smoke ahead. Still too far away to discern its origin, Terry marched into the night, until rain and difficult terrain made it impossible to proceed further. In the predawn hours the following morning, Terry's chief of scouts, Lieutenant James Bradley, and several Crow warriors set out in advance of the column in the direction of the Little Big Horn. As they rode, they came upon three Crows they soon identified as scouts who had been with Custer. These men, White-Man-Runs-Him, Hairy Moccasins, and Goes Ahead, tears running down their cheeks, related shocking news of the Boy General's destruction at the hands of the Sioux. Except for a detachment surrounded on a nearby hill, the Crows believed that the entire command had been wiped out. Bradley hurried back to the column with the news, which Terry's officers greeted with derision, unable to accept that Custer's force would have met such a fate. Terry, himself, "took no part in these criticisms, but sat on his horse silent and thoughtful, biting his lower lip. . . ." Bradley guessed that he was thinking that if the Crows' stories were true, and the Indians had defeated Custer with his six hundred men, what would they do to Terry's smaller force of four hundred? But compelled to investigate, Terry directed his men forward into the valley. As they rode, the smoke they had seen over the past two days became denser and, by afternoon, Indians began to appear at their front, first in small groups and then in greater and greater numbers. Shots were exchanged, but the Indians did not attack. As dusk approached, Terry deemed it prudent to go into camp. After an uneasy night, the soldiers woke at dawn to find the valley empty of Indians. Resuming their march, they soon reached the abandoned Sioux village, a mass of debris—old firearms, cooking pots, blankets, and ominously, wounded cavalry horses, pieces of military equipment, and, hanging from an upright pole, three human heads burnt beyond recognition. Several tipis remained standing among the litter. They were found to house dead warriors in full regalia.[4]

While the troops attempted to comprehend the meaning of the tableau before them, Bradley returned from the other side of the river with news that he had seen white objects on a hillside above the river. At first, he thought they were the skinned carcasses of slaughtered buffalo or perhaps white rocks. Upon closer investigation, the troops were horrified to discover that they were the naked, mutilated bodies of 197 dead soldiers, one-third of Custer's command. As the troopers moved toward the spot, they saw upon a distant hilltop figures they assumed were Indians or ponies, but which, it developed, were the men of Major Marcus Reno's and Captain Thomas Benteen's battalions, all that remained of Custer's force. They now realized that the Sioux and Cheyennes had struck a decisive blow at the very heart of military pride.[5]

On Goose Creek, Sunday, June 25 dawned quietly. Crook was in the mountains hunting, while Captain Mills and his staff fished the creeks around the camp, landing, it was said, a hundred trout that day.[6] Two days later, a rumor would float through the camp that Custer had a big fight with Sitting Bull and that "many were killed on both sides."[7] And on the day of the battle, several officers and journalists would later report sighting smoke from the direction of the Little Big Horn, creating, in hindsight, an awareness, or at least a premonition, among the soldiers that something of moment had occurred. But there is no reliable documentation that anyone tried to follow up on these mysterious sightings.[8]

On July 1, Crook set out to explore the little-known Big Horn Mountains and do some hunting. But neither the magnificent scenery nor the search for gold, which occupied some of the company, diverted the general's anxiety about Terry's whereabouts. He stopped frequently to scan the surrounding country with his binoculars in the hope of sighting the general's column, but saw neither blue coats nor Indians, leaving him "greatly distressed," according to one of his companions.[9] But his angst seems not to have affected the hunting. When he returned to camp on July 4 to celebrate the nation's centennial with his troops, he had the remains of two mountain sheep and a huge buffalo, killed by Finerty, tied on his mules.

Any temporary elevation of his mood that might have resulted from the hunt faded quickly when, on arriving in camp, he was presented with a fresh communiqué from Sheridan, dated June 28. Writing before he had received word of Custer's defeat, Sheridan urged Crook to take the fight to the enemy and hit him hard, a not so subtle reminder to get a move on. Crook, his nerves raw from uncertainty and isolation, privately grumbled that "I wish Sheridan would come here himself and show us how to do it. It is rather difficult to surround three Indians with one soldier."[10] The next day, he repaired to a nearby stream where he sought to relieve his tension in an orgy of angling, landing seventy trout in an afternoon. Before casting his line, he had instructed Grouard and Big Bat to mount a scouting mission. Two nights previously, several parties of Indians had been reported about twenty miles from camp, and Crook wanted the two men to reconnoiter in the direction in which the Indians had been seen in an attempt to ascertain their location and strength. They were to take along an escort of twenty-five troopers under the command of Lieutenant Fredrick Sibley.[11]

As the area in question was believed to be teeming with Sioux, the patrol would be risky, and so would subject Crook's motives in ordering it to later scrutiny. The general, himself, allowed that he simply desired a reconnaissance of the area, and Bourke and Finerty, who had apparently witnessed the general's conversation with Grouard, agreed that was his intention. Grouard and Pourier would later claim that Crook sent them out to find and escort a contingent of Crow scouts into the camp. Either rationale would have justified the effort, but Captain Noyes, perhaps harboring some bitterness from his court-martial, had his own take. Interviewed many years later, he averred that "the real object of the scout was to furnish 'copy' for the newspaper correspondents with whom General Crook always was well provided."[12]

Whatever Crook's objective, the detachment left Goose Creek about noon on the 6th, a daylight departure at variance with Crook's usual practice of leaving after dark and, as it turned out, a mistake.[13] They immediately suspected that Sioux spies were observing their movements, and at nightfall, found evidence confirming their suspicions. By noon the next day, arriving at the headwaters of the Little Big Horn, they were positive that they were being hunted by a very large war party.[14] Taking shelter in some timber, they exchanged fire with their pursuers; and, when darkness fell, abandoned their horses and escaped on foot into the steep, heavily wooded mountains. With no food and carrying only their carbines and ammunition, over the next two days they endured an exhausting fifty-mile trek through trackless wilderness. On July 10, weak from hunger and fatigue, they stumbled upon soldiers from the camp hunting in the vicinity and were rescued. Though Finerty complained bitterly about losing his tack, horse, pipe, and blankets, and worst of all, his toothbrush, he had gotten off relatively lightly. Two of Sibley's soldiers were apparently driven mad by fear, hunger, and exhaustion. One, it was said, never recovered.[15]

The harrowing escape of the Sibley scout raised concerns among Crook's officers about the general's security, as he was away hunting in the same area at the time Sibley's men returned to camp. Colonel Royall, in command in Crook's absence, hurriedly dispatched a cavalry patrol to fetch him. The next morning, while the patrol continued its search for the general, Louis Richard and Ben Arnold arrived in camp with dispatches from Sheridan bringing the command its first word of the fight at the Little Big Horn.[16]

The calamitous news, wrote Bourke, "made every lip quiver and every cheek blanch with terror and dismay. Grief—Revenge, Sorrow and Fear stalked among us." The night before, Indians had raided the infantry camp, and the surrounding prairies had been set afire to deprive the troops of forage. These events, coupled with the news of the Custer battle, heightened concern about the general's safety to a fever pitch, causing Bourke to record a rare criticism of Crook in his diary. "The general has set an example of recklessness that cannot too strongly be condemned. . . . Else some day, his mutilated corpse will be found and this whole scheme of Sioux pacification fall to the ground."[17]

To the relief of all, the errant hunter returned to camp at dusk. Told first of the Sibley scout, he accepted the tale "with his customary placidity," though the large number of Indians awakened a premonition that "disaster [had] befallen a portion of Terry's command, and he fear[ed] the impetuous Custer [was] the victim." Then he read Sheridan's dispatch. Watching the general's face as he absorbed the news, Captain Mills thought he detected, "particularly in General Crook's expression, a feeling that the country would realize that there were others who had underrated the valor and numbers of the Sioux."[18]

The entire country had been stunned by the news of Custer's defeat, and the military establishment was no exception. At the time most officers learned of it, not a word from Crook had been received since his June 19 report on the Rosebud fight; and many suspected that he had met a similar fate. Sheridan, aware of his friend's reticent nature, had dismissed these worries out of hand, assuring Sherman that "Crook never sends a courier unless he has something important to say or wants something." Nevertheless, he took steps to reinforce both Crook's and Terry's commands, ordering Merritt's eight troops of the Fifth Cavalry, previously sent to Fort Laramie to refit, to proceed immediately to join Crook at Goose Creek. At the same time, he directed elements of the Fifth Infantry to join Terry on the Yellowstone.[19] With these additional troops, together with other previously designated reinforcements, the lieutenant general was confident that Terry and Crook could handle the situation.[20] Reiterating his earlier advice to "give [the Sioux] a good hard blow," Sheridan urged Crook to move quickly to join Terry's column. Now, he advised, was the time to do so, as the Indians had to be considerably weakened by their losses at the Rosebud and Little Big Horn.[21]

With the experience of the Sibley scout fresh in his mind, Crook took little comfort from Sheridan's armchair analysis. But he was heartened by word of reinforcements, and more particularly, by accompanying news of the pending arrival of a supply train from Fetterman, due at Goose Creek within the next couple of days with an escort of seven infantry companies. He was further encouraged to hear that a force of Washakie's Shoshones was due in camp shortly, to be followed by a contingent of Utes. On July 12, the Shoshones rode in, 213 in number, including Washakie's two sons, all in full battle dress. Their arrival was regarded as fortuitous as the Sioux had become increasingly bold, stepping up their efforts to steal horses and harass the camp.[22]

Despite his promise to Sheridan that he would go on the offensive as soon as he had been resupplied, and though reinforced by the Shoshones and the soon-to-arrive infantry, Crook was still not prepared to leave the safety of Goose Creek. To Sheridan, in a dispatch dated July 12, he explained that even with reinforcements, he continued to believe his force outnumbered by a factor of three to one. He could whip the enemy, he wrote, but, to quote his commander, "it would be a victory . . . barren of results." To enable him to "end the campaign with one crushing blow," he wanted the extra strength and mobility that would be afforded by Merritt's cavalry. Until they arrived, he would remain in place. "My advises," he added, referring to Sibley's report, "indicate that the Indians are camped along the Little Big Horn near the base of the Big Horn Mountains, and will probably remain there until my reinforcements come up."[23]

Without waiting for Sheridan's reply, Crook telegraphed Merritt, urging him to report to Goose Creek "with the least possible delay." But as the general well knew, even under the best of circumstances, Merritt's column would not arrive for some time. They carried forage for the horses, as well as 250 rounds of ammunition for each man, and so would have to use wagons, guaranteed to slow them down. The distance to be traveled was over two hundred miles, and since Crook wanted Merritt's horses to "reach here in the best possible condition," the trip would necessarily consume the better part of two weeks. In fact, Crook wrote to Terry (after communications by courier had been opened) that he did not anticipate Merritt's arrival until "about the last of the present month [July]."[24] As he also knew that Indians were inclined to move fast and frequently in the face of their enemy, it stretches credibility to assume, as he had assured Sheridan, that he really believed they would remain in place until Merritt's reinforcements arrived.

On the 13th, as he discussed tactics with Chief Washakie in front of his tent, Crook saw three men, dressed in faded and travel-stained army blue, trotting their jaded horses toward him. Couriers from Terry's camp, they had risked their lives to carry firsthand information to Crook about the Little Big Horn fight.[25] Reading Terry's dispatch, Crook must have taken particular interest in the latter's estimate that the Sioux and Cheyennes had fielded not less than twenty-five hundred warriors at the Little Big Horn, and Terry's report that upon leaving the big village, the Indians had divided into two bands, one headed into the mountains to the southwest and the other to the south and east. The dispatch noted that Terry had evacuated the wounded from the battle by riverboat to Fort Lincoln and now awaited the steamer's return, with supplies and reinforcements, which were expected on or about the 18th. Then, he planned to join Crook, since "the great and, to me, wholly unexpected strength which the Indians have developed . . . make it important and indeed necessary that we should unite or at least act in close cooperation." Without illusions regarding his qualifications as an Indian fighter, he added that he expected Crook to devise a plan for the pursuit of the Sioux, which he, Terry, would follow. With characteristic humility, he added, "I shall assume nothing by reason of my seniority, but shall be prepared to co-operate with you in a most cordial and hearty manner, leaving you entirely free to pursue your own course."[26]

The tone and substance of the dispatch reflected Terry's background and personality. Born to a wealthy and privileged Connecticut family, an attorney by training, he was a man of unfailing politeness and a kindly and sensitive nature. His troops found him attentive to their needs, and his tender care of the wounded at the Little Big Horn had won him the affection of all. Most of his experience with the Sioux had come through lawyerly negotiations with their chiefs, first over the Fort Laramie Treaty and, more recently, during the Black Hills council. In these discussions, he evidenced a sympathetic understanding of the Indian position. But, like Crook, he now believed that only defeat in battle would induce them to abandon their warrior culture and accept reservation life. Though Terry had made his lack of qualifications clear, Sheridan had insisted that Terry, who outranked Crook, should now command the joint force. Despite their common ideas about operations against the Sioux, how Crook would react to campaigning in a position subordinate to this lawyerly, genteel, but inexperienced officer, remained to be seen. However, in his response to Terry's dispatch, Crook gave every appearance of courteously acceding to Sheridan's wishes, writing that "should the two commands come together, . . . if you think the interests of the service will be advanced by combination, I will most cheerfully serve under you."[27]

Not long after Terry's couriers arrived, the wagon train from Fetterman rolled in, bringing supplies, news, and Crook's old friend Major Alexander Chambers, commanding the promised seven infantry companies. To Crook's annoyance, the column was accompanied by a whisky peddler and two soiled doves dressed as mule skinners, as well as a paymaster with $50,000 in back pay for the troops. Newly flush with cash, the presence of the doves (or "abandoned females" as Finerty delicately referred to them) and whisky aroused great interest in the ranks. Though not in the habit of imposing his temperance views on others, Crook speedily quelled this threat to good order and discipline by seizing the whisky and placing the ladies under confinement.[28]

The establishment of communications with Terry and the arrival of the infantry contingents and Shoshones apparently did little to calm Crook's nerves. Like the plagues that bedeviled Pharaoh, a succession of events ratcheted up the tension at Cloud Peak. The weather was oppressive. The air turned sultry and black storm clouds formed "a leaden mantle pall[ing] the sky," unleashing rain, thunder, and lightning upon the troops. Accompanying the deluge, biblical swarms of grasshoppers swept through the camp, darkening the sky and filling the air with their whirring racket.[29] Couriers from Fetterman arrived at intervals, bringing a flood of unwanted advice from Sheridan and press clippings dissecting Crook's performance on the Rosebud. To add to Crook's woes, Nickerson sent a wire dimming hopes of aid from the Utes. It appeared that the agent on their reservation had intervened to prevent them from joining the campaign.[30] Though Nickerson strove to correct the situation, it remained another nagging worry for the beleaguered general. Overshadowing all else was the ever-present menace of the Sioux, lurking in the hills about the camp—in great numbers, he supposed—harassing his pickets, threatening his livestock, and setting fire to the surrounding prairie. Billowing clouds of black smoke and ash filled the humid air, choking the troops and signaling the destruction of forage badly needed by the mules and horses.[31]

And, just when it seemed that nothing further could go wrong, on July 16, Sheridan telegraphed to inform Crook that "your wife met with a railroad accident coming back from Hot Springs, but is doing well." Crook was forced to await the arrival of local papers describing the incident to learn the details. Mary, accompanied by her brother, C. J. Dailey, had been en route by train from Wyoming to Oakland, Maryland, her family's home, when the sleeping car in which they had been riding jumped the track at a siding and turned over. She had suffered a broken arm and other painful injuries. These wounds were a mere annoyance compared to her anxiety about the fate of her husband, from whom she had heard nothing since the news of the Rosebud battle reached her in late June. Hopefully, though there is no record of it, the general took the time to send her a reassuring letter.[32]

On the heels of the news of Mary's accident came word that Merritt's arrival would be even later than anticipated. En route to Fort Laramie to refit before joining Crook, the colonel had received word that "eight hundred Cheyenne and a number of Sioux" were rumored to have fled the Red Cloud Agency to join Sitting Bull's people. Accordingly, he had deviated from his route to intercept the fleeing Indians.[33] On July 17, Merritt's force laid an ambush for the Cheyennes on the rolling prairie near Warbonnet Creek, a stream on the southern edge of the Black Hills about twenty-five miles northwest of the Agency. In the brief engagement that ensued, Merritt's scout, the redoubtable showman Buffalo Bill Cody, shot and scalped a warrior named Yellow Hair, and, according to legend, held the trophy aloft, crying, "the first scalp for Custer!"[34] Cody's victim was the only casualty of the skirmish. The rest of the Indians wheeled their ponies and, eager to get their women and children to safety, fled back toward the reservation, breaking into ever smaller groups and abandoning their possessions in their efforts to avoid capture. The soldiers chased them back to the proximity of the Agency, thus ending the attempted breakout.

Sheridan applauded Merritt's action. Notwithstanding the fact that it delayed the latter's arrival at Goose Creek, the lieutenant general considered the time well spent. To him, it was a blow struck to avenge Custer and a valuable lesson to any agency Indians contemplating a breakout. Additionally, it probably provided the army with the excuse needed to transfer control of the Red Cloud Agency from the Indian Bureau to the military. The Agency was placed under the supervision of the troops at Camp Robinson just five days after the skirmish.[35]

After he had learned of the delay, tension and even a touch of despair began to creep into Crook's dispatches. On July 16, he wrote, "I am getting anxious about Merritt's ability to reach me soon as the grass is getting very dry and the Indians are liable to burn it any day." The following week, he complained, "I find myself immeasurably embarrassed by the delay of Merritt's column. . . . The whole country is on fire and filled with smoke. I am in constant dread of an attack; . . . They set fire to the grass, but as much of it was still green, we extinguished it without difficulty; but should it be fired now, I don't see how we could stay in the country." And, in a rare moment of indecision, he plaintively confessed, "I am at a loss what to do; I can prevent their attack by assuming the aggressive, but as my effective strength is less than twelve hundred exclusive of Indian allies, I could do but little beyond scattering [the Sioux]."[36]

It was during this period that Crook received confirmation from four Crow scouts, who had ridden in from Terry's camp on the Yellowstone, of signs that the main body of Sioux was drifting toward the Big Horn Mountains, reinforcing intelligence he had gotten from his own scouts. The Crows believed that if confronted by too large a force, the Sioux and Cheyennes would retreat either to the Agencies or into Canada beyond the reach of the army.[37] Fear of such a dispersal was an ever-present concern to Crook and other Indian-fighting officers, and was the basis of Custer's decision to hastily attack the village on the Little Big Horn. Crook visualized the Indians camped high in the Big Horns, and from their mountain redoubt, spying "the approach of Terry's column for a distance of at least (50) fifty miles . . . ; this will prevent a union of our columns, without their becoming aware of it." Seeing the danger, he predicted, they would scatter to the winds. To avoid such an eventuality, he advised Sheridan, he would *not* join Terry in a cooperative operation. Instead, he proposed a pincer movement in which he and Terry would advance toward each other, trapping the hostiles between them. Such a strategy would require Crook to fight the Indians without Terry's troops, and risk being outnumbered. That made him all the more firmly committed to wait for Merritt's Fifth Cavalry; thus his "embarrassment" at the colonel's delay.[38]

Crook's angst about the campaign seemed to have increased his sensitivity to the press reports he had been reading, anger and hurt fostering paranoia. He wrote to Sheridan that Davenport, the *New York Herald* reporter, was guilty of writing "villainous falsehoods" about the Rosebud fight. He suspected a conspiracy. "There was a correct account furnished from here to the *NY Tribune*, but it never reached its destination and it is supposed here that it was suppressed in the Telegraph Office at Fetterman," an allegation vigorously denied by both the reporter and telegrapher.[39] But even as he railed against Davenport in his dispatches, he avoided demonstrating any anger toward him at Goose Creek, leaving retribution to his loyal aides, whose barbed comments left the correspondent "prowling about camp like a whipped cur."[40]

The same day he wrote to Sheridan of his change of plans, Crook drafted a dispatch to Terry about his new strategy, his tone continuing to reflect his uneasiness. "I am in constant dread of being attacked and burnt out, as the grass here is like tinder, and I may have to take the aggressive with my present force, which is under 1200 troops, in self-defense."[41] Two days later, Sheridan again wrote Crook. As yet unaware of Crook's altered plan, Sheridan explained that Merritt would arrive on August 1 and suggested that, "When he reaches you, if you do not feel strong enough to attack and defeat the Indians, it is best for you to form a junction with General Terry at once. I have sent to you and Terry every available man that can be spared in the Division, and if it has not made the column strong enough, Terry and you should unite your forces."[42] Though Sheridan's message was generally positive, Crook could not help but discern an undertone of impatience with his inaction.

To newsman Finerty, the pressure appeared to undermine Crook's usual decisiveness. "He seemed to swing like a pendulum between the desire to fight at any cost and an innate feeling that to risk a battle with an outnumbering band of savages, so recently and signally victorious, would be very rash and might, as in the case of the gallant Custer, result in disaster."[43] As July drew to a close, the pendulum swung toward an offensive, with or without Merritt, but his initial movements were so tentative as to betray his indecision. Instead of a decisive thrust forward, he ordered a series of cautious patrols followed by minuscule advances in the direction of the Little Big Horn. On the 25th, his Shoshones confronted a small band of Sioux on a scout. The two parties exchanged insults before the Shoshones fled back to camp. The encounter occasioned a transitory ripple of excitement, but brought the command no closer to the main body of tribesmen. So Crook continued to cautiously feel his way west toward the Big Horns.

On July 30, Richard and a party of Shoshones, riding north to check on reports that the Sioux had pursued a buffalo herd into the Big Horn Basin, found traces of a large deserted village strewn with various Custer artifacts, indicating the village had been occupied after the battle, but how long after, no one appeared to know. Numerous dog bones indicated that hunger now stalked these Indians, the great buffalo herds having apparently gone elsewhere.[44] While Richard rode north, Tom Cosgrove, accompanied by his Shoshones and Grouard, scouted northwest along the base of the mountains. Here, too, were signs of a large encampment. And again, evidence of the Custer fight was scattered among the detritus of camp life, remnants of Seventh Cavalry uniforms and equipment. The scouts believed that this village was probably the base from which the warriors who attacked Sibley's men had come. Trails leading eastward now indicated that the Sioux and the Cheyennes had, as the Crows predicted, divided into smaller bands before departing for the Powder River country, following the buffalo to their traditional late summer hunting grounds.[45] John Gray, whose careful historiography and cool logic produced one of the better analyses of the Sioux War, figured that these camps were abandoned considerably before their discovery. That would mean that the main camp had already dispersed while Crook sat at Goose Creek, leaving behind only small war parties to harass the camp and fire the surrounding grassland. Now, at the beginning of August, confronted by that embarrassing possibility and spurred to action by Sheridan's prodding, the general prepared to engage in what would become a grueling and ultimately fruitless "stern chase" after an enemy far more mobile and familiar with the country than he could ever hope to be.[46]

CHAPTER TWENTY-THREE

Merritt Joins the Campaign

August 3–10, 1876

After the Warbonnet skirmish, Merritt had refitted at Fort Laramie. Provisioning his column and reshoeing his tired horses delayed his departure for Goose Creek until July 23.[1] Even then, though Sheridan assured Sherman that "Merritt has made no delay since receipt of Crook's order to join him," the colonel appeared to be in no great hurry. Writing to his wife, Carr grumbled, "we are marching very slowly. Gen. Merritt . . . worries his animals by slow marching and contracted camps." As a consequence, the command would take well over a week to arrive at Camp Cloud Peak.[2]

En route, a number of reporters joined Merritt, bent on firsthand coverage of the expedition "to avenge Custer." These journalists would eventually end up with Terry's column in the ensuing weeks. Two were veteran correspondents, Cuthbert Mills of the *New York Times*, described by Bourke as "a very quiet but at the same time genial young man with an old head," and Barbour Lathrop, "garrulous and opinionated, but very good-hearted, decidedly bright," a veteran reporter for the *San Francisco Bulletin*. Bourke dismissed the rest as having journalistic pretensions, but not the real thing.[3]

At Goose Creek on the afternoon of August 2, Crook sought momentary distraction from his woes by attending an awkward demonstration of the new game of baseball put on by his soldiers. The game abruptly halted when a beefy man with a pockmarked face and long hair galloped into camp, calling for the general. Quickly recognized as a long-time associate of Buffalo Bill named Jonathan White, popularly known as Buffalo Chips, he brought welcome news. Merritt's regiment was only two days away.[4] Rather than wait for the colonel's arrival, Crook ordered his command to mount up immediately to meet him on the trail.

Merritt, a tall, lanky man with a round, boyish, and almost hairless face and piercing gray eyes, had brought with him eight hundred mounted soldiers, or ten troops of cavalry, together with seventy-six recruits to fill out the ranks of Crook's own cavalry regiments.[5] Lieutenant Charles King, riding with Merritt, described the senior officer who came out to meet his reinforcements, a man dressed in "a worn hunting jacket, slouch felt hat, and soldier's boots, with ragged beard braided and tied with tape." This unmilitary apparition greeted Colonel Carr, whom he seemed to know from prior service, "with twinkling eyes and half-shy, embarrassed manner."[6] At the moment, Carr was not in the best of spirits, disgruntled that Sheridan had appointed Merritt rather than himself as head of the Fifth Cavalry contingent. A veteran Indian fighter, he had commanded the Fifth, in the absence of its aging colonel, William Emory, who had been absent on assignment during most of his tour. When Emory finally retired, Carr had assumed he would replace him. Hence his disappointment when Sheridan decided otherwise. Nor was he particularly well disposed toward Crook, for that, indeed, was the identity of the senior officer who came forward to greet him. Carrie had served a difficult tour on the general's staff in Arizona. But all that baggage seemed forgotten for the moment, and the colonel cordially reciprocated his former commander's greeting.[7] Crook then turned to King, clasping his hand so firmly that the officer winced, and gave him a greeting for which, in the lieutenant's words, "I'd make that march twice over."[8]

Mills, the *Times* reporter, saw through Crook's bonhomie. He had observed the general seated "on a small hill, silently watching the long column of reinforcements filing by. When an officer inquired of him whether he was not glad to see this little army, he responded, "Oh, if they had come before!—if they had come before!,"[9] obviously struggling with his displeasure at Merritt's delay. Unlike Sheridan, he ascribed little importance to the Warbonnet skirmish, the cause of the Fifth's tardiness. Bourke probably spoke for Crook's thoughts when he wrote in his diary, "I have never been able to see the wisdom of

[Warbonnet]. The Indians were turned back, it is true, with the loss of one warrior killed, but they never staid [*sic*] at the Agency; every one of them was in our front within three weeks."[10]

But Crook had no time to waste brooding. He was impatient to get moving. Within hours of joining Merritt, he had outlined the organization of the column for the forthcoming campaign. Designating Merritt chief of cavalry, he placed Carr in charge of the Fifth Regiment and Royall at the head of the Second and Third. Chambers, Crook's steady infantry commander and veteran of the Rosebud fight, would lead a combined detachment drawn from three infantry regiments. Paymaster Stanton, who arrived with Merritt, was given command of the few civilian irregulars and volunteers accompanying the expedition.[11]

The general had given considerable thought to his chances for success in the short and long term. To his staff, he expressed an optimistic assessment that the Indians were probably camped in force only two days' march to the north. But to Sheridan he confessed that he believed "all hostile Indians left the foot of the Big Horn Mountains and moved back in the direction of the Rosebud Mountains. . . . I am fearful they will scatter as there is not sufficient grass in that country to support them in such large numbers." But he was still hopeful, writing that "if we meet the Indians in strong force, I will swing around and unite with General Terry."[12]

To move fast, his column would have to travel light. So, as he had before the Powder River and Rosebud fights, he left his wagons in camp, this time on the north fork of the Tongue, where they would form his supply base, and relied on his pack train to carry ammunition and rations.[13] Unfortunately, the number of mules available for his original command was insufficient to accommodate the needs of Merritt's reinforcements, whose presence almost doubled the size of the column. As the pack train could not carry enough supplies and forage for the increased force, the livestock would have to rely on available grazing.[14]

To avoid overburdening the mules and their own mounts, the men were limited to the barest essentials—four days' rations and one hundred rounds of ammunition, with an additional fifteen days' rations and one hundred fifty rounds per man transported by the pack train. Officers and men were allowed no extra clothing, not even so much as a change of underwear. Aside from the clothes on their back, they were authorized an overcoat, a blanket and, if they had one, an India rubber poncho or shelter half. As to camp equipment, Crook set the example. His mess of eleven shared one sheet-iron mess pan, one frying pan, one carving knife and fork, one coffeepot, one tin platter, and one large and two small tin ladles or spoons. Personal eating utensils, other than a tin cup tied to the pommel of each man's saddle, were banned. A bemused Cuthbert Mills found "just a little tinge of ostentation in the extreme primitiveness of [the staff's] style of living," observing that "it would have been as easy to carry half a dozen tin plates, forks and spoons, as to carry one solitary specimen of each of them and pass it around the mess." Davenport, always eager to find fault with Crook, agreed, but took it a step further. He alleged that Crook secretly accepted extra bedding and food from the packers while "ostentatiously . . . setting an example of self-denial," a canard refuted by Mills and later by Crook himself in a rare burst of loquacity.[15] While reporters found good copy in Crook's frugality, veterans among the enlisted men received his orders with dread, recalling privations on past spartan campaigns.

The night of August 4, on the eve of the expedition's departure, served as a portent of things to come. Heavy winds swept the camp, blowing down many of the shelter halves, while the Sioux set fires in the mountains to the west, filling the air with gusts of choking smoke and burning embers. Scores of wild animals, fleeing the flames, thundered around the tents, filling the darkness with their fearful cries.[16] But the misery of the night disappeared when the new day dawned, a fine, cloudless, mountain summer morning.

On Crook's orders, the infantry departed camp an hour before the cavalry, sparing the foot soldiers the ordeal of marching through choking dust raised by the horsemen.[17] Looking back over the long line of his cavalry from his vantage point at the head of the column, the general must have experienced some uneasiness at the obviously weakened condition of his mounts. After two months without grain or corn, and, in the case of Merritt's horses, a month of hard use without respite, they were a scrawny, tired-looking lot. But there was solace in the size and quality of his force. He had on hand over 2,000 men, no longer raw recruits, but battle-hardened, well-trained, and toughened veterans with two months' field duty under their belts. To these, he could add his Indian allies, Chief Washakie's Shoshones and a contingent of Crows, as well as the possible addition of the Utes if Nickerson's mission succeeded. All that remained was to locate the Sioux.

For three days, his men moved north along the Tongue, fording its winding loops no less than seventeen times. These frequent plunges into icy water were no problem for the cavalry, but torture for the infantry, who found themselves frequently wading through breast high water and then continuing their march in sopping clothing and wet boots. Aware of their discomfort, Crook ordered a battalion of cavalry to ride alongside them, carrying their packs and rifles at river crossings and offering a lift to any who wished it.[18]

Leaving the Tongue, with Crook far in the lead, the column turned west, crossed the divide into the valley of the Rosebud, and camped on the site of a huge village that had once stretched more than ten miles up the river. Dampening Crook's earlier expectations of catching up to the Sioux, his scouts estimated that the site was probably two weeks old. But such a determination, based on the moisture content of pony manure, was uncertain, as the 105 degree heat during the day dried the manure quickly, making an accurate reading of its age difficult.[19]

The cool waters of the streams they forded now provided relief to men and horses as they marched north down the Rosebud, passing the battlefield on which many of them had fought only weeks before, then crossing the divide into the valley of the Little Big Horn. Along the trail, they saw signs that a large body of Indians had come that way four to six days before. The freshness of the trail once again raised hopes of a quick decisive battle. But it was not to be. The Indians disappeared from their front, and smoke and fog obscured the soldiers' vision, slowing their progress through rough, burnt-out country.[20] Then, abruptly, on August 9, the weather changed. A cold, dreary drizzle replaced the heat, and that night the temperature plunge, a harbinger of fall weather. The column now passed through a Sioux burial site, "a great number of Indian corpses slung in branches of trees," which the Shoshones stopped to rob, knowing them to be the bodies of warriors who had died at the Rosebud and Little Big Horn.[21]

The next morning, the troops found thin sheets of ice along the edges of the stream and on the water in their cups.[22] After a noon halt to feed and rest the horses, the column sighted a huge dust cloud on the horizon to their front. Even the rawest recruit could see that it marked the approach of a large body of men and animals. Many in the command immediately tensed. Was this the final hoped-for confrontation with the Sioux? Cody, with apparent reckless abandon, detached himself from the column and galloped down the trail to investigate.

CHAPTER TWENTY-FOUR

Uniting with Terry

August 11–23, 1876

At the end of July, General Terry had concentrated his forces at the confluence of the Yellowstone and the Rosebud to await the arrival of riverboats carrying the supplies and reinforcements that he needed for the campaign. While the delay provided his troops a much-needed respite, it gave many, still suffering from the shock of Custer's defeat, too much time to think. Memories of the fierce battle and of the ordeal of burying the dead continued to prey upon them, deepening their depression and fear. An epidemic of scurvy, brought on by the lack of fresh or dried fruits and vegetables in their diet, caused further demoralization.[1]

On August 1, six companies of the Twenty-Second Infantry arrived by steamer. The following day, they were joined by six more companies, men from the Fifth Infantry under Colonel Nelson Miles, a close friend of General Terry. The two officers had served together during the war, and Terry was groomsman at Miles's wedding to Mary Sherman, General Sherman's niece, in 1867.[2] The Infantry brought the total of Terry's forces, which included a contingent of Crow and Arikara scouts, to 1,620 men, enough manpower, he thought, to take on any force that the hostiles might array against him.

On August 8, the column finally moved out, covering only nine and a half miles before sunset, their progress encumbered by a 240-wagon supply train and artillery. The next day, even with a predawn start, the column inched forward only another eleven miles in twelve hours, its snail-like pace raising serious doubts whether Terry would ever catch the hostiles. In a pessimistic letter to his family, the general expressed the hope that the failure of his campaign would not be noticed amid the excitement of the presidential campaign then being waged.[3]

On the afternoon of the 10th, his column moving at its usual glacial speed, Terry was aroused by the appearance of his Crow scouts racing down the valley toward him, raising clouds of dust in the shimmering heat haze. As they neared, he heard their piercing cries and watched warily as they slowed to run their ponies in circles, signaling the approach of an enemy in force. At the sight, the Indians who had remained with the column hastily flung aside their clothing and began donning their war paint, while Terry, with grim determination, formed his cavalry into a skirmish line and deployed the artillery across the valley floor.[4]

Suddenly, out of the haze appeared, not the Sioux nation, but a lone horseman galloping toward him. Terry now saw that he wore a white sombrero, his long hair and buckskin fringes streaming in the wind. Some moments later, he found himself politely, though with some chagrin, greeting the flamboyant Cody. Buffalo Bill was unperturbed. Like many of Crook's veterans, he had been fully aware when he gallantly spurred his horse ahead of the column, that he would find Terry's horse soldiers beneath the choking dust cloud. He quickly apprised Terry of Crook's presence. Then, wheeling his horse about, he escorted the scholarly general forward to meet his fellow commander, seated patiently in the shade of a cottonwood grove awaiting his approach. At that moment, it was painfully obvious to both officers that Crook's plan to trap the Indians between the jaws of their two forces had failed.[5]

At least on the surface, Terry's troops, including remnants of Custer's Seventh under Major Reno, looked impressive. They were clad in fresh uniforms, astride fat horses, and supported by wagons brimming with provisions and equipment. Their parade ground appearance stunned Crook's unshaven, filthy, ragged men, mounted on bone-thin, worn-out nags. But the two columns quickly overcame their initial surprise, mustered a brief cheer to mark their meeting, and broke into small groups to renew old friendships.

A new crop of journalists accompanied Terry's column, having arrived by Yellowstone riverboat to join him after the Custer fight.

They seemed as fiercely partisan in behalf of their general as Crook's correspondents (with the exception of Davenport) were toward him. Among them rode James O'Kelley of the *New York Herald*, an Irish soldier of fortune and a tough veteran of the French Foreign Legion who had fought his way through North Africa, Mexico, and France before becoming a war correspondent for the *Herald*. Covering the aftermath of the Little Big Horn, he had become a vigorous proponent of those who blamed Reno and Benteen for Custer's defeat. Like Davenport, he enthusiastically shared his paper's bias against Crook, losing no opportunity to attack him. Throughout the campaign, O'Kelley would characterize Crook's behavior as "to say the least, peculiar," suggesting, "perhaps Terry's volunteer background and Crook's West Point background" set them at odds with one another. To illustrate his contention that Crook treated Terry with hostility, he noted that Crook failed to leave his camp to meet his senior officer on his arrival, implying that this was an intentional snub.[6]

Others described Crook's welcome of Terry as courteous. It included an invitation "given with a full heart" to share in his meager lunch of hardtack and bacon. And his officers, recognizing the importance of the occasion, made "every exertion to receive our guests with the best in our possession: messengers were dispatched down to the pack-trains to borrow every knife, fork, spoon, and dish available."[7]

The two men were a study in contrasts—General Terry, resplendent in a clean blouse; the distinctly seedy-looking Crook, clad in his usual worn and stained hunting gear. And, though O'Kelly may have erred in perceiving rudeness in Crook's welcome, it would be a mistake to ignore the tension that underlay the relationship between the two men. Both were surprised and not a little disappointed that they had met each other instead of the Sioux. And even the briefest of consultations between them must have made it readily apparent that they had different agendas in pursuing the campaign. Each saw it through the prism of his own responsibilities. General Terry, commander of the Department of Dakota, feared the Indians would turn north and escape, ultimately crossing into Canada and safety, reinforcing Sitting Bill and threatening peace in Dakota Territory. Crook, commander of the Platte, was more concerned that they would break south and return to the Black Hills or to the Red Cloud Agency, where, under the protection of the reservation authorities, they could resume raiding the settlements in

Wyoming and Nebraska. Differing campaign priorities aside, the two officers were, in many ways, the antithesis of each other. As Bourke put it, while Terry "would be the more pleasing companion," Crook was "reticent to the extreme of sadness, brusque to the verge of severity." The lieutenant professed to see "indecision, vacillation and weakness" in Terry's face, compared to the "stolidity, rugged resolution and bull dog tenacity" of Crook's visage.[8] It is not difficult to imagine such contrasting personalities at loggerheads, especially where ego was involved. And there can be little doubt that Crook resented having to serve under a neophyte like Terry, or for that matter, anybody else.

But initially, the most important issue was whether Terry's column would be able to move fast enough to catch the Indians before they scattered. With a train of 240 heavily laden wagons, it was a legitimate concern. As Cody bluntly framed the issue, "were we going to catch Indians with such lumber as that?"[9] Crook confided his doubts to a fellow officer: "We shall find no Indians while such a force sticks together."[10] That evening, however, the matter was easily resolved. Crook had joined Terry in his tent for an amiable supper over which they engaged in a delicate minuet over who would take command. Terry graciously offered leadership of the joint command to Crook, and Crook, equally courtly for the moment, declined, leaving Terry free to take it. With that point settled, Terry confessed, to Crook's relief, that he knew that he would never catch the Indians burdened by his overloaded wagon train. With Crook nodding in hearty agreement, he outlined plans to send the train back to the Yellowstone escorted by Colonel Miles and his Fifth Infantry. Miles would remain on the river to block the Sioux from moving north, while Terry accompanied Crook on the Sioux trail.[11] In emulation of Crook's reliance on mule power, Terry planned to shift his supplies and equipment to a pack train, assigning one of his infantry regiments to serve as mule skinners for the duration of the campaign.

On August 11, Crook's men replenished their rations from Terry's wagons and packed up their mules. The combined column, now numbering about 4,000 men, the largest assemblage of troops that had ever served together on the plains, lumbered eastward on the Indian trail up the Valley of the Tongue. And so began what few guessed would become a ten-week campaign that still stands as among the most arduous ever undertaken by an American military unit.[12]

The march did not begin on a propitious note. Terry's newly minted muleteers, who had never so much as saddled a mule, watched enviously as Crook's experienced packers swiftly and efficiently packed their loads on well-trained animals. Then, it was their turn. Dealing with their own untutored and fractious beasts, they found the task far more difficult than they had supposed. Their efforts resulted in a day marked by frequent halts to pack and repack loads, many of which soon littered the trail. The column made only fifteen miles, crossing the divide between the Rosebud and the Tongue, before Crook's column was forced to go into camp around one o'clock in the afternoon to allow Terry's force to catch up.[13]

They had barely settled in when the heavens opened and a torrential rain began to fall. Some of Crook's troops, without tents or a change of clothing, built wickiups of saplings and ponchos. In search of alternatives, other soldiers, without regard for Indian sensibilities, sought shelter beneath Sioux burial platforms that lined that section of the trail.[14] For most, sleep was impossible. But General Crook and a few of his experienced veterans slept soundly, impervious to the elements.[15]

During the week that followed, the exhausted troops marched and rode through viscous Montana gumbo, following the broad Indian trail up the Tongue to the Mizpah to the Powder, and finally, north toward the Yellowstone, with only monotonous meals of soggy hardtack, alkali-flavored coffee, and raw bacon for sustenance. Each day, reports of fresh Indian sign goaded them on.[16] But their quarry continued to elude them, and the disappointment and general misery of the troops and their officers began to fracture the unity of the command, pitting Crook's men against Terry's.

As the weather deteriorated, so did the health of the troops, particularly the infantry, contributing to the general demoralization of the column. Their diet of salt pork and hardtack increased the incidence of scurvy and dysentery, and the newer recruits, unused to the hard marching, suffered from exhaustion, blistered feet, and bleeding and swollen legs. The weaker ones were mounted on Indian ponies so they would not be left behind and the column could keep moving. By the 15th, the livestock, particularly the government horses, enfeebled by insufficient grain and overwork, were in shocking condition. Finerty, whose own mount was so fatigued he could not ride it most of the time, reported that the marchers barely covered two miles in an hour.

"Very frequently, a played-out horse would fall, as if shot, and the rider was compelled either to abandon the equipments [*sic*] or pack them on a mule. . . . Our whole line of march from the Rosebud to the Powder and Yellowstone rivers was dotted with dead and abandoned horses."[17]

On the whole, Crook's troops, toughened by long campaigning in the field, fared better than Terry's. But given the condition of both horses and men, Crook soon realized that, though the Indian trail continued to point east from the Yellowstone, they could not go on without rest and resupply. So, on August 17, much to the troops' relief, the expedition camped at the confluence of the Powder and the Yellowstone. Though "a bleak desolate region, with poor grass, much of which had been burnt off by the Indians," it was accessible to the river steamers that carried supplies and reinforcements from the Missouri to the Yellowstone and the Big Horn.[18] The first of these boats, the *Far West*, the steamer that had carried the wounded from the Little Big Horn, arrived that evening with Colonel Miles aboard, carrying badly needed rations. Miles had scouted east along the Yellowstone as far as O'Fallon's Creek, without seeing any sign that the Sioux had crossed the river. But Terry, still concerned that they would break for Canada, ordered additional patrols eastward to check for Indian sign.[19]

For the next five days, the expedition's two commands huddled in their respective campsites on the riverbank awaiting a supply train from Terry's depot on the Rosebud. A few sunny days afforded the men the opportunity to dry their soaked clothing, but contributed to the spread of a prairie fire that burnt off the remaining grass around the camp, forcing the men to move downstream. General Terry visited Crook at his campsite during this brief respite and was charmed to find the general, "with several of his staff serenely seated in the water, washing their only set of garments." On the 18th, sutlers landed at the campsite, their boats loaded with produce, canned goods, and clothing, offered at outrageous prices. The soldiers, starved for an alternative to bacon and hardtack, willingly parted with their hard earned pay to procure such exotic delicacies as beans, canned fruit, and clean underwear.[20] On August 20, the rains returned and fell continuously for five days, leaving the column in a state of sodden misery.

As the riverbank now hosted two department generals, each with his own headquarters and high-ranking subordinates, there was a need to signify the location of each in the sprawling campsite. Terry had marked his headquarters with a personal standard and Crook now decided to do the same. His officers soon obliged, fashioning a guidon showing "two horizontal bands, white above, red beneath, with a blue star in the centre." Consistent with the make-do atmosphere of the command, the red came from a flannel undershirt, the white from a towel, and the star from an officer's old blouse. The flag was mounted on a staff made from a travois pole tipped with a metal cartridge.[21]

To soldiers and correspondents alike, the chase now seemed futile. Surely, the Indians had too great a head start to be caught before they reached sanctuary, either in Canada or on the reservation. The sense that they were enduring all of this hardship for nothing weighed heavily on the expedition's morale. The general gloom affected the Indian scouts as well as the soldiers. The Crows were the first to go. Already disgruntled with what they saw as the mismanagement of the expedition, they were anxious to return to their villages to hunt meat for the winter and to receive their annual distribution of government annuities. The Shoshones had urged Crook not to wait on the Yellowstone for supplies but to push ahead without Terry or lose any chance of catching the Sioux. As Terry, the senior officer, wanted to keep the command together, Crook was forced to decline their advice. Disappointed, they too decided to leave the expedition, so that only Terry's Arikaras and Crook's mixed-blood and white scouts remained.[22] Then Cody declared his intention to leave, expressing the opinion that there was no chance of a fight so long as the two forces remained together. The Indians would never make a stand against such a large number of troops.[23] Several of the correspondents, certain that the campaign would not generate any further news, joined the general exodus. Even Finerty, the redoubtable Irishman, contemplated departure. "By remaining I shall see very little else than mud, misery and rough country," he wrote. . . . "I fear very much that the last shot of this section of the campaign has been fired." But in the end, he, Strahorn, Wasson, and Davenport decided to stick it out.[24]

Some of the officers shared Finerty's doubts. Carr suffered from poor health and a continuing case of bilious resentment toward Merritt that by now had swelled to include Crook and Terry. He wrote his wife on August 24. "It has reached beyond a joke that we should be kept out and exposed because two fools do not know their business. I would leave the expedition today, if I could. There is no likelihood of our doing anything under present auspices."[25] Colonel Miles, who had become increasingly contemptuous of the leadership provided by Terry, Crook, and Gibbon, wrote letters of complaint to *his* wife. In a letter dated August 12, he assured her that the Indians were headed north at a rate too fast for the slow-moving column to catch them. On the 20th, he portrayed Crook's effort as "senseless and ill advised as it was fruitless."[26] While Carr and Miles complained to their wives about the futility of the campaign, the enlisted men, preoccupied with ill health, hunger, fatigue, and eternal rain, were impatient to move on, motivated, their officers guessed, by the erroneous belief that they were headed back to their posts rather than further down the trail.

Demoralization was accompanied by a widening rift between the officers of Terry's comparatively well-off command and Crook's shabby veterans, exacerbated by enforced idleness that provided fertile ground for internal dissension. Bourke observed that, "We have two Brigadiers; consequently we have two rival organizations in all the signification of acrimonious and splenetic jealousy." The fault lay, in his opinion, not with the commanders, whom he termed "noble-minded men," but with their subalterns.[27]

CHAPTER TWENTY-FIVE

The Horsemeat March

August–September 1876

Crook ignored all detractors, convinced that he had "work to do before going into winter quarters."[1] Relying on reports indicating that, at least for the time being, the Indians had not dispersed, he still believed that the enemy could be brought to bay.[2] Miles, after scouting east along the Yellowstone, had found no signs that the Sioux had crossed the river heading for Canada. The Arikaras, following the Indian trail eastward, reported that it continued undivided in the direction of the Little Missouri.[3]

The delay at the Yellowstone was frustrating but, as Crook well knew, necessary. He had reluctantly agreed to it because he could not go on without a resupply of grain for the livestock. He also desperately needed shoes for his infantry, and anxiously awaited a detachment of Crows whom he hoped would join the column on the river. If they came, their tracking abilities and knowledge of the country would immeasurably speed the column.[4]

At last, on the 23rd, a riverboat arrived with its cargo of shoes and some, but not enough, provender for the horses. To Crook's consternation, the Crows did not appear. They had encountered their discontented brothers on the trail en route home and had been convinced to turn back rather than join the expedition.[5] Along with the supplies came couriers with reports from Glendive, one of Miles's outposts on the Yellowstone, that Indians were present in some strength around the camp, news that both Crook and Terry seem to have dismissed as unimportant.[6]

As darkness fell and the command prepared to move out the next morning, yet another storm struck, soaking the unprotected soldiers and dampening whatever enthusiasm they had mustered for the coming ordeal. For much of the night, the horses, driven to a frenzy by the flashes of lightning and peals of thunder, stampeded through the muddy campsite, while the men huddled in wretched groups, "vainly trying to keep in some animal heat."[7] Even the normally stoic Crook bowed to the onslaught. Cuthbert Mills, who sought out the general for a final interview before hitting the trail, found him standing beneath a cottonwood wrapped in his army overcoat, some yards from a rude shelter made from an old tent fly. Resisting the temptation to take cover under the fly, Crook remained under the tree, chatting with Mills for a few moments, as the rain increased in intensity.

> At last, as if the thought had just struck him, the general said—"Why don't you get under shelter, Mr. Mills?"
>
> "I had scarcely thought it worthwhile, general—a mere shower (indifferently)!"
>
> He was silent for a time, until a sudden gust of wind shook the tree, and it poured a perfect deluge on us. This brought a surrender.
>
> "The rain is increasing. I think we had better get under cover," said the general, and he made tracks for the canvas, lively, and I followed him.[8]

The next morning, dawn broke clear over the Yellowstone. The new day seemed to have rejuvenated Crook's self-confidence, and with it, his faith in the superiority of his judgment. Waiting for his supplies to arrive, he had been like a bloodhound straining at the leash in his desire to resume the chase. Now, putting the storm's chaos behind him, he rationed his troops for fifteen days and, without informing General Terry of his intentions, marched them out of camp, eastward along the Powder.[9]

And so began the infamous and variously named Hunger, Mud, Horsemeat, and to some, Starvation March, each designation incorporating a different aspect of the coming ordeal. Even Bourke, usually loath to criticize his hero, would later declare that "no one who followed Crook during those terrible days was benefited in any way." Such were the hardships they endured, according to Bourke, that by 1892, only sixteen years after the event, over 50 percent of the officers who accompanied the expedition were gone from the military rolls, either dead or retired because of disability, among them Crook himself, felled by congestive heart failure at the age of sixty-two, attributed by his doctors to the stress of the campaign.[10]

It has been commonly assumed that Crook's decision to depart without informing the senior commander of the expedition was motivated by his desire to free himself of Terry's control and what he had come to see as a drag on the mobility of his column.[11] First Lieutenant Charles King, a Crook aide, and later close friend and chronicler, offered a different explanation. In a letter to a fellow officer many years later, he reminisced that "somebody had given Crook a line to the effect that both Terry and Miles had started a move to bring about Crook's relief from duty in the field in order to get his officers and men and start on a new hunt for Sitting Bull and his warriors. . . . Crook believed it and determined to checkmate the scheme by pulling out at once and getting far on the way to the Black Hills before reply could come from Washington." Crook apparently told King some years later that "some such game was afoot and that by prompt action he had blocked it."[12]

Whatever motivated his departure, his rate of march was somewhat less than speedy. The first day, he made only eleven miles in the gummy Montana ooze.[13] Only after making camp did he belatedly dispatch a note to Terry announcing his exodus. The latter, choosing to ignore Crook's embarrassing and rude breach of protocol, sent him a message announcing his intention to leave at six the next morning (the 25th) to join Crook's column, mildly expressing the hope that "your march will not be so long as to prevent my overtaking you."[14] But Crook had something else in mind.

The next day, Terry pressed through the mud for seventeen miles, reaching a juncture where he had expected Crook to await him, only to find that the general had continued several miles farther down the trail. As the frustrated Terry prepared to make camp, Cody, who had temporarily delayed his departure for the east, arrived with news of recent Indian sightings eastward on the Yellowstone, including a brief attack on one of the river steamers. Though these incidents were no more than annoying pinpricks, they bolstered Terry's conviction that Sitting Bull was making a break to the north.[15] Eager to enlist Crook's column in the chase, he wearily remounted, and with Cody by his side, rode out to find his wayward colleague.

When he finally caught up with him late that night, the two men awkwardly confronted one another with their fundamentally incompatible ideas of how the remainder of the campaign ought to be conducted. Terry maintained that Cody's intelligence indicated Sitting Bull's intention to cross the river and escape into Canada. If they worked together, he told the bemused Three Stars, the two columns could trap the hostiles in an ever-popular pincer movement. Terry considered Sitting Bull's people the "heart and soul of the Indian mutiny." Consequently, if this nucleus of recalcitrant tribesmen could be destroyed, "this thing would be over," or so he thought.[16]

Crook was unmoved by Terry's theory that Sitting Bull was headed for the Missouri and Canada. Nor did he subscribe to the notion that Sitting Bull was the "heart and soul" of Indian resistance, and he considered the raids on the Yellowstone a mere diversion. He was convinced that, at minimum, the Oglalas, whose numbers equaled those of Sitting Bull's band, would soon turn south toward the agencies and the Black Hills and Wyoming settlements, his own area of responsibility.[17] He also believed that now, desperate for food, they would delay long enough to hunt the antelope grazing along the Powder River, and there, he would bring them to bay.[18] If he was wrong and the trail fragmented or turned north, as Terry supposed, he would concede that Sitting Bull and Crazy Horse were making a break for Canada. In that event, he promised Terry, "you can calculate on my remaining with you until this unpleasantness ends or we are ordered to the contrary."[19]

Realizing that he would never be able to change Crook's mind, and unwilling to force his opinions on his more experienced fellow commander, Terry resignedly accepted Crook's reasoning. After agreeing to establish a resupply center for Crook's column at the mouth of Glendive Creek, he returned to his depot on the Powder to conduct his own search for Sitting Bull north of the Yellowstone. Only later would he learn that he had misread the situation and that Crook had been correct about the raids on the Yellowstone. Rather than signifying a general exodus to the north, they were simply an independent foray by a small band of Hunkpapas. Terry would mount a fruitless search for this band until early September, when he received orders from Sheridan to return to Fort Abraham Lincoln as part of a new strategy the lieutenant general had designed to end the war.[20]

From his Chicago vantage point, Sheridan had become increasingly skeptical that either Crook or Terry would be able to catch up with the Sioux.[21] From the outset, he had advocated tactics similar to those he had employed during the Red River War and Crook had used in Arizona. He would station troops in the Sioux hunting grounds to continually harass the Indians, using fear and hunger to drive them onto the reservation. Simultaneously, he would block agency Indians from joining the hostiles in the Powder River country by confiscating their guns and ponies.

Now, with Crook and Terry bogged down in the Montana mud, Sheridan decided to implement his plan. As a first step, he ordered both departmental commanders to establish temporary cantonments, Terry's at the confluence of the Tongue and the Yellowstone and Crook's at Goose Creek, part of a string of posts that would hem the Sioux into an area south of the Yellowstone. Goose Creek would be manned by Crook's troops. Miles would garrison the Tongue River cantonment. From there, his fifteen hundred infantrymen and cavalry would patrol the Yellowstone all winter, giving the hostiles no respite.[22] Concurrently, Sheridan would mount an operation to disarm the agency Indians and confiscate their ponies. Terry was to immediately initiate this policy on the Standing Rock Reservation, hence his recall to Fort Abraham Lincoln. With winter coming on, General Terry was all too happy to abandon the discomforts of the campaign and obeyed with alacrity. For his part, Crook stubbornly continued his pursuit of the now scattering Oglalas.[23]

During the waning days of August, Crook's column plodded eastward through burnt-out country, crossing the Powder and O'Fallon's Creek, marching toward the Little Missouri. For ease of movement, they traveled on the Fort Lincoln Road, which paralleled the track of the fleeing Indians. At the outset, they anticipated an encounter with the Sioux at any moment. To avoid alerting them to their presence, hunting was forbidden, as were bugle calls. As time wore on and the weather worsened, Crook's initial optimism began to dissipate. On August 28, it rained, turning the path to a muddy swamp in which the horses sank "to their knee joints." The next day, they found what appeared to be fresh sign, but it was a false lead, though Crook delayed the column for two days while his scouts explored its possibilities.[24]

The column continued its pursuit, "feeling out for the enemy, and looking for signs of the Indians' passage."[25] On August 31, the trail began to divide, indicating that the tribal coalition was disintegrating and the bands scattering. Though the incessant rain made following the tracks difficult, indications were that a substantial body of tribesmen was headed for the Little Missouri. Crook guessed that after crossing that river, it would turn south in the direction of the Black Hills in search of food, breaking into smaller groups for the hunt. Hopefully, they would reunite at some point after replenishing their meat supplies.[26]

Grouard, sent ahead to reconnoiter the Little Missouri, returned to the column on September 1. His report caused a resurgence of excitement. He had found four abandoned ponies and Indian sign on the riverbanks, indicating that a large village, estimated at 2,000 lodges, had camped there before breaking up "into squads of ten lodges to two hundred, going to the Agencies probably." He surmised that the hostiles had divided generally into two groups, one headed north and the other south toward the Black Hills.[27] Crook, who continued to place great faith in Grouard, saw the report as confirming his belief that the Sioux were splintering to hunt game before either returning to the Agencies or going into camp for the winter. With renewed optimism, he ordered a resumption of the march.

While Crook was energized by Grouard's report, his men, their nerves frayed by the hardships of the march and the lack of tangible success, failed to share his optimism. Absorbed in the chase, the general seemed oblivious or perhaps indifferent to their demoralized state. And as conditions worsened, he withdrew more and more into himself, not even informing his disheartened men where the column was headed or why. His reticence drew the ire of his soldiers, especially those who had joined him most recently, the men of the Fifth Cavalry. A trooper in the Fifth wrote his father, "I have never heard Crook's name mentioned but with a curse." Another commented, "Custer . . . still remain[s] unavenged, and the Indian Question is further from solution than ever." Some, like Carr, began to speculate that Crook had no idea where he was going. One private wrote in a dispatch to a Kansas paper that the general suffered from "slight attacks of aberration of the mind, to which [he] has of late evidently been subject.[28]

Deteriorating health continued to contribute to low morale. Marching, each day in sodden clothes through viscous mud in increasingly cold weather without adequate rations, took its toll. The older veterans suffered from rheumatism, neuralgia, and dysentery. Their boots, soaked in the persistent rains, dried on their feet, shrank, and became impossible to remove, causing sores and blisters that could not be treated. Struggling through the mud, day after cheerless day, some of the men went mad from exhaustion. An officer described hardened veterans who sat down and cried like children "because they could not hold out." Fuel was scarce and the small fires that could be kindled were insufficient to dry the soldiers' clothing or properly cook their rations, now reduced to pitifully small portions of bacon and hard tack, washed down with alkaline coffee. And even this rudimentary fare was diminishing at an alarming rate, adding malnutrition to scurvy and dysentery. The troops got some relief when, in an attempt to prevent scurvy, Crook suggested that they eat a number of local plants, a remedy that had some good effect.[29]

The horses suffered more than the men. Half-starved and covered with sores, most were too weak to carry their riders. Crook's decision to halt on the 29th to reconnoiter the area had provided an opportunity for the stock to rest and graze, but it did little good.[30]

On the afternoon of September 4, the column finally reached the Little Missouri, and a halt was called while the soldiers gorged themselves on the profusion of wild plums that grew on its banks, an impromptu feast that banished the threat of scurvy and somehow relieved their dystentery.[31] Prior to crossing the river, Carr had been disdainful of Grouard's assertion that the Indian camp lay somewhere in this region. "Of course, it is not east of us, and all the scouts and officers who are posted know that, but he [Crook] doesn't." Yet now he admitted there had been "a brush" with a small war party to their front. Were these warriors the rear guard of the big village, as Bourke speculated? If so, they managed to elude the troops in a dense fog. Nevertheless, Bourke concluded that, "this encounter satisfied every fair minded soldier that General Crook had adopted the proper course in hanging to the trail." The use of the qualifier, "fair minded," implied that perhaps others were not so convinced. And, though Crook might have been on the right trail, even Bourke considered further pursuit "a gloomy prospect" for 2,000 men "left without rations, in the midst of a desert, unknown to the maps and hundreds of miles from any habitation of civilized people."[32]

But the next day, encouraged by the brief skirmish, Crook pushed his tired troops another thirty miles to the Heart River, a tributary of the Little Missouri. Here, on September 5, confronted with a sorely depleted food supply, he was forced to put his command on half rations.[33] That evening, in a rare break from his normal taciturnity, he sat down to share his thoughts with Finerty regarding the remainder of the campaign. The rations on hand, he told the reporter, were only sufficient for an additional two and a half days, and Fort Abraham Lincoln, his nearest point of resupply, was one hundred miles, or a five-day ride, to the east. If he chose that option, as there were no signs of any Indians having headed in that direction, it would delay pursuit by at least two weeks. Although he did not mention it to Finerty, it would also bring the column into the Department of Dakota, with the attendant risk of subordinating his command to General Terry. Thus, he preferred to continue to follow the Sioux south toward the Black Hills. Though that meant traveling twice as far to a source of resupply, it presented at least the possibility of catching some of the bands before they reached the agencies or attacked the settlements. Such a victory, though small, might, he thought, justify the suffering and expense of the summer-long chase.[34] While he did not choose to say so, he was also moved by concern for the miners in the Hills, whom he had come to know and admire, and whom he felt a genuine obligation to protect.[35]

To Finerty, Crook's plan strained credulity. Unable to contain himself, he exclaimed, "You will march two hundred miles in the wilderness with used up horses and tired infantry on two and one half days' half rations!" That was exactly what he proposed, Crook admitted. He planned to send the Arikaras to Fort Lincoln to arrange for supplies to be delivered to the column at Custer City, in the Black Hills. In the meantime, he added with chilling calm, "if necessary, we can eat our horses."[36] That evening, he wrote to Sheridan, outlining the rationale for his decision and asking for twenty days' rations of fresh vegetables for his troops and 200,000 pounds of grain for the horses that survived the march.[37]

Crook's determination to head for the Black Hills caused the column's morale to plummet to a new low. According to Lieutenant Burt, the plan "was opposed by nearly all of his rank officers."[38] Most of the soldiers had anticipated an end to the campaign and had been looking forward to the relative comfort of Fort Abraham Lincoln. Now, they learned that instead, they would be marching south in pursuit of a will-o'-the-wisp. Waves of apprehension and revulsion ran through their ranks when it was further announced that they would soon be dining on their mounts. Many old cavalry hands equated eating horseflesh with cannibalism. But, as Finerty pointed out, they had no choice in the matter. "'I'd as soon think of eating my brother,'" he quoted one cavalry officer, "but, hunger," he predicted, "is a great sauce." Sure enough, in a few days, the men were wolfing down the meat from swayback mules and played-out horses with nary a backward glance, eating them "up clean, even the heart, liver, and lights, and not a bit of salt."[39]

Diet aside, the march exceeded their grimmest expectations. Continuous rains over the next two days turned the trail into a slough of deep, viscous mud, crisscrossed with flooded ravines. Anson Mills, as commander of the rearguard, was assigned the heart-rending task of shooting "all played out horses." "Every little while, the report of a pistol or carbine would announce that a soldier had shot his horse rather than leave it behind."[40] When the march ended on the Belle Fourche River on September 13, one-half the horses had broken down beyond rehabilitation, one-fourth of them dead, dozens butchered to sustain the column.[41]

The disheartened troops focused their discontent on their general. Some blamed Crook for incompetence, attributing their shortage of provisions to the time they thought he wasted on short marches and prolonged bivouacs.[42] Others claimed Crook lived better than his men. The *Herald*'s Davenport wrote that Crook had a hoard of extra blankets and messed with the packers, who managed to eat better than the rest of the command. He probably got this nugget of misinformation from the hungry men in the Fifth Cavalry, who had now named the general "Rosebud George" and composed a song memorializing their resentments.

But 'twas out upon the Yellowstone we had the damnedest
time,
Faith, we made the trip wid Rosebud George, six months
without a dime.
Some eighteen hundred miles we went through hunger, mud,
and rain,
Wid backs all bare, and rations rare, no chance for grass or
grain.
Wid 'bunkies shtarvin' by our side, no rations was the rule,
Shure 'twas at your boots and saddles, you brutes, but feed the
packer and mule.
But you know full well that in your fights no soldier lad was
slow,
And it wasn't the packer that won ye a star in the Regular
Army, O.[43]

Those closest to Crook recorded a different reality. They recounted that he shared all of their privations. Like them, he ate hard tack and half-cooked horsemeat and slept in wet and muddy clothes on the damp ground.[44] As Grouard put it, "There was one distinctive characteristic of Gen. Crook's—he would not take any advantage of his command. If they starved, he starved with them."[45] A mule skinner who had previously served with Crook in Arizona recalled that "on the Hunger March, [the general] shared his last mouthful with his men. When we would make camp, he would take care of his mule and help rustle wood and water for the night."[46]

James O'Kelly, the *Herald* reporter, though acknowledging the truth of the mule skinner's words, was unimpressed, accusing Crook of "theatrical" and "sensational" campaigning and of inflicting unnecessary suffering on his troops. "That a man possesses an exceptional constitution and an ostrich-like stomach does not constitute him a great general," he declared. "The mere fact that soldiers sleep in the rain and get dysentery and rheumatism will not make them better Indian fighters. The sooner this sensational campaigning is put an end to the better it will be for the health of the army and the purse of the nation."[47]

CHAPTER TWENTY-SIX

Slim Buttes

September 9, 1876

By September 7, the men had neared the limits of their endurance. The night before, they had camped by a lake so alkaline that neither horses nor men would touch it; during that day's march, many men had fallen by the wayside, sprawling like corpses along the trail for a distance of twenty miles, immobilized by fatigue, hunger, illness, and depression. Grain for the mounts had disappeared, and though grazing could be found in places, many horses were too broken to benefit from it. Mills shot seventy mounts that day, providing the column with their only sustenance. Fuel for cooking was so limited that Crook placed a guard on a half dozen rose bushes so that the sick would have fuel for a warm meal.[1] Without resupply, it was clear that the column would be unable to cover the remaining distance to the Black Hills, still about seventy-five miles away. Two thousand men, horses, and mules could not live off country where the Sioux and the August sun had burned off the grass and driven off all game, but for a few elusive jack rabbits and prairie dogs. Even tobacco had become scarce, an especially painful privation for the troops, who resorted to smoking coffee grounds and prairie grass in its place.[2]

At the evening halt, Crook summoned Anson Mills to his fireside, ordering him to select fifteen of his best men and horses from each of the ten companies of his regiment. Accompanied by Tom Moore, his packers, and the surviving pack animals, he was to ride for Deadwood in the Black Hills to pick up supplies for the column. To carry out Crook's order, Mills divided the detachment into two battalions, one commanded by First Lieutenant Emmett Crawford, who had served under Crook in Arizona, and the other by First Lieutenant Adolphus H. von Leuttwitz, a mercurial Civil War veteran and former officer in the Prussian Army.[3] Grouard and Captain Jack Crawford, known as the "Poet-Scout of the Black Hills," who was intimately familiar with the Hills' roads and trails, would serve as scouts.[4] Reporters Strahorn and Davenport decided to tag along in the hope of finding a topic other than misery and starvation to feed their readers. Their articles, together with writings by Lieutenant Frederick Schwatka, Crawford, Mills, and Grouard, and the diaries kept by several enlisted men, would assure the mission exceptional coverage.

Mills would later insist that, prior to departing, Crook told him that if he encountered a village, he should attack and hold it. Grouard had the same understanding, quoting Crook as saying he would send enough men with Mills to "jump any village we would come across."[5] It is likely that Crook meant to limit his instructions to *small* villages, as a major engagement would surely jeopardize Mills's resupply mission. Lieutenant Bubb, the expedition's commissary officer, supported this interpretation, claiming to have overheard Crook tell Mills to avoid a fight and "cut around it," should he come upon a large village. Such an order would have been consistent with the fact that Mills's troopers each carried only fifty rounds of ammunition for their carbines.[6]

As the food situation was critical, Mills's detachment set out as darkness fell, riding in the usual evening downpour. Grouard, relying on little more than his unerring sense of direction and the flickering light of a match, kept the soldiers on the track in this blackest of nights. Somehow, in the darkness, he discovered fresh pony tracks on the trail, an indication that Indians had recently passed this way. To avoid accidentally blundering into a village, the column made camp well before sunrise. At dawn, they resumed their journey in a dense fog that reduced visibility to almost zero. At about one o'clock that afternoon, as the fog began to lift, Grouard spotted a herd of ponies to his front, signaling the presence of a village ahead. Mills halted the command and pulled them out of sight in the thick brush to consider his next move.[7]

Crook had correctly divined the direction of the Indians. During the latter part of August and early September, the people of the great village had drifted eastward toward the Missouri River. According to Red Horse, a Miniconjou chief interviewed in 1877, they had moved at a pace just slow enough to keep the army interested, hoping to wear out the soldiers' horses, while avoiding battle with the huge force. After Crook and Terry had split up at the end of August, the Sioux had prepared an ambush, but the soldiers had unaccountably passed them by without making contact. After this, as Crook had surmised, the village had begun to fragment, the southern bands scattering to hunt game or drift into the White River Agencies. At the same time, Sitting Bull's people moved north of the Yellowstone toward Fort Buford. Red Horse had moved his village, a mixed group of southerners—Brules, Miniconjous, Oglalas, and Cheyennes—numbering about thirty-eight lodges, to an area known as Slim Buttes, not more than twenty miles south of Crook's column and directly in Mills's path. There, they camped along a small creek in a wooded depression near a number of other bands that remained in the vicinity to hunt. It was the pony herd of this village that Grouard stumbled upon.[8]

Mills, uncertain as to the size of the village, feared drawing closer lest the dogs or ponies, alerted by the scent of white men, betray his presence. Instead, he withdrew about half a mile into a deep gorge and sent Grouard to reconnoiter.[9] As darkness fell, the scout disguised himself as an Indian and infiltrated the village. He would later claim that while in the camp, he spotted two likely ponies tethered by a tipi and stole them and then rode back to report that the village was small enough for the detachment to strike.[10] Mills would dispute this account. Though he had great respect for Grouard's scouting abilities, unlike Crook, he considered him fundamentally unreliable—a coward and a liar. As Mills told it, Grouard returned from his scout of the village astride a fresh Indian pony and told the waiting captain that the camp was too big to attack with the force at hand.[11]

The Custer fight still fresh on their minds, Mills's officers were opposed to attacking the village without knowing its exact size. But Mills's blood was up. Overriding his officers' opposition, he determined to carry out the attack immediately, ignoring Bubb's suggestion that he notify Crook of the discovery of the village in case reinforcements were needed.[12] Relying on the shock of a surprise dawn assault to make up for any disparity in the size of the opposing forces, he divided his command into three detachments. When the command was close enough to charge, the right and left detachments, under Crawford and von Leuttwitz, would move to envelop the village to prevent the Indians from fleeing, while the third, under Schwatka, charged through its center, stampeding the ponies and sowing confusion among the tipis.[13]

They moved out at 3 A.M., after an uncomfortable night in the ravine. By dawn they were in their assigned positions just north of the village. But before the sky had lightened sufficiently to give clear visibility, the pony herd scented the soldiers and stampeded through the camp, forcing the troops to charge prematurely before the enveloping columns were completely in place.

The Indians, around 250 in number, were taken completely by surprise. But as the soldiers began to fire into the lodges, the warriors quickly recovered, grabbing their rifles and hastily exiting their tipis, cutting their way through the hide walls with their skinning knives.[14] Once outside, in the chaos of the attack, they herded the women and children toward bluffs that arose at the south end of the village, cliffs that gave the locale, and the ensuing battle, its name—Slim Buttes. Escaping through a gap in the troopers' lines, they fled into thick brush covering the slope. A small number, including some women and children, sought cover in a steep ravine and kept their attackers at bay with accurate rifle fire. The remainder of the band retreated into the hills to the south and west.[15]

His casualties were light—one killed, five wounded—but Mills regarded his position as precarious. Indians continued to fire from the bluffs into the village, and he could see a number of warriors riding back and forth on surrounding ridges.[16] Others had vanished over the bluffs to the west, probably, he surmised, to seek assistance from other villages in the vicinity. His conjecture was confirmed when warriors on the ridges shouted down to the troops that more Sioux would soon be arriving. With his men low on ammunition and fearing an imminent counterattack, Mills belatedly dispatched a courier with an urgent message to Crook that he "had the village and was trying to hold it." He then had his men dig entrenchments for defense pending the column's arrival.[17]

As soon as the soldiers' suppressing fire had forced the Indians to withdraw out of rifle range, the captain allowed his men to scavenge for food in the village. They found large quantities of dried meat and berries conveniently packed in rawhide sacks for use during the coming winter, as well as buffalo robes and hides of all kinds. There was no question this time of destroying valuable plunder. The troopers began collecting food and supplies, later burning only what could not be used. They took a grim satisfaction in their plundering, particularly after unearthing plentiful evidence of this village's participation in the Little Big Horn fight. A Seventh Cavalry guidon, an officer's overcoat, and several saddles belonging to Custer's troopers turned up, in addition to three horses in the pony herd with Seventh Cavalry brands.[18]

While Mills's troopers rummaged through the Sioux tipis, his courier found Crook, much nearer the village than anticipated. After Mills had departed on the 7th, the general had decided to remain in place for a day to allow the men and horses to rest. But he changed his mind, probably realizing that he could ill afford to dally with his rations running out and perhaps concerned for Mills's safety after his scouts reported an increase in Indian sign along the trail.[19] So he moved out in Mills's wake, and by nightfall on the 8th, he was camped only twenty miles from the village.

That night, the general decided to celebrate his forty-eighth birthday.[20] In what Bourke described as "the thinnest birthday celebration" he had ever attended, Crook marked the occasion by inviting several men to gather about his campfire. To the surprise of his guests, the renowned teetotaler withdrew a pint flask of whisky from the breast pocket of his worn overcoat and handed it around, requesting that they drink to his health. In a chill rain, the men huddled around the meager fire, eating the crumbs of hard tack that constituted their evening meal and washing it down with sips from the flask. If Crook partook, and Bourke's diary makes no mention of it, he could certainly have justified the lapse as medicinal.[21]

While his officers toasted their commander, others in the column cursed him—behind his back, of course. Having endured fatigue, the mud, cold rain, and lack of wood and potable water, his troops now faced the very real treat of starvation. They were on quarter rations, living on slivers of horse meat fried in the remains of their bacon ration, supplemented with six hard tack biscuits per man per day, "and Deadwood still five (5) days away."[22]

The following day dawned damp and cheerless. The men rose early from their soggy blankets and, according to Bourke, covered five miles of muddy trail by seven o'clock, before encountering Mills's courier, a packer named George Herman, in the swirling fog. Galloping down the line, he sought out Crook and announced that Mills had taken a village at Slim Buttes with six casualties.[23] A second courier followed, reporting that the captain expected a counterattack momentarily and urgently needed reinforcements.[24] The village was still some seventeen miles south of Crook's present position. Aware that the captain had only limited ammunition, and with images of Custer fresh in his mind, he did not delay. Selecting a detachment of one hundred cavalrymen mounted on the best horses available, he rode at their head to Mills's assistance, leaving instructions for the remaining cavalry and the infantry to follow at all possible speed.[25]

Bourke reported that Crook was more than a little disturbed that Mills "had discovered the village the previous evening, but had not sent back word as he should have done."[26] His anger was not mere pique at being deprived of glory, but fear that Mills's rashness might have robbed the column of a decisive victory. As Strahorn pointed out in hindsight, if Mills had sent for reinforcements before attacking the village, "there [would have been] plenty of time to have got the entire command there and so effectually surrounded the village."[27] But as he had at Powder River, Crook repressed his anger, all too aware that not only had Mills presented him with the only significant success in an otherwise fruitless campaign, but that the captured village would provide fresh mounts and, more importantly, provisions that could save the column from starvation. In the end, he let the matter rest, satisfying himself with an ambiguous commendation. Mills, he concluded, "is entitled to praise for the plucky manner in which he attacked and carried in the darkness of morning, a village of unknown strength and resources."[28]

Energized by the chance to engage the elusive enemy at last, the troops set a rapid pace, arriving at Slim Buttes a little after eleven o'clock.[29] Mills welcomed them, telling Crook that his men continued to receive sporadic fire from the Indians on the ridgeline and, of greater concern, from the deep ravine that wound into the hillside just beyond the camp. The general immediately took command and, seemingly oblivious to Sioux sniper fire, strode through the village, sizing up the situation and searching for a likely site for his headquarters. He then quickly deployed troops to drive the warriors on the heights out of rifle range and ordered a defensive line established along ridges to the north and west to guard against an anticipated counterattack. The remainder of his force he assigned to the task, begun by Mills, of unearthing and sorting through the vast amount of provisions found in the lodges.[30]

Sniping from warriors in the ravine slowed the work. The declivity in which the warriors lay concealed was narrow, in some places only six feet wide, with steep sides and thick brush cover. To fire accurately into it required that the soldiers expose themselves at its edge. For the Indians it was a perfect sniper's lair.[31] Already several mules had been killed and a number of troopers had had close calls while wandering among the lodges. The troops made one attempt to storm the ravine, but were driven off by heavy fire. Small groups now gathered in its vicinity, blindly shooting into its depths.[32]

To neutralize the threat, Crook led an attack on the west side of the ravine, again exhibiting what Finerty would term "his eccentric contempt for danger."[33] On the opposite bank, William Cody's friend, Buffalo Chips, became reckless in his eagerness to gain another scalp for Custer. He paid for it with a bullet in the chest that killed him instantly. A fusillade of shots from the ravine followed, wounding two troopers and killing a third. Big Bat, demonstrating the kind of individual courage that earned the admiration of friend and foe alike, shot one of the Sioux and then leapt into the ravine, scalped him, and escaped safely with his grisly prize. The troopers, infuriated by their casualties, redoubled their efforts, surrounding the opening and pouring a heavy volume of fire into the redoubt.

Above the crackling sound of massed volleys, an eerie wail rose from the gully, mingling with the screams of women and frightened children. These heartrending cries were Crook's first indication that noncombatants were in the ravine, prompting him to call an immediate ceasefire. After the firing tapered off, he instructed Grouard and Big Bat to tell the Indians that they would not be harmed if they surrendered. A pathetic scene ensued as the officers beat back soldiers bent on revenge, while Big Bat entered the ravine. He soon emerged, leading one haggard old woman, covered with blood and mud. When she saw Crook awaiting her on the ravine's rim, water dripping from his slouch hat into his untrimmed beard, she somehow recognized him as the leader of the force and clung to his hands and clothing, while he tried to calm her with assurances of safety. Eleven more women and six children followed.[34]

From the women, Crook learned that the village chief, a Miniconjou named American Horse, or Iron Shield as he was also called, remained in the gully with a few surviving warriors. Despite calls for their surrender, the Indian men held out for another two hours. Even the hate-filled soldiers were impressed with their courage. Finally, responding to a second call for their surrender and reassurances from the captive women, they cautiously emerged from their redoubt. His features set in an impassive expression, American Horse painfully climbed the steep slope of the ravine, leaning on the arm of a young warrior. In one hand, he held his rifle, butt forward, to signify his surrender. The other clutched his intestines, bulging from a jagged wound in his abdomen. The "fine looking, broad chested Sioux with a handsome face and a neck like a bull," impossibly maintained the formality of the moment while gripping his bleeding bowels. For his part General Crook struggled to preserve his own dignity—an "undeniably shabby-looking man in a private soldier's light blue overcoat, standing ankle-deep in mud and in a far-gone pair of private soldier's boots, crowned with a most shocking bad hat." That night, despite the column's surgeons' best efforts to save him, the chief died, stoically enduring his pain until the end.[35]

Soldiers who entered the ravine after the chief's surrender were confronted by a horrific scene. Among the dead, covered in blood and gore, were the bodies of the warrior killed by Big Bat, a woman, her skull blown to smithereens, another "so riddled by bullets that there appeared to be no unwounded part of her person left," and still another, shot through the breast, a dead infant by her side. Yet an amazing twenty-three of the twenty-eight Indians in the ravine had survived. Unhappily, the officers were unable to prevent several soldiers and a scout named Ute John from scalping the dead in a final act of barbaric vengeance repellent to most of the command.[36]

From the prisoners, Crook learned that Crazy Horse was camped in the vicinity and was expected to attack before the afternoon was out. A crackle of rifle fire from the bluffs surrounding three sides of the village soon announced his presence. The soldiers, veterans of many such attacks, scrambled into well-ordered skirmish lines to protect the wounded, the horses, pack train, and supplies. The attackers, numbering between six hundred and a thousand warriors, had anticipated a confrontation with only Mills's small command. Instead, they now found themselves facing two thousand disciplined troops, including infantry. The latter used their long range Springfield rifles to keep the Sioux at bay while cavalry charges drove them off the ridgelines. By sundown, the Indians had withdrawn from the field.[37]

That evening, the troopers, satiated at last with dried meat and berries, slept soundly, some lucky ones luxuriating in the warmth of captured buffalo robes. The remainder huddled in their wet blankets, their fatigue and a full stomach allowing them rest despite the steady rain and cold mud. By the next morning, in a gray mist that blanketed the village, Crook ordered the completion of its destruction. Everything not of value to the command was burned, utterly impoverishing the band. For the troops, it was now time to bury their dead. They had suffered two dead among their thirty casualties. (A third would later die of his wounds.) Wrapping both bodies in blankets and canvas, the troops buried them in a single pit dug on the trail. To conceal the site, a fire was built over the spot and the ashes scattered. The command then marched over the grave to obliterate any remaining signs.[38]

The column was ill-equipped to handle prisoners. So, after treating their wounds, Crook freed those captives who wished to return to their people. Surprisingly, a number of women and children and one warrior remained with the column on its march to Deadwood. The warrior, Charging Bear, subsequently enlisted as an army scout and would serve in the coming winter campaign against Crazy Horse.[39]

As the column prepared to depart, the Sioux gave them a last send-off, firing into the soldiers' camp from the ridgeline. But they were too few and too distant to pose a serious threat. Colonel Carr, commanding the rearguard, scattered them with little difficulty.[40]

Slim Buttes, the army's sole victory over the Sioux to date, was a meager triumph. Among his own officers were many who were highly critical of the general, including his admirer, Charles King.[41] Cuthbert Mills, whose reports on the expedition were generally favorable to Crook, aptly summed up this culminating battle of the campaign. "The general impression in this command is that we have not much to boast of in the way of killing Indians."[42] According to historian Jerome Greene, author of the definitive work on the battle, Slim Buttes may actually have prolonged the war, frightening the Indians with the specter of brutal retribution when and if they surrendered.[43] But most of the country was content to give Crook grudging credit for his stubborn pursuit and unhesitating destruction of the village.[44]

Captured provisions and meat from Indian ponies did not suffice to get the column to Deadwood. Because of the weakened condition of the men and animals, the rain, and the mud, it would take the men an additional four days to make the march. By the end of the second day, the food supply was depleted to the point that Crook once again ordered Mills and fifty troopers, now astride captured Indian ponies, to ride ahead to fetch provisions from the town.

That evening, prior to Mills's departure, Crook penned his official report to Sheridan describing the march and the action at Slim Buttes. Dated September 10, it was as usual brief, leaving it to his subordinates to fill in the details. For obvious reasons, he preferred to focus, not on the marginal results of the single engagement or the painful and fruitless summer campaign, but on his plans for the next stage in the war. After providing a cursory description of the fight, ignoring his own role in it, Crook noted that he had learned from his captives that most of the Sioux were now headed for the agencies, "with the exception of Crazy Horse and Sitting Bull with their immediate followers." The former, according to his sources, intended to remain at the headwaters of the Little Missouri, while the latter had gone north of the Yellowstone, presumably preparing to run for the Canadian border. He recommended that Terry's column take care of Sitting Bull, while he went after Crazy Horse. Briefly summarizing the severity of the campaign, he remarked that, "a great many animals gave out and had to be abandoned" and as a result, he required five hundred fresh mounts for the coming expedition, "preferably the half-breed horses raised on the Laramie plains."[45]

Wary of the press because of their coverage of the Rosebud fight, Crook cautioned Grouard, whom he chose to deliver the report to the nearest telegrapher, to wire it before any of the journalists' articles. He was unaware that Reuben Davenport had given Jack Crawford $500 to beat Grouard to the punch with the *Herald*'s story. Crawford and Grouard subsequently engaged in a horse-killing race to be the first to post their patron's version of the campaign. While Crawford got to a telegrapher first, the race turned out to be meaningless as Sheridan had arrived at Fort Laramie and personally received Crook's report directly from the courier who carried it to the post. He, in turn, forwarded it to department headquarters in Omaha and from there, it was disseminated to papers throughout the country. On September 17, the story of the battle was featured in papers from San Francisco to New York, with firsthand reports by not only Davenport, but Strahorn and Mills, who quoted liberally from the general's report.[46]

Back on the trail, the next two days were a nightmare. The march of September 12 in particular was remembered as among the worst of the campaign. It was a day, Charles King wrote, "when scores of our horses dropped exhausted on the trail—when starving men toiled piteously through thick clinging mud or flung themselves, weeping and worn out, upon the broad flooded prairie. . . . Men would sink hopelessly in the mire and never try to rise themselves; travois mules would plunge frantically in bog and quicksand, and pitch the wounded screaming from their litters."[47] From dawn to well after dark, the troops lurched forward, covering an incredible thirty-five miles in a cold drizzle before bedding down in the muck on the banks of rain-swollen Crow Creek. They were now only a few miles from the Belle Fourche River, with the Black Hills beyond.

Despite the hardship, Crook continued his relentless prosecution of the chase. Discovering an Indian trail on the evening of the 11th, he sent out a detachment to search the back trail for a village. The effort proved useless and cost the life of one more soldier. What these exhausted men on their used-up horses would have accomplished had they actually found a village, is difficult to say.[48]

On the morning of the 13th, the column, with men clinging to the tails and stirrups of the remaining horses, staggered the final five miles to the Belle Fourche. On arrival, those with sufficient strength struggled to high ground, hoping to spot Mills's supply wagons. Suddenly, the distant lowing of oxen and the cry "Rations coming!" electrified the command, causing several Gray Fox loyalists to cheer, "Hurrah for Old Crook!"[49] As the wagons, trailed by a herd of fifty cattle, hove into sight, the men, no longer able to contain their hunger, rushed forward, hurling boxes of crackers and tinned fruit to the ground and scrambling in the mud for their contents. In the melee, Lieutenant King snatched three ginger snaps from the sodden ground, declaring them to be "the sweetest morsels we had tasted in years."[50] That evening, surfeited on fresh beef, a welcome relief from unsalted horse meat, and flour and water flapjacks, the men rested secure in the knowledge that the Big Horn Expedition and Yellowstone had at last come to an end.[51]

CHAPTER TWENTY-SEVEN

Dealing with the Agency Sioux

September–October 1876

On September 15, a courier arrived in camp with dispatches from Sheridan. Additional food and grain for the horses were on their way to Custer City. The lieutenant general indicated that he would be traveling to Fort Laramie and expected to meet Crook there on the 17th. Having not as yet received Crook's report, he had devised his own plan for a winter occupation of the Yellowstone country that he thought would bring prompt closure to the Sioux conflict. Anticipating objections, Sheridan displayed a pliant attitude toward his fractious departmental commander, offering to "change my views to meet yours on any plan you may have."[1] Obediently, Crook turned over command of the column to Merritt, toasted his officers with a tin cup of champagne, and departed for Fort Laramie.[2]

His route took him through the raw mining towns that now dotted the Black Hills—Crook City, Deadwood, and Custer City. The miners in the region, who had been virtually under siege since the beginning of the Sioux War, had long admired the general for his intercession in their behalf the year before and now regarded him as their deliverer from the Indians. While they genuinely wished to thank him, they also saw his presence as an opportunity to lobby for the establishment of a military post in the Black Hills.[3]

The general's first port of call, Crook City, was the northernmost settlement in the Black Hills and one of the few places in the West that bore his name. Its population, a "fair sized crowd of hairy men and bilious women," emerged from the log shanties lining its rutted and muddy main street and overwhelmed Crook's entourage with raucous welcoming shouts.[4] At Deadwood, the "metropolis" of the Black Hills, a similarly uproarious greeting awaited them, replete with a thirteen-gun salute, "much in the way of bonfires . . . and no small portion of hard drinking."[5] Strolling down the main thoroughfare, Crook, displaying a latent talent for politics, "shook hands with everybody along the way and remembered everybody he ever had seen before, even those he had escorted out of the Hills the year before."[6] Then, in response to gentle hints from the city fathers, he and his officers trekked to a nearby bathhouse to remove several layers of dirt before attending a grand fete hosted by the town. Afterward, speaking from the balcony of the Grand Central hotel, the general expressed his warm affection for the miners and, in words that today's politicians have turned into a cliche, he urged those present to "let the private soldier feel that he is remembered by our people as the real defender of his country."[7]

The next morning, after gently disengaging himself from the adoring clutches of Deadwood's populace, he rode south to Custer City, where he was met by Captain James Egan and his troop of matching gray horses, escorting a supply column from Fort Laramie with provision for Crook's men. Swapping his jaded mounts for several of Egan's relatively fresh grays, the general left his escort and pack animals behind and galloped off on a nonstop twenty-four-hour, hundred-mile marathon to Fort Laramie, stopping briefly at Camp Robinson en route.[8]

Tired and trail-worn, the forty-eight-year-old general arrived at the Fort on September 24. Some of the euphoria from his exuberant reception in the Black Hills had been dampened by his encounter at Camp Robinson with a group of easterners, several of whom he recognized as former agents of Grant's peace initiative. Troubled by recollections of their disruption of his campaign against the Apaches in Arizona and memories of his old nemesis, "Vincent the Good," he had a premonition that their presence at Robinson signaled a similar initiative on the northern plains.

His concerns were well founded. The government had not forgotten that the casus belli of the Sioux War was acquisition of the Black Hills and the unceded lands. Encouraged by the public thirst for revenge for the Little Big Horn "massacre" that swept the nation that summer, Congress blithely ignored the troublesome questions of compensation and the requirements of the Treaty of 1868. Instead, it simply decreed that, unless the agency chiefs surrendered the Black Hills and the hunting lands in the Powder River and Big Horn countries, no more funds would be forthcoming for the purchase of rations for the Sioux Reservation. In other words, sign or starve. Concurrently, the government had decided to remove the Sioux from the White River agencies to points on the Missouri River, where they could be supplied cheaply by riverboat and kept safely distant from white settlements.[9]

The easterners whom Crook met at Camp Robinson represented the Black Hills Commission, charged with securing the chiefs' agreement to the government's wishes. At the time, the chiefs who, faced with the specter of a long winter without food, were on the verge of capitulating, which they did not long after the general rode off to his meeting with Sheridan. Though they signed away their rights to the land under duress, they stubbornly resisted the plan to remove them to the Missouri River or to Indian Territory—today, the State of Oklahoma—a similarly unpalatable alternative offered by the Commission. While they lacked the leverage to simply refuse relocation, they stalled implementation to gain time to come up with a strategy to kill the plan.[10] Though unaware of it at the time, Crook would become an integral part of that strategy.

Commission members had briefed Crook on their efforts before he hurriedly boarded the ambulance that would transport him to Fort Laramie, and he likely brooded over their words as his wagon rolled over the plains.[11] His mounting concern was not at the time focused on the obvious inequity of the Commission's actions—that would come later—but on his fear that these civilian meddlers would intrude on the conduct of the war and attempt to engineer a negotiated end to hostilities. Like Sheridan, he still considered such a resolution anathema, clinging to the belief that a decisive victory on the battlefield was an essential prelude to permanent resettlement on the reservation.

On arrival at Fort Laramie, though eager to see Sheridan, Crook paused to deliver Captain Andrew Burt, who accompanied him, to his wife, who resided at the fort. Mrs. Burt, grateful for the safe return of her husband, graciously invited the general to share her crowded home for the length of his stay. Years later, she recalled him as "not a great talker," but "a most agreeable guest, adapting himself readily to any inconvenience that arose."[12]

After exchanging niceties with Mrs. Burt, Crook at last joined Sheridan who, accompanied by Colonel Ranald Mackenzie, had been impatiently waiting to unfold his plan for ending the war, a strategy that he had devised and shared with General Sherman the month before.[13] "Our duty," he told the army's chief, "will be to occupy the game country and make it dangerous and when [the Sioux] are obliged from constant harassing and hunger to come in and surrender, we can then dismount, disarm and punish them at the Agencies as was done with the Southern Indians in the last campaign."[14] The plan would use Colonel Miles's infantry to patrol north of the Yellowstone from his cantonment on the Tongue, focusing on Sitting Bull's Hunkpapas, while Crook and Mackenzie campaigned south of the river, in search of Crazy Horse and his Oglalas. Crook voiced no objection, suggesting only that he be allowed to operate from a base in the Black Hills, a recommendation that Sheridan ignored.[15]

Sheridan then turned his attention to the agency Sioux, whom he, together with many of his officers, viewed as allied to Sitting Bull's people during the fighting. Though the majority had remained on the reservation, he believed that they had supplied their relatives in the field with reinforcements, weapons, and ammunition. Now, as winter approached, he was concerned that they would provide sanctuary for the returning warriors during the cold weather, allowing them a respite to prepare for another spring offensive. A more immediate worry was the possibility that the agency Indians, apprehensive that the government would wreak vengeance on them for the Custer defeat and haunted by the specter of a winter of starvation, might attempt a mass breakout. To guard against this threat, Sheridan had taken several measures, including the movement of large numbers of soldiers from nearby posts onto the White River Agencies.[16] And, though the commissioners from the East had assured the chiefs at Red Cloud and Spotted Tail that their people could keep their guns and ponies, Sheridan intended to disarm and dismount them as soon as he had sufficient troops on hand and the weather had turned bad enough to prevent the Indians from scattering into the wilderness.[17] In the interim, he banned the sale of arms and ammunition at the agencies. Ultimately, disarming the Sioux would render them completely dependent on government rations, as game on the reservation had become too scarce and scattered to hunt with bow and arrow. Sheridan's plan also included orders to apprehend any Indians returning to the reservation and treat them as prisoners of war. Viewing these measures in their entirety, it seems clear that Sheridan's objective was not only to render the agency Sioux harmless, but to make surrender so unattractive that a military solution to the war would become inevitable.[18]

Crook and Mackenzie were to be responsible for confiscating the arms and ponies at Spotted Tail and Red Cloud, while General Terry and the Seventh Cavalry would do the same at the Dakota Agencies.[19] Crook knew Mackenzie, having served briefly with him during the Civil War. The colonel had been assigned to the Department of the Platte since August, as Sheridan, feeling the need to inject new blood into the Sioux campaign, had appointed him to head the District of the Black Hills.[20] Headquartered at Camp Robinson and responsible for both the Oglala and Brule agencies, he had at his disposal a substantial force of cavalry, infantry, and artillery, backed by a contingent of Pawnee scouts.[21] Intense, audacious, and utterly fearless, newsman Finerty described Mackenzie as "a noble specimen of the *beau sabreur*—tall, well built, and with a frank, handsome face."[22]

An 1862 graduate of West Point, Mackenzie had ended the Civil War as a brigadier general of volunteers with a brevet rank of major general, and Grant's blessing as "the most promising young officer in the Army," having achieved his rank "upon his own merit without influence."[23] Reduced to colonel in the postwar service, he was assigned to the southern plains, where he gained a measure of renown by subduing an assortment of notably ferocious tribes, including the Commanches, Kiowas, and Southern Cheyennes, who called him "Bad Hand" as a consequence of a Civil War wound that cost him two fingers.

Unfortunately, the Indian wars revealed a dark side to the man. Quick-tempered, a rigid and harsh disciplinarian, he seemed more interested in upholding the reputation of his regiment than the welfare of his troops. As a consequence, he was feared, but not greatly loved, by his men.[24] Thin-skinned and moody under the best of circumstances, he quickly took offense at what he deemed attacks on his honor. As a consequence, his career was peppered with petty feuds and squabbles with fellow officers and civilians. Among these, it may be recalled, was his altercation with the hapless Colonel Reynolds of Powder River fame, whom Mackenzie accused of colluding with traders to cheat the Indians. In 1875, his mood swings and unpredictable behavior became more pronounced after he suffered a head injury in a fall from a wagon that fogged his mind for days. Sheridan's decision to transfer him to the Platte came just in time to extricate him from a cloud of controversy that seemed to cloak his actions at every turn. Crook, however, who had his own problems, probably warmly welcomed the addition of this tested Indian fighter to his command.

The three men were in complete agreement regarding the president's Black Hills commission. Civilians had no business trying to negotiate a peaceful end to the Sioux War. They also found the commission's proposal to remove the Sioux to Indian Territory ill-advised, fearing it would only spread resistance and sow confusion among the peaceful Indians already settled in the Territory. Together, they worked out a strategy that they hoped would undercut the easterner's authority. Mackenzie, as the junior officer, would write a letter to the president advancing their shared views, and the senior officers, including Sherman, would endorse it as it made its way up the chain of command. It would accuse the agency Indians of being openly defiant of the military and of signing the agreement with the commissioners only as a delaying tactic. With breathtaking arrogance, the authors would advise the president to suspend the congressionally mandated agreement and prohibit the commission from any "further communication with the Sioux at Red Cloud and Spotted Tail Agencies except through the military authorities."

When the letter arrived on Crook's desk, he gleefully appended an endorsement expressing his long-standing contempt for civilian administration of Indian agencies, and painted the agencies as "the head and front of all the trouble and hostilities which have been in progress." He also characterized the Sioux Reservation as a "regular depot of recruits and supplies" for tribes' warring cousins to the north. Sheridan added a vigorous condemnation of civilian interference in military matters, while Sherman iced the cake by enthusiastically backing the opinions of "three such able men and officers." Predictably, the administration wisely allowed the letter to sink into the bowels of the War Department, where it disappeared without a trace.[25]

After concluding their meeting at Fort Laramie, the three officers parted. Mackenzie returned to Camp Robinson, while Sheridan and Crook entertained a visiting delegation of Japanese officers. The lieutenant general then departed for Chicago, confident that he and his commanders had reached a meeting of the minds.[26] For his part, Crook, as he often did during periods of stress, sought to clear his mind by having a go at the local wildlife. With the help of officers at the post, he organized a weeklong "grand hunt" to Laramie Peak, returning on October 10, his mules laden with the carcasses of over sixty deer and antelope.[27]

Having temporarily slaked his blood lust, Crook turned his attention to the potentially incendiary task of disarming and dismounting the Indians at the White River (Spotted Tail and Red Cloud) Agencies. Chief Red Cloud had complicated the already delicate operation by moving his camp from the vicinity of Camp Robinson to Chadron Creek, some twenty-three miles from the post, in an effort to escape military oversight. Red Leaf, a Brule and former peace chief now allied with Red Cloud, followed, settling his people about a mile away from the Oglala camp. Both men refused to return to their former site despite the military's threat to withhold their rations. Their intransigence worried both Crook and Mackenzie, who feared that it presaged a mass breakout to join the northerners. To reinforce Mackenzie's troops, Crook sent for Wesley Merritt, still in the Black Hills. But then, concerned that the breakout was imminent, he decided not to wait for Merritt's arrival and to move immediately to disarm Red Cloud's people.[28]

Mackenzie had 982 soldiers at the post and a formidable detachment of one hundred Pawnee scouts organized, trained, and led by Frank North. North, with his brother, Luther, had formed the unit after Congress authorized the recruitment and service of Indian scouts in 1864. Following the Custer battle, Sheridan had requested that the Norths take a contingent of the Pawnees to Camp Robinson to be available to Crook for his campaign against the Sioux. The Pawnees leapt at the chance to return to their Nebraska homeland from Indian Territory, where their tribe had recently been banished and where they were being decimated by poverty and disease. Their enthusiasm was heightened by the opportunity to fight their traditional enemies, the Sioux, and to capture many ponies. Though many of the warriors had been weakened by malaria, the Norths selected the most healthy and sent them to Camp Robinson, where they arrived just in time to take part in the impending action against Red Cloud and Red Leaf.[29]

On the night of October 22, Mackenzie's troops, accompanied by fifty of the Pawnees, rode to Red Cloud's camp. While the soldiers surrounded the village in the predawn darkness, the Pawnees swept forward, gathering up the pony herd before the sleeping Indians were aware of their presence. The surprise was so complete that the scouts captured over seven hundred ponies without firing a shot. The Sioux, surrounded by an overwhelming force, then surrendered their arms. Allowing only the elderly and infirm to retain their mounts, Mackenzie marched the rest of the humiliated band on foot to Camp Robinson, where General Crook awaited them.[30]

Assembled on the post parade ground, Red Clouds' stunned followers listened as the Gray Fox bluntly informed them that, henceforth, they must submit to the will of the government, pointing to Bad Hand's heavily armed troops to underscore his point. He then announced that he was replacing Red Cloud with Spotted Tail as principal chief. The latter, he declared, was "the only important leader who has the nerve to be our friend." The shocked tribesmen then learned that many of their finer ponies were to be awarded to their enemies, the Pawnees, while others would be given to Sioux warriors recruited from the reservation to serve as scouts in the winter campaign against their northern cousins. The rest would be sold at auction, with the proceeds held by the government to pay for the purchase of future livestock for the Sioux.[31]

Up to this point, Crook had punctiliously adhered to Sheridan's instructions. But now, wishing to reward the cooperation of the agency Indians who had not followed Red Cloud to the Chadron, he allowed Spotted Tail and his followers to keep their guns and ponies. In so doing, he deliberately contravened Sheridan's order that he treat all agency Indians as hostile and punish them equally. Not surprisingly, Crook made no reference to his decision in his report to the lieutenant general the day following the seizure.[32] But a week later, he detailed the rationale for his action in a letter to the assistant adjutant general:

> The bands not disarmed . . . have been loyal to us, and to have disarmed them with the others [Red Cloud's and Red Leaf's] would simply have arrayed the white man against the Indian. . . . By not doing this they were convinced in the

> most decided manner that such was not our intention, and no amount of talk about "our friendship" and "the friendship of the Great Father" would have so thoroughly impressed it upon their minds. . . . This good effect was at once manifested in the desire of the warriors from these bands [to] enlist and enlistments have since been going on there in large numbers. . . . These enlistments will have a decided effect in inducing the hostiles to accept the terms offered for their surrender. . . . One thing is certain, it is the starting wedge by which the tribal organization is broken up.[33]

To reporter Cuthbert Mills, he emphasized that his desire to induce Sioux scouts to enlist for his upcoming campaign drove his decision to ignore Sheridan's orders. Attributing the failure of the Big Horn and Yellowstone Expedition to the absence of scouts familiar with the country, he told the journalist that he did not intend to repeat that mistake. He also explained to the reporter why he considered it important to have scouts recruited from the tribe with whom he was fighting. "Some people say it's wrong to use the people of a tribe against itself, but *pshaw!*—if I can kill one rattlesnake by making another bite him, I shall do it."[34]

Sheridan was singularly unimpressed by Crook's reasoning, never having had much use for Indian scouts, believing them to be fundamentally untrustworthy. Disregarding Crook's explanation, he fumed, "There must be no halfway work in this matter."[35] Two weeks later, still angry at his subordinate's disobedience, he wrote the secretary of war: "[Crook's] neglect to disarm and dismount other bands at the Agency is disapproved, and all the theories in this report [to the AAG] seem to be given as a plea for not having performed what he promised and what was expected of him."[36]

But the deed was done and it would widen the rift between the two former friends and classmates. Up to now, though Sheridan found Crook's performance during the spring and summer campaigns disappointing, he had continued to support him because he regarded him as personally loyal and because he thought they agreed on the management of the Indian problem. Now it seemed that Crook was prepared to go his own way, a course of action Sheridan could not tolerate. In a dispatch on October 30, he mounted an ill-disguised flank attack on his erstwhile friend, reprimanding him for submitting dispatches that were "not sufficiently detailed."[37] In pointedly chastising an officer famous for the cursory nature of his reports, Sheridan could have intended nothing less than a demonstration of his intense displeasure with Crook's decision.

Crook either chose to ignore or was oblivious to Sheridan's pique. He was delighted with the results of his decision. When his column finally departed from Fort Fetterman, among its Indian scouts were seventy-three Arapaho, nine Cheyenne, and seventy-three Oglala and Brule warriors, all enlisted from the White River Agencies, armed with army-issue pistols and carbines, and mounted on ponies seized from the bands of Red Cloud and Red Leaf.[38]

CHAPTER TWENTY-EIGHT

The Second Powder River Expedition

Winter 1876–1877

On October 24, while preparing for his new campaign, Crook assembled the travel-worn veterans of the Big Horn and Yellowstone Expedition on the Camp Robinson parade ground, where they had been reassigned under Colonel Merritt's command to keep watch over the Red Cloud Agency. Praising them for their pluck in the face of extraordinary hardship, the general expressed his gratitude and appreciation, knowing that, as soldiers on the remote frontier, this would probably be the only recognition they would receive.[1] He then turned to the work of assembling their replacements, a force dubbed the Powder River expedition. His objective remained to find and defeat Crazy Horse's Oglalas, recently reported to have moved south of the Yellowstone to hunt buffalo on the Rosebud and the Powder.[2] The general and his officers were not looking for a surrender, but a fight, "to atone and compensate for our trials, hardships and dangers for more than eight months."[3]

The size of the force would reflect both the army's exaggerated perceptions of Sioux military power following the Rosebud and Little Big Horn battles, and its determination to awe the enemy with a demonstration of its overwhelming strength. Over seventeen hundred troops would participate. A number were green recruits, sardonically referred to as "Custer's Avengers," men who had joined up in reaction to the Little Big Horn defeat.[4] The force included Mackenzie's eleven companies of cavalry—over eight hundred horsemen—accompanied by an equal number of infantry, reinforced by four companies of artillery. That latter would serve as foot soldiers, as their guns would have slowed the column down in the rough, roadless country in which they would be campaigning. The infantry would be led by Lieutenant Colonel Richard Irving Dodge, who had commanded the Jenney Expedition's escort the previous year. Well regarded by Crook and more particularly by Lieutenant Bourke, his selection proved fortunate for future historians. As a literate and conscientious diarist, he would provide a running commentary on the campaign from a jaundiced perspective that counterbalanced Bourke's hagiographic writings.[5]

With the troops rode 350 scouts—Indian, mixed-blood, and white. To the Sioux, Cheyennes, and Arapahoes recruited from the agencies were added the North brothers' Pawnees and a contingent of Crows. A Shoshone band would join the column at old Fort Reno. Elderly Chief Washakie, whose rheumatism precluded winter campaigning, had designated his sons to represent him in his stead. Organized by tribe, each band was captained by a white civilian or military officer. While, as Crook had hoped, their presence would prove valuable, the Sioux did not mix well with their traditional enemies, the Pawnees, Shoshones, and Crows, and it required all of Crook's knowledge and skill to cool tempers and prevent mayhem.[6]

This was to be no spartan effort. Neither Crook nor the government had any interest in duplicating the hardships of the Horsemeat March. With substantial appropriations from Congress and in anticipation of the rigors of a winter campaign, the general acquired lavish quantities of various stores and equipment and, according to at least one report, 168 wagons and 400 pack mules to carry them.[7] The troops were issued an elaborate array of winter clothing and equipment that included "heavy underwear; over that a suit of perforated buckskin, a blouse and cardigan jacket; leggings and moccasins (made by the Indians with the hair inside), . . . overcoat . . . heavily lined . . . with fur collar and wristlets, a sealskin cap and gloves." To ensure their warmth at night, the men carried three blankets each and a poncho or buffalo robe, and were to be housed in tents with Sibley stoves to heat them.[8] Ammunition was abundant—250 rounds for each carbine and rifle, and an additional 100 rounds for pistols.

Many wagons carried military equipment but most were loaded with forage and food, ensuring that neither man nor beast would starve, at least for the first thirty days. The column would then be resupplied in the field from the old Fort Reno and Tongue River cantonments. The need for forage for a winter campaign was so overwhelming that Crook ordered grain stripped from the surrounding posts to the extent that they seriously depleted the resources of the region. Unfortunately, the quantity of forage, large as it was, would prove inadequate, eventually crippling the campaign.[9]

Newspaper reporters did not flock to this column as they had during the spring and summer, whether through lack of interest, fear of the weather, or simply happenstance. Only one reporter, Jerry Roche of the *New York Herald*, joined the expedition. But several officers would write articles on the campaign, including paymaster Stanton.[10]

The column departed Camp Robinson on November 1, reaching Fort Laramie after a four-day march. Crook was in a hurry and set the men on the road to Fetterman at first light the following morning. The impetus for his abrupt departure from Laramie seems to have been the receipt of a wire from Sheridan announcing that on October 22, Colonel Miles had successfully engaged Sitting Bull's band. The battle, the lieutenant general enthusiastically informed Crook, would undoubtedly lead to the surrender "of all the hostile Indians belonging to the Missouri River Agencies."[11] His wildly optimistic prediction may well have been calculated to light a fire under Crook, who had now come to view the ambitious and aggressive Miles as his chief rival in the race to achieve victory over the Sioux. But in reality, the impact of Miles's attack was somewhat less than Sheridan imagined. Though the colonel's audacity in attacking almost a thousand Sioux with fewer than four hundred infantry greatly impressed Sitting Bull's followers, only a scattering of Miniconjou and Sans Arc lodges surrendered as a result. The remainder successfully eluded the troops and fled north toward Canada.[12]

On November 7, Crook and his cavalry completed the trek to Fetterman in bitter cold weather. The rest of the expedition trickled in over the next several days. While awaiting them, Crook held the first of several councils with the scouts. Tensions had developed between the rival Pawnees and Sioux over the distribution of the ponies taken from Red Leaf and Red Cloud. Crook intervened to calm the situation, guaranteeing the Lakotas a share of the confiscated ponies and reassuring the agency Indians, concerned about the welfare of their families on the reservation, that they would be well cared for during the campaign.[13]

With temperatures plummeting, the column finally marched out of Fort Fetterman on the 14th, fording the Platte through the ice floes that now drifted downriver, and headed north on the Bozeman Trail. Their destination was Cantonment Reno, which had been constructed near old Fort Reno and would be their first supply base.

After only two days on the trail, Dodge's diary entries began to signal a growing irritation with Crook. Grumpily, he complained that the general gave his Indians and packers the best campsites, leaving [Colonel Ranald] Mackenzie and himself to scramble for what was left. "The Cavy & Infy are nobodies. The Indians & pack mules have all the good places. He scarcely treats Mackenzie & I decently, but he will spend hours chatting pleasantly with an Indian or a dirty scout. . . ."[14] Not content with damning Crook's choice of companions, Dodge, like Davenport before him, railed against the general's supposed hypocrisy, fantasizing that Crook maintained a façade of spartan living while secretly indulging himself with all sorts of luxuries. The man, he wrote, "is a humbug—who hopes to make reputation by assuming qualities foreign to him." Not only that, he continued, "he is the very worst mannered man I have ever seen in his position. Though his ill manners seem to be the result rather of ignorance than of deliberate will—I believe him to be warm hearted—but his estimate of a man will I think be discovered to be founded not on what that man can or will do for the Service, but what he can or will do for Crook." Nevertheless, Dodge managed to find his way to Crook's tent most evenings for a convivial game of whist. And, gradually, his attitude softened.[15]

Manners aside, Crook was all business. The column reached the Fort Reno cantonment on November 18. Intended as a staging area for troops conducting winter patrols into Sioux and Cheyenne hunting grounds, it had been hastily constructed by an advance party under Captain Edwin Pollock about three miles upstream of the ruins of old Fort Reno. It offered little in the way of luxury. The troops were quartered in rude log huts and dugouts excavated in the clay bank on a bend in the river.[16]

From Cantonment Reno, Crook wasted no time in dispatching Sioux and Arapaho scouts north to the Crazy Woman Fork of the Powder in search of Crazy Horse's camp. While awaiting their return,

Crook met with the remaining scouts, including the newly arrived Shoshones, to counsel them regarding their behavior on the campaign, particularly warning against the killing of women and children. He also addressed the continuing friction between the Sioux and Pawnees, ostensibly over the distribution of ponies, but really having more to do with ancient enmities. In his effort to get the tribes to set aside their differences, he was greatly aided by several of the Sioux leaders, particularly Three Bears, who had been among those most upset about the ponies. By offering a Pawnee sergeant the gift of his best pony, this diplomatic warrior did much to defuse the situation and foster amity among the scouts.[17] While the meeting successfully eased tensions between the two historical enemies, whether it would have any impact on the killing of noncombatants remained to be seen.[18]

When Crook's scouts returned from Crazy Woman Fork on November 21, they brought with them a young Cheyenne captive who had been tricked into revealing that Crazy Horse had moved west toward the Big Horns and that the united Cheyenne and Oglala village was now camped on the Rosebud near the June battle site.[19] This bit of intelligence inspired Crook to move his camp to Crazy Woman's Fork, where he planned to leave his wagons and, carrying ten days' rations, make a rapid march against the Oglalas to catch them unawares.[20] But upon reaching the Fork, he obtained additional information that caused him to abruptly change course.

Shortly after sunrise on the 23rd, a figure appeared on a bluff outside the camp waving a white flag. The man was Sitting Bear, an agency Cheyenne. He had just returned from Crazy Horse's camp, where he had been sent by the officers at Fort Laramie to spy on the band and, if possible, induce them to surrender. According to Sitting Bear, Cheyenne scouts had spotted Crook's command and warned Crazy Horse. He further reported that a large Cheyenne village under Chief Morning Star, or Dull Knife as the Sioux knew him, was camped in the Big Horn Mountains not far from Crook's present location.

Having lost the element of surprise with respect to Crazy Horse, Crook decided instead to redirect his attention to the Cheyenne encampment. As speed was essential to catch Dull Knife off guard, he ordered Mackenzie, the scouts, and all but one company of cavalry to move forward as a strike force that same afternoon. He enjoined them to avoid a fight if possible, but in any case, to destroy the village. He anticipated that their mission would take five or six days.[21] While they were away, he and the balance of the column would remain in camp.[22]

Following Mackenzie's departure, the general whiled away the hours by having his officers conduct skirmish drills with the infantrymen, while he rode alone into the countryside around Crazy Woman's Fork, hunting buffalo. When that proved unproductive, he went after rabbits who infested the thick brush in the vicinity. In the evenings, he played whist with Dodge, the latter fuming as he, like Bourke, found Crook's solitary hunting adventures into hostile territory reckless and irresponsible.[23]

On the 26th, a courier rode into the camp to report that Mackenzie's men had attacked and taken Dull Knife's village and most of its ponies. But nearly all of the Indians had managed to escape into the hilly terrain north of the village and, from there, held off his troopers with accurate fire from their long-range rifles. Armed with much-shorter-range cavalry carbines, the cavalrymen had been unable to close with them, and Mackenzie asked that Crook send up the infantry with their long-barreled rifles to break the stalemate.[24] Crook lost no time in wiring Sheridan news of Mackenzie's attack and then ordered Dodge to march his infantry against the village to "take the Indians & finish the matter."[25] Soon after Dodge's departure, the general followed with his headquarters escort, catching up with Dodge after a grueling twelve-hour, twenty-six-mile trek along the Red Fork of the Powder. The march was an exercise in futility because the following day, they picked up Mackenzie's trail and saw that he was on his way back to the Crazy Woman campsite. Assuming this meant that the Cheyennes had fled the area, Crook reversed course and returned to the Crazy Woman, where the colonel awaited him.[26]

Mackenzie's report of the battle showed it was everything that Reynolds's engagement on the Powder River had not been. Though the two battles were fought under similar circumstances, the results were decidedly different. In this case, Crook had relied upon a far cooler and more experienced commander and equipped him with Indian scouts. The scouts, notably absent at the Reynolds fight, made up about one-third of Mackenzie's eleven hundred–man force, and their contribution was critical to the success of the venture.[27] They had guided Mackenzie's column in complete darkness to the Cheyenne camp, which lay in a canyon that could only be entered through a narrow defile, a site so inaccessible that without the scouts, the soldiers never would have found it.[28]

The scouts also played a major role in the ensuing battle. Mackenzie had assumed that a dawn attack would take the Cheyennes completely by surprise. But it should not have. According to Cheyenne accounts, their scouts had spotted the soldiers several days before and knew they were in the vicinity. But they had not moved or prepared a defense because a powerful chief, for reasons best known to himself, had ordered the village to hold an all-night dance. So, as Mackenzie's force gathered for their charge, the Cheyennes were just retiring wearily to their lodges after dancing the night away, unprepared for the storm that was about to engulf them.[29]

With the Indians still awake, a surreptitious predawn attempt to surround the encampment prior to an attack would have been futile. Instead, Mackenzie ordered an immediate charge with his scouts in the van. In a nod to Crook's instructions, he ordered them not to fire on the tribesmen unless the Indians fired first. Charging through the defile, they emerged on an open plain bisected by a stream. The command divided as the Pawnees followed the stream's left bank into the camp while the troopers held the ground to the right.[30]

Over twelve hundred Indians, including about three hundred warriors, were in the village. They occupied 173 lodges on both sides of the stream, scattered among the leafless cottonwoods that dotted the canyon bottom. Of course, they immediately began firing at the charging intruders, triggering an eager response from the soldiers and scouts.[31] Slowed by rough terrain and a muddy creek bottom, the attackers were unable to prevent the warriors from getting the women and children to safety in the hills and ravines at the north end of the village. But the attack had come so swiftly that the fleeing warriors had only enough time to snatch up their rifles and some ammunition. Very few were able to grab a buffalo robe or blanket to protect their families from the biting cold. As soldiers and Pawnees swept into the village, several Cheyennes had frantically attempted to save the pony herd by forming a defensive line in a ravine, firing on the oncoming soldiers to slow the attack. Most of these warriors were soon killed and the herd captured, but at the cost of the command's heaviest losses, including a highly regarded first lieutenant, John McKinney, mortally wounded at this time.[32]

Within fifteen minutes of the initial attack, most of the Cheyenne warriors had withdrawn into the hills and gullies to the north. From this vantage point, beyond the range of cavalry carbines, they poured accurate fire on the soldiers and auxiliaries. Mackenzie had no hesitancy about personally exposing himself to enemy fire, but he had no wish to incur unnecessary casualties in a frontal assault on these well-entrenched positions. Consequently, he had dispatched the courier to Crook requesting infantry reinforcements. He then moved the captured pony herd, about six hundred mounts, to the rear and ordered the destruction of the village.[33]

The results met Crook's fondest hopes for a winter campaign. Burning the villages and confiscating the horses of a nomadic people had a devastating impact on them, particularly in winter. The twin disasters robbed the Indians of their mobility and means to fight, and left them destitute and demoralized, struggling to survive in the subzero temperatures that prevailed on the northern plains at this time of year. Dull Knife's village was particularly affluent, making the pain of destruction so much worse. Bourke enthused that, "never had so rich and complete a prize fallen into the hands of the Regular Army from the day of its first organization." The soldiers and scouts carried off great quantities of buffalo robes and skins, looting a few objects that took their fancy. As Bourke remarked with notably less enthusiasm, they destroyed the rest, "wiping off the face of the earth many products of aboriginal taste and industry which would have been gems in the cabinets of museums." Using stored buffalo fat as an accelerant, the troops torched the lodges, broke surviving lodge poles into splinters, burned metal tools and weapons to destroy their temper, knocked the bottoms from kettles, pans, and canteens, smashed saddles, slashed bridles, and broke bits, tossing the pieces on what Bourke called "the funeral pyres of Cheyenne glory."[34]

As had been the case at Slim Buttes, the fierce energy with which the troopers and scouts carried out their task was fueled by the discovery of many relics of the Custer and Rosebud fights and other bloody encounters with whites—a Seventh Cavalry guidon and roster, saddles, nosebags, curry combs, photos, a gold pencil case, silver watch, and sums of money, both coin and paper. A bloodstained fringed shirt, thought to have belonged to Tom Custer, was unearthed in one of the tipis. The Pawnees, and more particularly the Shoshones, found their own motivation in grisly trophies of past victories over their people—a necklace adorned with human fingers, numerous scalps, including one identified as having been taken from the young Shoshone herder killed at the Rosebud, a bag filled with the right hands of twelve Shoshone babies, and the hand and arm of what was thought to have been a Shoshone woman.[35]

From their positions in the ravines and breaks north of the camp, the Cheyennes viewed the devastation, bitterly noting that among the perpetrators were fellow tribesmen and former allies. In desperation, they called out to the Cheyenne, Lakota, and Arapaho scouts, "Go home, you have no business here. We can whip the white soldiers alone, but can't fight you, too." Their words went unheeded. So they fought on, though low on ammunition.[36]

By late afternoon, the fighting had reached a stalemate, neither side able to gain an advantage. Mackenzie's forces had suffered six killed (an additional trooper died on the way back to camp) and twenty-two wounded, including a Shoshone scout. Cheyenne casualties, more difficult to estimate, were later said to exceed a hundred dead or wounded.[37] As night fell, the temperature plunged to between twenty-five and thirty below zero and it began to snow heavily. While the soldiers and scouts, warmed by the robes and blankets left by their fleeing enemy, dined on captured buffalo meat, the Cheyennes huddled in their hillside redoubts, half-naked, barefoot, unprotected from the killing cold. For warmth, they slaughtered several ponies, slicing open their bellies to allow the women and children to warm their hands and feet in the steaming entrails. Despite such desperate measures, several babies and youngsters died of exposure that night and in the days that followed.[38]

At sunrise, the soldiers completed the destruction of the village, loaded the wounded on travois, and headed out through deep snow on the return march to rejoin Crook's command. Watching from concealed positions in the surrounding hills, the surviving Cheyenne chiefs acknowledged the hopelessness of their position and decided to withdraw over the mountain northward, scattering into ever smaller bands to evade capture. Only a few rode, the rest walked, most without footwear, robes, or blankets, shepherding their women, children, and aged through deep snow and biting wind. Their ordeal lasted eleven days until they reached Crazy Horse's camp on the Tongue.[39]

The Oglalas did what they could to care for them, but they had little to share. Some of the Cheyennes, noting the scant rations and rude accommodations, perceived in them a lack of generosity. Their lingering bitterness would explain their later decision to volunteer as scouts in the army's final campaign against Crazy Horse.[40] With no alternative, the refugees would remain with the Oglalas over the winter, participating in yet another battle in the Wolf Mountains and suffering yet another defeat. While some were briefly able to resume their lives as free-roaming Indians of the Plains, most would surrender the following spring.[41] Cheyenne participation in the Sioux War, marked by an accumulation of devastating encounters with the white soldiers, had come to an end.

Overall, Crook was pleased with Mackenzie's report, characterizing the attack and its aftermath in a dispatch to Sheridan as "brilliant achievements."[42] Inexplicably, despite Three Stars' fulsome praise, Mackenzie reacted by sinking into a deep depression, reproaching himself for his "defeat" at the Indian village. Dodge confided to his diary that "he talked more like a crazy man than the sane Comdr of a splendid body of Cavalry," a prophetic insight considering that insanity would soon overwhelm the colonel. Deeply troubled by Mackenzie's depression and not knowing what else to do, Crook attempted to cheer him up with conversation and a game of whist. This rudimentary therapy may have had a positive effect, for over the next several weeks, Mackenzie's mood seemed to improve.[43]

As the expedition progressed, Dodge complained bitterly to his diary of Crook's extreme reticence. He provided so little information to his subordinates that they were unable to plan their daily schedules. The colonel's exasperation peaked when, on December 1, the general entered Dodge's tent unannounced while the latter was speculating with Mackenzie about Crook's next move and airing his usual complaints about being left in the dark. The embarrassed colonel "asked [Crook] to sit, but he said, 'I've only a moment to stay. You will march tomorrow & should make arrangements tonight for crossing the river.' 'What River?' I asked. 'This' he replied. I said 'I have heard we are to march back to Reno. Is it so?' He said, 'Yes.' Just then, Mackenzie made a motion as if to ask a question, when Crook abruptly left the tent without saying 'by your leave, or D—— your soul or any such pleasantry." Dodge was furious. The following evening, after a difficult march, the command arrived back at Cantonment Reno, as Crook had promised. Dodge, exhausted from the ride, had planned to sleep in the next morning, relying on Crook's announcement that it would be a day of rest. Instead, he was awakened at 7 A.M. and ordered to hit the trail. The exasperated colonel could only conclude that "[Crook] really does not know ahead what he intends to do. Makes up his mind at the last moment and then acts at once—expecting everybody else to do the same."[44]

It was on this morning that the Shoshones chose to bid farewell to the column. They had been overcome with grief and apprehension ever since the grisly discovery of the remains of their tribesmen in the Cheyenne camp. Fearing that these relics had been obtained on a recent raid, they were anxious to see to the safety of their families. Immediately prior to their departure, the scouts lined up in parade formation and presented Crook and various other members of the command with mementos of the campaign, artifacts looted from the Cheyenne village.[45]

On December 4, "[a] bad camp, water and grass miserable" put Dodge, who remained ignorant of Crook's intentions, in a foul temper; his mood only deepened when the general announced his intention to remain at this forlorn site for two additional days. By doing so, he hoped to avoid being caught on the open plains in an impending blizzard, but Dodge interpreted the sudden change in plans as a reaffirmation that "[Crook] has [no] definite plan or expectation." Enough was enough. Gathering his courage, the colonel approached Crook in his tent in what he fully anticipated would be a fruitless attempt to learn the general's plans for the next thirty days. To Dodge's "surprise and pleasure," Crook responded with uncharacteristic openness. Calmly, as if it were an everyday occurrence, he fully explained his agenda for the next month. As Crook explained his intentions, illustrating them on maps of the area, Dodge realized that he had devoted a great deal of thought to developing a strategy, and the necessary logistics, for the campaign against Crazy Horse's band. It made perfect sense.[46]

In precise terms, Crook explained that he had concluded that after Mackenzie's attack, Crazy Horse would not remain on the Tongue, but would probably flee northeast into the badlands around Slim Buttes. After resupplying the column at the cantonment, the general intended to march to the Belle Fourche, a little over midway between his present camp and the area where he suspected the Oglala village lay. From there, he would dispatch his scouts and spies to ascertain Crazy Horse's exact whereabouts and then attack him.[47] But logistics complicated his plan. With snow covering the grass, the column needed a minimum of 30,000 pounds of grain per day. Congress had failed to appropriate sufficient funds to purchase that quantity, and what was available could not be moved through the heavy snows that blocked the trails to Fort Fetterman and thence to the field. As a result, Crook anticipated a severe shortfall in the supply that ultimately would force him to terminate the expedition. But, for now, he intended to make at least a show of strength to demonstrate "that [the hostiles] are having the hot end of the poker"—that they were not safe, even in their winter quarters.[48]

As Crook predicted, the forage situation proved intractable. The progressive weakening of the stock due to poor nutrition, coupled with increasingly inclement weather and the failure of the Indian scouts and spies to locate Crazy Horse's village, undermined the column's ability to remain in the field.[49] But in the end, it was Sheridan who dealt the campaign its deathblow. In a dispatch received on December 19, he criticized Crook for substantially overspending his monthly appropriation, primarily for feed purchases. As Bourke noted in his diary, this meant that the campaign "must terminate speedily."[50]

Accompanying Sheridan's message was word that Major Julius Mason, the commanding officer at Red Cloud, had begun disarming and confiscating the ponies of the Indians whom Crook had previously exempted as a reward for their loyalty. Convinced that Sheridan was behind the move, Crook feared it would sabotage not only his present relations with the Arapahoes, Cheyennes, and Sioux who served faithfully on this campaign, but his future plans for assimilating the tribes into white society. According to Dodge, the news "completely knocked the 'old man' up." "He knows more about the management of Indians than Sheridan will ever know," Dodge allowed, "& it is very hard after working so long & indefatigably to get things in shape, to have all overturned in a moment."[51]

Stripped of other options, a disappointed Crook wearily announced that the column would begin its countermarch to Fetterman the next day.[52] Unlike their commander, Crook's officers and men, Indians and white, were delighted; thoroughly sick of winter campaigning, they were eager to return to their posts.[53] Their elation was short-lived.

Extreme cold, icy trails, and poor water marked the return journey. Christmas Day was the worst of the trip. While the expedition's two mercury thermometers froze at 26 degrees below, an alcohol thermometer at nearby Deadwood recorded forty below. To Bourke, it seemed as though "the fury of the elements . . . [was] eager to devour us. Beards, moustaches, and eye-lashes were frozen masses of ice. The keen air was filled with minute crystals, each cutting the tender skin like a razor, while feet and hands ached as if beaten with clubs."[54] Crook accompanied the column until the 28th and then departed for Cheyenne, where he faced the unpleasant duty of attending Colonel Reynolds's court-martial scheduled for January 5. The remainder of his troops continued on to Fetterman, leaving various contingents, both Indian and white, along the way.

Given the jaundiced views he recorded in his diary during the campaign, in the last analysis, Colonel Dodge's assessment of the expedition's impact was surprisingly positive.

> Taken in its entirety, our campaign has been a marked success. The Cheyenne have received a blow such as they have never had before, & from which they will not soon recover. While the hostile Sioux under Crazy Horse have been compelled . . . to leave the game region of the Rosebud in which they had pitched their winter camp, and to take refuge in the barren inhospitable and comparatively gameless bad land of the Little Missouri. They have learned by sad experience that at no time & in no place are they safe from the pursuit of the Troops.[55]

Dodge's words would prove prescient. While Crook's winter campaign did not cause the immediate collapse of Indian resistance, the destruction of Dull Knife's village, together with Colonel Miles's Yellowstone campaign into the heart of Sitting Bull's hunting grounds (see Chapter 29), had a cumulative demoralizing effect that weakened the resistance of the bands. This would become apparent the following spring.

Despite his several grievances against the general, all dutifully recorded in his diary, in the end, Dodge, an acute observer of human nature, was able to summon the objectivity to provide an insightful and, overall, positive summary of his commander's character and attainments. As his commentary was confined to the pages of his diary, his opinions were more candid than would otherwise be the case for a military officer writing about his superior. For that reason alone, his observations deserve careful attention.

> [Crook] has a most wonderful knowledge of the Indian character & this knowledge gives him a power over them which I have never before seen possessed by any one. Nor can I for the life of me understand it, even after seeing him time & again among the Indians & holding intercourse with them. Among Indians eloquence is a great power. All their instructions must necessarily be oral. Manner also has influence. Genl C. has the worst manner I ever saw—He has generally, very little to say at any "talk" and that little is said in a few words, his eyes downcast, his hands in the pockets of his old gray pants—voice low & hesitating—& in all respects he looks & acts far more like a schoolboy trying to fabricate an excuse for delinquency than like a general comdg an army.
>
> In spite of all this there is no shadow of a doubt as to the high estimation in which he is held by the Indians. He is a good strategist, has wonderful tenacity of purpose, will & pluck, & is entirely careless of his personal discomfort. He lacks but one thing to be a very great man—that is *Administrative ability.*
>
> He can decide how many & what troops to take into the field with him, but there his power ends. How to fit them out, & care for them afterwards is a problem, which, to him, has no solution. His ignorance of such things is remarkable & painful. It is even ludicrous for he carries it to such an extent, as to regard with the most profound admiration any man who evinces even a moderate ability in this direction. He must be fully aware of his own deficiency in this respect for having selected officers to do this work for him, he never interferes in any way, by order or suggestion, & when he gets hold of a man who does tolerably well, he can never admire him sufficiently or praise him enough. This would be admirable did he only get hold of first class men, but though a fair judge of human nature, he yet in the nature of things sometimes gets a man unequal to his work. . . . On the purely Military Organization of our

> Winter Expedition, I have no comments to make, except that at its start, General C had not yet succeeded in divesting himself of a certain contempt for—or rather an undervaluing of the Infantry Arm.[56]

As one might expect, Dodge aimed his most telling barbs at the general's apparent unwillingness to share his plans and strategies with his subordinates. Prior to the winter campaign, the colonel wrote, Crook failed to inform his Omaha staff, responsible for arranging logistics for the column, of the size of the force he intended to take on the expedition, how long he expected to be out, and where his base of operations would be. As a consequence, they were unable to determine the quantity of supplies needed or the locations to which they should be sent. According to Dodge, the staff had to extrapolate and aggregate this information from copies of orders issued by Crook's aides to the various companies who took part in the expedition. Before leaving Omaha to join the column, Dodge quoted Crook's adjutant general as pleading with him [Dodge] to keep the adjutant informed of the column's size, "'for,' he said, 'we are now working entirely in the dark & by guess, & any item you may give us may be of great service to us & you.'" However, while for Dodge, Crook's reticence may have created logistical problems, at least he no longer saw it as an indication of ignorance or a failure to plan.[57]

More surprising was Dodge's criticism of Crook's oversight of the supply train, given the general's reputation as a master of pack train management. Bourke, in an article on the winter expedition, had characterized Crook as a virtuoso in this area of command, applauding his packers for attending "with an assiduity almost devotion to the wants of the animals under their care."[58] Dodge had a markedly different view. He wrote on several occasions that Crook appeared to care nothing for his stock, relentlessly pushing his column forward regardless of the impact on their fitness. As a result, Dodge thought their condition was deplorable—half-starved and nearly played out from long hours in harness and poor care by the packers. At one point, he noted, "it will be a miracle if more than half of us do not have to walk back." His concern led him to confront Crook, telling him "of [the mules'] condition, of their lack of food, of their constant work & no care." Crook responded that he was aware of the situation, but refused to discuss it further, cryptically noting that "he had a certain problem to work out & had to do the best he could with his materials."[59]

The packers became Colonel Dodge's favorite whipping boys. In addition to their poor treatment of the animals, he accused them of carrying so much in the way of rations and personal conveniences (almost three times the amount carried by the troops) that they left insufficient room in the wagons for the forage needed for the livestock. He held Crook responsible for tolerating this situation, insisting that he was "too tender with his teamsters," failing "to force them to do the extra work needed to ensure better care of the stock. . . ."[60] Reconsidering, Dodge later concluded that the fault really lay with the teamsters and the quartermaster, Captain John V. Furey, who seemed to make no effort to control them. But in the final analysis, he believed Crook accountable for not properly ensuring that the packers toed the line.[61]

In all likelihood, Dodge had put his finger on a serious problem, one that may have been unique to the summer and winter campaigns of 1876. Indeed, the teamsters and mule skinners, civilian employees long favored by Crook, had grown accustomed to the privileged position he accorded them. Taking advantage of his good nature and a weak quartermaster, they may have gotten lazy and self-indulgent. There was evidence from multiple sources that they were better supplied with food and clothing than the soldiers, probably as a consequence of their far higher pay. However, deep in Indian country, with the command entirely dependent on their skills and experience, they acquired a degree of immunity from discipline, particularly as they were known to have the general's favor. Any attempt to punish one might result in the mass resignation of the lot, leaving the expedition stranded.[62] Perhaps this was what Crook had referred to when he told Dodge he had a "certain problem" that he had to work out.

CHAPTER TWENTY-NINE

Surrender

January–May 1877

On an afternoon in May 1877, expectant tribesmen, Indian police, and blue-coated soldiers gathered in clusters on the greening prairie that surrounded the stockade and outbuildings of the Red Cloud Agency, their eyes fixed on the pine-covered buttes that framed their northern horizon. Suddenly, a ripple of motion, a turning of heads, a straightening of backs, alerted the crowd to movement on the ridgeline. A line of horsemen, ant-like in the distance, appeared on the trail leading over the hills and wound its way slowly down the near slope into the valley. As the riders neared the agency, the waiting crowd could distinguish the figure of Lieutenant William Philo Clark, White Hat to the Oglalas, followed by Chief Red Cloud and a squad of Indian police, their faces frozen into dignified masks. Behind them rode a warrior on a white horse. Of medium size and slight build, he wore a single feather braided into his hair. All knew that this was Crazy Horse, leader of the Oglala resisters, at the head of his warriors and trailed by the women, children, and tribal elders of the band, all clad in their most colorful garb. Some rode; others came afoot, leading their mounts, their wealth lashed to travois poles or stuffed into painted buffalo skin parfleches thrown across their ponies' withers. The agency Indians, gathered around the weathered wooden outbuildings, observed with satisfaction, and not a little envy, the dignified spectacle they presented. Over eleven hundred proud Indians paraded in their finery, the sun reflecting off the beads and metal ornaments on their persons and clothing, filling the air with the measured chanting of the Oglala peace song. It seemed more a show of victory than a surrender; but for all intents and purposes, it signaled the end of the Great Sioux war.[1]

Lieutenant Clark, the officer in the white hat, was another of the bright young men selected by Crook to serve as his aides. Officially designated chief of scouts at Camp Robinson, his primary function was to serve as the general's eyes and ears on the reservation. His obvious interest in Indian folkways had won him the trust of the agency Sioux chiefs, and earned him the right to welcome Crazy Horse and his people to the White River Agencies. He had ridden out to meet the band with wagonloads of provisions for the near-starving column. In return, He Dog, the war chief's most trusted ally, had presented Clark with a war bonnet and scalp shirt, a buffalo robe, and a fine pony, as tokens of goodwill and friendship. Then, the young lieutenant had ridden at Crazy Horse's side on the last leg of the long journey into captivity.[2]

Now, while the women set up their tipis in a large crescent along the banks of the White River, Clark's troopers carried out Sheridan's orders, confiscating the warriors' mounts, over 2,200 in number, and their guns, collecting 170 rifles, carbines, and pistols belonging to the 300 fighting members of the band. Leaving nothing to chance during this delicate maneuver, Clark had stationed a company of Cheyenne scouts behind a nearby hill in case of trouble. But the warriors offered no resistance, though it can be assumed that some warily secreted weapons against a future threat.[3]

Ironically, Crook, the man ultimately responsible for engineering this spectacle, was absent. He was in Washington, arguing against the removal of the Oglalas and Brules to agencies on the Missouri River or to Indian Territory, the government's dumping ground for its unwanted aboriginal peoples. Crook's Washington visit, while sincerely motivated by his opposition to removal, had been part of a bargain to gain Spotted Tail's assistance in convincing his nephew, Crazy Horse, to bring his people peacefully into the reservation. To Crook, the chief's surrender was a key element in his campaign to secure the honor of attaining victory in the Sioux War, an objective that had involved him in a bitter competition with his fellow officer, Colonel Nelson Appleton Miles.

Though they had fought in some of the same battles during the Civil War, no record exists of Colonel Miles meeting George Crook face to face until the late summer of '76 when, commanding the Fifth Infantry, the colonel had joined Crook and Terry on the Yellowstone. Nevertheless, he had viewed the Gray Fox as a rival ever since the latter's appointment to brigadier general in Arizona in 1871, having been one of the colonels passed over by the War Department in order to secure Crook's promotion.[4] He was further irked when Crook was appointed commanding general of the Platte, believing Crook's service in Arizona was overrated and that he, himself, was far more qualified for the position.[5]

Miles had been employed as a clerk in his uncle's crockery establishment in Boston when the Civil War broke out. Dreaming of glory, he had raised a regiment that he envisioned leading into battle. His hopes were dashed when another man was given the position, and he was demoted from captain to lieutenant.[6] But he swallowed his disappointment and, by dint of his ability, courage, and initiative in combat, together with a talent for political maneuvering and self-promotion, rose rapidly through the ranks, becoming a major general by the age of twenty-six. He had an avid supporter in General Sheridan, with whom he shared several qualities, including his bulldog aggressiveness, tenacity in combat, towering ambition, and unabashed self-regard.

Awarded the rank of colonel after the war, he served briefly as Jefferson Davis's jailer and married the daughter of John Sherman, a US senator and brother of William Tecumseh Sherman, commanding general of the post–Civil War army.[7] He exploited this connection relentlessly, but with questionable success. He was a prolific letter writer, and his correspondence with his spouse and powerful in-laws starkly reveals a swollen ego, boundless ambition, and a vindictiveness that engaged him in the bitter rivalry with George Crook that redounded to the credit of neither man.[8]

Assigned to Fort Hayes in the spring of 1869, he assumed command of the Fifth Regiment of Infantry. There he joined George Custer, the ranking officer of the Seventh Cavalry at the same post. The two officers became fast friends, hardly surprising, as they were remarkably similar in character. While stationed at Hayes, Miles earned his credentials as an Indian fighter in the Red River War, a series of engagements that ultimately destroyed the resistance of the southern tribes and led the colonel to conclude that Indians needed a firm hand and a strong dose of civilization.[9]

Upon his transfer to Terry's command on the Yellowstone, Miles quickly concluded that he was far better suited to lead the campaign against the Sioux than either Terry or Crook. Though a close friend of Terry's, Miles had little patience with the scholarly general as a field commander, finding him too slow and indecisive and lacking enthusiasm for the campaign. He had even less use for Crook, recording his impressions in a series of letters to his wife. "General Crook was going to get ready to move—he has been doing that for a year." and, "General Crook makes no comments or gives General Terry any information." And "we lost seven days in coming up, we will lose at least five here [on the Rosebud] and during this time I presume Crook will make his move so that the same miserable lack of cooperation will be witnessed. No one knows where Crook is or the Indians. . . ." His contempt for the man seemed boundless; he sarcastically described one of his "magnificent" scouting expeditions as being as "senseless and ill-advised as it was fruitless."[10]

Ultimately, Terry, possibly tiring of Miles's attitude, acceded to his request for an independent command, and set him to patrolling the fords on the Yellowstone to prevent the escape of Sitting Bull's people to the north.[11] For several weeks, while Crook pushed grimly southward toward the Black Hills on the Hunger March, Miles had steamed up the Yellowstone on board the paddle wheeler, *Far West*, encountering some Indians but failing to engage them. In early September, Sheridan had ordered the construction of posts along the Yellowstone to deny the Sioux their fall and winter hunting grounds with the aim of starving them into submission. The task of building and garrisoning a cantonment at the confluence of the Tongue and the Yellowstone fell to Miles.

At the end of that dismal summer, as Crook prepared and mounted his elaborate fall expedition against Crazy Horse, Miles pursued his own operations against Sitting Bull's northern Lakotas, known to be hunting in his area of responsibility. Experience had convinced Miles, like Crook, "that winter was the best time for subjugating . . . Indians."[12] Of his own troops, Miles later exulted, "they expected us to hive up, but we were not the hiving kind."[13] And no one could deny the truth of these words. Using the primitive Tongue River cantonment, soon to be renamed Fort Keogh, as a base, Miles deployed his

Fifth Infantry, reinforced by two additional companies of foot soldiers from the Twenty-Second, into the frigid snow-covered countryside. Together with an additional six companies of the Twenty-Second stationed at Glendive Creek and an equal number of infantry from Fort Buford on the Missouri, Miles's small force represented the government's entire military presence in the vast hunting grounds north of the Yellowstone.[14] Arrayed against him were a loose coalition of several thousand northern Sioux—Hunkpapas, Miniconjous, and Sans Arcs—under Sitting Bull. They were joined by an influx of warriors who had recently fled the Missouri River Agencies after hearing that the military planned to confiscate their guns and ponies, and by the Oglalas and Cheyennes under Crazy Horse.[15]

In mid-October, Sitting Bull's warriors attacked one of Miles's supply trains, and the colonel retaliated. Leading a force of 394 riflemen, reinforced by an artillery piece, he caught up with the Sioux two days after the raid. Facing a band of about a thousand warriors, he offered to talk. Sitting Bull agreed, and Miles showed up wrapped in a huge winter overcoat of bearskin, moving the Indians to christen him "Bear Coat."[16] The encounter marked "the first occasion in the Sioux War that a federal representative had confronted a major leader of the non-treaty bands," though the participants appeared unimpressed by the historical import of the moment.[17] The discussions were rancorous, neither side showing any willingness to budge from its inflexible position. Sitting Bull only wished that the whites immediately depart his hunting grounds while Miles, speaking for Sheridan, countered that the Sioux must surrender their weapons and ponies and permanently remove to the reservation. In return the government would provide rations and amnesty for past sins.[18]

With the talks stalemated, Miles shifted abruptly to the offensive. His disciplined infantry, reinforced by his cannon, drove the more numerous Sioux from the field, forcing them to abandon large amounts of food, equipment, and even some ponies. The troops continued their pursuit for three days and were rewarded when a majority of the Indians, low on both ammunition and food, broke away from Sitting Bull and agreed to a parley. While some four hundred loyalist Hunkpapas fled before the meeting, several major chiefs and two thousand of their followers agreed to surrender. As Miles could not guard them and continue his campaign against Sitting Bull, he took five of their chiefs hostage to guarantee that their people would adhere to the terms of the surrender.[19]

But the agreement did not hold. Promises made on both sides were broken, and fewer than forty lodges actually surrendered at the Cheyenne River Agency, the remainder joining Crazy Horse. Much later, one of the Indian leaders admitted that his people had only acquiesced to Miles's terms as a ruse to buy time to go on a buffalo hunt. Miles, for his part, had intentionally made pledges beyond his authority to keep, establishing a pattern that would characterize his negotiating tactics for the remainder of the Sioux War and later in Arizona.[20]

Despite the breakdown of the surrender agreement, Miles had dealt a hard blow to the Sioux, while enhancing his own reputation as an aggressive Indian fighter. He had confirmed that trained and conditioned infantry could successfully pursue and defeat mounted Indians on their own terrain, even in winter. In so doing, his tough walks-a-heaps had demoralized Sitting Bull's followers and greatly eroded the chief's prestige by demonstrating the fragility of his coalition and his inability to protect his people.

In a letter to his wife, Miles boasted of his successes, contrasting them with Crook's. "From the reports of the disgraceful failures of late I judge that the country sooner or later will understand the difference between doing something and doing nothing."[21] To Sherman, he announced his intentions to continue hunting the Sioux on foot, advising the bemused commander-in-chief, "If you expect me to be successful, see that I am supported or give me command of this whole region and I will soon end this Sioux war, and I would be very glad to govern them afterwards."[22]

Miles continued his aggressive pursuit of Sitting Bull's people despite subzero temperature and blizzard conditions, combing the tributaries of the Missouri in search of the northerners' encampment. In December, one of his columns found and destroyed it, driving the occupants into the deep snows to seek shelter with Crazy Horse's Oglalas.[23] Unfortunately, they arrived at Crazy Horse's village at almost the same time as the refugees from Dull Knife's village. These extra mouths to feed severely strained the Oglalas' meager food reserves, much diminished by a poor fall hunt.[24] Close to starvation and hounded by the army, elements within the camp, led by the Oglala chief Sitting Bull of the South, sent a peace delegation to meet with General Miles. The effort failed after the delegation was attacked by vengeful Crow scouts who killed five of the Sioux leaders. An angry Miles immediately disarmed the Crows, turning twelve of their ponies over to the Sioux as reparations. But the damage had been done. Crazy Horse, who had opposed the peace initiative, now imposed harsh discipline on his people to prevent any further efforts to surrender, and reopened hostilities with harassing raids on the Tongue River cantonment.[25]

Miles retaliated. Despite temperatures hovering at thirty below and continued snowfall, his troops tracked the Oglalas south, and on January 8, in the foothills of the Wolf Mountains along the Tongue, engaged them and their Cheyenne allies in a desperate pitched battle in a blinding blizzard. The conflict raged for several hours until the Indians, running low on ammunition and unable to maintain contact with the enemy in the blowing snow, withdrew from the field. The soldiers followed, but ultimately gave up the pursuit, overwhelmed by cold and exhaustion. Despite a huge expenditure of ammunition and the intensity of the fighting, there were few casualties on either side.[26] Low on supplies, the force returned to the cantonment, ending the winter campaign. Miles eagerly proclaimed the battle a victory, pronouncing it "one of the most successful in [the] history of Indian warfare."[27]

While far from the triumph that Miles proclaimed it, the Wolf Mountain fight continued the disintegration of the great coalition of Teton Sioux and Cheyennes that had held the army at bay over the spring, summer, and early fall. Their cohesiveness dissolved under the combined weight of savage winter weather, persistent campaigning by Crook and Miles, and finally, the temptations afforded by diplomatic initiatives from the agencies.[28] Though Sitting Bull and Crazy Horse had fought with courage and skill, the fighting had cost them most of their winter clothing, blankets, lodges, and the vital store of nourishing dried food that would, under normal circumstances, have allowed them to weather the winter months.[29] In the process, their prestige had eroded, rendering Crazy Horse, in particular, less able to hold his people on a path of resistance, while the peace faction, despite the setback suffered when its leaders had been murdered by the Crows, grew in influence. Now, as the coalition weakened, each tribal unit felt freer to pursue its own ends, the Oglalas and Cheyennes moving east to the Little Powder, the Miniconjous and Sans Arcs to the Little Missouri, while the Hunkpapas followed Sitting Bull into Canada.

Word traveled slowly on the northern plains in winter, and Crook did not learn of Miles's Wolf Mountains victory until after his return from his winter campaign, reading of it in the newspapers on February 7 at Camp Robinson.[30] To the weary Three Stars, the news must have seemed a confirmation of Sheridan's November 5 telegram, trumpeting Miles's earlier triumph over Sitting Bull and predicting the imminent surrender of all the Indians from the Missouri River Agencies. Coming close on the heels of the Reynolds and Moore courts-martial in January, word of Miles's success at the Wolf Mountains must have left Crook worrying whether Sheridan now compared his performance to the colonel's and found it wanting. It was certainly apparent to Crook that the ambitious Miles was bent on winning exclusive recognition for ending the Sioux War. Crook's staff, reflecting their commander's mood, was plunged into gloom. "The newspapers of this date," Bourke wrote in his diary, "were blazoned with the wonderful achievements of General Miles' command on the Tongue river; to reason from the accounts we read, it was vain to hope for any further chance of distinction. Miles had evidently whipped the last of the Indian bands into fragments: or at least, so his telegraphic dispatches asserted. Still we hope for the best."[31]

News of Miles's successes, together with intelligence that Crazy Horse's people had now descended to a level of destitution and demoralization conducive to their surrender, energized Crook to mount his own peace initiative. Up to now, he had been fixed on a military solution to the war. A decisive engagement with Crazy Horse had been his Holy Grail since his initial expedition to the Powder River. Following the Dull Knife fight, he had brought his troops into winter camp, with the expectation that come spring, he would launch another expedition against the Sioux, the idea of a negotiated settlement of the war far from his mind. But in early January, Major Julius Mason, commanding officer of Camp Sheridan at the Spotted Tail Agency, alerted him to a possible alternative.

The previous month, on his own initiative, Mason had sent out his own peace feelers. But the mission was poorly timed. The two Miniconjou sub-chiefs who carried his proposal arrived at Crazy Horse's camp only days after the Crow attack on the peace delegation. Further, they could only offer the army's usual terms, unconditional surrender and the attendant loss of guns and ponies, in return for assurances of amnesty for the Custer defeat. Crazy Horse dismissed these conditions out of hand and, displaying his new militancy, issued orders that, if any of his people attempted to surrender, he would kill their ponies and confiscate their guns. Crazy Horse's harsh reaction drove a wedge between his militant followers and more accommodating non-Oglala factions.[32] Prominent among those favoring peace were the Cheyennes, who had lost the most in the war and were resentful of what they regarded as the Oglalas' lack of hospitality. Mason's spies and a trickle of warriors returning to the agencies carried word of the rift in Crazy Horse's encampment back to Camp Sheridan. They also reported that a peace initiative might be welcomed if it came from Spotted Tail, the agency chief most trusted and respected by the northern Lakota. On January 6, Mason telegraphed Crook in Omaha, requesting permission to ask Old Spot, with whom he had developed a close relationship, to carry peace proposals to the chief's nephew, Crazy Horse.[33]

Spotted Tail had led the Brules since 1865, guiding them through the tumultuous period of Sioux relations with the white man that resulted in their confinement to a reservation a fraction of the size of the country they had once proudly occupied. Though a redoubtable warrior—during his fighting years, he counted twenty-eight coups against enemies both white and Indian—his trips to the East had taught him that the whites were far too numerous and powerful to overcome in battle. Consequently, he had become a staunch advocate of peace. Considered "perfectly loyal to the government" by the military,[34] sometimes called a collaborator by his own people, in reality, he was a traditionalist who intelligently employed diplomacy to preserve what he could of native culture, to slow government attempts to force the Lakotas onto the white man's road, and to prevent their removal to distant reservations.[35] His people repaid his effectiveness with loyalty. During the Great Sioux War of 1876–77, the Brules remained at peace, and very few joined the northerners in the Powder River country.

In the halcyon summer of the war, when the Sioux and Cheyennes seemed able to check the army's every move, Spotted Tail's popularity with the war faction, particularly with such hardliners as Crazy Horse, ebbed, while his star rose among the whites who affectionately, if patronizingly, called him "Old Spot." Crook, in particular, contrasting the chief's behavior with that of the more fractious Red Cloud, held him in high regard. The previous fall, he had appointed him over Red Cloud as head chief of both Oglala and Brule Agencies.[36] Though this action caused a rift between the two Lakota leaders, it solidified Spotted Tail's importance as an Indian leader and spokesman.

After Crook's return from the Powder River in December, he spent much time at Camps Robinson and Sheridan and shared his mess with the Brule chief on many occasions. Bourke, who often attended these meals, "found Spotted Tail a man of great dignity, but at all moments easy and affable in manner; not hard to please, sharp as a briar, and extremely witty. . . . His conversational powers were of a high order, his views carefully formed, clearly expressed." Bourke concluded that he "was one of the great men of this country, bar none, red, white, black or yellow."[37]

Already invested in Spotted Tail's loyalty and effectiveness, Crook quickly seized on Mason's idea of using him as an emissary to Crazy Horse. But the chief was not yet prepared to leap at the offer. A shrewd negotiator, he recognized that the need for his assistance as a peacemaker might give him leverage to force cancellation of the government's plans to move the Brules and Oglalas to reservations on the Missouri. The Brules dreaded such a move, having been relocated to a site near the River in 1868. Conditions there had been so bad—many had died of disease or succumbed to the temptations of whisky peddlers—that the Interior Department transferred them to the White River in 1870.[38] Aware that previous negotiations had foundered because the government offered little but unconditional surrender, Spotted Tail thought that promising to cancel the move might make peace more palatable to Crazy Horse's people. Aware of Crook's friendship with President Hayes, he initially withheld his assistance unless it was accompanied by Three Stars' commitment to intercede in behalf of his people on the removal issue.[39]

In mid-January, while Crook suffered through the Reynolds court-martial in Cheyenne and Old Spot held out for concessions, Major Mason, with the general's approval, sent another emissary, George Sword, a nephew of Red Cloud and a prominent Oglala warrior, to present peace terms to Crazy Horse's camp.[40] Sword, like Spotted Tail, hoped to use the removal issue as a lever to persuade the Oglala leader to come into the reservation. Only if the chief came in, he argued, could he use his influence in conjunction with the agency Sioux to oppose the government's plan to relocate them to the Missouri. Crazy Horse was noncommittal, but allowed Sword to discuss surrender with the other chiefs. They, in turn, expressed an interest in ending the fighting.

On February 10, only days after Crook had learned of Miles's success at Wolf Mountains, couriers from Crazy Horse's camp arrived at Camp Robinson. As a result of Sword's visit, they announced, many Sioux and Cheyennes were now prepared to talk peace if Crook would send Spotted Tail as an emissary, bringing tobacco as a token of Crook's sincerity.[41] The general was delighted. While the army's campaigns of the previous year had not inflicted the kind of crushing defeat he thought necessary to guarantee peace, he believed that the incremental damage to Sioux and Cheyenne society had substantially undermined their fighting spirit. At last, he, as well as other thoughtful officers, had come to believe that force was no longer the only, or even the best, means to resolve the Indian problem on the Great Plains. A successful diplomatic initiative would avoid another bloody spring campaign; and perhaps of greater importance for the ambitious general, it would eclipse Miles's efforts and win the general the honor of ending the war. As Spotted Tail's participation was obviously essential, he approached his meeting with the chief at Camp Sheridan in a receptive frame of mind.[42]

If securing Spotted Tail's assistance meant lending his support to the chief's crusade to prevent removal to the Missouri, Crook could do so with a clear conscience. Only a year before, he had supported the removal for reasons of security.[43] But now, security was not such an issue. The Sioux had been humbled and no longer presented a realistic threat to the whites who now occupied their country; further, he had come to respect and trust some of their important chiefs and saw the justice of their cause. A cynic might dismiss this reasoning as rationalizations because he needed Spotted Tail's help. But that would ignore his history with the Apaches in Arizona and the Paiutes in Idaho. In those instances, he had fought for fair and decent treatment for his former enemies as the sole means to a lasting peace. Only a grant of sufficient arable land of their own choosing in a country free of disease, coupled with adequate rations to ease their transition to a sedentary agrarian society, would ensure that they achieved self-sufficiency and assimilation, Crook's goals for the Indians. He had previously advocated this position to the administration. But lacking the political will or any real interest in its new wards, the government responded by consigning them land no white wanted with as little material support as possible. Misery, starvation, and mismanagement had followed, leading, as Crook predicted, to renewed warfare, with the military bearing the brunt of it. So despite the odds against success, he was committed to the justness of his position and thus could wholeheartedly support Spotted Tail's initiative.

With Crook's promise to oppose removal, Spotted Tail agreed to lend his prestige to the peace initiative. The chief believed the Gray Fox to have been fair and honorable in his past dealings, and had personally profited from his relationship with the general. Given the white chief's friendship with the Great Father in Washington, if anyone could get the government to reconsider its intention to remove the Oglalas and Brules to the Missouri River, it was Crook.[44]

In agreeing to support Spotted Tail, Crook was taking far more of a risk than the chief. When he had opposed moving the Apaches from Camp Verde, he had challenged government policy at a time when his prestige had been high and the stakes had been commensurately lower, posing far less of a threat to his reputation and career. Now, the situation had reversed. His prestige was on the wane and his opponents were more powerful, both inside and outside government, raising the ante substantially.

In the private sector, removal was supported by wealthy and well-connected Dakota cattlemen, miners, and farmers who coveted the land on the White River, site of the present agencies. They were joined by businessmen—whisky traders and the like—who stood to gain substantial financial benefits from the move to the Missouri. These constituencies had allied themselves with powerful forces within the government. The Interior Department was, as usual, strongly committed to consolidating the Sioux on the Missouri for reasons of economy. Their position was wholeheartedly supported by the army's top brass. Sheridan and Sherman favored the Missouri River location for reasons of both security and economy. As even Crook had once acknowledged, the new agencies would be far enough east of the Black Hills and the immigrant trails to prevent trouble with white settlers and miners. And reservations on the river would be easier and cheaper to supply than the remote White River Agencies.[45] Further, neither Sherman nor Sheridan saw much advantage in placating hostile Indians by acceding to their wishes regarding the location of their reservation. Both men still distrusted a negotiated peace with the Sioux, believing that agency Indians continued to present a threat to the frontier settlement, wintering on the reservation, and striking out against the whites as soon as their ponies fattened on spring grass. Crook had concurred with this point of view as late as the previous October, and like Sheridan had advocated a decisive campaign in the spring and summer of 1877 to end the war permanently.[46] While he had changed his mind, as Sioux power had declined, Sheridan had not, and continued to press Crook to prepare to fight in the spring.[47]

Not only were the army's top generals opposed to Crook's position, but his influence with them had eroded considerably in recent months as he was no longer regarded as the authority on Indian matters he once was. Though the generals continued to support him in public, privately they were highly critical of the performance of both Crook and Terry. Sheridan in particular was irate with Crook because of his failure the previous fall to disarm the friendly agency Sioux at Red Cloud. He was further infuriated by an article that appeared in January in the *Chicago Tribune*. Penned by Crook's journalist friend Strahorn, it blamed "higher authorities" (read "Sheridan") for delaying Crook's departure from Goose Creek to join General Terry on the Yellowstone after the Little Big Horn fight. Outraged by the insinuation that he was responsible for Crook's overly long sojourn at Goose Creek, Sheridan lashed out in a letter to him written only days before Three Stars had returned to Camp Robinson following the Dull Knife fight.[48] He also shared the contents of the offending article with General Sherman, who responded irritably that Crook bore blame for the Custer debacle, having failed to pursue the hostiles following the engagement of the Rosebud. "In this matter," he wrote, "he [Crook] seems to have thought more of his own personal command than the grand object aimed at by the combined campaign."[49]

Sheridan had been so disappointed by both Crook and Terry that he and Sherman now contemplated handing over combat command for the anticipated spring campaign to the more aggressive Mackenzie and Miles, reassigning Crook and Terry to administrative duties. Explaining his reasoning to Sherman, Sheridan wrote, "The fact of the case is the operations of Generals Terry and Crook [during the summer of 1876] will not bear criticism, and my only thought has been to let them sleep. I approved what was done, for the sake of the troops, but in doing so, I was not approving much, as you know.[50]

While Crook may have been unaware of Sheridan's plan to remove him from field command, he certainly knew of the sentiments behind it. Perhaps sensing his vulnerability, during his discussions with Spotted Tail, he vetoed the chief's suggestion that Crazy Horse's people be allowed to keep their ponies if they surrendered, a concession that he knew would be sure to further inflame Sheridan. But then, throwing caution to the winds, he agreed to Spot's alternative suggestion that the ponies be confiscated, but then turned over to the Agency scouts as a reward for their service, knowing full well that they would promptly gift the mounts back to Crazy Horse's people.[51] In an even bolder challenge to Sheridan's authority, Crook also committed to recommending to the president that Crazy Horse's band be granted a separate reservation in the formerly unceded lands not far from the Black Hills.

Accepting Crook's assurances, Spotted Tail departed Camp Sheridan on February 13 bound for Crazy Horse's village. With him rode 250 of his best warriors, an entourage intended to impress the northerners, and a pack train of army mules laden with gifts.[52] Crook knew that if the mission failed, the concessions and promises he had made might end his career. But he had sufficient faith in the Brule chief that he wrote Sheridan that he thought preparations for a spring campaign could be deferred and would in all likelihood prove unnecessary. Sheridan shared Crook's commentary with Sherman on March 17, noting skeptically that he thought "it best to defer to his [Crook's] opinion *for a little while yet*" (emphasis added).[53] Yet his faith in Crook had been revived to the extent that he changed his mind about removing Crook from field command in the spring, should a campaign prove necessary.

On the Tongue River, Miles watched the developing peace initiative with a jaundiced eye. In January, he had thought that his triumph at the Wolf Mountains would be rewarded with an independent command and reinforcements sufficient to allow him to finish off Sitting Bull and Crazy Horse in one last campaign. And it appeared that he was close to achieving his ambition. General Sherman had been pleased by Miles's victory and had written Sheridan, "I think . . . Miles is in the best position and possessed of [the] most mental and physical vigor to exercise this command. I think that you should assign him the exclusive task of hunting down the hostile Sioux."[54] Sheridan agreed, and reinforced Miles's command, increasing it to more than 2,000 troops in preparation for the final campaign.[55]

But precisely at the moment that the glory of a military victory seemed within his grasp, Miles learned of Sword's mission. And just as Crook had been spurred to action by news of Miles's success in the Wolf Mountains, Miles was galvanized by the possibility that Crook might now step in and end the war, even though, he muttered to his wife, "he has no more to do with it than if he had been in Egypt."[56] Hastily, Miles mounted his own mission, sending an emissary to Crazy Horse's camp with an invitation to come to the Tongue Cantonment to talk peace. A delegation of Cheyennes and Sioux responded and, after meeting with Miles, agreed to surrender their people to him. But before they could do so, they were overtaken by Spotted Tail's representatives who, according to Miles, offered them more lenient terms, "including the right to retain their guns and ponies, and to obtain ammunition."[57] Miles insisted that the delegation then tried to exact similar concessions from him. When he refused, they chose to surrender at the Red Cloud and Spotted Tail Agencies, leaving the aggrieved colonel convinced that Crook had robbed him of the glory that was his just due.

In his frustration, Miles engaged in a public campaign to discredit Crook. In a letter to the *Chicago Times*, he wrote that Spotted Tail's emissaries had seduced the surrendering Indians with gifts of gunpowder and tales that the troops would be removed from the country.[58] At least one historian, Harry Anderson, found Miles's allegations about the guns and ammunition suspect because "Spotted Tail had been told explicitly [by Crook] not to make any such assurances. . . . [He] was far too intelligent to throw away Crook's friendship by offering what the General had distinctly forbidden."[59] Even Miles would not accuse Crook of involvement in such machinations, admitting to his wife, "I do not believe they got the powder from Crook, but that the traders sent it out with word that the Indians could trade for all the powder they want if they go in."[60]

While Miles broadcast charges about the inducements offered by Spotted Tail, it seems the ambitious colonel may have been up to some tricks of his own. Bourke, as always a Crook partisan, confided to his diary that he had heard that Miles had told the hostiles "that they should give up their old guns and ponies so he could tell the Great Father that he had taken their arms and ponies from them but their good arms and good horses they could keep." A statement by Miles in his annual report lends credence to Bourke's accusation. Discussing his meeting with the chiefs at the Tongue River Cantonment, he wrote that he told them they would only have to give up "such ponies and arms *as I might require*" (emphasis added), a condition that gave him considerable wiggle room.[61] Bourke also recorded that Miles told the Tongue River delegation that "if they came in to Red Cloud Agency, the people here would take the last thing they had."[62] This allegation was probably based on Bourke's interpretation of a statement made by Iron Shield, one of Miles's former spies in the Sioux camp. The spy had told officers at Fort Robinson that Miles informed Crazy Horse's people that "if they came in to the [Red Cloud] Agency they would be badly treated, but if they came in to him [Bear Coat] they would be treated well."[63]

In May, after hearing of Crazy Horse's surrender, Miles would make one last attempt to discredit Crook's achievement, passing along to Sheridan by way of Terry's AAG a rumor "that it is the intention of a large number of the Indians who have gone to the Agencies to make only a pretense of peace, and after securing information, supplies, etc., to resume hostilities, joining any hostile Indians who may be away from the Agencies." Sheridan forwarded the allegation to Crook without comment, perhaps indicating he did not put much stock in it.[64] In any event, history proved the rumor baseless.

In the end, Miles's peace campaign produced only meager results. Three hundred Cheyennes and a scattering of Sioux surrendered to his soldiers on the Tongue, an outcome that paled by comparison to the Crook/Spotted Tail mission. As the *Chicago Tribune* reported: "This [Crazy Horse's surrender] makes a total of nearly 4,000 Indians who have surrendered at Red Cloud and Spotted Tail agencies during the past ten weeks. That they have been influenced almost wholly by the efforts of military in this department under the direction of such field officers as Gen. Mackenzie, and by Gen. Crook's fine manipulation of the leading warriors, is a fact beyond question."[65]

Like the Chicago paper, the *New York Tribune* also described Crook's energetic campaigning as the decisive factor in bringing about the surrenders.[66] But both papers were remiss in failing to credit Miles's role, overlooking his infantry's indefatigable winter campaign that, together with Mackenzie's destruction of the Dull Knife camp, seriously eroded the bands' capacity to survive the winter and decisively demonstrated the army's commitment to their total defeat. Absent the pressure generated on the northerners by these campaigns, it is doubtful that Spotted Tail's initiative would have borne fruit, notwithstanding his charisma and influence. On the other hand, Spot's success owed much to Crook's reputation with the hostiles as both a persistent campaigner *and* someone who would keep his word. In sum, both Miles and Crook made substantial contributions to the surrender of the Sioux and Cheyennes during the spring of 1877, a surrender that was now delayed to allow the Indians' ponies to fatten for the journey into the White River Agencies.

The success of Spotted Tail's mission was apparent even before the exhausted chief returned to his agency on April 5. On March 15, Crook reported the surrender of several bands of Indians at Red Cloud, 133 destitute Cheyennes on the 13th, 130 Sioux the following day.[67] These capitulations were a hopeful sign. But the grass was turning green on the prairie, and if any of the bands were going to return to the warpath, it would be now. So on April 11, Crook arrived on the reservation to personally monitor the arrivals, including, he hoped, the all-important surrender of Crazy Horse's people.[68]

Three days later, the Miniconjous and Sans Arcs bands who had originally agreed to surrender to Miles, came in to the Spotted Tail Agency. Knowing the importance of martial show to these warriors of the Great Plains, Crook permitted them to make a grand entrance in the Indian fashion. As a result, Camp Sheridan witnessed the spectacle of painted fighters in full battle regalia, mounted on their best war ponies, charging onto the post, rifles blazing, their war cries echoing across the parade ground. Crook awaited them, standing erect, his troops in formation behind him, morning sunlight flashing from their polished weaponry. Led by the Miniconjou chief, Touch the Clouds, a huge figure of a man almost seven feet in height, the warriors yanked their mounts to a halt in front of the general and dismounted. Shaking his hand, each lay his weapon at Crook's feet, a gesture of submission. He, in turn, addressed each as *Kola* (friend). Lest the Indians interpret his generous decision to allow a grand entrance as a sign of weakness, when the Miniconjous turned in only 38 guns, Crook drew Spotted

Tail aside and told him that unless the tribe turned in all their weapons, "the troops would take them from their tipis." An additional 34 government carbines miraculously appeared the following day.[69]

After their guns had been confiscated, Crook counseled with the chiefs. In the course of these discussions, he made a promise that, while seemingly innocuous at the time, would haunt him later. "When you all come in and [are] peaceable, if you wanted sometime to go out to hunt the buffalo, I would send soldiers out with you, to look after you and take care of you." These words were greeted (and remembered) with enthusiastic "hous," the universal sign of approbation on the Plains.[70]

Toward the end of the council, Spotted Tail spoke at length, addressing the issue of removal, in a manner perhaps intended to force Crook into a public commitment and certainly to bolster the chief's own reputation. "You [General Crook] are one of the Great Father's men—sent here to do his business. . . . I want you to send word to my Great Father not to ask me to move to the Indian Country [Oklahoma] any more. I want to live here where I am." Unwilling to make a promise he might be unable to keep, Crook replied, "You asked me a lot of these things before you went away and I have not forgotten them. . . . I will remember what you ask and I will do the best I can. I have it all down on paper, but can't say how much I can do, it will depend on whether all Indians come in or not."[71]

As the council adjourned, Chief Red Cloud, jealous of the accolades now being conferred on Spotted Tail and wishing to carve out a role for himself in the peace process, approached Crook, offering to lead a delegation to Crazy Horse's village to ensure that the war chief honored his agreement. Crook had been monitoring the band's painfully slow approach to the reservation and had grown weary of fending off an increasingly impatient Sheridan, who still hinted at a spring campaign.[72] So he saw an advantage to the offer, though aware of Red Cloud's desire for self-aggrandizement. Straddling the issue, he told the chief he could go if he wanted to, but not as the general's representative. At the same time, he offered to provide him with quantities of rations to ensure that the surrendering band would be able to travel to the Agency without the need to hunt along the way. With the rations came a warning. Every day Crazy Horse delayed would bring him closer to the moment when the troops would "sally out and attack and kill his warriors wherever found."[73]

The following week, Dull Knife, at the head of 524 Cheyennes, surrendered at Camp Robinson. Bourke and others were shocked by their destitute appearance. "They are almost without blankets and with only a very scant supply of robes. They have many widows and many people with frozen feet: both these are melancholy souvenirs of their fight with Mackenzie." In resignation, they surrendered their arms to Crook and retired to a campsite designated for their use, erecting pitiful lodges, covered with remnants of canvas, old hides and robes, and a few pieces of gunnysacks salvaged from deserted army camps. Surprisingly, many would soon enlist as scouts against the Sioux. Bourke attributed their willingness to do so to bitterness toward Crazy Horse for his supposedly inhospitable treatment of the Cheyennes following Mackenzie's attack. They themselves explained it in terms of their anger at the chief for his heavy-handed attempts to prevent them from surrendering in January and February.[74]

Sheridan, who had fought the Southern Cheyennes and respected their martial abilities, now feared that if their proud northern cousins were allowed to remain in the North, they would only foment unrest among the other northern tribes. And though Cheyenne resistance during the war had largely been confined to fighting back when their villages had been attacked, Sheridan was determined to punish them for their supposed transgressions. Ignoring their expressed desire to remain in their northern homeland, he demanded that they be banished to Indian Territory to join the southern branch of their tribe. Knowing that most of the Northern Cheyennes were adamantly opposed removal to these disease-ridden lands, Crook and Mackenzie attempted to circumvent Sheridan's orders and instead presented the tribe with a range of options. They could, of course, go south. Alternatively, they could choose to join the Shoshones on their reservation at Camp Brown, or remain at Camp Robinson for a year, or until a permanent resolution could be devised. Though a majority favored the last alternative, a faction within the tribe favored joining their cousins in the south, among whom they had relatives and friends. This faction included Standing Elk, who appeared to have gained some influence with Crook, probably because of his compliant nature.[75] Against the wishes of the majority of the northerners, Standing Elk informed the military that the tribe would willingly move south. Crook and Mackenzie then put great pressure on the tribal chiefs who opposed the move—Little Wolf, Dull Knife, and Wild Hog—ultimately, it was said, promising that if they did not find Indian Territory agreeable, they could return north within a year. (Crook denied making this promise, stating that it was undoubtedly the result of a misunderstanding caused by an interpreter.) Reluctantly, on May 28, the Cheyennes began their long trek south.[76]

Having successfully, though as it would later develop, temporarily, swept the Northern Cheyennes under the rug and while awaiting the surrender of Crazy Horse's people, Generals Sherman and Sheridan turned to the Oglalas and Brules. As previously mentioned, both officers agreed with the Department of the Interior that removal to the Missouri was necessary. In late March, they signaled their continued commitment to the move, rejecting a proposal from Colonel Mackenzie to settle the Sioux bands of Young Man Afraid, American Horse, and Yellow Bear on the Tongue, as a reward for their loyalty to the army during the latter days of the war.[77] To the senior generals, the only outstanding issues were the timing of the move and how to bring General Crook, the man who would be responsible for its implementation, on board. On April 22, Sheridan wrote Crook, suggesting the move be scheduled for June and recommending that Spotted Tail be sent in advance to the Missouri River location to select a site.[78]

Sheridan's dispatch crossed a letter from Crook written on August 20 and probably drafted in consultation with the Brule and Oglala chiefs. In it, Crook proposed relocating the White River bands to the Yellowstone country rather than to the Missouri. He suggested that two agencies be created, one at the mouth of the Powder and the other on the Tongue. In support of his recommendation, Crook emphasized not only the interests of the Indians, but considerations important to the white establishment, a tactic he had used in opposing the Verde removal. He had drawn the boundaries of the proposed agencies so as to "open all the mineral country to [white] settlement." Security concerns had been addressed by insuring the remoteness of the agencies from the immigrant trails and white settlements. Nor had he neglected the economies afforded by the site, noting that the proposed reservations lay along navigable streams, enabling them to be supplied cheaply by steamer. Finally, to foster self-sufficiency, the locations selected had an abundance of game and arable land. Foreseeing the conversion of tribal land to private ownership to promote assimilation, he added that the country was sufficiently rich that "each Indian family can have set aside to it a portion of the land upon which to erect a ranch for itself."[79]

On receiving Sheridan's April 22 letter, Crook must have realized that his own recommendation had come too late.[80] But rather than concede, he requested an audience to discuss the matter in person. Sheridan agreed and Crook departed Camp Robinson for Chicago on April 28 in the company of Major Sandy Forsyth, Sheridan's senior aide, whom the lieutenant general had assigned to report on the surrenders.[81] Evidently, Crook had co-opted Forsyth who, as a veteran Indian fighter himself, would have some influence with Sheridan. "[Crook's proposal]," wrote Forsyth, "would be a capital move and would certainly get them [the Sioux] out of the way of the miners in the Black Hills and the Big Horn Mountains."[82]

The May 2 meeting between Crook and Sheridan did not go well. The lieutenant general criticized the leniency of Crook's surrender terms. He favored a far harsher approach that included imprisonment of the principal war leaders. Further, committed to the Missouri Reservation, he refused to entertain Crook's arguments for agencies in the Yellowstone country. However, he did consent to allow Crook to go to Washington to argue his case with the Interior Department, undoubtedly aware that it would be a futile effort.[83]

As expected, Crook's meeting with Interior's commissioner of Indian affairs also went poorly. Without a positive endorsement from the War Department, the commissioner hid behind the legal fiction that an agreement approved by Congress in March provided no alternative but to remove the Sioux to the Missouri. The fact that many of the bands reputedly covered by the agreement had no knowledge of it, and certainly would not have approved it if they had, appeared to carry no weight with him.[84]

Though he rejected Crook's Yellowstone proposal, Sheridan had agreed to support his request to postpone the move until October, and the commissioner duly consented. The delay would give Crook more time to plead his case or, as the commissioner and Sheridan viewed it, more time to get the Sioux used to the idea of removal. It was also agreed that a delegation from the Red Cloud and Spotted Tail Agencies would be allowed to present its case against removal in Washington to the new Great Father, Rutherford Hayes.[85]

While Crook was meeting with the commissioner of Indian affairs, Miles led his troops in the last military engagement of the Sioux War, an attack on one of the last holdouts, a village of about three hundred Miniconjous, Northern Cheyennes, and Sans Arcs under Chief Lame Deer. They had refused to surrender and were on a buffalo hunt in Miles's area of operations. In a dawn attack on May 7, Miles took the band by surprise, killing a small number, including Lame Deer, while the remainder fled into the brush, leaving behind the bulk of their food and possessions to be destroyed by the troops. The survivors eluded Colonel Miles's troops for three months before finally surrendering at Red Cloud.[86] The destruction of Lame Deer's village virtually ended Indian resistance on the Great Plains, though remnants of the band would continue raiding into the Black Hills well into the latter part of July.

CHAPTER THIRTY

Loose Ends

May–July 1877

Although the army had originally regarded Crazy Horse as a relatively unimportant leader, Crook had become convinced early on that he was the key to resolving the Sioux problem. But while the Gray Fox had played a prominent role in engineering the great war chief's surrender, the two men did not meet until May 25, 1877, upon Crook's return from Washington. The occasion was a military review of the Sioux and Cheyenne scouts at Camp Robinson. Recruited only days before, the scouts, organized by White Hat Clark into eighteen companies, had readily adapted to cavalry drill and now rode single file onto the post parade ground, wheeling in unison to face the general and his fellow officers. With Crazy Horse in the lead, the warriors dismounted and approached the general on foot, hands extended. At the last moment, Crazy Horse knelt theatrically in submission to take the general's hand.[1]

At the time Crazy Horse arrived at the Red Cloud Agency, John Bourke described him as "quite young, not over thirty years old [he was actually thirty-seven], five feet eight inches tall, lithe and sinewy, with a scar on his face," his bearing dignified, "but morose, dogged, tenacious, and melancholy. He behaved with stolidity, like a man who realized he had to give in to Fate, but would do so as sullenly as possible." With his light complexion and long, sandy brown hair, settlers had often mistaken him for a white man, a circumstance that must have displeased him. The scar, running from the corner of his nose to his jaw line, was the result of a bullet wound inflicted by an irate Oglala warrior named No Water, whose wife Crazy Horse had wooed away from him.[2]

His own people found the chief odd and often referred to him as the "Strange One." His nephew, Black Elk, characterized him as "a queer man [who] would go about the village without noticing people or saying anything. In his own tipi he would joke . . . but around the village he hardly ever noticed anybody, except little children. . . . He never joined a dance [not even the sacred Sun Dance], and . . . nobody ever heard him sing."[3] Nor was he a skilled orator, and he rarely spoke in council.

Putting his people's welfare before his own, he signaled his self-abnegation by leading an ascetic lifestyle and strictly adhering to the Lakotas' cardinal virtue, generosity, giving away most of his possessions, even when to do so meant enduring personal privation.[4] He refused to wear the war bonnet and scalp shirt that defined a warrior's status, and instead rode into combat clad only in a simple cotton shirt and breech clout, with a single feather in his hair. But, profoundly mystical, before each fight he engaged in an elaborate ritual that included painting symbolic patterns on himself and his mount and tying a small stone behind his ear, a talisman that prevented bullets from striking him. Once on the field of battle, he underwent a metamorphosis. The modest ascetic became a skilled tactician and charismatic leader who captured the profound respect of his people and the jealousy of the Sioux leadership.[5]

After his surrender, he entertained white officers in his lodge and accepted the rank of sergeant in the scouts. Yet he remained suspicious of the white man's intentions, and was deeply concerned about the plan to move his people to the Missouri River. While coming reluctantly around to the concept of a reservation, he adamantly opposed the unhealthy Missouri River sites and had selected an alternative site on the Tongue River that he believed Crook could help him obtain.[6] He immediately raised the topic at a council that Crook called following the parade ground review.

Crook had gathered over two hundred Indians, the principal chiefs and warriors of the Oglalas and Brules, in an attentive semicircle. Crazy Horse was the first to address the group. As was his habit, his utterance was both brief and direct. "In coming this way, I picked out a place [in the Yellowstone country] where I wish to live hereafter. I put a stake in the ground to mark the spot. There is plenty of game in that country. All of my relatives here approve my choice. I want them to go back with me and always live there together. That is all I have to say." Other prominent Sioux—Spotted Tail, Red Cloud, No Water, Man Afraid of His Horse—added their voices to the chorus opposing the move to the Missouri.[7]

When Crook addressed the assemblage, he spoke cautiously, not mentioning his disappointing failure to persuade Washington to alter its determination. He saw no reason to cause turmoil among the chiefs while there still remained a chance, albeit a slim one, to change the administration's position. Believing that the chiefs might achieve what he could not, he now aimed to convince Spotted Tail, the most accomplished diplomat among the Sioux, to take Crazy Horse, the most irreconcilable of the northerners, to Washington to meet with Crook's friend and patron, President Hayes. He hoped that Spot's oratory and Crazy Horse's presence might tip the balance, demonstrating that even the most adamant of the former hostiles now welcomed an equitable peace. With these thoughts in mind, he told the chiefs, "You asked for a reservation in the upper country. . . . I cannot decide these things myself. They must be decided in Washington. The commissioner promised he would let some of you go and talk to him at Washington. If you get this permission, I would like to have representative men go and see how it is for themselves. . . . I will try and be in Washington myself so I can hear both sides."[8]

Organizing the Washington delegation, and securing Crazy Horse's agreement to join it, now became one of Crook's primary objectives. But in the intervening months, events would occur—most critically, intratribal rivalries that roiled the Red Cloud and Spotted Tail Agencies—that would complicate and delay its attainment.

And, just as these events were unfolding, Crook found himself pulled away from his duties. Sheridan wished his company on a survey of Sioux country scheduled for mid-June through mid-July. The official reason for the trip was to give Sheridan the opportunity to survey the land recently taken from the Sioux and to ascertain the number, placement, and size of posts needed to hold it.[9] But judging from the boyish enthusiasm with which Sheridan viewed the occasion, it was to be more an adventure than the sober learning experience described in official documentation.[10] His choice of Crook to join the expedition was an obvious one. He knew the area that the expedition would cover and was highly experienced at arranging logistics for such excursions; and perhaps both men saw it as a chance to mend an old and increasingly battered friendship. The *Omaha Republican*, obviously partial to their hometown commander, chose to interpret Crook's selection as a token of Sheridan's "faith in the completeness of the conqueror's [Crook's] work."[11] Crook raised no objection to joining the expedition. The opportunity to hunt in such beautiful country and perhaps to mend fences with Sheridan was irresistible, though in hindsight, the expedition would remove him from the scene at a time that now appears inopportune.

The party included Sheridan's aide, Sandy Forsyth, and Crook's aides, Schuyler and Bourke. To garner support from important leaders in the press and business, Sheridan had invited a Chicago railway executive, and the editor of the city's *Evening Journal*. Of course, there were also servants, and a cavalry escort of sufficient size "to prevent the slightest anxiety about hostile Indians."[12] As he had for many such hunts, Three Stars arranged for Tom Moore, his pack master, to shepherd the mule train, while Grouard and Baptiste "Big Bat" Pourier, and several Arapaho and Sioux warriors acted as guides. On June 26, Crook joined the expedition, boarding Sheridan's train at the Omaha depot.[13]

During the first two weeks, the party enjoyed the magnificent scenery of the Wind River Range and the Big Horn country, while concentrating their energies on the decimation of huge quantities of game, including numerous buffalos from one of the last surviving herds in North America. A newsman covering the event noted that the buffalo slaughter bothered Sheridan, but supposedly he sanctioned it to please the Indians with the expedition, "who slew the beasts for pure wantonness and love of sport."[14] Even Bourke, who did his fair share of the killing, was chagrined by the improvident slaughter. "A great waste," he grimly wrote. "On this march we have left on the ground four times as much meat as we took for consumption."[15] Of course Crook contributed to the tally, killing a grizzly bear in addition to numerous elk and deer.[16]

The expedition's mood sobered as it neared the Custer battlefield, the Sioux War locale Sheridan was most eager to visit. There is no record of the thoughts that passed through Crook's mind as the column rode past the rude crosses marking the spot where Captain Myles Keogh's Company had been obliterated or the knoll further on where Custer's troopers had died while Crook's command had fished for trout on Goose Creek. The battlefield was in deplorable condition despite the fact that two weeks previously, Sheridan's brother and aide, Colonel Michael Sheridan, had visited the area to clean it up for his sibling's visit. Over the intervening year, wolves and weather had done their work, exposing bodies hastily buried by Gibbon immediately after the battle. A horrific tangle of bones of horses and men lay about the field, intermingled with "pieces of clothing, soldiers' hats, boots with the legs cut off, but *the human feet and bones still sticking in them*" (emphasis Bourke's).[17] Little Phil busied his escort, locating and burying as much as could be found of this human flotsam. Among their discoveries were the remnants of seventeen troopers, ten of whom had never been buried, and, in a ravine adjacent to the knoll, a body half risen from the soil clad in ragged buckskins and a bullet-riddled hat. These were said to be the remains of Mitch Bouyer, the mixed-blood scout who had warned Custer that if they entered the valley of the Little Big Horn they would never come out alive.[18] To protect the battlefield from future desecration, on his return to Chicago, Sheridan would successfully press the government to declare the battlefield a national cemetery.[19]

The following day, with images of the carnage still fresh in their minds, the expedition moved downriver to inspect Fort Keogh, soon to be renamed Fort Custer, which Sheridan had ordered built at the confluence of the Big Horn and Little Big Horn Rivers. There, they boarded steamboats, one of them ironically christened the *Rosebud*, to begin their return east. On board, they joined Generals Sherman and Terry, who were engaged in an inspection of the new posts on the Yellowstone. Though the weather turned hot and the travelers were attacked by mosquitos "the size of jack snipes," the five-day trip downriver to Bismarck was a marked contrast to Crook's starvation march the year before.[20]

In Bismarck, the expedition learned that a general strike by railway workers had halted the railroads east of Omaha. While Sheridan had been touring the West; riots had broken out in Chicago, as police, state militia, and strikebreakers—thugs hired by the city's financial elite—clashed with striking rail workers. The railroads and the military had a symbiotic relationship, the former providing transport for officers and men, while the latter furnished security to surveyors and construction gangs. The arrangement was further lubricated with free rail passes and luxurious accommodations for military officers on the one hand, and lavish hunts at government expense for railroad executives and allied businessmen. So it was no surprise that the railroads turned to the army for help to crush the rioters or that the army complied.[21]

The Northern Pacific generously put on a special train to whisk Sheridan and his fellow travelers from Bismarck to Chicago so that the lieutenant general could take charge. Regulars, including a contingent of troopers from the Platte, had been sent to restore order. Fortunately, they were assigned to guard government facilities and hence were not involved in the vicious street battles that ensued.[22] By the time Sheridan and Crook's train pulled into the Chicago Northwestern depot, little remained for them to do. The strike had been broken, inspiring the *Chicago Tribune* to inanely proclaim that "the fight with Communism is at an end."[23] The next day, Crook, satisfied that his further presence in Chicago was unnecessary and anxious to return to his headquarters, gratefully boarded a train back to Omaha.[24]

CHAPTER THIRTY-ONE

The Death of Crazy Horse

August–September 1877

The general remained at his Omaha headquarters only for a few days before taking leave to escort Mary to Oakland, Maryland, for a brief visit with her family. The fact that he could take leave immediately following his extended trip with Sheridan is a tribute not only to his regard for his wife but also to his firm, though mistaken, conviction that with the surrender of Crazy Horse, peace had finally come to the Department of the Platte. And it speaks to the misplaced faith he had in the staff who would handle matters in his absence.

Chief among those who would keep an eye on reservation affairs while the general was on leave was his aide, Lieutenant Philo "White Hat" Clark. Clark, who had hosted Crazy Horse at his surrender in May, was a 1868 graduate of West Point, a New Yorker who had joined Crook on the Yellowstone and quickly become one of his trusted aides. A handsome, "jaunty" personality who favored buckskin, he was, in Lieutenant King's opinion, the "show-figure" of Crook's staff.[1] He had an intelligent, inquiring mind and an abiding interest in the lifeways of the Plains Indians, becoming so proficient in their sign language that he would later be commissioned by Sheridan to write a book on the subject for use as a military manual. His facility in communicating with the scouts, whom he commanded, would earn him their loyalty; and, as their leader, he distinguished himself at the battle of Slim Buttes. Like Crook, he was said to think like an Indian, which he thought gave him insight into the byzantine twists and turns of agency politics. Utterly ruthless, he had no hesitation in manipulating his friends among the Indians in the interests of performing his duty as he saw it.[2]

As chief of scouts at Camp Robinson and interim agent at Red Cloud, Clark became Crook's eyes and ears on the reservation, spending much time in Crazy Horse's lodge, attempting to influence him to cooperate with the army, and passing on information to the general regarding the chief's on again, off again adaptation to reservation life. Crook relied heavily on his protégé and assumed that the young lieutenant "virtually controlled the Indians at the Spotted Tail and Red Cloud Agencies."[3] And perhaps both men believed that he really did.

During the early days of Crazy Horse's sojourn at the agency, Clark observed that the chief seemed to adjust to his new circumstances. With White Hat's encouragement, he wooed the pretty daughter of a mixed-blood interpreter at the fort, forming a liaison that Clark hoped would help to settle down the wild warrior from the north. As an added benefit, the lieutenant engaged the young lady to keep him apprised of the goings-on in Crazy Horse's lodge.[4] Having attended to the chief's domestic tranquility, Clark proceeded to persuade him to wear the uniform of the Indian scouts, and boasted that, without any objection from the chief, he had successfully employed some of his Sioux scouts to hunt down the remnants of Lame Deer's band.[5] To Crook in Maryland, he reported that "the rumors that small bands of Indians are leaving the agencies are utterly without any foundation in fact," optimistically concluding that "Indian affairs at both agencies [Spotted Tail and Red Cloud] are in satisfactory condition," and that "the influence of the Agency Indians over those who have recently come in from the north is particularly good." Lieutenant Colonel Luther P. Bradley, commanding officer at Camp Robinson, endorsed this rosy view, assuring the general, "We are as quiet here as a Yankee village on a Sunday."[6]

However, as Clark continued his courtship of Crazy Horse and attended feasts at his side, undercurrents of discontent were beginning to emerge at the Brule and Oglala Agencies. Tribal conflicts had been awakened by the sudden introduction of the northerners—Cheyennes, Miniconjous, Sans Arcs, and Crazy Horse's Oglalas—into the mix of agency Indians on the White River, a place already known for its tumultuous politics. The agency chiefs, Red Cloud in particular,

loud, exciting & emotional

observed how assiduously the army courted Crazy Horse, and feared his appointment as paramount chief of the agencies, a circumstance that would seriously diminish the chiefs' own influence and power.[7]

While his mere presence disrupted the delicate balance of agency politics, there were growing signs showed that Crazy Horse's adaptation to reservation life was far more superficial than previously supposed. Beneath his aloof façade, he remained the proud traditionalist, determined to lead his people on their own independent path rather than the white man's road. Though presenting a cordial face to Clark, Bourke, and other young officers who called at his tipi, he never overcame his basic distrust of whites or his well-founded fear that the government planned to relocate his people to the Missouri. His anxiety was heightened by Sheridan's forcible removal of the Northern Cheyennes to Indian Territory. Fearful of government treachery, he now refused to make his mark on any government paper, including ration receipts. And he began to equivocate about joining the delegation to visit the Great Father in Washington, influenced by dire rumors that he would be poisoned or imprisoned once he arrived in the East, or that his people would be secretly moved to the Missouri in his absence.[8]

By early August, the Indian agent at Red Cloud, James Irwin, who favored Red Cloud and feared Crazy Horse's influence, was describing the latter to his superiors as "silent, sullen, lordly and dictatorial."[9] His unyielding attitude, captured by Irwin, and efforts to bend his people to his will, estranged many, including his own lieutenants, He Dog, who had moved to Red Cloud's camp, and Little Big Man, who had aspirations of his own.[10] Frank Grouard would also join the list of the disaffected. Grouard, who knew the chief well from his sojourn in his camp in the years before he had become an army scout, had initially been supportive of him, advising him during his difficult adjustment to agency life.[11] Now, it was said, he had grown fearful of his old friend, worried that he might inform the army of alleged depredations the scout had participated in while living with the Sioux.[12] Grouard would play a prominent role in the tragic events that began to unfold during the late summer of 1877.

In this atmosphere of fear and distrust, Lieutenant Clark, influenced by information received from warriors he had sent to spy in Crazy Horse's camp, continued to believe that he could control events and manipulate the war chief to do his bidding. But his spies, many of whom had their own grievances against Crazy Horse, played a double game, and their reports, rather than truthful, were distorted by their attempts to undermine Crazy Horse's credibility with the white establishment.[13]

In early August, Crook returned to Omaha, seemingly unaware of recent developments. Buoyed by positive reports he had received throughout July, he judged the time ripe to fulfill his promise to the chiefs, made the previous May, to allow the Indians a buffalo hunt in late summer.[14] In hindsight, it seems odd that Crook would contemplate unleashing a large number of armed northern Sioux on the Powder River country with the army in pursuit of the Nez Perces and Sitting Bull's people poised on the Canadian border. Several factors, in addition to his officers' optimism about Crazy Horse's adaptation to reservation life, influenced his decision. The first was the significant importance he attached to keeping his word, a principle he had always held sacrosanct in his dealings with Indians. When he had made the original commitment to allow the hunt, he had given his word contingent on the surrender of all of the warring bands. Now, with the remnants of Lame Deer's people heading into the reservation, that precondition had been fulfilled and, in his mind, the promise needed to be honored. Honor combined with more pragmatic concerns. There was a severe meat shortage at the agencies and the tribes' tipis were in shabby condition. A hunt would ensure a sufficiency of meat and hides to provide food and shelter during the harsh winter to come.[15] Finally, and perhaps of greatest moment, was Crook's conviction that if he satisfied his pledge, the chiefs, including Crazy Horse, would be persuaded to join the Washington delegation that he viewed as critical to his efforts to prevent the removal of the Sioux to the Missouri.

At Crook's behest, Clark called a council at Red Cloud on July 27 to read a message from the Gray Fox announcing a hunt of forty days' duration, followed by the mission to Washington. His emphasis was on the latter, admonishing the chiefs to select only the men who could most favorably represent them in Washington. He closed the meeting by announcing that a feast would be held in connection with the council and, at the suggestion of Young Man Afraid, that it would be hosted by Crazy Horse.

To the Crazy Horse faction, word of the hunt eclipsed any thought of the Washington mission. Probably without giving the matter much thought, the Strange One again refused to definitely commit himself to the trip, though he hinted that he was still favorably disposed. Distracted by thoughts of the hunt, he probably failed to notice that when Clark announced that he was to host the feast, Red Cloud had risen and stalked angrily from the room.[16]

At ten o'clock that evening, two Indians arrived surreptitiously at Irwin's door. They had come to apprise the Indian agent that Red Cloud was disturbed by the decision to allow Crazy Horse to host the council feast, an honor he, and they, felt should go to him as the paramount chief of the Oglalas. They then launched into a diatribe against Crazy Horse, whom they accused of creating discord on the reservation. "Once away on the hunt," they warned, "he with his band of at least 240 braves, well armed and equipped, would go on the warpath and cause the government infinite trouble and disaster."[17] Irwin and his houseguest, Benjamin Shopp, an Interior official from Washington, both distrusted Crazy Horse and so were predisposed to accept the truth of this accusation without further investigation. Within a few days, Irwin wrote his superiors, recommending that the hunt be canceled. Shopp also sent a letter to the department endorsing Irwin's recommendation.[18]

On the 28th, Crook, who was still in Omaha and unaware of the growing furor surrounding the hunt, issued an order permitting agency traders to sell ammunition to the Indians in anticipation of the event. Meanwhile, Washington authorized the selection of "a delegation of 15 or 20 Indians from Red Cloud and Spotted Tail Agencies" to come east to discuss the removal. It was to proceed to Washington after the completion of the hunt.[19]

Spotted Tail and Red Cloud picked this moment to publicly announce their adamant opposition to the hunt, declaring it a danger and a distraction from the main issue, the proposed relocation of the Oglala and Brule Agencies. Spotted Tail, whose opinion carried great weight with Crook, argued that "trouble might ensue, and many would slip away and join Sitting Bull. . . ."[20] His followers and the chiefs who supported Red Cloud agreed. Their arguments, supported by the Interior Department representatives, left Crook little choice but to postpone the hunt until after the delegation had returned from Washington, a delay that would inevitably mean its cancellation because of the advent of winter.[21]

Though Colonel Bradley reported that "there will be no trouble about postponing the hunt,"[22] the decision profoundly affected Crazy Horse, who was angry, suspicious, and defiant. His fear of the whites was magnified by rumors fed to him by his mixed-blood mistress and others, and he now flatly refused to join the delegation to Washington, convinced that it was merely a pretext to arrest or kill him. Filled with despair by the desertion of his long-time friends and allies and the shift of power toward the agency chiefs, he became increasingly obdurate and dictatorial. When, on August 18, Clark met again with the Sioux leadership, the Strange One not only refused to go to Washington, but insisted that he ought to name the entire delegation, excluding all but northerners from the group.[23] Though Clark was angered by the war chief's attempt to dictate government policy, he held his temper and asked him calmly to rethink his position. Crazy Horse snapped in reply that "he had already stated he was not going."[24]

The chief's adamant refusal to go to Washington created a permanent rift between himself and Clark. Shocked and disillusioned, the lieutenant wrote Crook that

> force is the only thing that will work out a good condition in this man's mind; kindness he only attributes to weakness. . . . he has a large reputation and influence, but this power could be easily broken at the present time—and I believe it necessary. I am very reluctantly forced to this conclusion because I have claimed and felt all along that any Indian could be "worked" by other means, but absolute force is the only thing for him.[25]

Given the trust Crook reposed in Clark's judgment, he must have been taken aback by this sudden reversal in his lieutenant's reading of the situation. But, distracted by developments in the Nez Perce war, he failed to give the deteriorating state of affairs at Red Cloud his full attention.

War with the Nez Perces had broken out in June. The causes were the usual unstable mix of broken government promises, forced removal, and hot-blooded warriors. As the fighting was initially confined to the Department of the Columbia, to the west of the Platte, for the time being Crook was not directly involved. However, General Howard, the department's commander, was doing such a poor job managing the campaign that President Hayes contemplated sending Crook to replace him.[26] Only a last-minute engagement in early July in which Howard's troops could claim marginal success, caused Hayes to change his mind. Yet, throughout July and August, the tribe continued to elude Howard's troops, leading them on an embarrassing and costly chase across Idaho and inflicting heavy casualties.

On August 23, reports reached Crook that, having attacked Howard's forces at Camas Meadows three days before, the Nez Perces were now driving toward Yellowstone National Park in the northwest corner of Wyoming, fleeing toward sanctuary in Canada.[27] Sheridan responded by ordering Terry in the Department of Dakota and Crook on the Platte to mobilize their troops to block the advance, intending the type of enveloping action he so favored in Indian warfare. Crook planned to respond, using elements of the Fifth and Third Cavalries stationed at Camp Brown on the Wind River (Shoshone) Agency.[28] Believing that Clark had the situation at the White River Agencies well in hand, he intended to assume personal leadership of the campaign.

Crook had hoped to use Shoshones, who had performed so well at the Rosebud, as scouts for the campaign. But Sheridan, eager to test the loyalty of the newly surrendered Sioux and aware of their traditional enmity with the Nez Perces, insisted that he add a contingent from the White River Agencies. So Crook dutifully ordered Clark to recruit a hundred warriors from among the bands at Spotted Tail and Red Cloud.[29] Pursuant to Crook's instructions, the lieutenant summoned the chiefs, including Crazy Horse, to a council on the evening of August 30. Translating for White Hat were Louie Bordeaux, a scout of mixed French and Sioux parentage, and Frank Grouard. A third interpreter, William Garnett, joined the meeting after it was already underway.[30]

Billy Garnett, as he was known at Camp Robinson, would become one of the principal informants on events transpiring on the reservation throughout this period. His father was Richard Garnett, who served as commanding officer at Fort Laramie before the Civil War. In 1861, Garnett, a Virginian, went east to serve in the Confederate Army and was killed at Gettysburg. Billy's mother, an Oglala Sioux named Looks At Him, had stayed with her people and raised Billy as a Sioux. At the time of Crazy Horse's surrender, he was still a young man of twenty-two, intelligent, fluent in both Lakota and English, and comfortable in both cultures. He had come to know almost everyone in the environs of the Red Cloud and Spotted Tail Agencies and served as chief of Indian scouts, acting as both guide and interpreter. Throughout his life, he would remain on the reservation, a much-respected figure to both the Sioux and the army, regarded on all sides as reliable and trustworthy.[31]

According to Garnett, who was not present at the outset of the meeting but learned of it by talking with the other participants, Clark asked for volunteers to join the troops fighting the Nez Perces. The agency Sioux stepped forward without hesitation, but the northerners balked at the idea. The Miniconjou chief Touch the Clouds and Crazy Horse considered the request a betrayal of trust by the government. With inexorable logic, Crazy Horse pointed out, "You have asked us to become peaceful, how can you ask us now to go to war again?"[32] But as the conversation progressed, Crazy Horse grudgingly consented to consider Clark's proposal. The meeting broke up on that note.[33]

Colonel Bradley, post commander at Camp Robinson and an officer generally sympathetic to the Sioux, was worried. He sensed that the northern chiefs were concerned about more than a perceived breach of faith by the military. He knew that rumors were afloat that Sitting Bull had crossed the border from Canada and believed that many of these men suspected they would be used against him rather than the Nez Perces. Fearing "serious results if the scouts are held to this service," he wired Crook, requesting a suspension of the movement of any of the volunteers, including the agency Indians. Crook concurred with Bradley and agreed to his request. When Sheridan heard of the decision, he angrily telegraphed the general, demanding that it be countermanded and the scouts moved off to Camp Brown immediately.[34]

Crook received Sheridan's wire while aboard a Union Pacific train bound for Green River, Wyoming, where he planned to catch the stage to join his troops at Camp Brown. Responding coolly to Sheridan's bristling tone, he advised the lieutenant general that unless he was "particularly anxious to have it otherwise," the scouts would not be leaving at this time.[35] On September 3, Sheridan, by now aware of the volatility of the situation, sensibly backed off.

While this exchange of telegrams was underway, Clark called a second council on the Nez Perce issue. Crazy Horse attended in a combative mood. After reconsidering Clark's proposal, he had come prepared to offer what seemed to him a face-saving compromise. He would go out to hunt the buffalo first, taking his entire village, and then, "when overtaken [by the soldiers] would help to fight the Nez Perce." Clark and Garnett saw this remark as nothing more than an attempt to use the Nez Perce war as "an excuse which [Crazy Horse] thought would enable him to get away and go north. . . ."[36] Irate, White Hat engaged Crazy Horse through his interpreters in an angry war of words, which climaxed when the chief truculently conceded, "we will go north and fight until there is not a Nez Perce left." Whether deliberately or in error, Frank Grouard fatefully mistranslated his statement as "We will go north and fight until not a white man is left."[37] To Clark, in the context of a heated exchange, this must have seemed like a declaration of war. The two men continued their verbal jousting until at last Crazy Horse rose and stalked out of the meeting, exclaiming to his interpreter, "I told him [Clark] what I wanted to do. We are going to move, we are going out there to hunt." To Clark, he spat out, "You are too soft; you can't fight," and then, "if you want to fight the Nez Perce, go out and fight them; we don't want to fight; we are going out to hunt." Clark shouted back, "You cannot go out there, I tell you." With Clark's words still ringing in his ears, Crazy Horse angrily departed.[38]

Though Bordeaux and others earnestly tried to explain the mistranslation, Clark refused to heed them, so firmly had he become fixated in his hostility toward Crazy Horse. Without referring to the possibility of a mistranslation, he reported to Colonel Bradley that "Crazy Horse and Touch the Clouds with High Bear . . . told me that they were going north on the warpath."[39] Bradley, rattled by Clark's statement, immediately telegraphed Crook's adjutant in Omaha that the northerners were "going out with their bands: this means all of the hostiles of last year. I think General Crook's presence might have a good effect."[40]

Seated in the swaying Union Pacific car that bore him west toward war with the Nez Perces, Crook's attention was focused entirely on the upcoming campaign. He regarded Crazy Horse and the events at Red Cloud as a sideshow, one that he thought was being managed by Bradley and Clark. This misconception was shattered when the train pulled into its first stop along the route and a messenger boarded the train with a copy of Bradley's wire. Rather than react immediately, the general slept on Bradley's request before concluding the next morning that he did not want to become personally involved in the crisis, perhaps fearing its effect on his credibility with the Sioux (see note 46). Having made this decision, he scrawled a response outlining a strategy that, he was confident, would resolve the matter in his absence. The colonel, he wrote, should employ agency Indians, assisted by the troops at both Spotted Tail and Red Cloud, to simultaneously surround the respective bands of Crazy Horse and Touch the Clouds, disarm and then detain them. To avoid panicking the northerners, he suggested that the surrounds be made stealthily during the night, with the actual roundups occurring at dawn. If Bradley needed additional soldiers, he could request them from Fort Laramie. Action should be taken quickly. "Delay," he cautioned, "is very dangerous in this business."[41]

Sheridan, who had anxiously viewed the developments at Camp Robinson from afar, was not pleased with Crook's refusal to personally attend to the crisis. Tartly, he wired his subordinate that the Nez Perce affair was "but a small matter" compared to the repercussions of an outbreak by the northerners, which might signal a resumption of the Sioux War. So grave did Sheridan regard this situation, he ordered Crook to detrain at Sidney, Nebraska and go to Red Cloud at once.[42] Unable to do otherwise, Three Stars detrained at Sidney, and set off by wagon, with Bourke at his side, on the 120-mile ride to Camp Robinson. He would arrive just as events were reaching their climax.[43]

Lieutenant Jesse Lee, temporary agent at the Spotted Tail Agency, had come to know both Touch the Clouds and Crazy Horse well. He had discussed the substance of the critical August 31 meeting with Touch and with the interpreters who had been present, and he now believed that the rumors of a breakout by the northerners, at least with respect to Touch, were false. When Crook arrived at Camp Robinson on September 2, Lee attempted to share his conclusions with Crook. The latter, unwilling to be briefed piecemeal, directed him to Clark, who remained immovable in his conviction that Crazy Horse planned to resume hostilities. But Lee's presentation did raise doubts in Crook's mind about Touch the Clouds's possible involvement. Lee later recalled Crook as saying, "Mr. Lee, I don't want to make any mistake in this situation for it would, to the Indians, be the basest treachery to make a mistake in this matter."[44]

Though he now decided to give Touch the Clouds the benefit of the doubt, Crook, influenced by Clark, continued to distrust Crazy Horse.

To prevent his leading an outbreak, the general now determined to carry out the plan he had outlined to Bradley, to surround and disarm the chief's village the next morning.[45] That evening, however, he learned that the survivors of Lame Deer's band, over five hundred strong, had been sighted approaching the reservation to surrender. Fearing that a move against Crazy Horse might cause the new arrivals to bolt, he reversed course. Instead of the arrest, he scheduled a council at White Clay Creek for the following day to give Crazy Horse "one last chance for self-vindication."[46]

The next morning, Crook boarded an ambulance, accompanied by Clark and several others, for the two-mile trip to the council site. His route took him past the agency trading post. As the wagon jolted down the rutted path, he could see Billy Garnett, Big Bat Pourier, and an Oglala scout with the improbable name of Woman Dress, deep in conversation in front of the store. As the wagon approached, Pourier detached himself from the group and ran out to it, evidently having a message of some urgency to impart.[47]

For the events that ensued, historians rely heavily on information provided by Billy Garnett, who interpreted for the army over the next few days. Unfortunately, he gave three separate interviews on the subject that were inconsistent in several important respects. Using his stepfather's name, Hunter, Garnett first told his story in 1878 at Bourke's request to Lieutenant George Dodd of the Third Cavalry at Camp Robinson. In 1907, he was again interviewed, this time by historian Eli Ricker. A third and last exchange occurred with General Hugh Scott in 1920. The earliest interview differed substantially from the two later ones, particularly with regard to matters bearing directly on the involvement of both Crook and the army in the tragedy that followed. This first interview was given while Garnett still worked for the army and Crook remained commanding general of the Platte. As we shall see, this version of events seems to have been shaped to allay suspicions of the military's involvement in the death of the revered war chief. This could have been part of an effort to prevent further turmoil on the already restive Sioux reservation or simply to protect Crook's reputation. Either of these objectives render this version of events less credible than the ones that followed. The later interviews, thirty and then forty-three years after the event, though potentially suffering from inaccuracies due to memory lapses over time, were recorded long after any reason for concealment had passed, making them less suspect. They are also richer in detail, possibly for the same reason.

The three accounts agree that Pourier halted the wagon to allow Woman Dress, a scout and a nephew of Red Cloud, to speak with the soldiers. With Garnett interpreting, Woman Dress told the officers that, "Crazy Horse is going to come in there [Clay Creek] with sixty Indians, and catch General Crook by the hand . . . and those sixty Indians are going to kill Crook and whoever he has with him."[48] Crook appeared unfazed by the news. He was no stranger to threats on his life. Nor, aware of the false rumors that routinely swept the reservation, did he want to jump to any conclusions based on the wild tale of a single individual, a nephew of Red Cloud at that. So he interrogated Woman Dress to learn the source of his information. The scout admitted it was thirdhand, overheard by spies outside Crazy Horse's tipi and then relayed to another scout who then related it to Woman Dress.[49] To assess the reliability of his informant, Crook turned to Garnett. "What do you know about this man, Woman Dress?" The young interpreter deferred to Big Bat, related to the scout by marriage. Pourier, without hesitation, told Crook, "General, I want to tell you this man is a truthful man and whatever he tells you is the truth."[50] Crook regarded Big Bat as a man of integrity and his endorsement carried conviction. So he was persuaded to accept the veracity of Woman Dress's story. He now had to decide whether, despite the threat, he would attend the council.

Danger to his person was not the issue. This was not the first time in his long career as an Indian fighter that he had been informed that a council meeting would be used as a pretext to murder him. During his service on the Pacific coast and again in Arizona he had encountered similar situations and had turned them to his advantage. So, after pausing to digest the information, he cryptically announced his intention to proceed, remarking, "I never start any place but what I like to get there."[51]

Clark, more concerned than Crook about the danger, now intervened. Recalling to his commander the recent loss of General Custer, he pleaded with him to change his mind. "There is no use for you to start in there when you have no protection, just like that other [Custer] was." Clark's words, and a likely fear that his attendance would precipitate a bloody conflict between the Indian factions at the council, caused Three Stars to reconsider. But he worried about possible damage to his reputation should he fail to appear at the council. Would the chiefs interpret this as cowardice? This was not an issue of vanity, but of governance. An officer seen as faint of heart could not expect to command the respect and obedience of these warlike people. Again, Clark stepped forward, suggesting that Garnett carry word to the council that the general had received an important message that precluded his attendance. Satisfied that this subterfuge would solve the problem, Crook ordered the party to turn back to the post.[52]

In the initial 1878 interview, Garnett told Dodd that as he, Garnett, prepared to depart for White Clay, General Crook told him to ask "all the headmen to come up to the post as he wanted to talk to them." Garnett then added, "They all came except Crazy Horse," implying that the war chief had been included among the invitees, a construct that would have absolved Crook of any intention to plan to murder the chief at the meeting.[53] Compare this tale to Garnett's much later statement to Scott, made thirty years after Crook's death, in which he asserted that, prior to his departure, Clark gave him a hastily scribbled list of chiefs loyal to the military and told him to quietly summon *these* men to Camp Robinson as soon as possible to meet with the general.[54] This description appears to more accurately reflect the circumstances, but at the same time, makes the incident appear far more sinister and conspiratorial.

When Garnett arrived at the place where the council with Crazy Horse was to have been held, he saw many Indians, but neither the war chief nor his people were among them. The chief's absence, in light of subsequent events, would lead the interpreter to conclude that Woman Dress's account had been fabricated, a plot by Red Cloud to discredit Crazy Horse in Crook's eyes and turn him against the chief.[55] According to Garnett, Crook would later reach the same conclusion, stating frankly that he should have gone to the council and not listened to Clark, and admitting that he fell for Woman Dress's lies, having foolishly relied on Big Bat's affirmation of the scout's honesty.[56] He might have added that he had been predisposed to believe the warrior's tale as it neatly dovetailed with his own thinking, based on Clark's information—that Crazy Horse could not be trusted and should be arrested before he could resume his war against the white man.

Garnett told Scott that the meeting Crook held that afternoon at Camp Robinson was attended by only those Indian leaders whom the interpreter described as of "loyal brand"—Red Cloud and other Oglala chiefs considered reliable by the army. Frank Grouard, Pourier, and Garnett acted as interpreters. While Crook's aides were also present, Bradley, the post commander known to be sympathetic toward Crazy Horse, had not been invited to attend, though the meeting was held in his quarters.[57]

In the 1878 interview, Garnett described Crook as opening the meeting by informing the assembled chiefs that Crazy Horse had led them astray and "they must take him prisoner." Upon hearing this, "the Indians proposed killing him [Crazy Horse], a proposition agreed to by the others; but General Crook told them it must not be done as it would be murder, but insisted rather that he must be taken prisoner."[58] In *On the Border with Crook*, Bourke would repeat that Crook had firmly vetoed the plan to murder the war chief, apparently basing his information on Garnett's 1878 interview. He further described Crook as telling the assembled chiefs that he counted upon the loyal Indians themselves to make the arrest, "as it would prove to the nation that they were not in sympathy with the non-progressive elements of their tribe."[59] That statement seems an accurate reflection of Crook's Machiavellian strategy of playing off one faction against the other to break down tribal unity. It also harks back to his plan to persuade President Hayes to prevent the removal of the Oglalas and Brules to the Missouri. At the same time, this scenario absolves the Gray Fox of involvement in the plan to murder Crazy Horse and places the onus on Red Cloud and his cohorts so as to avoid the appearance of army involvement and protect the general's reputation.

The 1878 account provides no details about the assembled chiefs' plans to arrest Crazy Horse, probably intentionally, as such information would have inflamed his adherents. However, in 1907, when this was no longer an issue, Garnett provided Ricker with details:

> The business transacted [at the council] all related to the disarming of Crazy Horse and the scouts in his camp. . . . Crook put the question to these chiefs how the movement against Crazy Horse should be planned and managed. It was their opinion which was finally adopted that each chief present should pick two of his best men . . . all to go in the night to Crazy Horse's camp and surround it, and call out the chief

> and his scouts . . . and require them to give up their guns and revolvers, and if he refused, they were to be taken even at the cost of Crazy Horse's life.

Crook then ordered ammunition issued to the chiefs, who were dismissed with instructions to "go to their camps to prepare for the work that night."[60] The plain meaning of the plan Garnett outlined was to capture the chief, but if he died in any fighting that might ensue, that was acceptable to the army. Of the interpreter's three depictions of events, this one seems the closest to the truth. The plan would give Crook what we now term "plausible deniability" if the chief died during the arrest. And it seems to accurately reflect the general's growing determination, stoked by Clark's reports, to eliminate Crazy Horse, who, in his mind, now represented a threat to a lasting peace and, dearer to Crook's heart, his efforts to prevent removal of the Oglalas and Brules to the Missouri.

The 1920 interview with General Scott embroidered and perhaps overdramatized the events that Garnett described to Ricker. Garnett now insisted that Crook had planned the night attack with the stated objective of killing the war chief. To support his contention, Garnett described an offer by the military to pay $300 to the Indian who actually killed him, but left the matter of who made the offer hanging in the air. The Crazy Horse biographer, Kingsley Bray, who believed that Crook vetoed the chiefs' plan to kill Crazy Horse, wrote that the offer of the bounty was made by Clark, after Crook left the council and, according to Bray, without consulting him.[61]

After the council disbanded, Bradley confronted Garnett. Though the colonel had not attended the meeting, he had subsequently learned of the plan. Much disturbed, he told Garnett that it would be "bad to get after a man of the standing of Crazy Horse in this manner in the nighttime without his knowing anything about it." He apparently repeated his concerns to Clark, who then cancelled the dangerous night raid and, in its place, substituted a plan to arrest the chief the following morning. There is no evidence that Crook was involved in any way with this decision or that he wanted to be.[62] Like Pontius Pilate, he now seems to have washed his hands of the affair.

How does one explain such uncharacteristic behavior? Was the general so focused on his role in the coming Nez Perce campaign that he willingly walked away from the crisis, leaving it entirely in the hands of Bradley and Clark? A more plausible, albeit more unflattering, explanation is that, based on Clark's reports, Crook had concluded that Crazy Horse was one of the major obstacles to peace and, of more immediate concern, a potentially serious impediment to the general's campaign to prevent the removal of the Sioux to the Missouri. He would have to be eliminated, either arrested and deported to the East, or killed. But the chief's charisma among his people was such that if the action were attributed to Crook, his reputation among the Indians, a reputation that he cherished, would conceivably suffer irreparable damage. To avoid this outcome, he likely would have been anxious to disassociate himself from the inevitable flow of events to come. Surely, his trusted subordinate could handle the matter. Clark, an officer with a remarkable aptitude for behind-the-scenes manipulation and sang-froid to match, was the perfect man to accomplish this end. In any event, the next morning Crook and Bourke boarded an ambulance and headed off across the prairie to catch the train that would carry them to the Wind River Country and the Nez Perce war, leaving the fate of Crazy Horse in the hands of others.

the ability to stay calm in dangerous situations

Of course, the affair did not unfold as Crook expected. At 9:30 A.M., well after the Gray Fox had ridden off into the sunrise, Bradley, seeking to avoid carnage by the use of overwhelming force, dispatched eight troops of cavalry and infantry, two Gatling guns, a brass field piece, and four hundred "loyal" Sioux, to surround the village of Crazy Horse's remaining supporters.[63] They found it deserted, its residents having "scattered like a frightened covey of quail."[64] Crazy Horse had been forewarned. Depressed and abandoned by many of his followers, he had fled with his most faithful warriors to Spotted Tail's camp, seeking sanctuary. But the Brule chief, fearing that the Strange One's presence would disrupt the tranquility of his agency, refused to allow him to remain there. In desperation, Crazy Horse turned to his friend, Lieutenant Lee at nearby Camp Sheridan, who offered his protection, but only if the chief returned to Fort Robinson under military escort the next day. Crazy Horse, assured of his safety and promised the opportunity to present his grievances to Colonel Bradley on arrival at the post, reluctantly agreed.

On board the train headed for the Wind River Country, Crook, unable by nature to completely abdicate responsibility for events under his aegis, kept close tabs on the situation by telegraph. On the morn-

the power to protect, control or support something or someone

ing of September 5, responding to a message from Bradley describing Crazy Horse's "capture" at the Spotted Tail Agency, he wired the colonel, instructing him to send the chief under guard to Omaha following his transfer to Camp Robinson.[65] He then sent a telegram to Sheridan, emphasizing that he was now convinced that Crazy Horse would never be co-opted by the military. As long as the chief remained at the White River Agencies, he would continue to act as a magnet for unrest and would never cooperate in the relocation of his people to anywhere other than the Powder River country. After describing the orders he had sent to Bradley, he confessed to Sheridan, "I wish you would send him [Crazy Horse] off where he will be out of harm's way. . . . The successful breaking up of Crazy Horse's band has removed a heavy weight off my mind and I leave here feeling perfectly easy."[66] Sheridan, equally anxious to be rid of the fractious Oglala, replied that Crook should transfer Crazy Horse from Omaha to Sheridan's headquarters in Chicago as soon as possible. From there, the army would send him to Florida, probably to Fort Marion or the Dry Tortugas for incarceration.[67] This exchange of wires makes it clear that with Crazy Horse in custody, the generals no longer considered killing him an option.

Unaware that the military had already decided on his arrest and removal, Crazy Horse rode to Camp Robinson, anticipating that, as promised, he would have an opportunity to plead his case to the post commander. But Colonel Bradley, who had so recently fought to secure the chief's safety, now became the unwitting agent of his fate. When Crazy Horse arrived at the post at three o'clock that afternoon, the colonel refused to see him, believing that nothing he could say would change the outcome of events already ordained by higher authority. Obedient to Crook's instructions, he ordered the chief held in the post guardhouse, pending his transfer to Omaha. Initially, Crazy Horse went willingly with his military escort by his side. But as he neared the building, in Lieutenant Lee's words, "he saw the dungeon doors, the small grated window, and some prisoners in irons. . . . To his mind he was, then and there, at last brought face to face with what the white man had in store for him. No doubt feeling that he was abandoned by his friends, alone in his extremity . . . , he sprang, with the desperation of an infuriated tiger into the main guardroom." A struggle ensued and Little Big Man, his former lieutenant, seized him from behind in an attempt to restrain him. As the two men grappled with one another, the captain of the guard shouted, "Kill him! Kill him!" and one of the soldiers plunged a bayonet in his side.[68]

The wound was mortal. Attended by his father, Worm; his loyal friend, Touch the Clouds; and post surgeon, Valentine McGillycuddy, who administered morphine to ease the pain, the great chief died near midnight, lying on a blanket placed on the floor of the adjutant's office. The following morning, his father and Touch the Clouds quietly removed the body for burial in an unknown location. Born in 1840, he was only thirty-seven at the time of his death.[69]

CHAPTER THIRTY-TWO

Removal

September–October 1877

Word of Crazy Horse's death spread rapidly, creating deep divisions at the Red Cloud and Spotted Tail Agencies and threatening violence. But wiser heads prevailed with the chiefs' realization that internal strife was not only pointless, but undermined the united front needed to fight removal. Within a week of the slaying, the atmosphere calmed as the tribes united behind their leadership. Meanwhile, General Crook had found upon his arrival at Camp Brown that the fighting with the Nez Perces had passed him by, moving northeast into the Department of Dakota. With his troops out of the fighting, Crook saw no need to remain on the Wind River and returned to Omaha to assist the White River bands in their struggle against removal.[1]

With Crazy Horse out of the picture and the agencies apparently quiescent, Washington thought the time was ripe to proceed with the move. But the Brules and Oglalas, with Crook's support, refused to budge until the government fulfilled its promise to allow them to present their case in person to the president.[2]

Both Crook and the Indians knew that it would be a tough sell. The Interior Department was more deeply than ever committed to the Missouri River location. To make room for the Brules, the Department had already banished the Poncas, a small, inoffensive tribe, to Oklahoma, uprooting them from their tiny reservation at the confluence of the Missouri and Niobrara Rivers. The tribe, peaceful farmers who had always maintained good relations with the whites, suddenly found themselves occupying an arid wasteland in Indian Territory where they would soon face disease and malnutrition.[3]

The designated site on the Niobrara was not far from the old Whetstone Agency where the Brules had been resettled in 1868–69. They had found the hot, moist climate of these Missouri River lowlands, to which the Poncas were acclimated, to be lethal, accustomed as they were to the high, dry plains of western Nebraska and Wyoming. At the time, they had been fortunate. Their plight and Spotted Tail's protests had convinced the government to move them west to the White River. Now they faced similar conditions on the adjacent Niobrara.[4] But neither the opposition of the chiefs nor health concerns dampened the Interior Department's resolve to remove the tribes.[5] There were too many reasons in favor of removal for it not to proceed as planned. In particular, the previous year, unbeknownst to the Indian leaders, Congress had passed appropriations legislation requiring that all supplies intended for Spotted Tail and Red Cloud be delivered to the Missouri location. Now, with the goods in place on the river, neither the Interior nor the War Department wanted to incur the additional expense of moving them to another location. Furthermore, contracts had already been let for construction of agency buildings at the sites chosen for the new agencies.[6]

Obsessed with security, the military wholeheartedly supported the Interior Department. Unconvinced that they had knocked the fight out of the Sioux, Sherman and Sheridan still worried that, on the White River, the Indians presented a continuing threat to white settlements in western Nebraska and the Black Hills and might provide support to Sitting Bull should he return from Canada.

Though opposed by both the Interior Department and his own superiors, Crook refused to back down. Hammered by his persistent lobbying and the chiefs' stubborn resistance, the Washington bureaucrats reluctantly agreed to delay the move to allow the chiefs their promised meeting with the president. With Crazy Horse gone, the administration saw little harm in the exercise, believing the Indians would be so overawed by an audience with the Great Father that any opposition to removal would evaporate on the spot.[7]

Before noon on September 27, a mere three weeks after Crazy Horse had been slain, a delegation of Oglala notables, representing both Red Cloud and Crazy Horse factions, together with assorted Brule and

Arapaho chiefs, ceremonially painted and clad in their tribal finery, gathered in the East Room of the White House. At their side stood the Gray Fox, with his aide, White Hat Clark, their presence intended to reassure the tribesmen that they would receive a fair hearing. President Hayes, who anticipated a brief, largely symbolic meeting, greeted them with a glittering array of cabinet officials intended to overwhelm his native children. Included were the new secretary of the interior, German-born reformer Carl Schurz (known to the Sioux as Owl because of his hairy face and round glasses), the secretaries of state and war, the attorney general, and the postmaster general. Hayes had also invited his wife, teetotaling "Lemonade" Lucy. As the two women were longtime friends, Crook brought Mary. To speak for the Indians, Bishop Henry B. Whipple and William Welsh, humanitarian backers of the Indian cause, had also been invited.[8]

The august assemblage failed to distract the chiefs, and the council proved neither brief nor symbolic. It spilled over from the first afternoon into the next day and, after a brief respite to allow the Indians to explore the nation's capital, into yet a third morning. The Sioux and their allies presented their case with impressive unanimity and passion. Perhaps playing upon Lucy Hayes's well-known antipathy to alcohol, Red Cloud began by declaiming, "The Missouri River is the whiskey road, and if I went there I would not do good; I would come to nothing at all." Whipple chimed in, adding that though he believed that the Indians genuinely desired to become civilized, it would be impossible to do so on the Missouri, "as their women would become corrupt, and other evils follow to the men by the influence of bad white men." Spotted Tail and other chiefs spoke in a similar vein.[9] Crook's contribution was the soul of brevity. Perhaps hoping to wield his influence behind the scenes, he limited his public contribution to praising the Sioux for their cooperation over the past summer and fall and urging the president to attend carefully to the delegation's claims.[10]

When the president spoke, it was apparent that he had been moved by the delegation's fervor and unity of opposition. It was too late to avoid sending them to the Missouri over the winter, he told the chiefs. But if the bands would go there peacefully now, come spring, they could choose another site elsewhere on the reservation as a permanent home. Crook had earlier suggested an agency on the Tongue in accordance with Crazy Horse's wishes. This, Hayes said, was unacceptable.

But a site on the White River, in healthy country and well away from the Missouri, might be worthy of consideration.[11]

The chiefs were pleased with the president's offer and showed it by appearing at the White House for their next meeting wearing suits, a symbol of their desire to follow the white man's road. But with undeniable logic, they stubbornly insisted that they already knew where they wanted to live and didn't need to spend a winter on the Missouri to think about it. Spotted Tail preferred Wounded Knee Creek for his Brules, while Red Cloud had selected a site on White Clay Creek. Their supplies, they announced, could be moved there. Then, without missing a beat, the chiefs produced a laundry list of additional demands, ranging from teachers and cattle for their people, to a gift of forty dollars each, pocket money for the delegation's Washington visit. Unwilling, and perhaps unable, to respond directly to the chiefs' declared preferences for their agency locations, the president passed the buck, telling them that they had to move closer to their supplies and that "General Crook will help you." The interior secretary, he said, would look into their other demands. The gathering then adjourned in a flurry of handshakes.[12]

At a final meeting with Schurz, the delegation repeated its united opposition to the move. The Owl, refusing to be drawn into further discussions on the subject, distributed thirty dollars and an overcoat to each of the delegates and packed them off to the train station. Though outwardly satisfied that their voices had been heard, significantly, when the chiefs boarded the train, each carried a printed copy of the minutes of their meetings with the president, his promises neatly underlined in colored pencil.[13] Crook had scored something of a victory. A permanent move to the Missouri had perhaps been averted, but at a price. He now had the burden of convincing the wary Sioux chiefs that they must spend the winter on the Missouri, trusting that, come spring, the president would allow them to move to a site of their own choosing.

Crook spent most of October laboring to persuade the Indians to accept the temporary move. Since the government refused to transport the supplies on the Missouri to the White River, there was really no alternative. It was the same old choice: either go or starve.[14] Nevertheless, they balked, justifiably afraid that once they were on the Missouri, the government would renege and leave them stranded there. Only by pledging his personal honor to hold the government to its word could Crook finally convince them to make the journey.[15]

Sheridan was of little help, remaining at odds with his old friend. Still concerned about the threat to security, he continued to favor the Missouri River site, or better yet, Indian Territory. And once the chiefs agreed to the temporary move, he argued that Crook should assign three companies as escorts to prevent trouble on the march. But Crook resisted, first assigning only one company and then, reluctantly, two, convinced that a larger military escort would only exacerbate tensions.[16] He preferred to rely on the Indians to police themselves, enlisting three hundred of their number for the purpose, carefully chosen from both Crazy Horse and Red Cloud factions.[17]

To move the Indians and transport their possessions, a fleet of wagons was needed. But the Interior Department did not have them on hand. Crook knew that the Department would spend weeks procuring them, delaying the journey to the heart of winter when deep snows and subzero temperatures would turn the journey into a tragic ordeal similar to the trek from Camp Verde. So he shuttled frantically back and forth between the agencies, procuring the necessary wagons from the military's own stock and a herd of cattle to serve as the primary source of food during the march.[18] The *Army and Navy Journal* ironically noted that "cattle on the hoof, some 15,000, were . . . strange to say, the best they have ever been issued. The reason given was, the contractors had not time to find bad ones, as no delay was allowed."[19]

While plunging temperatures and driving snow plagued the eight thousand Indians who made the journey, the march proceeded fairly smoothly, if not strictly according to government plan. A contingent of northerners adamantly opposed the move. They included Miniconjous and Sans Arcs who had taken refuge with Spotted Tail's people after the death of Crazy Horse, warriors who, it was said, carried their leader's body with them. They proved a "hard and difficult element to control," burning the prairie behind them. An officer commanding one of the escorting troops thought that, but for the friendly agency Indians and scouts, "they would have attempted to have inflicted some damage on my command."[20] On November 17, a group of these northerners led by Chief Red Bear of the Sans Arc absconded from the column, heading north toward the Cheyenne River, hoping to join Sitting Bull across the Canadian line. Touch the Clouds, a Miniconjou moderate who had opted to remain with the agency Indians, was dispatched to attempt to dissuade them. But, though he reached them, they refused to listen to his entreaties and continued on their course, evading troops sent after them by Colonel Miles and eventually reaching Sitting Bull's camp.[21] Two days later, several more northerners attempted to break out, but this time their escape was foiled by agency police. In the end, of the eight thousand Indians making the journey, only two hundred failed to complete it, far fewer than Sheridan anticipated. Nor does it appear that additional troops would have made any difference. Perhaps recognizing these facts, Sheridan and Sherman refrained from criticizing Crook's handling of the march, including the events that followed.

Much to the generals' consternation, instead of proceeding to their designated sites on the Missouri, both Spotted Tail and Red Cloud stopped well short of the river, adamantly refusing to go further. Instead, the Oglalas settled down to winter on White Clay Creek, some eighty miles west of their assigned location, while Spotted Tail's Brules camped on Rosebud Creek, a tributary of the South Fork of the White River.[22] Not coincidentally, these sites were not far from the locations for which they had previously expressed a preference. Sherman and Sheridan, concerned that they now posed a threat to the Black Hills settlements, wanted to cut off their rations to force them to move to the Missouri. Crook joined Indian Agent Irwin in opposing this measure. The two men, on the same side for once, argued that the president had agreed to allow the chiefs to choose the location of their agencies and suggested that cutting off their rations in winter would only exacerbate unrest, for which the army was ill-prepared. The Interior Department backed their agent, and the decision was made to ship rations from the Missouri to the new camps for the remainder of the winter.[23] No one seemed happy with the arrangement. Though the Indians themselves provided the labor, the additional cost of the shipping added to Washington's general displeasure, while the Indians, as Crook pointed out in his annual report, continued to regard the removal as "a source of great dissatisfaction."[24]

While the Brules and Oglalas settled down for the winter, the government vacillated over whether to honor President Hayes's promise and allow the Indians to remain where they were when spring came. A strong faction opposed this course, Sheridan and others continuing to advocate banishment to Indian Territory. That idea, however, died when Schurz replaced John Q. Smith, the commissioner of Indian affairs, a staunch proponent of Indian Territory, with Ezra A. Hayt, who favored the Missouri.[25] Missouri River merchants, of course, eagerly attached themselves to Hayt's position. For Crook, it was the Arizona Ring all over again. In December, he pointedly reminded his superiors of the president's commitment to the Sioux to allow them to select their own locations and cautioned of serious consequences should his promise be ignored. In late January, he privately wrote to Webb Hayes, the president's son with whom he regularly corresponded, warning of a "combined effort on the part of certain parties on the Missouri" to have the Indians located on the River. Suspecting "latent opposition" would prevent his coming to Washington in the spring to present his case to the president, he asked Webb to intercede with his father on behalf of the Sioux.[26]

He also sought to enlist the press in his cause. Over the past several months he had come to know Thomas Henry Tibbles, a newspaperman in Omaha. Upon learning that they were both members of the Soldier Lodge secret society of the Omaha tribe, reputedly the only whites so honored up to that time, they formed a unique bond with one another.[27] In February 1877, Crook came to the editor's office to share the disheartening news that Commissioner Hayt had determined that President Hayes did not mean for the Indians to chose the location of their agency after all. A committee of "proper persons"—and by this Hayt meant whites—would select the sites. He, of course, had in mind the Missouri, and now planned a trip to visit Spotted Tail and Red Cloud to convince the Indians to go along with his interpretation of the president's promise.[28]

In Tibbles's words, the general was "heartsick." "He had given those Indians his word; now he felt sure that this new treachery would result in a general war that would involve all the northern tribes." A few days later, the general returned to Tibbles's office, this time in a far better mood. He had a plan, he explained. The editor was to convey a message to Old Spot, urging the chief "to refuse even to discuss [removal to the Missouri] at all—and to make some sort of a demonstration which would strike terror to the hearts of the 'men from Washington.'" Tibbles cheerfully did as requested, and Spotted Tail, his well-known sense of humor tickled by the idea, agreed. In June,

Congress authorized the commission's appointment; and in July, when the commissioners finally arrived at Spotted Tail's agency, they were met by a Brule delegation painted for war and looking "as frightful and dangerous as possible." After allowing the balding Hayt to spin out his tale of the advantages of life on the Missouri, Spotted Tail roared out his answer. "I have made . . . many treaties with men who came from Washington. Never has one of those been kept. All the men from Washington are liars, but the worst liars among them are the bald-headed ones! This last treaty must be kept! . . . If everything here is not on wheels and moving inside of ten days, I shall turn my young men loose, and they will make a desert of all the country between here and the Platte." The ruse worked. The Secretary of the Interior tersely noted in his annual report for 1878, "The Indians were found to be quite determined to move westward, and the promise of the Government in that respect was faithfully kept."[29]

The move took place in mid-November. The Brules settled on a new agency on the Rosebud, and the Oglalas on White Clay Creek. At Hayt's insistence, since "not one in a hundred can spell Ogalala [*sic*] correctly," the new Oglala agency was named Pine Ridge, though there were few pines and no ridges in the wide valley where Red Cloud had chosen to settle.[30]

Epilogue

The removal of the Sioux to their new agencies marked the end of the Great Sioux War and the final capitulation of the free-roaming tribes. Among the Sioux and their allies, only Sitting Bull and his loyal followers, unwanted refugees in the land of the Grandmother, as the Sioux referred to Canada, remained at large. They, too, would soon surrender. With the end of hostilities, responsibility for the management of Indian affairs reverted to the Department of the Interior's Indian Bureau, thus marking an end to Crook's dominant role in Indian affairs in the Department of the Platte.

The Bureau, charged with protecting the legal rights of their wards and providing "every assistance practicable . . . to advance them in agricultural pursuits and the arts of civilized life," seemed incapable of doing either.[1] Inadequate congressional appropriations, coupled with mismanagement and outright theft, quickly reduced the Indians to a state of destitution and desperation, which the army was helpless to ameliorate. Only when the tribes had been reduced to such dire straits that they saw no alternative but to break out of the reservations, could the military intervene. To many officers, including Crook, this latter duty was especially dispiriting, given that most such outbreaks could have been avoided had the Indian Bureau simply treated their charges with the dignity and fairness that had been promised.

The Sioux, who had experienced army control during the war, may have resented the rigid discipline of military governance, but they appreciated the probity of its officers. So, in the face of civilian corruption and incompetence, and ignorant of bureaucratic niceties, they turned to Crook for help. Unhappily, while sympathetic, the general was forced to admit that he could offer them little. "You know that I am your friend and friends must help each other . . . ," he wrote, "[however,] the grievances of which you now complain ought to be redressed by the Secretary of the Interior, as I cannot do much to assist you about them."[2]

Behind the scenes, he tried to use what influence he had. In the winter of 1878, for example, he wrote to General Sheridan on the matter of property stolen from the Indians:

> So long as white men steal from the Indians with impunity, and so long as the Indians are not afforded proper protection, this state of affairs [will] . . . eventually lead to hostilities with these tribes. . . .
>
> I . . . urge that the property of the Indians be protected, or that the terms of the treaty with them, by which they are to be reimbursed for such losses, be promptly and fully carried out.[3]

Receiving little in the way of response, he turned to sources outside the army for assistance, angering Sheridan and further eroding their already frayed relationship. On occasion, allied with the Indian Rights Association, an organization of white progressives engaged in a struggle for equitable treatment for its constituency, he fought a prolonged and ultimately futile battle against government neglect and private and public sector greed. His humanitarian efforts during the last decade of his life will be the subject of another work, the final volume of this project.

Was Crook the "greatest Indian fighter the United States Army ever had"? Martin Schmitt, the editor of the general's autobiography, claimed that General Sherman thought so.[4] The wide spectrum of opinions expressed both during Crook's lifetime and subsequently by historians attests to the controversial nature of his military leadership. His reticent and often deliberately opaque personality frequently obscured his intentions and motivations, leaving others to interpret his actions. He had a polarizing personality, and not unnaturally, the assessments of others were all too often colored by the observer's sentiments regarding him. Among Crook's superiors, Grant, whose private opinions about the general were apparently never set to paper, publicly praised him as "the best, the wiliest Indian fighter in this country."[5] Sherman ostensibly agreed, although in private correspondence with Sheridan, he was highly critical of Crook's performance in the Sioux War. Sheridan, himself, went from admirer to doubter after the Rosebud battle and its aftermath, which to him demonstrated that his old friend had lost his former aggressiveness in the face of the enemy. Sheridan's opinion continued to plummet as Crook's loyalty toward him waivered and he repeatedly disregarded his superior's demands for punitive actions against the Indians.

Among the officers who campaigned with Crook in the field, Carr and Miles were openly contemptuous of his reputation as an Indian fighter. Both had personal issues that shaded their opinions, but as high-ranking veterans of the Indian wars, their views cannot be entirely discounted. Dodge was originally infuriated by Crook's reticence, believing it covered indecision; but he ultimately endorsed the general's foresight and performance as a campaigner, confining his criticism to Crook's administrative abilities. General Howard, who had his own issues with Crook, but was ordinarily fair-minded, lauded his skills as a frontiersman and his early record in the West, which owed much to the fact that "he fought the Indians in their own way." But, referring to his 1880s efforts to capture Geronimo, Howard wrote, in the end, that he "put too much faith in his 'good Indians' guides, and General Miles . . . succeeded where he had failed."[6] Bourke, King, Stanton, Nickerson, and other junior officers openly worshipped the general, providing assessments of his capabilities that were sometimes as overblown as those of Miles were tainted by jealousy and venom.

One might expect a modicum of objectivity from newsmen. But this was a rare quality in nineteenth-century journalism. The *Herald*'s reporters, Davenport and Roche, whose paper was politically biased against the general, were highly critical of Crook's performance and rarely lost the opportunity to denigrate him. Strahorn, Wasson, Finerty, and to a lesser extent Mills campaigned with Crook and ultimately became his friends and admirers. Their relationships with the general did not provide the best foundation for objectivity, but their reports reflect a unanimity concerning his qualities as a leader that lend great credibility to their observations.

Temporal distance from the subject seems to have hardly made a difference. Historians, too, have failed to agree on an evaluation of Crook's performance as a fighting general. John Carroll, a leading Custer scholar, described him as "the most over-rated officer in the U.S. Army, and one who deserves censure for his retreat in 1876."[7] Charles Robinson, a Crook biographer, was critical of his subject, but more balanced than Carroll. He found Crook's Sioux War campaigns demonstrated that while he "might have understood the Indian mentality, he was not always able to convert that understanding into military action." Yet "in dealing with the Apaches . . . he was without peer."[8] Paul Hutton, a Sheridan biographer of note, found Crook "unconventional," a characteristic that "paid rich dividends in Indian warfare."

"Unconventional," as Hutton used the term, may refer to both his military innovations and his sympathy for the Indians. His humanity ultimately caused him to oppose the more severe and inequitable aspects of army policies and to some degree tempered the brutality of his campaigns.[9] Joseph Porter, author of the foreword to the paperback edition of Crook's autobiography, and an insightful chronicler of John Bourke's life, found Crook to be both an "aggressive and innovative campaigner," an evaluation that owed much to his reliance on Indian scouts. His effectiveness, Porter believed, was due to his understanding of Indian psychology and tribal structure.[10]

But perhaps the final arbiters of Crook's effectiveness as a fighting soldier should be those who faced him on the battlefield. And it is clear that the Indians both feared and respected his abilities. Crazy Horse merely echoed what many of the western tribes had expressed upon surrendering to the general after his unremitting campaigns against them. Crook, he declared, was more "feared by the Sioux than all other white men."[11] Yet, upon hearing of the general's death, Red Cloud, who was no great friend of the army, would sadly profess: "He, at least, never lied to us. His words gave the people hope. He died. Their hope died again. Despair came again." That was an epitaph that the old general would surely have appreciated.

Notes

PREFACE

1. Azor H. Nickerson, "Major General George Crook and the Indians," 1. Nickerson was wrong about Crook's age. Born in September 1828, he had just turned thirty-eight. Schmitt, ed., *General George Crook, His Autobiography*, xx.

2. Nickerson, "Major General George Crook," 1–2.

3. Crook to R. B. Hayes, Jan. 4, 1871. George Crook Letter Books, George Crook Collection, typescript, Rutherford B. Hayes Library, Presidential Center, Fremont, OH.

4. Juarez, *The Tarnished Saber.*

5. Nickerson, "Major General George Crook," 3–4.

6. Opler, *An Apache Life-way.*

7. Paul Hedren casts these officers' experiences in a somewhat more positive light. See *Great Sioux War Orders of Battle*, 26–27.

8. Magid, *George Crook, From the Redwoods to Appomattox.*

CHAPTER 1

1. The two men traveled without their spouses. Nickerson, though he never mentioned it, apparently left his wife behind in San Francisco and sent for her at a later date. Crook had left his spouse, Mary, whom he had married immediately after the war, in Maryland with her family, planning to send for her when he was settled into his new assignment. Schmitt, ed., *General George Crook*, 155.

2. Nickerson, "Major General George Crook," 5.

3. Ibid.

4. Bancroft, *History of Oregon*, 30:527n.

5. Nickerson, "Major General George Crook," 8; Bancroft, *History of Oregon*, 30:521; Bourke, "George Crook in Indian Country," reprint, 2.

6. Nickerson, "Major General George Crook," 9.

7. Peterson, *Idaho*, 58–59.

8. *Owyhee Avalanche*, Dec. 8, 1866, quoted in Michno, *The Deadliest Indian War*, 191. "Lo" was a sarcastic reference, much favored in the West, to the eastern establishment's romantic view of Indians, exemplified in a poem by Alexander Pope about the Noble Savage that begins, "Lo, the poor Indian . . ."

9. Michno, *Deadliest Indian War*, 5.

10. Walker, *Indians of Idaho*, 87–102.

11. Hopkins, *Life Among the Paiutes*, 5.

12. Canfield, *Sarah Winnemucca of the Northern Paiutes*, 19.

13. U.S. Docs. Serial 1324, 71, 74, quoted in Keith and Donna Clark, "William McKay's Journal, 1866–67: Indian Scouts, part 1, 121–22.

14. Egan, *Sand in a Whirlwind*, 79–103.

15. For details, see Michno, *Deadliest Indian War*, 65–66; Clark and Clark, "William McKay's Journal," part 1, 139.

16. Bancroft, *History of Oregon*, 30:531.

17. Idaho State Historical Society, "The Snake War, 1864–1868," no. 236, 1; Michno, *Deadliest Indian War*, 63; Bourke, "George Crook in Indian Country," 1–2.

18. *Owyhee Avalanche*.

19. Athearn, *William Tecumseh Sherman and the Settlement of the West*, 223.

20. See map, ibid., 23.

21. Bancroft, *History of Oregon*, 30:519; Utley, *Frontier Regulars*, 19–23.

22. The son of Robert E. Lee's sister, Marshall had chosen, much to his uncle's disgust, to serve in the Union Army. Even worse, in Lee's opinion, he had been an aide to General Pope, whom Lee regarded with utter disdain. As a staff officer, Marshall's wartime career involved little combat experience and proved undistinguished. Michno, *Deadliest Indian War*, 143.

23. In July 1866, President Johnson signed a law authorizing the recruitment of an additional four regiments of cavalry. One such regiment, the Eighth, was formed in California and included many Civil War veterans. Companies of the Eighth, commanded by John Gregg, who had served under Crook in the Appomattox campaign, were sent to garrison the posts in the Boise District. Ibid., 174, 208; for Crook and Gregg in the Appomattox campaign, see Magid, *George Crook*, 306.

24. Bancroft, *History of Oregon*, 30:521; "The Snake War, 1864–1868," in Michno, *Deadliest Indian War*, 153–57.

25. Hanley, *Owyhee Trails*, 61; Michno, *Deadliest Indian War*, 150.

26. Schmitt, *General George Crook*, 142–43.

27. William Parnell, "Operations against Hostile Indians with General Crook, 1867–1868," in Cozzens, ed., *Eyewitnesses*, 2:9.

28. Schmitt, *General George Crook*, 142–43.

29. Ibid., 144.

30. Bourke, "George Crook in Indian Country," 2.

31. Ibid.

32. Nickerson, "Major General George Crook," 9.

33. Michno, *Deadliest Indian War*, 190.

34. Bancroft, *History of Oregon*, 30:532; Report of the Secretary of War, 1868, 58, quoted in Schmitt, *General George Crook*, 144n. There is some confusion as to the identity of the two civilians because their names are not given in the reports. Michno identi-

fies them as Archie McIntosh and Sinora Hicks. But Crook wrote in his autobiography that his chief scout on this leg of the expedition was Cayuse George Rundell, who had previously scouted for Marshall and whom Crook soon found "utterly worthless and demoralized." The author believes that the two scouts were Hicks and Rundell and that McIntosh joined the column after their first engagement. Schmitt, *General George Crook*, 142; Michno, *Deadliest Indian War*, 193–94.

35. *Rancheria* was a term commonly used to describe an Indian encampment in the Southwest. Military officers serving in other parts of the West adopted the terminology.

36. U.S. House of Representatives, Report of the Secretary of War, 1867, 1:77.

37. Michno, *Deadliest Indian War*, 194.

38. Schmitt, *General George Crook*, 145.

39. Dunlay, *Wolves for the Blue Soldiers*, 46.

40. Clark and Clark, "William McKay's Journal," part 1, 129–30.

41. 14 Stat. 332–38, July 28, 1866; Utley, *Frontier Regulars*, 54–56; Bancroft, *History of Oregon*, 30:530; Dunlay, *Wolves for the Blue Soldiers*, 46.

42. Reuben Maury to Benjamin Alvord, Feb. 17, 1864, quoted in Clark and Clark, "William McKay's Journal," part 1, 130.

43. Clark and Clark, "William McKay's Journal," part 1, 141. General Steele was a recent convert. When Governor George Woods of Oregon had first requested that he enlist Warm Springs tribesmen to serve in independent units, but in conjunction with the military, Steele had refused. As he favored the extermination of Indians regardless of sex or age, he was not troubled by the scouts' mode of warfare. Rather, he thought that Wood's proposal exceeded the parameters of the law, believing that Congress intended scouts to serve as part of regular army units, rather than independently. Steele was overruled by the secretary of war. Bancroft, *History of Oregon*, 30:531; Michno, *Deadliest Indian War*, 100.

44. The Warm Springs had their incentive for hunting the Paiutes. The latter had made repeated horse-stealing raids on the Warm Springs Agency, and had killed a Warm Springs chief while negotiating with him under a flag of truce. See Clark and Clark, "William McKay's Journal," part 1, 126, and part 2, 330.

45. Darragh was "a morose, backward, unsocial man, . . . esteemed highly by those who knew him best, but they were very few, for he encouraged but few to come near enough to know him." He would return to New York in the 1880s and go into the building trades, working on both New York's first skyscraper and the Waldorf Astoria. Elizabeth Lord, *Reminiscences of Eastern Oregon*, quoted in Clark and Clark, "William McKay's Journal," part 1, 133. McKay was short, stocky, with dark skin—the color of snuff, according to a contemporary—and the dark hair and eyes of an Indian. He was known for his kindly and gentlemanly manner and his fondness for whisky. On the reservation, he served in many capacities, including as a coroner for the tribe. *Owyhee Avalanche*, Aug. 3, 1867, quoted in Clark and Clark, part 2, 312; Clark and Clark, "William McKay's Journal," part 1, 132–35.

46. Joseph Wasson, "Colonel Crook's Campaign," *Owyhee Avalanche*, Aug. 3, 1867, in Cozzens, *Eyewitnesses*, 2:38.

47. Dunlay, *Wolves for the Blue Soldiers*, 46.

48. Schmitt, *General George Crook*, 145–46.

49. Ibid.; Report of Secretary of War, 1867, 71.

50. Schmitt, *General George Crook*, 147.

51. Thrapp, *Encylopedia of Frontier Biography*, 2:908–909.

52. Schmitt, *General George Crook*, 147–48.

53. Ibid., 148.

54. Ibid., 148–49; Bancroft, *History of Oregon*, 30:533; Michno, *Deadliest Indian War*, 202.

55. Report of Secretary of War, 1867, 77; Schmitt, *General George Crook*, 149; Bancroft, *History of Oregon*, 30:533.

56. Michno cites the extermination order at 199, but indicates in an ensuing footnote that a copy of the order has never been located. Michno, *Deadliest Indian War*, 205n13.

57. Bancroft, *History of Oregon*, 30:531n20; Clark and Clark, "William McKay's Journal," part 2, 329.

58. Gilliss and Gilliss, *So Far from Home*, 166. Attempts were made to blame the deaths of women and children on Indian scouts, but such accusations were by no means always justified. The Shoshone scouts opposed the practice, fearing retaliation against their own families. Bancroft, *History of Oregon*, 30:531n20.

59. Bancroft, 30:533. Crook does not mention this engagement, and there is no indication how he knew that the men in the camp had been involved in prior depredations. It is entirely possible that the warrior shot for violating his parole was executed simply for defending himself when the soldiers attacked.

60. Schmitt, *General George Crook*, 149; Michno, *Deadliest Indian War*, 210.

61. Schmitt, *General George Crook*, 150.

62. Ibid., 150–51.

63. Ibid; Crook to Strong, Aug. 2, 1867, quoted in Gilliss and Gilliss, *So Far from Home*, 314n3.

64. Crook to Steele, Apr. 2, 1868, quoted in Michno, *Deadliest Indian War*, 214; Schmitt, *General George Crook*, 152.

65. Michno, *Deadliest Indian War*, 223.

66. Bancroft, *History of Oregon*, 30:533; Michno, *Deadliest Indian War*, 200–202.

67. Report of Secretary of War, 1867, 78.

68. Ibid., 79.

69. Ibid., 74.

70. Halleck referred to Crook by his brevet rank in the regular army conferred in recognition of his services during the Civil War. In 1869–70, Congress abolished the use of brevet ranks in official communications. Utley, *Frontier Regulars*, 22.

CHAPTER 2

1. Wasson, "Colonel Crook's Campaign," *Owyhee Avalanche*, July 27, 1867, in Cozzens, *Eyewitnesses*, 2:33.

2. Knight, *Following the Indian Wars*, 36.

3. *Rocky Mountain News*, Aug. 8, 1876, quoted in ibid., 169.

4. Bourke, *On the Border with Crook*, 95.

5. *Owyhee Avalanche*, Aug. 2 and Sept. 28, 1867, in Cozzens, *Eyewitnesses*, 2:39.

6. Knight, *Following the Indian Wars*, 43.

7. Schmitt, *General George Crook*, 141.

8. Wasson, *Owyhee Avalanche*, Sept. 21, 1867, in Cozzens, *Eyewitnesses*, 2:56.

9. A troop was the cavalry equivalent of an infantry company. Utley, *Frontier Regulars*, 37n8.

10. Wasson, "Colonel Crook's Campaign," *Owyhee Avalanche*, Aug. 3, 1867, in Cozzens, *Eyewitnesses*, 2:35.

11. Ibid., July 27, 1867, 2:34. Though Wasson did not mention it, Crook further obscured his movements by never marching the same distance on any two consecutive days, a tactic he had employed in West Virginia when operating behind enemy lines during the war. Bourke, "George Crook in Indian Country," 3.

12. Wasson, "Colonel Crook's Campaign," 2:35.

13. Ibid., 2:36.

14. Bourke, "George Crook in Indian Country," 3; Wasson, "Colonel Croook's Campaign"; Clark and Clark, "William McKay's Journal," part 2, 277; Essin, *Shavetails and Bell Sharps*, 89.

15. Essin, *Shavetails and Bell Sharps*, 14–15, 3.

16. Schmitt, *General George Crook*, 5–6; ibid., 4.

17. Essin, *Shavetails and Bell Sharps*, 93–94; Bourke, *On the Border*, 150.

18. Essin, *Shavetails and Bell Sharps*, 97.

19. Bourke, "George Crook in Indian Country," 13.

20. Wasson, *Owyhee Avalanche*, Aug. 17, 1868, 43, in Cozzens, *Eyewitnesses*; Michno, *Encyclopedia of Indian Wars*, 204.

21. Parnell, "Operations," in Cozzens, *Eyewitnesses*, 2:12; Wasson, *Owyhee Avalanche*, Sept. 21, 1967, in Cozzens, *Eyewitnesses*, 2:57.

22. See Cozzens, *Eyewitnesses*, 2:720n1, quoting Thrapp, *Encyclopedia*, 3:1116–17.

23. Parnell, "Operations," in Cozzens, *Eyewitnesses*, 2:113.

24. In his autobiography, Crook, writing an account of the previous winter's campaign, noted that he had arrived at [old Camp] Warner from C. F. Smith in a blizzard. He had waited for the storm to abate, and "a couple of days later," had "moved down to Lake Warner so I could operate against the Indians, as that country was comparatively free from snow." Schmitt, *General George Crook*, 151. While it appeared from his choice of words that he had built the new post that winter, that was not the case. See Crook to R. P. Strong, AAG, Dept. of Columbia, Portland, Aug. 2, 1867, NA, Letters Received, Records of the U.S. Army Continental Commands, 1821–1920, Record Group 393.

25. Schmitt, *General George Crook*, 151; Crook to Strong, Aug. 2, 1867; *Owyhee Avalanche*, Aug. 17, 1867, quoted in Gilliss and Gilliss, *So Far from Home*, 213n1. Wasson, who accompanied Crook on the scouting party, was enthusiastic about Crook's decision, writing that "the new site will have the advantages over that of any post now occupied in the district. . . ." Wasson, *Owyhee Avalanche*, Aug. 17, 1867, in Cozzens, *Eyewitnesses*, 2:47.

26. Crook to Strong, Aug. 2, 1867.

27. Gilliss and Gilliss, *So Far from Home*, 213n1; Michno, *Deadliest Indian War*, 236.

28. Wasson, *Owyhee Avalanche*, Aug. 17, 1868, in Cozzens, *Eyewitnesses*, 2:46.

29. Crook to Strong, Aug. 2, 1867.

30. Ibid.

31. Bancroft, *History of Oregon*, 30:537; Michno, *Deadliest Indian War*, 237.

32. Wasson, *Owyhee Avalanche*, Nov. 2, 1867, in Cozzens, *Eyewitnesses*, 2:49.

33. Schmitt, *General George Crook*, 154n4. General William F. Harney was a noted Indian fighter in his own right.

34. Bancroft, *History of Oregon*, 30:535–36; Wasson, *Owyhee Avalanche*, Nov. 1, 1867, in Cozzens, *Eyewitnesses*, 2:73–74; Magid, *George Crook*, 71–86.

35. Michno, *Deadliest Indian War*, 250; Wasson, *Owyhee Avalanche*, Sept. 21, 1867, in Cozzens, *Eyewitnesses*, 2:58; Clark and Clark, *McKay's Journal*, 2:288.

36. Wasson, *Owyhee Avalanche*, Sept. 21, 1867, 2:57–58.

37. Bourke, "General Crook in Indian Country," 5.

38. Wasson, *Owyhee Avalanche*, 64, in Cozzens, *Eyewitnesses*; Clark and Clark, "William McKay's Journal," 2:292n219.

39. Wasson, in Cozzens, *Eyewitnesses*, 2:64.

40. Parnell, "Operations," in Cozzens, *Eyewitnesses*, 2:13.

41. Wasson, in Cozzens, *Eyewitnesses*, 2:67.

42. Michno, *Deadliest Indian War*, 255.

43. Ibid.

44. See ibid., 255–56; Parnell, "Operations," in Cozzens, *Eyewitnesses*, 2:14; Wasson, in Cozzens, *Eyewitnesses*, 2:68; Richard I. Eskridge, "The Battle of the Infernal Caverns," in Cozzens, *Eyewitnesses*, 2:84; Bancroft, *History of Oregon*, 30:540.

45. Wasson, *Owyhee Avalanche*, Nov. 8, 1867, in Cozzens, *Eyewitnesses*, 2:68; Parnell, "Operations," in *Eyewitnesses*, 2:14.

46. Parnell, "Operations," in Cozzens, *Eyewitnesses*, 2:15.

47. Wasson, in Cozzens, *Eyewitnesses*, 2:70.

48. Parnell, "Operations," in Cozzens, *Eyewitnesses*, 2:15–16; Wasson, in Cozzens, *Eyewitnesses*, 2:71.

49. Bancroft, *History of Oregon*, 30:542.

50. Schmitt, *General George Crook*, 154.

51. Report of Brevet Major General George Crook, Oct. 14, 1868, in Annual Report of the Secretary of War, 1868, Part 1, 69. Crook's own estimate was that twenty Indians had been slain and twelve wounded. Regarding his own casualties, these too may have been underestimated. Wasson put the number of casualties at eight soldiers killed and twelve wounded. Bancroft and Michno used Wasson's figures rather than Crook's. Bancroft, *History of Oregon*, 30:544; Michno, *Encyclopedia of the Indian Wars*, 211.

52. Wasson, in Cozzens, *Eyewitnesses*, 2:74–75.

53. Ibid. It should be noted that neither regulars nor Indians had any scruples about disfiguring the bodies of the dead. Parnell, for example, mentioned without censure that one of his troopers was killed while attempting to enter a cave to scalp a dead warrior whose body he had spotted within. Parnell, "Operations," in Cozzens, *Eyewitnesses*, 2:17. And, as shall be seen, troopers on occasion tore down and looted the burial scaffolds of the Plains Indians.

54. Bancroft, *History of Oregon*, 30:544; Wasson, quoted in Michno, *Deadliest Indian War*, 252.

55. Bancroft, *History of Oregon*, 30:544.

56. Wasson, in Cozzens, *Eyewitnesses*, 2:70.

57. Ibid., 2:73.

58. Gilliss and Gilliss, *So Far from Home*, 148.

59. Ibid., 153–54.

60. Schmitt, *General George Crook*, 155; see also Gilliss and Gilliss, *So Far from Home*, 155, for a description of her cabin; Bourke, "George Crook in Indian Country," 6; Anonymous, "In Memoriam, 'Jim,'" Nov. 1874, Bourke File, Nebraska Historical Society, Box 10–2.

61. "In Memoriam"; Schmitt, *General George Crook*, 155. Jim would sadly meet his maker in Arizona, killed by a Mohave Apache, who was apparently unaware of or indifferent to the fact that he belonged to the military commander of the district.

62. Parnell, "Operations," in Cozzens, *Eyewitnesses*, 2:20; Schmitt, *General George Crook*, 155–56.

63. Gilliss and Gilliss, *So Far from Home*, 183, 170–71, 174, 177.

CHAPTER 3

1. Bancroft, *History of Oregon*, 30:548. Having nothing to do with Santa's reindeer, the region was supposedly named by an early explorer after he witnessed a violent thunderstorm there. Schmitt, *General George Crook*, 156n6.

2. See Michno, *Deadliest Indian War*, 283–87, 289, 295.

3. Parnell, "Operations," 2:19.

4. Michno, *Deadliest Indian War*, 275. One bone of contention was the division of the captives who were to be sold into slavery. Though a bloody civil war had just been fought over slavery, the question of condemning these hapless souls to involuntary servitude did not appear to trouble either Crook or the War Dept. (277).

5. Ibid., 295–96.

6. Parnell, "Operations," in Cozzens, *Eyewitnesses*, 2:24.

7. See ibid., 21–25, for a vivid description of the hardships of the campaign.

8. Ibid., 24–25.

9. Michno, *Deadliest Indian War*, 296.

10. Crook to AAG, Feb. 24, 1868, RG 363, Dept. of Columbia, Letters Received, Box 4.

11. Parnell, "Operations," in Cozzens, *Eyewitnesses*, 2:26–28. In his annual report to the secretary of war, Crook indicated that his return to Warner on this occasion was due to his supplies being exhausted, perhaps confusing this expedition with the earlier one. Report of Brevet Major General George Crook, Oct. 14, 1868, Report of the Secretary of War, 1868, Part 1, 40th Cong., 3rd Sess., 70.

12. Parnell, "Operations," in Cozzens, *Eyewitnesses*, 2:28–29.

13. Ibid., 30.

14. Michno, *Deadliest Indian War*, 308–309, 324–26.

15. Utley, *Frontier Regulars*, 180.

16. Magid, *George Crook*, 84.

17. Report of the Secretary of War, 1868, 44.

18. Report of the Secretary of War, 1867, 77–79.

19. Letters in George Crook ACP File, NARA, Microform, M1395; Charles M. Robinson III, *General Crook and the Western Frontier*, 101.

20. Crook to Dept. of Columbia, May 29, 1868, RG 393, Dept. of Columbia, Letters Received, Box 4.

21. Juarez, *Tarnished Saber*, 38.

22. Lieutenant William McCleave to Post Adjutant, Camp Harney, June 24, 1868, Dept. of Columbia, Letters Received, Box 5; Michno, *Deadliest Indian War*, 325–26.

23. McCleave to Kelly, June 4, 1868, Dept. of Columbia, Letters Received, Box 5.

24. Crook to AAG, June 6, 1868, Dept. of Columbia, Letters Received; Crook, Report of the Secretary of War, 1868, 71.

25. Michno, *Deadliest Indian War*, 326.

26. Kelly to Nickerson, June 24, 1868, Dept. of Columbia, Letters Received.

27. Crook to AAG, June 6, 1868; Michno, *Deadliest Indian War*, 327.

28. Michno, *Deadliest Indian War*, 327.

29. Gilliss and Gilliss, *So Far from Home*, 176–77; Nickerson, "Major General George Crook," 11.

30. Nickerson, "Major General George Crook," 11–12.

31. See Magid, *George Crook*, 67.

32. Crook to AAG, July 6, 1868, Dept. of Columbia, Letters Received, Box 5; see also Nickerson, "Major General George Crook," 11.

33. Bancroft, *History of Oregon*, 30:550; Nickerson, "Major General George Crook," 13; see also Dunlay, *Wolves for the Blue Soldiers*, 124; Parnell, "Operations," in Cozzens, *Eyewitnesses*, 2:31, 32.

34. Bancroft, *History of Oregon*, 30:551.

35. Schmitt, *General George Crook*, 159.

36. George Crook, "Race with the Indians," *Daily Oregonian*, July 29, 1868, in Cozzens, *Eyewitnesses*, 2:86.

37. Ibid.

38. Crook to AAG, Aug. 22, 1868, RG 393, Dept. of Columbia, Letters Received, Box 5; Michno, *Deadliest Indian War*, 340–41.

39. Crook to AAG, Oct. 24, 1869, RG 393, Dept. of Columbia, Letters Sent 1866–69.

40. Schmitt, *General George Crook*, 158.

41. Crook to AAG, Oct. 24, 1869, RG 393, Dept. of Columbia, Letters Sent 1866–69; Michno, *Deadliest Indian War*, 339.

42. Crook to AAG, Aug. 22, 1868, Letters Sent.

43. Nickerson for Crook to Elmer Otis, Oct. 9, 1869, Letters Sent.

44. Nickerson, "Major General George Crook," 13.

45. Utley, *Frontier Regulars*, 8.

46. Cited as "Military Correspondence, Dec. 7, 1869" and quoted in Bancroft, *History of Oregon*, 30:553n46.

47. Michno, *Deadliest Indian War*, 342.

CHAPTER 4

1. Utley, *Frontier Regulars*, 16.

2. Ibid., 192.

3. Schmitt, *General George Crook*, 160.

4. Ralph H. Ogle, *Federal Control of the Western Apaches, 1848–1886*, 78–79.

5. Ibid. By assigning Crook at his brevet rank, the president hoped to finesse the problem of the waiting colonels.

6. Quoted without naming his source by Dan Thrapp in the introduction of Summerhayes, *Vanished Arizona*, xiii.

7. Nickerson, "Major General George Crook," 13.

8. Summerhayes, *Vanished Arizona*, 43.

9. Schmitt, *General George Crook*, 162.

10. Bourke, *On the Border*, 9.

11. Strikers like Peisen were a common fixture in the nineteenth-century army, particularly in the homes of officers with families. While maintaining their military status, they were compensated by the officers for whom they worked, who, in return, were relieved of the responsibility of maintaining their uniforms, cooking, and taking care of a

myriad of other time-consuming housekeeping chores. Peisy would remain with Crook for the remainder of the general's career, demonstrating both the desirability of the position and his commitment to the family. Schmitt, *General George Crook*, 162n3.

12. Crook's mood was undoubtedly further soured by the knowledge that the army had failed to tell Mary of her husband's assignment to Arizona before she had embarked from her family's Oakland, Maryland home. Thus, she traveled west believing that she was to join him in San Francisco, only to have to immediately return east because of Crook's sudden assignment in Arizona, where he would be unable to accommodate her presence at the time. Fanny Daily to War Dept., May 5, 1871, Crook ACP File, Microfilm Records M 1395, National Archives.

13. Schmitt, *General George Crook*, 162.

14. The so-called ambulance was a wagon originally developed to carry the wounded during the Civil War, hence its name. "The ambulance resembles an omnibus, is entered by two steps in the rear, contains seats for eighteen persons—fourteen inside and four on the front seat. By raising the flaps of the inside seats and supporting them by the uprights attached, and removing the cushions from the backs of the permanent seats, a bed is arranged which will accommodate one, two, or, on an emergency, three men lying down." "Civil War Ambulance Wagons," www.civilwarhome.com/ambulancewagons .html, Oct. 19, 2006.

15. Bourke, *On the Border*, 56; John Ross Browne, *Adventures in the Apache Country*, 131.

16. Bourke, *On the Border*, 108, 138; Schmitt, *General George Crook*, 163.

17. Worcester, *Apaches, Eagles of the Southwest*, 7.

18. Goodwin, *Western Apache Raiding*, 12.

19. Lockwood, *Apache Indians*, 53.

20. Goodwin, *Western Apache Raiding*, 14.

21. Lockwood, *Apache Indians*, 5. "Papagos" is used here to describe that tribe rather than the more anthropologically correct Tohono O'odham; the former name was commonly in use at the time of Crook's service in Arizona. See Jacoby, *Shadows at Dawn*, 13–14.

22. The Apaches were not entirely averse to using horses as mounts, recognizing that under some circumstances they provided greater mobility. But with brutal practicality, when pursued, they often rode their mounts to death and then ate them. See Worcester, *Apaches*, 10.

23. Ibid., 38.

24. Ibid., 19.

25. Thrapp, *Conquest of Apacheria*, 7.

26. For a fascinating account of the pre–Civil War and Civil War period, as well as a contemporary Anglo's interpretation of Apache ways of life, see Cremony, *Life Among the Apaches*.

27. For a detailed discussion of the Yavapais, see Braatz, *Surviving Conquest*.

28. Lockwood, *Apache Indians*, 92–99.

29. Utley, *Frontier Regulars*, 199.

30. For more on Stoneman's performance at Chancellorsville, see Sears, *Chancellorsville*, 367–70.

31. California State Museum, *George Stoneman, Jr.*, www.militarymuseum.org/stone man.html.

32. Ogle, *Federal Control*, 77.

33. Ibid., 76–77; Lockwood, *Apache Indians*, 174–76.

34. Walker and Bufkin, *Historical Atlas of Arizona*, 37.

35. Whitman participated in Sheridan's Shenandoah expedition as commander of the Thirtieth Maine, which was then attached to the Nineteenth Corps. Though Crook played a prominent role in that campaign, there is no evidence that the two men ever encountered one another at the time. HQ USMA to George Pittman, Dec. 30, 1864, Pittman Papers; see also Thrapp, *Conquest*, 80.

36. Thrapp, *Conquest*, 80.

37. Andrew H. Cargill, "The Camp Grant Massacre," reprinted in Cozzens, *Eyewitnesses*, 1:64.

38. Second Lieutenant W. W. Robinson, Jr., to Vincent Colyer, Indian Commissioner, Sept. 10, 1871, Appendix A *b*, No. 3 to Board of Indian Commissioners, Peace with the Apache Indians of Arizona and New Mexico, Report of Vincent Colyer.

39. Bourke, *On the Border*, 104; Thrapp, *Conquest*, 87.

40. Thrapp, *Conquest*, 80. Oury, born in Virginia, had gone to Texas as a teenager, where he became one of the few survivors of the Alamo, having been assigned by Travis to carry dispatches out of the post before the mission was besieged. He subsequently served as a Texas ranger, mined gold in California, and arrived in Tucson in 1856, where he rapidly became a prominent figure in the community (87n13).

41. Lockwood, *Apache Indians*, 180.

42. William S. Oury, "Historical Truth: The So-called 'Camp Grant Massacre' of 1871," *Arizona Daily Star*, June 29 and July 1, 1879, reprinted in Cozzens, *Eyewitnesses*, 1:61.

43. This is one historian's estimate, but the body count has varied widely. Ogle, *Federal Control*, 81. For a breakdown on the casualties and number of participants as they have been reported over the years, see Colwell-Chanthaphonh, "The 'Camp Grant Massacre' in the Historical Imagination," 349–69.

44. Dunn, Jr., *Massacres of the Mountains*, 621–22.

45. For samples of newspaper reports on the massacre from across the West, see Terrell, *Apache Chronicle*, 280.

46. Ultimately, in December 1871, a grand jury did indict five of the Anglos and twenty Mexicans responsible for the murders, together with seventy-five unnamed Papagos. The trial lasted for five days and, to no one's surprise, the defendants were acquitted by a jury after nineteen minutes' deliberation. Cargill, "The Camp Grant Massacre," in Cozzens, *Eyewitnesses*, 1:66; Thrapp, *Conquest*, 92–93.

47. Crook to Commanding Officer, Fort Whipple, June 19, 1871, Records of the U.S. Army Continental Command, RG 393, Fort Whipple Letters Received, 1866–71.

CHAPTER 5

1. See Bourke, *On the Border*, 108–109.
2. Schmitt, *General George Crook*, 165.
3. Porter, *Paper Medicine Man*, 1–4.
4. Ibid.
5. Bourke, *On the Border*, 29.
6. Ibid., 105.
7. Ibid., 110.
8. Ibid., 109–10.

9. Ibid., 111–12.

10. See Magid, *George Crook*, 264, 284.

11. Porter, *Paper Medicine Man*, 4.

12. Ibid.

13. Ibid., 272.

14. Bourke, *On the Border*, 136; Corbusier, *Verde to San Carlos*, 14–15. Also see Braatz, *Surviving Conquest*, 13–14, for an extensive discourse on the Americans' erroneous habit of considering the Apaches and Yavapais to be one people.

15. Bourke, *On the Border*, 137.

16. Crook to AGO, July 10, 1871, RG 75, M234, R4, quoted in Sweeney and Debo, *Great Apache Chiefs*, 319. See Thrapp, *Conquest*, 77, and Worcester, *Apaches*, 144. The latter has suggested that Crook's initial march across the 110 miles of desert to Fort Bowie was intended as "a gesture of warning to Cochise."

17. Bourke, *On the Border*, 145–46.

18. Jacoby, *Shadows at Dawn*, 80; Schmitt, *General George Crook*, 163; Bourke, *On the Border*, 137.

19. Bourke, *On the Border*, 137–38; Crook to AG, Sept. 4, 1871, Headquarters, Dept. of Arizona, Letters Sent, RG 393, vol. 1; also in George Crook Letterbook, no. 1, Rutherford Hayes Library.

20. For more on frontier uniforms, see Utley, *Frontier Regulars*, 75–79.

21. Bourke, *On the Border*, 137; McChristian, *Fort Bowie*, 3.

22. Bourke, *On the Border*, 139.

23. Crook to AAG, Sept. 4, 1871; Schmitt, *General George Crook*, 164.

24. Bourke, *On the Border*, 141; Schmitt, *General George Crook*, 164.

25. Schmitt, *General George Crook*; Thrapp, *Conquest*, 98–99.

26. Affecting a frontier coarseness not uncommon in his memoir, Crook referred to Miguel as Old One-Eyed Mcgill, despite using his correct name in his Sept. 4, 1871, report to the AAG; Schmitt, *General George Crook*, 166.

27. Bourke, *On the Border*, 142–44.

28. Crook to AAG, Sept. 4, 1871.

29. Colyer, Report, 12. According to Thrapp, this idea was planted in Colyer's mind by a Mexican alcalde named Trujillo, who bore a grudge against Crook, making his allegation suspect. See Thrapp, *Conquest*, 100n14. Colyer, like Crook, had his own preconceptions and his own agenda.

30. Downey and Jacobsen, *The Red/Bluecoats*, 106; see also Perry, *Apache Reservation*, 105–107.

31. Crook to Price, Aug. 19, 1871, Hq. Dept. of Arizona, Letters Sent, RG 393, Vol. 1; Blanca Apache Chief, Friend of Fort Apache Whites, Counselor to Indian Agents. Dobyns, *Apache People (Coyoteros)*, 41. For more on Alchesay, see Wharfield, *Alchesay*.

32. Crook to AAG, Sept. 4, 1871. According to John Staggs of Bowie, Arizona, who has extensively studied these tags, or ration tokens, they were made of copper, had a hole punched in them so they could be worn, and were stamped with symbols denoting the tribe to whom they had been issued.

33. Dobyns, *Apache People*, 40.

34. Crook to AAG, Sept. 4, 1871; Colyer, Report, 10, 12; Sladen, *Making Peace with Cochise*, 14–15. The Mexican official would later retaliate by informing Colyer that Crook had coerced the White Mountains into becoming army scouts. See note 29.

35. See Crook to AAG, Sept. 4, 1871.

36. Thrapp, *Conquest*, 100.

37. Schmitt, *General George Crook*, 166; see also Bourke, *On the Border*, 145–48; Crook to AAG, Sept. 4, 1871.

38. Bowman, "Development of the General Crook Trail."

CHAPTER 6

1. Report of Brevet Major General E. O. C. Ord, Sept. 27, 1869, in Report of Secretary of War, 1969, vol. 1, 41st Cong., 2nd Sess., Ex. Doc. No. 1, 124.

2. Lockwood, *Apache Indians*, 178.

3. Thrapp, *Conquest*, 86.

4. Bancroft, *History of Oregon*, 17:561.

5. Ogle, *Federal Control*, 69.

6. Ibid., 86–87.

7. Cowen, B. R., Acting Secretary of Interior, July 21, 1871; Colyer, Report, Appendix A *b*, no. 5.

8. Bancroft, *History of Oregon*, 17:562.

9. Colyer, Report, 29.

10. Colyer reported that Governor Safford believed the average Arizonan was so ill-disposed toward the peace commissioners that he thought it necessary to issue a proclamation in the *Arizona Citizen* saying, "If they [the commissioners] come among you entertaining erroneous opinions upon the Indian question and the condition of affairs in this Territory, then, by kindly treatment and fair, truthful representation, you will be enabled to convince them of their errors." Ibid., 19.

11. Thrapp, *Conquest*, 103n22.

12. Colyer, Report, 1.

13. Crook to AG, Sept. 28, 1871, George Crook Letterbook, vol. 1.

14. See Porter, *Paper Medicine Man*, 74–81, for an extensive discussion of the nineteenth-century ethnology theories to which Crook and John Bourke subscribed.

15. Schmitt, *General George Crook*, 167.

16. Ibid., 168.

17. Colyer, Report, 11.

18. Schmitt, *General George Crook*, 167–68; Bourke, *On the Border*, 160.

19. Bourke, *On the Border*.

20. Crook to AG, Sept. 19, 1871, George Crook Letterbook, vol. 1; Bourke, *On the Border*, 160.

21. Crook to AG, Sept. 28, 1871, George Crook Letterbook, vol. 1.

22. Ibid., letters of Sept. 4 and Sept. 28, 1871.

23. Ibid., letter of Sept. 4, 1871.

24. Ibid., letter of Sept. 28, 1871.

25. Ibid.

26. Lockwood, *Apache Indians*, 189; Bourke, *On the Border*, 150.

27. Crook to AAG, Dec. 11, 1871, Dept. of Arizona, Fort Whipple, Letters Sent, Records of the U.S. Army Continental commands, RG 393.

28. Bourke, *On the Border*, 154,

29. Vaughn, *Reynolds Campaign*, 30. Moore's sister was Carry Nation, famous for her axe-wielding temperance campaigns. Tom remained close to his ferocious sibling despite

her fanaticism and his habit of visiting her over the years with a jug of whisky ever close at hand. Henry Daly, "The Warpath," *American Legion Monthly* (Apr. 1927), 16.

30. Crook to AG, Sept. 28, 1871.

31. Marion, "'As Long as the Stone Lasts'"; Colyer, Report, 14.

32. Colyer, Report, 14.

33. Crook to Nelson, Sept. 22, 1872, Dept. of Arizona Fort Whipple, Letters Sent.

34. See Crook to AAG, Dec. 11, 1871, Dept. of Arizona, Letters Sent.

35. Crook to illegible, Sept. 12, 1871, Letters Sent; Crook, letter to illegible, Oct. 17, 1871.

36. For details of Whitman's indiscretions, see Cunningham, "Calamitous Career of Lieutenant Royal Whitman."

37. An example of the distorted nature of the allegations was the editor's reference to the lieutenant's fondness for "dusky maidens." These, it developed, were the five elderly Apache women who had initially approached Whitman to determine whether it was safe to come into Camp Grant for purposes of trade. Thrapp, *Conquest*, 93.

38. Court Martial of Lieutenant Royal Whitman, Cases Tried by General Court Martial, Camp Lowell, Dec. 4, 1871. NARA, Court Martial Files, #PP 2309.

39. Crook to Whitman, Dec. 5, 1871, Dept. of Arizona, Fort Whipple, Letters Sent.

40. Crook to AAG, Dec. 11, 1872.

41. Colyer, Report, 21–22; Braatz, *Surviving Conquest*, 123.

42. Colyer, Report, 28.

43. Schmitt, *General George Crook*, 168.

44. Colyer, Report, 28.

45. Crook to Schofield, Oct. 10, 1872, quoted in Ogle, *Federal Control*, 94–95.

46. Ogle, *Federal Control*, 94.

47. Lockwood, *Apache Indians*, 187.

48. Ogle, *Federal Control*, 95.

CHAPTER 7

1. Thrapp, *Conquest*, 101. Hubert Bancroft, the historian, had seen Loring in San Francisco the day before his departure, and the latter had jokingly remarked that his short haircut would pose a challenge for any Indian seeking to scalp him. Bancroft, *History of Oregon*, 30:560n14.

2. "The Wickenburg Massacre: First Authentic Account from an Eyewitness," *New York Times*, Jan. 1, 1872.

3. Thrapp, *Conquest*, 105.

4. Crook to Date Creek Commander, Nov. 12, 1871, Fort Whipple, Letters Sent.

5. Thrapp, *Conquest*, 105; Farish, *History of Arizona*, 8:298–305; Worcester, *Apaches*, 131.

6. Crook to Hayes, Nov. 28, 1871, George Crook Letterbook, Hayes Library.

7. Sherman to Schofield, Nov. 9, 1871, quoted in Ogle, *Federal Control*, 96. Similar orders went out to Sheridan, who commanded the Division of the Missouri, which included New Mexico.

8. General Order No. 10, Division of the Pacific, Nov. 21, 1871, quoted in Ogle, *Federal Control*, 100.

9. General Order No. 32, Dec. 11, 1871, and General Order No. 35, Dec. 27, 1871, Dept. of Arizona Issuances, General Orders, Circulars, and Court Martial Orders, 1870–93, RG 393.

10. Bancroft, *History of Oregon*, 17:563.

11. Ogle, *Federal Control*, 102; Crook to AAG, Jan. 8, 1872, Fort Whipple, Letters Sent.

12. Crook to Hayes, Jan. 4, 1872, George Crook Letterbook, Hayes Library.

13. Stanton, "Arizona in the Winter of 1871–1872," typescript, no. 70393, Thaddeus Stanton Papers.

14. Ogle, *Federal Control*, 103; Schofield to Crook, Dept. of the Pacific, Circular Mar. 8, 1872, Dept. of Arizona, Circulars and Court Martial Orders, 1870–93, RG 393.

15. Circular, Mar. 27, 1872, Dept. of Arizona, Circulars and Court Martial Orders.

CHAPTER 8

1. Bancroft, *History of Oregon*, 17:564.

2. Warner, *Generals in Blue*, 237.

3. Quoted in Marion, "'As Long as the Stone Lasts,'" 109.

4. Howard to Grant, Apr. 15, 1872, Appendix E, Report of the Commissioner of Indian Affairs, 1872, Washington, D.C., GPO, 1872, 160.

5. Ibid.

6. Howard, *My Life and Experiences*, 149.

7. In his report Howard wrote, "It will take unremitting activity by troops to secure those who are badly disposed." Report of the Commissioner for Indian Affairs, 1872, 151. See also comments, 168.

8. Howard, *My Life and Experiences*, 151–52; Howard, "Major General George Crook," 326–28.

9. Schmitt, *General George Crook*, 169–70.

10. Report of the Commissioner for Indian Affairs, 151.

11. This was in accordance with General Schofield's General Order No. 10.

12. Thrapp, *Conquest*, 109; Marion, "'As Long as the Stone Lasts,'" 114. Ultimately Whitman was acquitted of these charges and returned to Camp Grant. Court Martial Records, Headquarters, Military Division of the Pacific, General Order no. 6, June 26, 1872. Charges were brought against Whitman a third time in August 1872. Crook's role in this prosecution is not known, but the specifications again included allegations of conduct unbecoming an officer, in particular, drunkenness, threatening a post surgeon with a pistol, and, perhaps most telling, referring to General Crook as "a damned son of a bitch." On this occasion, the court found him guilty of conduct unbecoming and sentenced him to six months' suspension from duty and confinement to post during that period. Both findings and sentence were sustained by General Schofield. General Order no. 12, Sept. 21, 1872, Court Martial Records, Div. of the Pacific. Whitman continued to serve in the army until 1879, when he retired for disability reasons. He died in 1913 in Washington, D.C. Letter from U.S. Military Academy to George H. Pittman, Dec. 30, 1964, Pittman Papers.

13. Marion, "'As Long as the Stone Lasts,'" 117.

14. Ibid.

15. Report of the Commissioner for Indian Affairs, 1872, 151.

16. L. Lamprey typescript, 15–16, New York Public Library, Acquisition #270128A, quoted in Marion, "'As Long as the Stone Lasts,'" 120.

17. Marion, "'As Long as the Stone Lasts'"; Report of the Commissioner, 152.

18. Marion, "'As Long as the Stone Lasts.'"

19. Magid, *George Crook*, 7. John Bourke in his diary entry for Dec. 11, 1872, referred to Dailey's presence, noting that he accompanied Crook as a "volunteer bacon chawer" on an expedition into the Tonto Basin. Robinson, ed., *Diaries of John Gregory Bourke*, (hereafter *Bourke Diaries*), 1:35.

20. Howard, *My Life and Experiences*, 152.

21. Howard to Crook, May 9, 1872, Report of the Commissioner, appx. K, 169.

22. Schmitt, *General George Crook*, 170.

23. Worcester, *Apaches*, 125; Cunningham, "Calamitous Career," 156.

24. Howard, *My Life and Experiences*, 150.

25. Schmitt, *General George Crook*; Cunningham, "Calamitous Career," 150; Thrapp, *Conquest*, 109. Marion correctly points out that Whitman was in Tucson for his court-martial on May 20, the day before the council commenced. So this incident may have occurred sometime toward the end of the talks. See court-martial records, ibid.; Marion, "'As Long as the Stone Lasts,'" 140n18.

26. Marion, "'As Long as the Stone Lasts,'" 124.

27. Report of the Commissioner, 155.

28. Schmitt, *General George Crook*, 171.

29. These articles from the *Arizona Citizen*, May 25, June 1, and June 8, 1872, were quoted with minor editing in Marion's article, "'As Long as the Stone Lasts'"; see 140n16.

30. Marion, "'As Long as the Stone Lasts,'" 130–31, quoting from *Arizona Citizen*.

31. Schmitt, *General George Crook*, 171.

32. Ibid.; Marion, "'As Long as the Stone Lasts,'" 131.

33. President Grant would later make the decision to return the children to the Apaches. Howard, "General Howard's Treaties," in Cozzens, *Eyewitnesses*, 1:121.

34. Schmitt, *General George Crook*, 172.

35. Ibid., 173; Annual Report of the Secretary of the Interior, 1872, 533–39.

36. Howard to Crook, May 26, 1872, Report of the Commissioner, appx. N, 172.

37. For a firsthand account of Howard's negotiations with Cochise, see Sladen, *Making Peace with Cochise*. See also Sweeney, *Cochise*, 340–66.

38. Crook to AAG, Feb. 11, 1873, George Crook Letterbook, vol. 1, 25–27.

CHAPTER 9

1. In his eagerness to discredit Colyer, Crook may have been too hasty in his judgment. Evidence pointed to bandit rather than Indian involvement, including a report from a settler who lived near the site and had sent two of his Indian employees to Date Creek to look into the cause of the massacre. They had returned with assurances that no Indian from the reservation had been involved. Further, items were left at the scene and others taken that did not reflect normal Indian practice. Clothing and blankets attractive to Indians were left behind, while some cash, normally of no interest, was taken. Tracks leaving the scene did head toward Date Creek, but then turned abruptly in another direction. According to some sources, eventually it was determined that a group of Mexican

woodcutters was responsible, and some of the gang were hanged by vigilantes. See Braatz, *Surviving Conquest*, 133–34; Genung statement in Farish, *History of Arizona*, 8:299–301. According to Farish, Crook may have changed his mind afterward about the Yavapais' involvement, since he later employed the same Indians he had sought to arrest at Date Creek as scouts to hunt down others (301).

2. Farish, *History of Arizona*, 8:305.

3. Charles Genung, who employed several Yavapais on his ranch and found them trustworthy, thought Irataba's allegations highly suspect, claiming the chief was acting out of jealousy because his people were given less favorable treatment than the Date Creek Yavapais. Ibid., 316.

4. Magid, *George Crook*, 97–98.

5. Farish, 304–306; Crook to AAG, Sept. 18, 1872, George Crook Letterbook; Bourke, *On the Border*, 169–70. In Bourke's version of the incident, the Yavapais planned to kill Crook's men at a signal from their chief. Learning of the plot, Crook devised a plan to counter it.

6. Crook to AAG, Sept. 18, 1872, Crook Letterbook.

7. Bourke, *On the Border*, 170; ibid. Crook's version of the incident is very similar to that of Genung, who was also present; see Farish, *History of Arizona*, 8:314.

8. Bourke, *On the Border*. There was another attempt on Crook's life, according to John Mahony, the stage keeper at one of the stations near Wickenburg. Mahony, who claimed to have been present, said that an Indian tried to stab Crook from behind and was stopped by Genung, who restrained the man and was ready to shoot him. Crook ordered him not to, but after the fracas was over, the Indian was found dead, a small knife wound in his side. Mahony alleged in a newspaper interview in 1927 that he saw Crook "step over light as a flash and stick a dirk into him." He then warned the others not to say anything. "Spin Yarns of Old Indian Fights," *The Sun* (Fort Covington, N.Y.), Oct. 13, 1927. Genung never recorded the incident. Nor did anyone else mention anything remotely similar, leading the author to doubt the story.

9. Crook to AAG, Sept. 18, 1872, Crook Letterbook; Farish, *History of Arizona*, 8:308, 314.

10. Farish, *History of Arizona*, 8:308; Thrapp, *Al Sieber*, 98–99.

11. Genung, in Farish, *History of Arizona*, 8:314–17.

12. Thrapp supports Crook's contention, claiming that more than fifty raids and forty murders could be "attributed to the Apaches and other hostile Indians" during the year following Colyer's peace mission. Thrapp, *Conquest*, 114.

13. George Crook, Annual Report, Headquarters, Dept. of Arizona, Sept. 21, 1872, Crook Letterbook.

14. Crook to AG US, Dec. 13, 1872, Crook Letterbook; Thrapp, *Conquest*, 113.

15. Corbusier, *Verde to San Carlos*, 245; "Al Sieber," in Cozzens, *Eyewitnesses*, 1:667n1. A detailed accounting of Sieber's colorful life and career is found in Thrapp, *Al Sieber*.

16. Dept. of Arizona, General Order 32, Sept. 27, 1872, Lieutenant Walter Schuyler to his father, Sept. 29, 1872, Schuyler Papers.

17. Crook AG, Dec. 13, 1872; Bourke, *On the Border*, 171.

18. Schofield to AG, Oct. 18, 1872, quoted in Ogle, *Federal Control*, 113–14.

19. Schmitt, *General George Crook*, 175.

20. General Order No. 10, Nov. 21, 1871, paraphrased in Opler, *Apache Life-way*, 100. Thrapp mistakenly indicated that Crook had originated the order; see Thrapp, *Al Sieber*, 107.

21. Thrapp, *Conquest*, 119.
22. Crook to AAG, Dec. 13, 1872.
23. Schmitt, *General George Crook*, 179.
24. Ibid., 175.
25. Bourke, "George Crook in Indian Country," 44.
26. Bourke, *On the Border*, 203.
27. Ibid.
28. Thrapp, *Al Sieber*, 107; Bourke, *Diaries*, 1:34.
29. Bourke, *On the Border*, 182.
30. Thrapp, *Conquest*, 120; Bourke, "George Crook in Indian Country," 16; Bourke, *On the Border*, 176.
31. Bourke, *On the Border*, 181.
32. Schmitt, *General George Crook*, 176; Walker and Bufkin, *Historical Atlas of Arizona*, 37; Crook to AAG, Dec. 13, 1872; Thrapp, *Conquest*, 122.
33. Nickerson, "Major General George Crook," 18; Crook to AAG, Dec. 13, 1872.
34. Crook to AAG, Dec. 13, 1872.
35. Ogle, *Federal Control*, 194.
36. General Order No. 14, Apr. 9, 1873, quoted in Thrapp, *Al Sieber*, 116.
37. Bourke, *On the Border*, 213; Schmitt, *General George Crook*, 179–80.
38. Nickerson, "Major General George Crook," 18.
39. Anonymous, "Early Days in Arizona with the Fifth Cavalry," in Cozzens, *Eyewitnesses*, 1:144; Bourke, "General Crook in Indian Country," 17; Bourke, *On the Border*, 185.
40. Corbusier, *Verde to San Carlos*, 135. Delche's name has been spelled differently by almost every author who has written about him, but all seem to agree that it means "Red Ant" in the Yavapai language.
41. Schmitt, *General George Crook*, 180. Crook was not alone in his opinion. Dr. Corbusier, army surgeon at Camp Verde, no Indian hater but one who knew Delche well, considered him the "only Indian whom [he] thoroughly disliked and mistrusted." "He played hide and seek with the soldiers, and, when the notion struck him he would go to an agency, promise to be a good boy, get well fed and ammunitioned—and then light out." *Verde to San Carlos*, 57.
42. Bourke, *Al Sieber*, 114.
43. Braatz, *Surviving Conquest*, 115, 118; "Talk with Delche," by Captain William McC. Netterville, Camp McDowell, Nov. 2, 1871, in Colyer, Report, 25.
44. Thrapp, *Al Sieber*, 115; Bourke, *On the Border*, 184; Bourke, *Diaries*, 39.
45. Mike, whose Yavapai name was Hoo-moo-thy-ah, or Wet Nose, was adopted by James Burns and later educated at the Carlisle School. He left a lengthy manuscript on his people's history, customs, and beliefs. Included is a detailed and tragic description of the cave fight, much of it reprinted in Corbusier, *Verde to San Carlos*, 75–81.
46. The description and the quotes used relating to the engagement at Salt River Cave come from Bourke's narratives in *On the Border*, 188–201; his article "With General Crook in the Indian Wars," 50–56; and his *Diaries*, 1:45–52.
47. Bourke, *On the Border*, 202–207; Braatz, *Surviving Conquest*, 139.
48. Nickerson, "Major General George Crook," 17.
49. Bourke, *On the Border*, 208.
50. Nickerson, "Major General George Crook," 16–17; ibid.

51. Schmitt, *General George Crook*, 178. After viewing the topography of the area, Thrapp concluded that at least some of those who leaped over the rim probably survived, escaping down the slope of the mountain. Thrapp, *Al Sieber*, 112.

52. Post returns from the action indicate that twenty-three Indians were killed and ten captured, while the Chronological List of Actions shows thirty-three killed and thirteen captured. See Thrapp, *Al Sieber*, 112, regarding confusion over actual number of casualties, quoting Returns Camp Apache, for Mar. 27, 1873. U.S. War Dept., Chronological List of Actions, from Jan. 1, 1866 to Jan. 1891.

53. Schmitt, *General George Crook*, 179.

54. Ibid.

55. Bourke, *On the Border*, 213.

56. General Order No. 13, Headquarters, Dept. of Arizona, Prescott, Apr. 8, 1873, General Orders, Circulars, Court Martial Orders, Dept. of Arizona Issuances, 1870–1873, RG 393.

57. Bourke, *On the Border*, 212–14. Tiswin, or "gray water," was a weak beer made from fermented corn and served on social occasions. If no food is taken beforehand, it can induce drunkenness. Tiswin-intoxicated Indians had caused so much trouble fighting among themselves and with others that Crook thought it wise to prohibit the making and drinking of it entirely. On tiswin in Apache culture, see Opler, *Apache Life-way*, 369–70.

58. Bourke, *On the Border*, 212–14; for an eyewitness description of the surrender, see "Peace at Last," *Arizona Miner*, Apr. 12, 1873.

59. Bourke, *On the Border*, 225.

60. General Order No. 12, Apr. 7, 1873.

61. Schmitt, *General George Crook*, 180; Braatz, *Surviving Conquest*, 141; Thrapp, *Al Sieber*, 115–16.

62. General Order No. 14, Ap. 9, 1873; Crook to AAG, Apr. 12, 1873, Crook Letterbook 1.

63. Crook to AAG, July 7, 1873.

64. Annual Report of Brigadier General George Crook, U.S. Army, Commanding Dept. of Arizona, Sept. 22, 1873.

65. John Bourke, "A conference with Cochise," in Cozzens, *Eyewitnesses*, 1:152–54; Account of the Interview between Post Major Brown, Captain, 5th Cavalry, and the Indian Chief Cochise, Feb. 3, 1873, Bourke Papers, Nebraska Historical Society, Lincoln.

66. Crook to AAG, July 7, 1873.

67. General Order No. 7, Division of the Pacific, Apr. 28, 1873, quoted in Bourke, *On the Border*, 220–21.

68. Thrapp, *Conquest*, 143.

69. "A Great Event in Arizona," Sept. 6, 1873, *Arizona Miner*; First Telegrams in Arizona, Nebraska Historical Society, Lincoln, RG 2996, Box 10.

70. NARA, Crook ACP File; see also Robinson, *General Crook*, 137–38.

71. Utley, *Frontier Regulars*, 198.

72. Ogle, *Federal Control*, 114.

73. Noted anthropologist Morris Opler quoted a Chiricahua informant: "Gray Fox . . . is connected with death. If at dark, Fox goes near some camps, that means that someone in that group is going to die." *Apache Life-way*, 226.

74. Crook to McCormick, Secretary of the Territory, Apr. 11, 1873, *Tucson Citizen*, May 24, 1873.

CHAPTER 10

1. Schmitt, *General George Crook*, 183.
2. Annual Report of Brigadier General George Crook, U.S. Army, Commanding Dept. of Arizona, Aug. 31, 1874, Crook Letterbook. Between the date of Cha-lipan's surrender at Camp Verde and Crook's departure from Arizona in March 1875, the Chronological List of Actions with Indians noted thirty-five hostile encounters in Arizona and New Mexico, resulting in the deaths of over 240 Indians, the capture of about an equal number, and the deaths of several soldiers and scouts, an indication of the number and mood of Indians who continued to remain off the reservation. Chronological List, Lockwood, *Apache Indians*, 204.
3. Schmitt, *General George Crook*, 184.
4. Ibid., 185; Crook, Annual Report, Sept. 22, 1873.
5. Schmitt, *General George Crook*.
6. Apparently, at the behest of the Ring, a sergeant had written a "scurrilous letter against Howard" and signed Agent Stevens's name to it. Stevens was dismissed before the forgery was discovered. Ogle, *Federal Control*, 138n65.
7. Both Thrapp, *Conquest*, 146, and Ogle, ibid., 139, identify the agent as R. A. Wilbur, but his correct name is given in the commissioner of Indian affairs annual report, 1873, serial 1601, 289–90, as H. R. Wilbur. There were two agents named Wilbur in Arizona at the time. R. A. Wilbur was the agent at the Tohono O'odham Agency during this period.
8. Thrapp, *Conquest*, 148, 152.Why Almy disregarded his orders and approached the hostile crowd without protection will never be known. Thrapp speculated that Almy's Quaker background may have led him to intervene in the hope of defusing the situation without resort to violence. For a detailed description of the incident based on the investigative report, see Thrapp, *Conquest*, 146–55; see also Ogle, *Federal Control*, 138–40; and "Sad and Bad News from the San Carlos Indian Agency," *Arizona Miner*, June 7, 1874.
9. Crook to AAG, Div. Pac., July 3, 1873, Hayes Library.
10. Crook to AG, Apr. 10, 1874; Thrapp, *Conquest*, 154.
11. Nickerson to Brown, Prescott, July 3, 1873, NARL, Indian Bureau Microfilm, RG 75, quoted in Thrapp, *Conquest*, 154; Ogle, *Federal Control*, 141.
12. See Thrapp, *Al Sieber*, 101, for a summary of Schuyler's career.
13. Crook to Schuyler, Sept. 15, 1873, Schuyler Papers.
14. Thrapp, *Al Sieber*, 124–25; Braatz, *Apache Indians*, 142–43.
15. The reasons for Eskiminzin's arrest have never been clearly determined, but Randall apparently acted with Crook's hearty approval. The general continued to mistrust the Aravaipa chief, and perhaps suspected him of involvement in Delche's outbreak. See Crook to AAG, Apr. 10, 184, Hayes Library.
16. Ibid.
17. Thrapp, *Conquest*, 157–59.
18. George Crook, Annual Report for 1874, Aug. 31, 1874, Crook Letterbook.
19. Schmitt, *General George Crook*, 181.

20. At the time, Crook publicly attempted to soften the tone of his ultimatum by claiming that he had told the Indians they were to bring in the murderers "dead or alive"; Crook to AG, Apr. 10, 1874, Crook Letterbook. Nickerson's version of the event appeared to contradict Crook's. He wrote that the general informed the Indians that if they wished to return to the reservation, "when they came, they must bring the heads of their leaders." Nickerson, "Major General George Crook," 15. On the other hand, John Clum, agent at San Carlos, supported Crook's version. When three Indians delivered the head of a renegade to Clum, they informed him that, "General Crook had told them they could not return unless they brought with them the renegade, dead or alive. They had not been able to bring him alive, they said, and his body was too heavy to carry forty miles; so they brought only his head." Perhaps Crook tailored his message according to his audience.

21. Thrapp, *Conquest*, 160.

22. Crook, Annual Report, 1874.

23. Crook to Schuyler, June 23, 1874, Schuyler Papers.

24. Thrapp, *Conquest*, 161.

25. *Tucson Citizen*, Aug. 22, 1874.

26. Corbusier, *Verde to San Carlos*, 139.

27. Schmitt, *General George Crook*, 181–82.

28. Crook, Annual Report 1873, Aug. 31, 1874, Crook Letterbook.

CHAPTER 11

1. Thrapp, *Conquest*, 165; Ball, *An Apache Odyssey Indeh*, 37.

2. Annual Report of the Commissioner of Indian Affairs for the Year 1872 (Washington, D.C., Government Printing Office, 1872), 177.

3. See Braatz, *Surviving Conquest*, 170–71; Thrapp, *Conquest*, 165; Wellman, *Death in the Desert*, 1987), 150; Bourke, *On the Border*, 213.

4. Magid, *George Crook*, 67.

5. Braatz, *Surviving Conquest*, 146; Crook to Superintendent of Indian Affairs, Apr. 9, 1873, Crook Letterbook.

6. Braatz, *Surviving Conquest*, 146–47.

7. Crook, Annual Report for 1873, Sept. 22, 1873.

8. Crook, Annual Report for 1874, Aug. 31, 1874.

9. Crook to AG, Apr. 10, 1874.

10. Dunn, *Massacres of the Mountains*, 633.

11. Crook, Annual Report for 1874.

12. Corbusier, *Verde to San Carlos*, 266–69.

13. Agent L. E. Report to Commission of Indian Affairs, quoted in Corbusier, *Verde to San Carlos*, 261.

14. For Mike Burns's story, see Braatz, *Surviving Conquest*, 173.

15. Eaton, "Stopping an Apache Battle," 12–18. Corbusier recorded that there were only fifteen soldiers assigned as escorts; *Verde to San Carlos*, 271.

16. See Eaton, "Stopping an Apache Battle," 17. It is possible that Crook was in a really bad mood that day, or that Eaton's recollection, recorded when the officer was in his 80s, was inaccurate. Numerous other assertions at variance with the recollections of Surgeon Corbusier cast some doubt on the accuracy of Eaton's memory.

17. As a consequence of Crook's decision to have Corbusier accompany the transfer, historians have three distinctly different accounts of the journey. Dudley wrote an official

report of the move, quoted in Corbusier, *Verde to San Carlos*, 261–62. It was so riddled with "absurdities and inaccuracies" (Corbusier's words) that it hardly merits mention. Eaton and Corbusier also set down their recollections, and these in many respects contradict one another as well as Dudley's account. Eaton described the weather as intensely hot ("Stopping an Apache Battle," 16), while Corbusier referred constantly to the cold and snow (*Verde to San Carlos*, 273–74). From that unpromising beginning, the two narratives continue to diverge. According to Eaton, Crook told him that he was to have command of the move and referred to Dudley as an inspector from the bureau present only to report on the move ("Stopping an Apache Battle," 15). Corbusier's narrative asserts that Dudley was in charge of the move (as does Dudley's report), making all of the decisions about route and movement, often to the detriment of the Indians (*Verde to San Carlos*, 272–77). In any event, Dudley and Eaton seemed to have gotten along famously, while Corbusier repeatedly crossed swords with the commissioner while trying to ameliorate the suffering of the Indians that resulted from Dudley's callous decisions.

18. Corbusier, *Verde to San Carlos*, 270.

19. Eaton, "Stopping an Apache Battle," 16; ibid., 276–77.

20. Clum, *Indian Agent, The Story of John P. Clum*, 150. Dudley, noting that the Indians claimed seven dead and ten wounded, stated, "Not a great loss where so much blood was expended." Dudley report in Corbusier, *Verde to San Carlos*, 262.

21. Schmitt, *General George Crook*, 184.

CHAPTER 12

1. Bourke, *Diaries*, 1:89–90.

2. Ibid.

3. Bourke, *On the Border*, 221–22.

4. Bourke, *Diaries*, 1:90.

5. Clum, *Indian Agent*, 130. Dr. Corbusier, visiting San Carlos in the fall of 1921, found conditions on San Carlos to be much the same as they had been in 1875. "Most of [the Apaches] were living in round huts . . . thatched with grass, old canvas, and pieces of tin. . . . Some had ragged blankets, but most slept directly on the ground as less likely to attract lice. They cooked mostly in tin cans, over an open fire. They had learned . . . English, and a few had some schooling." *Verde to San Carlos*, 280.

6. Bourke, *On the Border*, 230–31.

7. The Mormons at this time were on unfriendly terms with the U.S. government and allied with the Utes on occasion against the gentiles, non-Mormon whites. For more details, see Denton, *American Massacre*.

8. Bourke, *Diaries*, 1:102.

9. Schmitt, *General George Crook*, 183. Bourke came to the same conclusion; *On the Border*, 230.

10. Bourke, *Diaries*, 1:114.

11. Ibid., 1:118.

12. Quoted in Wagoner, *Arizona Territory*, 141.

13. Bourke, *Diaries*, 1:134.

14. Quoted in *Cumberland (Md.) Daily News*, Apr. 30, 1875.

15. Bourke, *Diaries*, 1:134.

16. "An Outpouring of People," *Arizona Miner*, Mar. 25, 1875; Lieutenant Bourke referred to the building as Katz's Restaurant, *Diaries*, 1:137.

17. Bourke, *Diaries*, 1:137–38.
18. Juarez, *Tarnished Saber*, 51–52.

CHAPTER 13

1. Bourke, *Diaries*, 1:157.
2. Magid, *George Crook*, 248–49; Schmitt, *General George Crook*, 134n7.
3. Hutton, *Phil Sheridan and His Army*, 123.
4. General Philip Sheridan to Secretary of War Belknap, Mar. 4, 1875, Box 11, Sheridan Papers.
5. Hutton, *Phil Sheridan and His Army*, 128.
6. Sheridan Report, Sept. 26, 1868, Box 83, Sheridan Papers.
7. Black Kettle, a peace chief of the Cheyennes, had offered to bring his band in to Fort Cobb for their protection. General Hazen had rejected his offer and sent him back to his camp on the Washita where, a little more than a week later, Custer struck the village, killing over one hundred men, women, and children, including Black Kettle and his wife. See Hoig, *Peace Chiefs of the Cheyenne*, 118–20.
8. Schmitt, *General George Crook*, 187; Bourke, *Diaries*, 1:146–56.
9. General Order No.10, Headquarters Dept. of the Platte, Omaha, Apr. 27, 1873, reproduced in *Bourke Diaries*, 1:476.
10. Sajna, *Crazy Horse, the Life*, 11; Ostler, *The Plains Sioux and U.S. Colonialism*, 21; Utley, *Lance and the Shield*, 3.
11. Two other divisions of the Sioux nation, the Santees, who had remained in Minnesota, and the Yanktonais, who dwelled on the eastern plains, would be only peripherally involved in the ensuing conflict. Utley, *Lance and the Shield*, 4.
12. For an excellent account of the massacre, see Bray, *Crazy Horse, A Lakota Life*, 98–101.
13. The complete text of the treaty can be found at 15 Stats. 635, Apr. 29, 1868, reprinted in Kappler, *Indian Affairs*, 998–1003.
14. Article 2, in Kappler, *Indian Affairs*, 998.
15. Article 12, in ibid., 1002.
16. Article 16, in ibid., 1002–1003.
17. In 1881, as the government engaged in a belated effort to preserve the last remnants of the northern buffalo herd, Sheridan wrote his superiors, "If I could learn that every buffalo in the northern herd were killed I would be glad. The destruction of this herd would do more to keep Indians quiet than anything else that could happen." Sheridan to AG, Oct. 13, 1881, Box 29, Sheridan Papers, quoted in Hutton, *Phil Sheridan and His Army*, 246.
18. Article 11, in Kappler, *Indian Affairs*. See chapter 14.
19. Hyde, *Red Cloud's Folk*, 168–69.
20. Utley, *Lance and the Shield*, 87.

CHAPTER 14

1. Hyde, *Spotted Tail's Folk*, 146–86.
2. Buecker, *Fort Robinson*, 18–19; Larson, *Red Cloud*, 157–58.
3. Larson, *Red Cloud*, 21.

4. Interview in the *National Republican* (Washington, D.C.), Nov. 30, 1875.

5. Utley, *Lance and the Shield*, 115.

6. Hassrick, *The Sioux, Life and Customs*, 9.

7. For an excellent account of the slaughter of the southern herd during the period 1871–74, see McHugh, *Time of the Buffalo*, 271–75.

8. Utley, *Lance and the Shield*, 114.

9. Sheridan to Congressman Wheeler, Nov. 24, 1874, Box 6, Sheridan Papers.

10. John S. Gray, *Centennial Campaign*, 16–17.

11. Hutton, *Phil Sheridan and His Army*, 291.

12. *Cheyenne Daily Leader*, Mar. 3, 1870.

13. Wert, *Custer: The Controversial Life*, 316.

14. Connell, *Son of the Morning Star*, 271.

15. Guy V. Henry, "A Winter March to the Black Hills," in Cozzens, *Eyewitnesses*, 4:183–87.

16. Bourke, *Diaries*, 1:162.

17. Crook to AAG, Aug. 16, 1875, Crook Letterbook.

18. Quoted in Gray, *Centennial Campaign*, 18.

19. Sheridan, for one, shared these reservations. In March, he wrote an article for the *Army and Navy Journal* that, while expressing confidence in Custer's statements that gold had been found in the Hills, noted, "there has not been any fair test yet made to determine its existence in large quantities. . . . The geological specimens brought back by the Custer expedition are not favorable indications of the existence of gold in great quantities." Philip H. Sheridan, "The Black Hills," in Cozzens, *Eyewitnesses*, 4:189. The expedition's geologist, Newton H. Winchell, shared Sheridan's skepticism, reporting that he had seen no evidence of gold in the Black Hills and doubted its presence. Kime, ed., *Black Hills Journals*, 5.

20. Mattes, *Indians, Infants, and Infantry*, 200; Kime, *Black Hills Journals*, 6.

21. Kime, *Black Hills Journals*, 8n13. In addition to reporters, Lieutenant Bourke, Captain Burt, and Surgeon J. R. Lane, who formed part of the escort, also contributed articles for major newspapers.

22. Sheridan to Sherman, July 3, 1875, NARA, Division of the Missouri, Letters Sent, RG 393.

23. Kime, *Black Hills Journals*, 7; see Bourke's report to Crook on the expedition's progress, June 15, 1875, Box 11, Sheridan Papers.

23. Bourke, *Diaries*, 1:161.

24. Kime, *Black Hills Journals*, 97.

25. *Chicago Tribune*, Aug. 21, 1875, quoted in Kime, *Black Hills Journals*, 19n28.

26. For a description of Dodge, see *Chicago Tribune*, Aug. 21, 1875, quoted in Kime, *Black Hills Journals*, 19–28. For Dodge's opinion of Indians, see Dodge, *Our Wild Indians*, 56, quoted in Smith, *View from Officers' Row*, 20.

27. Magid, *George Crook*, 114; Kime, *Black Hills Journals*, 172.

28. Bourke, *Diaries*, 1:190; Hedren, ed., *Ho for the Black Hills*, 25–26.

29. Kime, *Black Hills Journals*, 64.

30. Ibid., 86.

31. Dodge to Crook, NARA, Dept. of the Platte, Letters Received, RG 98, Boxes 36 and 37; Dodge to Crook, Aug. 7, 1875; Kime, *Black Hills Journals*, 55.

32. Kime, *Black Hills Journals*, 164.

33. Ibid., 139. Dodge must have had some inkling beforehand that the Sioux would not prove troublesome, as he brought along his teenage son, Fred, as a guest of the expedition. Bourke, *Diaries*, 1:164.

34. Roy Morris, Jr., *Sheridan, The Life and Wars*, 356; Hutton, *Phil Sheridan and His Army*, 273–76; Bourke, *Diaries*, 1:157n3. Robinson states that Bourke also attended the wedding, which took place on June 3, 1875. According to Bourke's diary, he was on the Janney expedition that day, deep in the Black Hills. Bourke, *Diaries*, 1:180.

35. He further restrained himself in his memoir, confining his commentary on the wedding to mentioning that it was "a quiet affair." Schmitt, *General George Crook*, 187.

36. Crook to Sheridan, Aug. 16, 1875, Crook Letterbook.

37. Crook to AAG Omaha, Sept. 15, 1875, Crook Letterbook.

38. Hedren, *Ho for the Black Hills*, 32–33.

39. Schmitt, *General George Crook*, 189.

40. "A Vain Search for Gold," *New York Times*, Apr. 30, 1876, in Abrams, *Newspaper Chronicle*, 5:110.

41. Kime, *Black Hills Journals*, 153.

42. Proclamation, General George Crook, July 29, 1875, Dept. of the Platte, Letters Received, RG 98.

43. Ibid.

44. Crook to AAG, Aug. 16, 1875, Crook Letterbook; Dodge to Crook, Aug. 10, 1875, Dept. of the Platte, Letters Received, Crook Letterbook; see also Crook to AAG, Sept. 15, 1875, Crook Letterbook. Crook neglected to mention to Dodge this side agreement with the miners to allow seven men to stay in the hills. When the miners met in August and told the colonel about the arrangement, he tactfully allowed them to implement it, knowing that if they were lying, they would be exposed in short order. Kime, *Black Hills Journals*, 167–68; Dodge to Pollack, Aug. 10, 1875, and Dodge to Crook, Aug. 10, 1875, Dept. of the Platte, Letters Received.

45. Columbus Delano, Dept. of the Interior, to the President, Sept. 14, 1875.

46. Kime, *Black Hills Journals*, 155–57; Hedren, *Ho for the Black Hills*, 32.

47. Mining Committee to Crook, Aug. 2, 1875, Dept. of the Platte, Letters Received; Kime, *Black Hills Journals*, 167.

48. Kime, *Black Hills Journals*, 168–69.

49. Dodge to Crook, Sept. 4, 1875, Dept. of the Platte, Letters Received.

50. See Slough Diary, entries for Aug. 27 and Sept. 8, 1875.

51. Ibid., entries for Sept. 27–29 and Oct. 5–11, 1875.

52. Crook to AAG, Aug. 16, 1875, Crook Letterbook; Captain Jack Crawford had estimated that there were 500 to 1,000 in the Hills prior to Crook's arrival. The following January, he indicated that the number currently in the Hills was 1,000, with another 300 in Custer City waiting to go in. Hedren, *Ho for the Black Hills*, 30, 46.

53. Gray, *Centennial Campaign*, 24; Bray, *Crazy Horse*, 190.

CHAPTER 15

1. According to the scout, Frank Grouard, Sitting Bull's response to the invitation was to declare war against the white man. DeBarthe, *Life and Adventures of Frank Grouard*, 274.

2. Utley, *Lance and the Shield*, 125.

3. Schmitt, *General George Crook*, 190; Crook received an invitation to attend the meeting from Jonathan Collins, Secretary of the Sioux Commission, to Crook, Aug. 20, 1875, Dept. of the Platte, Letters Received, 1875, RG 98. Crook responded by note, stating that he would "not be able to be present at the time and place specified."

4. Schmitt, *General George Crook*, 190; Mills, 168.

5. Gray, *Centennial Campaign*, 23.

6. Hutton, *Phil Sheridan and His Army*, 298–99; ibid., 24.

7. Gray, *Centennial Campaign*, 24–25.

8. Chandler had replaced Delano as secretary the previous month after investigation of misdoings at the Red Cloud Agency found sufficient evidence of corruption at the highest level of the department, which forced Delano's resignation. Ibid.

9. Schmitt, *General George Crook*, 189.

10. Sheridan to Terry, Nov. 9, 1875, Sheridan Papers.

11. Bray, *Crazy Horse*, 192.

12. Gray, *Centennial Campaign*, 26.

13. The Watkins Report of Nov. 9, 1875, is found in its entirety in "Military Expedition Against the Sioux," H. Ex. Doc., No. 184, 44th Cong., 1st Sess. Sections are quoted in Gray, *Centennial Campaign*, 27–30.

14. Ibid.

15. Sheridan to Sherman, Jan. 3, 1876, Sheridan Papers.

16. Ibid.

17. Annual Report of the Secretary of the Interior for 1875, H. Ex. Doc. 1, 1875, 44th Cong., 1st Sess., 506.

18. See, for example, Lieutenant Crawford's Aug. 17, 1875, report from Sydney Barracks. He had responded to word of an attack near Redington's Ranch but "could find no trail or any sign of Indians having been there for a long time." Dept. of the Platte, Letters Received. On Sept. 2, the same officer chased several Sioux, but had no evidence that they were raiding, although they were in the vicinity of Chimney Rock, an area outside the unceded lands.

19. Gray's *Centennial Campaign* contains a lucid and well-documented account of the machinations that led to the issuance of the proclamation. See 30–32.

20. J. Q. Smith, Indian Commissioner, to Zachariah Chandler, Secretary of the Interior, January 21, 1876. Sheridan's endorsement is quoted in Gray, *Centennial Campaign*, 33.

21. Some of the Cheyenne and Sioux warriors, interviewed well after the war, insisted that they had actually begun to move toward the reservation. Sandoz to Vaughn, letter dated Oct. 7, 1958, in J. W. Vaughn, *Reynolds Campaign*, 127. Wooden Leg, who was in the Powder River camp at the time of the attack, indicated that his people had received word the soldiers would attack them unless they moved onto the reservation. They did not believe the news at first, but simply sought to stay away from the whites to avoid a confrontation. Marquis, *Wooden Leg*, 160–61. See also ch. 16, n136.

22. Bray, *Crazy Horse*, 193; see also Hyde, *Red Cloud's Folk*, 251.

23. On January 3, upon receiving word of the ultimatum, Sheridan wrote to Sherman stating he had already canvassed his generals, Terry and Crook, and that both expressed readiness to undertake operations against the Sioux as soon as they had been notified that "such action becomes necessary." Sheridan to Sherman, Jan. 3, 1876, Sheridan Papers.

CHAPTER 16

1. Sheridan to Terry, Feb. 8, 1876, Sheridan Papers; Vaughn, *Reynolds Campaign*, 8.

2. Strahorn, "General Crook's Expedition," *Weekly Rocky Mountain News*, Mar. 1, 1876, in Abrams, *Newspaper Chronicle*, 5:32.

3. McChristian, *U.S. Army in the West*, 165–66; Bourke, *On the Border*, 268.

4. Bourke, *On the Border.*

5. Among other sources, Sioux references to Three Stars (Wichahpi Yamni) are found in Neihardt, *Black Elk Speaks*, 99; and Eleanor Hinman, Interview with He Dog, July 7, 1930, "Oglala Sources on the Life of Crazy Horse," www.nebraskahistory.org/lib-arch/research /manuscripts. See also Larson, *Red Cloud*, 201.

6. Bourke, *On the Border*, 247.

7. Annual Report of the Secretary of the Interior for 1875, H. Ex Doc. 1, 44th Cong., 1st Sess., 506. The following year, the department reported that, "The number of this so-called band [the winter roamers] was estimated last winter [1875–76] to be not over 3,000. From this number not more than six or eight hundred warriors could have been mustered." Annual Report of the Secretary of the Interior for 1876, HR Ex Doc. 1, 2, 44th Cong., 2nd Sess., 392. It is evident that the secretary had overlooked the probability that the northern forces would be reinforced by an influx of agency Sioux.

8. Robinson, *A Good Year to Die*, 59.

9. Alter Ego [Strahorn], "General Crook's Expedition, The Eve of an Important Winter Campaign," *Rocky Mountain News*, Mar. 1, 1876, in Abrams, *Newspaper Chronicle*, 5:30.

10. Bourke, *On the Border*, 246; Stanton, "Big Horn Expedition," *New York Tribune*, Apr. 4, 1876, in Abrams, *Newspaper Chronicle*, 5:60. Modern estimates continue to vary. But Gray is probably the most reliable source. After an exhaustive analysis of the numbers at the Little Big Horn fight, he concluded that the largest aggregation of Indians in one place during the entire Sioux War had included about 3,400 northern roamers (including men, women, and children). He arrived at this figure by relying on Strahorn's estimate plus four hundred Cheyennes. To that number he then added 8,000 reservation Sioux who he estimated were present in the village that Custer attacked. About one in four of these Indians were warriors, according to Gray, making the number of fighters at the Little Big Horn, and hence the number of warriors with whom the army would contend, no more than 2,800. Gray, *Centennial Campaign*, 308–20. In sum, Strahorn's source seems to have been pretty accurate.

11. Bourke, *Diaries*, 1:206; Stanton, "General Crook, The Column Begins its March," *New York Tribune*, Mar. 1, 1876, in Abrams, *Newspaper* Chronicle, 5:31.

12. Bourke, *Diaries*, 1:217–18.

13. Chun, *United States Army in the Plains Indian Wars*, 69–70; Utley, *Frontier Regulars*, 72; McChristian, *U.S. Army in the West*, 113.

14. A serious drawback to the Springfields was their tendency to jam, a problem caused when their copper shell casings reacted with the tannin in the leather of the ammunition pouch, forming verdigris on the shell. When heated by firing, the verdigris coated the firing chamber, causing the shell to stick in the breech. Removing the casing with a knife or ramrod consumed precious seconds that in an attack could mean the difference between life and death. Chun, 69; Vaughn, *Reynolds Campaign*, 28; McChristian, *U.S. Army in the West*, 114–15.

15. McChristian, *U.S. Army in the West*, 192.

16. Vaughn, *Reynolds Campaign*, 29–30.

17. Gray, *Centennial Campaign*, 47.

18. For references to the need for secrecy, see Bourke, *Diaries*, 1:226; Alter Ego, "Crook Expedition," 30.

19. DeBarthe, *Life and Adventures*, 178.

20. Bourke, *Diaries*, 1:220; Vaughn, *Reynolds Campaign*, 41.

21. Daly, "Scouts—Good and Bad," 24.

22. Though there has been much speculation about Grouard's origins, it appears that this version, contained in DeBarthe's biography, is correct. See Gray, "Frank Grouard," 57.

23. Letter from Club Foot Boyd appearing in the *Bismarck Tribune*, Nov. 8, 1876, referenced in Gray, "Frank Grouard," 59.

24. DeBarthe's biography was written in 1891 following a series of conversations with Frank at Grouard's ranch near Sheridan, Wyoming. Grouard's reliability as a witness to history is suspect, and his reputation for inscrutability and taciturnity rivaled Crook's. DeBarthe calls him a "veritable sphinx." DeBarthe, *Life and Adventures*, 14. Others knew him as "the silent man of the plains"; ibid., 27. Moreover, when he did speak out, his accounts, including those in the memoir, often varied from the accounts of others. As for DeBarthe, he admitted to exaggerating and inventing incidents in the book to make it a more lively read. So, sections of the memoir should be treated cautiously.

25. Ibid., 76–77.

26. Ibid., 154.

27. Ibid., 112–17.

28. Ibid., 172–76.

29. Ibid., 178.

30. Strahorn, "Ninety Years of Boyhood," 119.

31. See note 25 above referencing letter from Club Foot Boyd.

32. Bourke, *On the Border*, 254.

33. Goodwin, *As I Remember Them*, 312.

34. Walter M. Camp, Papers, The Hammer Collection, Series 671/04, Walter Mason Camp Files, Little Big Horn National Monument Archive, Crow Agency, Mont., 789; Reid, *Ohio in the War*, 799–804. How Reid, in New York, would have known of Stanton's presence at Fort Fetterman is a question that has never been addressed.

35. Vaughn, *Reynolds Campaign*, 29.

36. Strahorn, "Ninety Years," 116.

37. Knight, *Following the Indian Wars*, 170.

38. Werner, *The Soldiers Are Coming*, 45.

39. George Crook, Official Report [of the Powder River battle], May 7, 1876, reproduced in Vaughn, *Reynolds Campaign*, appx. B, 200–202.

40. Crook to Hayes, Mar. 1, 1876, Crook Letterbook.

41. Bourke, *Diaries*, 1:212.

42. Crook, Official Report, May 6, 1876.

43. See Hedegaard, "Colonel J. J. Reynolds and the St. Patrick's Day Celebration," Master's thesis; and Kapaun, "Major General J. J. Reynolds and His Division."

44. Robinson and Hoig, *Bad Hand*, 52–53.

45. As an example of Reynolds's contentiousness, Captain Anson Mills alleged in a letter written at the turn of the century that Reynolds conducted a vendetta against Mills and Captain Henry, another officer on the expedition, that split the command into

factions. Letter from Mills to Walter Camp, Dec. 7, 1917, Little Big Horn N.M. Archive; Warner, *Generals in Blue*, 398.

46. Bourke, *On the Border*, 270.

47. Bourke, *Diaries*, 1:210.

48. Alter Ego, "The Indian War, Movements of the Big Horn Expedition," Mar. 29, 1876, *Rocky Mountain News*, in Abrams, *Newspaper Chronicle*, 5:56; Bourke, *On the Border*, 250.

49. Bourke, *Diaries*, 1:219.

50. Crook to Custer, Feb. 27, 1876, George Crook Papers; ibid., 1:211.

51. Alter Ego, "The Indian Wars."

52. Ibid.

53. See chapter 5 herein.

54. Bourke, *On the Border*, 257; *Diaries*, 1:220.

55. Alter Ego, "Northwestern Wyoming, General Crook in the Wake of the Plundering Sioux," Apr. 12, 1876, *Rocky Mountain News*, in Abrams, *Newspaper Chronicle*, 80.

56. Bourke, *Diaries*, 1:226.

57. Ibid., 229–30; Alter Ego, "Northwestern Wyoming," 82.

58. Bourke, *Diaries*, 1:230.

59. Ibid., 238.

60. Alter Ego, "The Big Horn Expedition, An Indian Encampment Destroyed," *Rocky Mountain News*, Apr. 4, 1876, in Abrams, *Newspaper Chronicle*, 60.

61. Ibid.; Bourke, *On the Border*, 264–65; Bourke, *Diaries*, 1:237.

62. Bourke, *Diaries*, 1:233.

63. Ibid., 239.

64. For years, Grouard insisted that the Indians in the village were Crazy Horse's people; DeBarthe, *Life and Adventures*, 98. But it was later established that they were primarily Northern Cheyennes with a sprinkling of Oglala Sioux under He Dog, together with a few Miniconjous, who had come to the camp to trade. See Vaughn, *Reynolds Campaign*, 100; Gray, *Centennial Campaign*, 56.

65. Bourke, *Diaries*, 1:245; Alter Ego, "The Big Horn Expedition, Some Interesting Data for Ambitious Gold Seekers," *Rocky Mountain News*, Apr. 12, 1876, in Abrams, *Newspaper Chronicle*, 82.

66. DeBarthe, *Life and Adventures*, 185–86.

67. Alter Ego, "Big Horn Expedition," 83–84; Vaughn, *Reynolds Campaign*, 61. In his autobiography, Crook stated that "Our pack mules' shoes were so smooth I was afraid to take them into the rough country the village was likely to be in." Schmitt, *General George Crook*, 191. At his court-martial, Reynolds questioned Crook's decision to split the command, in particular his judgment about the mules. He declared that they were rough shod, in good shape, and could move as fast as or faster than horses over bad terrain. Court-martial testimony quoted in Vaughn, *Reynolds Campaign*, 176. If a post facto determination of the correctness of Crook's decision comes down to a question of mule management, this author would have to side with the general, given his well-documented expertise in such matters.

68. Alter Ego, "Big Horn Expedition."

69. Bourke, *On the Border*, 270; Strahorn, "Ninety Years," 123. It is unclear whether Bourke and Strahorn referred to Reynolds's unwise involvement in Texan politics or to his clash with Mackenzie, which occurred after Bad Hand received a shipment of corn rations that had been adulterated with dirt. He refused to pay for it and accused Reyn-

olds of involvement in fraudulent contracting practices. Mackenzie sought to have him court-martialed, but nothing came of it as Sheridan ignored the charge. Nonetheless he subsequently relieved Reynolds as departmental commander and returned him to his regiment. Robinson and Hoig, *Bad Hand*, 53.

70. Official Report of General George Crook, May 17, 1876, set out in Vaughn, *Reynolds Campaign*, appx. B, 200.

71. Reynolds Court Martial Transcript, Walter Camp files, The Hammer Collection, Series 671/04, Walter Mason Camp Files. See also Stanton, "Column Begins Its March," 229. Though Reynolds would testify at his trial that he did not receive these instructions, his statement was flatly contradicted by a number of witnesses. Grouard, who claimed to have been present at the time, testified that Crook sent Reynolds off, telling him "to keep any meat or horses he might capture." Walter Mason Camp Files, 751. He repeated this to DeBarthe, who wrote that Reynolds had orders to "jump the village and capture the horses, take all the dried meat we could get, and keep the Indian saddles and burn the village, and to hold the village until we could get a courier back to [Crook]." DeBarthe, *Life and Adventures*, 188. Strahorn provided testimony to the same effect, stating he overheard Crook tell Reynolds that "if Indians were found and an attack made he wanted him to save the ponies and the meat and the buffalo robes. Said the soldiers were on rather slim rations and he wanted the meat and wanted the robes to keep the men warm and these (meat and robes) should be placed upon the ponies." Walter Mason Camp Files, 770. Major Stanton, who was not present at the briefing, nevertheless reported substantially the same information in a dispatch to the *New York Tribune*, though he may have simply been repeating what Strahorn told him. Stanton, "A Review of the Reynolds Campaign," *New York Tribune*, Apr. 7, 1876, in Cozzens, *Eyewitnesses*, 4:229.

72. DeBarthe, *Life and Adventures*, 754.

73. Official Report of Colonel Joseph J. Reynolds, in Vaughn, *Reynolds Campaign*, appx. B, 208.

74. DeBarthe, *Life and Adventures*, 189; Bourke, *On the Border*, 271; Alter Ego, "The Fight with Crazy Horse," *Rocky Mountain News*, Apr. 12, 1876, in Abrams, *Newspaper Chronicle*, 85.

75. Reynolds Report, in Vaughn, *Reynolds Campaign*.

76. DeBarthe, *Life and Adventures*, 193; Bourke, *Diaries*, 1:255.

77. Vaughn, *Reynolds Campaign*, 66; DeBarthe, *Life and Adventures*, 95.

78. For a good map of the battle site, see Vaughn, *Reynolds Campaign*, 71; for a description, see Werner, *Soldiers Are Coming*, 21.

79. DeBarthe, *Life and Adventures*, 191; Walter Camp Files, Stanton testimony, 739.

80. See Vaughn, *Reynolds Campaign*, 68; Alter Ego, "The Fight with Crazy Horse," 86–87.

81. Alter Ego, "The Fight with Crazy Horse"; Vaughn, *Reynolds Campaign*, 70, Reynolds Report, 208.

82. Alter Ego, "The Fight with Crazy Horse."

83. Walter Camp File, Egan court martial testimony, 771; Walter Camp File, Bourke testimony, 748.

84. Walter Camp File, Bourke court martial testimony, 747; Stanton testimony, 742–43; see also Mills testimony to same affect, 758. For Moore's self-justification, see First Official Report of Captain Alex Moore, Mar. 22, 1876, in Vaughn, *Reynolds Campaign*, 225. Grouard would later testify that he had cautioned Moore to remain on the ridge until Egan attacked, lest he ruin the element of surprise, Walter Camp File, 753;

but Mills, following the same trail, was able to get far closer to the village than Moore without being seen, Walter Camp File, 758.

85. Bourke, *On the Border*, 274.

86. Walter Camp File, Mills testimony, 760–61.

87. Court Martial Records in Camp File, testimony by Bourke, 751; Stanton, 744; Eton, 773; and Mills, 760. At his court-marital, Reynolds insisted that it would have taken the entire command to load the ponies with the meat and supplies, leaving the soldiers unprotected if the Indians pressed their attack. His argument seems to have been predicated on the quantities of supplies present in the camp. But he then apparently contradicted that reasoning when he claimed to have been unaware of "the large amounts of meat, robes, . . . etc. that have been reported." Court Martial Records in Camp File, testimony by Reynolds, 803. The only officer who seemed to agree with Reynolds's assessment was Noyes, a fellow defendant in the court-martial. Noyes testified that "we did not have men enough to catch ponies and pack them and at same time protect ourselves from Indians." He contended that the ponies were skittish around whites and difficult to handle, which might have further complicated the task. However, even Noyes was of the opinion that the troops could have held the camp overnight. Ibid., testimony by Noyes, 785, 787.

88. Ibid., Bourke testimony, 749; Vaughn, *Reynolds Campaign*, 98. An account of the battle by Wooden Leg of the Northern Cheyennes claims that the Indians had few guns and not much ammunition, but journalists and a number of soldiers commented on the numerous casks of gunpowder and lead found in the tipis. See, for example, Stanton, "The Big Horn Expedition, an Indian Encampment Destroyed," *New York Tribune*, Apr. 4, 1876, in Abrams, *Newspaper Chronicle*, 60; Strahorn, *Rocky Mountain News*, Mar. 18, 1876, quoted in Vaughn, *Reynolds Campaign*, 98.

89. Vaughn, *Reynolds Campaign*, 99; Bourke, *On the Border*, 276.

90. Bourke, *Diaries*, 1:255; DeBarthe, *Life and Adventures*, 193.

91. Marquis, *Wooden Leg*, 161; Hyde, *Red Cloud's Folk*, 259.

92. Werner, *Soldiers Are Coming*, 35; Greene, *Lakota and Cheyenne*, 3–8 (Wooden Leg account), 12 (Kate Bighead account).

93. Bourke, *Diaries*, 1:253.

94. Court Martial Records, Camp File, Egan testimony, 772.

95. Court Martial Records, Camp File, Mills testimony, 764; see McChristian, *U.S. Army in the West*, 16, for a description of these items of apparel. That evening, after arriving in camp, Assistant Surgeon Curtis Munn treated sixty-six cases of frostbite. Vaughn, *Reynolds Campaign*, 122.

96. Official Report of Captain Anson Mills, in Vaughn, *Reynolds Campaign*, appx. B, 219–20; Brown, "Reynolds Attack on Crazy Horse's Village."

97. Mills report, in Vaughn, *Reynolds Campaign*; Walter Camp File, Egan testimony, 772, 774, Mills testimony, 763, and testimony of Privates Michael Hummelsbough, George Mailland, and Jeremiah Murphy, 774–76.

98. Walter Camp File, Stanton testimony, 741.

99. DeBarthe, *Life and Adventures*, 190, 194; Walter Camp File, Egan testimony, 773; Stanton, "Correspondence of the Washington Chronicle," *Omaha Daily Herald*, Apr. 3, 1876, in Cozzens, *Eyewitnesses*, 4:233.

100. Bourke, *Diaries*, 1:255.

101. DeBarthe, *Life and Adventures*, 195.

102. Greene, *Lakota and Cheyenne*, 3–15.

103. Bourke, *Diaries*, 1:257; Camp File, Stanton testimony, 741.

104. Vaughn, *Reynolds Campaign*, 145; DeBarthe, *Life and Adventures*, 195–96.

105. Bourke, *Diaries*, 1:257.

106. Court Martial Records, Camp Files, Mills testimony, 766–67. The timing of Reynolds's decision to move out became an issue at his court-martial, and officers gave conflicting testimony. Estimates ranged from noon to 1:30. And Mills testified that while Reynolds implied his destination was Fort Reno, he never actually said so. Camp Files, Mills testimony; Vaughn, *Reynolds Campaign*, 146.

107. Ultimately, Crook learned that the scouts' error had been due to their habit of reckoning distance in terms of time rather than miles. Vaughn, *Reynolds Campaign*, 150.

108. Ibid., 151; Bourke, *Diaries*, 1:258.

109. Vaughn, *Reynolds Campaign*, 152; Camp File, Alexander Chambers testimony, 746.

110. DeBarthe, *Life and Adventures*, 197.

111. Bourke, *Diaries*, 1:258.

112. See Vaughn, *Reynolds Campaign*, 156; Crook to Sheridan, Telegram, Mar. 22, 1876, reproduced in Court Martial Records, Camp File, 799.

113. Sheridan to War Dept., May 16, 1876, Sheridan Papers; Sherman, Report of the General of the Army in Report of the Secretary of War, 1876, 44th Cong., 2nd Sess., 1, 29.

114. Schmitt, *General George Crook*, 192; see also Nickerson, "Major General George Crook," 21–22.

115. Camp File, Chambers testimony, 745–46.

116. Vaughn, *Reynolds Campaign*, 166.

117. Ibid., 168–69.

118. Ibid., 170.

119. Dread of capture and mutilation by the Indians had always been a major psychological burden for soldiers fighting on the frontier. Under the circumstances, to these troops, Reynolds's conduct, especially leaving the wounded Private Ayers to the mercies of the Cheyennes, appeared a realization of their worst nightmares. Bourke noted in his diary that eleven troopers, veterans of the Powder River expedition, deserted, saying that "they would not fight under men who would leave their dead and dying to fall into the hands of a savage foe." Bourke, *Diaries*, 1:265. In May, while marching from Fort D. A. Russell to Fetterman to join the spring campaign, an additional sixty-five troopers from the column deserted, reputedly believing that an order had been issued to leave the wounded on the field, a policy said to stem from the Reynolds precedent. "Facing the Foe," *Chicago Times*, May 20, 1876, in Abrams, *Newspaper Chronicle*, 5:147. Captain Noyes reported seeing more drunkenness among the men in the months after Powder River than at any previous time in his experience. Noyes to Townsend, May 11, 1876, Laramie Letters Received, quoted in Hedren, *Fort Laramie and the Great Sioux War*, 90–91.

120. Crook to Sheridan, Sheridan to Crook, May 8, 1876, Dept. of the Platte, Telegrams, RG 393.

121. Vaughn, *Reynolds Campaign*, 170–71.

122. Strahan to Mrs. Crook, Feb. 4, 1877, George Crook Papers.

123. Bourke, *Diaries*, 1:265.

124. Strahan to Mary Crook, George Crook Papers.

125. Vaughn, *Reynolds Campaign*, 172–73.

126. Ibid.

127. Court Martial Records, Camp File, Reynolds testimony, 805.

128. Captain Andrew Burt, for example, reported for the *New York Herald* during the Jenney Expedition in the summer of 1875, doing so with the full knowledge of his commanding officer, Colonel Dodge. Burt had been sufficiently comfortable in the role of reporter that he had the temerity to ask Dodge to delay a supply train back to Fort Fetterman in order to allow him time to complete his dispatches, a request that Dodge indignantly denied. Kime, *Black Hill Journals*, 100. Lieutenant Bourke wrote articles for the *San Francisco Alta California* and the *Cincinnati Gazette* on the same expedition, certainly with Crook's approval.

129. Court Martial Records, Camp File, 798. Ironically, Reynolds, in an effort to impugn Captain Mills's testimony, pointed out earlier in the proceedings that Crook had court-martialed the captain several years before in Arizona for publishing an account of an expedition against the Apaches and later denying having done so. Mills was convicted and reprimanded, although in that instance, Crook was probably more troubled by Mills's prevarication than by his scribblings. Vaughn, *Reynolds Campaign*, 175.

130. Vaughn, *Reynolds Campaign*, 178.

131. Quoted in ibid.

132. Ibid., 185–86.

133. Ibid., 187.

134. Ibid., 95.

135. Ibid., 93.

136. As Wooden Leg put it, "We were not looking for [the white men]. We were trying to stay away from all white people, and we wanted them to stay away from us." And when the village heard of the approach of Crook's soldiers, "The council of old men decided we should keep away from the soldiers and not try to fight them." Two Moons, the Cheyenne chief, would also claim that at the time of the attack, his band was en route to Fort Laramie to avoid any trouble with the soldiers. Marquis, *Wooden Leg*, 160, 163.

137. Ibid., 169, 179, 185.

138. Ibid., 179.

139. Vaughn, *Reynolds Campaign*, 135; Utley, *Lance and the Shield*, 133.

CHAPTER 17

1. "Custer Sacrificed," *New York Herald*, May 6, 1876, in Abrams, *Newspaper Chronicle*, 5:120; "Grant's Revenge," May 10, 1876, in Abrams, *Newspaper Chronicle*, 5:125; Sherman to Terry, May 8, 1876, quoted in Gray, *Centennial Campaign*, 70.

2. "The Starving Indians," *New York Times*, Apr. 23, 1876, in Abrams, *Newspaper Chronicle*, 5:99.

3. Crook to Sheridan, Telegram, Apr. 2, 1876, Dept. of the Platte, Press Copies of Telegrams, RG 393.

4. Hedren, *Fort Laramie*, 79; Gray, *Centennial Campaign*, 91; Sheridan to Crook, Telegram, Apr. 29, 1876, ibid.; Hedren, *Fort Laramie*, 73.

6. Bourke, *Diaries*, 1:267.

7. "Depredations by Indians," *New York Times*, and "Raids and Murders," *New York Tribune*, Apr. 24, 1876, in Abrams, *Newspaper Chronicle*, 5:100–101; "Raiding Redskins," *Rocky Mountain News*, May 17, 1876, in Abrams, *Newspaper Chronicle*, 5:139.

8. Bourke, *Diaries*, 1:265; Gray, *Centennial Campaign*, 91; Hedren, *Fort Laramie*, 78; Nadeau, *Fort Laramie and the Sioux*, 271–72; "Indian Matters," *Rocky Mountain News*, Apr. 26, 1876, in Abrams, *Newspaper Chronicle*, 103.

9. Crook to Sheridan, Telegram, Apr. 27, 1876, Dept. of the Platte, Press Copies of Telegrams, RG 393.

10. Crook to Sheridan, May 29, 1876, Military Division of the Missouri, Telegrams, RG 393.

11. Jordon to Townsend, Commander, Ft. Laramie, June 2, 1876, Military Division of the Missouri, Special File, 1876.

12. Sheridan to Sherman, May 29, 1876, Military Division of the Missouri, Letters Sent, RG 98; Gray, *Centennial Campaign*, 94.

13. See Hedren, *Great Sioux War Orders of Battle*, 50–52, for details on composition of the force.

14. Utley, *Frontier Regulars*, 260; Gray, *Centennial Campaign*, 110; Bourke, *Diaries*, 1:288–89; Bourke, *On the Border*, 290–91; Hedren, *Fort Laramie*, 88.

15. Bourke, *Diaries*, 1:275.

16. Bourke, *On the Border*, 286; Hyde, *Red Cloud's Folk*, 260.

17. Bourke, *Diaries*, 1:267.

18. Ibid., 267–68; Larson, *Red Cloud*, 200–201.

19. Bourke, *Diaries*, 1:269.

20. Ibid., 271.

21. Larson, *Red Cloud*, 201.

22. Hyde, *Red Cloud's Folk*, 257–59; Bourke, *Diaries*, 1:272–73. Grouard later supported Crook's suspicions regarding Hastings's involvement, informing the general that the agent's clerk had admitted that Hastings had indeed instructed the chiefs not to let their young men accompany the expedition and had sharply rebuked Sitting Bull of the South for speaking to Crook without first consulting with him. Bourke, *Diaries*, 1:275.

23. Bourke, *On the Border*, 288; Bourke, *Diaries*, 1:284–85; "A Close Shave for Crook," *Rocky Mountain News*, May 24, 1876, in Abrams, *Newspaper Chronicle*, 5:157; Strahorn, "Ninety Years," 138–39.

24. Linderman, *Plenty Coups*, viii–vix. The spelling of Absarokee has many variants.

25. This point is illustrated by a story told by his biographer. In 1869, in his seventy-first year, he overheard some young men of his band arguing over who would succeed him, thinking he was too old to lead in battle. "Giving no evidence he had heard them, he mounted his horse and disappeared, no one knew where. After an absence of 'two moons' he reappeared with seven scalps." Dramatically holding the scalps aloft, he announced, "Let him who would take my place count as many scalps." As none among his dumbstruck warriors accepted his challenge, he continued to reign as chief of the Eastern Shoshones until his death in 1900. Hebard, *Washakie, Chief of the Shoshone*, 137, 283.

26. Ibid., 24–25.

CHAPTER 18

1. Schmitt, *General George Crook*, 141; Magid, *George Crook*, 254, 282; see Robinson, *General Crook and the Western Frontier*, xvii, comparing Crook to Douglas McArthur in regard to his assiduous cultivation of his public image.

2. Robinson, *General Crook and the Western Frontier*, xvii.

3. Porter, *Paper Medicine Man*, 13.
4. Finerty, *John F., War Path and Bivouac*, 4.
5. Strahorn, "Ninety Years," 136.
6. Knight, *Following the Indian Wars*, 172.
7. Kime, *Black Hills Journal*, 56.
8. Charles King, *Campaigning with Crook*, 154.
9. Knight, *Following the Indian Wars*, 172. Dodge noted in his diary that Davenport was "not blessed with a vast amount of courage, . . . Last night they persuaded him that the hooting of an owl was the songs of Indian women over an approaching fight, & scared him almost to death by predicting a hard fight today." Kime, *Black Hills Journal*, 56. For his part, Charles King, then a lieutenant, but later an author of many books on the West, accused Davenport of cowardice at the battle of Slim Buttes in the first edition of his book, *Campaigning with Crook*, 155. He retracted the accusation in a later edition after learning that the man had actually displayed "cool courage" in battle. King, reprint edition, 146.
10. Knight, *Following the Indian Wars*, 172.
11. Kime, *Black Hills Journal*, 57.
12. Knight, *Following the Indian Wars*, 171.
13. Finerty, *War Path and Bivouac*, 22.
14. Knight, *Following the Indian Wars*, 169.
15. King, *Campaigning with Crook*, 144; ibid., 173; Finerty, *War Path and Bivouac*, xvi, 4.
16. See Charles Rankin and Oliver Knight, introduction to reprint edition of Finerty, *War Path and Bivouac*, v–xviii.
17. Finerty, *War Path and Bivouac*, 6, 12, 31.
18. DeBarthe, *Life and Adventures*, 211.
19. Bourke, *Diaries*, 1:291.
20. Ibid.; DeBarthe, *Life and Adventures*, 213.
21. Mills, *My Story*, 401.
22. The incident may have been caused by the absence of a safety on the cavalry pistol. James E. H. Foster, "From Fort Fetterman to the Rosebud," in Cozzens, *Eyewitnesses*, 4:269.
23. DeBarthe, *Life and Adventures*, 215.
24. Finerty, *War Path and Bivouac*, 53; Bourke, *Diaries*, 1:299.
25. Maketa, ed., *Marching with General Crook*, 9–10.
26. Bourke, *Diaries*, 1:303.
27. Finerty, *War Path and Bivouac*, 55.
28. Maketa, *Marching with General Crook*, 16.
29. Foster, "From Fort Fetterman to the Rosebud," in Cozzens, *Eyewitnesses*, 4:269–70, 274.
30. Finerty, *War Path and Bivouac*, 56; Bourke, *Diaries*, 1:303; ibid., 269.
31. Finerty, *War Path and Bivouac*, 57; Crawford, *Exploits of Ben Arnold*, 243; Bourke, *Diaries*, 1:303; Maketa, *Marching with General Crook*, 11.
32. A dispatch from Reuben Davenport of the *Herald* reported that the warriors from Red Cloud numbered about three thousand. Davenport, "An Indian Battle. The Warring Sioux Attack General Crook's Command," *New York Herald*, June 16, 1876, reprinted in Abrams, *Sioux War Dispatches*, 70.

33. Hutton, *Phil Sheridan and His Army*, 312–13.

34. Foster, "From Fort Fetterman to the Rosebud," in Cozzens, *Eyewitnesses*, 4:269–70.

35. Finerty, *War Path and Bivouac*, 59–61; Bourke, *Diaries*, 1:305; Foster, "From Fort Fetterman," in Cozzens, *Eyewitnesses*, 4:273; Strahorn, "Ninety Years," 142–43; Wasson, "General Crook's Expedition, July 6, 1876, Alta California," in Abrams, *Newspaper Chronicle*, 5:266–67.

36. Bourke, *Diaries*, 1:305; Vaughn, *With Crook at the Rosebud*, 19.

37. Wasson, *Alta California*. Information provided by the Cheyennes years later proved Crook wrong about both the purpose of the attack and the identity of the attackers. In reality, the raiders were not Sioux, but a party of about two hundred Northern Cheyennes under their chief, Little Hawk, who, upon learning of the whereabouts of the camp from a hunting party, set out to reconnoiter it, probably hoping to steal horses if the opportunity arose. Utley, *Lance and the Shield*, 135; Marquis, *Wooden Leg*, 192–97; Gray, *Centennial Campaign*, 332; McDermott, 20.

38. Bourke, *Diaries*, 1:307–308.

39. Foster, "From Fort Fetterman," in Cozzens, *Eyewitnesses*, 4:274; Mangum, *Battle of the Rosebud*, 42; Maketa, *Marching with General Crook*, 16; Bourke, *Diaries*, 1:309.

40. Bourke, *Diaries*, 1:310; Finerty, *War Path and Bivouac*, 64–66; DeBarthe, *Life and Adventures*, 218.

41. Bourke, *Diaries*, 1:312; DeBarthe, *Life and Adventures*, 217–20; Davenport, "Looking for Sioux," *New York Herald*, June 21, 1876, in Abrams, *Newspaper Chronicles*, 5:217; Strahorn, "Ninety Years," 147. The exact number of Crow volunteers has been subject to dispute. Bourke and Strahorn gave the number as 176. Davenport's estimate was 180, and Grouard's, 159.

42. Mangum, *Battle of the Rosebud*, 43; Gray, *Centennial Campaign*, 118. Grouard believed that, seeing the white canvas tents of the soldiers, the Crows thought he had led them to a Sioux village. DeBarthe, *Life and Adventures*, 220; Finerty, *War Path and Bivouac*, 66.

43. Though Washakie was with the contingent, because of his age, he had delegated responsibility to his sons to lead the detachment in battle. See DeBarthe, *Life and Adventures*, 221.

44. Bourke, *Diaries*, 1:314; Finerty, *War Path and Bivouac*, 66.

45. Crook aide C. S. Roberts quoted the general as saying, "They [Indian scouts] know better how to obtain the information which is needed . . . than we do, and should be allowed to use their own methods in getting it." C. S. Roberts to W. S. Shipp, Aug. 14, 1885, in Bigelow, *On the Bloody Trail of Geronimo*, 43–44.

46. Ibid., 313. This report apparently referred to an incident occurring on May 26–27 described by Lieutenant James Bradley in *March of the Montana Column*, 123–26.

47. Official Report of General Crook, Camp Cloud Peak, June 20, 1876, in Vaughn, *With Crook at the Rosebud*, 215; Gray, *Centennial Campaign*, 118–19; Bourke, *Diaries*, 1:313; DeBarthe, *Life and Adventures*, 223.

48. DeBarthe, *Life and Adventures*. Anson Mills was also skeptical. He did not believe that either the Crows or Crook had any clear idea where the Sioux were. *My Story*, 402.

49. Official Report of General Crook, Camp Cloud Peak, June 20, 1876.

50. Bourke, *Diaries*, 1:313.

51. Nickerson, "Major General George Crook," 24.

52. Finerty, *War Path and Bivouac*, 74; Strahorn, "Ninety Years," 148; DeBarthe, *Life and Adventures*, 222.

53. Finerty, *War Path and Bivouac*, 78.

54. Crook was not the only man in the column in a glum mood. Two of the correspondents were similarly long-faced. Strahorn, thrown from his horse and dragged through a patch of prickly pears, would be extracting thorns from various portions of his anatomy for the next several weeks. Strahorn, "Ninety Years," 151. For his part, Finerty had accidentally discharged his pistol, narrowly missing his leg and blowing the cantle off his saddle. When a passing officer inquired whether he was wounded, stunned and mortified, he blurted out, "I don't know, Colonel." "Then, by Jove, it is about time you found out," the officer retorted, riding off in a gale of laughter. Finerty, *War Path and Bivouac*, 77.

55. Maketa, ed., *Capron Diary*, entry of Jun. 16, 1876; Vaughn, *With Crook at the Rosebud*, 36; Mangum, *Battle of the Rosebud*, 49.

56. Finerty, *War Path and Bivouac*, 79.

57. Debarthe, *Life and Adventures*, 223.

CHAPTER 19

1. Vaughn, *With Crook at the Rosebud*, 39; Utley, *Lance and the Shield*, 134.

2. Little Hawk indicated that he arrived at the camp at daybreak on the 17th and that the subsequent battle commenced about noon. Chronologically, this recollection is so badly out of sync with white accounts, it would seem that Little Hawk's memory was faulty in this regard. See Little Hawk's Reminiscences, in Greene, ed., *Lakota and Cheyenne*, 21–26.

3. Marquis, *Wooden Leg*, 198–99; Utley, *Lance and the Shield*, 138, 140; McDermott, *1876 Campaigns*, 134. Confirming the decision to preempt Three Stars' attack, a relative of one of the Crow warriors who rode with Crook recounted in an interview with Walter Camp that Lakotas with whom he had spoken, asserted that the Sioux were aware of Custer's approach toward their camp. When they discovered Crook's approach, they decided it was better to meet him in battle to prevent him from joining forces with Custer. Ironically, according to this account, it appears that the chiefs adopted a strategy to defeat the white columns in detail, just as Crook had planned to defend the Indians once the big village had broken up. Camp File, BYU, 361.

4. "Little Hawk's Reminiscence," in Greene, *Lakota and Cheyenne*, 25. Most white participants estimated that there were between 1,500 and 3,000 Indians at the fight on the Rosebud. The higher estimates probably represent some inflation to account for the battle's outcome. In fairness, an accurate accounting based on battlefield estimates would have been difficult given the mobility of the Indians and the broken nature of the terrain. Gray estimates that there were 1,000 Cheyenne and Sioux warriors in the village and that one-quarter remained behind to guard the women and children, leaving 750 to attack Crook's column. John Stands in Timber, grandson of Lame White Man, a Cheyenne chief present at the battle, told Vaughn that the Indians numbered 1,500, with 100 being Cheyennes. Vaughn, *With Crook at the Rosebud*, 46. See also Utley, *Lance and the Shield*, 140; Vestal, *Warpath, The True Story of the Fighting Sioux*, 187.

5. Vaughn, *With Crook at the Rosebud*.

6. Vestal, *Warpath*, 187.

7. Vaughn, *With Crook at the Rosebud*, 48.

8. Reuben Davenport, "The Battle of Rosebud Creek," *New York Herald*, July 6, 1878, in Abrams, *Newspaper Chronicle*, 5:269; but see Strahorn, who stated it was believed that it was only "a small hunting party discovered." "Crook: The Battle of the Rosebud," *Rocky Mountain News*, July 5, 1876, in Abrams, *Newspaper Chronicle*, 5:260.

9. James Foster, "Battle of the Rosebud," *New York Daily Graphic*, July 13, 1876, in Abrams, *Sioux War Dispatches*, 93.

10. Mills, *My Story*, 404; Lemly, "Fight on the Rosebud," 8; Mangum, *Battle of the Rosebud*, 52.

11. Crook's Official Report, June 20, 1876, in Vaughn, *With Crook at the Rosebud*, 214; Mangum, *Battle of the Rosebud*; Davenport, article of June 6, in Abrams, *Sioux War Dispatches*; Lemly, "Fight on the Rosebud," 7.

12. Vaughn, *With Crook at the Rosebud*, 48–49.

13. Mills, *My Story*, 404.

14. Finerty, *War Path and Bivouac*, 83–84.

15. Ibid., 84.

16. Mills, *My Story*, 405.

17. Nickerson, "Major General George Crook," 26.

18. DeBarthe, *Life and Adventures*, 224.

19. Official Report of Major Andrew Evans, in Vaughn, *With Crook at the Rosebud*, 217–19.

20. Lemly, "Fight on the Rosebud," 8; Bray, *Crazy Horse*, 209; Powers, *Killing of Crazy Horse*, 184. Crook would later be criticized for disbursing his troops too widely about the field, two examples being the placement of Van Vliet and Henry's battalions. In his autobiography and in public statements made subsequent to the battle, he correctly denied responsibility for these deployments, but mistakenly attributed them to orders from Nickerson. This error, to which Nickerson never publicly responded, was an unwarranted slap at an aide who served him faithfully for many years. It contributed to the eventual dissolution of their friendship, a circumstance to which Crook, in his later years, appeared oblivious. See Schmitt, *General George Crook*, 194; Crook's Official Report, June 20, 1876, in Vaughn, *With Crook at the Rosebud*, 217.

21. Bourke, *On the Border*, 312.

22. Finerty, *War Path and Bivouac*, 86; Bray, *Crazy Horse*, 209.

23. McDermott, *1876 Campaigns*, 26. Though the allies had been instructed to tie red cloth around their arms to distinguish them from the hostiles, this tactic foundered on the fact that among the Plains Indians, red was a commonly favored color, so that many of the Sioux and Cheyennes wore similar adornments. Lemly, "Fight on the Rosebud," 10–11; Robinson, *Good Year to Die*, 149.

24. Nickerson, *1876 Campaigns*, 26; Mills, *My Story*, 406.

25. Finerty, *War Path and Bivouac*, 85. Racism may have also been the reason that Finerty's account omitted the vital and courageous role played by the Crows and Shoshones only moments before the charge.

26. McDermott, *1876 Campaigns*, 27.

27. Davenport, "The Battle of Rosebud Creek," *New York Herald*, July 6, 1876, in Abrams, *Newspaper Chronicle*, 5:261.

28. Vaughn, *With Crook at the Rosebud*, 57; Willert, *Little Big Horn Diary*, 164.

29. Official Report of Lieutenant Colonel W. B. Royall, June 20, 1876, in Vaughn, *With Crook at the Rosebud*, 229.

30. Vaughn, *With Crook at the Rosebud*, 167; Mangum, *Battle of the Rosebud*, 67.

31. DeBarthe, *Life and Adventures*, 316; Bourke, *Diaries*, 1:328. The horse recovered and was fit enough for Crook to ride in August and loan to Finerty at the end of the Hunger March. Finerty, *War Path and Bivouac*, 205.

32. Lemly, "Fight on the Rosebud," 12.

33. Mills, *My Story*, 407.

34. Foster, "From Fetterman to the Rosebud," *Chicago Tribune*, July 5, 1876, in Cozzens, *Eyewitnesses*, 4:279; Finerty, *War Path and Bivouac*, 90; Mangum, *Battle of the Rosebud*, 71.

35. McDermott, *1876 Campaigns*, 28.

36. Davenport, *New York Herald*, July 6, 1876, in Abrams, *Newspaper Chronicle*.

37. McDermott, *1876 Campaigns*, 28–30; Vaughn, *With Crook at the Rosebud*, 115. Davenport later contended that had Crook not ordered Royall to move to rejoin the main body of troops, the colonel would have been able to take to a crest above him and save his own men from disaster, perhaps driving the Sioux from the field. The fact that Royall's force came close to being annihilated seems to contradict this assertion. Crook angrily responded to Davenport's version of events in a dispatch to General Sheridan. Davenport, "Battle of Rosebud Creek," *New York Herald*, July 13, 1876, in Abrams, *Newspaper Chronicle*, 6:23; Crook to Sheridan, July 23, 1876, quoted in Vaughn, *With Crook at the Rosebud*, 124.

38. Strahorn, "Ninety Years," 153.

39. Finerty described the canyon as a "dark and winding defile," and others, including Bourke, painted it in equally lurid and dramatic colors. Finerty, *War Path and Bivouac*, 90; Bourke, *On the Border*, 31. These ominous perceptions may have been a purely psychological phenomenon conjured up after the fact. Today, if one rides along the road that descends through the canyon, the scene seems entirely different. The valley floor appears far broader and the slopes on either side much gentler than contemporary accounts would have it. See Mangum, *Battle of the Rosebud*, 86; Willert, *Little Big Horn Diary*, 164–65.

40. DeBarthe, *Life and Adventures*, 229. Today we know that Grouard was referring to felled timber and brush along the sides of the ravine that only looked like barricades, but that were, in reality, barriers the Sioux had thrown up to keep their ponies from wandering. Hyde, *Red Cloud's Folk*, 266.

41. Finerty, *War Path and Bivouac*, 91.

42. Ibid., 92; Bourke, *On the Border*, 316; Mills, *My Story*, 408; Porter, *Paper Medicine Man*, 45.

43. Mills, *My Story*, 408. Of course, Mills was in error; he was never anywhere near the village.

44. Crook, Official Report, in Vaughn, *With Crook at the Rosebud*, 214. The *Herald*'s Davenport, in an account of the battle filled with explicit and implied criticisms of the general's handling of the fight and finger-pointing at the Indian allies, provided an alternate, and uncorroborated, reason for Mills's recall. In a piece datelined June 19, he wrote that Crow scouts had come to Crook after Mills's departure, stating that the Sioux village was in the entirely opposite direction from where Crook thought it to be. Accordingly, Crook then canceled Noyes's marching orders and sent Nickerson to retrieve Mills. Davenport's report is suspect since no other participant recorded this version of events, and is in error in stating that Noyes's orders were canceled, as the

latter joined Mills at the bend in the Rosebud as originally instructed. Davenport, "The Indian War," *New York Herald*, June 24, 1876, in Abrams, *Newspaper Chronicle*, 5:224.

45. DeBarthe, *Life and Adventures*, 231–32.

46. Crook, Official Report, in Vaughn, *With Crook at the Rosebud*, 216; Nickerson, "Major General George Crook," 28; Lemly, "Fight on the Rosebud," 10; see also Ricker interview with Baptiste Pourier, Jan. 6–7, 1907, quoted in Vaughn, *With Crook at the Rosebud*, 99.

47. R. E. Strahorn to Brininstool, in Benteen, "The Custer Fight," ed. Brininstool, privately published by E. A. Brininstool, 20–30; Crook, Official Report, in Vaughn, *With Crook at the Rosebud*, 214. Years later, writing for posterity, Crook conveniently overlooked these considerations, crediting his savvy alone for the decision. "I noticed some Indians who were just above where [Mills] passed, and who could have inflicted much damage on his troops without any danger to themselves. Instead of doing this, they sneaked off the hill . . . , which showed me plainly that we were doing just what they wanted us to do. So I recalled the squadron." Schmitt, *General George Crook*, 195.

48. While on a visit to the site in the fall of 1876, Crook told Mills that he ought to be thankful to him for returning [Mills] from that canyon as they were as well or better equipped to destroy [him] as they were to destroy Custer." Mills, *My Story*, 409. This belief was shared by others in the command who embellished it over the years. In his 1891 work, Bourke wrote that Crazy Horse had 6,500 warriors waiting to attack Crook, and had turned the canyon into a cul de sac, "the front being closed with a dam and abatis of broken timber . . . the rear, of course, to be shut off by thousands of yelling murderous Sioux and Cheyenne." *On the Border*, 311. Nickerson wrote that, two years after the battle, while visiting the field with Crook and General Sheridan, "the Indians [scouts accompanying the visitors] pointed out where . . . they had a thousand more warriors in ambush down the cañon in a position where, once in, we could not possibly have gotten out and had Mills or the whole command continued down the cañon to attack the village, not a man could have escaped." Nickerson, "Major General George Crook," 28–29. For a detailed analysis regarding the existence of the village and possibility of an ambush, see Vaughn, *With Crook at the Rosebud*, 84–86.

49. For Crazy Horse interview, see Vaughn, *With Crook at the Rosebud*, 135–36; Powers, *Killing of Crazy Horse*, 294–95; Bourke, *On the Border*, 311; DeBarthe, *Life and Adventures*, 230–31; Bray, *Crazy Horse*, 206, 208; and Hyde, *Red Cloud's Folk*, 266. Marie Sandoz in her highly imaginative biography indicates that Crazy Horse came up with the ambush idea late in the battle; but it is questionable whether the chief could have controlled such a large group of individualistic warriors from different bands in a manner that would have allowed him to execute this maneuver. See also Sajna, *Crazy Horse, Life Behind the Legend*, 280–81.

50. See Lazy White Bull's account in Greene, *Lakota and Cheyenne*, 21.

51. There is no agreement on the casualty figures, as Plains Indians usually carried off their dead. Though only thirteen were left upon the field, a substantially greater number must have died or been severely wounded. See Crook, Official Report, for the number of hostiles left on the field. Indians returning to Red Cloud after the battle reported that "Sitting Bull had two thousand Indians in [the] Rosebud fight and lost five killed and

thirty wounds." Major John P. Hawkins, Acting Assistant Adjutant General to AAG, Military Division of Missouri, Records of the War Dept., Military Division of Missouri, Special File, 1876, NARA. Red Feather, a brother-in-law of Crazy Horse, later put the loss at four Sioux and one Cheyenne killed. William Garnett to McGillycuddy, Valentine, Mar. 6, 1922, in Robert A. Clark, ed., *The Killing of Chief Crazy Horse*, 110. An article from the Fifth Cavalry Camp (the Fifth was not in the battle) dated July 19 estimated the Indian losses at one hundred wounded and eighty-six killed; Crazy Horse gave the total Cheyenne and Sioux losses at thirty-six killed and sixty-three wounded, a number deemed reasonable by Vaughn based on interviews with surviving participants. Vaughn, *With Crook at the Rosebud*, 67.

52. Vaughn, *With Crook at the Rosebud*, 147. Carroll Friswold wrote the commentary for the book *The Killing of Chief Crazy Horse*, which included correspondence between Valentine McGillycuddy, a surgeon who joined the Big Horn and Yellowstone Expedition at Goose Creek, and Billy Garnett, the half Sioux interpreter. The latter concluded from the exchange that Crazy Horse "quit the fight to get some food and rest." Clark, *Killing of Chief Crazy Horse*, 103.

53. Grinnell, *The Fighting Cheyennes*, 344; Eli Ricker, "Interview with Respects Nothing," Nov. 9, 1906, Ricker Tablet #29; Vaughn, *With Crook at the Rosebud*, 147.

54. Crook, Official Report, in Vaughn, *With Crook at the Rosebud*. Bourke, *Diaries*, 1:329. The number of Crook's casualties, like those of the Indians, has been variously reported. Contemporary accounts, including Crook's after-action report, identified nine soldiers dying in action. As memories faded, the numbers grew. In later accounts, Grouard recalled twenty-eight dead. DeBarthe, *Life and Adventures*, 233. Crook in his memoir put the number at "over a dozen." Schmitt, *General George Crook*, 195. As to the Indian allies, official reports and private accounts based on Crow and Shoshone tallies indicated that only one of their number died, a young Shoshone pony herder, while seven were wounded. An affidavit from Big Bat, executed much later, affirmed that four Crows were wounded and disabled in battle. The remainder were Shoshones. Dept. of the Interior, U.S. Indian Service document executed at Crow Agency, MT, on Oct. 17, 1908, White Swan Library.

55. Finerty, *War Path and Bivouac*, 93. Finerty's estimate may be exaggerated. Pourier noted that during the battle, many soldiers left unspent cartridges on the ground and never recovered them. Pourier interview, Ricker Papers. On the matter of ammunition, Wasson, too, had unkind words regarding the soldiers' aim. "There was ammunition enough expended on our side to have killed the entire Sioux race and the circle of fire was at one time at least three miles in length." Wasson, "The Sioux War," *New York Tribune*, July 6, 1876, in Abrams, *Newspaper Chronicle*, 5:278. He also criticized Indian marksmanship, and Davenport claimed to have noticed that toward the end of the fight, several Sioux warriors who had wounded soldiers, salvaged their cartridges rather than wasting time scalping the troopers, indicating that they were running short of ammunition. Davenport, "Battle of Rosebud Creek," July 6, 1876, in Abrams, *Newspaper Chronicle*, 5:268; see also Lemly, "Fight on the Rosebud," 12.

56. Finerty, *War Path and Bivouac*, 95.

57. Lemly, "Fight on the Rosebud," 10.

58. Bourke, *Diaries*, 1:317.

59. Only a year later, Henry resumed his duties, and ultimately rose to the rank of general, and later, governor of Puerto Rico during the Spanish-American War. Nickerson, "Major General George Crook," 28; Connell, *Son of the Morning Star*, 91–92.

60. Davenport, "The Battle of Rosebud Creek," *New York Herald*, July 6, 1876, in Greene, ed., *Battles and Skirmishes*, 38; "The Indians: Interview with a Returned Officer [Captain A. H. Nickerson]," *Chicago Tribune*, June 12, 1876, in McDermott, *1876 Campaigns*, 144; interview with Sweet Mouth, a Crow woman who witnessed the battle, "Indian Maid's Vengeance in Early Montana Days," *Billings Gazette*, Sept. 20, 1911, in McDermott, *1876 Campaigns*, 136–37.

61. Regarding Crow discontent, see Mattes, *Indians, Infants, and Infantry*, 220; "Crook's Fight," *Washington Evening Star*, June 24, 1876, in McDermott, *1876 Campaigns*, 144.

62. Finerty, *War Path and Bivouac*, 97; Maketa, *Marching with General Crook*, 21, 23; Juarez, *Tarnished Saber*, 76–77.

63. Bray, *Crazy Horse*, 212; Marquis, *Wooden Leg*, 204–206.

CHAPTER 20

1. Annual Report of the Secretary of War, 1876, quoted in Mangum, *Battle of the Rosebud*, 92.

2. Crook, Official Report, in Vaughn, *With Crook at the Rosebud*, 214.

3. Interview at Red Cloud Agency, Oct. 26, 1876, appearing as "Crook's Conclusions," *Chicago Times*, Nov. 4, 1876.

4. Bourke, *Diaries*, 1:328; Bourke, *On the Border*, 316.

5. *New York Times*, June 24, 1876.

6. *Army and Navy Journal* (Sept. 16, 1876): 86, quoted in Vaughn, *With Crook at the Rosebud*, 165.

7. Mills, *My Story*, 409.

8. The incident is described in the diary of Lyman W. V. Kennon, U.S. Military History Institute, Carlisle, PA, and is set forth in Schmitt, *General George Crook*, 196, and repeated verbatim in Vaughn, *With Crook at the Rosebud*, 166–67.

9. Porter, *Paper Medicine Man*, 46; Strahorn, "Ninety Years," 156; Thomas C. MacMillan, *Chicago Inter-Ocean*, July 12, 1876, quoted in Vaughn, *With Crook at the Rosebud*, 162.

10. Davenport, "Battle of the Rosebud," *New York Herald*, July 6, 1876, in Abrams, *Newspaper Chronicle*, 5:273. While their indiscipline prior to the engagement has been documented, most reports from the field found the Indian allies both courageous and reliable during the battle itself.

11. The *Herald* editorial appears in Abrams, *Newspaper Chronicle*.

12. "Indian War," *St. Louis Times*, reprinted in *Augusta Chronicle*, June 30, 1875; *Georgia Weekly Telegraph* (Macon), July 4, 1876. "General Crook's Position," *New York Times*, July 14, 1876.

13. Vaughn, *With Crook at the Rosebud*, preface. Archaeological evidence indicates that of those Indians who fought Custer eight days after the Rosebud, fully two-thirds were armed with either rifles or pistols. They were probably as well armed against Crook. See McDermott, *1876 Campaigns*, 38. The terrain consisted of a confusion of steep hills and ravines that covered a field four miles long and two miles wide.

CHAPTER 21

1. Bourke, *On the Border*, 321. Ben Arnold, a scout, estimated that no fewer than 15,000 fish were taken from the surrounding creeks, Crawford, *The Exploits of Ben Arnold*,

254; the more scientifically minded Bourke surveyed the men and officers, and computed that an average of four hundred a day were caught during the first twenty-one days spent in camp. Bourke, *Diaries*, 358.

2. "In Bivouac on Pumpkin Creek," *Cincinnatti Commercial*, Sept. 11, 1876, in Cozzens, *Eyewitnesses*, 4:371; Davenport, "Crook's Command, Inactivity of the Troops in the Presence of the Hostile Sioux," *New York Herald*, Aug. 3, 1876, in Abrams, *Newspaper Chronicle*, 6:230.

3. For more on Crook's mental state, see Gray, *Centennial Campaign*, 200. Crook to Sheridan, July 13, 1876, in Bourke, *Diaries*, 1:369. Crook expanded on this theme in a subsequent letter to Sheridan, writing that, "I learned that the hostiles had received reinforcements." Crook to Sheridan, July 16–17, in Bourke, *Diaries*, 1:369. As to actual numbers, see Gray, *Centennial Campaign*, 346–57, for analysis of numbers at Little Big Horn. For Rosebud, Grinnell estimated that there were "nearly 1,000 warriors," Grinnell, *Fighting Cheyennes*, n332; "about a thousand," Hyde, *Red Cloud*, 262. Of the reporters on the scene, one put the numbers as high as 2,500 (Davenport) but most agreed upon about 1,500. Abrams, *Sioux War Dispatches*, 103.

4. Sheridan to Crook, July 10 and July 28, 1876, Sheridan Papers.

5. Davenport, "Crook's Command," *New York Herald*, Aug. 3, 1876, in Abrams, *Newspaper Chronicle*, 6:230.

6. (Helena, Montana) *Daily Independent*, June 30, 1876, quoted in McDermott, *1876 Campaigns*, 36.

7. Schmitt, *General George Crook*, 195.

8. Schuyler letter to his father, July 2, 1876, Schuyler Papers; Bourke, *Diaries*, 1:342.

9. Sheridan to Crook, Jun. 18, 1876, NARS, RG 98, Letters Sent, Military Division of the Missouri.

10. Bourke, *Diaries*, 1:343.

11. Ibid., 1:339–65.

CHAPTER 22

1. After the Custer battle, Terry twice tried to send couriers to Crook, only to have them turned back. King, "George Crook at Camp Cloud Peak, 124.

2. These are Gray's numbers. He lists Custer's regimental strength as 33 officers and 718 men, but notes that 152 troopers were detached in the field, leaving him with the troop strength noted. Gray, *Centennial Campaign*, 285–86.

3. See Gray, *Centennial Campaign*, 142–47, for a detailed account of Terry's plan of attack.

4. James Bradley, *March of the Montana Column*, 153–59; Connell, *Son of the Morning Star*, 1–3.

5. Lieutenant Bradley to the *Helena Herald*, July 25, 1876, in Bradley, *Montana Column*, 172; Connell, *Son of the Morning Star*, 3–4. According to Gray, 16 officers and 242 enlisted men died in the battle or from wounds suffered during the engagement. Fourteen civilians also died with Custer. Gray, *Centennial Campaign*, 285–86. By Bradley's count, 208 men had died with Custer, and another 56 with Reno. However, his figures relied only on the bodies found at the time. Bradley, *Montana Column*, 164.

6. Bourke, *Diaries*, 1:343.

7. "Crook's Camp After the Retreat," *New York Herald*, July 12, 1876, in Abrams, *Sioux War Dispatches*, 168.

8. According to Finerty, Mills, hunting in the Big Horn Mountains on the 25th (remember, Bourke has him fishing in a nearby creek), later claimed he saw "a great smoke" to the northeast at a distance of thirty-five to forty miles. Finerty noted that Mills's fellow officers dismissed the captain's report as smoke from a prairie fire, a not uncommon phenomenon in those parts. Finerty, *War Path and Bivouac*, 103–104. Mills would later assert that his sighting occurred on the 28th, and insisted that he and his fellow officers "realized there had been a fight." He further claimed that he reported the sighting to Crook, but he offered no hint of Crook's reaction. Mills, *My Story*, 410. Notwithstanding these recollections, there is no contemporary documentation indicating that Crook or any of his officers had an inkling of Custer's fate for another two weeks. Bourke's diary, the only contemporaneous source, made no mention of smoke on the 25th, Bourke, *Diaries*, 1:345. Years later, Finerty opined that the smoke came from grassfires ignited by sparks from guns used during the Custer battle. Finerty, *War Path and Bivouac*, 103–104. The historian Gray, using the date given by Mills for the smoke sighting, thought the smoke resulted from Gibbon burning debris in the Indian village on the 28th. Gray, *Centennial Campaign*, 198. Topping all other narratives for sheer inventiveness, DeBarthe, Grouard's creative biographer, ignoring the fact that the Custer battle occurred in the afternoon, wrote that around ten o'clock on the morning of the 25th, Groaurd spotted smoke signals that told of a big fight with the soldiers. He relayed this information to officers of the command, but they ridiculed the idea of a battle. To prove he was right, according to DeBarthe, Grouard rode seventy miles to the battlefield, viewed the dead of Custer's command, and then infiltrated the Indian village, remaining there until dawn. Two days later, which would have been the 27th, he showed up in Crook's camp. DeBarthe, *Life and Adventures*, 255, 258. As seems obvious, this story was pure fiction, an invention, perhaps one of those stories the author admitted including in his book without Grouard's consent to spice up the narrative. See Ricker interview with E. E. Server at Crow Agency.

9. King, "George Crook at Camp Cloud Peak," 119; Strahorn, "Ninety Years," 182.

10. Strahorn, "Ninety Years," 158.

11. Bourke, *Diaries*, 1:355; Finerty, *War Path and Bivouac*, 113; Crook to Sheridan, July 16, 1876, quoted in Bourke, *Diaries*, 1:374–75.

12. Crook to Sheridan, July 16–17, 1876, quoted in Bourke, *Diaries*, 1:374–75; Finerty, *War Path and Bivouac*; Bourke, *Diaries*, 1: 356; De Barthe, *Life and Adventures*, 266; Pourier, in Greene, *Battles and Skirmishes*, 65; letter from Noyes to Walter Camp, June 28, 1914, Walter M. Camp Papers, Robert Ellison Collection, Denver Public Library. While Noyes provided no supporting evidence for his allegation, it is evidence of the belief harbored by at least some of Crook's officers that the general conducted his campaigns with at least one eye on the press.

13. Finerty charitably attributed this daylight departure to the general's impatience to learn definite information about the whereabouts of the Sioux. Finerty, *War Path and Bivouac*, 114.

14. According to Bourke, Sibley reported that the war party had been "from 300 to 400 strong, altho' the calculation of Frank Grouard . . . was that the enemy was as strong forces as at the Rosebud fight." Bourke, *Diaries*, 1:359.

15. Strahorn, "Ninety Years," 192. The entire affair, known as the Sibley Scout, is described in detail in Finerty's *Warpath and Bivouack*, 113–28, and in Grouard's biography, DeBarthe, *Life and Adventures*, 264–82.

16. Bourke, *Diaries*, 1:361. Sheridan himself only learned the news from an AP wire story he read while attending the nation's July 4 centennial celebrations in Philadelphia. Initially, he disbelieved it, but it was confirmed the following day when he received Terry's official report of the event. Only then had Sheridan sent the dispatch to Crook at Goose Creek. Hutton, *Phil Sheridan and His Army*, 318.

17. Bourke, *Diaries*, 1:362, 363.

18. Bourke, ibid., 1:359; Finerty, *War Path and Bivouac*, 129; Mills, *My Story*, 410–11.

19. Hutton, *Phil Sheridan and His Army*, 318.

20. Sheridan to Sherman, July 7, 1876, quoted in Hutchins, ed., *The Army and Navy Journal on the Battle of the Little Big Horn*, 43.

21. Summarized by Bourke, *Diaries*, 1:362.

22. Finerty, *War Path and Bivouac*, 143; ibid.

23. Telegram, Crook to Drum, dated July 12, 1876, but dispatched from Fetterman on July 15, Crook Papers, University of Oregon.

24. Telegram, Crook to Merritt, July 12, 1876, Crook Papers; Crook to Terry, July 16, 1876, ibid.

25. Bourke, *Diaries*, 1:365.

26. Terry to Crook, July 9, 1876, quoted in ibid., 1:365–68.

27. Crook to Terry, July 16, 1876, Crook Papers.

28. Finerty, *War Path and Bivouac*, 143–44.

29. Bourke, *Diaries*, 1:384–86.

30. Ibid., 2:23.

31. Ibid., 2:25.

32. Sheridan to Crook, July 16, 1876, Sheridan Papers; "Mrs. General Crook," *Boston Globe*, July 12, 1876, in Abrams, *Newspaper Chronicle*, 6:56.

33. Merritt to Crook, July 19, 1876, quoted in Bourke, *Diaries*, 1:387; Stanton to Merritt, July 15, 1876, quoted in Hedren, *First Scalp for Custer*, 55–57. An accompanying dispatch indicated that of the 800 Cheyennes, only 150 were warriors, the rest being women and children. William Jordan to Merritt, in Hedren, *First Scalp*; see also Gray, *Centennial Campaign*, 349; Greene, *Lakota and Cheyenne*, 80; see also Buecker, *Fort Robinson and the American West*, 83.

34. For a firsthand account, see King, *Campaigning with Crook*, 34. Cody would embellish the tale, which became a staple of his Wild West show, claiming that he had killed the man, a warrior named Yellow Hair (often called Yellow Hand) in hand-to-hand combat. See Hedren, *First Scalp for Custer*, 78–80. In the Cheyenne account of the fight, provided by Beaver Heart, a young warrior who was part of Yellow Hair's party, the warrior was killed by a volley fired by a line of soldiers. Two men, one a soldier and the other in civilian dress, then dismounted, and one of the men, whom Beaver Heart did not know, scalped the corpse. Greene, *Lakota and Cheyenne*, 81–82; Marquis, *Wooden Leg*, 85.

35. Buecker, *Fort Robinson*, 84. With the benefit of hindsight, some historians have come around to Sheridan's view that the psychological impact of Merritt's action had a profound effect on the reservation Indians and discouraged any more major defections. Hedren, *First Scalp*, 83–84; King, "Cloud Peak," 162.

36. Crook to Sheridan, July 16, 1876, Crook to Sheridan, July 23, 1876, Crook Papers.

37. Fredrick Schwatka, "With Crook's Expedition," *Chicago Inter-Ocean*, Aug. 3, 1876, quoted in Cozzens, *Eyewitnesses*, 4:350.

38. Crook to Sheridan, July 23, 1876; Crook to Terry, July 16–17, 1876, quoted in Bourke, *Diaries*, 1:375–76.

39. Crook to Sheridan, July 23, 1876.

40. Bourke, *Diaries*, 1:383.

41. Crook to Terry, July 23, 1876, NARA, Dept. of Dakota, Letters Received, 1876, RG 98; Crook to Sheridan, July 23, 1876.

42. Sheridan to Crook, July 25, 1876, quoted in Bourke, *Diaries*, 1:386–87; Sheridan to Sherman, July 16, 1876, quoted in King, *War Eagle*, 160.

43. Finerty, *War Path and Bivouac*, 150.

44. Bourke, *Diaries*, 2:32–33.

45. Schwatka, "With Crook's Expedition," quoted in Cozzens, *Eyewitnesses*, 4:352.

46. Gray, *Centennial Campaign*, 212–20.

CHAPTER 23

1. Hedren, *First Scalp*, 81.

2. Sheridan to Sherman, July 27, NARA, Military Division of Missouri, Letters Sent, RG 98, quoted in King, *War Eagle*, 163, 163–64.

3. King, *War Eagle*, 184–85; see also Watson, "A Checklist of Indian War Correspondents 1866–1890," 310–12; Bourke, *Diaries*, 2:42; Bourke, *On the Border*, 346.

4. Bourke, *Diaries*, 2:34. Chips, a thirty-five-year-old plainsman, was said to have served under J. E. B. Stuart during the Civil War and then drifted west, where his path crossed Buffalo Bill's. Infected by a severe case of hero worship, he imitated the flamboyant scout in every possible respect and accompanied him on many assignments, including his stint with Merritt's Fifth Cavalry. Legend has it that Chips received his unusual nickname one day when General Sheridan summoned Cody for a council. The famed scout being absent, Mr. White presented himself to the general, who promptly inquired as to who the hell he was. The man replied that when Cody was not around, he was Buffalo Bill. To which Sheridan allegedly responded, "The devil you are! Buffalo Chips, you mean!" To Mr. White's everlasting chagrin, the name stuck. Finerty, *War Path and Bivouac*, 151; Hedren, *First Scalp*, 38.

5. Bourke, *On the Border*, 344; Finerty, *War Path and Bivouac*, 153.

6. C. King, *Campaigning with Crook*, 52.

7. J. King, *War Eagle*, 135, 166.

8. C. King, *Campaigning with Crook*, 52.

9. Anson Mills, "Seeking an Indian Fight," *New York Times*, Aug. 18, 1876, in Abrams, *Newspaper Chronicle*, 6:354.

10. Bourke, *Diaries*, 2:23. Carr, who participated in the engagement, agreed. "There were a few sacks of flour destroyed, three Indians killed, 12 ponies captured and a few went back to the Agency—probably to go north and depredate the settlements." But then, Carr had his own grudge against Merritt. Carr to his wife, July 19, 1876, quoted in J. T. King, *War Eagle*, 162.

11. Bourke, *Diaries*, 2:44.

12. C. King, *Campaigning with Crook*, 52; Crook to Sheridan, Aug. 4, 1876, quoted in Bourke, *Diaries*, 2:45; Gray, *Centennial Campaign*, 207; Bourke, *On the Border*, 347.

13. Wasson, "Merritt's Cavalry Join the Command," *Daily Alta California*, Aug. 9, 1876, in Abrams, *Newspaper Chronicle*, 6:287.

14. See Mills, "The Indian Campaign, The Part Taken by General Crook's Command," *New York Times*, Oct. 11, 1876, in Abrams, *Newspaper Chronicle*, 7:214. Mills saw the inadequate size of the pack train as one of the major shortcomings of the campaign.

15. Strahorn, "Ninety Years," 153–54; Bourke, *Diaries*, 2:46–48; Mills, "Notes on the Indian Wars," *New York Times*, Sept. 14, 1876, in Abrams, *Newspaper Chronicle*, 7:89; Davenport, "Crook's Campaign," *New York Herald*, Oct. 2, 1876, in Abrams, *Newspaper Chronicle*, 7:175; Mills, "The Pursuit of the Sioux," *New York Times*, Sept. 28, 1876, in Abrams, *Newspaper Chronicle*, 7:165. For Crook's defense, see Finerty, "The Fellows in Feathers: An Interview with General Crook," *Chicago Times*, Nov. 4, 1876, quoted in Abrams, *Sioux War Dispatches*, 218.

16. Finerty, *War Path and Bivouac*, 152.

17. Bourke, *Diaries*, 2:47.

18. Hedren, *We Trailed the Sioux*, 35; Bourke, *Diaries*, 2:48.

19. Bourke, *Diaries*, 2:49.

20. Schwatka, "With Crook's Expedition," in Cozzens, *Eyewitnesses*, 4:356; C. King, *Campaigning with Crook*, 68–69; Finerty, *War Path and Bivouac*, 158.

21. Bourke, *Diaries*, 2:55; "Crook's Campaign," *New York Herald*, Oct. 2, 1876, in Abrams, *Newspaper Chronicle*, 7:175.

22. Schwatka, "With Crook's Expedition," in Cozzens, *Eyewitnesses*, 4:357.

CHAPTER 24

1. Stevenson, *Deliverance from the Little Big Horn*, 129–30.

2. Johnson, *Unregimented General*, 34.

3. Bailey, *Pacifying the Plains*, 164.

4. James J. O'Kelly, "The Sioux War," *New York Herald*, Aug. 24, 1876, in Abrams, *Newspaper Chronicle*, 6:388. O'Kelly notes that in their haste to deploy, twelve raw recruits in the Seventh Cavalry fell from their horses, two breaking their legs.

5. Gibbon, *Adventures on the Western Frontier*, 160; Bailey, *Pacifying the Plains*, 164; C. King, *Campaigning with Crook*, 73; Bourke, *Diaries*, 2:56.

6. O'Kelly, "The Sioux War," in Abrams, *Newspaper Chronicle*, 6:388. In contrast to O'Kelly, Bourke reported no friction during this initial encounter, commenting that the meeting between the two generals was "most cordial." Bourke, *Diaries*, 2:56.

7. Bourke, *On the Border*, 351. Captain King and Finerty also described the meeting as friendly. C. King, *Campaigning with Crook*, 76; Finerty, *War Path and Bivouac*, 162.

8. Bourke, *Diaries*, 2:57.

9. Finerty, *War Path and Bivouac*, 162.

10. Ibid., 165.

11. Though Miles had just arrived on the northern plains, he had already begun carping about the campaign's leadership. While unhappy about the inexperience of his old friend Terry, he saved most of his venom for General Crook who, as Miles never forgot, had been promoted to general over Miles and other colonels. Thus, even Virginia Johnson, author of a hagiographic biography of General Miles, admits that Miles's departure

was greeted with relief by the officers of the command. For his part, Miles was equally eager to leave the expedition, which he judged correctly was doomed to fail. Like Crook, he always sought opportunities for independent command. Johnson, *Unregimented General*, 100; Wooster, *Nelson A. Miles*, 81.

12. Finerty, *War Path and Bivouac*, 165.

13. Gibbon, *Adventures*, 162.

14. C. King, *Campaigning with Crook*, 80.

15. Hedren, *We Trailed the Sioux*, 36.

16. Maketa, *Marching with General Crook*, 48.

17. Finerty, *War Path and Bivouac*, 167.

18. Gibbon, *Adventures*, 164.

19. Greene, *Yellowstone Command*, 50.

20. C. King, *Campaigning with Crook*, 86; Schuyler to his father, Nov. 1, 1876, quoted in Schmitt, *General George Crook*, 203; ibid.

21. Bourke, *On the Border*, 356–57. For additional detail, see Hedren, "More on the Personal and Designating Flags," in Hart, ed., *Custer and His Times*, 5:139–52.

22. Bourke, *Diaries*, 2:68–69, 75.

23. C. Mills, "Steaming up the Yellowstone," *New York Times*, Sept. 12, 1876, quoted in Abrams, *Dispatches*, 222. Captain King, a great admirer of Cody's, remembered that the scout "reluctantly" broke away from the campaign because of theatrical engagements in the East. C. King, *Campaigning with Crook*, 94.

24. Finerty, *War Path and Bivouac*, 169–70.

25. J. T. King, *War Eagle*, 172.

26. Miles to his wife, Aug. 10 and Aug. 20, 1876, Johnson, *Unregimented General*, 102–103.

27. Andrew Burt, "Dispatches from Crook's Column," *Cincinnati Commercial*, Sept. 11, 1876, in Cozzens, *Eyewitnesses*, 4:372; Bourke, *Diaries*, 2:75.

CHAPTER 25

1. Burt, "Dispatches from Crook's Column."

2. Ibid.

3. Terry to Crook, quoted in Gray, *Centennial Campaign*, without further attribution, 224.

4. Bourke, *Diaries*, 2:76.

5. Greene, *Yellowstone Command*, 51; Bourke, *Diaries*, 2:81.

6. Gray, *Centennial Campaign*, 229.

7. Finerty, *War Path and Bivouac*, 172.

8. Mills, "Notes of the Indian War," *New York Times*, Sept. 14, 1876, in Abrams, *Newspaper Chronicle*, 89–90.

9. Finerty, *War Path and Bivouac*, 174; Gray, *Centennial Campaign*, 238.

10. Bourke, *On the Border*, 359; *The Republican*, Oakland, Md., Mar. 29, 1890.

11. See, for example, Gray, *Centennial Campaign*, 230.

12. King to Eaton, July 24, 1924, King Papers.

13. Burt, "Dispatches," 373; Bourke, *Diaries*, 2:86.

14. Gray, *Centennial Campaign*, 230.

15. Greene, *Yellowstone Command*, 54–55.

16. Terry to Crook, Aug 25, 1876, quoted in Bourke, *Diaries*, 2:88.

17. Bourke, ever the loyal subordinate, believed Terry's interpretation of the situation "insane," claiming that an "alarming number of the officers of Terry's command" supported it, but that all the officers in Crook's column ridiculed it. Bourke, *Diaries*, 2:82, 89; Gray, *Centennial Campaign*, 233; Greene, *Yellowstone Command*, 55.

18. Burt, "Dispatches," 372.

19. Crook to Terry, Aug. 25, 1876, Crook Papers; Burt, "Dispatches"; Greene, *Yellowstone Command*, 55.

20. Gray, *Centennial Campaign*, 233–38.

21. See Sheridan to Sherman, Aug. 10, 1876, NARA, Division of Missouri, Letters Sent, RG 393.

22. Hutton, *Phil Sheridan and His Army*, 322–23; Sheridan to Crook, Aug. 17, Aug. 23, and Sept. 8, 1876, quoted in Bourke, *Diaries*, 2:123–26; Utley, *Frontier Regulars*, 278; Gray, *Centennial Campaign*, 234.

23. Telegram, Sheridan to Crook, Aug. 23, 1876, Sheridan Papers.

24. C. King, *Campaigning with Crook*, 90; Finerty, *War Path and Bivouac*, 175; Bourke, *Diaries*, 2:92–93.

25. Mills, "In Camp Beaver Creek," *New York Times*, Sept. 14, 1876, in Abrams, *Newspaper Chronicle*, 89–91.

26. Telegram, Crook to Sheridan, Sept. 5, 1876, NARA, Office of the AG Consolidated File 3770, AGO 1876; Gray, *Centennial Campaign*, 238.

27. Burt, "Dispatches," 375; Bourke, *Diaries*, 2:93; DeBarthe, *Life and Adventures*, 296.

28. Jame Frew in letter to his father, quoted in Hedren, *We Trailed the Sioux*, 56; Pvt. Alfred McMachin letter, quoted in *We Trailed the Sioux*, 61; Carr to his wife, in J. T. King, *War Eagle*, 173; Pvt. McMachin, quoted in Dobak, "Yellow Legs Journalists."

29. Surgeon Bennett A. Clements's report on medical conditions during the Horsemeat March, quoted in Bourke, *Diaries*, 2:476–77; Schuyler, letter to his father, Nov. 1, 1876, quoted in Bourke, *Diaries*, 2:466–74; Bourke, *Diaries*, 2:91–92; Finerty, *War Path and Bivouac*, 175–76.

30. C. King, *Campaigning with Crook*, 92.

31. Clements's report, quoted in Bourke, *Diaries*, 2:95.

32. J. T. King, *War Eagle*, 174–75; Bourke, *Diaries*, 2:94, 97.

33. Bourke, *Diaries*, 2:97.

34. Finerty, *War Path and Bivouac*, 182–83.

35. Greene, *Slim Buttes*, 37.

36. Finerty, *War Path and Bivouac*, 183.

37. Telegram, Crook to Sheridan, Sept. 5, 1876.

38. Burt, "Dispatches," 376.

39. Finerty, *War Path and Bivouac*, 184; James Frew, quoted in Hedren, *We Trailed the Sioux*, 54.

40. Greene, *Slim Buttes*, 42.

41. Finerty, *War Path and Bivouac*, 184; C. King, *Campaigning with Crook*, 96.

42. Greene, *Slim Buttes*, 40.

43. C. King, *Campaigning with Crook*, 149–50.

44. Finerty, "The Fellow in Feathers, An Interview with General Crook," *Chicago Times*, Nov. 4, 1876, in Cozzens, *Eyewitnesses*, 4:289.

45. DeBarthe, *Life and Adventures*, 301–302.

46. Glover, "Reminiscences."

47. James J. O'Kelly, "The Sioux War, Unfortunate Result of Theatrical Campaigning," *New York Herald*, Sept. 12, 1876, in Abrams, *Newspaper Chronicle*, 7:75.

CHAPTER 26

1. Bourke, *Diaries*, 2:100; Mills, *My Story*, 170.
2. Hedren, *We Trailed the Sioux*, 54–55.
3. Greene, *Slim Buttes*, 46–47; Report of Mills to George F. Chase, Sept. 9, 1876, NARA Records of the War Dept., Office of the AG, From the Annual Report of Secretary of War, 1876; Mills, *My Story*; orders to Lieutenant John Bubb, expedition commissary, quoted in Greene, *Slim Buttes*.
4. A teetotaler, Crawford dressed as flamboyantly as his theatrical friend and colleague, Buffalo Bill, but was said to be otherwise modest and free of affectation. He would soon form a friendship with the *Herald* reporter, Davenport. Wheeler, *The Old West*, 223. For more on Crawford, see Hedren, *Ho for the Black Hills*.
5. Mills, *My Story*, 170; DeBarthe, *Life and Adventures*, 302.
6. Greene, *Slim Buttes*, 48.
7. DeBarthe, *Life and Adventures*, 302; Official Report of Captain Mills, Sept. 9, 1876, quoted in Greene, *Slim Buttes*, appx. C, 132.
8. Red Horse interview with Colonel W. H. Wood, Feb. 27, 1877, quoted in Greene, *Lakota and Cheyenne*, 86; Strahorn, "Ninety Years," 202; Greene, *Slim Buttes*, 50.
9. Mills Official Report, in Greene, *Slim Buttes*, 132; *Slim Buttes*, 51.
10. DeBarthe, *Life and Adventures*, 305.
11. Mills, "Mills on Slim Buttes," *Chicago Tribune*, Sept. 20, 1876, quoted in Greene, *Slim Buttes*, 54.
12. Greene, *Slim Buttes*, 56; Mills, "Mills on Slim Buttes"; Fredrick Schwatka, "Big Horn and Yellowstone Expedition in Camp on Whitewood Creek," *Chicago Inter-Ocean*, Oct. 4, 1876, in Cozzens, *Eyewitnesses*, 4:362.
13. See Mills Official Report in Greene, *Slim Buttes*; Schwatka, "Big Horn and Yellowstone."
14. Schwatka, "Big Horn and Yellowstone."
15. Mills, *My Story*, 171; Greene, *Slim Buttes*, 60–63. Greene's work is a masterful synthesis of the many eyewitness accounts of the battle.
16. The wounded included Leuttewitz, whose knee was shattered by a bullet. Mills, Official Report, in Greene, *Slim Buttes*, 134; Bourke, *On the Border*, 370; Jack Crawford, "Crook's Campaign," *Omaha Weekly Bee*, Sept. 27, 1876, quoted in McDermott, *1876 Campaigns*, 184–86.
17. John W. Bubb to Walter Camp, Sept. 17, 1917, quoted in Greene, *Slim Buttes*, 64; Jack Crawford, "More About Crook's Last Fight," *Cheyenne Daily Leader*, Sept. 24, 1876, in McDermott, *1876 Campaigns*, 199–200; Greene, *Slim Buttes*, 65.
18. The troopers were outraged to also discover, among the papers scattered about the camp, two passes from Indian agents at the Spotted Tail and Whetstone agencies, assuring any readers that the bearers were friendly Indians. Crawford, *Omaha Weekly Bee*, Sept. 27, 1876, in McDermott, *1876 Campaigns*.
19. Greene, *Slim Buttes*, 67; Bourke, *Diaries*, 2:102.
20. Crook's birth date is generally believed to have been Sept. 28. See Magid, *George Crook*, 350n1.
21. Bourke, *Diaries*, 2:102.

22. Ibid., 106.

23. Bourke, *On the Border*, 369–70; both King, *Campaigning with Crook*, 97, and Finerty, *War Path and Bivouac*, 186, wrote that the courier arrived just as they were breaking camp, but this seems unlikely given the distance traveled and arrival time of Crook's column.

24. Greene, *Slim Buttes*, 68–69.

25. Finerty, *War Path and Bivouac*, 186.

26. Bourke, *Diaries*, 2:106.

27. Strahorn, *Daily Rocky Mountain*, Sept. 17, 1876, quoted in Greene, *Slim Buttes*, 69.

28. Bourke, *Diaries*, 2:108.

29. Finerty, *War Path and Bivouac*, 189; Bourke, *On the Border*, 370; Bubb to Camp, quoted in Greene, *Slim Buttes*, 70.

30. Greene, *Slim Buttes*, 70–71.

31. Ibid., 74.

32. Bourke, *Diaries*, 2:108–109.

33. Finerty, *War Path and Bivouac*, 189.

34. Greene, *Slim Buttes*, 75–76; ibid., 190, 192; C. King, *Campaigning with Crook*, 112; Ricker interview with Big Bat Pourier in which he alleges that Grouard remained as far out of the line of fire as possible. Jensen, ed., *Voices of the American West*, 269.

35. Bourke, *On the Border*, 372–73; Burt, "Dispatches," Sept. 17, 1876, in Cozzens, *Eyewitnesses*, 376–77; Greene, *Slim Buttes*, 76–80; Finerty, *War Path and Bivouac*, 190; C. King, *Campaigning with Crook*, 111.

36. Finerty, *War Path and Bivouac*, 191–92.

37. Greene, *Slim Buttes*, 82; Burt, "Dispatches," in Cozzens, *Eyewitnesses*, 377.

38. Two troopers and the scout, Buffalo Chips, died in the engagement. Official reports by Mills and Carr, quoted in Greene, *Slim Buttes*, 132, 136. Only two were buried on the field, the third, Private John Wenzel, dying later of his wounds. Hedren, *We Trailed the Sioux*, 53.

39. Bourke, *Diaries*, 2:114; Greene, *Slim Buttes*, 89, 92.

40. J. King, *War Eagle*, 179.

41. Quote from a Charles King letter in Greene, *Slim Buttes*, 113. Crook's unpopularity with the officers and men was acknowledged by Finerty, *War Path and Bivouac*, 204, and evidenced by the sarcastic ditty composed by an unidentified officer of the 5th, ending:

> Too few are left who care to tell
> How starved men fought and ponies fell;
> But "Crook was right," the papers yell
> To George's great felicity.

From Camp papers, quoted in Greene, *Slim Buttes*, 119–20.

42. Mills, "Among the Black Hills," *New York Times*, Oct. 12, 1876, in Abrams, *Newspaper Chronicle*, 7:218.

43. Greene, *Slim Buttes*, 115.

44. Finerty, *War Path and Bivouac*, 204. For a full analysis of the battle and its impact, I recommend to the reader Greene, *Slim Buttes*.

45. Crook, Official Report of Battle of Slim Buttes, Sept. 10, 1876, in Greene, *Slim Buttes*, 130–31.

46. For the details of the complicated but ultimately meaningless Grouard-Crawford race, see Hedren's account in *Ho for the Black Hills*, 226–35; DeBarthe, *Life and Adventures*, 314–35; Walter Camp interview with Lieutenant Bubb in Greene, *Slim Buttes*, quoted at 174n26; *Slim Buttes*, 107.

47. C. King, *Campaigning with Crook*, 131.

48. Bourke, *Diaries*, 2:117; see Gray, *Centennial Campaign*, 251–52, who was highly critical of this latest "stern chase."

49. Finerty, *War Path and Bivouac*, 202.

50. C. King, *Campaigning with Crook*, 133.

51. McGullycuddy, *Blood on the Moon*, 61.

CHAPTER 27

1. Sheridan to Crook, Sept. 11, 1876, quoted in Bourke, *Diaries*, 2:126.

2. Finerty, *War Path and Bivouac*, 206.

3. Bourke, *Diaries*, 2:130.

4. Finerty, *War Path and Bivouac*, 207.

5. Bourke, *On the Border*, 381.

6. Bennett, *Old Deadwood Days*, 132.

7. *Chicago Times*, Sept. 23, 1876, quoted in Greene, *Slim Buttes*, 109.

8. See Bourke, *Diaries*, 2:131–44, for details of Crook's colorful passage through the Black Hills.

9. Hyde, *Red Cloud's Folk*, 280–83; Gray, *Centennial Campaign*, 261.

10. For the particulars of the commission's sordid terms, see Gray, *Centennial Campaign*, 262.

11. Hedren, *Fort Laramie and the Great Sioux War*, 170.

12. Mattes, *Indians, Infants, and Infantry*, 232.

13. Ibid., 233; Hutton, *Phil Sheridan and His Army*, 323.

14. Sheridan to Sherman, Aug. 10, 1876, NARA, Division of the Missouri, Letters Sent, RG 393.

15. Hutton, *Phil Sheridan and His Army*, 322–25; Hedren, *Fort Laramie and the Great Sioux War*, 170.

16. Hyde, *Red Cloud's Folk*, 278–79.

17. Clow, "General Philip Sheridan's Legacy," 460–77, 462; Gray, *Centennial Campaign*, 259–60; Hutton, *Phil Sheridan and His Army*, 322.

18. Gray, *Centennial Campaign*, 260; Sheridan to Crook, Aug. 23, 1876, in Bourke, *Diaries*, 2:124.

19. Hutton, *Phil Sheridan and His Army*, 325.

20. Hedren, *Fort Laramie*, 171.

21. Robinson and Hoig, *Bad Hand*, 201.

22. Finerty, *War Path and Bivouac*, 219. He was actually only 5'9" tall.

23. Grant, *Personal Memoirs of U. S. Grant*, 451.

24. Robinson and Hoig, *Bad Hand.*

25. Sources pertaining to the letter include Mackenzie to Crook, Sept. 30, 1876, in Manypenny, *Our Indian Wards*, 348; Gray, *Centennial Campaign*, 265; Robinson and Hoig, *Bad Hand*, 202; Olson, *Red Cloud and the Sioux Problem*, 231.

26. Hedren, *Fort Laramie*, 171.

27. Mattes, *Indians, Infants, and Infantry*, 233. The hunt occasioned some discontent among the disgruntled troops of the Big Horn and Yellowstone expedition who were still stationed in the Black Hills. Though the men were now well rested and fed, their horses were not; and they took a dim view of Crook's "hunting and picnicking around Laramie Peak" while their mounts grew weaker by the day from a diet still deficient in grain. Hedren, *Fort Laramie*, 181.

28. Crook to Merritt, Sept. 25, 1876, Crook Letterbook; Crook to Sheridan, Oct. 23, 1876; Hyde, *Red Cloud's Folk*, 285; Olson, *Sioux Problem*, 232; Greene, *Morning Star Dawn*, 19.

29. Crook to Sheridan, Oct. 23, 1876, Crook Letterbook; Crook to AAG, Oct. 30, 1876; see North, *Man of the Plains*, 195–98, 202; Grinnell, *Two Great Scouts and Their Pawnee Battalion*, 244–45, 249–50.

30. North, *Man of the Plains*, 204.

31. Compensation for the ponies taken from Red Cloud and Red Leaf was not finalized until 1944. For details on the long and unsavory history of the Sioux pony claims, see Clow, "Sioux Pony Campaign of 1876," 470–74.

32. Crook to Sheridan, Oct. 23, 1876, Crook Letterbook.

33. Crook to AAG, Oct. 30, 1876, Crook Letterbook.

34. Mills, "The Indian Campaign, the Part Taken by General Crook's Command," *New York Times*, Oct. 11, 1876, in Abrams, *Newspaper Chronicle*, 7:216.

35. Sheridan to Crook, Oct. 25, 1876, NARA, Dept. of the Platte, Letters Received, RG 393.

36. Sheridan to Secretary of War, Nov. 6, 1876, Sheridan Papers.

37. Sheridan to Crook, Oct. 30, 1876, NARA, Dept. of the Platte, Letters Received, RG 393, quoted in Greene, *Morning Star Dawn*, 26.

38. Greene, *Morning Star Dawn*, 29. The number of scouts fluctuates depending on whose report you read. Hyde thought the recruitment disappointing. According to him, only fifty-nine Sioux, many of them mixed bloods, and a few northern Cheyennes and Arapahoes rode with the column. Hyde, *Red Cloud's Folk*, 287. A *New York Herald* reporter, Jerry Roche, wrote from Fetterman on Nov. 7 that there were fifty-seven Sioux, ninety-six Arapahoes, and six Cheyennes, in an article "Our Indian Allies," Nov. 16, 1876, quoted in McDermott, *1876 Campaigns*, 217.

CHAPTER 28

1. General Orders No. 8, Camp Robinson, NE, Oct. 24, 1876, quoted in King, *Campaigning with Crook*, 157–58.

2. Crook to Sheridan, Jan. 8, 1877, NARA, Sioux War Papers, Reel 280.

3. Bourke, *Diaries*, 2:162.

4. Wheeler, *Buffalo Days*, 127. A second lieutenant in the Fifth Cavalry, Wheeler recalled that half the men of his troop (company) were recruits.

5. Kime, ed., *Powder River Expedition Journals*, 9–12; Greene, *Morning Star Dawn*, 28–29.

6. John Bourke, "Mackenzie's Last Fight with the Cheyennes," 2–3.

7. Bourke, *Diaries*, 2:160–63. The reported number of wagons and mules varies widely. See ibid., 4; but see Hedren, *Fort Laramie*, 196; and Greene, *Morning Star Dawn*, 31.

8. Wheeler, *Buffalo Days*; Greene, *Morning Star Dawn*.

9. Kime, *Powder Expedition Journals*, 63; Greene, *Morning Star Dawn*, 33; Crook to AAG, Jan. 8, 1877, Crook Letterbook.

10. Bourke considered Roche "a far more presentable, scholarly and genial gentleman" than his predecessor, Mr. Davenport, Bourke, *Diaries*, 2:177; Hedren, *Fort Laramie*, 196.

11. Telegram, Sheridan to Crook, Nov. 5, 1876, Dept. of the Platte, Letters Received, RG 393, quoted in Greene, *Morning Star Dawn*, 35.

12. Utley, *Lance and the Shield*, 172–73.

13. Bourke, *Dairies*, 2:159–60; Greene, *Morning Star Dawn*, 38–39.

14. Kime, *Powder Expedition Journals*, 69.

15. Ibid., 65–66.

16. Greene, *Morning Star Dawn*, 72–74.

17. Bourke, "Mackenzie's Last Fight," 10.

18. Grinnell, *Two Great Scouts*, 263; Smith, *Sagebrush Soldier*, 35; see Bourke, *Diaries*, 2:170–74 for a detailed account of the council; Greene, *Morning Star Dawn*, 77.

19. Telegram, Crook to Sheridan, Nov. 21, 1876, quoted in Bourke, *Diaries*, 2:176.

20. Grinnell, *The Fighting Cheyennes*, 362; Bourke, "Mackenzie's Last Fight," 13.

21. Wheeler, *Buffalo Days*, 129; Crook to AAG, Jan. 8, 1877; Bourke, *Diaries*, 2:179; Grinnell, *Fighting Cheyennes*, 362; Bourke, "Mackenzie's Last Fight," 13; Dodge Diary, 81–82; see also Greene, *Morning Star Dawn*, 84–85. Dodge speculated that after Mackenzie had destroyed the Cheyenne village, Crook planned to go after Crazy Horse on the Rosebud, but the general never made his intentions clear in this regard. See Kime, *Powder Expedition Journals*, 82–83; Greene, *Morning Star Dawn*, 84–85.

22. Kime, *Powder Expedition Journals*, 82; Bourke, *Diaries*, 2:179. Writing in 1890, Bourke recalled that Crook was to follow Mackenzie "as promptly as possible on the trail. . . ." However, Crook made no move to do so, and there seems to have been no reason for him to have done so. Bourke must have been in error, or the general changed his mind. Bourke, "Mackenzie's Last Fight," 14.

23. Kime, *Powder Expedition Journals*, 84–85.

24. Ibid., 85; Bourke, *Diaries*, 2:185; Bourke, "Mackenzie's Last Fight," 27.

25. Greene, *Morning Star Dawn*, 156; Kime, *Powder Expedition Journals*, 85–86; Collins, *My Experiences in the West*, 161.

26. Greene, *Morning Star Dawn*, 156; Kime, *Powder Expedition Journals*, 85–92.

27. Greene, *Morning Star Dawn*, 85; Bourke, "Mackenzie's Last Fight," 4.

28. The march to the village is described in Wheeler, *Old West*, 130; Bourke, "Mackenzie's Last Fight," 13, 19; Greene, *Morning Star Dawn*, 86; Jerry Roche, "The Dull Knife Fight," *New York Herald*, Dec. 11, 1876, in Cozzens, *Eyewitnesses*, 4:418; Greene, *Morning Star Dawn*, 97–101.

29. Grinnell, *Fighting Cheyennes*, 1915, 370–75; Beaver Heart's account of Dull Knife Battle is in Greene, *Lakota and Cheyenne*, 119.

30. Greene, *Morning Star Dawn*, 103; Bourke, "Mackenzie's Last Fight," 22; North, *Man of the Plains*, 212; Grinnell, *Fighting Cheyennes*, 364.

31. Greene, *Morning Star Dawn*, 92.

32. North, *Man of the Plains*, 213; ibid., 111–17.

33. Bourke, *Diaries*, 2:185; Bourke, "Mackenzie's Last Fight," 27.

34. Bourke, "Mackenzie's Last Fight," 28–29.

35. Ibid., 31; Roche, "Dull Knife Fight," 424.

36. Bourke, "Mackenzie's Last Fight," 27; Roche, "Dull Knife Fight," 429.

37. Greene, *Morning Star Dawn*, 139–40.

38. North, *Man of the* Plains, 217; Bourke, "Mackenzie's Last Fight," 28; Beaver Heart account, in ibid., 120.

39. Dr. Thomas Marquis's comments on pictograph showing the battle, in Greene, *Lakota and Cheyenne*, 123.

40. Greene, *Morning Star Dawn*, 163.

41. Smith, *Sagebrush Soldier*, 130.

42. Crook to Sheridan, Nov. 28, 1876, quoted in Bourke, *Diaries*, 2:194–95; Kime, *Powder River Journal*, 97.

43. Kime, *Powder River Journal*, 98, 135.

44. Ibid., 100, 103.

45. Bourke, *Diaries*, 2:197.

46. Kime, *Powder River Journal*, 105–107.

47. Crook to AAG, Jan. 8, 1877, Crook Letterbook.

48. Bourke, "Mackenzie's Last Fight," 36; Bourke, *Diaries*, 2:104; Interview with General Crook, Dec. 9, 1876, *Army and Navy Journal* (Dec. 30, 1876), reprinted in Kime, *Powder River Journal*, 116n130.

49. Kime, *Powder River Journal*, 135.

50. Bourke, *Diaries*, 2:218; Bourke, "Mackenzie's Last Fight," 38.

51. Kime, *Powder River Journal*, 132.

52. Crook to Sheridan, Dec. 21, 1876, quoted in Bourke, *Diaries*, 2:224–26; Kime, *Powder River Journal*, 135–36.

53. Bourke, *Diaries*, 2:223; Kime, *Powder River Journal.*

54. Bourke, "Mackenzie's Last Fight," 42.

55. Kime, *Powder River Journal*, 171–72.

56. Ibid., 172–73. Dodge's opinion regarding Crook's tendency to undervalue infantry does not appear to be supported by the general's record. Crook, an old infantry officer, had learned early on the value of foot soldiers in Indian warfare, having led them in battle in California and Oregon. At the Rosebud, he had depended on the accuracy and range of their long rifles. Nor could their durability on the Hunger March have escaped his notice. And his disposition of troops on the march evidenced a concern for their welfare, a lifelong preoccupation dating back to his years on the Pacific coast and his Civil War service. See Magid, *George Crook*, 39, 116, 346.

57. Kime, *Powder River Journal*, 175.

58. Bourke, "Mackenzie's Last Fight," 41.

59. Kime, *Powder River Journal*, 114–15.

60. Ibid., 116.

61. Ibid., 147.

62. Ibid.

CHAPTER 29

1. Bourke, *On the Border*, 412; Hyde, *Red Cloud's Folk*, 290–92; "Surrender of Crazy Horse," *New York Tribune*, May 7, 1877, 207–208, reprinted in Hardorff, *The Death of Crazy Horse*; "End of the Sioux War," *New York Sun*, May 23, 1877, reprinted in Hardoff, *Death of Crazy Horse*, 209–12.

2. Hyde, *Red Cloud's Folk*, 291; "Surrender of Crazy Horse," in Hardoff, *Death of Crazy Horse*, 208.

3. Hyde, *Red Cloud's Folk*, 292; Buecker, *Fort Robinson*, 94–95.

4. Wooster, *Nelson A. Miles*, 77.

5. Johnson, *Unregimented General*, 75.

6. Ibid., 5–7.

7. Amchan, *Most Famous Soldier in America*, 30–46.

8. Although her biography is largely hagiographic, historians are indebted to Virginia Johnson, author of *The Unregimented General*, for the publication of a great deal of the prolific correspondence between Miles and his wife.

9. Miles, *Personal Recollections*, 1:179–80.

10. Letters from Miles to his wife, July 29, 1876; Aug. 2, 1876; Aug. 4, 1876; and Aug. 20, 1876, quoted in Johnson, *Unregimented General*, 90, 91, 94, 102.

11. Miles to his wife, Aug. 12, 1876, ibid., 101.

12. Miles, *Personal Recollections*, 217.

13. George E. Pond, "Major General Nelson A. Miles," *McClure's Magazine*, Nov. 1895, quoted in Johnson, *Unregimented General*, 110.

14. Greene, *Yellowstone Command*, 70.

15. Colonel W. H. Wood to AAG, Dept. of Dakota, Mar. 1, 1877, NARA, Sioux War Papers, Microfilm.

16. The estimates as to the number of Indians come from Miles, *Personal Recollections*, 1:225; Utley, "Crook and Miles, Fighting and Feuding on the Indian Frontier."

17. Greene, *Yellowstone Command*, 94.

18. Wood to AAG, Mar. 1, 1877; Miles, *Personal Recollections*, 1:225–27.

19. Greene, *Yellowstone Command*, 100–108.

20. Ibid., 109; Miles, *Personal Recollections*, 228; Wood to AAG, Mar. 1, 1877; Utley, *Frontier Regulars*, 272–74; Hyde, *Spotted Tail's Folk*, 261–62.

21. Miles to his wife, Oct. 25, 1867, in Johnson, *Unregimented General*, 125.

22. Miles to William Sherman, Nov. 18, 1876, quoted in Johnson, *Unregimented General*.

23. Miles, *Personal Recollections*, 229; Utley, *Frontier Regulars*, 274.

24. Greene, *Yellowstone Command*, 150.

25. Hyde, *Spotted Tail's Folk*, 261–62; Greene, *Yellowstone Command*, 150–51; Bray, *Crazy Horse, A Lakota Life*, 250–51; Anderson, "Indian Peace-talkers," 287.

26. Greene, *Yellowstone Command*, 155–58. Miles reported one killed and nine wounded. While accounts of Indian losses vary, the most liberal estimates put the death count for the Sioux and Cheyennes at about twelve or fifteen. Ibid., 176.

27. Miles to his wife, Jan. 19, 1877, quoted in Johnson, *Unregimented General*, 155. But at least one historian, Kingsley Bray, has concluded that the Wolf Mountains battle, rather than being a great victory, actually represented a "tactical breakthrough for Crazy Horse and his war leaders" and boosted Lakota morale. Bray, *Crazy Horse, A Lakota Life*, 259.

28. Greene, *Yellowstone Command*, 182; Bray, *Crazy Horse, A Lakota Life*.

29. Anderson, "Indian Peace-talkers," 239.

30. Bourke, *Diaries*, 2:243.

31. Ibid., 2:242.

32. Anderson, "Indian Peace-talkers," 235, 238–39.

33. Ibid., 239–40.

34. Mills, *My Story*, 158.

35. Hyde, *Spotted Tail's Folk*, xiii, xv, 240.

36. "The Indian Question," *New York Herald*, Nov. 4, 1876, in Abrams, *Newspaper Chronicle*, 7:263; interview with Crook, *New York Herald*, Oct. 25, 1876, quoted in Anderson, "Indian Peace-talkers," 240n13.

37. Bourke, *On the Border*, 401.

38. Hyde, *Spotted Tail's Folk*, 219–57.

39. Anderson, "Indian Peace-talkers," 240–41; Hyde, *Spotted Tail's Folk*, 266.

40. Bourke, *Diaries*, 2:241. At the time, Sword was known as Hunts the Enemy. He was an *akicita* (camp police) leader in the Oglala Bad Face band. Bray, *Crazy Horse, A Lakota Life*, 265.

41. Bray, *Crazy Horse, A Lakota Life*, 301; Sajna, *Crazy Horse, Life Behind the Legend*, 305.

42. Bourke, *Diaries*, 2:244.

43. *New York Tribune*, Feb. 28, 1876.

44. Anderson, "Indian Peace-talkers," 243.

45. Endorsement by General Sherman, Oct. 17, 1876, added to letter from Mackenzie to Crook, Sept. 30, 1876, quoted in Manypenny, *Our Indian Wards*, 350; NARA, Sherman to Sheridan, Apr. 9, 1877, Sioux War File, Microfilm.

46. Crook to Sheridan, endorsement of Mackenzie letter, Oct. 2, 1876, in Mannypenny, *Our Indian Wards*, 33–34.

47. Sheridan to Sherman, Feb. 10, 1877, and Mar. 17, 1877, Sheridan Papers.

48. Sheridan to Crook, Jan. 27, 1877; Hutton, *Phil Sheridan and His Army*, 327.

49. Sherman to Sheridan, Feb. 17, 1877.

50. Sheridan to Sherman, Feb. 10, 1877.

51. Bray, *Crazy Horse, A Lakota Life*, 266; Anderson, "Indian Peace-talkers," 243–44.

52. Hyde, *Spotted Tail's Folk*, 264.

53. Sheridan to Sherman, Mar. 17, 1876.

54. Sherman to Sheridan, Feb. 2, 1876, quoted in Greene, *Yellowstone Command*, 183.

55. Greene, *Yellowstone Command*, 184.

56. Miles to his wife, Mar. 17, 1877, quoted in Johnson, *Unregimented General*, 161; Greene, ibid., 187.

57. Annual Report of the Secretary of War for 1877; Miles, *Personal Recollections*, 1:241.

58. *Chicago Times*, Apr. 20, 1877, quoted in Bourke, *Diaries*, 2:270–71.

59. Anderson, "Indian Peace-talkers," 248n29; Knight, "War or Peace."

60. Miles to his wife, Mar. 17, 1877, in Johnson, *Unregimented General*, 162; Statement of Iron Shield, messenger from General Miles, made at Camp Robinson, Apr. 7, 1877, NARA Sioux War file, Microfilm.

61. Annual Report of the Secretary of War for 1877, 496, quoted in Anderson, "Indian Peace-Talkers," 249n30.

62. Bourke, *Diaries*, 2:266–67.

63. "Statement of Iron Shield."

64. Miles to AAG, Dept. of Dakota, May 24, 1877, NARA, Dept. of the Platte, Letters Received, RG 393.

65. *Chicago Tribune*, May 8, 1877, quoted in Buecker, *Fort Robinson*, 95.

66. "End of a Successful Campaign," *New York Tribune*, Apr. 28, 1877, in Abrams, *Newspaper Chronicle*, 8:95.

67. Crook to Sheridan, Mar. 15, 1877, Crook Letterbook.

68. Anderson, "Indian Peace-talkers," 250–51.

69. *Chicago Times*, Apr. 17, 1877, quoted in Anderson, ibid. While the Indians may have appreciated Crook's orchestration of the event, Sheridan did not. Referring to the surrender ceremony, he acidly informed Crook, "the papers this morning make it look as if we had surrendered to them." Sheridan to Crook, Apr. 17, 1877, NARA, Dept. of Missouri, Letters Sent, quoted in Schmitt, *General George Crook*, 216n9.

70. Bourke, *Diaries*, 2:258.

71. Ibid., 259–61.

72. Sheridan to Crook, Mar. 30, 1877, Sheridan Papers.

73. Bourke, *Diaries*, 2:266; see also Knight, "War or Peace," 532.

74. Crook to Sheridan, Apr. 21, 1877, NARA, Dept. of the Platte, Telegrams Sent, RG393; Bourke, *Diaries*, 2:273–74; Anderson, "Indian Peace-talkers," 245.

75. Grinnell, *Fighting Cheyenne*, 400.

76. Lieutenant Charles Johnson to J. Q. Smith, Commissioner of Indian Affairs, June 4, 1877, reprinted in Hardorff, *The Death of Crazy Horse*, 163; Sandoz, *Cheyenne Autumn*, 12; Monnet, *Tell Them We Are Going Home*, 21–24. For Crook's supposed promise to the Cheyennes, see Wild Hog's testimony, Select Committee on Removal of N. Cheyennes, 160, in Monnet, *Tell Them*, 23–24. In February 1880, Crook laid out a different scenario in a letter to the chairman of the Senate Select Committee. In the letter, he noted that the Interior Department had decided to remove all of the Indians at the Red Cloud Agency to the Missouri. None were more opposed than the Cheyennes. "Upon being consulted (by whom he does not say), the Interior Dep't consented to allowing these Northern Cheyennes to go to Indian Territory if they so desired." Crook wrote that he then met with the tribe and gave them the options of accompanying the Sioux to the Missouri or of joining the Southern Cheyennes in Indian Territory. "I was careful not to advise them in any particular, as I knew nothing about that country and preferred to let them form conclusions among themselves." Admitting there was disagreement among themselves, he noted that they "had many councils . . . before coming to tell me that they had decided to go." Crook to Senator S. S. Kirwood, Committee Chairman, Fort Omaha, Feb. 22, 1880, Crook Letters, Hayes Library.

77. Mackenzie to Commissioner of Indian Affairs with Crook endorsement, Mar. 19, 1877, requesting reservation on the Tongue River, NARA, Division of the Missouri, Letters Received, RG 393; Smith, Commissioner of Indian Affairs, to Carl Schurz, Secretary of the Interior, Apr. 9, 1877, noting that Sheridan had rejected Mackenzie's request and indicating that Interior should do the same. NARA, Special Files (Sioux War), Microfilm M1495.

78. Sheridan to Crook, Apr. 22, 1877, Sheridan Papers.

79. Crook to Sheridan, Apr. 20, 1877, NARA, Special File (Sioux War) M1495; see also Bourke, *Diaries*, 2:272.

80. In fact, as Crook must have suspected, the government had long considered removal to the Missouri a done deal and made no secret of it. A newspaper article in the *New York Tribune* as early as February 1876 noted that the government had decided that economics dictated the move. "Hence, as soon as the Northern Indians are driven in, it is understood that these latter must also go to the Missouri." "General Crook Expedition," *New York Tribune*, Feb. 28, 1876.

81. Sheridan to Crook, Apr. 23, 1877, NARA, Dept. of the Platte, Telegrams in the Field, RG 393; Bourke, *Diaries*, 2:279.

82. Forsyth to Sheridan, Apr. 22, 1877, NARA, Special File (Sioux war), M1495.

83. Bray, *Crazy Horse, A Lakota Life*, 302.

84. Smith to Schurz, Apr. 9, 1877; Sherman to Sheridan, May 7, 1877, NARA, Division of the Missouri, Letters Received, RG 393.

85. Sherman to Sheridan, May 7, 1877, NARA, Division of the Missouri, Letters Received, RG 393; Bray, *Crazy Horse, A Lakota Life*, 302.

86. See Greene, *Yellowstone Command*, 201–19, for a detailed description of the engagement.

CHAPTER 30

1. *Cheyenne Daily Leader*, May 27, 1877; *Black Hills Daily Times*, May 28, 1877, both quoted in Hardorff, *Death of Crazy Horse*, 220; Bray, *Crazy Horse, A Lakota Life*, 303.

2. Bourke, *On the Border*, 415; Bray, *Crazy Horse, A Lakota Life*, 144–45.

3. Neihardt, *Black Elk Speaks*, 86–87.

4. Ibid.

5. A number of writers have captured Crazy Horse's enigmatic personality. See Bray, Sandoz, Neihardt, and Powers, all cited in the bibliography and footnotes of this work.

6. Bray, *Crazy Horse, A Lakota Life*, 275–76.

7. "The Great Council," *Chicago Times*, May 26, 1877, quoted in Hardorff, *Death of Crazy Horse*, 226.

8. Ibid., 231.

9. Hedren, *After Custer*, 28. The author devotes an entire chapter to the Sheridan expedition (27–49), providing far more detail than is usually accorded to this interesting event.

10. Bourke, *Diaries*, 2:306; Hutton, *Phil Sheridan and His Army*, 328–29; see also Sheridan's letter of invitation to Babitson (?), May 17, 1877, Sheridan Papers.

11. *Omaha Republican*, June 15, 1877.

12. Sheridan to Crook, June 1, 1877, Sheridan Papers.

13. "Buffalo Phil," *Chicago Times*, July 30, 1877.

14. Ibid.

15. Bourke, *Diaries*, 2:329.

16. "Buffalo Phil."

17. Bourke, *Diaries*, 2:341.

18. Connell, *Son of the Morning Star*, 272.

19. Hutton, *Phil Sheridan and His Army*, 329.

20. Bourke, *Diaries*, 2:351.

21. Hutton, *Phil Sheridan and His Army*, 175. Bourke reflected the contempt of the officer class for the strikers, characterizing the poverty that had moved the workers to strike as the result of "dry Goods clerks [who] try to live in the style of European bankers and our day laborers as merchants only should." Their sympathies would probably not have been aroused by learning that the cause of the strike was a decision by the Baltimore and Ohio to cut the wages of its workers by 10 percent in the midst of an economic depression and on the heels of two similar reductions. Bourke, *Diaries*, 2:352.

22. Ibid., 2:353.

23. Hutton, *Phil Sheridan and His Army*, 176–77.

24. Hedren, *After Custer*, 48.

CHAPTER 31

1. C. King, *Campaigning with Crook*, 121.

2. See R. A. Clark, *Killing of Chief Crazy Horse*, 137, for an excellent thumbnail sketch of the lieutenant; W. P. Clark, *The Indian Sign Language*, 6.

3. Crook Report quoted in R. A. Clark, *Killing of Chief Crazy Horse*, 138.

4. Bray, *Crazy Horse, A Lakota Life*, 319.

5. W. P. Clark to AG, July 13, 1877, quoted in Hardorff, *Death of Crazy Horse*, 162; Garnett account in R. A. Clark, *Killing of Chief Crazy Horse*, 76.

6. W. P. Clark to AG, July 13, 1877, quoted in Hardorff, *Death of Crazy Horse*, 164; L. P. Bradley to Crook, July 16, 1877, NARA, Division of the Missouri, Letters Received, RG 393.

7. See Larson, *Red Cloud*, 212; Buecker, Fort Robinson, 107.

8. See William Garnett interview, Ricker Collection, in Hardorff, *Death of Crazy Horse*, 28–29.

9. James Irwin, Indian Agent, to J. Q. Smith, Commissioner of Indian Affairs, Aug. 4, 1877, printed in Hardorff, *Death of Crazy Horse*, 167.

10. Bourke, *Diaries*, 3:68–69.

11. Ibid., 68.

12. Louis Bordeaux interview in Hardorff, *Death of Crazy Horse*, 102.

13. Jesse M. Lee, "The Capture and Death of an Indian Chieftain," in Cozzens, *Eyewitnesses*, 4:531; Buecker, *Fort Robinson*, 108; Bourke, *Diaries*, 3:69.

14. Clark to Crook, Aug. 1, 1877: "Everything has gone on well at both agencies since I last wrote you"; Telegram, AAG Williams to Crook, Aug. 4, 1877, Division of the Missouri, Letters Received, RC 939: "Everything [at Camp Sheridan] is moving splendidly." See Bourke, *Diaries*, 3:69, regarding buffalo hunt.

15. Benjamin K. Shopp, Special Agent, to J. Q. Smith, Aug. 15, 1877, in Hardorff, *Death of Crazy Horse*, 169–70; Sajna, *Crazy Horse, Life Behind the Legend*, 311; Buecker, *Fort Robinson*, 105.

16. The substance of the council is taken from a report by Benjamin Shopp to the Commissioner of Indian Affairs, Aug. 15, 1877, quoted in Bray, *Crazy Horse, A Lakota Life*, 320–21.

17. Shopp Report.

18. Irwin to Commissioner Smith, Aug. 4, 1877, in Hardorff, *Death of Crazy Horse*, 166–67; Shopp letter, Aug. 15, 1877, in Hardorff, *Death of Crazy Horse*, 168; Bray, *Crazy Horse, A Lakota Life*, 321–22.

19. Bray, *Crazy Horse, A Lakota Life*, 323; Jesse Lee statement, in Brininstool, "Chief Crazy Horse, His Career and Death," 4–78, 9.

20. Lee statement, in Brininstool, "Chief Crazy Horse, His Career and Death."

21. Bray, *Crazy Horse, A Lakota Life*, 324–25; Bourke, *Diaries*, 3:69–70.

22. Bradley to Williams, AG, Aug. 5, 1877, quoted in Hardorff, *Death of Crazy Horse*, 167.

23. Bourke, *Diaries*, 3:70.

24. Clark to Crook, Aug. 18, 1877, in Hardorff, *Death of Crazy Horse*, 173–74; Buecker, *Fort Robinson*, 108; Bray, *Crazy Horse, A Lakota Life*, 331.

25. Clark to Crook, Aug. 18, 1877; Billy Hunter's [Garnett] statement, in Hardorff, *Death of Crazy Horse*, 61; Buecker, *Fort Robinson*, 109.

26. Brown, *The Flight of the Nez Perce*, 209–10.

27. Yellowstone was set aside as a national park of 2.2 million acres by President Grant on Mar. 1, 1872, for the benefit and enjoyment of the public. http://yellowstone.net/history/timeline/the-early-years-1872-1915.

28. Bourke, *Diaries*, 3:71; Greene, *Nez Perce Summer*, 203.

29. Buecker, *Fort Robinson*, 110.

30. Bourke, *Diaries*, 3:71; Lee statement in Brininstool, "Chief Crazy Horse," 12.

31. Nadeau, *Fort Laramie*, 86; Clark, *Killing of Chief Crazy Horse*, 73; Hardorff, *Death of Crazy Horse*, 25. Garnett died at Pine Ridge in 1929.

32. Garnett interview quoted in Bray, *Crazy Horse, A Lakota Life*, 337.

33. Ibid., 338. For further accounts of the meeting, see Lee, "Capture and Death," 532–33; Louis Bordeaux version of Crazy Horse's speech in Sajna, *Crazy Horse, Life Behind the Legend*, 312.

34. Bradley to Crook, Aug. 30, 1877, and Sheridan to Crook, Aug. 31, 1877, NARA Dept. of the Platte, Telegrams to Crook in the Field RG 393.

35. Crook to Sheridan, Aug. 31, 1877, ibid.

36. Billy Hunter (Garnett) statement, in Hardorff, *Death of Crazy Horse*, 61.

37. Dr. McGillicuddy's statement in Brininstool, "Chief Crazy Horse," 38; Bray, *Crazy Horse, A Lakota Life*, 339–40. McGillicuddy, the post surgeon at Fort Robinson who was present, suspected the mistake was deliberate. So did the interpreter, Bordeaux. Bordeaux interview in Hardorff, *Death of Crazy Horse*, 102; see also Sandoz, *Cheyenne Autumn*, 392.

38. Garnett interview, in Hardorff, *Death of Crazy Horse*, 32; Bray, *Crazy Horse, A Lakota Life*, 342.

39. Lee in Cozzens, *Eyewitnesses*, 532.

40. Williams, AAG, to Crook, Aug. 31, 1877, quoted in Bourke, *Diaries*, 3: appx. 2, 504.

41. Powers, *Killing of Crazy Horse*, 357–58; Telegram, Crook to Bradley, Sept. 1, 1877, reprinted in Bourke, *Diaries*, 3:505.

42. Telegram, Sheridan to Townsend, Sept. 1, 1877, quoted in Bourke, *Diaries*, 3:504; Telegram, Sheridan to Crook, Sept. 1, 1877, in Bourke, *Diaries*, 3:505. See also Buecker, *Fort Robinson*, 111.

43. Powers, *Killing of Crazy Horse*, 359.

44. Lee in Cozzens, *Eyewitnesses*, 533–34; Lee account in Brininstool, "Chief Crazy Horse," 16.

45. Bray, *Crazy Horse, A Lakota Life*, 348.

46. Garnett 1907 interview, in Hardorff, *Death of Crazy Horse*, 32; Bourke, *Diaries*, 3:73. Crook may also have had another, equally important, reason for canceling his arrest order and giving Crazy Horse a last opportunity to reconsider. To Three Stars, his reputation for integrity among the Indians was vital. The Sioux had lost respect for Miles because they thought he had murdered Lame Deer after luring him into peace negotiations. According to Bourke, who remained close to the general during this time, Crook wished to avoid having his own actions seen in a similar light. See Bradley's Report to Sheridan, Sept. 7, 1877, reprinted in Hardorff, *Death of Crazy Horse*, 184; Bourke, *Diaries*, 3:72–73; and Bray, *Crazy Horse, A Lakota Life*, 351.

47. Bray, *Crazy Horse, A Lakota Life*, 354.

48. Scott Interview, 1920, quoted in R. A. Clark, *Killing of Chief Crazy Horse*, 77.

49. Hardorff, *Death of Crazy Horse*, 23; Bourke, *Diaries*, 3:74. According to Garnett, one of Clark's spies, Little Wolf, heard it while eavesdropping outside Crazy Horse's tipi and reported it to Lone Bear, who, in turn, told Woman Dress. Garnett account in R. A. Clark, *Killing of Chief Crazy Horse*, 77; Bray, *Crazy Horse, A Lakota Life*, 354.

50. Scott interview in R. A. Clark, *Killing of Chief Crazy Horse*, 78.

51. Ibid., 77.

52. Ibid., 78.

53. Dodd interview in Bourke, *Diaries*, 3:516. Bourke undoubtedly used this interview as the basis for his statement in his later book on General Crook that "Crazy Horse paid no attention to the message." Bourke, *On the Border*, 420.

54. Scott interview in R. A. Clark, *Killing of Chief Crazy Horse*, 77–78.

55. Ricker interview with Garnett, reprinted in ibid., 35. According to Marie Sandoz in her biography of Crazy Horse, Charles Eastman, a western-educated Sioux, also believed that Woman Dress was acting as an agent of Red Cloud and his subchiefs. Sandoz, *Cheyenne Autumn*, 428.

56. Scott interview in R. A. Clark, *Killing of Chief Crazy Horse*, 99.

57. Ricker 1907 interview in Hardorff, *Death of Crazy Horse*, 38.

58. Dodd interview in Bourke, *Diaries*, 3:516.

59. Bourke, *On the Border*, 420. It must be assumed that Bourke here relied on the Dodd interview recorded in his diary.

60. Ricker interview in Hardorff, *Death of Crazy Horse*, 41.

61. Scott interview in R. A. Clark, *Killing of Chief Crazy Horse*, 79; Bray wrote that Clark sweetened the offer by adding his own sorrel race horse as a bonus, but offers no source for this information. Bray, *Crazy Horse, A Lakota Life*, 355.

62. Ricker interview in Hardorff, *Death of Crazy Horse*, 41; Bray, *Crazy Horse, A Lakota Life*, 355.

63. Powers, *Killing of Crazy Horse*, 382.

64. Telegram, Clark to Crook, Sept. 4, 1877, quoted in R. A. Clark, *Killing of Chief Crazy Horse*, 177.

65. Bradley to Crook, Sept. 5, 1877, quoted in Bourke, *Diaries*, 3:507; Crook to Bradley, Sept. 5, 1877, quoted in Hardorff, *Death of Crazy Horse*, 180.

66. Crook to Sheridan, Sept. 5, 1877.

67. Sheridan to Crook, Sept. 5, 1877, quoted in Hardorff, *Death of Crazy Horse*, 180–81; Buecker, *Fort Robinson*, 115.

68. Lee in Cozzens, *Eyewitnesses*, 537–39.

69. Bray, *Crazy Horse, A Lakota Life*, 5.

CHAPTER 32

1. Greene, *Nez Perce Summer*, 205; Report of General Crook, Sept. 23, 1878, in the Report of the Secretary of War, 1878, 1:90.

2. Larson, *Red Cloud*, 219.

3. In his annual report for 1878, the Indian agent at the Ponca Agency in Oklahoma noted with remarkable candor, "malaria has been particularly fatal to them and many deaths have resulted. The poncas now number 639 people . . . which shows a decline of 45 [since the 1877 report]." Report of William Whitman, Indian Agent, in Annual

Report of the Commissioner of Indian Affairs to the Secretary of the Interior for the year 1878 (Washington, D.C., Government Printing Office, 1878), 65. Crook's role in the Ponca story is best told in Tibbles, *Buckskin and Blanket Days.*

4. See letter from Pinckney Ludenbeck, First Infantry, to AG, Dept. of Dakota, Aug. 14, 1877, NARA, Division of the Missouri, Letters Received, RG 393.

5. The commissioner of Indian affairs maintained that neither he nor the secretary of the interior had any choice in the matter, that it was mandated by act of Congress, Stat. 19, 191. Whitman, Annual Report of the Commissioner of Indian Affairs, 18.

6. Hyde, *A Sioux Chronicle*, 5.

7. Olson, *Red Cloud and the Sioux Problem*, 248. Also see Tibbles, *Buckskin and Blanket Days*, 188–89.

8. Hyde, *Spotted Tail's Folk*, 292; "The President Receives the Sioux and Arapaho Indian Delegations," *Omaha Republican*, Sept. 28, 1877; "Arapaho and Sioux Chiefs Have Another Talk with the President," *Omaha Republican*, Sept 28, 1877; Olson, *Red Cloud and the Sioux Problem*, 249.

9. Olson, *Red Cloud and the Sioux Problem.*

10. Ibid., 25; *Omaha Republican.*

11. *Omaha Republican.*

12. Olson, *Red Cloud and the Sioux Problem*, 252.

13. Hyde, *Sioux Chronicle*, 6.

14. Hyde, *Red Cloud's Folk*, 299.

15. Crook to AAG, Division of the Missouri, Dec. 6, 1877, in Annual Report of Secretary of War, 1878 (Washington, D.C., Government Printing Office, 1878), 91–92; Olson, *Red Cloud and the Sioux Problem*, 254; Tibbles, *Buckskin and Blanket Days*, 189.

16. Telegram, Crook to Sheridan, Oct. 8, 1877, NARA, Press Copies of Telegrams, Dept. of the Platte, RG 393.

17. Telegram, Crook to Sheridan, Oct. 18–19, 1877, NARA.

18. Crook to AAG, Division of the Missouri, in Report of Secretary of War, 1878.

19. *Army and Navy Journal* 15, no. 14 (Nov. 10, 1877).

20. Report of Lieutenant Joseph Lawson to Headquarters, Dept. of the Platte, Dec. 4, 1877, Dept. of the Platte, Letters Received, RG 393.

21. Hyde, *Spotted Tail's Folk*, 287; Hedren, *After Custer*, 150–51.

22. Hyde, *Spotted Tail's Folk*, 288; Hedren, *After Custer*, 150–51.

23. Sheridan Report in Annual Report of the Secretary of War Rep. 1878; Olson, *Red Cloud and the Sioux Problem*, 255–56; Hedren, *After Custer*, 151.

24. Crook Report, in Annual Report of the Secretary of War, 1878, 92.

25. Hyde, *Sioux Chronicle*, 10.

26. Crook to AG, Dec. 13, 1877, Crook Letterbook; Crook to Webb Hayes, Jan. 26, 1878, Webb Hayes Papers, Hayes Library.

27. Tibbles, *Buckskin and Blanket Days*, 187.

28. Olson, *Red Cloud and the Sioux Problem*, 258–59.

29. Tibbles, *Buckskin and Blanket Days*, 190–92.

30. J. H. Hammon to Commissioner of Indian Affairs, Dec. 8, 1878, quoted in Olson, *Red Cloud and the Sioux Problem*, 263.

EPILOGUE

1. Circular Letter from Ely Parker, Commissioner of Indian Affairs, to Superintendents and Agents of the Indian Dept., June 12, 1869, NARA, Military Division of Missouri, Letters Received, RG 393.

2. Crook to Chiefs of the Sioux Nation, Dec. 17, 1879, quoted in Schmitt, *General George Crook*, 220–21.

3. Crook to Sheridan, Dec. 4, 1878, Crook Letterbook.

4. Schmitt, *General George Crook*, xix. Actually, what Sherman said to a reporter when informed of Crook's death was, "[George Crook] was the most [effective] man in dealing with the Indians that the United States ever had in its service. The Indians respected and trusted him, and he could bring them around or make them amenable to reason where every one else failed." "Death of General Crook," *Dayton Daily*, Mar. 21, 1890.

5. Quoted in Hutton, *Phil Sheridan and His Army*, 128.

6. "Death of General Crook," *New York Times*, Mar. 22, 1890. This conclusion would be much disputed today when it has become clear that Apache scouts were essential to the ultimate surrender of Geronimo.

7. Carroll, ed., *Custer's Chief of Scouts*, 62–63n86.

8. Robinson, *General Crook and the Western Frontier*, 311.

9. Hutton, *Phil Sheridan and His Army*, 128.

10. Schmitt, *General George Crook*, xi–xiii.

11. Ibid., xi.

Bibliography

MANUSCRIPTS AND ARCHIVAL SOURCES

Bourke, John. File. Nebraska Historical Society, Omaha.

Camp, Walter Mason. The Hammer Collection, Series 671/04, Walter Mason Camp Files. Little Big Horn National Monument Archive, Crow Agency, Mont.

Camp, Walter M. Papers. Robert Ellison Collection. Denver Public Library.

Crook, George. Letterbooks. George Crook Collection. Typescript. Rutherford B. Hayes Library, Rutherford B. Hayes Presidential Center, Fremont, Ohio.

Crook, George. Papers. Special Collections and University Archives, University of Oregon Libraries, Eugene.

Glover, James. "Reminiscences as told to Mrs. George F. Kitt in 1928." Arizona Historical Society Library, Tucson.

Hedegaard, Michael J. "Col. J. J. Reynolds and the St. Patrick's Day Celebration on the Powder River: Battle of Powder River (Montana, Mar. 17, 1876)." Master's thesis. U.S. Army Command and General Staff College, Ft. Leavenworth, Kans., 2001.

Kapaun, David. "Major General J. J. Reynolds and His Division at Chicamauga: A Historical Analysis." Master's thesis. U.S. Army Command and General Staff College, Ft. Leavenworth, Kans., 1999.

Kennon, Lymon. Diary. U.S. Military History Institute, Carlisle, Pa.

King, Charles. Papers. Huntington Library, Pasadena, Calif.

National Archives, Washington, D.C.

Cases Tried by General Court-Martial, Court-Martial Files.

Department of Arizona. General Orders, Circulars, and Court-Martial Orders, 1870–93, RG 393.

Department of Arizona, Fort Whipple. Letters Received, 1866–71. Records of the U.S. Army Continental Commands, RG 393.

Department of Arizona, Fort Whipple. Letters Sent. Records of the U.S. Army Continental Commands, RG 393.

Department of Columbia. Letters Received. Records of the U.S. Army Continental Commands, 1821–1920, Record Group (RG) 393.

Department of the Pacific. Letters Sent, 1866–69. Records of the U.S. Army Continental Commands, 1821–1920, RG 393.

Department of the Platte. Letters Received. Records of the U.S. Army Continental Commands, RG 98.

Department of the Platte. Press Copies of Telegrams, RG 393.

George Crook. Appointments, Commissions, and Personal File, Microfilm Records M1395.

Military Division of the Missouri. Letters Received, RG 393.

Military Division of the Missouri. Letters Sent, RG 393.

Military Division of the Missouri. Special File, 1876.

Military Division of the Missouri. Telegrams, RG 393.

Sioux War Papers. Microfilm.

Nickerson, Azor H. "Major General George Crook and the Indians." Crook Files. U.S. Military History Institute, Carlisle, Pa.

Pittman, George. Pittman Papers. Arizona Historical Society, Tucson.

Ricker, Eli. Papers. White Swan Library and Monument Archives, Little Big Horn Battlefield Monument, Crow Agency, Mont.

Schuyler, Walter. Schuyler Papers. Huntington Library, Pasadena, Calif.

Sheridan, Philip. Sheridan Papers. Library of Congress, Washington, D.C.

Slough, John P., Slough Diary, Slough Papers. Montana Historical Society Research Center, Helena.

Stanton, Thaddeus. Papers. Huntington Library, Pasadena, Calif.

Strahorn, Robert E. "Ninety Years of Boyhood." Strahorn Library, College of Idaho, Caldwell, 1942.

PUBLISHED DOCUMENTS

Board of Indian Commissioners. Peace with the Apache Indians of Arizona and New Mexico and Arizona. Report of Vincent Colyer, Member of Board of Indian Commissioners. 1871. Reprint, Freeport, N.Y., Books of Libraries Press, 1971.

Bowman, Eldon G. "Development of the General Crook Trail: Arizona's First Designated State Historic Trail." Paper presented to the Arizona Historical Convention, Apr. 28, 1978, Fort Huachuca, Ariz.

Chronological List of Actions, etc. with Indians from January 15, 1837–January, 1891. 1891. Reprint, Fort Collins, Colo., Old Army Press, 1979.

Kappler, Charles. *Indian Affairs Laws and Treaties.* 1913. Reprint, Washington, D.C., Government Printing Office, 1927.

U.S. House of Representatives. *Report of the Secretary of the Interior, 1875*, HR Ex Doc. 1, 1 Sess. 44 Cong., 506.

———. *Report of the Secretary of the Interior, 1876*, HR Ex Doc. 1, 2 Sess. 44 Cong., 392.

———. *Report of the Secretary of War, 1867.* Part 1, 40th Cong., 2nd Sess., 1867. Exec. Doc. No. 1. Washington, D.C., Government Printing Office, 1867.

———. *Report of the Secretary of War, 1868*, Part 1, 40th Cong., 3rd Sess., 1868. Exec. Doc. No. 1. Washington, D.C., Government Printing Office, 1868.

———. *Report of the Secretary of War, 1869*, Part 1, 41st Cong., 2nd Sess., 1869. Exec. Doc. No. 1. Washington, D.C., Government Printing Office, 1869.

———. *Report of the Secretary of War, 1876*, 44th Cong., 2nd Sess., 1876, Exec. Doc. No. 1. Washington, D.C., Government Printing Office, 1876.

———. *Report of the Secretary of War, 1878*. 46th Cong., 2nd Sess., 1878, Exec. Doc. No. 1. Washington, D.C., Government Printing Office, 1878.

U.S. Office of Indian Affairs. *Annual Report of the Commissioner of Indian Affairs, 1872*. Washington, D.C., Government Printing Office, 1872.

———. *Annual Report of the Commissioner of Indian Affairs to the Secretary of the Interior for the year 1877*. Washington, D.C., Government Printing Office, 1877.

NEWSPAPERS

Arizona Miner
Arizona Republican
Army and Navy Journal
Augusta (Ga.) Chronicle
Billings Gazette
Bismarck Tribune
Black Hills Daily Times
Cheyenne Daily Leader
Chicago Inter-Ocean
Chicago Times
Chicago Tribune
Cincinnati Commercial
Cincinnati Enquirer
Cumberland (Md.) Daily News
Daily Alta California
Georgia Weekly Telegraph (Macon)
Helena (Mont.) Daily Independent
National Republican (Washington, D.C.)
New York Daily Graphic
New York Herald
New York Sun
New York Times
New York Tribune
Omaha Daily Bee
Omaha Republican
Owyhee Avalanche
(Oakland, Md.) Republican
Rocky Mountain News
Washington Evening Star

PAMPHLETS AND ARTICLES IN PERIODICALS

Anderson, Harry H. "Indian Peace-talkers and the Conclusion of the Sioux War of 1876." *Nebraska History* 44 (1963): 233–54.

Benteen, Fredrick W., and E. A. Brininstool, eds."The Custer Fight, Captain F. W. Benteen's Story of the Battle of the Little Big Horn, June 25–26, 1876." Privately published by E. A. Brininstool, Hollywood, Calif., 1940.

Bourke, John G. "George Crook in Indian Country." *Century Magazine*, Mar. 1891; reprint, Palmer Lake, Colo., Filter Press, 1997.

———. "Mackenzie's Last Fight with the Cheyennes: A Winter Campaign in Wyoming and Montana." 1890. Reprint, New York, Argonaut, 1966.

Brininstool, E. A., "Chief Crazy Horse, His Career and Death." *Nebraska History Magazine* 12, no. 1 (Jan.–Mar. 1929): 4–78.

Brown, W. C, "Reynolds Attack on Crazy Horse's Village on Powder River, March 17, 1876." *Winners of the West* 11, no. 5 (Apr. 30, 1934).

Clark, Keith, and Donna Clark. "William McKay's Journal, 1866–67: Indian Scouts, Part I." *Oregon Historical Quarterly* 79, no. 2 (Summer 1978): 121–71.

———. "William McKay's Journal, 1866–67: Indian Scouts, Part II." *Oregon Historical Quarterly* 79, no. 3 (Fall 1978): 269–333.

Clow, Richmond L. "General Philip Sheridan's Legacy: The Sioux Pony Campaign of 1876." *Nebraska History* 57 (1976): 460–77.

Colwell-Chanthaphonh, Chip. "The 'Camp Grant Massacre' in the Historical Imagination." *Journal of the Southwest* 45 (Autumn 2003): 340–69.

Cunningham, Bob. "The Calamitous Career of Lt. Royal E. Whitman." *Journal of Arizona History* 29, no. 2 (Winter 1979): 423–44.

Daly, Henry W. "Scouts—Good and Bad." *American Legion Monthly* 5, no. 2 (Aug. 1928): 24–25, 66–70.

Dobak, William A. "Yellow Legs Journalists: Enlisted Men as Newspaper Reporters in the Sioux Campaign, 1876." *Journal of the West* 13 (Jan. 1974).

Eaton, George O. "Stopping an Apache Battle." 1905, ed. Don Russell. *Journal of the U.S. Cavalry Association* XLII, no. 178 (July–Aug. 1933): 12–18.

Gray, John S. "Frank Grouard: Kanaka Scout or Mulatto Renegade?" *The Westerners Brand Book* 16, no. 8 (Oct. 1959): 57–64.

Hedren, Paul L. "More on the Personal and Designating Flags of the Sioux War." In John P. Hart, ed. *Custer and his Times*. Vol. 5, 139–52. Cordova, Tenn., Little Big Horn Association, 2008.

Howard, Oliver O. "Major General George Crook, USA." *Chatauquan* 11 (June 1890): 326–70.

Idaho State Historical Society. "The Snake War, 1864–1868." No. 236. Boise, Idaho State Historical Society, 1966.

King, James T. "George Crook at Camp Cloud Peak: 'I Am at a Loss What to Do.'" *Journal of the West* 11, no. 1 (Jan. 1972): 114–27.

———. "George Crook Indian Fighter and Humanitarian." *Journal of the Southwest* 9, no. 4 (Winter 1967): 333–48.

Knight, Oliver. "War or Peace: The Anxious Wait for Crazy Horse." *Nebraska History* 54, no. 4 (Winter 1973): 521–45.

Lemly, H. R. "The Fight on the Rosebud, By Valor and Arms." *Journal of American Military History*, 1, no. 4 (Summer 1975): 7–12.

Marion, Jeanie. "'As Long as the Stone Lasts': General O. O. Howard's Peace Conference." *Journal of Arizona History* 35, no. 2 (Summer 1994): 109–40.

McDermott, John D. *General George Crook's 1876 Campaigns, A Report prepared for the American Battlefield Protection Program*. Sheridan, Wyo., Frontier Heritage Alliance, 2000.

Utley, Robert L. "Crook and Miles, Fighting and Feuding on the Indian Frontier." *Quarterly Journal of Military History* 2, no. 1 (Autumn 1989): 81–91.

Watson, Elmo Scott. "A Checklist of Indian War Correspondents 1866–1890." *Journalism Quarterly* (Dec. 1940): 310–12.

Wharfield, H. B. *Alchesay, Scout with General Crook, Sierra Blanca Apache Chief, Friend of Fort Apache Whites, Counselor to Indian Agents.* El Cajon, Calif., privately printed, 1969.

BOOKS

Abrams, Marc. H. *Sioux War Dispatches, Reports from the Field, 1876–1877.* Yardley, Pa., Westholme, 2012.

———, ed. *Newspaper Chronicle of the Indian Wars.* Vols. 4–9. Brooklyn, Abrams, 2010.

Adams, Kevin. *Class and Race in the Frontier Army, Military Life in the West, 1870–1890.* Norman, University of Oklahoma Press, 2009.

Amchan, Arthur J. *The Most Famous Soldier in America, A Biography of Lt. Gen. Nelson A. Miles, 1839–1925.* Alexandria, Va., Amchan, 1989.

Athearn, Robert G. *William Tecumseh Sherman and the Settlement of the West.* Norman, University of Oklahoma Press, 1956.

Bailey, John W. *Pacifying the Plains—General Alfred Terry and the Decline of the Sioux, 1866–1890.* Westport, Conn., Greenwood, 1979.

Ball, Eve. *An Apache Odyssey Indeh.* Norman, University of Oklahoma Press, 1988.

Bigelow, John S. *On the Bloody Trail of Geronimo. Los* Angeles, Western Lore, 1958.

Bancroft, Hubert Howe. *History of Oregon, 1848–1888.* San Francisco, History Company, 1890.

———. *The Works of Hubert Howe Bancroft.* 39 vols. San Francisco, A. L. Bancroft & Company and The History Company, 1883–91.

Bennett, Estelline. *Old Deadwood Days.* 1928. Reprint, Lincoln, University of Nebraska Press, 1982.

Bourke, John G. *On the Border with Crook.* 1891. Reprint, New York, Time-Life, 1980.

———. *With General Crook in the Indian Wars.* 1891. Reprint, Palo Alto, Calif., Lewis Osborne, 1968.

Braatz, Timothy. *Surviving Conquest, A History of the Yavapai Peoples.* Lincoln, University of Nebraska Press, 2003.

Bradley, James. *The March of the Montana Column.* 1896. Reprint, Norman, University of Oklahoma Press, 2001.

Bray, Kingsley M. *Crazy Horse, A Lakota Life.* Norman, University of Oklahoma Press, 2006.

Brown, Mark H. *The Flight of the Nez Perce, a History of the Nez Perce War.* New York, G. P. Putnam's Sons, 1967.

Browne, John Ross. *Adventures in the Apache Country: A Tour Through Arizona and Sonora with notes on the Silver Regions of Nevada.* 1871. Reprint, New York, Promontory, 1974.

Buecker, Thomas R. *Fort Robinson and the American West, 1874–1899.* Norman, University of Oklahoma Press, 1999.

Canfield, Gae W. *Sarah Winnemucca of the Northern Paiutes.* Norman, University of Oklahoma Press, 1983.

Carroll, John M., ed. *Custer's Chief of Scouts, The Reminiscences of Charles A. Varnum.* Lincoln, University of Nebraska Press, 1987.

Chun, Clayton. *The United States Army in the Plains Indian Wars, 1865–1890* (Battle Orders). Oxford, UK, Osprey Publications, 2004.

Clark, Robert A., ed. *The Killing of Chief Crazy Horse.* Lincoln, University of Nebraska Press, 1988.

Clark, William P. *The Indian Sign Language.* 1885. Reprint, Lincoln, University of Nebraska Press, Bison Books, 1986.

Clum, Woodworth. *Indian Agent, the Story of John Clum.* 1936. Reprint, Lincoln, University of Nebraska Press, 1978.

Collins, John S. *My Experiences in the West.* 1904. Reprint, Chicago, Lakeside, 1970.

Connell, Evan S. *Son of the Morning Star.* San Francisco, North Point, 1984.

Corbusier, William T. *Verde to San Carlos, Recollections of a Famous Army Surgeon and His Observant Family on the Western Frontier, 1869–86.* Tucson, Dale Stuart King, 1968.

Cozzens, Peter, ed. *Eyewitnesses to the Indian Wars.* Vols. 1–4. Mechanicsburg, Pa., Stackpole Books, 2001.

Crawford, Lewis F. *The Exploits of Ben Arnold, Indian Fighter, Gold Miner, Cowboy, Hunter, & Army Scout.* 1926. Reprint, Norman, University of Oklahoma Press, 1999.

Cremony, John C. *Life Among the Apaches.* 1868. Reprint, New York, Indian Head Books, 1991.

DeBarthe, Joe. *The Life and Adventures of Frank Grouard.* 1894. Reprint, New York, Time-Life, 1982.

Denton, Sally. *American Massacre, The Tragedy at Mountain Meadows, September 1857.* New York, Alfred A. Knopf, 2003.

Dobyns, Henry F. *The Apache People (Coyoteros).* Phoenix, Indian Tribal Series, 1971.

Downey, Fairfax, and Jacques Noel Jacobsen, Jr. *The Red/Bluecoats, the Indian Scouts, U.S. Army.* Fort Collins, Colo., Old Army Press, 1973.

Dunlay, Thomas W. *Wolves for the Blue Soldiers, Indian Scouts and Auxiliaries with the United States Army, 1860–1890.* Lincoln, University of Nebraska Press, 1987.

Dunn, J. P., Jr. *Massacres of the Mountains, A History of the Indian Wars of the Far West, 1815–1875.* New York, Archer House, 1958.

Egan, Ferol. *Sand in a Whirlwind, the Paiute War of 1860.* Garden City, N.Y., Doubleday, 1972.

Essin, Emmett M. *Shavetails and Bell Sharps, The History of the Army Mule.* Lincoln, University of Nebraska Press, 1997.

Farish, Thomas E. *History of Arizona*, vol. 8, San Francisco, Filmer Brothers Electrotype, 1918.

Finerty, John F. *War Path and Bivouac or The Conquest of the Sioux.* 1890. Reprint, Norman, University of Oklahoma Press, 1977.

Gibbon, John. *Adventures on the Western Frontier.* Bloomington and Indianapolis, Indiana University Press, 1994.

Gilliss, Julia, and Charles Gilliss. *So Far From Home: An Army Bride on the Western Frontier.* Portland, Oregon Historical Society Press, 1993.

Goodwin, Charles. C. *As I Remember Them.* Salt Lake City, Special Committee of the Salt Lake Commercial Club, 1913.

Goodwin, Grenville. *Western Apache Raiding and Warfare*, ed. Keith H. Basso. Tucson, University of Arizona Press, 1983.

Grant, Ulysses S. *Personal Memoirs of U. S. Grant.* Boston, 1885. Reprint, Boston, Da Capo Press, 1982.

Gray, John S. *Centennial Campaign, the Sioux War of 1876.* 1976. Reprint, Norman, University of Oklahoma Press, 1988.

Greene, Jerome A., ed. *Battles and Skirmishes of the Great Sioux War, 1876–1877, the Military View.* Norman, University of Oklahoma Press, 1993.

———, ed. *Lakota and Cheyenne, Indian Views of the Great Sioux War, 1876–1877.* Norman, University of Oklahoma Press, 1994.

———. *Nez Perce Summer, 1877.* Helena, Montana Historical Society Press, 2000.

———. *Slim Buttes, 1876, An Episode of the Great Sioux War.* Norman, University of Oklahoma Press, 1982.

———. *Yellowstone Command, Colonel Nelson A. Miles and the Great Sioux War, 1876–1877.* Lincoln, University of Nebraska Press, 1991.

Grinnell, George Bird. *The Fighting Cheyennes.* 1915. Reprint, Norman, University of Oklahoma Press, 1956.

———. *Two Great Scouts and their Pawnee Battalion.* Edited by Donald F. Danker. Lincoln, University of Nebraska Press, Bison Book edition, 1973.

Gump, James O. *The Dust Rose Like Smoke, The Subjugation of the Zulu and the Sioux.* Lincoln, University of Nebraska Press, 1994.

Hanley, Mike. *Owyhee Trails, The West's Forgotten Corner.* Caldwell, Idaho, Caxton Printers, 1975.

Hardorff, Richard G., ed. *The Death of Crazy Horse, A Tragic Episode in Lakota History.* Lincoln, University of Nebraska Press, 2000.

Hart, John P., ed. *Custer and His Times.* Vol. 5, Cordova, Tenn., Little Big Horn Association, 2008.

Hassrick, Royal B. *The Sioux, Life and Customs of a Warrior Society.* Norman, University of Oklahoma Press, 1964.

Hebard, Grace Raymond. *Washakie, Chief of the Shoshone.* 1930. Reprint, Lincoln, University of Nebraska Press, Bison Book edition, 1995.

Hedren, Paul L. *After Custer, Loss and Transformation in Sioux Country.* Norman, University of Oklahoma Press, 2011.

———. *First Scalp for Custer, the Skirmish at Warbonnet Creek, Nebraska, July 17, 1876.* 1980. Reprint, Lincoln, University of Nebraska Press, 1987.

———. *Fort Laramie and the Great Sioux War*, 1988. Reprint, Norman, University of Oklahoma Press, 1998.

———. *Great Sioux War Orders of Battle: How the U.S. Army Waged War on the Northern Plains, 1876–1877.* Norman, Okla., Arthur C. Clark Co., 2011.

———, ed. *Ho for the Black Hills: Captain Jack Crawford Reports the Black Hills Gold Rush and Great Sioux War.* Pierre, South Dakota Historical Society Press, 2012.

———. *We Trailed the Sioux, Enlisted Men Speak on Custer, Crook, and the Great Sioux War.* Mechanicsburg, Pa., Stackpole Books, 2003.

Hoig, Stanley. *Peace Chiefs of the Cheyenne.* Norman, University of Oklahoma Press, 1980.

Hopkins, Sarah Winnemucca. *Life Among the Paiutes, Their Wrongs and Claims.* 1883. Reprint, Reno, University of Nevada Press, 1994.

Howard, Oliver O. *My Life and Experiences Among Our Hostile Indians: A Record of Personal Observations, Adventures, and Campaigns Among the Indians of the Great West.* Hartford, Conn., A. D. Worthington, 1907.

Hutchins, James S., ed. *The Army and Navy Journal on the Battle of the Little Big Horn and Related Matters, 1876–1881.* El Segundo, Calif., Upton & Sons, 2003.

Hutton, Paul A. *Phil Sheridan and His Army*. Lincoln, University of Nebraska Press, 1985.

Hyde, George E. *Red Cloud's Folk, A History of the Oglala Sioux Indians*. Norman, University of Oklahoma Press, 1937.

———. *A Sioux Chronicle*. Norman, University of Oklahoma Press, 1956.

———. *Spotted Tail's Folk, A History of the Brule Sioux*. 1961. Reprint, Civilization of the American Indian Series, University of Oklahoma, Norman, 1974.

Jacoby, Karl. *Shadows at Dawn, A Borderlands Massacre and the Violence of History*. New York, Penguin, 2008.

Jensen, Richard E., ed. *Voices of the American West, The Settler and Soldier Interviews of Eli Ricker, 1903–1919*. Lincoln, University of Nebraska Press, 2005.

Johnson, Virginia W. *The Unregimented General*. Boston, Houghton Mifflin, 1962.

Josephy, Alvin M., Jr. *500 Nations, An Illustrated History of North American Indians*. New York, Alfred A. Knopf, 1994.

Juarez, Angelo D. *The Tarnished Saber, Major Azor Howett Nickerson, USA, His Life and Times*. Chatham, Mass., The Nickerson Family Association, 1993.

Kappler, Charles J., ed. *Indian Affairs*. Vol. 2, *Laws & Treaties*. Washington, D.C., Government Printing Office, 1904.

Kime, Wayne R., ed. *The Black Hills Journals of Colonel Richard Irving Dodge*. Norman, University of Oklahoma Press, 1996.

———. *The Powder River Expedition Journals of Colonel Richard Irving Dodge*. Norman, University of Oklahoma Press, 1997.

———. *Richard Irving Dodge: The Life and Times of a Career Army Officer*. Norman, University of Oklahoma Press, 2006.

King, Charles. *Campaigning with Crook*. 1890. Reprint, Norman, University of Oklahoma Press, 1989.

King, James T. *War Eagle, A Life of General Eugene A. Carr*. Lincoln, University of Nebraska Press, 1963.

Knight, Oliver. *Following the Indian Wars*. Norman, University of Oklahoma Press, 1960.

Larson, Robert W. *Red Cloud, Warrior-Statesman of the Lakota Sioux*. Norman, University of Oklahoma Press, 1997.

Linderman, Frank. *Plenty Coups, Chief of the Crows*. 1930. Reprint, Lincoln, University of Nebraska Press, 1962.

Lockwood, Frank C. *The Apache Indians*. 1938. Reprint, Lincoln, University of Nebraska Press, 1987.

Magid, Paul. *George Crook, From the Redwoods to Appomattox*. Norman, University of Oklahoma Press, 2011.

Maketa, Ray, ed. *Marching with General Crook, Diary of Lt. Thaddeus H. Capron, Company C, 9th Infantry*. Douglas, Alaska, Cheechako, 1983.

Mangum, Neil C. *Battle of the Rosebud: Prelude to the Little Big Horn*. El Segundo, Calif., Upton & Sons, 1996.

Manypenny, George W. *Our Indian Wards*. 1880. Reprint, Boston, Da Capo, 1972.

Marquis, Thomas B. *Wooden Leg, A Warrior who Fought Custer*. 1931. Reprint, Lincoln, University of Nebraska Press, 2003.

Mattes, Merrill J. *Indians, Infants, and Infantry, Andrew and Elizabeth Burt on the Frontier*. 1960. Reprint, Lincoln, University of Nebraska Press, 1988.

McChristian, Douglas C. *Fort Bowie, Arizona, Combat Post of the Southwest, 1858–1894.* Norman, University of Oklahoma Press, 2005.

———. *The U.S. Army in the West, 1870–1880, Uniforms, Weapons, and Equipment.* Norman, University of Oklahoma Press, 1995.

McGullycuddy, Julia B. *Blood on the Moon, Valentine McGillycuddy and the Sioux.* 1941. Reprint, Lincoln, University of Nebraska Press, Bison Book edition, 1990.

McHugh, Tom. *The Time of the Buffalo.* New York, Alfred A. Knopf, 1972.

Michno, Gregory F. *The Deadliest Indian War in the West, the Snake Conflict, 1864–1868.* Caldwell, Idaho, Caxton, 2007.

———. *Encyclopedia of Indian Wars, Western Battles and Skirmishes, 1850–1890.* Missoula, Mont., Mountain Press, 2003.

Miles, Nelson A. *Personal Recollections and Observations of General Nelson A. Miles.* 1896. Reprint, Lincoln, University of Nebraska Press, Bison Paperback, 1992.

Mills, Anson. *My Story.* 1918. Reprint, Mechanicsburg, Pa., Stackpole Books, 2003.

Monnet, John H. *Tell Them We are Going Home.* Norman, University of Oklahoma Press, 2001.

Morris, Roy, Jr. *Sheridan, The Life and Wars of General Phil Sheridan.* New York, Random House, 1992.

Nadeau, Remi. *Fort Laramie and the Sioux.* Lincoln, University of Nebraska Press, 1967.

Neihardt, John G. *Black Elk Speaks.* 1932. Reprint, Lincoln, University of Nebraska Press, 1972.

North, Luther, *Man of the Plains: Recollections of Luther North, 1856–1882.* Edited by Donald F. Danker. Lincoln, University of Nebraska Press, 1961.

Ogle, Ralph H. *Federal Control of the Western Apaches 1848–1886.* Albuquerque, University of New Mexico Press, 1970.

Olson, James C. *Red Cloud and the Sioux Problem.* Lincoln, University of Nebraska Press, 1965.

Opler, Morris E. *An Apache Life-way.* New York, Cooper Square Publishers, 1965.

Ostler, Jeffrey. *The Plains Sioux and U.S. Colonialism From Lewis and Clark to Wounded Knee.* Cambridge, UK, Cambridge University Press, 2004.

Perry, Richard J. *Apache Reservation, Indigenous Peoples and the American State.* Austin, University of Texas Press, 1993.

Peterson, F. Ross. *Idaho.* New York, W. W. Norton, 1976.

Porter, Joseph C. *Paper Medicine Man, John Gregory Bourke and His American West.* Norman, University of Oklahoma Press, 1986.

Powers, Thomas. *The Killing of Crazy Horse.* New York, Alfred A. Knopf, 2010.

Pumpelly, Raphael. *Travels and Adventures of Raphael Pumpelly.* 1870. Reprint, New York, Henry Holt & Co., 1920.

Reid, Whitelaw. *Ohio in the War: Her Statesmen, Generals, and Soldiers.* Cincinnati, Moore, Wilstach & Baldwin, 1868.

Robinson, Charles M., III, ed. *The Diaries of John Gregory Bourke.* Vols. 1–3. Denton, University of North Texas Press, 2003–2007.

———. *General Crook and the Western Frontier.* Norman, University of Oklahoma Press, 2001.

———. *A Good Year to Die, The Story of the Great Sioux War.* New York, Random House, 1995.

Robinson, Charles M. III, and Stanley E. Hoig. *Bad Hand: A Biography of General Ranald S. MacKenzie*. Abilene, Tex., State House Press, 2005.

Sajna, Mike. *Crazy Horse, The Life Behind the Legend*. New York, John Wiley & Sons, 2000.

Sandoz, Mari. *Cheyenne Autumn*. New York, McGraw-Hill, 1953.

———. *Crazy Horse, the Strange Man of the Oglalas*. New York, Alfred A. Knopf, 1942.

Schmitt, Martin F. *General George Crook, His Autobiography*. 1946. Reprint, Norman, University of Oklahoma Press, 1986.

Sears, Stephen W. *Chancellorsville*. Boston, Houghton Mifflin, 1996.

Sladen, Frank J., Jr. *Making Peace with Cochise: The 1872 Journal of Captain Joseph Alton Sladen*, ed. Edwin Sweeney. Norman, University of Oklahoma Press, 1997.

Smith, Sherry L. *Sagebrush Soldier, Private William Earl Smith's View of the Sioux War of 1876*. Norman, University of Oklahoma Press, 1989.

———. *View from Officers' Row: Army Perceptions of Western Indians*. Tucson, University of Arizona Press, 1991.

Stevenson, Joan Nabseth. *Deliverance from the Little Big Horn, Doctor Henry Porter and Custer's Seventh Cavalry*. Norman, University of Oklahoma Press, 2012.

Summerhayes, Martha. *Vanished Arizona, Recollections of the Army Life of a New England Woman*. Lincoln, University of Nebraska Press, 1979.

Sweeney, Edwin R. *Cochise: Chiricahua Apache Chief*. Norman, University of Oklahoma Press, 1995.

Sweeney, Edwin R., and Angie Debo. *Great Apache Chiefs, Cochise and Geronimo*. New York, MJF Books, 1991.

Terrell, John Upton *Apache Chronicle, the Story of the People*. New York, World Publishing, 1972.

Thrapp, Dan L. *Al Sieber, Chief of Scouts*. Norman, University of Oklahoma Press, 1964.

———. *The Conquest of Apacheria*. Norman, University of Oklahoma Press, 1967.

———. *Encyclopedia of Frontier Biography*. Vol. 2. Lincoln, University of Nebraska Press, 1988.

Tibbles, Thomas Henry. *Buckskin and Blanket Days, Memoirs of a Friend of the Indians*. New York, Doubleday, 1957.

Utley, Robert M. *A Clash of Cultures, Fort Bowie and the Chiricahua Apaches*. Washington, D.C., National Park Service, 1977.

———. *Frontier Regulars, the United States Army and the Indians, 1866–1891*. New York, Macmillan, 1973.

———. *The Lance and the Shield, the Life and Times of Sitting Bull*. New York, Henry Holt, 1993.

Vaughn, J. W. *The Reynolds Campaign on the Powder River*. Norman, University of Oklahoma Press, 1961.

———. *With Crook at the Rosebud*. Mechanicsburg, Pa., Stackpole Books, 1994.

Vestal, Stanley. *Warpath, The True Story of the Fighting Sioux Told in a Biography of Chief White Bull*. 1934. Reprint, Lincoln, University of Nebraska Press, 1984.

Wagoner, Jay. *Arizona Territory, 1863–1912, A Political History*. Tucson, University of Arizona Press, 1970.

Walker, Deward E. *Indians of Idaho*. Moscow, University Press of Idaho, 1978.

Walker, Henry P., and Don Bufkin. *Historical Atlas of Arizona*. Norman, University of Oklahoma Press, 1979.

Warner, Ezra. *Generals in Blue: Lives of the Union Commanders.* 1964. Reprint, Baton Rouge, Louisiana State University Press, 1992.

Werner, Fred H. *The Soldiers Are Coming, the Story of the Reynolds Battle, March 17, 1876,* Greeley, Colo., Werner Publications, 1882.

Wert, Jeffry D. *Custer: The Controversial Life of George Armstrong Custer.* New York, Simon & Schuster, 1996.

Wellman, Paul. *Death in the Desert, The Fifty Years' War for the Great Southwest.* 1935. Reprint, Lincoln, University of Nebraska Press, 1987.

Wheeler, Homer W. *Buffalo Days.* 1925. Reprint, Lincoln, University of Nebraska Press, Bison Book edition, 1990.

Wheeler, Keith. *The Old West: Scouts.* Alexandria, Va., Time-Life, 1978.

Willert, James. *Little Big Horn Diary, A Chronicle of the 1876 Indian War.* El Segundo, Calif., Upton and Sons, 1997.

Wooster, Robert. *Nelson A. Miles and the Twilight of the Frontier Army.* Lincoln, University of Nebraska Press, 1993.

Worcester, Donald E. *The Apaches, Eagles of the Southwest.* Norman, University of Oklahoma Press, 1979.

ELECTRONIC SOURCES

California State Military Museum. *California and the Military, George Stoneman, Jr., Civil War General and California Governor.* www.militarymuseum.org/stoneman.html.

Civil War Medicine. *Civil War Ambulance Wagons.* www.civilwarhome.com/ambulance wagons.html. Last updated 10/19/2003.

Interview with He Dog, July 7, 1930. *Oglala Sources on the Life of Crazy Horse.* www .nebraskahistory.org/lib-arch/research/manuscripts.

http://yellowstone.net/history/timeline/the-early-years-1872-1915.

Acknowledgments

One of the happiest circumstances in writing Crook's biography has been the people I have met and the places I have visited along the way. Publication of my first book, *George Crook: From the Redwoods to Appomattox*, earned me an introduction to writers and researchers whom I had known only through their works and by reputation. Among these individuals, historians of the National Park Service historians stand out, serving both as role models and guides to a store of knowledge about the period covered in my writing and the techniques and resources needed to unearth documentation important to my work. I continue to be impressed by the single-mindedness with which they pursue truth and accuracy in their writing, their enthusiasm for their subject matter, and their generosity in sharing information brought to light through their labors. I would single out two for special mention, Paul Hedren, to whom I have dedicated this book, and Jerome Greene, whose histories of the various aspects of the Sioux War are referred to again and again in the endnotes of this work. And I would be remiss in not mentioning Robert Utley, the dean of western historians, whose works are referenced in practically every modern history of the frontier West. I have not had the privilege of knowing him, but his works are the standard to which I aspire.

A second category of historians are those with academic affiliations, men like Robert Larson, the late Charles Robinson, Paul Hutton, and Wayne Kime. Unlike many university professors, these authors seem to have successfully avoided the pitfalls of stuffy, obscure language to produce books that are both accessible and a pleasure to read. Hutton's work on Sheridan was especially useful to me, as were Robinson's edited volumes of John Bourke's diaries, and Kime's editing work on Richard Irving Dodge.

Finally, there exists a parallel universe of writers and researchers, to whom I feel a special kinship, individuals who labor in the annals of history for the sheer joy of acquiring knowledge and making it available to others. These writers pursue their craft without academic recognition, and for very little compensation, frequently making outstanding contributions to the history of the Old West. Among these men and women, I am especially indebted to Gregory Michno, whose research into the Paiute wars is referenced often in the early chapters of this book, and Ed Sweeney, a recognized pioneer in the history of the Chiricahua Apaches. Another independent researcher and writer to whom I owe much is Marc Abrams, who has produced an invaluable multivolume compilation of contemporaneous newspaper articles on the Sioux War, as well as a book that synthesizes the work of early reporters covering that conflict. Like the late Charles Robinson's efforts with the Bourke diaries, his painstaking labors have made history readily accessible to those without the patience or resources to read these materials in their original form or in microfiche.

In this connection, I would be remiss in not recognizing such organizations as the Order of the Indian Wars and the Western Writers of America that support both professional and amateur students of western history.

Working alone, I continue to value the contributions of those who read my work in progress, providing feedback on whether it was clear and comprehensible. In writing this book, I continued to receive support from the Johns Hopkins Writers Program and from my former mentor at the school, Mary Collins, who, despite a busy schedule, took time to review some of my chapters. My writers group on Martha's Vineyard, under the supportive tutelage of Cynthia Riggs, patiently listened to the book from beginning to end, providing helpful and constructive commentary, as did John Hough for a brief but extremely fruitful period.

Like many who write about the West, my work has been facilitated by the archivists and librarians at the National Archives and the Library of Congress who helped me access hard-to-find materials and figure out the complexities of microfilm readers, and the many volunteers and professionals who work at the Arizona Historical Society in Tucson and the Nebraska Historical Society in Lincoln, the Rutherford Hayes Library in Fremont, Ohio, the Military History Institute in Carlisle, Pennsylvania, the Swan Library at Little Big Horn Battlefield, the Huntington Museum in Pasadena, and numerous public libraries around the country, including my own West Tisbury Free Public Library.

Finally, I would like to extend my sincere thanks and appreciation to Charles Rankin, Editor in Chief of the University of Oklahoma Press, and his hardworking staff, and my editors, Steven Baker and Gary Von Euer. Without their efforts, this book would never have been published.

Index

References to illustrations appear in italic type.